Interdisciplinary Studies in Human Rights

Volume 15

Human rights are one of the normative cornerstones of contemporary international law and global governance. Due to the complexities of actual or potential violations of human rights and in light of current crises, new and interdisciplinary research is urgently needed. The series Interdisciplinary Studies in Human Rights recognizes the growing importance and necessity of interdisciplinary research in human rights. The series consists of monographs and collected volumes addressing human rights research from different disciplinary and interdisciplinary perspectives, including but not limited to philosophy, law, political science, education, and medical ethics. Its goal is to explore new and contested questions such as the extraterritorial application of human rights and their relevance for non-state actors, as well as the philosophical and theoretical foundations of human rights. The series also addresses policy questions of current interest including the human rights of migrants and refugees, LGBTI rights, and bioethics, as well as business and human rights.

The series editors are Members of the Centre for Human Rights Erlangen-Nürnberg (CHREN), an interdisciplinary research center at Friedrich-Alexander-University Erlangen-Nürnberg. The Advisory Board brings together human rights scholars from a wide range of academic disciplines and regional backgrounds. The series welcomes suggestions for publications of academic research falling into the series subject matter.

Lene Guercke

Failure of the State

Organised Crime and Mexico's Disappeared

Springer

Lene Guercke
Human Rights Center
Faculty of Law, University of Berkeley
Berkeley, CA, USA

ISSN 2509-2960 ISSN 2509-2979 (electronic)
Interdisciplinary Studies in Human Rights
ISBN 978-3-031-83716-6 ISBN 978-3-031-83717-3 (eBook)
https://doi.org/10.1007/978-3-031-83717-3

This work was supported by H2020 European Research Council (677955).

This Springer imprint is published by the registered company Springer Nature Switzerland AG
The registered company address is: Gewerbestrasse 11, 6330 Cham, Switzerland

'I am now 47 years old and ever since I was a [child] I have heard my parents talk about disappearances. My parents lived through the period of the dirty war during the 70s, the [1968 Tlatelolco massacre] in Mexico, this terrible crime of the State that we still talk about today. I mean, that tells you how this has marked all of us. […] I hope that the generations that will come after us won't have to go on living like this, won't have to continue hearing this, and how it has marked all of us, that generation and the children of that generation. So, this is nothing new, it is not something that happened all of a sudden, but something that has already been deeply rooted in the territory and in the way authorities act. They have killed so many innocent persons, and we are here to give them a voice. We might not have their names, we do not have a wall with all the victims' names, we don't know, because many of them, well, there are no registers, they were killed, buried, burned, who knows. But that these people have a right to restitution, that they may one day be vindicated by those of us who are here now'. (Interview 11)

This book is dedicated to all those who continue to search for their loved ones, in Mexico and elsewhere. And to those who accompany them in their struggle.

'[Yo] actualmente tengo 47 años y desde que yo era niña, he oído a mis padres hablar de desaparición. A mis padres les tocó el movimiento de la guerra sucia en los años setenta, el 68 en México, este crimen de estado atroz que sucedió en México, y del que hoy en día seguimos hablando. O sea, eso te dice, de qué manera nos marcó, cómo nos marcó a todos. [...] Espero que las generaciones que vienen detrás de nosotros no tengan que seguir viviendo así, ni tengan que seguir oyendo esto, y cómo nos marcó a todos, a esa generación, y a los hijos de esa generación. Entonces, no es algo novedoso, no es algo que sucedió de pronto, si no que ya tiene rato así enraizado en el territorio y en el ... actuar de las autoridades. Y que asesinaron a muchas personas inocentes, y que nosotros estamos aquí para darles voz. Que nosotros no tenemos nombres, no tenemos una pared donde diga los nombres de las víctimas, no lo sabemos, porque muchos de ellos, pues no hay registros, fueron asesinados, enterrados, quemados, no sé. Pero que esas personas tengan derecho a una restitución, o sea a ver que algún día esas personas podrán ser reivindicadas, por quienes estamos ahora aquí'. (Entrevista 11)

Dedico este libro a todas las personas que continuan buscando a sus seres querides, en México y en otras partes del mundo. Y a las personas que les acompañan en su lucha.

Preface

This book is based on research conducted for my PhD thesis in Law, which was carried out in the framework of the ERC-funded project '"We are All Ayotzinapa": The Role of Digital Media in the Shaping of Transnational Memories on Disappearance' (2016–2021).[1] This interdisciplinary research project was based at the KU Leuven Faculty of Arts and aimed at researching the effect of digital media on collective memories of enforced disappearances. Its main focus was the case of 43 students from a rural teacher's college in Ayotzinapa, in the Mexican state of Guerrero, whose 2014 disappearance drew national and international attention, triggering protests and demands for justice across the globe. The particularity of this case lies in the prior absence of such attention and mobilisation despite a significant rise in disappearances in the country since 2006, when the government declared a 'war on drugs'. Further, despite a history of state-sponsored repression through enforced disappearances during the country's 'dirty war' in the 1970s, Mexico is conspicuously absent from the transnational memory of enforced disappearance in Latin America. Given that today there exist both an international and a regional legal framework specifically aimed at addressing and ending enforced disappearances, as well as international monitoring mechanisms, the project contained a legal dimension aimed at examining the phenomenon of (enforced) disappearances in Mexico from an international legal perspective. The PhD thesis was completed and defended in 2021 and has been modified and updated in 2024 for the purpose of publication.

Berkeley, CA, USA — Lene Guercke

[1]European Union's Horizon 2020 research and innovation programme (grant agreement n° 677955). For more information on the project, see http://digitalmemories.be.

Acknowledgements

This book is based on my PhD thesis, which I wrote between 2017 and 2021. During those 4 years, I received support, encouragement, and inspiration from many persons without whom I would not have been able to complete my dissertation. Since then, life and work have taken me on different paths, and even more persons have contributed to making this book a reality. I thank my PhD supervisors, Prof. Stephan Parmentier and Prof. Silvana Mandolessi at KU Leuven for giving me the freedom and support to design and steer my research project according to my interests and ideas and trusting me to see it through. I am grateful for your guidance and encouragement throughout this process and beyond. Equally, I would like to thank the members of my supervisory committee, Dr. Elisenda Calvet and Prof. Koen Lemmens, and especially Dr. Calvet for her support and guidance from the very beginning onwards. I am also thankful for comments and questions received by members of the evaluation committee, Prof. Barbara Frey, Prof. Letizia Paoli, and Prof. Jan Wouters. Furthermore, I want to thank Dr. Karina Ansolabehere for welcoming me at the Instituto de Investigaciones Jurídicas (UNAM), for supporting me throughout my research stay, for sharing your insights with me, and for your interest and comments on my research.

Over the course of my research, I had the privilege of getting to know many inspiring professionals who work on the issue of disappearances in Mexico, and I want to thank all those persons who gave me their time and shared their experiences and views with me during informal meetings, interviews, and presentations of my research. I sincerely appreciate your time and hope that my work can be of some use to the important work that you do. Moreover, I especially want to thank the NGOs who allowed me to accompany them (without knowing me beforehand): Centro de Derechos Humanos de las Mujeres (CEDEHM), Ciudadanos en Apoyo a los Derechos Humanos (CADHAC), Centro para los Derechos Humanos Fray Juan de Larios, Centro de Justicia para la Paz y el Desarrollo (CEPAD), and Tlachinollan, Centro de Derechos Humanos de la Montaña. My stays with you opened my eyes to many things and I am extremely grateful for your trust and openness to let me look over your shoulders for a week. I deeply admire your work and hope that our paths will cross again. I would especially like to thank Alejandra Nuño, who encouraged me to travel outside of Mexico City during my fieldwork. During my stay in Mexico, I also had the opportunity to meet relatives who are searching for their loved ones, and who shared parts of their stories with me. All of these stories have stayed with me, and I am grateful to all those individuals for sharing them.

Through my affiliation with two faculties at KU Leuven (Law and Arts), I was able to meet and exchange with many researchers and I am particularly grateful to the members of the Research Line on Human Rights and Transitional Justice, whose fascinating projects it was a pleasure to engage with. Special thanks to Dr. Olivia Herman, whom I am glad to have been able to share the PhD journey with. Thanks also to my colleagues from the Digital Memories project, especially Dr. Martín Zícari, whose company throughout the years, as a colleague and as a friend, has meant a lot to me. Seeing you complete and defend your thesis gave me a lot of motivation. I also want to particularly thank Dr. Katia Olalde, whose support and advice have meant a lot to me. Different chapters of my thesis were read and commented on by Ana Srovin Coralli, Zoe Slade, and Dr. María de Vecchi Gerli, and I want to thank all of them for taking the time to engage with my research and provide such helpful comments. María, thank you also for the chats and advice on fieldwork in Mexico. I am also grateful to Prof. Lea Sgier, who not only inspired me to become a thorough qualitative interviewer and researcher, but also took the time to comment on my interview guide. A big thank you also to Dr. Amalie Trangbæk, Dr. Audrey Gagnon, Dr. Jenny Rademann, and Dr. Larissa Versloot for reading and commenting on different parts of my thesis and for sharing your own fascinating research with me. Our exchanges were a true source of motivation and inspiration for me and were one of the best things to come out of the pandemic. Thanks also to Dr. Grażyna Baranowska for her feedback and support and to everyone else who commented on my work when I had the occasion to present parts of it: Dr. Julie Fraser, Dr. Maria Chiara Campisi, Dr. Miryam Rivera Holguín, Ahmed Gumusbas, and James Rischbieth (especially for the discussion on terminology). Moreover, I would like to thank Eva Nudd for her insights into the African human rights system.

Additionally, I would like to thank Prof. Alexa Koenig for welcoming me at the UC Berkeley Human Rights Centre, for giving me excellent feedback on the text and for providing me with time and space to work on the book manuscript. It is a great privilege to work with you. A big thanks also to the brilliant HRC team for sharing your combined brainpower to come up with a title for the book.

Last, but certainly not least, I want to thank all those who have been supporting me in different ways outside of work. My parents, who have supported me in pursuing the studies and career path that I chose (and wherever I chose); my friends, who have listened and encouraged me always, with a special shout-out to Nick and his —very biased— unwavering confidence in my abilities, and Laura for the pandemic walks and conversations. And to my husband, Arturo — I cannot thank you enough for bearing with me throughout the PhD —and again when finishing the book manuscript— for being there when I needed you and for leaving when I had to focus; for moving to Belgium, for believing in me, for trusting me, and for your love. I am lucky to have you in my life.

Contents

Abbreviations

ACHR	American Convention on Human Rights
African Guidelines	Guidelines on the Protection of All Persons from Enforced Disappearance in Africa
ALS	Areas of limited statehood
ARSIWA	Articles on Responsibility of States for Internationally Wrongful Acts
Basic Principles	Basic Principles and Guidelines on the Right to a Remedy and Reparation for Victims of Gross Violations of International Human Rights Law and Serious Violations of International Humanitarian Law
CAT	Committee against Torture
CED	Committee on Enforced Disappearances
CEAV	Commission for Victims' Assistance/Comisión Ejecutiva de Atención de Víctimas (Mexico)
CEDAW	Committee on the Elimination of Discrimination against Women
CNB	National Search Commission/Comisión Nacional de Búsqueda (Mexico)
DEA	United States Drug Enforcement Agency
DPPED	UN Declaration on the Protection of All Persons from Enforced Disappearance
ECHR	European Convention on Human Rights
ECtHR/European Court	European Court of Human Rights
EFM	Extraordinary Forensic Mechanism/Mecanismo Extraordinario Forense (Mexico)
FEMOSPP	Special Prosecutors' Office for the Attention of Matters Allegedly Related to Federal Crimes Committed Directly or Indirectly by Public

	Servants Against Persons Linked to Social or Political Movements of the Past/Fiscalía Especial para la Atención de Hechos Probablemente Constitutivos de Delitos Federales Cometidos Directa o Indirectamente por Servidores Públicos en Contra de Personas Vinculadas con Movimientos Sociales y Políticos del Pasado (Mexico)
FGR	National Prosecutor's Office/Fiscalía General de la República (Mexico)
GIEI	Interdisciplinary Group of Independent Experts/ Grupo Interdisciplinario de Expertos Independientes
Guiding Principles	Guiding Principles for the Search for Disappeared Persons
HRC	Human Rights Committee
IACFDP	Inter-American Convention on Forced Disappearance of Persons
IACHR	Inter-American Commission on Human Rights
IACtHR/Inter-American Court	Inter-American Court of Human Rights
ICJ	International Court of Justice
ICL	International Criminal Law
ICPPED	International Convention for the Protection of all Persons from Enforced Disappearance
ICC	International Criminal Court
ICCPR	International Covenant on Civil and Political Rights
IHL	International Humanitarian Law
IHRL	International Human Rights Law
LEDDCPI/General Law on Disappearances	General Law on Enforced Disappearances, Disappearances committed by Private Individuals and the National Search System/Ley General en Materia de Desaparición Forzada de Personas, Desaparición Cometida por Particulares y del Sistema Nacional de Búsqueda de Personas (Mexico)
LGV/Victims' Law	General Law on Victims/Ley General de Víctimas (Mexico)
MEH	Mechanism for Truth and Historical Clarification/ Mecanismo para la Verdad y el Esclarecimiento Histórico (Mexico)
Minnesota Protocol	Minnesota Protocol on the Investigation of Potentially Unlawful Death
MPJD	

	Movement for Peace with Justice and Dignity/Movimiento por la Paz con Justicia y Dignidad (Mexico)
MNDM	Movement for Our Disappeared in Mexico/Movimiento por Nuestros Desaparecidos en México (Mexico)
NIAC	Non-international armed conflict
NGO	Non-governmental organisation
OCG	Organised criminal group
OHCHR	Office of the High Commissioner for Human Rights
SNAV	National System for Victims' Assistance/Sistema Nacional de Atención a Víctimas (Mexico)
Trafficking Rapporteur	UN Special Rapporteur on trafficking in persons, especially women and children
UN	United Nations
UNCAC	United Nations Convention against Corruption
UNTOC	United Nations Convention against Transnational Organised Crime
WGEID	Working Group on Enforced or Involuntary Disappearances

Terminology for the Mexican Context

Colectivo	Term to refer to a group of relatives of disappeared persons in Mexico.
Agent of the prosecutor's office	Translation for 'ministerio público', which in Mexican Spanish refers to the person, usually with legal training, who is in charge of leading criminal investigations.

Chapter 1
Introduction

In September 2014, 43 students from a rural teacher's college in Ayotzinapa, a town in the Mexican state of Guerrero, were disappeared. As in previous years, the students had commandeered buses in order to travel to Mexico City and participate in the annual commemoration march of the 1968 'Tlatelolco' student massacre.[1] However, on September 26th, 2014, they were stopped and attacked by police forces in the town of Iguala, Guerrero. During the course of the night between September 26 and 27, there were multiple attacks on the students, as well as on a bus carrying a local football team and some other passing-by vehicles. These attacks resulted in six deaths, over 40 injured persons, and the disappearance of the 43 students.[2] The case of 'Ayotzinapa', as it became known, drew national and international attention, triggering protests and demands for justice across the globe. Additionally, it led to the creation of several unprecedented bodies and institutions in Mexico, including an international support mechanism.[3] Nonetheless, ten years later, the fate and whereabouts of the students continue to remain unknown.[4] At the same time, the case of

[1] The Tlatelolco massacre is one of the most prominent and most widely known examples of an attack by Mexican security forces on students who were peacefully protesting in the zone of Tlatelolco in Mexico City on October 2nd, 1968. See, for example, Aguayo (2015).

[2] GIEI (2015), pp. 7–8.

[3] In November 2014, the Mexican state signed an agreement with the Inter-American Commission on Human Rights (IACHR) to set up a team of international experts (Grupo Interdisciplinario de Expertos Independientes/ Interdisciplinary Group of Independent Experts, GIEI) to support the Mexican government's investigation of the case. The experts' mandate expired in early 2016 and a Special Follow-up Mechanism based at the IACHR was created, which formally monitored developments until 2018. In 2020, the GIEI was reinstated. Its sixth and final report was released in July 2023.

See https://www.oas.org/en/IACHR/jsForm/?File=/en/iachr/giei/ayotzinapa/default.asp# (accessed 26 November 2024); GIEI (2023).

[4] So far, the remains of three of the students have been identified, two of which by the University of Innsbruck in Austria. The remains of the second student were identified in June 2021. See Gibler (2023).

L. Guercke, *Failure of the State*, Interdisciplinary Studies in Human Rights 15,
https://doi.org/10.1007/978-3-031-83717-3_1

Ayotzinapa is only the proverbial tip of the iceberg of the present-day phenomenon of disappearances in Mexico, where, according to the most recent numbers available, over 103,500 persons have disappeared or gone missing since the onset of the so-called 'war on drugs' in late 2006.[5] Despite the formation of and advocacy by *colectivos* ('groups') of relatives of the disappeared in northern parts of the country since at least 2009,[6] it was not until the case of the 43 students from Ayotzinapa that the issue of disappearances in Mexico gained global attention and sparked mass mobilisations at national level.[7] Among the particularities of the Ayotzinapa case, which arguably contributed to its mobilising force, was the clear involvement of state agents in the abduction of the students, which made it impossible for the Mexican government to deny that this was an *enforced* disappearance and thus a human rights violation for which the state held responsibility.[8] In fact, the Ayotzinapa case highlighted the direct involvement of state agents from different levels of the state's security forces in a disappearance case, as well as the collusion between state and criminal actors and a prominent call during the protests following the disappearance of the 43 students, an artistic intervention on Mexico City's main square[9] and a hashtag of online mobilisations was '*Fue el Estado*' ('It was the state').[10]

In the context of Mexico's 'war on drugs', denial of state responsibility is facilitated because perpetrators of disappearances, and other infringements of human rights, are not just state agents but also members of organised criminal groups (OCGs) and, to a lesser extent, other non-state actors.[11] While cases like Ayotzinapa show that the state can be directly or indirectly involved, state participation in disappearances is not always as easily identifiable, which makes the determination of the scope of the state's responsibility legally—and conceptually—

[5] Data retrieved from the National Register on Disappeared and Missing Persons (Registro Nacional de Personas Desaparecidas y No Localizadas, RNPDNO): https://versionpublicarnpdno.segob.gob.mx/Dashboard/Sociodemografico. Accessed 4 November 2024. However, this official number should be taken with caution due to significant flaws in the data and registration (see further Chap. 5).

[6] For example, in the north-eastern state of Coahuila, the *colectivo* FUUNDEC (Fuerzas Unidas por Nuestros Desaparecidos en Coahuila) was founded in 2009. See Sánchez Valdés et al. (2018). In the neighbouring state of Nuevo León, the *colectivo* that is now AMORES also began meeting in 2009. See CADHAC (2014), p. 16. Since then, additional *colectivos* have been formed in both states.

[7] See, for example, BBC Mundo (2014); de Vecchi Gerli (2018), p. 196. For an overview of different protests around the world, see also https://blogsarchive.sites.haverford.edu/disappeared-students/international/. Accessed 22 November 2024.

[8] See Anaya Muñoz (2013).

[9] See https://infoactivismo.org/fueelestado/. Accessed 22 November 2024. For a description and analysis of this particular action, see Zícari (2021).

[10] For an analysis of this intervention from a Memory Studies perspective, see ibid.

[11] See, for example, Inter-American Commission on Human Rights (2015) Situation of Human Rights in Mexico. OEA/Ser.L/V/II.Doc. 44/15, paras 34–52; Committee on Enforced Disappearances (CED) (2022) Report of the Committee on Enforced Disappearances on its visit to Mexico: Findings. UN Doc. CED/C/MEX/VR/1 (Findings).

challenging when OCGs, or other non-state actors, are the direct perpetrators (see below). A lack of clarity regarding the scope of the state's responsibility creates uncertainty regarding the extent to which victims of disappearances committed by OCGs, and their relatives, are protected by the specialised international legal framework concerning the protection of persons from enforced disappearance and International Human Rights Law (IHRL) more generally.

This book explores the protective capacity of IHRL[12] vis-à-vis victims of disappearances committed by OCGs, and their relatives, thereby spotlighting the issue of OCGs as perpetrators of human rights violations and the ensuing legal and non-legal questions, particularly in view of the relationship between such groups and state agents through corruption. To do so, the book combines two disciplinary perspectives: a doctrinal legal analysis of state obligations and responsibility for disappearances committed by non-state actors and OCGs on the one hand, and, on the other hand, an exploratory qualitative study of the present-day issue of disappearances in Mexico and the experiences of human rights practitioners working on this topic. By adding a qualitative perspective to the theoretical analysis, the book provides a richer understanding of the challenges faced by human rights practitioners 'on the ground' who work in a context where OCGs commit human rights violations alongside, or in collusion with, state forces. Furthermore, and in line with much human rights scholarship that is ultimately aimed at improving human rights protection,[13] the book aims to provide an analysis that could be utilised in litigation efforts relating to OCGs as perpetrators of human rights violations.

In the remainder of this Introduction, I introduce the issue of disappearances committed by non-state actors from the perspective of IHRL, which constitutes the 'puzzle' upon which the research is based. I then discuss the methodological approach, outline the book's structure and define key terms that I will use throughout the book.

[12] I understand 'protection by international law' to mean that there are clear standards in relation to a) the state's obligations towards victims, b) the determination of responsibility of the state if it fails to comply with its obligations, and c) the legal possibility of claiming reparations for the harm suffered. That is, I refer to the extent to which victims and their representatives can draw on international standards to demand accountability and reparations, including guarantees of non-repetition, for the harm suffered.

[13] See, for example, McInerney-Lankford (2017), p. 38. The author argues that legal human rights research is 'essential for upholding human rights norms and ensuring the realization of human rights.' Additionally, Brems has highlighted that much legal human rights scholarship is aimed at improving the protection for human rights, yet authors often fail to make this aim explicit. See Brems (2009), p. 86.

1.1 Enforced Disappearances in IHRL

Enforced disappearances are considered one of the most heinous crimes and human rights violations that exist today.[14] While first applied in an official manner by the Nazi regime against certain types of political prisoners,[15] the practice of making people disappear with the aim of causing terror among the population became particularly notorious during the 1960s and 1970s, when it was prominently employed as a repression technique by dictatorships in Latin America.[16] Strong advocacy by groups of relatives during that period, especially from Latin America, led not only to the invention of the term 'enforced disappearance',[17] but also to the creation of international mechanisms tasked with supporting relatives in establishing the whereabouts of the disappeared, such as the Working Group on Enforced or Involuntary Disappearances (WGEID),[18] and, eventually, the adoption of regional and international legal instruments aimed at countering the practice of enforced disappearance.[19] At the international level, due to the persistence of both the practice of enforced disappearance and a number of gaps in the existing international legal framework relating to the particular characteristics of this crime,[20] in 2006 the International Convention for the Protection of All Persons from Enforced Disappearance (ICPPED) was adopted, which entered into force in 2010.[21] In addition to this progressive codification in IHRL, the prohibition of enforced disappearance is considered a customary norm of International Humanitarian Law (IHL)[22] and, when practiced as 'part of a widespread or systematic attack' it amounts to a crime against

---

[14] Cançado Trindade (2012), p. 508.

[15] See, for example, Huhle (2014).

[16] Scovazzi and Citroni (2007), pp. 7–13.

[17] Frey (2009); Dulitzky (2019).

[18] See https://www.ohchr.org/en/issues/disappearances/pages/disappearancesindex.aspx. Accessed 24 November 2024.

[19] For an overview of the different General Assembly resolutions adopted on the issue of enforced disappearances, see Scovazzi and Citroni (2007), p. 245 ff. In 1992, the UN Declaration on the Protection of all Persons from Enforced Disappearance (DPPED) was adopted by the UN General Assembly, followed by the adoption of the first legally binding instrument, the Inter-American Convention on Forced Disappearances in 1994. See Declaration on the Protection of All Persons from Enforced Disappearance 1992 (A/RES/47/133); Inter-American Convention on Forced Disappearance of Persons 1994 (33 ILM 1529).

[20] Commission on Human Rights (2002) Report Submitted by Mr. Manfred Nowak, Independent Expert Charged with Examining the Existing International Criminal and Human Rights Framework for the Protection of Persons from Enforced or Involuntary Disappearances. UN Doc. E/CN.4/2002/71; Scovazzi and Citroni (2007), pp. 257–263.

[21] International Convention for the Protection of All Persons from Enforced Disappearance 2006 (1726 UNTS 3) (ICPPED).

[22] See Rule 98 of the International Committee of the Red Cross' Customary IHL Database: https://ihl-databases.icrc.org/customary-ihl/eng/docs/v1_rul_rule98. Accessed 24 November 2024.

humanity under International Criminal Law (ICL).[23] According to some authors, and the African Commission on Human and Peoples' Rights, the prohibition of enforced disappearance has by now reached the status of a peremptory norm of international law.[24]

Despite these important advances at the international legal level, enforced disappearances continue to occur and be employed by governments as a repressive tactic against opponents.[25] However, today (enforced) disappearances occur in a variety of different contexts not traditionally associated with the repression of political opponents, and even in democratic regimes.[26] For example, one 'new' form of enforced disappearance were the so-called 'extraordinary renditions' carried out by the United States in collaboration with European (and other) countries following the terrorist attacks of 11 September 2001 and in the context of the 'war on terror'.[27] Current contexts in which disappearances occur often involve non-state actors as perpetrators. For example, disappearances can occur in the context of armed conflicts involving both state and non-state actors, where non-state armed groups might act on behalf of a state or their own motives and disappear opponents.[28] At the same time, victims of human trafficking can also become victims of disappearances, and migrants can disappear *en route* while being smuggled from one country into another.[29] Moreover, in contexts of generalised (criminal) violence, disappearances may result from dead bodies being disposed of in order to leave no trace.[30]

It is in the latter situations that OCGs play a particularly prominent role as perpetrators of disappearances.[31] The situation in Mexico is one example where

---

[23] Article 7 Rome Statute of the International Criminal Court 1998 (2187 UNTS 90), Article 5 ICPPED.

[24] Cançado Trindade (2012); Sarkin (2012); African Commission on Human and Peoples' Rights (2022) Guidelines on the Protection of All Persons from Enforced Disappearances in Africa, p. 9.

[25] See, for example, Citroni (2014); Payne and Abouharb (2016); Human Rights Watch (2024). See also Human Rights Council (2024) Enforced disappearances and elections: Report of the Working Group on Enforced or Involuntary Disappearances. UN Doc. A/HRC/57/54.

[26] See Dulitzky (2019); Ansolabehere et al. (2021).

[27] See, for example, Ott (2011), p. 6; Pervou (2023), pp. 57–59.

[28] On enforced disappearances committed by paramilitary groups, see, for example, Scovazzi and Citroni (2007), pp. 21–24; Ott (2011), p. 5; Vermeulen (2012), pp. 6–18; Sarkin and Baranowska (2018), pp. 19–25. Note, however, that in the context of armed conflicts there is a difference between those who are 'missing' as a result of the conflict and those who are forcibly disappeared. See Sarkin (2017), pp. 3–4. For an overview of the differences between 'disappeared' and 'missing' persons, see also CED (2023) Report of the Committee on Enforced Disappearances on its visit to Iraq: Information on the visit and findings. UN Doc. CED/C/IRQ/VR/1 (Findings), para. 51.

[29] See Human Rights Council (2017) Report of the Working Group on Enforced or Involuntary Disappearances on Enforced Disappearances in the Context of Migration. UN Doc. A/HRC/36/39/Add.2; Baranowska (2020); CED (2023) General Comment No. 1 on Enforced Disappearance in the Context of Migration. UN Doc. CED/C/GC/1; Fischer and Duhaime (2024).

[30] Inter-American Commission on Human Rights (IACHR) (2015) Violence, Children and Organized Crime. OEA/Ser.L/V/II. Doc. 40/15, paras 329–330.

[31] See Global Initiative Against Transnational Organized Crime (2020).

criminal groups have become extremely powerful actors that engage in war-like battles against each other and against the state.[32] The northern countries of Central America are another example,[33] as are Haiti[34] and some countries in the Caribbean.[35] In these contexts, the level of atrocities is comparable to that experienced in armed conflicts, yet whether these situations can be categorised as non-international armed conflicts (NIAC) from an international legal perspective continues to be a matter of debate.[36] In some cases, disappearances committed by non-state actors, including OCGs, can amount to an enforced disappearance, yet this depends on the relationship between the non-state actor concerned and authorities (see below). From a legal perspective, the participation of non-state actors thus adds complexity to an already complex human rights violation.

1.1.1 Non-State Actors as Perpetrators of Disappearances

The ICPPED defines enforced disappearances as:

> the arrest, detention, abduction or any other form of deprivation of liberty by agents of the State or by persons or groups of persons acting with the authorization, support or acquiescence of the State, followed by a refusal to acknowledge the deprivation of liberty or by concealment of the fate or whereabouts of the disappeared person, which place such a person outside the protection of the law.[37]

This definition indicates that, under IHRL, disappearances carried out by non-state actors are not *enforced* disappearances unless it can be shown that they were committed with the 'authorization, support or acquiescence of the State.' The question of whether or not to include non-state actors as perpetrators of *enforced* disappearances in the definition was one of the most difficult aspects during the negotiation process of the ICPPED[38] and it was ultimately agreed to include a separate article (Article 3) that obliges states to 'take appropriate measures to investigate acts defined in article 2 committed by persons or groups of persons acting *without* the authorization, support or acquiescence of the State and to bring

[32] See Chap. 5 for an overview of the dynamics of disappearances in Mexico. See also ICRC (2023).

[33] On the issue of disappearances committed by gangs in El Salvador, for example, see Carcach and Artola (2016).

[34] See, for example, Pellegrini (2024).

[35] Freeman and Casij Peña (2023); UNODC (2024).

[36] In 2023, the International Committee of the Red Cross (ICRC) dedicated a full issue of its Review to these debates: ICRC (2023); Muggah (2023); Redaelli and Arévalo (2023); Kalmanovitz (2023); Freeman and Casij Peña (2023); Padin (2023). See also Peterke and Wolf (2016), pp. 403–404; Lambin (2018), p. 85. Given that debates around this question are ongoing, for the purpose of this book it will be assumed that IHRL is the principal applicable body of law in these situations.

[37] Article 2 ICPPED.

[38] See Scovazzi and Citroni (2007), p. 279; Ott (2011), pp. 23–26; Vermeulen (2012), pp. 54–56; Pervou (2023), p. 48.

those responsible to justice'.[39] The relative vagueness of this article, however, left a gap in the international human rights framework with regard to the specific obligations of states vis-à-vis victims of disappearances committed by non-state actors.[40] This gap extends beyond the direct victim of the disappearance to relatives, who are also considered victims of *enforced* disappearances according to Article 24 ICPPED[41] and in international jurisprudence[42] due to the detrimental impact that the disappearance of a loved one and the uncertainty regarding their fate have on relatives.[43] Importantly, under Article 5 ICPPED, when disappearances committed by non-state actors that would normally fall within the scope of Article 3 ICPPED are committed 'as part of a widespread or systematic attack against a civilian population' and meet the criteria established in ICL, they can amount to *enforced* disappearances as a crime against humanity.[44] This is because, following the definition contained in Article 7(2)(i) of the Rome Statute, enforced disappearances as crimes against humanity can be committed in pursuance of an 'organisational policy' by a 'political organisation', which could include non-state actors.[45]

---

[39] Article 3 ICPPED. Emphasis added.

[40] See Commission on Human Rights (2006) Report of the Intersessional Open-Ended Working Group to Elaborate a Draft Legally Binding Normative Instrument for the Protection of All Persons from Enforced Disappearance. UN Doc. E/CN.4/2006/57, paras 12–14; Anderson (2006); Pérez Solla (2006); Scovazzi and Citroni (2007); Ott (2011); Vermeulen (2012); Huhle (2013); de Frouville (2021).

[41] Article 24(1) ICPPED establishes that '"victim" means the disappeared person and any individual who has suffered harm as the direct result of an enforced disappearance'.

[42] See, for example, *Case of Blake v Guatemala (Merits)* [1998] Inter-American Court of Human Rights Ser C No 36, para. 114; *Varnava and Others v Turkey* [2009] European Court of Human Rights Applications nos. 16064/90, 16065/90, 16066/90, 16068/90, 16069/90, 16070/90, 16071/90, 16072/90 and 16073/90, para. 200; *Rosa María Serna et al v Colombia* [2015] Human Rights Committee UN Doc. CCPR/C/114/D/2134/2012, para. 9.8.

[43] See, for example, Commission on Human Rights (2002) Report Submitted by Mr. Manfred Nowak, Independent Expert Charged with Examining the Existing International Criminal and Human Rights Framework for the Protection of Persons from Enforced or Involuntary Disappearances. UN Doc. E/CN.4/2002/71, para 77.

[44] This was confirmed by the CED in its Statement on Non-State Actors: CED (2023) Statement on non-State actors in the context of the International Convention for the Protection of All Persons from Enforced Disappearances. UN Doc. CED/C/10, para. 17.

[45] See Commission on Human Rights (2002) Report Submitted by Mr. Manfred Nowak, Independent Expert Charged with Examining the Existing International Criminal and Human Rights Framework for the Protection of Persons from Enforced or Involuntary Disappearances. UN Doc. E/CN.4/2002/71, para 69; Anderson (2006), p. 274. This issue was also touched upon in the reports on the draft Convention against Crimes Against Humanity: International Law Commission (2015) First Report on Crimes against Humanity. UN Doc. A/CN.4/680, paras 145–150. However, not all scholars agree with this interpretation of Article 7 Rome Statute. For example, Ambos and Böhm argue that in the case of enforced disappearances, it is impossible for a non-state actor to commit this crime due to its special nature. They base this argument on the understanding that the main violation contained in an enforced disappearance is the legal and factual blocking of resources for investigation and access to justice. Consequently, the authors argue that only where an 'organisation' is in full control of a certain territory could it perpetrate enforced disappearances. See Ambos

The exclusion of non-state actors from the definition of enforced disappearance and uncertainty regarding obligations under Article 3 ICPPED, alongside growing involvement of non-state actors in the commission of disappearances, has posed challenges for international mechanisms. For example, the WGEID, which was established in 1980 as the first international mechanism to deal with the issue of enforced disappearance through its humanitarian role of assisting families in determining the fate and whereabouts of their loved ones, for many years did not admit cases where no direct or indirect state involvement could be established.[46] In 2019, however, it began to document cases 'tantamount to enforced disappearances' perpetrated by non-state actors who 'exercise effective control and/or government-like functions over a territory'[47] and has called on these non-state actors 'to immediately stop and prevent acts tantamount to enforced disappearances.'[48] Conversely, in 2023, the Committee on Enforced Disappearances (CED), which is the treaty body to the ICPPED, adopted a Statement on Non-State actors in the Context of the International Convention for the Protection of All Persons from Enforced Disappearances (Statement on Non-State Actors), in which it addressed some of the uncertainties surrounding disappearances committed by non-state actors. This Statement brought some much needed clarification in relation to the definition of 'authorization', 'support', and 'acquiescence', but did not remove all uncertainties regarding state obligations (see Chaps. 2 and 3).

This book provides a thorough analysis of the existing legal framework and gaps pertaining to disappearances committed by non-state actors and applies it to OCGs, who have not yet received much attention in scholarship. By focusing on the extent to which gaps in the international legal framework (discussed above) persist and can be addressed from within the international legal framework, the research contributes to the sparse scholarship on the issue of disappearances committed by non-state actors. By focusing exclusively on non-state actors and introducing an empirical perspective, the book adds to existing legal scholarship on enforced disappearances, which is principally doctrinal in nature and focused mainly on *enforced* disappearances committed by, or with direct involvement of, state agents.[49] While the

and Böhm (2009), pp. 246–248. On these discussions, see also de Frouville (2021); Wolffenbuttel (2021).

[46] Human Rights Council (2007) Report of the Working Group on Enforced or Involuntary Disappearances 2007: General Comment on the Definition of Enforced Disappearance. UN Doc. A/HRC/7/2 at para. 26, para. 1; Human Rights Council (2012) Report of the Working Group on Enforced or Involuntary Disappearances. UN Doc. A/HRC/19/58/Rev.1, Annex II, p. 139, para. 6.

[47] Human Rights Council (2019) Report of the Working Group on Enforced or Involuntary Disappearances. UN Doc. A/HRC/42/40, para. 94.

[48] Human Rights Council (2020) Report of the Working Group on Enforced or Involuntary Disappearances. UN Doc. A/HRC/45/13, para. 45. This decision reflects the WGEID's and other human rights mechanisms' stance that in situations where non-state actors exert *de facto* territorial control, they also hold human rights obligations. See OHCHR (2021).

[49] See Pérez Solla (2006); Scovazzi and Citroni (2007); Anderson (2006); Ott (2011); Citroni (2012); Vermeulen (2012); Sarkin (2012); Sarkin (2013); Genovese and van der Wilt (2014);

question of non-state actors as perpetrators of (enforced) disappearances has also received some attention,[50] only one author has examined the question of state responsibility in relation to such disappearances in more depth.[51] The persistence of enforced disappearance at a global level[52] and growing attention towards non-traditional types of (enforced) disappearances by human rights bodies, such as the disappearance of migrants and the issue of non-state actors as perpetrators,[53] indicate a need for research on this topic.

At the same time, however, under positive international law only states can commit human rights violations in a legal sense and be held accountable before international or regional human rights fora.[54] Consequently, while there is increasing discussion in scholarship on the question of whether different types of—increasingly powerful—non-state actors themselves may have human rights obligations,[55] victims who seek to obtain redress for violations through an international or regional human rights mechanism can still only present claims against states, both in legal fora but also beyond the strictly legal sphere.[56] Therefore, the extent of a *state's* responsibility in relation to acts committed by non-state actors remains important. This is to some extent reflected in the recently growing interest in the notion of due diligence in international legal scholarship, as illustrated by the publication of several books on this issue in recent years.[57] While this book does not focus on the notion of due diligence specifically, the research contributes to broader discussions of state responsibility in relation to acts committed by non-state actors.[58]

Citroni (2014); Sarkin and Baranowska (2018); Calvet Martínez (2018); Baranowska (2021); Pervou (2023).

[50] See Vermeulen (2012), Chap. 9; Huhle (2013); de Frouville (2021).

[51] See Vermeulen (2012), Chap. 9.

[52] Payne and Abouharb (2016); Tolbert (2017); OHCHR (2023).

[53] See Human Rights Council (2017) Report of the Working Group on Enforced or Involuntary Disappearances on Enforced Disappearances in the Context of Migration. UN Doc. A/HRC/36/39/Add.2; Sarkin (2017); Srovin Coralli (2021); CED (CED) (2023) General Comment No. 1 on Enforced Disappearance in the Context of Migration. UN Doc. CED/C/GC/1; CED (2023) Statement on non-State actors in the context of the International Convention for the Protection of All Persons from Enforced Disappearances. UN Doc. CED/C/10.

[54] See Kälin and Künzli (2009), p. 82; McCorquodale (2010), p. 97; Hamid and Wouters (2021a), p. 54; Mackenzie-Gray Scott (2022), pp. 22–24.

[55] Generally, the view is that non-state actors hold certain human rights obligations when they exercise *de facto* governmental authority or territorial control. See, for example, Kälin and Künzli (2009); McCorquodale (2010); Mackenzie-Gray Scott (2022), Chap. 2. For a 'stocktaking' of these discussions, see Clapham (2019). Moreover, non-state actors are considered to have obligations under IHL in the context of armed conflicts. See Clapham (2006); Sassòli (2010); Dudai and McEvoy (2012).

[56] See Gallagher (2010), pp. 218–219. See also Mackenzie-Gray Scott's overview of gaps in the international law on state responsibility when it comes to non-state actors. Mackenzie-Gray Scott (2022), p. 29 ff.

[57] See, for example, Monnheimer (2021); Krieger et al. (2020); Besson (2021).

[58] See Mackenzie-Gray Scott (2022).

By focusing specifically on the issue of disappearances committed by OCGs, the book introduces a non-state actor that has largely been overlooked in human rights scholarship. While there exists growing research on the obligations and accountability of many non-state actors that impact human rights in practice,[59] such as armed groups,[60] multinational companies,[61] NGOs,[62] international organisations,[63] and private security companies,[64] OCGs have received very little attention. This is despite the fact that OCGs are mentioned as a perpetrator that can infringe on human rights in human rights textbooks[65] and legal instruments[66] and that the 'organised crime' of human trafficking is indisputably a crime that directly affects several human rights.[67] Existing scholarship on the topic of organised crime and human rights is mostly concerned with either the obligations of states to protect individuals from human trafficking[68] or smuggling,[69] or with the question whether organised crimes could be considered as a particular type of human rights violation, such as torture.[70] Furthermore, in recent years the issue of organised crime as such, and the variety of legal questions related to it, have received more attention from scholars in international law more generally.[71] Given the growing power and influence of (transnational) organised crime, however, and the different ways its activities impact on human rights,[72] focusing attention on this particular non-state actor from a human rights law perspective is important.

---

[59] See, for example, Alston (2005); De Brabandere (2009); Clapham (2013); Weissbrodt (2013); Noortmann et al. (2015). On the question of subjects in international law more generally, see Klabbers (2009).

[60] See, for example, Clapham (2014); Murray (2016); Fortin and Clapham (2017).

[61] See, for example, de Schutter (2006); McCorquodale (2010); Deva and Bilchitz (2013); Olsen (2023).

[62] See, for example, Spiro (2011).

[63] See, for example, Von Bogdandy and Steinbrück Platise (2012).

[64] See, for example, van Genugten et al. (2011); Hoppe (2008); Torroja (2017).

[65] See, for example, Kälin and Künzli (2009), p. 82.

[66] African Commission on Human and Peoples' Rights (2015) General Comment No. 3 on the African Charter on Human and People's Rights: The Right to Life (Article 4), para. 2: 'Organised crime and terrorism can pose significant threats to the enjoyment of the right to life'.

[67] See, for example, Obokata (2005); Gallagher (2010). According to the IACtHR: '[...] owing to its nature and complexity, organized crime in all its different forms constitutes, per se, a serious threat for the international community, because it attacks the security, stability and democratic governance of the States, hinders their development, and impedes the realization of the human rights of the persons subject to their jurisdiction.' *Case of Alvarado Espinoza and Others v Mexico* [2018] Inter-American Court of Human Rights Series C No. 370, para. 178.

[68] See, for example, Obokata (2006); Gallagher (2010).

[69] See Obokata (2005).

[70] See, for example, McGregor (2014). On human trafficking as a human rights violation more generally, see also Office of the High Commissioner for Human Rights (2014), p. 5.

[71] See Obokata (2010); Letschert and Van Dijk (2011); Hauck and Peterke (2016); Decoeur (2018); ICRC (2023).

[72] See Van Dijk (2011); Dudai and McEvoy (2012), pp. 19–23.

At the same time, Chap. 5, which introduces the context of disappearances in Mexico that is mostly absent in legal literature on the subject, highlights a number of questions for the international framework on enforced disappearances that do not yet have clear answers. Although the empirical research conducted for this project solely explores the Mexican context, the legal questions are broader in nature and can therefore be of relevance beyond this context. The focus on OCGs particularly also goes beyond the Mexican context and can be equally relevant for other countries where OCGs, or gangs, as well as the fight against them, impact on the enjoyment of human rights and both the state and criminal groups are responsible for violations. Finally, the empirical analysis of this research may contribute to the emerging field of research concerned with the protection of human rights in so-called 'areas of limited statehood' in Political Science and International Relations scholarship on human rights.[73]

1.2 Methodological Approach

This research is based on the premise that the lack of clarity regarding the extent of international legal obligations of states towards victims of disappearances committed by non-state actors can be problematic. This is especially because of the great suffering that a disappearance inflicts on the relatives of the disappeared person, regardless of the identity of the perpetrator.[74] In this sense, the research contains the normative assumption that IHRL *should* provide protection to victims of disappearances committed by OCGs, and their relatives. If it is assumed that IHRL is meant to *protect* human rights,[75] international human rights standards must provide clarity with regards to states' obligations, the determination of responsibility of the state if it fails to comply with these obligations, and the legal possibility of claiming reparations for harm suffered as a result of this failure.

To explore IHRL's protective capacity vis-à-vis victims of disappearances committed by OCGs, and their relatives, this research combines a doctrinal legal analysis on the scope of state responsibility relating to such disappearances, containing descriptive, comparative, and normative elements, with an exploratory qualitative study of the situation of disappearances in present-day Mexico and the experiences of human rights practitioners working on this issue. The question of methods for human rights research has received growing attention in recent years.[76]A major criticism of purely legal human rights scholarship is that the latter implicitly assumes that law will have a positive impact, and that it often remains too removed from

[73] See, for example, Börzel et al. (2018); Baade et al. (2018); Risse (2017); Hamid and Wouters (2021b).

[74] See, for example, Scovazzi and Citroni (2007), p. 278; Calvet Martínez (2015), p. 84.

[75] Shaw (2008), p. 271.

[76] See, for example, Coomans et al. (2009); Andreassen et al. (2017).

reality.[77] On the other hand, explanatory social science research focused on the effectiveness or 'impact' of human rights norms, generally does not consider the nuances of these legal norms and risks 'ignoring or misrepresenting' them.[78] In so far as legal standards constitute the basis for assessing the extent to which they can be actualised, their content must also be analysed and understood. At the same time, while not without risks, combining different disciplinary perspectives and methods can provide a more nuanced understanding of human rights issues and contribute to advancing 'research frontiers'.[79] Thus, in trying to bridge the gap between 'internal' and 'external' human rights scholarship, this research seeks to address two 'sides' of the problem of disappearances being committed by OCGs, contrasting the content of the IHRL framework with an 'external' view on the legal and non-legal challenges of working towards ensuring the 'protection' of the rights of victims of disappearances committed by OCGs, and their relatives. For the purpose of (disciplinary) clarity, the research is divided in two parts, and the findings of both parts are discussed together in a concluding chapter.

1.2.1 Doctrinal Research

The doctrinal analysis is based on a non-exhaustive review of case law involving disappearances at the hands of non-state actors, as well as of cases concerning violations of human rights that can effectively overlap with a disappearance, such as the right to life. It also includes jurisprudence in which tribunals dealt with the question of acquiescence. The analysis focuses mainly on case law of the Inter-American Court of Human Rights (IACtHR) and the European Court of Human Rights (ECtHR), which have most extensively addressed questions of non-state actors, as well as case law of the International Court of Justice (ICJ) for general questions of attribution. Additionally, it includes views adopted by United Nations treaty bodies and the African human rights system where applicable.

1.2.2 Empirical Research

Conversely, and in view of the criticism of purely legal research mentioned above, to avoid making assumptions about the effect of legal norms, answering a question about the *protective capacity* of international legal standards warrants moving

[77] For such criticisms, see, for example, Forsythe (2009); Sano and Thelle (2009). For a discussion of existing criticisms of legal human rights scholarship and an argument for why it is still key to focus on such legal research, see McInerney-Lankford (2017).

[78] See Coomans et al. (2010), p. 181.

[79] Langford (2017), p. 163.

beyond the doctrinal level to examine how these standards are, or can be, used in the 'real world'.[80] This means exploring the experiences of those who use and draw on the relevant international legal framework in their work, with the aim of understanding the challenges they face, as well as whether and how the legal questions that persist at the international level actually come up in practice.

The empirical research is based on a critical realist position towards scientific inquiry. Critical realism, as defined by Maxwell, combines a combination of ontological realism with epistemological constructivism.[81] This means assuming the existence of a real world outside the researcher's own mind, which the latter can strive to comprehend, while accepting that any such comprehension will never be complete and will always be shaped by the researcher's own background and assumptions.[82] In taking this perspective, ontologically I take the view that there is an 'external reality'[83] that exists independently of our minds and means of knowledge-construction.[84] Thus, for the purpose of the research, I assumed that real legal and non-legal challenges to the protection of victims of disappearances committed by OCGs existed and that the experiences of human rights practitioners were also real and could provide insight into these challenges.[85] At the same time, epistemologically, I acknowledge that my own background, assumptions, and biases inevitably influenced the manner in which I understood and interpreted the data.[86] Consequently, I do not claim that my interpretation of the experiences of the human rights practitioners interviewed for this book represents a single 'truth' or the only possible understanding of the data.[87]

Due to the qualitative nature of the research and its critical realist underpinnings, the evaluation criteria of reliability, validity, and generalisability, which are generally used in quantitative research, are not appropriate for this research.[88] Rather, to ensure the quality of the empirical research, I focused on ensuring 'trustworthiness' of the methods for data collection and analysis.[89] A key component for assessing trustworthiness is demonstrating the systematicity of the research through a transparent incorporation of reflexivity.[90] Therefore, in what follows I provide an overview of the data collection and analysis process and reflect on my own positionality.

---

[80] See McInerney-Lankford (2017), p. 48.

[81] Maxwell (2018), p. 19.

[82] Ibid., p. 26.

[83] Braun and Clarke (2013), p. 27.

[84] Jackson describes this as 'mind-world dualism'. See Jackson (2010), pp. 31 and 37.

[85] See Braun and Clarke (2013), p. 27.

[86] Ibid., p. 21.

[87] Ibid., pp. 30–31.

[88] See Schwartz-Shea and Yanow (2012), pp. 94–95; Braun and Clarke (2013), pp. 278–282.

[89] See Schwartz-Shea and Yanow (2012), pp. 99–107; Braun and Clarke (2013), p. 279.

[90] See Schwartz-Shea and Yanow (2012), p. 104.

1.2.2.1 Data Collection and Analysis

Why Mexico?

The present-day context of disappearances in Mexico is well-suited for studying the issue of disappearances committed by OCGs 'in reality' for several reasons: first, OCGs are said to be among the main perpetrators of disappearances in the country. Second, in recent years there has been much mobilisation and effort by the relatives of the disappeared and human rights NGOs in response to the disappearance crisis, which has, among others, led to the adoption of a specific and unique domestic legal framework that complements the IHRL framework. Finally, as a state party to virtually all international and regional human rights treaties, Mexico has received substantial scrutiny from regional and international human rights bodies and courts, offering country-specific case law and expert opinions on the context.

Data Collection

In order to contrast the internal legal question about disappearances committed OCGs and state responsibility for such crimes with the real-life experience of those who *use* international standards to advance the protection of human rights, I chose to interview human rights practitioners. My main interest was to understand how practitioners who professionally engage with the defence of human rights and have an expertise in the applicable legal frameworks, experienced a situation where human rights violations were committed within a legal 'grey' area. I define human rights *practitioners* as persons who engage in the defence of human rights in some form of professional capacity.[91] In this, I distinguish practitioners from government officials who are tasked (directly or indirectly) with the protection of human rights, as well as from victims of human rights violations who have become human rights defenders in the course of their struggle for truth and justice. Including the latter's perspective would undoubtedly have added richness to the research, but for reasons of scope and feasibility I focused only on one of these groups, considering that there are significant differences in their position vis-à-vis legal standards and victims. The semi-structured interviews were conducted during a 3 month fieldwork stay in Mexico in 2019, half of which was spent in Mexico City and the other half I spent one week each with five human rights NGOs based in the states of Chihuahua, Nuevo León, Coahuila, Jalisco, and Guerrero.[92]

---

[91] Note that there is no single understanding of what constitutes a human rights 'practitioner'. See, for example, Redhead and Turnbull (2011).

[92] The stays with the five NGOs allowed me to gain a better understanding of the environment in which they worked on a day-to-day basis. It also gave me flexibility to adjust the interviews to the NGO members' schedules, which are often very busy and can change with little notice. The NGOs I stayed with were Centro de Derechos Humanos de las Mujeres (CEDEHM), Ciudadanos en Apoyo a los Derechos Humanos (CADHAC), Centro para los Derechos Humanos Fray Juan de Larios,

The decision not to interview relatives was methodologically and ethically[93] grounded. Nonetheless, during my fieldwork I questioned the exclusion of relatives of the disappeared ('victims') who have become human rights activists and doubted whether I was excluding a crucial perspective.[94] However, when visiting the NGOs in states, I re-gained confidence in the decision not to interview 'las doñas' ('the ladies', which refers to the—mostly female—group of relatives) because this approach was perceived as respectful by my contact persons.[95] Nonetheless, I was able to meet and converse with some relatives during my fieldwork and I am very grateful to the relatives I spoke to (mothers and fathers, a sister, brothers, wives), who trusted me and shared part of their stories. Some of the relatives I spoke to, generally briefly, thanked me for 'voltearnos a ver' ('looking at us'). Their experiences are not reflected in this book because, for the reasons explained above, their stories were not 'data' for the analysis. Nevertheless, I want to acknowledge the struggle of these individuals, as well as all the relatives of the disappeared more generally. Their pain is unimaginable for those of us who have not experienced it, and their love for and determination to find their loved ones and find out what happened to them cannot be put into words. Thus, while this book focuses on the experiences of practitioners who accompany relatives in their struggle, it is in no way intended to minimise the importance of the experiences and struggles of relatives themselves.

Data Analysis

Abduction

The qualitative analysis conducted for this research follows an abductive logic of inquiry. Abduction lies between deductive and inductive reasoning in that it begins neither entirely from theory (deduction), nor from observations (induction), but rather departs from a 'puzzle' or surprise that the researcher encounters and wishes to further understand or explain.[96] Given the exploratory nature of this research and the aim to combine doctrinal and empirical approaches, an abductive logic of inquiry was most appropriate. Abductive research begins with a researcher's prior

---

Centro de Justicia para la Paz y el Desarrollo (CEPA), and Tlachinollan, Centro de Derechos Humanos de la Montaña.

[93] The decision not to speak to relatives unless it was absolutely necessary for methodological reasons, was taken by the team of the 'Digital Memories' project, on which I worked, during the first year of working. The two main reasons for this were the lack of preparation of the team members to speak to victims and the risk of re-traumatisation during interviews on the one hand, and the difficulty of 'returning' anything to the relatives that could in some way benefit them on the other hand, given the geographical distance.

[94] In addition, I doubted whether it was not more important from an ethical perspective to include relatives. Field diary notes, for example 27 July 2019 and 30 July 2019.

[95] Field diary notes, 16 August 2019.

[96] See Schwartz-Shea and Yanow (2012), pp. 27–34.

knowledge and certain puzzles that emerge from either the researcher's experience or theoretical literature.[97] The process of abduction then implies an 'iterative engagement between lived experience and theory'.[98] In this book, the empirical part of the research builds on the doctrinal legal research presented in Chaps. 2–4, and the 'puzzle' of non-state actors, and more specifically OCGs, as perpetrators of disappearances. My aim was to understand how, if at all, the open legal questions materialised in practice and posed challenges for human rights practitioners in their work. This was partially motivated by my previous research and work experience in and on Mexico, where I was 'puzzled' by the rare engagement in human rights scholarship and NGO work with OCGs as perpetrators of violations, despite their clear involvement.[99] Following this abductive logic, I used the doctrinal analysis, as well as prior knowledge about the Mexican context and information obtained during a first brief fieldwork stay, as a framework of reference for the design of the interview guide.[100] At the same time, maintaining an abductive logic of inquiry during the fieldwork and coding of the interviews required me to stay open to 'surprises' and unexpected information, which led me to re-think and adjust the research questions.

Thematic Analysis

Given the descriptive and non-explanatory purpose of the data analysis, I opted for a thematic analysis of the interview data that involves identifying the main themes relevant to the topic of study and possible relations between them. A thematic analysis, which consists in determining and analysing patterns ('themes') across a dataset,[101] differs from other forms of qualitative analytic methods in that it is not 'theoretically bounded' and therefore allows for a better understanding of the experience of participants.[102] To facilitate the analysis, I coded the interviews following Boyatzis' method of thematic analysis, which involves creating an initial coding scheme based on summaries of interviews, followed by continuous revision and refinement throughout the coding and analysis process.[103] After identifying the

[97] Ibid., pp. 29–31.

[98] Ibid., p. 40.

[99] For example, NGO reports generally mention the involvement of OCGs in such acts, as well as collusion, but then only focus on violations committed by state agents. The exception to this are the Open Society Justice Initiative's publications that focus on the commission of crimes against humanity in the Mexican context. See Open Society Foundations (2016); Open Society Justice Initiative (2018). Conversely, scholars working on violence and security in Mexico, generally only mention human rights violations committed by state agents in passing and focus principally on violence committed by OCGs.

[100] See Kennedy and Thornberg (2018), p. 55.

[101] Braun and Clarke (2013), p. 79.

[102] Ibid., p. 80.

[103] Boyatzis (1998), p. 45 ff. On the interconnection between analysis and writing, see Braun and Clarke (2013), Chap. 11.

main themes in the data, I turned to existing theoretical literature about human rights protection with a view to linking my analysis to theoretical discussions, and the overall research question (see Chap. 7). The literature selection was based on aspects that most 'struck' me in the data,[104] as well as my previous knowledge relating to questions of human rights compliance and evasion of accountability. I then connected the interview themes to selected theoretical perspectives in order to critically examine the protective capacity of IHRL in relation to victims of disappearances committed by OCGs, and to identify avenues for further research.[105] Based on the realist assumption that the participants' experiences represent a form of reality and that the participants themselves are the 'ultimate authority' on their own experiences, I also conducted a light 'member checking' exercise with a number of participants to 'validate' my analysis and ensure that it did not misrepresent their experiences.[106]

1.2.2.2 Reflexivity

Reflexivity in qualitative research acknowledges the researcher's own role in the production of 'knowledge' and emphasises the subjectivity of the research process.[107] To ensure this, I kept journals and wrote down any reflection about my own assumptions and characteristics that could have an impact on the data collection and analytic processes. Based on these notes, especially the diary entries written during fieldwork in 2019, in this section I discuss my own position vis-à-vis the participants and the 'surprises' I encountered while conducting the interviews, as

[104] These included the potentially different meanings of the 'state' and its perceived absence in certain parts of the country, which pointed me to scholarship on 'areas of limited statehood', and the apparent intentionality of failure of the Mexican state, which reminded me of theories of denial and evasion of accountability, as well as of the notion of 'state criminality' in international legal scholarship.

[105] At this point my approach differs from 'typical' abductive research as described in the literature because it was not my aim to generate an explanatory theory or hypothesis to explain a phenomenon. See, for example, Schwartz-Shea and Yanow (2012), pp. 27–28; Timmermans and Tavory (2012), p. 171; Kennedy and Thornberg (2018), p. 52.

[106] See ibid., pp. 106–107; Braun and Clarke (2013), pp. 284–285. There are, however, general limitations to the extent to which qualitative data can be 'validated', see ibid., pp. 282–285. Due to the COVID-19 pandemic-related travel restrictions, it was not possible to conduct the exercise as thoroughly as I had intended. Ultimately, I held two virtual sessions with 14 participants in June 2021. The response by those who participated was overall positive, and nobody expressed strong disagreement with any of the information presented. However, participants made several comments to add to my analysis, some of which were also based on developments since 2019, when the interviews were conducted. To reflect these comments, I added them in footnotes where appropriate.

[107] See Schwartz-Shea and Yanow (2012), pp. 100–104; Braun and Clarke (2013), pp. 36–37; Maxwell (2018), pp. 24–26. On the particular importance of reflexivity in legal and socio-legal research, see also Nouwen (2014), pp. 233–234.

well as how what I learned during fieldwork impacted my empirical research questions.[108]

Positionality

The interviews were 'expert' interviews in the sense that I selected the participants because of their professional experience and considered all of them to be 'experts' in their own field of work.[109] This means that I was interviewing 'up', rather than 'down',[110] although to me it felt like a more equal level, possibly due to my own previous experience of working in Mexican civil society.[111] Nonetheless, as a white, female German researcher based in Belgium, it is important to include a brief reflection on my own position vis-à-vis the participants in the research. As a non-Mexican who has lived in the country for several years, I am familiar with the country, culture, language, and ways of communication. Having previously worked in Mexican civil society allowed me to establish rapport with participants quickly in most instances. Yet, despite my knowledge about the country and the topic, there are aspects that I am not deeply familiar with, and these include the Mexican judicial and legal system more generally. While this knowledge gap did not manifest significantly during the interviews, there were occasions where I may not have fully understood what participants were referring to and may not have picked up on certain nuances. Moreover, given the heterogeneity of the Mexican context, and my own 'chilangocentrismo' ('Mexico-City bias'),[112] in some of the interviews that I conducted outside of Mexico City I might have not been able to fully understand or capture local specificities. On the few occasions that participants used a word or term that I did not know, I asked to clarify its meaning immediately.

[108] This section is principally based on my 'field diary' or 'field notes' and I omit references to the specific entry dates.

[109] On expert interviews, see, for example, Bogner et al. (2018). The authors define experts as 'people who possess specific knowledge that relates to a clearly demarcated range of problems'. Ibid., p. 655.

[110] On constellations in interviews and potential implications, see ibid., pp. 600–661.

[111] There were only three interviews during which I felt sightly patronised by the (male) participants, and only in one interview did the participant start off by suggesting what he would talk to me about. I let him speak and then followed up with my own questions and, fortunately, we spoke for quite a while, which allowed me to ask most of the questions.

[112] This is a term that came up in a few interviews when discussing the differences between NGOs based in Mexico City and those in states. 'Chilango' is a colloquial term to describe everything related to Mexico City. Therefore 'chilangocentrismo' refers to a Mexico City-perspective or bias that perhaps fails to consider the realities outside of the capital.

Assumptions and 'Surprises'

Two main frameworks of reference guided my empirical work, which influenced both the design of the interview topic guide and my expectations towards what I would hear.[113] The first derived from the first part of this book, which is based on doctrinal legal research. Having commenced my research by examining the determination of international responsibility of the state for disappearances committed by OCGs and the issues and questions related to this matter from a theoretical perspective, one of my assumptions going into field research was that some of these questions would inevitably come up in reality. My empirical research questions were principally motivated by my aim to bridge the gap between legal and empirical human rights scholarship in contrasting law and reality in a single piece of research. Yet, while my empirical research—and the interview guide—were based on the legal analysis, due to my interdisciplinary academic human rights background I was also already familiar with what Risse terms the 'mainstream' in human rights research relating to compliance in Political Science and International Relations scholarship.[114] Much of this scholarship focuses on the interplay between local and international human rights actors, who are able to jointly exert pressure on governments to change practices and enhance compliance with international human rights norms. What initially sparked my research interest was how the existence of grey areas in the human rights norms and standards themselves would impact on these processes.

Thus, familiar with theories about the workings of transnational human rights advocacy based on such 'mainstream' research, I assumed that it could be an issue for human rights NGOs to work on cases that clearly involved only non-state actors (in the Mexican case OCGs) and that they might purposefully select other cases to litigate because of the direct involvement of state actors in these.[115] This assumption was partially based on the fact that reports issued by NGOs on the topic of disappearances in Mexico almost always describe in much more detail cases of enforced disappearances (or other types of human rights violations, such as extrajudicial executions) where state actors were involved. Secondly, prior to embarking on this research, I lived in Mexico City and worked in Mexican civil society. While the issues I worked on did not include disappearances directly, they were connected. This meant that I had certain assumptions, based on my work experience, of how NGOs worked strategically and selected topics and cases, and was even concerned that I would receive information that could potentially be used against NGOs. However, I barely received any information of this nature, which, in hindsight,

---

[113] On the impossibility of approaching research as a 'blank slate' with no prior knowledge, see Schwartz-Shea and Yanow (2012), p. 38.

[114] See Risse (2017), p. 135. This 'mainstream' includes the the 'boomerang effect' proposed by Keck and Sikking and the 'spiral model of human rights' proposed by Risse, Ropp and Sikkink. Ibid., p. 137.

[115] For an argument in this vein and the challenges of 'framing' the situation in Mexico as a human rights issue, see Anaya Muñoz (2013).

most likely relates to the reality of impunity in which most participants work where the vast majority of cases are not a judicial stage and only very few organisations actually engage in strategic litigation.

In this sense, when I was in Mexico and began conducting interviews, and especially when I started to travel and spend time with NGOs outside of Mexico City, I soon realised that my assumptions were quite removed from reality. While there are indeed some NGOs based in Mexico City who litigate cases before regional and international mechanisms and therefore select cases strategically depending on the structural changes their resolution might achieve,[116] the reality in the states, and for some Mexico City-based NGOs, is quite different: rather than strategically choosing cases to illustrate deficiencies in human rights protection, human rights NGOs based in states with high numbers of disappearances, committed by both state and non-state actors, have to tend to everyday urgencies and try different legal and non-legal routes to obtain responses from the state to the pressing demands and needs of victims. In fact, international legal questions seemed far away in this reality, even though international legal standards and mechanisms do play a role in the legal aspect of the NGOs' work.[117] This is linked to the prevailing impunity in Mexico, which applies irrespectively of the nature of a particular crime or human rights violation. This is clearly evidenced by the small number of convictions for disappearances and prevalence of 'generalised' impunity.[118] Quite probably, this is also the reason why I sometimes got either bemused or very short reactions when I asked about reparations during interviews. Despite my prior awareness of the generalised nature of impunity in Mexico, I had not made the connection between the lack of judicial advances and the relevance (or irrelevance) of the international legal questions which I examine in the first part of the book. Consequently, my fieldwork highlighted a link between systemic impunity and the (ir-)relevance of international legal questions. Moreover, it showed the differences in the work and experiences of participants based on their location in Mexico City or in one of the states, which I further reflect on in Chap. 6. These differences struck me during fieldwork because I had previously only spoken to, and therefore gotten an impression of the reality of, NGOs and experts based in Mexico City. These realisations led me to adjust the research focus and the interview guide, to which I added a question about the differences in work when interviewing participants based in states.

---

[116] On strategic litigation, see Gutiérrez Contreras et al. (2012).

[117] For example, the CEDEHM in Chihuahua litigated the case of *Alvarado Espinoza and others v Mexico* before the IACtHR (*Case of Alvarado Espinoza and others*) and Tlachinollan litigated the case of *Rosendo Cantú et al v Mexico* [2010] Inter-American Court of Human Rights Series C No. 216. Additionally, the Centro Diocesano de Derechos Humanos Fray Juan de Larios has been actively involved in submitting communications to the International Criminal Court (ICC).

[118] See Serrano (2024).

1.3 Structure of the Book

This book is structured as follows: the first part of the book (Chaps. 2–4) presents the doctrinal legal analysis. In Chap. 2, I examine states' obligations in relation to disappearances committed by non-state actors under IHRL. For this, I explore both obligations under general human rights instruments, as well as under the ICPPED. In Chap. 3, I analyse the determination of state responsibility in relation to disappearances committed by non-state actors, based on the rules of state responsibility enshrined in the Articles on Responsibility of States for Internationally Wrongful Acts (ARSIWA).[119] Moreover, I examine how state responsibility has been determined by regional and international human rights bodies in cases involving non-state actors as perpetrators of disappearances and/or other violations of the right to life. In this, I focus mainly on the jurisprudence of the European Court of Human Rights (ECtHR) and the Inter-American Court of Human Rights (IACtHR) and the issue of responsibility for a failure to prevent. Drawing on the findings of Chaps. 2 and 3, in Chap. 4 I specifically address the issue of disappearances committed by OCGs and apply the analysis of the previous chapters to this matter. Furthermore, I introduce the United Nations Convention against Transnational Organised Crime (UNTOC) and its Protocols on Human Trafficking and Smuggling,[120] and the United Nations Convention against Corruption (UNCAC)[121] as instruments of *lex specialis* to further specify state obligations in relation to disappearances committed by OCGs.

The second part of the book (Chaps. 5–7) presents the findings of the study on the issue of disappearances in Mexico in the context of the 'war on drugs'. First, in Chap. 5 I introduce the phenomenon of disappearances in Mexico and provide a brief overview of its main characteristics, including victims, perpetrators, and the country's ongoing forensic crisis. I also present the Mexican legal framework that deals with disappearances and the rights of victims, as well as, based on the findings from Chaps. 2–4, some of the questions arising specifically in the Mexican context from an international law perspective. Having thus introduced the Mexican context in Chap. 5, in Chap. 6 I present the analysis of experiences of human rights practitioners working on the issue of disappearances in Mexico based on the interviews conducted for this research. To this end, I describe three main, interrelated themes that I identified across the interviews: uncertainty, pragmatism, and frustration. Each theme and corresponding sub-themes are described in detail and illustrated with quotes from the interviews. The analysis indicates that the point at

---

[119] UN General Assembly (2002) Articles on Responsibility of States for Internationally Wrongful Acts. UN Doc. A/RES/56/83.

[120] United Nations Convention against Transnational Organized Crime 2000 (2225 UNTS 209); Protocol to Prevent, Suppress and Punish Trafficking in Persons, Especially Women and Children, supplementing the United Nations Convention against Transnational Organized Crime 2000 (2237 UNTS 319); Protocol Against the Smuggling of Migrants by Land, Sea and Air, supplementing the United Nations Convention Against Transnational Organized Crime 2000 (2241 UNTS 507).

[121] United Nations Convention against Corruption 2003 (2349 UNTS 41).

which the three themes converge is the overall protection failure of the Mexican state. Based on this finding, in Chap. 7 I explore how the experiences of human rights practitioners, and the notion of an overall protection failure of the state, can be drawn on to think critically about the protective ability of IHRL in relation to disappearances committed by OCGs. For this, I connect the themes to analytic perspectives from human rights compliance, sociological and legal scholarship. Despite the limitations of purely legal solutions to structural issues and in view of the continued importance of international legal standards as tools for human rights work on the ground, the standards need to be able to capture reality. In that sense, new concepts may need to be developed to capture overall protection failure. Re-visiting the notion of state criminality and exploring the concepts of 'state gross negligence' or 'state recklessness' may offer additional pathways for achieving this. In the Conclusion (Chap. 8) I bring together the findings from both parts of the book and reflect on avenues for further research.

1.4 Notes on Terminology

Throughout the book, I will use some key terms that can have multiple meanings. To avoid confusion, in this section I outline how I use these terms.

1.4.1 'Disappearances'

I consider 'enforced disappearances' and 'disappearances committed by non-state actors' (or by OCGs) as having different legal meanings. Throughout the book I use the phrase 'disappearances committed by non-state actors' as a means of distinguishing these from *enforced* disappearances. By using this phrase, I only refer to those disappearances where no 'authorization, support or acquiescence' by the state can be established and that would fall within Article 3 ICPPED. I consider victims of both crimes as 'disappeared'. While the use of the same word may create some confusion, this is in line with terminology used by human rights bodies, including the CED and the Inter-American Court of Human Rights.[122] As illustrated by the CED in the report on its visit to Iraq, there is a difference between victims of disappearances and persons who have gone 'missing'.[123] According to the

[122] *Case of González et al ("Cotton Field") v Mexico* [2009] Inter-American Court of Human Rights Serie C No. 205, para 2. The *Cotton Field* case dealt with the 'disappearance and subsequent death' of three women, possibly by members of an organised criminal group, and the failure to protect of the Mexican state. See also CED (2023) General Comment No. 1 on Enforced Disappearance in the Context of Migration. UN Doc. CED/C/GC/1, para. 4.

[123] CED (2023) Report of the Committee on Enforced Disappearances on its visit to Iraq: Information on the visit and findings. UN Doc. CED/C/IRQ/VR/1 (Findings), para. 51.

International Committee of the Red Cross, a '[m]issing person is a person whose whereabouts are unknown to his/her relatives and/or who, on the basis of reliable information, has been reported missing in accordance with the national legislation in connection with an international or non-international armed conflict, a situation of internal violence or disturbances, natural catastrophes or any other situation that may require the intervention of a competent State authority.'[124] This means that while the categories of 'missing' and 'disappeared' persons can overlap, they are nevertheless distinct because for a person to be considered as 'missing' no criminal activity is required. However, there are instances where 'missing' persons might also be a victim of a disappearance.[125]

1.4.2 *'Human Rights Violations'*

The term 'human rights violations' will be used throughout the book to refer also to acts committed by non-state actors. It thereby refers to the *de facto* violation of human rights and is not meant to imply that such acts are—or should be—considered human rights violations in a legal sense. The use of this terminology is in line with that used by the Inter-American Court.[126]

1.4.3 *Organised Criminal Group*

For the purpose of this research, I use the definition of OCG that is contained in the UNTOC:

> a structured group of three or more persons, existing for a period of time and acting in concert with the aim of committing one or more serious crimes or offences established in accordance with this Convention, in order to obtain, directly or indirectly, a financial or other material benefit.[127]

---

[124] Article 2.1 International Committee of the Red Cross (2009) Guiding Principles / Model Law on the Missing. https://www.icrc.org/en/document/guiding-principles-model-law-missing-model-law. Accessed 24 November 2024.

[125] See also Citroni (2016), pp. 17–18; Baranowska (2017), pp. 712–713. For a discussion of the use of terminology in relation to migrants, see Sarkin (2017), p. 4; Baranowska (2020); CED (2023) General Comment No. 1 on Enforced Disappearance in the Context of Migration. UN Doc. CED/C/GC/1, para. 4.

[126] 'An illegal act *which violates human rights* and which is initially not directly imputable to a State [...]'. Emphasis added. *Case of Velásquez-Rodríguez v Honduras (Merits)* [1988] Inter-American Court of Human Rights Ser. C No. 4, para. 172.

[127] Article 2(a) UNTOC.

This definition is very broad, which means that it can encompass many different types of criminal organisations.[128] Moreover, scholarship on organised crime more generally underscores the wide diversity of organisations that can be considered as engaging in 'organised crime', which is in itself a contested concept with no universally agreed upon definition.[129] The implication for this research is that the general argument developed in relation to OCGs may not be equally applicable to all contexts due to existing differences among criminal groups. At the same time, using this definition also means that groups that do not fit this definition, but are nevertheless involved in the commission of disappearances, are excluded from the argument developed in this book. This does not mean, however, that the argument could not be equally applicable to such groups. An example are gangs, which do not necessarily meet the definition of OCG contained in Article 2 UNTOC because they do not necessarily operate for the purpose of obtaining a financial or material benefit, and because some gangs might not be sufficiently 'structured'.[130] Nonetheless, for the purpose of developing the argument, using the UNTOC definition as a basis and not engaging in depth with the (conceptual) issues that surround it, or the notion of 'organised crime' more generally, avoids some of the complexities inherent to any scholarly endeavour in the realm of organised crime.[131]

1.4.4 Impunity

Throughout the book, I occasionally refer to impunity. While cognisant of the complexity of the notion of impunity,[132] I use the term in its legal sense, as defined in the Principles for the Protection and Promotion of Human Rights through Action to Combat Impunity (Impunity Principles):

> [...] the impossibility, *de jure* or *de facto*, of bringing the perpetrators of violations to account - whether in criminal, civil, administrative or disciplinary proceedings - since they are not subject to any inquiry that might lead to their being accused, arrested, tried and, if found guilty, sentenced to appropriate penalties, and to making reparations to their victims.[133]

---

[128] See Fijnaut and Paoli (2008), paras 5–6. Indeed, the definition contained in the UNTOC has been criticised for being both too broad and to narrow at the same time. See Peterke and Wolf (2016), p. 382.

[129] For a collection of different definitions of organised crime, see the compilation of definitions by Klaus von Lampe: http://www.organized-crime.de/organizedcrimedefinitions.htm. Accessed 24 November 2024.

[130] For a discussion on gangs and organised crime, see Decker and Pyrooz (2014).

[131] For discussions on conducting research on organised crime, see, for example, Hobbs and Antonopoulos (2014); Windle and Silke (2019).

[132] For a socio-legal conceptualisation of impunity, see, for example, Umaña (2017). Umaña holds that '[i]mpunity is more easily recognised or proclaimed than defined and there is not a consistent effort of reflection and clarification of this issue.' Ibid., p. 227.

[133] See Commission on Human Rights (2005) Report of the Independent Expert to Update the Set of Principles to Combat Impunity, Diane Orentlicher: Updated Set of Principles for the Protection and Promotion of Human Rights through Action to Combat Impunity. UN Doc. E/CN.4/2005/102/Add.1, para. 6.

While *de jure* impunity refers to the existence of legislative impediments to carrying out prosecutions, such as amnesties, *de facto* impunity is understood as encompassing not just the absence of convictions and sanctioning of perpetrators of crimes, but also the failure to take adequate investigative steps to achieve such convictions, which can have multiple causes.[134] The consequences of impunity are manifold and can include the violations of human rights (such as the right to access to justice) and effectively prevent victims from obtaining reparations.[135] At the same time, the absence of punishment is often considered as a factor that perpetuates the commission of crimes.[136] In the Mexican context specifically, impunity refers principally, though not exclusively, to *de facto* impunity, which encompasses the under-reporting of crimes, a lack of effective investigations, and a lack of criminal convictions for perpetrators of crimes. Notably, available data on impunity in Mexico refer not only to impunity for grave human rights violations, but to all types of crimes.[137]

References

Aguayo S (2015) De Tlatelolco a Ayotzinapa: las violencias del Estado, Primera edición. Ediciones Proceso, Mexico City

Alston P (ed) (2005) Non-state actors and human rights. Oxford University Press, Oxford [England]; New York

Ambos K, Böhm ML (2009) La Desaparición Forzada de Personas como Tipo Penal Autónomo: Análisis comparativo-internacional y propuesta legislativa. In: Ambos K (ed) Desaparición Forzada de Personas: Análisis Comparado e Internacional. Deutsche Gesellschaft fürTechnische Zusammenarbeit (GTZ), Bogotá, pp 195–255

Anaya Muñoz A (2013) Non-state actors as violators in Mexico: a hard case for global human rights norms. In: Brysk A (ed) The politics of the globalization of law: getting from rights to justice. Routledge, Oxon, New York, pp 180–198

Anderson K (2006) How effective is the International Convention for the Protection of All Persons from Enforced Disappearance likely to be in holding individuals criminally responsible for acts of enforced disappearance. Melb J Int Law 7:245–277

Andreassen B-A, Sano H-O, Mclnerney-Lankford S (eds) (2017) Research methods in human rights: a handbook. Edward Elgar Publishing, Cheltenham, UK

Ansolabehere K, Payne L, Frey B (eds) (2021) Disappearances in the post-transition era in Latin America. Oxford University Press, Oxford, New York

---

[134] See Calvet Martínez (2016), pp. 148–152.

[135] Ibid., p. 146.

[136] See Human Rights Committee (2004) General Comment No. 31: The Nature of the General Legal Obligation Imposed on States Parties to the Covenant. UN Doc. CCPR/C/21/Rev.1/Add. 13, para. 18; Calvet Martínez (2015), p. 154.

[137] For a general overview on impunity in Mexico, see, for example, https://www.impunidadcero.org/index.php. Accessed 24 November 2024. On impunity in relation to enforced disappearances and other serious human rights violations, see, for example, Guevara Bermúdez and Chávez Vargas (2018); fidh and i(dh)eas (2020).

Baade B, Mührel L, Petrov AO (eds) (2018) International humanitarian law in areas of limited statehood: adaptable and legitimate or rigid and unreasonable? 1st edn. Nomos, Baden-Baden
Baranowska G (2017) Advances and progress in the obligation to return the remains of missing and forcibly disappeared persons. Int Rev Red Cross 99:709–733. https://doi.org/10.1017/S181638311800036X
Baranowska G (2020) Disappeared migrants and refugees: the relevance of the International Convention on Enforced Disappearance in their search and protection. Deutsches Institut für Menschenrechte, Berlin
Baranowska G (2021) Rights of families of disappeared persons: how international bodies address the needs of families of disappeared persons in Europe, 1st edn. Intersentia, Cambridge Antwerp Chicago
BBC Mundo (2014) Masivas protestas en México por desaparición de estudiantes. In: BBC News Mundo. https://www.bbc.com/mundo/noticias/2014/10/141009_mexico_protestas_estudiantes_desaparecidos_iguala_ao. Accessed 26 Nov 2024
Besson S (2021) La due diligence en droit international. Brill Nijhoff, Leiden
Bogner A, Littig B, Menz W (2018) Generating qualitative data with experts and elites. In: Flick U (ed) The SAGE handbook of qualitative data collection. SAGE Publications, London, pp 652–665
Börzel TA, Draude A, Risse T (2018) The Oxford handbook of governance and limited statehood. Oxford University Press, Oxford
Boyatzis RE (1998) Transforming qualitative information: thematic analysis and code development. SAGE Publications
Braun V, Clarke V (2013) Successful qualitative research: a practical guide for beginners. SAGE Publications
Brems E (2009) Methods in legal human rights research. In: Coomans F, Grünfeld F, Kamminga MT (eds) Methods of human rights research. Intersentia, Antwerp; Portland, Or, pp 77–90
CADHAC (Ciudadanos en Apoyo a los Derechos Humanos) (2014) Desaparición de personas en Nuevo León. Sistematización de experiencias en búsqueda de la justicia y la verdad. 1st edn. Monterrey
Calvet Martínez E (2015) Desapariciones forzadas y justicia transicional. La búsqueda de respuestas a través del derecho a la verdad, a la justicia y a la reparación. Dissertation, Universitat de Barcelona
Calvet Martínez E (2016) Impunidad. Eunomía Revista en Cultura de la Legalidad 10:144–157
Calvet Martínez E (2018) Desapariciones forzadas y justicia transitorial. Tirant lo Blanch, Valencia
Cançado Trindade AA (2012) Enforced disappearances of persons as a violation of jus cogens: the contribution of the jurisprudence of the Inter-American Court of Human Rights. Nord J Int Law 81:507–536. https://doi.org/10.1163/15718107-08104005
Carcach C, Artola E (2016) Disappeared persons and homicide in El Salvador. Crime Sci 5:13. https://doi.org/10.1186/s40163-016-0061-x
Citroni G (2012) When is it enough? Enforced disappearance and the “temporal element”. Droits fondamentaux 11
Citroni G (2014) Enforced disappearance: challenges to accountability under international law: Foreword. J Int Crim Justice 12:731–734. https://doi.org/10.1093/jicj/mqu055
Citroni G (2016) Missing persons and victims of enforced disappearance in Europe. Issue Paper. Council of Europe, France
Clapham A (2006) Human rights obligations of non-state actors in conflict situations. Int Rev Red Cross 88:491–523
Clapham A (ed) (2013) Human rights and non-state actors. Edward Elgar Pub, Cheltenham, UK
Clapham A (2014) Focusing on armed non-state actors. In: Gaeta P, Clapham A, Haeck T, Priddy P (eds) The Oxford handbook of international law in armed conflict. Oxford University Press, New York

Clapham A (2019) Human rights obligations for non-state actors: where are we now? In: Lafontaine F, Larocque F (eds) Doing peace the rights way: essays in international law and relations in honour of Louise Arbour. Intersentia, Cambridge, pp 11–36

Coomans F, Grünfeld F, Kamminga MT (eds) (2009) Methods of human rights research. Intersentia, Antwerp; Portland, OR

Coomans F, Grünfeld F, Kamminga MT (2010) Methods of human rights research: a primer. Hum Rights Q 32:179–186

De Brabandere E (2009) Non-state actors, state-centrism and human rights obligations. Leiden J Int Law 22:191–209. https://doi.org/10.1017/S0922156508005700

de Frouville O (2021) Criminalizing or trivializing enforced disappearances? The issue of 'non-state actors'. In: de Frouville O, Sturma P (eds) La pénalisation des droits de l'homme. Pedone, Paris

de Schutter O (ed) (2006) Transnational corporations and human rights. Hart Publishing, London

de Vecchi Gerli M (2018) ¡Vivxs lxs Queremos! The Battles for Memory around the Disappeared in Mexico. Doctoral Dissertation, University College London

Decker SH, Pyrooz DC (2014) Gangs: another form of organized crime? In: Paoli L (ed) The Oxford handbook on organized crime. Oxford University Press, pp 270–287

Decoeur H (2018) Confronting the shadow state: an international law perspective on state organized crime. Oxford University Press, Oxford, New York

Deva S, Bilchitz D (eds) (2013) Human rights obligations of business: beyond the corporate responsibility to respect? Cambridge University Press, Cambridge

Dudai R, McEvoy K (2012) Thinking critically about armed groups and human rights praxis. J Hum Rights Pract 4:1–29. https://doi.org/10.1093/jhuman/hus014

Dulitzky AE (2019) The Latin-American flavor of enforced disappearances. Chic J Int Law 19:423–489

fidh (International Federation for Human Rights), I(dh)eas (2020) Situation of impunity in Mexico. Report No. 750a. https://www.idheas.org.mx/wp-content/uploads/2020/05/Mexique750ang-1.pdf. Accessed 8 Nov 2024

Fijnaut C, Paoli L (2008) Transnational organized crime. Max Planck Encyclopedia of Public International Law

Fischer AR, Duhaime B (2024) "The Purloined Letter": migrant disappearances, systematic impunity, and states' risk awareness. Can Yearb Int Law/Annuaire canadien de droit international:1–52. https://doi.org/10.1017/cyl.2024.4

Forsythe DP (2009) Human rights studies: on the dangers of legalistic assumptions. In: Coomans F, Grünfeld F, Kamminga MT (eds) Methods of human rights research. Intersentia, Antwerp; Portland, OR, pp 59–76

Fortin K, Clapham A (2017) The accountability of armed groups under human rights law. Oxford University Press, Oxford, New York

Freeman M, Casij Peña M (2023) Negotiating with organized crime groups: questions of law, policy and imagination. Int Rev Red Cross 105:638–651. https://doi.org/10.1017/S1816383122000649

Frey BA (2009) Los Desaparecidos: the Latin American experience as a narrative framework for the international norm against forced disappearances. In: Forcinito A, Marrero-Fente R, McDonough K (eds) Human rights in Latin American and Iberian cultures. pp 52–72

Gallagher AT (2010) The international law of human trafficking. Cambridge University Press, Cambridge UK; New York

Genovese C, van der Wilt HG (2014) Fighting impunity of enforced disappearances through a regional model. Amsterdam Law Forum 6:4–22

Gibler J (2023) Cómo el gobierno dinamitó la investigación del caso Ayotzinapa. Quinto Elemento Lab. In: Quinto Elemento Lab. https://quintoelab.org/project/ayotzinapa-gobierno-instruccion-investigacion-iguala-normalistas. Accessed 6 Nov 2024

GIEI (Grupo Interdisciplinario de Expertos Independientes) (2015) Informe Ayotzinapa: Investigación y primeras conclusiones de las desapariciones y homicidios de los normalistas

de Ayotzinapa – Resumen. https://prensagieiayotzi.wixsite.com/giei-ayotzinapa/informe-. Accessed 22 Nov 2024
GIEI (2023) Informe Ayotzinapa VI: Hallazgos, avances, obstáculos y pendientes. https://comisionayotzinapa.segob.gob.mx/work/models/Comision_para_la_Verdad/Documentos/pdf/Informe_Ayotzinapa_VI.pdf. Accessed 26 Nov 2024
Global Initiative Against Transnational Organized Crime (2020) Disappearances through organized crime. https://resiliencefund.globalinitiative.net/wp-content/uploads/2020/09/disappearances_OC_infographic.pdf. Accessed 30 Oct 2024
Guevara Bermúdez JA, Chávez Vargas LG (2018) La impunidad en el contexto de la desaparición forzada en México = Impunity in the context of enforced disappearance in Mexico. Eunomía Revista en Cultura de la Legalidad:162–174. https://doi.org/10.20318/eunomia.2018.4161
Gutiérrez Contreras JC, Cantú Martínez S, Rincón Covelli T (2012) Litigio Estratégico en Derechos Humanos: Modelo para armar. Comisión Mexicana de Defensa y Promoción de los Derechos Humanos, Mexico City
Hamid L, Wouters J (2021a) De facto regimes in areas of limited statehood and the international rule of law. In: Hamid L, Wouters J (eds) Rule of law and areas of limited statehood. Edward Elgar Publishing, Cheltenham, UK, pp 47–72
Hamid L, Wouters J (eds) (2021b) Rule of law and areas of limited statehood: domestic and international dimensions. Edward Elgar Publishing, Cheltenham
Hauck P, Peterke S (eds) (2016) International law and transnational organised crime. Oxford University Press, Oxford, New York
Hobbs D, Antonopoulos GA (2014) How to research organized crime. In: Paoli L (ed) The Oxford handbook of organized crime. Oxford University Press, Oxford; New York, pp 96–117
Hoppe C (2008) Passing the buck: state responsibility for private military companies symposium: private military contractors and international law. Eur J Int Law 19:989–1014
Huhle R (2013) Non-state actors of enforced disappearance and the UN Convention for the Protection of All Persons from Enforced Disappearance. HuV-I/JILPAC 26:21–26
Huhle R (2014) Noche y niebla. Mito significado. In: Casado M, López Ortega JJ (eds) Desapariciones forzadas de niños en Europa y Latinoamérica: del convenio de la ONU a las búsquedas a través del ADN. Publicacions i Edicions de la Universitat de Barcelona, Barcelona, pp 251–278
Human Rights Watch (2024) "We will find you": a global look at how governments repress nationals abroad. Human Rights Watch
ICRC (International Committee of the Red Cross) (2023) Organized crime. Int Rev Red Cross 105
Jackson PT (2010) The conduct of inquiry in international relations: philosophy of science and its implications for the study of world politics. Routledge, London
Kälin W, Künzli J (2009) The law of international human rights protection. Oxford University Press, Oxford
Kalmanovitz P (2023) Can criminal organizations be non State parties to armed conflict? Int Rev Red Cross 105:618–636. https://doi.org/10.1017/S1816383122000510
Kennedy BL, Thornberg R (2018) Deduction, induction, and abduction. In: Flick U (ed) The SAGE handbook of qualitative data collection. SAGE Publications, London, pp 49–64
Klabbers J (2009) (I Can't Get No) recognition: subjects doctrine and the emergence of non-state actors. In: Bianchi A (ed) Non-state actors and international law. Ashgate, Surrey, Burlington (VT), pp 37–56
Krieger H, Peters A, Kreuzer L (2020) Due diligence in the international legal order. Oxford University Press, Oxford
Lambin J (2018) Mexico: armed gang violence sliding into armed conflict? In: Bellal A (ed) The War Report: Armed Conflicts in 2017. Geneva Academy of International Humanitarian Law and Human Rights, Geneva, pp 83–91
Langford M (2017) Interdisciplinarity and multimethod research. In: Andreassen B, Sano H-O, McInerney-Lankford S (eds) Research methods in human rights. Edward Elgar Publishing, Cheltenham, pp 161–191

Letschert R, Van Dijk J (eds) (2011) The new faces of victimhood. Springer, Dordrecht
Mackenzie-Gray Scott R (2022) State responsibility for non-state actors: past, present and prospects for the future. Hart Publishing, Bloomsbury Publishing Plc, Oxford, UK
Maxwell JA (2018) Collecting qualitative data: a realist approach. In: Flick U (ed) The SAGE handbook of qualitative data collection. SAGE Publications, London, pp 19–31
McCorquodale R (2010) Non-state actors and International Human Rights Law. In: Joseph S, McBeth A (eds) Research handbook on International Human Rights Law. Edward Elgar, Cheltenham, pp 97–114
McGregor L (2014) Applying the definition of torture to the acts of non-state actors: the case of trafficking in human beings. Hum Rights Q 36:210–241. https://doi.org/10.1353/hrq.2014.0000
McInerney-Lankford S (2017) Legal methodologies and human rights research: challenges and opportunities. In: Andreassen B, Sano H-O, McInerney-Lankford S (eds) Research methods in human rights. Edward Elgar Publishing, pp 38–67
Monnheimer M (2021) Due diligence obligations in International Human Rights Law. Cambridge University Press, Cambridge
Muggah R (2023) Organized crime in armed conflicts and other situations of violence. Int Rev Red Cross 105:569–574. https://doi.org/10.1017/S1816383123000036
Murray D (2016) Human rights obligations of non-state armed groups. Hart Publishing, Oxford
Noortmann M, Reinisch A, Ryngaert C (eds) (2015) Non-state actors in international law. Hart Publishing, Oxford; Portland (OR)
Nouwen SMH (2014) 'As You Set out for Ithaka': practical, epistemological, ethical, and existential questions about socio-legal empirical research in conflict. Leiden J Int Law 27:227–260. https://doi.org/10.1017/S092215651300071X
Obokata T (2005) Smuggling of human beings from a human rights perspective: obligations of non-state and state actors under International Human Rights Law. Int J Refug Law 17:394–415. https://doi.org/10.1093/ijrl/eei013
Obokata T (2006) Trafficking of human beings from a human rights perspective: towards a more holistic approach. Martinus Nijhoff Publishers, Leiden
Obokata T (2010) Transnational organised crime in international law. Hart Publishing, Oxford; Portland (OR)
Office of the High Commissioner for Human Rights (OHCHR) (2014) Human Rights and Human Trafficking. Fact Sheet No. 36. United Nations, New York, Geneva
OHCHR (2021) Joint Statement by independent United Nations human rights experts on human rights responsibilities of armed non-State actors. United Nations High Commissioner for Human Rights Press Release. https://www.ohchr.org/en/press-releases/2021/02/joint-statement-independent-united-nations-human-rights-experts-human-rights?LangID=E&NewsID=26797. Accessed 16 Nov 2024
OHCHR (2023) Enforced Disappearances. Fact Sheet No. 6, Rev. 4. United Nations, New York, Geneva
Olsen TD (2023) Seeking justice: access to remedy for corporate human rights abuse. Cambridge University Press, Cambridge
Open Society Foundations (2016) Undeniable atrocities: confronting crimes against humanity in Mexico. Open Society Foundations, New York
Open Society Justice Initiative (2018) Corruption that kills: why Mexico needs an international mechanism to combat impunity. Open Society Foundations, New York
Ott L (2011) Enforced disappearance in international law. Intersentia, Antwerpen
Padin JF (2023) Opening Pandora's Box: the case of Mexico and the threshold of non-international armed conflicts. Int Rev Red Cross 105:772–794. https://doi.org/10.1017/S1816383122000571
Payne CL, Abouharb MR (2016) The International Covenant on Civil and Political Rights and the strategic shift to forced disappearance. J Hum Rights 15:163–188. https://doi.org/10.1080/14754835.2015.1103158

Pellegrini S (2024) Viv Ansanm: living together, fighting united – the alliance reshaping Haiti's gangland. In: ACLED. https://acleddata.com/2024/10/16/viv-ansanm-living-together-fighting-united-the-alliance-reshaping-haitis-gangland/. Accessed 26 Nov 2024

Pérez Solla MF (2006) Enforced disappearances in international human rights. McFarland, Jefferson

Pervou I (2023) The right not to be subjected to enforced disappearance: concept, content and scope, 1st edn. Springer Nature Switzerland, Cham

Peterke S, Wolf J (2016) International humanitarian law and transnational organised crime. In: Hauck P, Peterke S (eds) International law and transnational organised crime. Oxford University Press, Oxford, New York, pp 381–405

Redaelli C, Arévalo C (2023) Targeting drug lords: challenges to IHL between *lege lata* and *lege ferenda*. Int Rev Red Cross 105:652–673. https://doi.org/10.1017/S1816383123000024

Redhead R, Turnbull N (2011) Towards a study of human rights practitioners. Hum Rights Rev 12: 173–189. https://doi.org/10.1007/s12142-010-0180-9

Risse T (2017) Human rights in areas of limited statehood: from the spiral model to localization and translation. In: Snyder J, Vinjamuri L, Hopgood S (eds) Human rights futures. Cambridge University Press, Cambridge, pp 135–158

Sánchez Valdés VM, Pérez Aguirre M, Verástegui González J (2018) Formación y Desarrollo de los Colectivos de Búsqueda de Personas Desaparecidas en Coahuila: Lecciones Para el Futuro. El Colegio de Mexico, Mexico City

Sano H-O, Thelle H (2009) The need for evidence-based human rights research. In: Coomans F, Grünfeld F, Kamminga MT (eds) Methods of human rights research. Intersentia, Antwerp; Portland, OR, pp 91–110

Sarkin J (2012) Why the prohibition of enforced disappearance has attained jus cogens status in international law. Nord J Int Law 81:537–584. https://doi.org/10.1163/15718107-08104006

Sarkin J (2013) Putting in place processes and mechanisms to prevent and eradicate enforced disappearances around the world. S Afr Yearb Int Law 38:20–48

Sarkin J (2017) Respecting and protecting the lives of migrants and refugees: the need for a human rights approach to save lives and find missing persons. Int J Hum Rights:1–30. https://doi.org/10.1080/13642987.2017.1354572

Sarkin J, Baranowska G (2018) Why enforced disappearances are perpetrated against groups as state policy: overlaps and interconnections between disappearances and genocide. Católica Law Rev 2:11–42

Sassòli M (2010) Taking armed groups seriously: ways to improve their compliance with international humanitarian law. J Int Humanit Leg Stud 1:5–51. https://doi.org/10.1163/187815210X12766020139767

Schwartz-Shea P, Yanow D (2012) Interpretive research design: concepts and processes. Routledge, New York, NY

Scovazzi T, Citroni G (2007) The struggle against enforced disappearance and the 2007 United Nations Convention. Nijhoff, Leiden

Serrano S (2024) Hacia la responsabilidad de los perpetradores: las sentencias por desaparición de personas. In: Ansolabehere K, Serrano S, Martos A (eds) Desapariciones y regímenes de violencia. Lecciones desde México, 1st edn. Universidad Nacional Autónoma de México (UNAM), Instituto de Investigaciones Jurídicas (IIJ), Mexico City, pp 137–162

Shaw MN (2008) International law, 6th edn. Cambridge University Press, Cambridge, UK; New York

Spiro PJ (2011) NGOs and human rights: channels of power. In: Joseph S, McBeth A (eds) Research handbook on International Human Rights Law. Edward Elgar, Cheltenham, UK, pp 115–138

Srovin Coralli A (2021) Non-state actors and enforced disappearances: defining a path forward. Geneva Academy Working Paper. https://www.geneva-academy.ch/research/publications/detail/608-non-state-actors-and-enforced-disappearances-defining-a-path-forward. Accessed 16 Nov 2024

Timmermans S, Tavory I (2012) Theory construction in qualitative research: from grounded theory to abductive analysis. Sociol Theory 30:167–186

Tolbert D (2017) To prevent enforced disappearances, rethink the justice and security equation. In: Huffington Post. https://www.huffpost.com/entry/to-prevent-enforced-disappearances-rethink-the-justice_b_59a5c794e4b05fa16286bdd8. Accessed 22 Nov 2024

Torroja H (ed) (2017) Public international law and human rights violations by private military and security companies. Springer International Publishing, Cham

Umaña C (2017) Impunity: in the search of a socio-legal concept elucidations from a state crime case study. Dissertation, University of Ottawa

UNODC (United Nations Office on Drugs and Crime) (2024) Caribbean Gangs: Drugs, Firearms, and Gangs Networks in Jamaica, Saint Lucia, Guyana and Trinidad and Tobago. https://www.unodc.org/documents/data-and-analysis/AOTP/Caribbean_Gangs_Drugs_firearms_and_gang_networks_in_Jamaica_Saint_Lucia_Guyanaand_Trinidad_an_July_2024_Final.pdf. Accessed 26 Nov 2024

Van Dijk J (2011) Transnational organized crime, civil society and victim empowerment. In: The new faces of victimhood. Springer, Dordrecht, pp 99–126

van Genugten W, van der Heijden M-J, Jägers N (2011) Protecting the victims of the privatization of war. In: The new faces of victimhood. Springer, Dordrecht, pp 253–278

Vermeulen ML (2012) Enforced disappearance: determining state responsibility under the international convention for the protection of all persons from enforced disappearance. Intersentia, Antwerp

Von Bogdandy A, Steinbrück Platise M (2012) ARIO and human rights protection: leaving the individual in the cold. Int Organ Law Rev 9:67–76. https://doi.org/10.1163/15723747-00901014

Weissbrodt D (2013) Roles and responsibilities of non-state actors. In: Shelton D (ed) The Oxford handbook of International Human Rights Law. Oxford University Press, Oxford

Windle J, Silke A (2019) Is drawing from the state 'state of the art'?: a review of organised crime research data collection and analysis, 2004–2018. Trends Organ Crim 22:394–413. https://doi.org/10.1007/s12117-018-9356-5

Wolffenbuttel AR (2021) Enforced disappearances: applicable to political organizations? Va J Int Law Online 61:159–174

Zícari M (2021) Fue el estado ('It was the state'): embodied practices of memory and the re-writing of Mexico's genealogy of violence. Mem Stud. https://doi.org/10.1177/17506980211017959

Chapter 2
State Obligations Relating to Disappearances Committed by Non-State Actors

States not only have obligations relating to actions by their own officials under IHRL, but they also need to take measures aimed at ensuring human rights protection against actions by non-state actors. Following a classical division of types of human rights obligations, these are considered 'positive' obligations. In relation to disappearances, human rights bodies have had to deal with cases of enforced disappearances and disappearances involving non-state actors prior to the adoption of an express prohibition or a specific legal framework against this crime.[1] This was possible because disappearances imply the violation or threat to multiple human rights, including the rights to life, liberty, humane treatment, freedom from arbitrary detention, and access to justice (see below). Moreover, as discussed in the Introduction, until the adoption of the International Convention for the Protection of All Persons from Enforced Disappearances (ICPPED), no legal instrument specifically addressed the issue of disappearances committed non-state actors.[2] As a result, state obligations in relation to such disappearances have mostly been articulated indirectly in case law or instruments focused on the protection of rights that can be violated as a result of a disappearance. This chapter outlines states' positive obligations in relation to disappearances committed by non-state actors based on international instruments[3] and examines how the content of these obligations has been developed in the

[1] The first binding legal instrument that explicitly addressed enforced disappearance as a stand-alone human rights violation was the Inter-American Convention on Forced Disappearance of Persons in 1994. Inter-American Convention on Forced Disappearance of Persons 1994 (33 ILM 1529) (IACFDP). The UN Declaration on the Protection of all Persons from Enforced Disappearance (1992 (UN Doc. A/RES/47/133)) (DPPED) was adopted in 1992 but is not a legally binding instrument.

[2] See Article 3, International Convention for the Protection of All Persons from Enforced Disappearance 2006 (1726 UNTS 3) (ICPPED).

[3] An examination of whether such obligations could also derive from other sources of international law, as listed in Article 38 of the Statute of the International Court of Justice (international custom and general principles of law) lies beyond the scope of this research. Consequently, the findings of this analysis may not apply if states are not parties to the instruments that I refer to.

L. Guercke, *Failure of the State*, Interdisciplinary Studies in Human Rights 15,
https://doi.org/10.1007/978-3-031-83717-3_2

jurisprudence of the Human Rights Committee (HRC), the European Court of Human Rights (ECtHR/European Court), the Inter-American Court of Human Rights (IACtHR/Inter-American Court), and, more recently, the African Commission on Human and Peoples' Rights (ACHPR/African Commission).[4] Subsequently, I explore how these obligations have been articulated in the ICPPED and by its treaty body, the Committee on Enforced Disappearances (CED/the Committee),[5] as well as by the Working Group on Enforced or Involuntary Disappearances (WGEID),[6] and outline the protection gaps that persist in this framework and beyond.

2.1 State Obligations Concerning Acts by Non-State Actors

Enforced disappearances imply the violation of a number of rights, including the right to life, the right not to be tortured or subjected to ill-treatment, the right to security and liberty of the person, the right to an effective remedy, and the right to access to justice, of both the disappeared person, as well as of their relatives.[7] Disappearances committed by non-state actors can equally lead to violations of these rights. Consequently, states that are parties to general international human rights instruments have obligations regarding disappearances committed by non-state actors (that would fall within Article 3 ICPPED), regardless of whether

[4] I omit an analysis of jurisprudence by the African Court on Human and Peoples' Rights for reasons of feasibility and because the African Court's jurisprudence is much more limited than that of the African Commission. On the difference, see (Nani) Jansen Reventlow and Curling (2019).

[5] Articles 28–36 ICPPED establish the functions of the CED. While the CED can also deal with individual complaints if states accept its jurisdiction, the CED has thus far not dealt with a case involving a disappearance committed by a non-state actor.

[6] The WGEID was established in 1980 as the first international mechanism to deal with the issue of enforced disappearances, primarily through its humanitarian role of assisting families in determining the fate and whereabouts of their loved ones. Moreover, it is the body tasked with monitoring adherence to the DPPED. For more information on the WGEID, see https://www.ohchr.org/en/issues/disappearances/pages/disappearancesindex.aspx (accessed 15 November 2024). While the WGEID's reports and General Comments therefore do not constitute interpretations of the ICPPED, they nevertheless provide guidance for the interpretation of state obligations in relation to enforced disappearances.

[7] For example, Article 1(2) of the DPPED states that: '[the practice of enforced disappearance] constitutes a violation of the rules of international law guaranteeing, inter alia, the right to recognition as a person before the law, the right to liberty and security of the person and the right not to be subjected to torture and other cruel, inhuman or degrading treatment or punishment. It also violates or constitutes a grave threat to the right to life.' For an overview of the different rights that can be violated as a result of a disappearance, of both the victim and their relatives, see also Commission on Human Rights (2002) Report submitted by Mr. Manfred Nowak, independent expert charged with examining the existing international criminal and human rights framework for the protection of persons from enforced or involuntary disappearances. UN Doc. E/CN.4/2002/71, paras 75–80. See also Preamble, African Commission on Human and Peoples' Rights (2022) Guidelines on the Protection of All Persons from Enforced Disappearances in Africa, p. 6 (Preamble).

they are states parties to the ICPPED. These obligations encompass measures to prevent and respond to disappearances committed by non-state actors and are part of states' positive human rights protection obligations. This section provides a brief overview of how positive obligations have been articulated in a general manner before examining how obligations of states regarding disappearances committed by non-state actors have been articulated directly and indirectly in jurisprudence dealing not just with such disappearances, but also with human trafficking, kidnapping, slave labour, as well as deprivation of life by non-state actors.

2.1.1 Positive Obligations

A common classification of human rights obligations holds that the obligations established in international human rights instruments are both negative, in the sense that states must refrain from directly violating rights, as well as positive, in that states must actively take measures to 'ensure'[8] or 'secure'[9] the rights established in international or regional human rights treaties.[10] It is by now well-established that positive obligations also encompass an obligation to protect rights from infringement by non-state actors.[11] This obligation has a preventive and a responsive component, the latter of which comprises obligations to investigate and provide redress for the

---

[8] Art 2(1) International Covenant on Civil and Political Rights 1966 (999 UNTS 171) (ICCPR); Art 1(1) American Convention on Human Rights 1969 (1144 UNTS 143) (ACHR).

[9] Art 1 European Convention on Human Rights 1950 (ETS 5) (ECHR).

[10] Human Rights Committee (2004) General Comment No. 31: The Nature of the General Legal Obligation Imposed on States Parties to the Covenant. UN Doc. CCPR/C/21/Rev.1/Add. 13, para. 6. For an overview of the development of positive and negative obligations, see also Shelton and Gould (2013).

[11] The term 'obligation to protect' derives from a characterisation of the nature of human rights obligations proposed by former UN Special Rapporteur on the right to food, Asbjørn Eide, who distinguished these three aspects of human rights obligations. Eide defined the three aspects as follows: 'The obligation to respect requires the State, and thereby all its organs and agents, to abstain from doing anything that violates the integrity of the individual or infringes on her or his freedom [...].'; 'The obligation to protect requires from the State and its agents the measures necessary to prevent other individuals or groups from violating the integrity, freedom of action, or other human rights of the individual [...].'; 'The obligation to fulfil requires the State to take the measures necessary to ensure for each person within its jurisdiction opportunities to obtain satisfaction of those needs, [...] which cannot be secured by personal efforts.' See Commission on Human Rights (1987) Report on the Right to Adequate Food as a Human Right Submitted by Mr. Asbjørn Eide, Special Rapporteur. UN Doc. E/CN.4/Sub.2/1987/23, paras 67–69. In relation to human rights violations committed by non-state actors the obligation to *protect* human rights is of particular relevance. See, for example, United Nations Office of the High Commissioner for Human Rights (OHCHR) (2011) Guiding Principles on Business and Human Rights: Implementing the United Nations "Protect, Respect and Remedy" Framework, HR/PUB/11/04. The 'respect, protect, fulfil' framework has become widely accepted as the frame of reference for describing dimensions of states' human rights obligations from a scholarly perspective. See, for example, de Schutter (2010), pp. 242 ff; Mégret (2010), p. 130; Alston (2024), pp. 156 ff.

harm caused.[12] The applicability of such protective obligations to disappearances committed by non-state actors was explicitly articulated by the HRC as early as 1982 in its first General Comment on the right to life. In it, the HRC emphasised that the protection of the right to life required not only the adoption of positive measures to 'prevent and punish deprivation of life by criminal acts',[13] but also of

> specific and effective measures to prevent the disappearance of individuals, something which unfortunately has become all too frequent and leads too often to arbitrary deprivation of life. Furthermore, States should establish effective facilities and procedures to investigate thoroughly cases of missing and disappeared persons in circumstances which may involve a violation of the right to life.[14]

Similarly, in relation to the right to liberty and security of the person (Article 9 ICCPR), the HRC held the following in in its General Comment No. 35:

> States parties have the duty to take appropriate measures to protect the right to liberty of person against deprivation by third parties. States parties must protect individuals against abduction or detention by individual criminals or irregular groups, including armed or terrorist groups, operating within their territory. [...][15]

Several other United Nations treaty bodies and special procedures dealing with specific issues that can overlap with disappearances committed by non-state actors have reaffirmed these obligations. These include the Committee against Torture (CAT),[16] the Committee on the Elimination of Discrimination against Women (CEDAW),[17] the Committee on the Protection of the Rights of All Migrant Workers and Members of Their Families,[18] and the UN Special Rapporteur on trafficking in persons, especially women and children (Trafficking Rapporteur).[19]

---

[12] See Human Rights Committee (2004) General Comment No. 31: The Nature of the General Legal Obligation Imposed on States Parties to the Covenant. UN Doc. CCPR/C/21/Rev.1/Add. 13, para. 8; *Mahmut Kaya v Turkey* [2000] European Court of Human Rights Application no. 22535/93, 2000–III, para. 85; *Case of Velásquez-Rodríguez v Honduras (Merits)* [1988] Inter-American Court of Human Rights Ser. C No. 4, para. 166.

[13] Human Rights Committee (1982) General Comment No. 6: Article 6 (Right to Life). Reproduced in UN Doc. HRI\GEN\1\Rev.1 (1994), p. 6, para. 3.

[14] Ibid., para. 4.

[15] Human Rights Committee (2014) General Comment No. 35: Article 9 (Liberty and Security of Person). UN Doc. CCPR/C/GC/35, para. 7.

[16] Committee against Torture (2008) General Comment No. 2: Implementation of Article 2 by States Parties. UN Doc. CAT/C/GC/2, para. 18.

[17] Committee on the Elimination of Discrimination against Women (2017) General Recommendation No. 35 on Gender-Based Violence against Women, Updating General Recommendation No. 19. UN Doc. CEDAW/C/GC/35, para. 24 (2) (b).

[18] Committee on the Protection of the Rights of All Migrant Workers and Members of Their Families (2013) General Comment No. 2 on the Rights of Migrant Workers in an Irregular Situation and Members of Their Families. UN Doc. CMW/C/GC/2, para. 21, relating to protection against violence.

[19] OHCHR (2002) Recommended Principles and Guidelines on Human Rights and Human Trafficking. UN Doc. E/2002/68/Add. 1, para. 2; See also UN General Assembly (2015) Report of the

At the level of regional human rights systems, the African Commission and Court on Human and Peoples' Rights, the ECtHR, and the IACtHR have also affirmed that states' positive obligations include taking measures to prevent violations of human rights at the hands of non-state actors, and to respond to them in a diligent manner by investigating and providing an effective remedy. A distinction that is often applied is what the ECtHR has termed 'substantive' and 'procedural' aspects of positive obligations in relation to a particular right. Broadly speaking, substantive obligations encompass measures that guarantee the right in question, such as the creation of legal frameworks and regulations, whereas procedural obligations relate to measures that ensure access to a remedy.[20] In relation to the right to life for example, the substantive aspect relates to the taking of life, or failing to prevent such taking of life, whereas the procedural aspect refers to the obligation to conduct an effective investigation into the death.[21] The exact distinction between substantive and procedural obligations is neither clear nor consistent in the ECtHR's case law and there are many instances where they overlap.[22] Nonetheless, the distinction is relevant when it comes to disappearance cases, especially where these involve non-state actors as perpetrators. This is because the distinction between the two types of obligations has permitted the ECtHR to assess states' failure to comply with their procedural obligation to investigate a potentially unlawful death even though the death itself—or disappearance—occurred before the acceptance by a state of its jurisdiction.[23]

The IACtHR also confirmed the obligations of states in relation to disappearances committed by non-state actors in the widely cited case of *Velásquez Rodríguez v Honduras*, which was one of the Court's first contentious cases and its first judgment on the Merits of a case. Although the IACtHR found that the state was directly responsible for the enforced disappearance of Manfredo Velásquez, it also addressed the hypothetical question of state responsibility if the disappearance had been committed by private individuals, based on the obligation of states under the ACHR to 'ensure [...] the full exercise of those rights and freedoms' (Article 1(1)):

Special Rapporteur on Trafficking in Persons, Especially Women and Children. UN Doc. A/70/260, on due diligence obligations of states in relation to human trafficking.

[20] Akandji-Kombe (2007), p. 16. For an in-depth discussion of the difference between substantive and procedural positive obligations, see Lavrysen (2016), p. 49 ff.

[21] *McCann and Others v the United Kingdom* [1995] European Court of Human Rights Application no. 18984/91, para. 161.

[22] Lavrysen (2016), p. 53 ff.

[23] *Varnava and Others v Turkey* [2009] European Court of Human Rights Applications nos. 16064/90, 16065/90, 16066/90, 16068/90, 16069/90, 16070/90, 16071/90, 16072/90 and 16073/90, paras. 136–150. See also Baranowksa's discussion of the ECtHR's judgment in the case of *Šilih v Slovenia,* in which the Court held that the procedural obligation to investigate arising from Article 2 ECHR applies from the moment of ratification onwards, even if a person's death occurred before the ECtHR had jurisdiction. Moreover, with regard to disappearance cases, the ECtHR has considered cases admissible *ratione temporis* based on the continuous nature of the violation. See Baranowska (2021), pp. 42–48.

> However, this does not define all the circumstances in which a State is *obligated to prevent, investigate and punish human rights violations*, nor all the cases in which the State might be found responsible for an infringement of those rights. An illegal act which violates human rights and which is initially not directly imputable to a State (for example, because it is the act of a private person or because the person responsible has not been identified) can lead to international responsibility of the State, not because of the act itself, but *because of the lack of due diligence to prevent the violation or to respond to it as required by the Convention.*[24]

While the IACtHR has also used the notion of substantive and procedural obligations and followed the ECtHR's distinction,[25] it has not done so consistently.

In its General Comment on the Right to Life, the African Commission on Human and Peoples' Rights (ACHPR) confirmed that states have a responsibility to protect 'individuals and groups from [arbitrary deprivations of life] at the hands of others'[26] and took up the distinction between substantive and procedural obligations,[27] which it reiterated in its Guidelines on the Protection of All Persons from Enforced Disappearance in Africa (African Guidelines):

> The right to life engages both a negative State obligation to refrain from arbitrary killings and a positive State obligation to protect life. It encompasses both substantive and procedural obligations.[28]

In the case of *Zimbabwe Human Rights NGO Forum v Zimbabwe*, the ACHPR further summarised the obligation to protect as '[entailing] the creation and maintenance of an atmosphere or framework of an effective interplay of laws and regulations so that individuals will be able to freely realize their rights and freedoms.'[29] Moreover, the ACHPR explicitly held that the IACtHR's statements made in *Velásquez Rodríguez* were applicable to interpreting obligations arising from the African Charter on Human and People's Rights.[30]

An important concept relating to positive obligations is that of due diligence, as indicated in the statements by both the HRC and the IACtHR cited above. Due diligence obligations are obligations of conduct, which means that states have to take

---

[24] *Case of Velásquez-Rodríguez v. Honduras (Merits)*, para. 172. Emphasis added.

[25] For example, the IACtHR has made explicit reference to the ECtHR's distinction between substantive and procedural aspects of obligations, as well as its own use of this distinction. See *Case of González et al ("Cotton Field") v Mexico* [2009] Inter-American Court of Human Rights Serie C No. 205, paras 292–4.

[26] African Commission on Human and Peoples' Rights (2015) General Comment No. 3 on the African Charter on Human and People's Rights: The Right to Life (Article 4), para. 2.

[27] Ibid., para. 12: '[...] Any deprivation of life resulting from a violation of the procedural or substantive safeguards in the African Charter, including on the basis of discriminatory grounds or practices, is arbitrary and as a result unlawful.'

[28] African Commission on Human and Peoples' Rights (2022) Guidelines on the Protection of All Persons from Enforced Disappearances in Africa, para. 3.1.

[29] *Zimbabwe Human Rights NGO Forum v. Zimbabwe* [2006] African Commission on Human and Peoples' Rights 245/02, para. 152.

[30] Ibid., paras 143–146.

reasonable measures to try and achieve a particular result.[31] Because they are obligations of conduct, however, a failure to achieve the result in question does not necessarily mean that the state did not act diligently.[32] An in-depth discussion of the concept of due diligence lies beyond the scope of this book. Nonetheless, and considering that the application of this concept in jurisprudence is not always clear, it is important to note for the purpose of this—and the following—chapters that not all positive obligations are obligations of due diligence.[33] The content of due diligence measures is always context-dependent.

2.1.2 The Obligation to Prevent

In view of the different ways in which persons can be disappeared by non-state actors (see Introduction), preventive obligations in relation to such disappearances effectively overlap with preventive measures relating to torture or inhumane treatment, violence against women, human trafficking, kidnapping or other forms of deprivation of liberty, and killings. Broadly speaking, the obligations of states to prevent violations of rights at the hands of non-state actors can be divided into two categories: first, there are obligations of a *general* nature, which refer to the general organisation of the state, the functioning of the judicial apparatus, and the adoption of (preventive) policies. Second, there can be an obligation to adopt *specific* measures in order to protect a person (or group of persons) from a concrete risk of harm.[34] While the terminology of 'general' and 'specific' preventive measures is not based on a consensus among scholars dealing with obligations of states in relation to harm caused by non-state actors,[35] all agree on the existence of a distinction. This becomes particularly relevant in relation to determining state responsibility for a failure to comply with preventive obligations, which I discuss in the following chapter (Sect. 3.2.1). There is no exhaustive list of either general or specific preventive measures, given that, as measures of due diligence, they are generally

[31] Koivurova (2010); Ferstman (2020); Monnheimer (2021).

[32] Crawford (2013), p. 227.

[33] In her recent book on the topic of due diligence, Monnheimer (2021) provides a detailed overview of the relationship between positive obligations and due diligence obligations. Nonetheless, there continue to be discussions about this relationship.

[34] On the difficulty of establishing the boundary of these specific measures, see Ebert and Sijniensky (2015), p. 344.

[35] Van der Have makes a distinction between such levels of prevention on the basis of different temporal moments. Her focus are obligations to prevent gross human rights violations, which, according to her, are not clear. van der Have (2018), pp. 2 and 12. Lavrysen refers to specific measures as 'ad hoc' measures. Lavrysen (2016), p. 112 ff. Monnheimer distinguishes between 'positive obligations of result, positive obligations of diligent conduct, and positive obligations of progressive realisation'. Monnheimer (2021), p. 55. Bauer distinguishes between 'systemic' and 'individual' due diligence obligations in relation to torture committed by non-state actors. Bauer (2021), pp. 817–818.

context-dependent and it is left up to states to decide which reasonable measures to adopt in order to protect the rights of individuals within their jurisdiction.[36] Nonetheless, there are certain fundamental elements which can be identified on the basis of jurisprudence of human rights courts and recommendations issued by United Nations treaty bodies.[37] The following sections thus provide examples of how both general and specific preventive measures have been articulated by international and regional human rights bodies.

2.1.2.1 General Measures

General preventive measures relating to harm committed by non-state actors are aimed at deterring the commission of crimes between individuals, as well as at reducing the likelihood for such acts to occur. On the one hand, such measures comprise formal legislative and administrative measures that ensure the prohibition of certain acts that can result in harm to other persons and provide for their prosecution.[38] Thus, they include the adoption of criminal law provisions against different forms violence, as well as of mechanisms to ensure their effective application. In its General Comment No. 36 on the right to life, for example, the HRC emphasised that in order to protect the right to life, states have to adopt 'protective legal frameworks' that should '[include] effective criminal prohibitions on all manifestations of violence or incitement to violence that are likely to result in a deprivation of life [...]'.[39] Similarly, for the ECtHR, the main elements for the general obligation to prevent are the existence of 'effective criminal-law provisions', as well as the existence of a 'law-enforcement machinery' to respond to crimes

[36] de Schutter (2010), p. 365. In its Advisory Opinion on the Environment and Human Rights, the IACtHR formulated this as follows: 'This Court has maintained that, in application of Article 1(1) of the American Convention, States have the obligation *erga omnes* to respect and guarantee protection standards and to ensure the effectiveness of human rights. In this regard, the Court recalls that the general obligations to respect and to ensure rights established in Article 1(1) of the Convention *give rise to special duties that can be determined based on the particular needs for protection of the subject of law, due to either their personal conditions or specific situation.*' IACtHR (2017) Advisory Opinion on the Environment and Human Rights. OC-23/17, para. 115. Emphasis added.

[37] While the recommendations of UN treaty bodies are less 'authoritative' than jurisprudence, they nevertheless provide an indication of what the bodies charged with interpreting particular human rights treaties consider to constitute preventive measures. See McCall-Smith (2016), pp. 27–28.

[38] Notably, Monnheimer refers to such obligation as positive obligations of *result* in the sense that a failure by a state to put in place such measures leads to the state's responsibility. See Monnheimer (2021), pp. 55–69. However, this distinction is not necessarily made by all scholars, especially when these measures are considered as part of a state's due diligence obligations. See sources cited above at note 35 and Mackenzie-Gray Scott (2021), p. 354.

[39] Human Rights Committee (2019) General Comment No. 36: Article 6: Right to Life. UN Doc. CCPR/C/GC/36, para. 20.

committed by non-state actors.[40] The *effectiveness* of criminal-law provisions depends on their implementation in practice. To exemplify, in the case of *Mahmut Kaya v Turkey*, which dealt with the disappearance and subsequent execution of a doctor in the context of the conflict between the Turkish government and the Kurdistan Workers Party (PKK) during the early 1990s,[41] the ECtHR assessed the Turkish government's argument that it had taken sufficient protective measures. To do so, the Court reviewed deficiencies in the application of the Turkish criminal-law framework and found a lack of independence in criminal investigations, which often led to inaction by authorities where state agents were alleged to be involved in a crime.[42] All of this was held to '[undermine] the effectiveness of the protection afforded by criminal law'.[43]

Beyond the adoption and effective implementation of laws, the obligation to take general preventive measures also includes the adoption of policies and other measures to address the underlying causes of particular violations at the hands of non-state actors. The HRC has articulated this broader content of the obligation to prevent in specifying that the obligation to protect life 'also implies that States parties should take appropriate measures to address the general conditions in society that may give rise to direct threats to life or prevent individuals from enjoying their right to life with dignity.'[44] Moreover, where such threats to life emanate from a particular non-state actor, states should take measures against this actor.[45] This illustrates that, in the view of the HRC, general measures encompass not just the adoption of laws, but also addressing underlying problems that may give rise to violations of the right to life at the hands of non-state actors.

The African Commission has expressed the view that the adoption of 'appropriate domestic laws' to protect the right to life is an important aspect of its protection.[46] In addition, similarly to the HRC, and adopting a broad interpretation of the right to life, the ACHPR stated that:

---

[40] *Osman v The United Kingdom* [1998] European Court of Human Rights Application no. 23452/94, 1998–VIII, para. 115; *Mahmut Kaya v Turkey*, para. 85; *Osmanoğlu v Turkey* [2008] European Court of Human Rights Application no. 48804/99, para. 72; *Medova v Russia* [2009] European Court of Human Rights Application no. 25385/04, para. 95; *Rantsev v Cyprus and Russia* [2010] European Court of Human Rights Application no. 25965/04, para. 218; *Tsechoyev v Russia* [2011] European Court of Human Rights Application no. 39358/05, para. 135; *Olewnik-Cieplińska and Olewnik v Poland* [2019] European Court of Human Rights Application no. 20147/15, para. 117.

[41] In this case, the ECtHR could not establish whether state agents were responsible for the victim's execution. See *Mahmut Kaya v Turkey*, para. 87.

[42] In practice, the ECtHR found that cases were not examined by sufficiently independent authorities (ibid., para. 95), nor were investigations carried out in a serious manner (or even started) (ibid., para. 96). Finally, the courts dealing with PKK crimes were not independent either (ibid, para. 97).

[43] Ibid., para. 98.

[44] Human Rights Committee (2019) General Comment No. 36: Article 6: Right to Life. UN Doc. CCPR/C/GC/36, para. 26.

[45] This is further discussed in Chap. 3, Sect. 3.2.1.3 and in Chap. 4, Sect. 4.1.1.3.

[46] African Commission on Human and Peoples' Rights (2015) General Comment No. 3 on the African Charter on Human and People's Rights: The Right to Life (Article 4), para. 10.

> [...] In cases where the risk has not arisen from malicious or other intent then the State's actions may not always be related to criminal justice. Such actions include, inter alia, preventive steps to preserve and protect the natural environment and humanitarian responses to natural disasters, famines, outbreaks of infectious diseases, or other emergencies.[47]

The ECtHR has not made statements of such a broad nature, but it has nevertheless interpreted Article 2(1) ECHR concerning the right to life in such a way that it entails an obligation to 'afford general protection to society' against potential risks from an identified source.[48] The IACtHR, on the other hand, has adopted a broad conception of preventive obligations since it first articulated the obligation to prevent in the seminal case of *Velásquez Rodríguez v Honduras:*

> [The state's] duty to prevent includes all those means of a legal, political, administrative and cultural nature that promote the protection of human rights and ensure that any violations are considered and treated as illegal acts, which, as such, may lead to the punishment of those responsible and the obligation to indemnify the victims for damages. It is not possible to make a detailed list of all such measures, since they vary with the law and the conditions of each State Party.[49]

This statement has been repeated in the IACtHR's case law relating to the disappearance and murder or sexual torture of women,[50] as well as in relation to modern day slavery.[51]

Applying General Preventive Measures to Disappearances

The general preventive measures listed above can equally apply to disappearances committed by non-state actors. Thus, states must ensure that their criminal legislation allows for the prosecution of perpetrators of such crimes and is applied in an

---

[47] Ibid., para. 41.

[48] *Mastromatteo v Italy* [2002] European Court of Human Rights Application no. 37703/97, 2002–VIII, para. 69. For a more in-depth discussion of risks stemming from an identified source, see Chap. 3 (Sect. 3.2.1.3).

[49] *Case of Velásquez-Rodríguez v. Honduras (Merits)*, para. 175.

[50] See, respectively: *Case of González et al. ("Cotton Field") v. Mexico*, para. 252; *Case of López Soto and others v Venezuela* [2018] Inter-American Court of Human Rights Series C No 362, para. 130.

[51] *Case of the Hacienda Brasil Verde Workers v Brazil* [2016] Inter-American Court of Human Rights Series C No. 318, para. 322. In addition, examples of general preventive measures can also be found in reparations orders of the IAtHR, especially in its assessment of guarantees of non-repetition. See, for example: *Case of González et al. ("Cotton Field") v. Mexico*, paras 474 ff; *Case of Velásquez Paiz and Others v Guatemala* [2015] Inter-American Court of Human Rights Series C No 307, paras 243 ff; *Case of Gutiérrez Hernández et al v Guatemala* [2017] Inter-American Court of Human Rights Series C No. 339, paras 210 ff; *Case of the Pueblo Bello Massacre v Colombia* [2006] Inter-American Court of Human Rights Series C No. 140, para. 269. In the case of the *Hacienda Brasil Verde Workers*, for example, the IACtHR reviewed the measures taken by the Brazilian government to counter slave labour and found them to be sufficient to prevent such practices in the future. *Case of the Hacienda Brasil Verde Workers v. Brazil*, paras 469–70.

effective manner. Given that preventive measures are always context-dependent, this does not necessarily mean that there exists a general requirement to criminalise disappearances committed by non-state actors through specific legislation.[52] However, if the perpetrators of such disappearances could not be adequately prosecuted under existing criminal legislation, then a general preventive measure could include the criminalisation of disappearances committed by non-state actors.[53] Moreover, if a particular context fosters the commission of such crimes, general preventive measures should aim at changing this context and addressing root causes.

The obligation to address root causes of violations committed by non-state actors is particularly clear in relation to obligations towards particular groups that can become victims of disappearances committed by non-state actors, especially women and migrants. For example, in relation to violence against women committed by non-state actors, the CEDAW has specified the need to adopt laws and create institutions to address violence against women by private actors, as well as to ensure their effective functioning.[54] Moreover, the obligation of due diligence 'require[s] […] the adoption and implementation of measures to eradicate prejudices, stereotypes and practices that are the root causes of gender-based violence against women.'[55] Instruments for the prevention of violence against women in regional human rights systems also articulate a variety of preventive measures.[56] Moreover, similar measures have been articulated in relation to victims of human trafficking[57] and, regarding disappearances specifically, migrants (see below,

---

[52] There is an open discussion about whether disappearances committed by non-state actors that are encompasses by Article 3 ICPPED should be considered as crimes in their own right. For a recent discussion on this topic, see de Frouville (2021).

[53] For example, in a report published in 2015, the IACHR made a series of recommendations to Mexico to improve the human rights situation in the country, which included the recommendation to adopt a General Law on Disappearances and Enforced Disappearances, underlining the need to address not only enforced disappearances, but also other types of 'disappearances' by legal means. See Inter-American Commission on Human Rights (2015) Situation of Human Rights in Mexico. OEA/Ser.L/V/II.Doc. 44/15, para. 223. However, the creation of two crimes has drawn some criticism in Mexico. See Chaps. 5 and 6 on Mexico.

[54] Committee on the Elimination of Discrimination against Women (2017) General Recommendation No. 35 on Gender-Based Violence against Women, Updating General Recommendation No. 19. UN Doc. CEDAW/C/GC/35, para. 1. 'Under the obligation of due diligence, States parties must adopt and implement diverse measures to tackle gender-based violence against women committed by non-State actors, including having laws, institutions and a system in place to address such violence and ensuring that they function effectively in practice and are supported by all State agents and bodies who diligently enforce the laws' (para. 24(2)).

[55] Ibid., para. 26. See also para. 30 for more specificity.

[56] See African Union (2003) Protocol to the African Charter on Human and People's Rights on the Rights of Women in Africa (Maputo Protocol), para. 2; Convention on preventing and combating violence against women and domestic violence ('Istanbul Convention') 2011 Council of Europe (CETS No. 210), Chapter III, Articles 12–17; Inter-American Convention on the Prevention, Punishment, and Eradication of Violence against Women ('Convention of Belém do Pará') 1994 (33 ILM 1534), Article 8.

[57] For a discussion of these measures, see Chap. 4, Sect. 4.1.1.1.

Sect. 2.2.3.1). General preventive obligations can thus be seen as quite comprehensive, especially if they are meant to address root causes of violations committed by non-state actors and can be quite detailed when they relate to specific violations or groups of (potential) victims.

2.1.2.2 Specific Prevention Measures

In addition to general measures which states must adopt to safeguard the human rights of individuals against acts by non-state actors, the ECtHR and IACtHR have also held that there can be an obligation to take specific preventive measures to protect the rights of a person who is at risk. This obligation was first articulated by the ECtHR in the case of *Osman v UK*, where the Court held that:

> [...] Article 2 of the Convention may also imply in certain well-defined circumstances a positive obligation on the authorities to take *preventive operational measures* to protect an individual whose life is at risk from the criminal acts of another individual.[58]

The obligation to adopt this second type of preventive 'operational' measures is very specific to each case and can encompass different elements, depending on the situation. Specific preventive obligations are always obligations of due diligence, which means that they are obligations of conduct that require states to take reasonable measures to prevent a particular violation of a right or multiple rights once they are aware of a risk. Moreover, these specific preventive obligations do not exist in all types of cases of risk to an individual, due to what the ECtHR summarised as 'the difficulties involved in policing modern societies, the unpredictability of human conduct and the operational choices which must be made in terms of priorities and resources'.[59] In view of this limitation, the European Court also elaborated a set of criteria that, if present, would trigger a state's obligation to take preventive operational measures, which are further discussed in the following chapter (Sect. 3.2.1.1).[60] This threshold, as first articulated in *Osman v UK*, has not only been taken up as a general principle by the European Court,[61] but has also been adopted by the IACtHR[62] and the HRC.[63]

---

[58] *Osman v. The United Kingdom*, para. 115. Emphasis added.

[59] Ibid., para. 116.

[60] Ibid.

[61] *Mastromatteo v. Italy*, para. 68; *Osmanoğlu v Turkey*, para. 74; *Medova v Russia*, para. 96; *Rantsev v. Cyprus and Russia*, para. 219; *Tsechoyev v. Russia*, para. 136; *Olewnik-Cieplińska and Olewnik v. Poland*, para. 119.

[62] *Case of the Pueblo Bello Massacre v. Colombia*, para. 124; *Case of González et al. ("Cotton Field") v. Mexico*, para. 280; *Case of Velásquez Paiz and Others v Guatemala*, para. 109; *Case of the Hacienda Brasil Verde Workers v. Brazil*, para. 323; *Case of López Soto and others v. Venezuela*, para. 140. On the use of this threshold by both courts, see Ebert and Sijniensky (2015).

[63] Human Rights Committee (2019) General Comment No. 36: Article 6: Right to Life. UN Doc. CCPR/C/GC/36, para. 21.

Given that the existence of specific preventive obligations, as well as their content are always case-dependent, it is not feasible or desirable to define a 'list' of specific preventive measures. This is because the requirements to act *reasonably* in order to prevent violations of human rights by non-state actors will vary depending on the substantive rights in question and the particular context.[64] A case-by-case assessment of the existence of specific prevention obligations means that it is usually intertwined with a tribunal's analysis of state responsibility in a particular case, which I discuss in Chap. 3. With this in mind, this section provides some examples of the content of specific preventive obligations as articulated in cases dealing with state responsibility for a failure to prevent non-state harm, which are illustrative and by no means exhaustive.

Notably, with the exception of some of the cases cited below, few cases involving disappearances committed by non-state actors have actually dealt with a failure to take operational measures to prevent the victim's initial deprivation of liberty that led to the disappearance. Rather, the preventive measures assessed by the respective courts deal with measures taken to prevent violations *after* the person had been deprived of liberty and disappeared. This is because in many cases of disappearances committed by non-state actors, the required level of awareness of risk for an obligation to take preventive operational measures to arise,[65] was only established once the disappearance had been reported to the authorities.[66] Consequently, it is difficult to discern more specific preventive obligations to prevent the initial disappearance.

Examples of Specific Preventive Measures

A first example of specific preventive measures to protect a person from a disappearance by a non-state actor are those aimed at preventing violence against a person who has received threats or belongs to a particularly vulnerable group. In such situations, the HRC has held that states must 'respond urgently and effectively' to protect 'persons in situation of vulnerability whose lives have been placed at particular risk because of specific threats or pre-existing patterns of violence', for example by taking the following measures:

> the assignment of around-the-clock police protection, the issuance of protection and restraining orders against potential aggressors and, in exceptional cases, and only with the free and informed consent of the threatened individual, protective custody.[67]

---

[64] Ferstman (2020), p. 465; Monnheimer (2021), p. 71. See also the discussion on how responsibility is determined in cases concerning a failure to act with due diligence by the ACHPR in *Zimbabwe Human Rights NGO Forum v. Zimbabwe*, paras 155–158.

[65] The requirement of awareness of risk is discussed further in Chap. 3, Sect. 3.2.1.

[66] The question of what this means for the determination of state responsibility is further discussed in Chap. 3, Sect. 3.2.1.2.

[67] Human Rights Committee (2019) General Comment No. 36: Article 6: Right to Life. UN Doc. CCPR/C/GC/36, para. 23.

In the case of *Medova v Russia* before the ECtHR, the victim and his captors had been taken into custody by authorities after the captors had refused to present their identity documents at a checkpoint. The ECtHR held that authorities should have been aware of a risk to the victim's rights based on the prevailing context and failed to take sufficient preventive measures by releasing the group without thoroughly identifying the captors' identity, which lead to the victim's disappearance.[68] The preventive measures that authorities could have taken, therefore, were to carefully verify the identity documents of suspicious individuals who had control over another individual.[69]

A second example of specific preventive measures relates to measures aimed at reducing an identified risk to the enjoyment of rights, even where no potential victim has been identified. For example, the ECtHR has dealt with a number of cases which concerned convicted criminals who committed homicides after being released from prison in the framework of reintegration schemes.[70] In these cases (discussed further in Chap. 3), the ECtHR assessed whether these schemes contained sufficient safeguards and had been effectively applied in practice, including a careful assessment by authorities of the risk posed by the particular prisoner.[71] The IACtHR took a similar approach in the case of the *Pueblo Bello Massacre*, which dealt with the disappearance of a group of 43 men and boys from the village of Pueblo Bello in Colombia, at the hands of a paramilitary group. The Court established that the Colombian state had been aware of the risk posed by paramilitary groups,[72] and found that the steps taken by the state to dismantle these groups had been ineffective.[73] For example, it found that the Colombian military had not sufficiently controlled the roads in the area surrounding Pueblo Bello, which allowed the paramilitary group to abduct the victims.[74] Thus, specific preventive measures would have included dismantling the paramilitary groups and setting up stronger controls in areas where they operated.

---

[68] *Medova v Russia*, paras 98–99.

[69] Note that such a case could now potentially fall within the definition of acquiescence adopted by the CED in 2023. See Chap. 3, Sect. 3.1.2.1.

[70] *Mastromatteo v. Italy*; *Maiorano and Others v Italy* [2009] European Court of Human Rights Application no. 28634/06; *Choreftakis and Choreftaki v Greece* [2012] European Court of Human Rights Application no. 46846/08.

[71] *Mastromatteo v. Italy*, paras 74–77; *Maiorano and Others v. Italy*, paras 114–121; *Choreftakis and Choreftaki v Greece*, paras 58–59. The basis of the ECtHR's reasoning in these cases was that imprisoning dangerous individuals constituted *per se* a measure to protect society, with the implication that states must ensure that any scheme involving the release of a prisoner contained sufficient safeguards to protect society. See *Mastromatteo v. Italy*, para. 72; *Maiorano and Others v. Italy*, para. 108; *Choreftakis and Choreftaki v Greece*, para. 49 and paras 54–56. These cases and the ECtHR's reasoning are discussed in more detail in Chap. 3 (Sect. 3.2.1.3).

[72] *Case of the Pueblo Bello Massacre v. Colombia*, para. 125.

[73] Ibid., paras 125–127.

[74] Ibid., paras 138–139.

A somewhat intermediary approach was taken by the ECtHR in the case of *Mahmut Kaya v Turkey*. The European Court found that the state was aware of a real and imminent risk to Hasan Kaya, a doctor who was suspected of supporting the PKK,[75] and determined that the state had failed 'to take reasonable measures available to them to prevent a real and immediate risk to the life of Hasan Kaya'.[76] This finding was based on the lack of an effective application of the criminal laws in place and the subsequent failure to investigate alleged links between security forces and other armed groups, which, in the opinion of the ECtHR, could have led to the adoption of other —unspecified— preventive measures.[77] While the Court did not specify the content of the 'wide range of preventive measures' that authorities could have taken, its reference to their complete failure to investigate suggests that 'reasonable' preventive measures would have included investigating ties between authorities and counter-guerrilla groups, and holding officials implicated in unlawful killings accountable.

2.1.3 The Obligation to Investigate, Search and Provide an Effective Remedy

The obligation to respond a disappearance or human rights violation by a non-state actor comprises obligations to investigate, prosecute, and provide an effective remedy. The obligation to provide an effective remedy contains a procedural aspect related to ensuring that persons can access courts and, through the courts, redress for the harm they have suffered, as well as an obligation to provide substantive reparation.[78] In relation to the first aspect of the obligation to provide an effective remedy, states must carry out an effective investigation into a particular human rights violation and to prosecute those responsible,[79] which effectively overlaps with the obligation to investigate and prosecute. Therefore, I examine the content of the obligations to investigate and remedy together, in so far as the latter has been interpreted as requiring an effective investigation. The question of whether states have an obligation to provide substantive reparations is examined separately.

[75] *Mahmut Kaya v. Turkey*, paras 89–91.

[76] Ibid., para. 101.

[77] Ibid., para. 100.

[78] Shelton (2020), p. 184.

[79] Human Rights Committee (2019) General Comment No. 36: Article 6: Right to Life. UN Doc. CCPR/C/GC/36, para. 27.

2.1.3.1 The Obligation to Investigate

Given that disappearances violate several rights, of both the victim as well as of relatives,[80] states' obligation to investigate disappearances committed by non-state actors can be derived from their obligation to protect these different rights.[81] For example, in relation to the right to life, the Human Rights Committee stated in its General Comment No. 36 that:

> An important element of the protection afforded to the right to life by the Covenant is the obligation on the States parties, where they know or should have known of potentially unlawful deprivations of life, to investigate and, where appropriate, prosecute such incidents [...].[82]

The obligation to investigate as a key component of procedural obligations to protect substantive rights has been similarly emphasized by the ECtHR and the IACtHR in their respective case law[83] and by the ACHPR in its Guidelines on Enforced Disappearance in Africa and its General Comment No. 3 on the Right to Life.[84] In cases involving disappearances at the hands of non-state actors, the obligation to investigate additionally derives from the substantive obligations to ensure access to an effective remedy and safeguard the relatives' right to integrity. This is because disappearances are continuous crimes that do not end until the disappeared person has been found alive or their remains located, which means that the obligations to search and investigate are crucial to ending the crime.[85] Moreover, in view of the particularly detrimental impact that a disappearance has on the relatives of the disappeared person, which has been deemed to constitute ill-treatment,[86] the

[80] See below and Chap. 3, Sect. 3.2.2.1.

[81] See Vermeulen (2012), pp. 314–318. Consequently, a state can be responsible for the violation of multiple rights when it fails to investigate a disappearance committed by a non-state actor. See Chap. 3, Sect. 3.2.2.

[82] Human Rights Committee (2019) General Comment No. 36: Article 6: Right to Life. UN Doc. CCPR/C/GC/36, para. 27.

[83] See, for example, *Mahmut Kaya v. Turkey*, para. 96; *Varnava and Others v. Turkey,* para. 191; *Rantsev v. Cyprus and Russia*, para. 288; *Case of the Pueblo Bello Massacre v. Colombia*, para. 142; *Carlos Moreno Zamora et alt v Mexico* [2019] Human Rights Committee Communication No. 2760/2016, CCPR/C/127/D/2760/2016, para. 12.5.

[84] African Commission on Human and Peoples' Rights (2022) Guidelines on the Protection of All Persons from Enforced Disappearances in Africa, para. 3.1; African Commission on Human and Peoples' Rights (2015) General Comment No. 3 on the African Charter on Human and People's Rights: The Right to Life (Article 4), para. 2.

[85] See Galvis Patiño and Huhle (2020).

[86] See, for example, *Molina et al v Colombia* [2015] Human Rights Committee UN Doc. CCPR/C/114/D/2134/2012, para. 9.8; *Carlos Moreno Zamora et alt. v Mexico*, para. 12.9; *Osmanoğlu v Turkey*, para. 98; *Varnava and Others v. Turkey*, paras 200–202; *Case of the Pueblo Bello Massacre v. Colombia*, paras 160–1; *Case of González et al. ("Cotton Field") v. Mexico*, para. 424. Note, however, that the European Court has taken an approach in which it did not consider all relatives as suffering equally. See Chap. 3, Sect. 3.2.2.1.

obligation to investigate acquires particular importance. In the case of *Aslakhanova and Others v Russia*, the ECtHR explained this importance as follows:

> Investigation into a disappearance does not serve the sole purpose of establishing the circumstances of the killing, and finding and punishing the perpetrator. The crucial difference in investigations into disappearances is that, by conducting an investigation, the authorities also aim to find the missing person or find out what happened to him or her.[87]

In this vein, the ECtHR has held that Article 13 ECHR, which establishes the right to an effective remedy, also creates an obligation on states to conduct an effective investigation based on the rights of the disappeared victim's next of kin, even where it is not proven that state officials were directly involved in the victim's disappearance.[88] This is because, in the absence of an effective investigation, relatives are effectively prevented from accessing other remedies.[89] Notably, in a number of cases involving disappearances or killings at the hands of non-state or unknown actors, in which the ECtHR dealt with violations of the right to provide an effective remedy under Article 13 ECHR, the Court has stated that the requirements of the obligation to carry out an effective investigation arising from Article 13 may be 'broader than the obligation to investigate imposed by article 2'.[90] Notwithstanding, the Court has not clarified in what way the obligation to investigate as derived from Article 13 would differ from that related to the procedural obligation to investigate.[91]

Similarly, the IACtHR has derived the obligation to investigate and prosecute principally from the rights to access to justice under Articles 8 (1) (fair trial/due process of law) and 25 (judicial protection), read in connection with the obligation of Article 1(1) ACHR to ensure the 'free and full exercise' of rights, both of the

---

[87] *Aslakhanova and Others v Russia* [2012] European Court of Human Rights Applications nos. 2944/06 and 8300/07, 50184/07, 332/08, 42509/10, para. 214.

[88] *Mahmut Kaya v. Turkey*, para. 126; *Toğcu v Turkey* [2005] European Court of Human Rights Application no. 27601/95, para. 137; *Medova v Russia*, para. 129.

[89] *Toğcu v Turkey*, para. 139; *Medova v Russia*, para. 130.

[90] *Toğcu v Turkey*, para. 139.

[91] The ECtHR generally determines the existence of a violation of Article 13 ECHR by referring to the respective paragraphs where it assessed the effectiveness of the investigation in relation to (procedural) obligations arising from Article 2, without taking into consideration any additional elements. Moreover, in several cases where the ECtHR found a violation of the procedural obligation to conduct an effective investigation in relation to Article 2 ECHR, it then found that it was not necessary to examine the allegation of a violation of Article 13 on the basis that it had already found a violation of the procedural limb of Article 2. See *Osmanoğlu v Turkey*, para. 111; *Varnava and Others v. Turkey*, paras 210–211; *Tsechoyev v. Russia*, para. 159. In the case of *Medova v Russia*, the ECtHR did find a violation of Article 13, but did so 'in conjunction' with the violation of Article 2, without clarifying what this meant. *Medova v Russia*, para. 131. This leaves some confusion about whether, for the ECtHR, the obligation to provide an effective remedy does indeed require more than the conduct of an effective investigation and, if so, what would be required—for example the prosecution of perpetrators as a means of enabling effective access to compensation. However, given that in most cases involving disappearances, especially at the hands of non-state or unknown perpetrators, there is no effective investigation, the question of prosecution is generally not addressed in these cases.

disappeared person, as well as of the relatives.[92] Despite criticism of the IACtHR's approach as blurring the source of the obligation to investigate,[93] the Court has continued to base the obligation to investigate on both the substantive right in question, as well as Articles 8 and 25 in its case law.

In addition, due to the specific nature of disappearances, carrying out a prompt search and an effective investigation can also constitute a means of preventing subsequent violations of rights, for example the rights to life or personal liberty. The ECtHR stated this clearly in the case of *Osmanoğlu v Turkey*:

> [...] It follows that the action which was to be expected from the domestic authorities was not to prevent the disappearance of the applicant's son – which had already taken place – but to take preventive operational measures to protect his life, which was at risk from the criminal acts of other individuals.[94]

In this manner, the obligation to investigate can effectively constitute a preventive obligation derived from the substantive limb of the (potentially) affected rights, such as the right to life under Article 2 ECHR, or the right to liberty and security of the person under Article 5 ECHR.[95] This approach has been criticised as blurring the distinction between the substantive and procedural aspects of the rights in question in cases involving disappearances, and thereby potentially leading to a lack of clarity as to the nature of the obligations.[96] However, as argued by Vermeulen, such blurring might be inevitable due to the particular nature of disappearances as continuous crimes.[97] The IACtHR has also derived the obligation to investigate from the substantive rights in question, such as the right to personal liberty (Article 7), life (Article 4), and the right to humane treatment (Article 5), read in conjunction with Article 1(1),[98] yet it does not apply a strict distinction between the substantive and procedural aspects of obligations. While there thus exists some vagueness in

---

[92] *Case of the Pueblo Bello Massacre v. Colombia*, paras 211–212; *Case of González et al. ("Cotton Field") v. Mexico*, paras 388–389.

[93] See the separate opinion of Judge Medina Quiroga in the *Case of the 19 Merchants*. Medina Quiroga argued that the obligation to investigate should be derived from the substantive rights directly, rather than from the inherently procedural rights guaranteed under Articles 8 (fair trial) and 25 (access to justice) ACHR. See Partially Dissenting Opinion of Judge Medina Quiroga, *Case of the 19 Merchants v Colombia* [2004] Inter-American Court of Human Rights Ser C No. 109, especially para. 11.

[94] *Osmanoğlu v Turkey*, para. 76.

[95] See *Medova v Russia*, paras 122–125. Notably, the approach taken by the ECtHR in *Medova* in relation to the right to liberty and security of the person differs from previous cases involving disappearances by unknown actors, where the ECtHR did not find a violation of article 5 because the victim was not deprived of liberty by state agents, or did not find it necessary to examine a possible violation of article 5 separately. See *Tahsin Acar v Turkey* [2004] European Court of Human Rights Application no. 26307/95, paras 241–243; *Toğcu v Turkey*, paras 132–133; *Osmanoğlu v Turkey*, paras 102–4.

[96] See Vermeulen (2012), pp. 408–410.

[97] Ibid., p. 409.

[98] *Case of the Pueblo Bello Massacre v. Colombia*, para. 145; *Case of González et al. ("Cotton Field") v. Mexico*, para. 287.

relation to the precise legal basis for the obligation to investigate disappearances committed by non-state actors in the European and Inter-American human rights systems, its existence is undisputed.

The Content of the Obligation to Investigate

The obligation to investigate is an obligation of due diligence and therefore generally considered to be an obligation of means rather than result, which implies that the failure of an investigation to identify the perpetrators, or even the failure to prosecute the perpetrators once they have been identified, does not automatically constitute a failure to meet this obligation.[99]

According to the HRC, investigations into potentially unlawful death should follow the criteria of the Minnesota Protocol and be aimed at 'bringing those responsible to justice'.[100] Moreover, the HRC further specified the content of the obligation to investigate in its General Comment No. 36 on the right to life.[101] In the case law of the ECtHR and the IACtHR it is equally possible to distinguish a set of

---

[99] See, for example, *Osmanoğlu v Turkey*, para. 88; *Rantsev v. Cyprus and Russia*, para. 288; *Tsechoyev v. Russia*, para. 150; *Olewnik-Cieplińska and Olewnik v. Poland*, para. 136; *Case of Velásquez-Rodríguez v. Honduras (Merits)*, para. 177; *Case of González et al. ("Cotton Field") v. Mexico*, para. 289; *Case of Gutiérrez Hernández et al. v. Guatemala*, para. 148; *Case of Velásquez Paiz and Others v Guatemala*, para. 143; *Zimbabwe Human Rights NGO Forum v. Zimbabwe*, para. 158. Note, however, that in the case of *enforced* disappearances, an argument has been made that the obligation to investigate, and especially the obligation to search, are in fact obligations of result, given that states have an obligation to ensure victims' right to know the truth about the 'fate of the disappeared person' (Article 24 (2) ICPPED). See the dissenting opinion by Helen Keller and Fabián Salvioli in the case of *Cifuentes Elgueta v Chile* before the Human Rights Committee. *Cifuentes Elgueta v Chile* [2009] Human Rights Committee UN Doc. CCPR/C/96/D/1536/2006, individual opinion of Committee members Hellen Keller and Fabián Salvioli (dissenting), para. 29. Whether this argument would equally apply in cases involving disappearances committed by non-state actors is less clear because it would first have to be established that there is an equal right to know the truth of relatives of persons who were disappeared by non-state actors. While such an argument could be made on the basis of the suffering caused to relatives of a disappeared person, if the state is not directly responsible for a disappearance, it could legitimately be objected that imposing an obligation of result on it in relation to the outcome of an investigation into a crime committed by a non-state actor would be too high of a burden.

[100] Human Rights Committee (2019) General Comment No. 36: Article 6: Right to Life. UN Doc. CCPR/C/GC/36, para. 27; *Carlos Moreno Zamora et alt. v Mexico*, para. 12.5. The Minnesota Protocol defines 'potentially unlawful deaths' as those arising from a violation of the duty to respect the right to life (a), death in custody (b), as well as situations where: '[t]he death occurred where the State may have failed to meet its obligations to protect life. This includes, for example, any situation where a state fails to exercise due diligence to protect an individual or individuals from foreseeable external threats or violence by non-State actors.' United Nations Office of the High Commissioner for Human Rights (OHCHR) (2017) The Minnesota Protocol on the Investigation of Potentially Unlawful Death (2016). HR/PUB/17/4, para. 2 (c). This section of the Protocol can be read as encompassing disappearances at the hands of non-state actors. See Frey (2021).

[101] Human Rights Committee (2019) General Comment No. 36: Article 6: Right to Life. UN Doc. CCPR/C/GC/36, para. 28.

criteria that would make an investigation of a disappearance committed by non-state actors *effective* in the view of these courts. While the ECtHR has held that the exact form that an investigation should take depends on the circumstances of each case, throughout its jurisprudence, the Court has used a number of criteria to determine the effectiveness of an investigation in cases concerning disappearances at the hands of non-state actors.[102] It is not entirely clear whether and to what extent the ECtHR considers that there exists a difference in relation to the effectiveness of an investigation of a disappearance or an unlawful death, and how the criteria for assessing effectiveness differ in cases involving non-state actors. At first sight, it appears as though the criteria are the same. Nevertheless, in the case of *Tahsin Acar v Turkey* the ECtHR stated that 'where an involvement of state agents or bodies is alleged, specific requirements as to the effectiveness of investigation may apply'.[103] Unfortunately the European Court failed to specify what these 'specific requirements' are and how they differ from the requirements for the effectiveness of investigations involving disappearances committed by non-state actors, thereby leaving some doubt about the Court's view on this issue.

The IACtHR articulated the basic criteria for an effective investigation in a more general manner and regardless of the perpetrator in the *Velásquez Rodríguez* case, holding that an investigation:

> [...] must be undertaken in a serious manner and not as a mere formality preordained to be ineffective. An investigation must have an objective and be assumed by the State as its own legal duty, not as a step taken by private interests that depends upon the initiative of the victim or his family or upon their offer of proof, without an effective search for the truth by the government. This is true regardless of what agent is eventually found responsible for the violation.[104]

A review of subsequent cases involving disappearances committed by non-state actors before the ECtHR and the IACtHR, as well as the HRC's General Comment No. 36 and the African Commission's Guidelines, indicates that the criteria enumerated by the IACtHR in *Velásquez Rodríguez* continue to be applied and have been expanded. As a result, it is possible to derive a general list of criteria for the effectiveness of an investigation into disappearances committed by non-state actors. These include the independence and impartiality of investigations;[105] the conduct of the investigation in such a manner as to allow for the identification and punishment

[102] *Tahsin Acar v. Turkey*, para. 221; See also Vermeulen (2012), p. 327.

[103] *Tahsin Acar v. Turkey*, para. 220.

[104] *Case of Velásquez-Rodríguez v. Honduras (Merits)*, para. 177.

[105] Human Rights Committee (2019) General Comment No. 36: Article 6: Right to Life. UN Doc. CCPR/C/GC/36, para. 28; *Tahsin Acar v. Turkey*, para. 222; *Medova v Russia,* para. 103; *Rantsev v. Cyprus and Russia*, para. 233; *Case of the "Mapiripán Massacre" v Colombia* [2005] Inter-American Court of Human Rights Serie C No. 134, para. 219; *Case of the Pueblo Bello Massacre v. Colombia*, para. 143; *Case of González et al. ("Cotton Field") v. Mexico*, para. 290; *Case of Velásquez Paiz and Others v Guatemala*, para. 143; *Case of Gutiérrez Hernández et al. v. Guatemala*, para. 148. African Commission on Human and Peoples' Rights (2022) Guidelines on the Protection of All Persons from Enforced Disappearances in Africa, para. 4.1.4 (ii).

of perpetrators;[106] the promptness of the investigation,[107] especially where there is a possibility that the victim can be rescued;[108] the participation of the relatives of the disappeared person in the investigation and protection of their interests,[109] as well as transparency,[110] or what the ECtHR has termed an 'element of public scrutiny'.[111] Furthermore, for the ECtHR the investigation must involve securing relevant evidence[112] by taking 'all reasonable steps available' to the authorities,[113] including, for example, taking eye-witness testimony.[114] For the IACtHR, states have to use 'all

[106] Human Rights Committee (2019) General Comment No. 36: Article 6: Right to Life. UN Doc. CCPR/C/GC/36, paras 27–28.

[107] Ibid., para. 28; *Tahsin Acar v. Turkey*, para. 224; *Toğcu v Turkey*, para. 111; *Osmanoğlu v Turkey*, para. 89; *Medova v Russia*, para. 103; *Rantsev v. Cyprus and Russia*, para. 233; *Olewnik-Cieplińska and Olewnik v. Poland*, para. 137; *Case of the Pueblo Bello Massacre v. Colombia*, para. 143; *Case of González et al. ("Cotton Field") v. Mexico*, paras 283 and 368.

[108] The ECtHR has stated this in cases concerning the prohibition of slavery and forced labour under Article 4 ECHR 'where the possibility of removing the individual from the harmful situation is available, the investigation must be undertaken as a matter of urgency'. *Rantsev v. Cyprus and Russia*, para. 288; *J and Others v Austria* [2017] European Court of Human Rights Application no. 58216/12, para. 107. This could equally apply to cases of disappearances committed by non-state actors where there is suspicion that the victim might have disappeared as a consequence of human trafficking. Similarly, in the *Cotton Field* case, the IACtHR established the standard of 'strict due diligence' for conducting search operations during the initial hours and days following the report of a woman's disappearance. See *Case of González et al. ("Cotton Field") v. Mexico*, para. 283. The notion of 'strict due diligence' is discussed further in Chap. 3 (Sect. 3.2.1.2).

[109] See, for example, Human Rights Committee (2019) General Comment No. 36: Article 6: Right to Life. UN Doc. CCPR/C/GC/36, para. 28; *Tahsin Acar v. Turkey* (n 169) para. 225; *Medova v Russia*, paras 103 and 109; *Rantsev v. Cyprus and Russia*, para. 233; *Olewnik-Cieplińska and Olewnik v. Poland*, para. 136; *Case of the Pueblo Bello Massacre v. Colombia*, para. 144; *Case of Velásquez Paiz and Others v Guatemala*, para. 144; *Case of the Hacienda Brasil Verde Workers v. Brazil*, para. 376.

[110] In its General Comment No. 36, the HRC refers to the transparency of investigations and further formulated a requirement to make information about the investigation public, which is only limited to the extent that there exists a 'compelling need to protect the public interest or the privacy and other legal rights of directly affected individuals.' See Human Rights Committee (2019) General Comment No. 36: Article 6: Right to Life. UN Doc. CCPR/C/GC/36, para. 28.

[111] *Tahsin Acar v. Turkey*, para. 225; *Olewnik-Cieplińska and Olewnik v. Poland*, para. 136.

[112] *Tahsin Acar v. Turkey*, para. 223; *Rantsev v. Cyprus and Russia*, para. 241; *Olewnik-Cieplińska and Olewnik v. Poland*, para. 136. While the IACtHR has not specifically mentioned an obligation to secure evidence in the cases analysed for this research, it has considered errors in the gathering of evidence as one example of irregularities occurring in an investigation. See *Case of González et al. ("Cotton Field") v. Mexico*, para. 333.

[113] *Tahsin Acar v. Turkey*, para. 223; *Osmanoğlu v Turkey*, para. 88.

[114] *Toğcu v Turkey*, para. 110; *Osmanoğlu v Turkey*, para. 88. For an overview of steps that in the ECtHR's view could have 'offered a reasonable prospect of success in finding the applicant's son', see ibid. (*Osmanoğlu*), paras 79–83. The HRC also explicitly requires the protection of witnesses, victims and relatives, as well as those conducting the investigation: 'States parties must also take the necessary steps to protect witnesses, victims and their relatives and persons conducting the investigation from threats, attacks and any act of retaliation.' Human Rights Committee (2019) General Comment No. 36: Article 6: Right to Life. UN Doc. CCPR/C/GC/36, para. 28.

available legal means'[115] in the investigation, which could be viewed as a similar obligation.[116] Finally, authorities must act 'of their own motion' (ECtHR), or 'ex officio' (IACtHR, HRC, African Commission) to start the investigation rather than wait for relatives to make a formal complaint.[117]

According to the HRC and the IACtHR the obligation to investigate potentially unlawful deaths also includes the identification of bodies.[118] This is relevant for disappearances committed by non-state actors, as the correct identification of bodies is one way of avoiding that a person who was killed by a non-state actor 'disappears' because the body was not properly identified.[119] As discussed in Chap. 5 (Sect. 5.1. 2.2), this is likely to be the case of many disappeared persons in Mexico today, where a lack of forensic capacity has meant that thousands of bodies have been buried in mass graves without having been identified, implying that thousands of 'disappearances' could have been avoided.[120] This overview indicates that, despite occasional vagueness of language in existing jurisprudence, human rights bodies generally view the content of the obligation to investigate disappearances committed by non-state actors and the criteria effectiveness as equal to those established in the Minnesota Protocol[121] and in the ICPPED (see below).

---

[115] *Case of the Pueblo Bello Massacre v. Colombia*, para. 143; *Case of González et al. ("Cotton Field") v. Mexico*, para. 290. In other cases, the IACtHR articulated this obligation in a slightly different manner. For example, in the case of *Velásquez Paiz v. Guatemala*, the IACtHR held that 'due diligence requires that the investigative agency takes all the steps and makes all the inquiries needed to obtain the desired result.' See *Case of Velásquez Paiz and Others v Guatemala*, para. 143; see also *Case of Gutiérrez Hernández et al. v. Guatemala*, para. 148.

[116] The HRC in turn refers to the 'credibility' of the investigation. See Human Rights Committee (2019) General Comment No. 36: Article 6: Right to Life. UN Doc. CCPR/C/GC/36, para. 28.

[117] The ECtHR has mostly made this statement in relation to investigations of unlawful death (see *Tahsin Acar v. Turkey*, para. 221; *Rantsev v. Cyprus and Russia*, para. 232; *Olewnik-Cieplińska and Olewnik v. Poland*, para. 136). However, it has also done so in cases of disappearances that occurred in *'life-threatening circumstances'*. See *Tahsin Acar v. Turkey*, para. 226. For the HRC, see Human Rights Committee (2019) General Comment No. 36: Article 6: Right to Life. UN Doc. CCPR/C/GC/36, para. 28. For the IACtHR, see *Case of González et al. ("Cotton Field") v. Mexico*, para. para 290. African Commission on Human and Peoples' Rights (2022) Guidelines on the Protection of All Persons from Enforced Disappearances in Africa, para. 4.1.4 (ii).

[118] Human Rights Committee (2019) General Comment No. 36: Article 6: Right to Life. UN Doc. CCPR/C/GC/36, para. 28; *Case of González et al. ("Cotton Field") v. Mexico*, para. 300. For the African Commission, the identification of bodies is part of the obligation to search. See African Commission on Human and Peoples' Rights (2022) Guidelines on the Protection of All Persons from Enforced Disappearances in Africa, para. 4.1.4 (i).

[119] See Chap. 5 on the situation in Mexico for an explanation of these types of 'disappearances', which may not fit precisely within the definition of either Article 2 or 3 ICPPED.

[120] Guercke (forthcoming).

[121] United Nations Office of the High Commissioner for Human Rights (OHCHR) (2017) The Minnesota Protocol on the Investigation of Potentially Unlawful Death (2016). HR/PUB/17/4.

2.1.3.2 The Obligation to Search[122]

A crucial aspect in cases of disappearances is the search for the victims, which is different in nature from the obligation to investigate in that it is aimed at establishing the whereabouts of the disappeared person rather than identifying the perpetrators.[123] Nonetheless, the investigation and search also mutually reinforce each other in that an investigation can contribute evidence for the location of victims and locating the disappeared person will likely also contribute to the investigation.[124] Importantly, if persons are disappeared by non-state actors in the context of an armed conflict, states also have obligations under International Humanitarian Law (IHL) to locate 'missing' persons and provide family members with information about the fate of their loved ones, regardless of the identity of the perpetrator.[125]

Case law dealing with disappearances committed by non-state actors indicates that states do have an obligation to search for the victim, but it is unclear whether, for the tribunals examined, this obligation derives from the obligation to investigate or from other obligations. The ECtHR, for example, has often omitted any reference to an obligation to search victims of disappearances.[126] However, when reviewing

[122] Jurisprudence by the HRC is omitted in this section, given that the HRC has not specifically dealt with the obligation to search in its jurisprudence involving disappearances committed by non-state actors. The HRC has, however included the search for the victim's remains in the case of death as part of the state's obligation to provide an effective remedy: 'assuming that Mr. Moreno Pérez is deceased, endeavour to find his mortal remains and return them to his family in dignified conditions'. See *Carlos Moreno Zamora et alt. v Mexico*, para. 14(e). In *Maria Eugenia Padilla García and others v Mexico*, the HRC ordered the Mexican state to conduct an effective investigation, including ensuring that authorities in charge of the search are well-trained, which can be read as implying an obligation to search. However, in this case the HRC found that state agents were directly involved in the disappearance. See *Maria Eugenia Padilla García et al v Mexico* [2019] Human Rights Committee UN Doc. CCPR/C/126/D/2750/2016, para. 11. The HRC made a similar statement in the case of *Hidalgo Rea and Rivera Hidalgo v. Mexico*, which was also a case where the HRC found sufficient evidence for the direct involvement of state actors, thus considering the case an *enforced* disappearance. *Hidalgo Rea and Rivera Hidalgo v. Mexico* [2021] UN Doc. CCPR/C/131/D/3259/2018, para. 11.

[123] For a discussion of the distinction between establishing the 'fate' and 'whereabouts' of a disappeared person, see Huhle (2022).

[124] Committee on Enforced Disappearances (CED) (2017) Report of the Committee on Enforced Disappearances. UN Doc. A/72/56, para. 63.

[125] On this, see Baranowska (2020), pp. 12–13. According to Rule 117 of the International Committee of the Red Cross's (ICRC) Database on Customary IHL, states have an obligation to account for missing persons: 'Each party to the conflict must take all feasible measures to account for persons reported missing as a result of armed conflict and must provide their family members with any information it has on their fate.' See https://ihl-databases.icrc.org/en/customary-ihl/v1/rule117. Accessed 16 November 2024.

[126] Indeed, while the Inter-American Court consistently orders a continuation of the search for the victim(s) as part of its reparation orders (see, for example, *Case of Gutiérrez Hernández et al. v. Guatemala*, para. 209), the ECtHR has not taken this approach. On this, see Citroni (2012), p. 62. For an analysis of ECtHR judgments and reparation orders, see Baranowska (2021), pp. 103–106.

whether a state failed to take protective measures to safeguard a victim's right to life once authorities had been made aware of a disappearance, one element taken into consideration by the ECtHR was whether the authorities took steps to *find* the person.[127] Thus, the obligation to search can be viewed as implicit in the obligation to investigate as a means of protecting a victim's right to life. For example, in the case of *Olewnik-Cieplińska and Olewnik v Poland*, which concerned the kidnapping and subsequent death of a businessman at the hand of private individuals, the Court found that once Mr. Olewnik had been kidnapped, the Polish authorities were aware of an immediate risk to his life and therefore had a positive obligation to take preventive measures. This was because, according to the Court, it could be 'assumed' in cases of kidnapping for ransom in Poland at the time, partially based on statistical evidence of the Polish government, that kidnappings 'involved particular torment, and included cases of damage to health, and cases of death of the victim'.[128] The state's obligation to prevent implied that 'the domestic authorities [...] do all that could reasonably be expected of them *in order to find Mr Olewnik as swiftly as possible* and identify the perpetrators of the kidnapping.'[129] This approach is in line with previous case law of the ECtHR, where it considered the context of 'life-threatening circumstances' in order to determine the scope of authorities' obligations to investigate a disappearance.[130]

The IACtHR, for its part, has held that in response to reports of disappearances authorities should carry out 'exhaustive search activities'.[131] This requires taking 'prompt immediate action by ordering, without delay, the necessary measures to determine the whereabouts of the victims'[132] by police, prosecutors, and judicial authorities. Further, states must establish '[a]dequate procedures [...] for reporting disappearances, which should result in an immediate effective investigation'.[133] In this, authorities must presume that the victim is still alive until their fate has been

[127] See *Osmanoğlu v Turkey*, paras 79–84.

[128] Ibid., para. 122.

[129] *Olewnik-Cieplińska and Olewnik v. Poland*, para. 125. Emphasis added. The extent to which such reasoning would be applicable to cases of disappearances committed by non-state actors, however, is not clear. This is because kidnappings usually involve the demand of ransom money in exchange for the victim, as was the case in *Olewnik-Cieplińska and Olewnik v. Poland* (ibid., para. 123), which means that while the whereabouts of the victim are unknown, there is less uncertainty about her fate than in cases of disappearances. Consequently, it could be argued that authorities are more aware of a specific risk to the victim's rights and have more possibilities of locating the victim than in cases where there is no information at all about her fate or communication with the perpetrators.

[130] See, for example, *Tahsin Acar v. Turkey*, para. 226; *Osmanoğlu v Turkey*, para. 75.

[131] *Case of the Hacienda Brasil Verde Workers v. Brazil*, para. 427.

[132] *Case of González et al. ("Cotton Field") v. Mexico*, para. 283.

[133] Ibid. See also *Case of the Hacienda Brasil Verde Workers v. Brazil*, para. 427; *Case of López Soto and others v. Venezuela*, para. 142.

clarified.[134] While this obligation was initially articulated in cases dealing with women who disappeared in a general context of violence against women, the Inter-American Court reiterated this standard in the case of the *Hacienda Brasil Verde Workers*, which dealt with the disappearance of two (male) adolescents who had escaped a farm where they had been held in slave-like conditions.[135] Moreover, the IACtHR repeatedly orders the continuation of search activities as a form of reparation. For example, in the case of *Pueblo Bello*, the IACtHR held that the lack of an effective search for the victims was a factor that produced suffering for their relatives[136] and ordered the Colombian state to carry out an effective search and identification of the victims as part of the reparations.[137] The foregoing suggests that, on the basis of the rights of relatives of the disappeared person to know about the fate of the victim, for the IACtHR states do have an obligation to search for the disappeared, regardless of the identity of the perpetrator.

The Continuous Nature of the Obligations to Investigate and Search

Given the nature of enforced disappearances as continuous crimes, the obligation to investigate and search for disappeared persons is also of a continued nature.[138] Both the ECtHR and the IACtHR have addressed this question in cases involving disappearances committed by non-state actors. In relation to the obligation to investigate, in the case of *Varnava and Others v Turkey*, which involved the disappearance of nine Cypriot men during Turkish military operations in Cyprus during the 1970s, the ECtHR stated that

> [w]here disappearances in life-threatening circumstances are concerned, the procedural obligation to investigate can hardly come to an end on discovery of the body or the presumption of death; this merely casts light on one aspect of the fate of the missing person.

---

[134] *Case of González et al. ("Cotton Field") v. Mexico*, para. 283; *Case of Velásquez Paiz and Others v Guatemala*, para. 122; *Case of the Hacienda Brasil Verde Workers v. Brazil*, para. 427; *Case of López Soto and others v. Venezuela*, para. 142.

[135] *Case of the Hacienda Brasil Verde Workers v. Brazil*, para. 427. Note that the IACtHR made this link in relation to the obligation to act with due diligence to investigate allegations of forced labour or slavery to which the victims had been subjected prior to their disappearance (ibid., para. 364), and not to their status a minors.

[136] *Case of the Pueblo Bello Massacre v. Colombia*, para. 256.

[137] Ibid., paras 270–273.

[138] Dulitzky and Anayanssi Orizaga (2019), p. 16; Galvis Patiño and Huhle (2020). See also *Case of Velásquez-Rodríguez v. Honduras (Merits)*, para. 181; *Case of Radilla-Pacheco v Mexico* [2009] Inter-American Court of Human Rights Series C No. 209, para. 143; *Case of the Hacienda Brasil Verde Workers v. Brazil*, paras 426–427; *Case of Alvarado Espinoza and Others v Mexico* [2018] Inter-American Court of Human Rights Series C No. 370, para. 165; African Commission on Human and Peoples' Rights (2022) Guidelines on the Protection of All Persons from Enforced Disappearances in Africa, para. 4.1.4 (i) regarding the obligation to search, (ii) and (iii) regarding the obligation to investigate, and (iv) regarding the obligation to prosecute.

> An obligation to account for the disappearance and death, and to identify and prosecute any perpetrator of unlawful acts in that connection, will generally remain.[139]

Additionally, in *Varnava* the ECtHR broadened its previous approach and held that the *procedural* obligation arising from Article 2 ECHR implied a 'continuing obligation on the respondent Government to account for the whereabouts and fate of the missing men in the present case; if warranted, consequent measures for redress could then be effectively adopted'.[140] The ECtHR explained this as follows:

> [i]t cannot therefore be said that a disappearance is, simply, an "instantaneous" act or event; the additional distinctive element of subsequent failure to account for the whereabouts and fate of the missing person gives rise to a continuing situation. Thus, the procedural obligation will, potentially, persist as long as the fate of the person is unaccounted for; the ongoing failure to provide the requisite investigation will be regarded as a continuing violation [...]. This is so, even where death may, eventually, be presumed.[141]

Given that in this particular case the Cypriot men had disappeared in the context of a military operation, even though it could not be established that they were in fact disappeared by Turkish forces, it is not clear whether this reasoning would equally apply in cases where the perpetrators were clearly not state agents or acting with state support or endorsement. While the ECtHR has repeated the statements made in *Varnava and Others* in a number of cases, these were cases in which the ECtHR found that the respective victims had been disappeared by state agents.[142] In other disappearance cases where the ECtHR did not find it established that state agents were directly responsible, such as the previously cited cases of *Tahsin Acar v. Turkey*, *Osmanoğlu v. Turkey*, or *Medova v. Russia,* it did not deal with the question of a continuing violation, or the continuous nature of the obligation to search. As a result, it is not entirely clear whether the obligation to investigate cases of disappearances committed by non-state actors and to account for the victims' whereabouts is equally considered as continuous by the ECtHR, or whether this will always depend on the circumstances of the case.

In the case-law of the IACtHR, the continuous obligation to investigate and search appears to apply to all types of disappearances. Thus, in the case of *Velásquez Rodríguez*, the IACtHR held that '[t]he duty to investigate facts of this type continues as long as there is uncertainty about the fate of the person who has disappeared'. Furthermore, '[...] the State is obligated to use the means at its

---

[139] *Varnava and Others v. Turkey*, para. 145.

[140] Ibid., para. 186.

[141] Ibid., para. 148. Note however that the European Court did not order to conduct an effective investigation as part of the reparations. This was criticized in the concurring opinion of Judge Spielmann, joined by judges Ziemele and Kalaydjieva, who considered that conducting an effective investigation should have been ordered as a form of restitution. See *Varnava and Others v. Turkey*, Concurring Opinion of Judge Spielmann joined by Judges Ziemele and Kalaydjieva, para. 3.

[142] See, for example, *Skendžić and Krznarić v Croatia* [2011] European Court of Human Rights Application no. 16212/08, para. 61; *Aslakhanova and Others v. Russia*, paras 122 and 124; *Zorica Jovanović v Serbia* [2013] European Court of Human Rights Application no. 21794/08, paras 47–48.

disposal to inform the relatives of the fate of the victims and, if they have been killed, the location of their remains'.[143] This is the case even if it should for some reason be the case that it is not possible to 'legally punish' the perpetrators[144] and the obligation to investigate exists in relation to 'every situation involving a violation of the rights protected by the Convention',[145] which includes acts by 'private persons or groups'.[146] In the case of the *Hacienda Brasil Verde Workers*, the IACtHR referred to its case-law that establishes a continuous obligation of states to investigate acts of *enforced* disappearance and punish those responsible.[147] This reference, despite the case clearly not being one of *enforced* disappearance, suggests that the IACtHR considers the continuous obligation to investigate as equally applicable in cases involving disappearances committed by non-state actors.[148]

The African Commission has also emphasised the continuous nature of the obligations to search, investigate, and prosecute.[149] While the Commission articulated the content of these obligations and their continuous nature in relation to enforced disappearances, it then added the following clarification to each obligation: 'For the avoidance of doubt, under international law the obligation to [search/identify/prosecute and punish] applies even where the disappearance was perpetrated by a non-State actor.'[150] This reference by the Commission to disappearances committed by non-state actors suggests that the content of the obligations remains the same, regardless of the presumed perpetrator.

2.1.3.3 The Obligation to Repair

While there is no question about the obligation of states to provide an effective remedy in cases of disappearances committed by non-state actors in the form of an effective investigation and, where possible, the prosecution of perpetrators, it is not

---

[143] *Case of Velásquez-Rodríguez v. Honduras (Merits)*, para. 181. Note that in the Spanish original version, the IACtHR actually refers to a right of the relatives to know about the victim's fate: 'el *derecho de los familiares de la víctima de conocer cuál fue el destino de ésta* y, en su caso, dónde se encuentran sus restos, representa una justa expectativa que el Estado debe satisfacer con los medios a su alcance' (emphasis added). This is interesting because the reference to a right to know of the relatives could arguably be understood as creating an even stronger obligation.

[144] Ibid.

[145] Ibid., para. 176.

[146] Ibid., paras 176–177.

[147] *Case of the Hacienda Brasil Verde Workers v. Brazil*, para. 426.

[148] Ultimately, the IACtHR found no violation because it was not clear whether the victims had indeed been victims of a disappearance, as a result of which the state could be held responsible for its failure to investigate and punish a disappearance (because it might not have been one in the first place). See Ibid., para. 433.

[149] African Commission on Human and Peoples' Rights (2022) Guidelines on the Protection of All Persons from Enforced Disappearances in Africa, paras. 2.4 and 4.1.4 (i–iv).

[150] Ibid., paras 4.1.4 and 4.1.6.

certain whether this also encompasses the more substantive component of remedies, i.e., reparations.[151] Even though the right to reparation for gross human rights violations is by now firmly established in IHRL,[152] disappearances committed by non-state actors are, legally speaking, not human rights violations. Logically then, they can also not be considered 'gross human rights violations'. The exception would be a situation where disappearances committed by non-state actors are committed on such a scale that they would constitute enforced disappearances as crimes against humanity in line with Article 5 ICPPED and the Rome Statute.[153] The question whether victims of crimes that do not constitute human rights violations, such as disappearances committed by non-state actors, have a self-standing right to reparation under international law still has no definitive answer and requires further research.

The Basic Principles and Guidelines on the Right to a Remedy and Reparation for Victims of Gross Violations of International Human Rights Law and Serious Violations of International Humanitarian Law (Basic Principles)[154] establish a clear duty to provide reparations for 'gross violations of International Human Rights Law'.[155] While the Principles establish that 'States should endeavour to establish national programmes for reparation and other assistance to victims in the event that the parties liable for the harm suffered are unable or unwilling to meet their obligations',[156] the wording of this paragraph ('should', rather than 'shall') indicates that the establishment of such programmes is not an obligation *de lege lata*.[157] Therefore, states currently do not have a self-standing obligation to provide 'full reparation' to victims of non-state actors. Indeed, according to Theo Van Boven, the question of reparations for acts committed by non-state actors was discussed during the negotiations of the Basic Principles and there was a general feeling 'that non-State actors are to be held responsible for their policies and practices, allowing

[151] See Shelton (2015), pp. 16–17; Calvet Martínez (2015), p. 305. For an overview of the different terminology used in human rights instruments (remedy/redress/reparation), see Shelton (2015), p. 17.

[152] Human Rights Committee (2004) General Comment No. 31: The Nature of the General Legal Obligation Imposed on States Parties to the Covenant. UN Doc. CCPR/C/21/Rev.1/Add. 13, para. 16; United Nations General Assembly (UNGA) (2006) Basic Principles and Guidelines on the Right to a Remedy and Reparation for Victims of Gross Violations of International Human Rights Law and Serious Violations of International Humanitarian Law. UN Doc. A/RES/60/147, para. 11.

[153] The CED has endorsed this view, as discussed later in the chapter.

[154] UNGA (2006) Basic Principles and Guidelines on the Right to a Remedy and Reparation for Victims of Gross Violations of International Human Rights Law and Serious Violations of International Humanitarian Law. UN Doc. A/RES/60/147.

[155] Ibid., para. 15.

[156] Ibid., para. 16.

[157] Shelton (2015), p. 75.

victims to seek redress and reparation on the basis of legal liability and human solidarity, and not on the basis of State responsibility.'[158]

Nonetheless, according to Shelton '[t]he inclusion of non-state actors, the scope of their liability, and the duties of the state respecting violations by them remain debated topics'.[159] While an in-depth analysis of these debates lies beyond the scope of this research, it is important to note that the truth commissions of Peru and Sierra Leone adopted the view that the states had a legal obligation to provide reparations to victims of all perpetrators, both state and non-state.[160] While truth commissions are not judicial bodies and their legal authority is weak, their approach is nevertheless important because it supports an argument that in situations of large-scale violations of human rights, the state obligation to provide reparation exists regardless of the identity of the perpetrator. Such an approach can be warranted in situations of mass violence where the sheer number of cases may require collective, rather than individualised approaches,[161] because it might not be feasible to identify individual perpetrators in order to determine whether a particular disappearance was an *enforced* disappearance or a disappearance committed by non-state actors.

According to the HRC, the obligation to provide an effective remedy also includes an obligation to 'make reparation to individuals whose Covenant rights

---

[158] Van Boven (2010), para. e. This view is also reflected in the 2021 *Joint Statement by independent United Nations human rights experts on human rights responsibilities of armed non-State actors*. Among the recommendations made by the experts is the following: 'provide appropriate redress, reparations and other assistance to victims, in cases of both direct and indirect responsibility for abuses committed by armed non-State actors, in particular in cases where armed non-state actors are unable or unwilling to meet their responsibilities in this regard.' See OHCHR (2021). The reference to '*cases of both direct and indirect responsibility*' supports the view that there is no self-standing obligation to repair. Rather, this obligation continues to be connected to the direct or indirect responsibility of the state. A separate discussion is whether the non-state actors themselves could have an obligation to provide reparations, which goes beyond the scope of this book. For a recent analysis of this question, see Herman (2024).

[159] Shelton (2015), p. 75.

[160] See Comisión de la Verdad y Reconciliación en el Perú (2003), p. 143, citing *Velásquez Rodríguez v. Honduras*. The Truth and Reconciliation Commission then held 'it follows that, given its role to maintain social and public order, *the duty of the State to repair extends to human rights violations committed by private actors, including subversive and terrorist groups*. Consequently, the Truth and Reconciliation Commission and its Comprehensive Reparations Plan recommends equal treatment of all victims, be they victims of crimes committed by State agents or subversive or terrorist groups' (own translation, emphasis in original). The Truth and Reconciliation Commission for Sierra Leone made the following statement in its report: 'The Commission took the view that the State has a legal obligation to provide reparations for violations committed by both state actors and private actors. The Commission is of the opinion that all victims should be treated equally, fairly, and justly. Given the nature of the conflict in Sierra Leone, it was not always possible to identify the perpetrators or the group they belonged to. States have the obligation to guarantee the enjoyment of human rights and to ensure that human rights violators are brought to justice and that reparations are made to victims.' Sierra Leóne Truth and Reconciliation Commission (2004), para. 21.

[161] For a general overview of challenges related to reparation in post-conflict societies, see Letschert and Van Boven (2011).

have been violated.'[162] This wording suggests that an obligation to provide reparation arises once a human rights violation has been committed. Consequently, if a disappearance committed by a non-state actor is not a human rights violation *per se*, which *de lege lata* it is not, unless committed with the authorisation, support or acquiescence of state agents, a narrow reading would imply that states do not have an obligation to repair. Nonetheless, it is notable that in its General Comment No. 31, the HRC stated that a state may incur international responsibility for 'failing to take appropriate measures or to exercise due diligence to prevent, punish, investigate *or redress* the harm caused by such acts by private persons or entities.'[163] Whether the due diligence obligation to redress harm caused by private persons only refers to the obligation to provide an effective (procedural) remedy, or whether it would also encompass substantive reparations, is not entirely clear and will likely depend on the circumstances of each case.[164] Given that the HRC explicitly mentions punishment, investigation, *or* redress, an argument could be made that redress here refers to reparations, or at least to compensation. Such an argument would be in line with the European Convention on the Compensation of Victims of Violent Crimes, which was adopted in 1983 due to the perceived necessity to

> introduce or develop schemes for the compensation of [victims of intentional crimes of violence who have suffered bodily injury or impairment of health and of dependants of persons who have died as a result of such crimes] by the State in whose territory such crimes were committed, in particular when the offender has not been identified or is without resources.[165]

Moreover, many countries have compensation schemes in place for victims of crimes, indicating state practice on this issue.[166] Notwithstanding, it is important to keep in mind that compensation is only one aspect of reparations, and there continue to exist discussions about whether IHRL always requires 'full' reparation.[167]

Notably, in its Guidelines on Enforced Disappearances, the African Commission clarified that the obligation to provide redress to victims of enforced disappearances encompasses 'effective and timely remedies, including reparations'. After outlining the content of effective remedies and reparations, as it did in previous paragraphs concerning the obligations to search, investigate, and prosecute, the Commission added:

---

[162] Human Rights Committee (2004) General Comment No. 31: The Nature of the General Legal Obligation Imposed on States Parties to the Covenant. UN Doc. CCPR/C/21/Rev.1/Add. 13, para. 16. Emphasis added.

[163] Ibid., para. 8. Emphasis added.

[164] I thank Prof. Barbara Frey for emphasising that the answer will be elaborated on a case by case basis.

[165] Preamble, European Convention on the Compensation of Victims of Violent Crimes 1983 (ETS No 116).

[166] See Shelton (2015), p. 5. For an overview of domestic practice by states, see ibid., pp. 316–321.

[167] Ibid., p. 17.

> For the avoidance of doubt, States shall ensure that victims of crimes analogous to enforced disappearances which have been carried out by non-State actors shall have access to effective remedies.[168]

If reparations are a component of effective remedies, this sentence can be read as implying that victims of disappearances committed by non-state actors also have a right to reparation under the African Guidelines. Read in this manner, the African Guidelines would be the most progressive instrument when it comes to reparations for victims of disappearances committed by non-state actors, which would be a welcome development from a victim-centred perspective. The Guidelines would also go beyond the obligations established in the ICPPED, which I discuss in the next section.

2.2 State Obligations under the ICPPED

Until the adoption of the ICPPED in 2006 (and its entry into force in 2010), existing international and regional instruments on enforced disappearances did not contain any specific obligations concerning disappearances committed by non-state actors. Both the (non-binding) DPPED[169] and the first legally binding regional instrument, the IACFDP, define the crime of enforced disappearance as committed by state agents or by 'persons or groups acting with the authorisation, support, or acquiescence of the State'[170] and do not contain any explicit obligations in relation to acts that do not amount to an *enforced* disappearance in accordance with these definitions. The exclusive focus on state actors as perpetrators (through direct or indirect involvement), was criticised as leaving a gap in the 'full protection' of persons from enforced disappearances prior to the negotiations of the ICPPED, due to the characteristic absence of evidence in disappearance cases that makes it difficult to identify the perpetrators.[171] This led to discussions during the negotiations of the Convention about whether or not to include non-state actors as possible perpetrators in the definition of enforced disappearance, as well as about how to determine state

[168] African Commission on Human and Peoples' Rights (2022) Guidelines on the Protection of All Persons from Enforced Disappearances in Africa, para. 4.1.9.

[169] In the preamble of the DPPED, enforced disappearances are defined as occurring where 'persons are arrested, detained or abducted against their will or otherwise deprived of their liberty by officials of different branches or levels of Government, or by organized groups or private individuals acting on behalf of, or with the support, direct or indirect, consent or acquiescence of the Government, followed by a refusal to disclose the fate or whereabouts of the persons concerned or a refusal to acknowledge the deprivation of their liberty, which places such persons outside the protection of the law'.

[170] Art II, IACFDP.

[171] See specifically Commission on Human Rights (2002) Report submitted by Mr. Manfred Nowak, independent expert charged with examining the existing international criminal and human rights framework for the protection of persons from enforced or involuntary disappearances. UN Doc. E/CN.4/2002/71, para. 73.

responsibility in such instances.[172] The final consensus reached was to exclude non-state actors from the definition of enforced disappearance as contained in Article 2 ICPPED, but to specify the obligations of states in relation to disappearances committed by non-state actors acting without the authorisation, support or acquiescence of state actors in a separate article.[173] Consequently, since the adoption of the ICPPED, states parties to the Convention have explicit obligations with regard to disappearances committed by non-state actors under Article 3 ICPPED:

> Each State Party shall take *appropriate measures to investigate* acts defined in article 2 committed by persons or groups of persons acting without the authorization, support or acquiescence of the State and to *bring those responsible to justice*.[174]

It is therefore unquestionable that the ICPPED establishes obligations for states to investigate and to prosecute disappearances committed by non-state actors. These obligations have also been affirmed by the WGEID in its General Comment on the definition of enforced disappearance, as well as in its recent Report on standards and public policies for an effective investigation of enforced disappearances[175] and by the CED in its 2023 Statement on Non-State Actors,[176] as well as in several concluding observations.[177]

---

[172] Commission on Human Rights (2003) Report of the Intersessional Open-Ended Working Group to Elaborate a Draft Legally Binding Normative Instrument for the Protection of All Persons from Enforced Disappearance. UN Doc. E/CN.4/2003/71, para. 35; Commission on Human Rights (2004) Report of the Intersessional Open-Ended Working Group to Elaborate a Draft Legally Binding Normative Instrument for the Protection of All Persons from Enforced Disappearance. UN Doc. E/CN.4/2004/59, paras 29–41; Commission on Human Rights (2005) Report of the Intersessional Open-Ended Working Group to Elaborate a Draft Legally Binding Normative Instrument for the Protection of All Persons from Enforced Disappearance. UN Doc. E/CN.4/2005/66, paras 29–35; Commission on Human Rights (2006) Report of the Intersessional Open-Ended Working Group to Elaborate a Draft Legally Binding Normative Instrument for the Protection of All Persons from Enforced Disappearance. UN Doc. E/CN.4/2006/57, paras 12–14.

[173] Commission on Human Rights (2006) Report of the Intersessional Open-Ended Working Group to Elaborate a Draft Legally Binding Normative Instrument for the Protection of All Persons from Enforced Disappearance. UN Doc. E/CN.4/2006/57, paras 12–15. There remain, however, some ambiguities as to the relationship between Articles 2 and 3. On this, see de Frouville (2021).

[174] Article 3, ICPPED. Emphasis added.

[175] Human Rights Council (2007) Report of the Working Group on Enforced or Involuntary Disappearances 2007: General Comment on the Definition of Enforced Disappearance. UN Doc. A/HRC/7/2 at para. 26, para. 2: 'The Working Group concurs with the provisions of article 3 of the International Convention, in connection with the fact that States shall take appropriate measures to investigate acts comparable to enforced disappearances committed by persons or groups of persons acting without the authorization, support or acquiescence of the State and to bring those responsible to justice.'; Human Rights Council (2020) Report of the Working Group on Enforced or Involuntary Disappearances on Standards and Public Policies for an Effective Investigation of Enforced Disappearances. UN Doc. A/HRC/45/13/Add.3, paras 90–92.

[176] CED (2023) Statement on non-State actors in the context of the International Convention for the Protection of All Persons from Enforced Disappearances. UN Doc. CED/C/10, para. 20.

[177] See, for example, CED (2015) Concluding Observations on the Report Submitted by Iraq under Article 29 (1) of the Convention. UN Doc. CED/C/IRQ/CO/1, para. 23; CED (2016) Concluding

Nonetheless, the exact content of the obligations enshrined in Article 3 continues to remain somewhat elusive, and several scholars have pointed to a need for further elaboration of what constitute 'appropriate measures' to investigate.[178] The CED's Statement on Non-State Actors, which reiterates the obligations in Article 3 ICPPED, also does not provide any further guidance in this regard. Therefore, the following section examines the content of the obligation to take 'appropriate measures' for the investigation and prosecution of disappearances committed by non-state actors from within the international framework on enforced disappearances, having in mind the standards from general IHRL discussed previously.

2.2.1 Content of the Obligations under Article 3

Article 3 ICPPED does not specify what exactly constitute 'appropriate measures' and the preparatory works indicate that states were reluctant to create a too stringent or too detailed obligation in this regard. Thus, the word 'appropriate' was chosen to replace a previous version of Article 3, which referred to the obligation of states to take the '*necessary* measures' (emphasis added) to investigate disappearances committed by non-state actors. The term 'necessary', however, was seen as placing 'excessively heavy obligations on States'.[179] The negotiations of the ICPPED thus indicate the intention of states to allow for a certain level of discretion in complying with the obligations under Article 3 and that the content of the obligation to investigate disappearances committed by non-state actors may not be equal to that of investigating *enforced* disappearances.[180] To a certain extent, this stance is reflected in Section V. of the Statement on Non-State Actors concerning 'Obligations of States parties in relation to disappearances committed by non-State actors falling within the scope of Articles 3 and 5' in which the CED clarifies that '[i]n the case of enforced disappearances falling under article 5 of the Convention, States parties must apply all the provisions of the Convention, specifically fulfilling their obligations set forth in articles 4 to 16, 24 and 25.'[181] Disappearances within the scope of Article 3 ICPPED are not included in this paragraph, suggesting that the

---

Observations on the Report Submitted by Colombia under Article 29 (1) of the Convention. UN Doc. CED/C/COL/CO/1, para. 24.

[178] McCrory (2007), p. 551; Huhle (2013), p. 24; Vermeulen (2012), pp. 92–93. For a brief discussion of the content of 'appropriate measures', see also Vermeulen (2012), pp. 401–402.

[179] Commission on Human Rights (2006) Report of the Intersessional Open-Ended Working Group to Elaborate a Draft Legally Binding Normative Instrument for the Protection of All Persons from Enforced Disappearance. UN Doc. E/CN.4/2006/57, para. 14.

[180] Some authors have nevertheless argued that certain articles of the ICPPED could and should apply to disappearances committed by non-state actors. See, for example, de Frouville (2021), p. 37; Huhle (2013), p. 25.

[181] CED (2023) Statement on non-State actors in the context of the International Convention for the Protection of All Persons from Enforced Disappearances. UN Doc. CED/C/10, para. 21.

articles cited do not apply, including Article 12 ICPPED on investigations.[182] Nonetheless, interpreting the investigation obligations of states deriving from Article 3 ICPPED as subject to different standards from those relating to enforced disappearances would not only run counter to the position of other human rights bodies examined in the previous section, but also make little sense from the perspective of the Convention itself. As noted by Vermeulen, it is logical to apply equal standards to disappearances committed by non-state actors, given the possibility that such investigations might reveal the involvement of state actors that would 'convert' a disappearance falling within Article 3 ICPPED into an enforced disappearance.[183] In a similar vein, in its Report on standards and public policies for an effective investigation of enforced disappearances, the WGEID stated that the ECtHR and IACtHR have considered the 'same requirements of *ex officio* investigations, promptness, effectiveness, involvement of family members, and impartiality of investigating entities apply in relation to enforced disappearances allegedly committed by non-State actors',[184] which suggests that the WGEID considers the standards as equally applicable to disappearances committed by non-state actors.

Regarding statements by the CED itself, it has been somewhat difficult to gauge the Committee's position on the content of obligations to investigate disappearances falling within Article 3 ICPPED, as it often referred to elements of an effective investigation only in relation to *enforced* disappearances. For example, in its 2015 concluding observations on Mexico, the CED referred to the Mexican state's obligation to undertake a prompt, thorough and impartial investigation on its own initiative 'where there are reasonable grounds for believing that a person has been

[182] Article 12 ICPPED outlines the obligation to investigate enforced disappearances:

1. Each State Party shall ensure that any individual who alleges that a person has been subjected to enforced disappearance has the right to report the facts to the competent authorities, which shall examine the allegation promptly and impartially and, where necessary, undertake without delay a thorough and impartial investigation. Appropriate steps shall be taken, where necessary, to ensure that the complainant, witnesses, relatives of the disappeared person and their defence counsel, as well as persons participating in the investigation, are protected against all ill-treatment or intimidation as a consequence of the complaint or any evidence given.
2. Where there are reasonable grounds for believing that a person has been subjected to enforced disappearance, the authorities referred to in paragraph 1 of this article shall undertake an investigation, even if there has been no formal complaint.
3. Each State Party shall ensure that the authorities referred to in paragraph 1 of this article:
   (a) Have the necessary powers and resources to conduct the investigation effectively, including access to the documentation and other information relevant to their investigation;
   (b) Have access, if necessary with the prior authorization of a judicial authority, which shall rule promptly on the matter, to any place of detention or any other place where there are reasonable grounds to believe that the disappeared person may be present.

[183] See Vermeulen (2012), pp. 482–483.

[184] Human Rights Council (2020) Report of the Working Group on Enforced or Involuntary Disappearances on Standards and Public Policies for an Effective Investigation of Enforced Disappearances. UN Doc. A/HRC/45/13/Add.3, paras 142 ff.

subjected to *enforced* disappearance.'[185] Yet the CED stayed silent on the obligation to investigate cases where such reasonable grounds may not exist.

In its more recently adopted documents, however, the CED has indirectly indicated that the same standards for conducting effective investigations apply to enforced disappearances and disappearances falling within Article 3 ICPPED, even though it has not yet explicitly discussed the meaning of 'appropriate' measures. In its General Comment on Enforced Disappearance in the context of Migration, the Committee, explicitly stated

> The Committee recalls that the obligations to search for disappeared persons, conduct effective investigations into cases of alleged disappearance, *including those falling within article 3 of the Convention*, and prosecute and punish perpetrators are fundamental to ending this heinous crime and preventing its reoccurrence.[186]

In addition, and given the prevalence of under-reporting of disappearances of migrants, it added that

> Authorities should initiate the search and investigation *ex officio* as soon as they become aware of or have indications, through any means, that a person has been subjected to disappearance. [...] The burden of proof should not be on the victims or relatives. [...][187]

The explicit reference to Article 3 of the Convention at the beginning of the paragraph, and the subsequent reference to authorities' awareness of a person's having been subjected to 'disappearance' (and not enforced disappearance), indicates that the obligation to conduct *ex officio* investigations also applies to disappearances falling within Article 3 of the Convention and that it is for the state to provide evidence. Moreover, the following paragraphs, which list the measures states should take to ensure that persons can report disappearances without fear of reprisals (para. 38), the effectiveness of investigations and searches (paras 39–41), the appropriate involvement of and sharing of information with relatives (para. 42), and the search, identification and return of 'remains of migrants who are found dead along migratory routes' (para. 43), refer to 'disappeared persons' in a comprehensive and inclusive manner. In that sense, it is unfortunate that the Committee did not engage with the applicability of Article 12 ICPPED to disappearances falling within Article 3 ICPPED in a more explicit manner in the Statement, which could have provided greater clarity in this regard.

Regardless of the applicability of Article 12 ICPPED, the General Comment confirms that the CED views state obligations regarding the search and investigation of disappeared persons as applicable regardless of the perpetrator. This is reflected in the General Comment's reference to the Committee's 2019 Guiding Principles for the Search for Disappeared Persons (Guiding Principles) and their content. In the

---

[185] CED (2015) Concluding Observations on the Report Submitted by Mexico. UN Doc. CED/C/MEX/CO/1, para. 28. Emphasis added.

[186] CED (2023) General Comment No. 1 on Enforced Disappearance in the Context of Migration. UN Doc. CED/C/GC/1, para. 37. Emphasis added.

[187] Ibid.

Guiding Principles, the CED stated that the principles were 'complementary' to the 2016 Minnesota Protocol on the Investigation of Potentially Unlawful Death (Minnesota Protocol).[188] Thus, the standards established in the Minnesota Protocol in relation to the conduct of an 'effective' investigation can be applied to obligations under the ICPPED, which would be consistent with the HRC's approach mentioned above. The criteria for an 'effective' investigation established by the Minnesota Protocol are that investigations must be '(i) prompt; (ii) effective and thorough; (iii) independent and impartial; and (iv) transparent'.[189] Moreover, for an obligation to investigate to arise, no formal complaint is required[190] and authorities must involve the relatives of the disappeared person in the investigation and protect them throughout this process.[191] These criteria are directly reflected in the CED's General Comment, which also makes explicit reference to the Minnesota Protocol and establishes that '[i]nvestigations of cases of the disappearance of migrants must be transparent, thorough and impartial'.[192] In addition, as mentioned above, investigations must be conducted *ex officio* (para. 37) and relatives of disappeared persons must be included throughout the investigation process (para. 42). While articulated in relation to disappearances of migrants, there is no reason why these standards would not be equally applicable other disappearances committed by non-state actors.

This is also supported by the CED's reports on its visits to Mexico and Iraq, where perpetrators include both state and non-state actors and not all disappearances can necessarily be categorised as 'enforced disappearances'.[193] In its recommendations to Mexico, the Committee named as a priority 'for the State party to establish a global and comprehensive search and investigation strategy for *cases of disappearance* to ensure that both recent and older cases are duly addressed',[194] thereby encompassing all disappearances. Similarly, in its recommendations to the Iraqi government, the Committee emphasised the urgent need to establish a 'comprehensive search and investigation strategy for cases of disappearances [...] *regardless* of the ethnic, religious or national background of the disappeared persons, the national

---

188 CED (2019) Guiding Principles for the Search for Disappeared Persons. UN Doc. CED/C/7, para. 3.

189 United Nations Office of the High Commissioner for Human Rights (OHCHR) (2017) The Minnesota Protocol on the Investigation of Potentially Unlawful Death (2016). HR/PUB/17/4, para. 22.

190 Ibid., para. 15.

191 Ibid., paras 35–36.

192 CED (2023) General Comment No. 1 on Enforced Disappearance in the Context of Migration. UN Doc. CED/C/GC/1, para. 39.

193 See CED (2023) Report of the Committee on Enforced Disappearances on its visit to Iraq: Information on the visit and findings. UN Doc. CED/C/IRQ/VR/1 (Findings), paras 49 ff; CED (2022) Report of the Committee on Enforced Disappearances on its visit to Mexico: Findings. UN Doc. CED/C/MEX/VR/1 (Findings), para. 13.

194 CED (2022) Report of the Committee on Enforced Disappearances on its visit to Mexico: Observations and Recommendations. UN Doc. CED/C/MEX/VR/1 (Recommendations), para. 14. Emphasis added.

origin of the alleged perpetrators, or the time, location and *circumstances of the disappearances*.'[195]

2.2.2 The Obligation to Search under the ICPPED

Due to the continuous nature of disappearances and the suffering that it implies for the relatives of the disappeared person, the search for the disappeared is crucial.[196] While closely connected to the obligation to investigate, the obligation to search victims of (enforced) disappearances is considered to be an autonomous obligation based on several articles of the ICPPED.[197] If the obligation to search is autonomous from that to investigate, a strict reading of the Convention implies that there is no explicit obligation to search for victims of disappearances committed by non-state actors that fall within the scope of Article 3 ICPPED. Notwithstanding, the CED has consistently taken the view that the obligation to search exists irrespective of the perpetrators. This stance is illustrated by the Committee's recommendations to countries where disappearances are committed by both state and non-state actors, such as Iraq, Colombia,[198] and Mexico.[199] For example, in its 2015 Concluding Observations on Iraq, the Committee formulated the following recommendation:

> Furthermore, the Committee recommends that the State party adopt the necessary measures to ensure that all persons deprived of liberty by these groups [the so-called Islamic State in Iraq and the Levant and affiliated groups] and whose fates remain unknown are searched for and located.[200]

Similarly, in its 2016 concluding observations on the report submitted by Colombia, the Committee recommended that 'the search is continued until the fate of the

---

[195] See CED (2023) Report of the Committee on Enforced Disappearances on its visit to Iraq: Observations and recommendations. UN Doc. CED/C/IRQ/VR/1 (Recommendations), para. 11. Emphasis added.

[196] Galvis Patiño and Huhle (2020).

[197] CED (2017) Report of the Committee on Enforced Disappearances. UN Doc. A/72/56, paras 61–63; Galvis Patiño and Arias Ávila (2019), pp. 5–6; Dulitzky and Anayanssi Orizaga (2019), p. 41.

[198] CED (2016) Concluding Observations on the Report Submitted by Colombia under Article 29 (1) of the Convention. UN Doc. CED/C/COL/CO/1, paras 25–26; CED (2021) Concluding observations on the additional information submitted by Colombia under Article 29 (4) of the Convention. UN Doc. CED/C/COL/OAI/1, paras 26–27.

[199] CED (2015) Concluding Observations on the Report Submitted by Mexico. UN Doc. CED/C/MEX/CO/1, paras 40–41; CED (2019) Follow-up Observations on the Additional Information Submitted by Mexico under Article 29 (4) of the Convention. UN Doc. CED/C/MEX/FAI/1, para. 19; CED (2022) Report of the Committee on Enforced Disappearances on its visit to Mexico: Observations and Recommendations. UN Doc. CED/C/MEX/VR/1 (Recommendations), paras 14–22.

[200] CED (2015) Concluding Observations on the Report Submitted by Iraq under Article 29 (1) of the Convention. UN Doc. CED/C/IRQ/CO/1, para. 23.

disappeared person is established',[201] without distinguishing between disappearances committed by state or non-state perpetrators. Finally, in its reports on the visits to Mexico and Iraq, the Committee also highlighted the obligation to search for all victims of disappearances by specifically addressing the responsibility of the state in cases where disappearances are committed by non-state actors without the authorisation, support or acquiescence of the state. According to the Committee, not only do states bear responsibility if they fail to investigate such disappearances and bring perpetrators to justice, but also 'if they fail to search for and locate disappeared persons and, in the event of their death, if their bodies are not returned to their families and relatives in a dignified manner [...].'[202] In the report on its visit to Iraq, the CED also made explicit that the state should establish a 'consolidated nationwide database of disappeared persons, *including of persons who have been subjected to enforced disappearance*',[203] which clearly indicates that all victims of disappeared must be registered and searched for.[204]

The Committee's Guiding Principles also refer to 'disappeared' persons in a general manner and state clearly that:

> Each State in which cases of enforced disappearance occur or disappearances are committed by persons or groups acting without the authorization, support or acquiescence of the State should have competent institutions with the capacity to search for disappeared persons.[205]

---

[201] CED (2016) Concluding Observations on the Report Submitted by Colombia under Article 29 (1) of the Convention. UN Doc. CED/C/COL/CO/1, para. 26(a).

[202] CED (2022) Report of the Committee on Enforced Disappearances on its visit to Mexico: Findings. UN Doc. CED/C/MEX/VR/1 (Findings), para. 41. The Committee repeated this statement in its report on the visit to Iraq. See CED (2023) Report of the Committee on Enforced Disappearances on its visit to Iraq: Information on the visit and findings. UN Doc. CED/C/IRQ/VR/1 (Findings), para. 53.

[203] CED (2022) Report of the Committee on Enforced Disappearances on its visit to Mexico: Findings. UN Doc. CED/C/MEX/VR/1 (Findings), para. 77. Emphasis added.

[204] Indeed, the wording is particularly interesting when contrasted with previous recommendations made by the Committee, which were often phrased in such a way as to suggest that data should be collected in order to identify cases of enforced disappearance, leaving doubts about obligations towards disappearances falling within Article 3. For example, in its 2016 concluding observations on Colombia, the CED made the recommendation to gather data on 'disappeared persons' (para. 14), but then further specified that Colombia should 'Take the necessary steps to generate statistical information that indicates the extent of the problem of enforced disappearances in the strict sense of the term, that is, disappearances where State agents were allegedly involved, directly or indirectly, in committing the offence.' (CED (2016) Concluding Observations on the Report Submitted by Colombia under Article 29 (1) of the Convention. UN Doc. CED/C/COL/CO/1, para. 14). The CED also criticised the definition of enforced disappearance in the Colombian Criminal Code as too broad because the latter includes individuals acting independently of the state as perpetrators of enforced disappearances: 'the inclusion of non-State actors in the definition of the crime of enforced disappearance dilutes the accountability of the State and that the broad definition of enforced disappearance contained in article 165 of the Criminal Code could have other types of consequences, such as a lack of clear statistics or inadequacies in searches for disappeared persons and in criminal investigations, as these require differentiated approaches and strategies' (ibid., para. 15).

[205] CED (2019) Guiding Principles for the Search for Disappeared Persons. UN Doc. CED/C/7, Principle 10(1).

Table 2.1 Content of the obligation to search according to the Guiding Principles for the Search for Disappeared Persons

Principle 1	'The search for a disappeared person should be conducted under the presumption that he or she is alive'
Principle 2	'The search should respect human dignity'
Principle 3	'The search should be governed by a public policy'
Principle 4	'The search should follow a differential approach'
Principle 5	'The search should respect the right to participation'
Principle 6	'The search should begin without delay'
Principle 7	'The search is a continuing obligation'
Principle 8	'The search should be conducted on the basis of a comprehensive strategy'
Principle 9	'The search should take into account the particular vulnerability of migrants'
Principle 10	'The search should be organized efficiently'
Principle 11	'The search should use information in an appropriate manner'
Principle 12	'The search should be coordinated'
Principle 13	'The search and the criminal investigation should be interrelated'
Principle 14	'The search should be carried out safely'
Principle 15	'The search should be independent and impartial'
Principle 16	'The search should be governed by public protocols'

This approach of the Committee was made explicit in the Statement on Non-State Actors:

> [...] As a corollary [to the explicit obligation under article 3 to investigate and bring perpetrators to justice], States have an obligation to search for disappeared persons in accordance with the Guiding Principles for the Search for Disappeared Persons [...].[206]

Thus, while the obligation to search is not explicitly mentioned in Article 3, the CED has interpreted the obligation to investigate as implying an obligation to search due to their mutually reinforcing nature.[207] Moreover, as explained by de Frouville, unless a search is carried out it is often impossible to identify the perpetrator(s) and determine with certainty whether there was direct or indirect state involvement that would make the disappearance an enforced disappearance.[208]

The Guiding Principles thus apply equally to enforced disappearances and disappearances committed by non-state actors falling within Article 3 ICPPED (see Table 2.1). Importantly, Principle 7 of the Guiding Principles establishes that the obligations to search and investigate are continuous obligations, regardless of the

[206] CED (2023) Statement on non-State actors in the context of the International Convention for the Protection of All Persons from Enforced Disappearances. UN Doc. CED/C/10, para. 20.

[207] See also CED (2019) Guiding Principles for the Search for Disappeared Persons. UN Doc. CED/C/7, Principle 13. For an in-depth discussion of the 'ambiguous' relationship between the search and investigation, and the meaning of the words 'fate' or 'whereabouts' in the definition of enforced disappearance, see Huhle (2022). For a study on the practical challenges of coordinating search activities and criminal investigations, see Srovin Coralli (2021a).

[208] de Frouville (2021), n. 90.

perpetrator of the disappearance. This also means that even where the search has been stopped, this should '[u]nder no circumstances [...] result in the search or criminal investigation being closed'.[209]

2.2.2.1 Urgent Actions

Finally, in addition to making the obligation to search for victims of disappearances—ostensibly—falling within Article 3 ICPPED explicit, in its Statement on Non-State Actors, the CED clarified the applicability of Article 30 ICPPED to such disappearances and provided additional guidance about the content of states' obligations. Article 30 ICPPED establishes an 'Urgent Action' procedure for relatives of a disappeared person or their legal representatives to submit an urgent search request to the Committee.[210] In the past, when the Committee has had to decide how to deal with Urgent Action requests where these mention the possible involvement of non-state actors as perpetrators,[211] it accepted the requests, given that until an investigation had been conducted, it was not possible to determine whether authorities were directly or indirectly involved in the disappearance or not, even if non-state agents had been the direct perpetrators.[212] However, the Committee previously decided to close the Urgent Action as soon as 'the information provided by the parties in the course of the urgent action procedure shows that there is no involvement of agents of the State, including through support or acquiescence'.[213] Notably, however, the wording of Article 30 refers only to 'disappeared persons' and not specifically to victims of *enforced* disappearance. Consequently, and if the obligation to search applies to all cases, an argument can and has been made that Urgent Actions should also encompass victims of disappearances committed by non-state actors without any indication or possibility of state involvement.[214]

---

[209] CED (2019) Guiding Principles for the Search for Disappeared Persons. UN Doc. CED/C/7, Principle 7(5).

[210] According to Article 30 (1) ICPPED 'A request that a disappeared person should be sought and found may be submitted to the Committee, as a matter of urgency, by relatives of the disappeared person or their legal representatives, their counsel or any person authorized by them, as well as by any other person having a legitimate interest.'

[211] CED (2017) Report of the Committee on Enforced Disappearances. UN Doc. A/72/56, paras 55–58.

[212] Ibid., para 58. The CED had already decided to accept Urgent Action requests where there was no indication of who the perpetrators were. For example, it accepted an Urgent Action concerning a disappearance in Mexico in an area where both soldiers and criminal gangs had a presence. See CED (2014) Report of the Committee on Enforced Disappearances. UN Doc. A/69/56, para. 61. Similarly, the CED also accepted an Urgent Action from Colombia where a person had disappeared after taking a taxi. See CED (2015) Report of the Committee on Enforced Disappearances. UN Doc. A/70/56, paras 53–55.

[213] CED (2017) Report of the Committee on Enforced Disappearances. UN Doc. A/72/56, para. 58 (b).

[214] An example is the argument by Prof. Clapham that the CED could receive requests under Article 30 if the perpetrators of the disappearance were armed groups. See Clapham (2017), p. 448.

The Committee has now endorsed this argument. According to the Statement on Non-State Actors, in relation to Urgent Actions requests under Article 30, the Committee 'may decide to register cases of disappearances allegedly committed by non-State actors falling within the scope of article 3 and 5, [...], and request the State to search for and locate the person as a matter of urgency.' Possibly foreseeing objections (or practical difficulties) related to state capacity or lack of territorial control, the Committee added:

> Even though the State may not immediately have the capacity to search for and locate the person – for instance, if the non-State actors alleged to be responsible for the disappearance have control over the territory in which the person was disappeared – the Committee may request the State party to take all reasonable measures, within the scope of their powers, that are necessary to do so, including interim measures, such as the following: registering the case in a specific database, securing mass graves and preserving evidence; collecting relatives' DNA; providing assistance to relatives, including legal and psychological assistance; and taking steps, to the extent possible, to obtain information from the non-State actor as to the fate or whereabouts of the disappeared person.[215]

The last part of this paragraph can thus be used as guidance to define the measures states should take with regard to the search for persons who were disappeared by non-state actors and whose disappearances fall within Article 3 ICPPED, even in situations where they might not be in control of the territory and cannot physically conduct searches.[216]

2.2.3 *Obligation Gaps under the ICPPED*

The CED's Statement on Non-State Actors has provided some much needed clarification of states' obligations relating to disappearances committed by non-state actors, especially those falling within Article 3 ICPPED. When read together with General Comment No. 1, it is clear that the Committee views the obligations to investigate and search as equally applicable to all disappearances. Nonetheless, when it comes to obligations to prevent or redress, the Statement does not provide further guidance—other than excluding disappearances falling within Article 3 from the realm of most other articles of the Convention, including Article 24 that concerns reparations (see above). This reflects Vermeulen's analysis that '[c]rimes that fall within the scope of [Article 3] are excluded from the obligations laid down in the remaining articles of the ICPPED.'[217] The exceptions are Articles 30 and 31, relating

[215] CED (2023) Statement on non-State actors in the context of the International Convention for the Protection of All Persons from Enforced Disappearances. UN Doc. CED/C/10, para. 24.

[216] This approach is consistent with the reasoning of the ECtHR regarding states' positive obligations in areas that are no longer under a state's full control. See, for example, *Ilaşcu and Others v Moldova and Russia* [2004] European Court of Human Rights Application no. 48787/99, 2004-VII, paras 332–352.

[217] Vermeulen (2012), p. 92.

to Urgent Actions and communications alleging violations of the ICPPED, respectively (see above). This section addresses obligations to prevent and redress regarding disappearances falling within Article 3 of the Convention from the perspective of the Convention and Committee.

2.2.3.1 The Obligation to Prevent under the ICPPED

Article 3 ICPPED does not establish an obligation to prevent disappearances committed by non-state actors[218] and the CED's Statement on Non-State Actors reinforces the interpretation that preventive obligations relating to enforced disappearances in the ICPPED are not applicable to such disappearances.[219] Indeed, several prevention obligations defined in the ICPPED, as well as in the IACFDP, the DPPED, and the African Guidelines are mainly based on 'classical' forms of enforced disappearance committed by agents of the state and initiate with a detention at the hands of security forces.[220] Therefore, the preventive measures set out in Articles 16–23 ICPPED,[221] Article XI of the IACFDP,[222] and paragraph 4.1.2 of the African Guidelines,[223] refer to preventive measures that would be difficult to apply to non-state actors. For example, Articles 16–23 ICPPED encompass the obligation not to return a person to a country where they might be at risk of being forcibly disappeared (non-refoulement, Article 16), safeguards relating to detention practices, such as the prohibition of secret detention, the requirement to keep official registers, the obligation to ensure access to lawyers and relatives (Article 17), obligations related to providing access to information (Articles 18–20), the orderly and transparent release from detention (Article 21), the penalisation of obstruction of remedies or failure to record detentions or provide information (Article 22), and the

---

[218] Ibid., p. 93.

[219] CED (2023) Statement on non-State actors in the context of the International Convention for the Protection of All Persons from Enforced Disappearances. UN Doc. CED/C/10, para. 21.

[220] See, for example, Berman and Clark (1982), pp. 532–533; Scovazzi and Citroni (2007), pp. 7–10. The more recent examples of enforced disappearances in the context of the 'war on terror', for example through 'extraordinary renditions', also involve detention by security forces. On this practice, see, for example, Pervou (2023), p. 53 ff.

[221] These are preventive measures according to the CED. See CED (2015) Concluding Observations on the Report Submitted by Mexico. UN Doc. CED/C/MEX/CO/1, para. 34.

[222] Article XI IACFDP establishes that: 'Every person deprived of liberty shall be held in an officially recognized place of detention and be brought before a competent judicial authority without delay, in accordance with applicable domestic law. The States Parties shall establish and maintain official up-to-date registries of their detainees and, in accordance with their domestic law, shall make them available to relatives, judges, attorneys, any other person having a legitimate interest, and other authorities.'

[223] Paragraph 4.1.2 of the African Guidelines concerns the obligation to prevent enforced disappearances and contains an extensive list of measures, which are mainly related to detention.

training of law enforcement personnel (Article 23). However, where a non-state actor exercises state-like functions, the measures could well be applicable.[224]

Other, more general measures, however, could also be considered as preventive measures in relation to disappearances that would fall within the remit of Article 3 ICPPED and are committed by non-state actors who do not exercise governmental functions. This is in particular the case for obligations relating to the criminalisation of the offense and prosecution of perpetrators (Articles 4 and 6–12), given that criminal prosecution is often understood as a form of deterrence and thus serves a (general) preventive function.[225] In that sense, it is unfortunate that the CED did not engage in more depth with the question of whether any of the preventive obligations enshrined in the Convention could apply to disappearances falling within Article 3.[226] At the same time, the Statement does not fully block the possibility for future development regarding the applicability of certain preventive obligations under the ICPPED in relation to disappearances falling within Article 3. This is because paragraph 21 of the Statement refers to the applicability of Convention obligations to disappearances falling within Article 5 and omits a reference to Article 3, rather than explicitly excluding disappearances falling within Article 3 from the reach of other Convention obligations.

Neither the CED nor the WGEID have dealt with the question of prevention of disappearances committed by non-state actors explicitly. Nonetheless, both have addressed situations where disappearances are committed by both state and non-state actors in their reports. In particular, both bodies have made references to preventive measures in relation to disappearances of migrants, that often involve non-state actors. In its 2017 Report on Enforced Disappearances in the Context of Migration, the WGEID included among its recommendations the gathering and systematisation of information about persons who go 'missing' during transit or within a country's territory.[227] Moreover, it also proposed additional preventive measures that could be

[224] In this vein, note the decision by the WGEID in 2019 to document cases 'tantamount to enforced disappearances' that are perpetrated by non-state actors 'that exercise effective control and/or government-like functions over a territory' (Human Rights Council (2019) Report of the Working Group on Enforced or Involuntary Disappearances. UN Doc. A/HRC/42/40, para. 94).

[225] This argument has also been made by Huhle (2013). The Committee Against Torture for example justifies the need to define the crime of torture as a specific crime by pointing to the deterrent and thereby preventive effect of criminalisation and the prospect of punishment for perpetrators. Committee Against Torture (2008) General Comment No. 2: Implementation of Article 2 by States Parties. UN Doc. CAT/C/GC/2, para. 11.

[226] The Committee's silence on the matter might also relate to its mandate and the fact that the Convention does not bind non-state actors, making it—to some extent—unnecessary for the CED to engage with this question. Notably, prevention obligations relating to enforced disappearances that amount to crimes against humanity are also applicable to disappearances committed by non-state actors. See CED (2023) Statement on non-State actors in the context of the International Convention for the Protection of All Persons from Enforced Disappearances. UN Doc. CED/C/10, para. 21.

[227] Human Rights Council (2017) Report of the Working Group on Enforced or Involuntary Disappearances on Enforced Disappearances in the Context of Migration. UN Doc. A/HRC/36/39/Add.2, para. 86(a).

specifically targeted at 'mitigat[ing] factors that may increase the risk of enforced disappearances of migrants', including measures against trafficking networks or other criminal groups that engage in the abuse or exploitation of migrants.[228] Finally, the WGEID recommended that states 'avoid adopting excessively rigid and strict migration policies, as they encourage the use of less travelled and more dangerous routes', and monitor migration routes in order to avoid loss of life and disappearances of migrants.[229] In its General Comment on Enforced Disappearances in the Context of Migration, the CED went further than the WGEID by comprehensively addressing the question of preventive measures regarding disappearances of migrants and outlining a series of general steps aimed at preventing all types of disappearances.

More specifically, measures that apply to all types of disappearances include standardised data collection and exchanges (paras 23–24), conducting contextual analysis in order to identify patterns in disappearances, as well as 'the underlying structural failures that enable these crimes, and possible ties between authorities and criminal networks involved in trafficking in persons and smuggling of migrants' (para. 26), adopting 'evidence-based policies to foster access to regular, safe and orderly migration' and '[enhancing] pathways for regular migration' (para. 27), ensuring that families are not separated, with a particular view to protecting children (para. 29), and non-criminalisation of migrants and those who assist them (para. 30). In particular, in recognising the often-prominent role played by non-state actors in the disappearance of migrants, the General Comment considers countering exploitation or trafficking in persons and abuses of power, including by implementing transnational crime suppression instruments as a form of prevention (para. 28).[230] In addition to these preventive measures, the CED considers investigations to have a preventive function.[231]

While these measures concern disappearances in the specific context of migration, they reflect the type of preventive measures that states could take also in other situations where non-state actors are involved in the commission of disappearances, and the general preventive measures discussed in the previous section of this chapter. In recommendations made by the CED to states parties where disappearances are committed by non-state actors, such as Iraq, Colombia and Mexico, the Committee has also emphasised the need to collect accurate data and maintain adequate registers

[228] Ibid., para. 65. I discuss this particular aspect in more detail in Chap. 4, Sect. 4.1.1.2.

[229] Ibid., para. 66. A similar recommendation has been made by the Special Rapporteur on Extrajudicial, Summary and Arbitrary Executions Agnes Callamard in her report on deaths of refugees and migrants in the course of their migration journeys. See UNGA (2017) Report of the Special Rapporteur of the Human Rights Council on Extrajudicial, Summary or Arbitrary Executions: Unlawful Death of Refugees and Migrants, UN Doc. A/72/335, para. 101.

[230] See also Chap. 4.

[231] See CED (2023) General Comment No. 1 on Enforced Disappearance in the Context of Migration. UN Doc. CED/C/GC/1, para. 37.

on disappeared and/or missing persons, as a basis for designing policies to prevent and address the issue of disappearances.[232]

In addition to these general preventive measures, the CED also included a nod to specific prevention obligations in its Statement on Non-State Actors. In para. 22, the Committee emphasises that

> States have strict obligations with regard to due diligence when they have knowledge of a case of disappearance, or of a real and imminent risk of disappearance, perpetrated by a non-State actor. These due diligence obligations are particularly strict where women or girls are involved, owing to the link that the disappearance may have with, inter alia, acts of sexual violence, femicide and trafficking in women.[233]

While this is a very general statement that does not mention any concrete measures, it is nevertheless important in that it illustrates the CED's stance on due diligence obligations in situations where a state has awareness of risk of the commission of a disappearance, which are especially strict in relation to women.[234] Moreover, the wording in this paragraph is notable in that it refers to the risk of a disappearance, and not an *enforced* disappearance, thereby distinguishing this paragraph from the definition of acquiescence.

2.2.3.2 The Obligation to Provide Reparations under the ICPPED

A key aspect of the ICPPED are the obligations it establishes in relation to reparations under Article 24. In his report on the existing framework on enforced disappearances prior to the commencement of ICPPED negotiations, independent expert Manfred Nowak emphasised the importance of reparations:

> In the case of enforced disappearance, which is a particularly serious and continuing human rights violation committed with the very intention of evading responsibility, truth and legal remedies, reparation is of the utmost importance, not only as a matter of redress for the individual victims, but also as a pre-condition for establishing truth, justice and peace in the societies affected by such practices.[235]

---

[232] See, for example, CED (2015) Concluding Observations on the Report Submitted by Mexico. UN Doc. CED/C/MEX/CO/1, para. 35; CED (2015) Concluding Observations on the Report Submitted by Iraq under Article 29 (1) of the Convention. UN Doc. CED/C/IRQ/CO/1, para. 12; CED (2016) Concluding Observations on the Report Submitted by Colombia under Article 29 (1) of the Convention. UN Doc. CED/C/COL/CO/1, para. 14; CED (2019) Concluding observations on the additional information submitted by Mexico under article 29 (4) of the Convention. UN Doc. CED/C/MEX/OAI/1, para. 31; CED (2022) Report of the Committee on Enforced Disappearances on its visit to Mexico: Observations and Recommendations. UN Doc. CED/C/MEX/VR/1 (Recommendations), paras 104–112; CED (2023) Report of the Committee on Enforced Disappearances on its visit to Iraq: Information on the visit and findings. UN Doc. CED/C/IRQ/VR/1 (Findings), para. 54.

[233] CED (2023) Statement on non-State actors in the context of the International Convention for the Protection of All Persons from Enforced Disappearances. UN Doc. CED/C/10, para. 22.

[234] This reflects the jurisprudence of the IACtHR, which I discuss further in Chap. 3, Sect. 3.2.1.2.

[235] Commission on Human Rights (2002) Report submitted by Mr. Manfred Nowak, independent expert charged with examining the existing international criminal and human rights framework for

Article 24 ICPPED defines 'victims' of enforced disappearance as both the direct victims, as well as 'any individual who has suffered harm as the direct result of an enforced disappearance'[236] and establishes the right of all victims to 'know the truth regarding the circumstances of the enforced disappearance, the progress and results of the investigation and the fate of the disappeared person'.[237] States also have an obligation to 'search for, locate and release disappeared persons', as well as to search for and return the remains of disappeared persons who have died.[238] Furthermore, Article 24 establishes the rights of victims to not only compensation for material and moral damages but also to measures of restitution, rehabilitation, satisfaction (including restoration of dignity and reputation) and guarantees of non-repetition.[239] Finally, the article instructs states to take measures in relation to the disappeared person's legal situation as a means to enable relatives' access to, for example, social benefits and financial matters of the disappeared person,[240] and to guarantee the freedom to participate in associations formed with the aim of locating disappeared persons or supporting victims.[241]

However, where a disappearance is committed by a non-state actor and therefore cannot qualify as an *enforced* disappearance, the reparation obligations are less clear because Article 24 is not applicable to the victims and their relatives.[242] Indeed, this point was emphasised by some delegations during the negotiations of the ICPPED, who argued that states should not be obliged to provide 'full reparation' to victims of disappearances committed by non-state actors.[243] By not including disappearances falling within Article 3 in paragraph 21 of the Statement (see above), the CED appears to reaffirm this stance. Notably, in its report on its visit to Mexico in 2021, the Committee stated that states not only bear responsibility if they fail to investigate disappearances falling within Article 3 ICPPED and bring perpetrators to justice, but also 'if they fail to search for and locate disappeared persons and, in the event of their death, if their bodies are not returned to their families and relatives in a dignified manner and, in general, if they fail to fulfil their obligations towards the victims (Art.

the protection of persons from enforced or involuntary disappearances. UN Doc. E/CN.4/2002/71, para. 84.

236 Article 24(1) ICPPED.

237 Article 24(2) ICPPED.

238 Article 24 (3) ICPPED.

239 Article 24 (4) and (5) ICPPED.

240 Article 24 (6) ICPPED.

241 Article 24 (7) ICPPED.

242 According to Vermeulen, '[c]rimes that fall within the scope of this article are excluded from the obligations laid down in the remaining articles of the ICPPED. As a result, the CED has an important task to clarify the scope and meaning of this article.' Vermeulen (2012), p. 92. See also Huhle (2013), p. 25.

243 Commission on Human Rights (2005) Report of the Intersessional Open-Ended Working Group to Elaborate a Draft Legally Binding Normative Instrument for the Protection of All Persons from Enforced Disappearance. UN Doc. E/CN.4/2005/66, para. 110.

24), including children (Art. 25).'[244] The reference to Articles 24 and 25 of the Convention in this paragraph, which is exclusively concerned with disappearances falling under Article 3, is noteworthy, because it implies that these articles apply to those disappearances.[245] Moreover, the first draft of the Statement on Non-State Actors, which was published on the CED's website for commentary in 2022, contained a paragraph stating that articles 4–16 and Articles 24 and 25 applied in relation to Article 3.[246] This sentence was, however, changed in the final version of the Statement, indicating a more conservative position by the Committee on this matter after the first draft was sharply criticised by some states parties.[247]

Consequently, the ICPPED leaves a protection gap regarding victims of disappearances committed by non-state actors falling within Article 3 ICPPED, and their relatives, in relation to states' obligations to provide reparations. From a victim's perspective, and in view of the detrimental impact that a disappearance has on the relatives of a disappeared person irrespective of the identity of the perpetrators,[248] this is an unfortunate division.[249] While a strict reading and interpretation of the Convention warrants such a distinction, whether and how it can be held up in practice raises some doubts. For example, certain disappearances committed by non-state actors fall within Article 3 ICPPED up until the point at which they reach the threshold of constituting crimes against humanity in line with Article 5, which then 'converts' them into enforced disappearances. Yet, disappearances are inherently characterised by a lack of investigation and search, which, as discussed, itself can constitute a violation of the rights of relatives of the disappeared. In contexts where it is not clear cut who the perpetrators are (state/

[244] CED (2022) Report of the Committee on Enforced Disappearances on its visit to Mexico: Findings. UN Doc. CED/C/MEX/VR/1 (Findings), para. 41.

[245] The statement was repeated in the Iraq visit report, but without the explicit reference to Articles 24 and 25 ICPPED. See CED (2023) Report of the Committee on Enforced Disappearances on its visit to Iraq: Information on the visit and findings. UN Doc. CED/C/IRQ/VR/1 (Findings), para. 53.

[246] CED (2022) Draft statement on 'non-State actors and enforced disappearances in the context of the International Convention for the Protection of All Persons from Enforced Disappearances': 'Under article 3, States parties have an obligation to investigate enforced disappearances perpetrated by non-State actors and to bring those responsible to justice. To that end, States parties shall apply, in relation to those disappearances, articles 4 to 16 of Convention, as well as articles 24 and 25.' Para. 16.

[247] The draft Statement also held that certain disappearances falling within Article 3 of the Convention could be considered as *enforced* disappearances, which was heavily criticised by States parties and relatives' organisations who submitted inputs to the draft Statement (ibid., para. 14). For a list of public inputs, see https://www.ohchr.org/en/calls-for-input/2022/call-inputs-comments-draft-statement-non-state-actors-and-enforced. Accessed 10 March 2025.

[248] On the impact of disappearances on relatives, see the contributions to the Torture Journal's 2021 Special Section on Enforced Disappearance as Torture: Vicente and Nudd (2021); Perez-Sales et al. (2021); Favre et al. (2021); Perez and Esgareño (2021); Bourguignon et al. (2021); Haq (2021); Madi (2021); Morales-Sáez and Espina (2021). See also Srovin Coralli (2021b). For an analysis of the main needs of relatives of disappeared persons, see Baranowska (2021).

[249] See also the critique of the Statement made in this regard by Reyes et al., who lament the Statement's '[upholding] of a hierarchy of victims'. Reyes et al. (2024), pp. 198 and 204.

non-state), maintaining separations between victims seems untenable.[250] In that sense, the Committee's position expressed in the General Comment and the Statement on Non-State Actors regarding the burden of proof resting with the state (para. 37 and para. 7 relating to acquiescence, respectively) gain particular importance: it is up to the state to investigate disappearances and show that there was no direct or indirect involvement by any of its officials. A question for the Committee to answer would be whether, in the meantime, there could be a presumption of state involvement for the purpose of victim protection and relatives' access to remedies, seeing that in either case it is up to the state to provide answers about the fate or whereabouts of their loved ones. Perhaps in this manner, a compromise could be reached among the negotiating states' position that states should not have to provide 'full reparation measures' (see above) and the reality that, even if states are not directly or indirectly involved in the commission of a disappearance, it is still their actions and omissions that affect the relatives on a day-to-day basis.

2.3 Conclusion: Chapter 2

Deriving from states' general positive obligation to protect the different rights that can be violated in the course of a disappearance—whether committed by a state or non-state actor, states hold obligations to prevent, investigate and remedy such disappearances. Due to the complex nature of this crime, state obligations in relation to disappearances committed by non-state actors may require multiple actions that persist over time. Further, given the overlap between disappearances and other human rights violations, obligations relating to the prevention and response to these crimes also overlap with those relating to the rights to life, liberty and personal integrity. Therefore, to analyse the obligations of states in this regard, it is necessary to include a wide range of instruments and jurisprudence relating to cases which are not strictly speaking disappearance cases or were not handled as such. As the analysis in this chapter illustrates, in cases of disappearances committed by non-state actors, the obligations to prevent, investigate and provide an effective remedy are interrelated. Thus, for example, an investigation into a disappearance can be a form of preventing subsequent violations of rights (although not the initial deprivation of liberty and therefore the disappearance itself), and both the search and investigation of a disappearance can be crucial to ending the suffering of both the victims and their relatives. Furthermore, an investigation can also be the basis for the possibility of relatives to access (judicial) remedies and reparation. Finally, reparations ordered in cases involving disappearances committed by non-state actors often involve searching for the victim and investigating the disappearance. This is due to the peculiar nature of disappearances as continuous crimes that violate multiple

[250] See also Gallagher (2020).

rights and have a detrimental impact not just on the disappeared person, but also on relatives.

States parties to the ICPPED have an explicit obligation to investigate disappearances committed by non-state actors and hold perpetrators accountable, based on Article 3 ICPPED. However, the ICPPED is silent on the obligations to prevent such disappearances and provide reparations for them to the relatives of the disappeared. The obligation of states to prevent violations of human rights at the hands of non-state actors is part of the general obligation to protect human rights, which encompasses a number of different elements, from general measures relating to the establishment of a well-functioning legal and judicial system and the criminalisation of acts by private individuals that amount to human rights violations, to specific measures based on either an individual victim's need for protection or the state's knowledge about a potential source of risk to all of society. Strictly speaking, these preventive obligations must be established in relation to the initial deprivation of liberty to constitute preventive measures against a disappearance, because otherwise the disappearance will already have occurred, and preventive obligations relate to (potential) subsequent rights violations (such as the rights to life, physical integrity, and access to justice). The jurisprudence that addresses the initial deprivation of liberty is limited, yet the CED's General Comment on Enforced Disappearance in the Context of Migration indicates that preventive measures should be thought of in broad terms and include addressing structural issues that increase risks of disappearances in general.

Beyond Article 3 ICPPED, the obligation to investigate cases of disappearances committed by non-state actors derives from a number of different rights, both of the victim and of the relatives.[251] A review of the criteria for an effective investigation established by the HRC together with case law from the ECtHR and IACtHR dealing with disappearances committed by non-state or unknown actors, and the African Guidelines shows, that there is a general convergence among these bodies as regards the content of the obligation to investigate. While in the jurisprudence of the ECtHR and IACtHR not all criteria are consistently mentioned in all cases of disappearances, and the exact investigative measures that are due will depend on each case, the general criteria of promptness, thoroughness, independence and transparency listed in the Minnesota Protocol should be considered as the minimum standards applicable for assessing the effectiveness of an investigation. In the same vein, the obligation to investigate and the obligation to search for a disappeared person are continuous obligations, which has been confirmed by the CED and the ACHPR and is reflected in the jurisprudence of the IACtHR and, to a lesser extent, the ECtHR. Finally, states have an obligation to provide an effective remedy, which is especially important in relation to the relatives of the disappeared person. This obligation also includes conducting an effective investigation, as well as ensuring access to judicial remedies for relatives of the disappeared person. However, with the

[251] It is beyond the scope of this book to analyse whether the content of the obligation to investigate and search differs depending on the right on which it is based.

exception of the African Guidelines, the obligation to provide an effective remedy is not currently considered as encompassing an obligation to provide substantive reparation and Article 24 ICPPED on reparations is not applicable to disappearances falling within Article 3 of the Convention. In that sense, states hold obligations to provide reparations to victims of non-state actors only to the extent that they are found to be responsible for having violated their protective obligations under general IHRL instruments. The question of how this responsibility can and has been established is the focus of the next Chapter.

References

Akandji-Kombe J-F (2007) Positive obligations under the European Convention on Human Rights: a guide to the implementation of the European Convention on Human Rights. Council of Europe

Alston P (2024) International human rights: text and materials. New York University School of Law, New York

Baranowska G (2020) Disappeared migrants and refugees: the relevance of the International Convention on Enforced Disappearance in their search and protection. Deutsches Institut für Menschenrechte, Berlin

Baranowska G (2021) Rights of families of disappeared persons: how international bodies address the needs of families of disappeared persons in Europe, 1st edn. Intersentia, Cambridge Antwerp Chicago

Bauer J (2021) Obscured by 'Willful Blindness': States' preventive obligations and e obligations and the meaning of acquiescence under the convention against torture. Colum Hum Rts L Rev 52:738–825

Berman MR, Clark RS (1982) State terrorism: disappearances. Rutgers Law J 13:531–577

Bourguignon M, Dermitzel A, Katz M (2021) Grief among relatives of disappeared persons in the context of state violence: an impossible process? Torture J 31:14–33. https://doi.org/10.7146/torture.v31i2.127344

Calvet Martínez E (2015) Desapariciones forzadas y justicia transicional. La búsqueda de respuestas a través del derecho a la verdad, a la justicia y a la reparación. Dissertation, Universitat de Barcelona

Citroni G (2012) Measures of reparation for victims of gross human rights violations: developments and challenges in the jurisprudence of two regional human rights courts. Inter-Am Eur Hum Rights J 5:49–71

Clapham A (2017) Armed non-state actors and the UN Convention on enforced disappearances. In: Réciprocité et universalité: sources et régimes du droit international des droits de l'homme: mélanges en l'honneur du professeur Emmanuel Decaux. Pedone, Paris, pp 443–448

Comisión de la Verdad y Reconciliación en el Perú (2003) Comisión de La Verdad y Reconciliación: Informe Final. Vol. IX, Reparations. http://www.cverdad.org.pe/ifinal/pdf/TOMO%20IX/2.2.%20PIR.pdf. Accessed 16 Nov 2024

Crawford J (2013) State responsibility: the general part. Cambridge University Press, Cambridge

de Frouville O (2021) Criminalizing or trivializing enforced disappearances? The issue of 'non-state actors'. In: de Frouville O, Sturma P (eds) La pénalisation des droits de l'homme. Pedone, Paris

de Schutter O (2010) International human rights law: cases, materials, commentary. Cambridge University Press, Cambridge; New York

Dulitzky A, Anayanssi Orizaga I (2019) ¿Dónde Están? Estándares internacionales para la búsqueda de personas desaparecidas forzadamente. International Bar Association, London

Ebert FC, Sijniensky RI (2015) Preventing violations of the right to life in the European and the Inter-American Human Rights Systems: from the Osman Test to a coherent doctrine on risk prevention? Hum Rights Law Rev 15:343–368. https://doi.org/10.1093/hrlr/ngv001

Favre P, Rauschenbach MC, Jimenez A et al (2021) Who are they to say? Experiences and legal recognition of victimhood of enforced disappearance in Colombia and El Salvador. Torture J 31: 50–67. https://doi.org/10.7146/torture.v31i2.125771

Ferstman C (2020) Human rights due diligence policies applied to extraterritorial cooperation to prevent "irregular" migration: European Union and United Kingdom support to Libya. German Law J 21:459–486

Frey BA (2021) Conceptualising disappearances in international law. In: Ansolabehere K, Frey BA, Payne LA (eds) Disappearances in the post-transition era in Latin America. British Academy Scholarship, London

Gallagher J (2020) (Enforced) disappearances – when state and criminal perpetrators blur. In: Völkerrechtsblog. https://voelkerrechtsblog.org/articles/enforced-disappearances-when-state-and-criminal-perpetrators-blur/. Accessed 6 Nov 2024

Galvis Patiño MC, Arias Ávila O (2019) Los Principios Rectores para la Búsqueda de Personas Desaparecidas: origen y contenido. Ideas verdes No. 19. Heinrich Böll Stiftung, Bogotá

Galvis Patiño MC, Huhle R (2020) The rights of the victims of enforced disappearance do not have an expiration date. In: Opinio Juris. http://opiniojuris.org/2020/07/07/the-rights-of-the-victims-of-enforced-disappearance-do-not-have-an-expiration-date/. Accessed 16 Nov 2024

Guercke L (forthcoming) Contemporary disappearances in Mexico: a conceptual challenge for the international framework on enforced disappearances. In: Baranowska G, Kolaković-Bojović M (eds) Enforced disappearances: on universal responses to a worldwide phenomenon. Cambridge University Press

Haq I (2021) The half-widows of Kashmir: a discourse of enforced disappearance. Torture J 31:92–98. https://doi.org/10.7146/torture.v31i2.123624

Herman O (2024) Reparations by non-state armed groups under international law: from conflict to repair in Colombia and beyond. Routledge, Abingdon, Oxon [UK]; New York, NY

Huhle R (2013) Non-state actors of enforced disappearance and the UN Convention for the Protection of All Persons from Enforced Disappearance. HuV-I/JILPAC 26:21–26

Huhle R (2022) Fate and whereabouts: the two elements that make up the right to know about the victims of forced disappearance. In: Mandolessi S, Olalde K (eds) Disappearances in Mexico: from the 'dirty war' to the 'war on drugs'. Routledge, Oxon, New York, pp 150–165

Koivurova T (2010) Due diligence. Max Planck Encyclopedia of Public International Law

Lavrysen L (2016) Human rights in a positive state: rethinking the relationship between positive and negative obligations under the European Convention on Human Rights. Intersentia, Cambridge; Antwerp; Portland

Letschert R, Van Boven T (2011) Providing reparation in situations of mass victimization-key challenges involved. In: Letschert R, Haveman R, De Brouwer A-M, Pemberton A (eds) Victimological approaches to international crimes. Intersentia, Antwerp, pp 153–184

Mackenzie-Gray Scott R (2021) Due diligence as a secondary rule of general international law. Leiden J Int Law 34:343–372. https://doi.org/10.1017/S0922156521000030

Madi A (2021) Analyzing long-term impacts of counterinsurgency tools in civil wars: a case study of enforced disappearances in Algeria. Torture J 31:83–91. https://doi.org/10.7146/torture.v31i2.128337

McCall-Smith K (2016) Interpreting international human rights standards: treaty body general comments as a chisel or hammer? In: Tracing the role of soft law in human rights. Oxford University Press

McCrory S (2007) The International Convention for the Protection of all Persons from Enforced Disappearance. Hum Rights Law Rev 7:545–566. https://doi.org/10.1093/hrlr/ngm021

Mégret F (2010) Nature of obligations. In: Moeckli D, Shah S, Sivakumaran S (eds) International Human Rights Law, 1st edn. Oxford University Press, Oxford, pp 124–149

Monnheimer M (2021) Due diligence obligations in International Human Rights Law. Cambridge University Press, Cambridge

Morales-Sáez N, Espina J (2021) The aftermath of enforced disappearance and concealment: a qualitative inquiry with families in Paine, Chile. Torture J 31:34–49. https://doi.org/10.7146/torture.v31i2.121224

(Nani) Jansen Reventlow Y-O, Curling R (2019) State obligations in the African System. In: Kadelbach S, Rensmann T, Rieter E (eds) Judging International Human Rights: Courts of General Jurisdiction as Human Rights Courts. Springer International Publishing, Cham, pp 313–341

OHCHR (2021) Joint Statement by independent United Nations human rights experts on human rights responsibilities of armed non-State actors. United Nations High Commissioner for Human Rights Press Release. https://www.ohchr.org/en/press-releases/2021/02/joint-statement-independent-united-nations-human-rights-experts-human-rights?LangID=E&NewsID=26797. Accessed 16 Nov 2024

Perez NH, Esgareño E (2021) Enforced disappearance as a form of psychological torture: evidence from the Ayotzinapa Case (México). Torture J 31:19–31. https://doi.org/10.7146/torture.v32i3.125248

Perez-Sales P, Duhaime B, Méndez J (2021) Current debates, developments and challenges regarding torture, enforced disappearances and human rights. Torture J 31:3–13. https://doi.org/10.7146/torture.v31i2.128890

Pervou I (2023) The right not to be subjected to enforced disappearance: concept, content and scope, 1st edn. Springer Nature Switzerland, Cham

Reyes J, Farbstein SH, Ochoa S et al (2024) Harmonizing legal approaches to enforced disappearances: evidentiary challenges, emerging developments, and the role of non-state actors. Harv Hum Rights J 37:169–205

Scovazzi T, Citroni G (2007) The struggle against enforced disappearance and the 2007 United Nations Convention. Nijhoff, Leiden

Shelton D (2015) Remedies in International Human Rights Law. Oxford University Press, Oxford

Shelton DL (2020) Advanced introduction to International Human Rights Law, 2nd edn. Edward Elgar Publishing, Cheltenham

Shelton D, Gould A (2013) Positive and negative obligations. In: Shelton D (ed) The Oxford handbook of International Human Rights Law. Oxford University Press, Oxford

Sierra Leóne Truth and Reconciliation Commission (2004) Witness to Truth: Final Report of the TRC. Vol. 2, Chapter 4 (Reparations). https://www.sierraleonetrc.org/index.php/view-report-text-vol-2/item/volume-two-chapter-four?category_id=20. Accessed 16 Nov 2024

Srovin Coralli A (2021a) Coordination between the search and criminal investigations concerning disappeared persons. Swisspeace. https://www.swisspeace.ch/assets/publications/downloads/Reports/Coordination-between-the-search-and-criminal-investigations-concerning-disappeared-persons.pdf. Accessed 6 Nov 2024

Srovin Coralli A (2021b) Non-state actors and enforced disappearances: defining a path forward. Geneva Academy Working Paper. https://www.geneva-academy.ch/research/publications/detail/608-non-state-actors-and-enforced-disappearances-defining-a-path-forward. Accessed 16 Nov 2024

van Boven T (2010) The United Nations Basic Principles and Guidelines on the Right to a Remedy and Reparation for Victims of Gross Violations of International Human Rights Law and Serious Violations of International Humanitarian Law: Introductory Note. In: United Nations Audiovisual Library of International Law. https://legal.un.org/avl/ha/ga_60-147/ga_60-147.html. Accessed 16 Nov 2024

van der Have N (2018) The prevention of gross human rights violations under International Human Rights Law. T.M.C. Asser Press, The Hague

Vermeulen ML (2012) Enforced disappearance: determining state responsibility under the international convention for the protection of all persons from enforced disappearance. Intersentia, Antwerp

Vicente A, Nudd E (2021) Addressing a forgotten struggle: victims of enforced disappearance in Africa. Torture J 31:68–82. https://doi.org/10.7146/torture.v31i2.125518

Chapter 3
State Responsibility for Disappearances Committed by Non-State Actors

States have obligations not to disappear persons and to protect them from disappearances committed by non-state actors. However, as discussed in the previous chapter, many of these are due diligence obligations and a failure to comply with them does not necessarily lead to a state's international responsibility. In the absence of obligations to prevent and provide reparations to victims and relatives of disappearances falling within Article 3 ICPPED, the question of state responsibility becomes especially important for analysing IHRL protection vis-à-vis victims of such disappearances and their relatives. How is state responsibility determined in cases involving disappearances—and other human rights violations—committed by non-state actors? That is the question this chapter answers. State responsibility for acts committed by non-state actors is not just a matter of IHRL but is also addressed in the law on state responsibility. The basic rules of state responsibility are contained in the Articles on Responsibility of States for Internationally Wrongful Acts (ARSIWA/Articles on State Responsibility), which were adopted by the International Law Commission in 2001.[1] The ARSIWA establish so-called 'secondary rules' relating to attribution of conduct and to the consequences of a breach, whereas the content of state obligations is a matter of the respective 'primary rules', comprised of legal instruments, general principles, or customary norms.[2] According to these rules, a state can be held responsible for an internationally wrongful act that can be attributed to the state, and if this attributable act constitutes a breach of the state's international obligations.[3] The determination of state responsibility in relation to disappearances committed by non-state actors therefore requires two steps: first, it

---

[1] UN General Assembly (2002) Articles on Responsibility of States for Internationally Wrongful Acts. UN Doc. A/RES/56/83 (ARSIWA).

[2] International Law Commission (ILC) (2001) Draft Articles on Responsibility of States for Internationally Wrongful Acts, with Commentaries. ILC Yearbook 2001, Vol. II, Part II, p. 31, paras 1–3. On the difference between primary and secondary obligations and criticism thereof, see also Crawford (2013), pp. 64–66.

[3] Article 2 ARSIWA.

L. Guercke, *Failure of the State*, Interdisciplinary Studies in Human Rights 15,
https://doi.org/10.1007/978-3-031-83717-3_3

must be established what conduct can be attributed to the state in line with the corresponding rules. Second, it must be determined whether attributable acts and omissions constitute a breach of the state's international obligations. Following these steps, this chapter first examines the conditions under which disappearances committed by non-state actors can be directly attributed to the state. Next, I turn to the question of breach and specifically examine how state responsibility has been established in case law in relation to states' obligations to prevent and respond, which are always attributable to the state.[4]

3.1 Attribution of Acts Committed by Non-State Actors

The first step in determining the international responsibility of a state for disappearances committed by non-state actors is the question of attribution.[5] In the case of disappearances, attribution can be based either on the general rules of attribution as established in the ARSIWA, or on the notions of 'authorisation, support or acquiescence' contained in the IHRL definition of 'enforced disappearance'[6] as *lex specialis* to these general rules of attribution.

3.1.1 Attribution under the ARSIWA

Articles 4–11 of the Articles on State Responsibility establish the general rules of attribution in international law. All conduct of state organs (Article 4), persons exercising governmental authority (Article 5),[7] or conduct of an organ 'placed at the disposal of a State by another' (Article 6) is attributable to a state, even where the person exceeds authority, contravenes instructions or acts otherwise *ultra vires* (Article 7).[8] Therefore, all actions or omissions committed directly by state officials, or persons officially carrying out state functions (Article 5 ARSIWA), are attributable to the state for the purpose of establishing responsibility. The conduct of groups that are not considered 'state organs' can be attributed to the state where it is shown that the latter 'directed or controlled' their conduct (Article 8), where a non-state

[4] See de Schutter (2010), p. 375.

[5] Article 2 (a) ARSIWA.

[6] See Preamble, Declaration on the Protection of All Persons from Enforced Disappearance 1992 (A/RES/47/133) (DPPED); Article II, Inter-American Convention on Forced Disappearance of Persons 1994 (33 ILM 1529) (IACFDP); Article 2, International Convention for the Protection of All Persons from Enforced Disappearance 2006 (1726 UNTS 3) (ICPPED).

[7] For a discussion on the meaning of governmental authority in line with Article 5 ARSIWA, see Mackenzie-Gray Scott (2022), p. 39 ff.

[8] I discuss this article in more depth in Chap. 4 in relation to corrupt acts of officials (see Sect. 4.2.1.1).

group exercises governmental authority in the absence of official authorities (Article 9), where an insurrectional movement becomes the government (Article 10), or where a state can be seen has having adopted the conduct of the non-state groups 'as its own' (Article 11).

The question of attribution of acts committed by non-state actors to a state has been dealt with in a number of cases before the International Court of Justice (ICJ) that provide further guidance about the meaning of these articles. Articles 8 and 11 ARSIWA are the most relevant for the purpose of this research, as they relate to situations where the non-state actor has not taken on governmental functions or become the government (Articles 9 and 10 ARSIWA).[9] In relation to the direction or control of activities by a non-state actor in line with Article 8, the main question centres around the exact level of 'control' that would be required for the purpose of attribution. The ICJ has set a rather high standard and established a requirement of 'effective control' by state organs over the conduct of non-state actors, or evidence that the state gave direct instructions to these actors to commit a specific act.[10] The ICJ first dealt with the question of attribution of acts by private actors to the state in the *Nicaragua* case,[11] where it assessed whether the activities of the *contras* rebel group in Nicaragua could be directly attributed to the United States, based on the latter's material support to this group. While there was evidence that the United States had trained the *contras* and provided financial and other support to them,[12] the ICJ found that it was not possible to attribute all of the *contras'* acts to the United States because their relationship was not one of 'complete dependence'.[13] The ICJ confirmed this high standard of attribution in the *Genocide* case[14] and also specified that a state would have to exercise 'effective control' in relation to the precise operation that led to a breach of obligations, rather than general control over all activities.[15] Since the adoption of the ARSIWA, and especially in relation to global terrorism, some scholars have suggested that the control standard of Article 8 is less stringent than that of 'effective control' established in the ICJ's jurisprudence, given that Article 8 only mentions 'control'.[16] Indeed, as shown by Mackenzie-Gray Scott, the International Law Commission never envisaged a standard of 'effective' control

[9] Contexts where the non-state actor has taken on governmental functions could fall within the discussion around situations where non-state actors exercise effective control, which is beyond the scope of this research. For a discussion on Article 9 ARSIWA in relation to OCG, see Chap. 4 (Sect. 4.2.1.1).

[10] *Military and Paramilitary Activities in and Against Nicaragua (Nicaragua v United States) (Merits)* [1986] International Court of Justice ICJ Rep 14, para. 115.

[11] Ibid.

[12] Ibid., paras 106–108.

[13] Ibid., paras 110–111.

[14] *Application of the Convention on the Prevention and Punishment of the Crime of Genocide (Bosnia and Herzegovina v Serbia and Montenegro)* [2007] International Court of Justice ICJ Rep 43, paras 400 and 406.

[15] Ibid., para. 400.

[16] On this, see Crawford (2013), pp. 156–157.

and the ICJ's 'invention' of this standard was not without criticism.[17] Far from being a universally agreed upon standard, the exact content of Article 8 remains a contested issue.[18]

The attribution criterion of Article 11 ARSIWA, which refers to the acknowledgement and adoption of the conduct of non-state actors as the state's own, was used by the ICJ in the *United States Diplomatic and Consular Staff in Tehran* case. According to the ICJ, acknowledgement means that the endorsement of an act committed by a non-state actor can 'transform [its] legal nature' into an act of state for the purpose of establishing responsibility.[19] In this case, the Iranian government openly endorsed the taking of hostages in the United States Embassy in Teheran by a group of Iranian militants.[20] According to the ARSIWA Commentary, the acknowledgement does not have to be express[21] but it is important to note that the standard goes beyond mere approval or endorsement of conduct in that it requires a state to 'adopt' the latter and not just to acknowledge an existing situation.[22] The standard for attribution following the ARSIWA and the jurisprudence of the ICJ is thus rather high. Where the non-state actor in question does not exercise governmental functions, its acts can only be directly attributed to the state if it can be evidenced that there is a strong relationship between the state and the non-state actor. However, several human rights instruments contain more specific rules on attribution than the general rules on state responsibility and can therefore be considered as *lex specialis* to the ARSIWA[23] in accordance with Article 55,[24]

[17] Mackenzie-Gray Scott (2022), p. 74 ff. The author presents an enlightening analysis of how the ICJ 'invented' the effective control test (ibid., pp. 74–81).

[18] Ibid., pp. 98–106. 'The debates surrounding Article 8 have contributed to ambiguity, inconsistency and uncertainty about its requirements.' (p. 106).

[19] *Case Concerning United States Diplomate and Consular Staff in Tehran (United States of America v Iran)* [1980] International Court of Justice ICJ Rep 3, para. 74.

[20] Ibid., paras 69–74.

[21] ILC (2001) Draft Articles on Responsibility of States for Internationally Wrongful Acts, with Commentaries. ILC Yearbook 2001, Vol. II, Part II, p. 54 para. 9.

[22] Ibid., p. 53 para. 6.

[23] The IACtHR articulated this as follows in the case of the *Mapiripán Massacre v Colombia*: '[The American Convention] constitutes *lex specialis* regarding State responsibility, in view of its special nature as an international human rights treaty vis-à-vis general International Law. *Therefore, attribution of international responsibility to the State, as well as the scope and effects of the acknowledgment made in the instant case, must take place in light of the Convention itself.* '*Case of the "Mapiripán Massacre" v Colombia* [2005] Inter-American Court of Human Rights Serie C No. 134, para. 107. Emphasis added.

[24] Article 55 of the ARSIWA deals with the question of *lex specialis*. It is important to note that, as long as there is no inconsistency between the rules of state responsibility and the primary rules, both are applicable. See ILC (2001) Draft Articles on Responsibility of States for Internationally Wrongful Acts, with Commentaries. ILC Yearbook 2001, Vol. II, Part II, p. 140, para. 4. The ICJ reaffirmed this in the *Genocide Case*: 'The rules for attributing alleged internationally wrongful conduct to a State do not vary with the nature of the wrongful act in question in the absence of a clearly expressed *lex specialis*.' *Application of the Convention on the Prevention and Punishment of the Crime of Genocide*, para. 401.

thereby opening the possibility of a lower attribution threshold. As discussed in the following section, the ICPPED is one of those instruments.

3.1.2 Attribution Based on Authorisation, Support or Acquiescence

To recall, the ICPPED defines enforced disappearance as follows:

> ... the arrest, detention, abduction or any other form of deprivation of liberty by agents of the State *or by persons or groups of persons acting with the authorization, support or acquiescence of the State*, followed by a refusal to acknowledge the deprivation of liberty or by concealment of the fate or whereabouts of the disappeared person [...].[25]

This definition contains three *lex specialis* criteria with regards to the general standards of attribution: authorisation, support and acquiescence. If it can be shown that a non-state actor who committed a disappearance acted with the 'authorisation, support or acquiescence' of state agents, these disappearances become *enforced* disappearances and thereby a human rights violation directly attributable to the state for the purpose of international responsibility.

The criteria of authorisation, support or acquiescence set a lower standard for attribution than that of 'effective control' or 'adoption of conduct' established in the ARSIWA or by the ICJ. Notably, none of these criteria are defined in the ICPPED, nor in any other IHRL enforced disappearance instrument, and the *travaux preparatoires* of the ICPPED do not indicate that there was a discussion about the meaning of any of these terms.[26] Prior to 2023, the CED had also not issued any interpretive guidance on the meaning of the three attribution criteria. This changed with the Committee's adoption of the Statement on non-State actors in the context of the International Convention for the Protection of All Persons from Enforced

[25] Article 2 ICPPED. Emphasis added. As already mentioned in Chap. 2, the definitions contained in the IACFDP (Article II) and DPPED (Preamble) contain very similar wording.

[26] During the negotiations of the ICPPED states discussed the definition of enforced disappearance and who the perpetrators could be, but this discussion centred around the question whether non-state actors could directly commit enforced disappearances. See Commission on Human Rights (2003) Report of the Intersessional Open-Ended Working Group to Elaborate a Draft Legally Binding Normative Instrument for the Protection of All Persons from Enforced Disappearance. UN Doc. E/CN.4/2003/71, para. 35; Commission on Human Rights (2004) Report of the Intersessional Open-Ended Working Group to Elaborate a Draft Legally Binding Normative Instrument for the Protection of All Persons from Enforced Disappearance. UN Doc. E/CN.4/2004/59, paras 27–41; Commission on Human Rights (2005) Report of the Intersessional Open-Ended Working Group to Elaborate a Draft Legally Binding Normative Instrument for the Protection of All Persons from Enforced Disappearance. UN Doc. E/CN.4/2005/66, paras 28–34. See also Vermeulen (2012), pp. 65–66. The Convention against Torture (CAT) also contains the term 'acquiescence' in the definition of torture but also does not provide a definition of it.

Disappearances (Statement on Non-State Actors),[27] in which it provided definitions of all three terms.

Authorisation and support are defined as follows:

> 3. "Authorization" means that the State, through its agents, has either orally or in writing given permission to persons or groups of persons to commit disappearance.
>
> 4. "Support" means that the State has provided some assistance to persons or groups of persons who have committed enforced disappearance, inter alia, through the sharing of information and/or the provision of means such as infrastructure, funding, weapons, training or logistics. For the purpose of attribution in this context, support does not have to be provided with the specific aim of committing enforced disappearance.[28]

The definitions of authorisation and support are broadly in line with the ordinary meanings[29] of both terms and indicate a requirement for some form of action on the part of state actors. Notably, in cases where human rights bodies have addressed direct attribution of acts by non-state actors to a state, their analysis has generally been limited to the notion of acquiescence, if at all, and there has not been explicit engagement with the notions of 'authorisation' or 'support'.[30] This may be because both notions warrant certain state actions, which, if present, might obviate the need for a more thorough analysis.

3.1.2.1 Acquiescence

The term 'acquiescence', on the other hand, is more complex because it refers to inaction and silence that expresses consent.[31] Perhaps due to the inherent difficulty of inferring consent from silence,[32] the application of this attribution criterion in case law of different human rights bodies (at UN and regional level) has by no means been consistent (see below) and it is therefore a welcome development that the CED has adopted an explicit definition of the concept. The Committee defines acquiescence as follows:

---

[27] Committee on Enforced Disappearances (CED) (2023) Statement on non-State actors in the context of the International Convention for the Protection of All Persons from Enforced Disappearances. UN Doc. CED/C/10, para. 3.

[28] Ibid., paras 3–4.

[29] Authorisation is defined as: 'official permission for something to happen, or the act of giving someone official permission to do something'. See https://dictionary.cambridge.org/dictionary/english/authorization?q=authorisation. Accessed 30 October 2024. Support is defined as: 'to agree with and give encouragement to someone'; 'If you support an activity or a habit, you provide the money needed to pay for it'; 'to provide the right conditions, such as enough food and water, for life'. See https://dictionary.cambridge.org/dictionary/english/support. Accessed 30 October 2024.

[30] I thank Prof. Stephan Parmentier for bringing my attention to this point.

[31] See Marques Antunes (2006), para. 2.

[32] See ibid., para. 19. On disappearances specifically, see Huhle (2013), pp. 21 and 24.

> 5. "Acquiescence" means that the State knew, had reasons to know or ought to have known of the commission or of the real and imminent risk of commission of enforced disappearance by persons or groups of persons, but that one of the following applies:
>
> (a) The State has either accepted, tolerated or given consent to this situation, even implicitly;
> (b) The State has deliberately and in full knowledge, by action or omission, failed to take measures to prevent the crime and to investigate and punish the perpetrators;
> (c) The State has acted in connivance with the perpetrators or with total disregard for the situation of the potential victims, facilitating the actions of the non-State actors who commit the act;
> (d) The State has created the conditions that allowed their commission.
>
> 6. In particular, there is acquiescence within the meaning of article 2 when there is a known pattern of disappearance of persons and the State has failed to take the measures necessary to prevent further cases of disappearance and to investigate the perpetrators and bring them to justice.[33]

Two things are noticeable about this definition. First, the definition in paragraph 5 is tautological because it requires state awareness of a risk of commission of *enforced* disappearance. Following the logic of the Convention, if acquiescence can be established, a disappearance that would otherwise fall within Article 3 ICPPED is effectively 'converted' into an enforced disappearance within the meaning of Article 2 ICPPED. Therefore, the wording at the beginning of paragraph 5 leads to an unfortunate blurring of the types of disappearances and should be interpreted as an unintentional oversight by the Committee, rather than an intentional blurring of concepts.

Secondly, the definition is split across two paragraphs (5 and 6) that address slightly different scenarios. For example, according to paragraph 5, the determination of acquiescence requires a level of foreseeability ('knew, had to reasons to know or ought to have known') in relation to 'the commission or [...] the real and imminent risk of commission' of a disappearance at the hands of a non-state actor, in addition to one of the situations described in sub-paragraphs a) to d). Conversely, paragraph 6 refers to the existence of a 'known pattern' of disappearances as a basis for establishing acquiescence if there is a failure to prevent or respond to disappearances committed by non-state actors. The separation of the two paragraphs implies that the criteria of foreseeability and existence of a real and imminent risk included in paragraph 5, are not necessary to establish acquiescence in line with the definition of paragraph 6. While it may be that the CED considers the existence of a '*known* pattern' (emphasis added) to encompass foreseeability and existence of risk, paragraph 6 seems to create a lower threshold for attribution.[34] Notably, the definition does not provide additional guidance about when a risk would be considered 'real and imminent'.

---

[33] CED (2023) Statement on non-State actors in the context of the International Convention for the Protection of All Persons from Enforced Disappearances. UN Doc. CED/C/10, paras 5–6.

[34] Guercke (2025).

Acquiescence in International Jurisprudence

Given that the CED's Statement on Non-State Actors provides the first-ever definition of acquiescence in the human rights context, it is worth examining it in light of prior jurisprudence by other UN human rights bodies,[35] the ECtHR, and the IACtHR that involved a determination of acquiescence by the state.[36] This —scarce— jurisprudence is not limited to disappearances, but also involves other rights violations committed by non-state actors, including torture and deprivation of liberty. The following section discusses this jurisprudence with a focus on the criteria used by tribunals to establish acquiescence.

The Committee Against Torture and Acquiescence

At the UN level, the treaty body that has most directly dealt with the topic of acquiescence is the Committee Against Torture (CAT). This is because, similarly to the definition of enforced disappearance in the ICPPED, the Convention Against Torture defines torture as committed by public officials or 'at the instigation of or *with the consent or acquiescence* of a public official.'[37] In its General Comment No. 2, the CAT made the following statement in relation to state responsibility:

> [...] where State authorities [...] know or have reasonable grounds to believe that acts of torture or ill-treatment are being committed by non-State officials or private actors and they fail to exercise due diligence to prevent, investigate, prosecute and punish such non-State officials or private actors consistently with the Convention, the State bears responsibility and its officials should be considered as authors, complicit or otherwise responsible under the Convention for consenting to or acquiescing in such impermissible acts.[38]

This statement suggests that for the CAT, in cases involving torture, a failure of the state to protect a victim by exercising due diligence to prevent or stop torture at the hands of non-state actors, can be viewed as constituting acquiescence.[39] The CED

[35] The CED is one of the 'youngest' UN treaty bodies and began working in 2011. So far, it has only issued three decisions on merits in individual communications submitted to it, none of which concern a disappearance committed by non-state actors. In the decision of *Berrospe Medina et al. v Mexico*, the state had alleged that perpetrators were most like members of organised crime. However, the Committee held that there was 'sufficient direct or circumstantial evidence of the involvement of State agents [,which] reverses the burden of proof and requires the State party to refute that evidence and the allegation that the disappearance is attributable to it'. *Berrospe Medina and Mendoza Berrospe v. Mexico* [2023] Committee on Enforced Disappearances CED/C/24/D/4/2021, para. 7.3.

[36] The author was unable to identify jurisprudence concerning acquiescence from the African human rights system.

[37] Article 1(1), Convention Against Torture and Other Cruel, Inhuman or Degrading Treatment or Punishment 1984 (1465 UNTS 85) (CAT). Emphasis added.

[38] Committee Against Torture (2008) General Comment No. 2: Implementation of Article 2 by States Parties. UN Doc. CAT/C/GC/2, para. 18.

[39] See Vermeulen (2012), p. 428. On failing to prevent amounting to acquiescence in relation to torture, see also Zach (2019), pp. 61–62; Bauer (2020), p. 781.

definition of acquiescence differs from the understanding of acquiescence as a 'simple' failure to act with due diligence because it requires not only a higher level of knowledge of risk ('know, had reason to know or ought to have known', rather than 'reasonable grounds to believe'), but also a certain level of state involvement, either through consent (including implicit consent) (para. 5 (a)), *deliberate* failure to take preventive measures (para. 5 (b)), connivance with perpetrators (para. 5 (c)), or involvement in creating the conditions for the act to occur (para. 5 (d)). Conversely, the CED definition is arguably broader because it refers to knowledge of *risk* of the commission of a disappearance, whereas the CAT refers to awareness of torture *being committed.*

In practice, cases where the CAT has established acquiescence have involved a combination of failures to prevent and investigate in situations where state actors could clearly have intervened. For example, in the case of *Hajrizi Dzemajl*, police officers in former Yugoslavia failed to intervene and stop an angry mob who attacked and burned down a Roma settlement. According to the CAT, the officers had acquiesced to the attack because they had not only been made aware of an immediate risk to the victims but were also physically present during the attack yet did nothing to stop it.[40] In the case of *Guerrero Larez v Venezuela*, the victim was a prison inmate at the time of his disappearance and was allegedly killed by a group of inmates. His body was then dismembered and buried. The CAT determined that the victim's disappearance was an *enforced* disappearance because the prison authorities failed to prevent violence among prison inmates and because they did not provide any information about the victim's whereabouts. Since the victim was in the direct care of the state, authorities had a 'special obligation' to take preventive measures to protect his rights from being violated.[41]

A decisive element in these cases, as well as in General Comment No. 2 cited above, is the required knowledge of a specific risk to an individual or group of individuals.[42] The degree of this knowledge, however, is not clear. For example, McCorquodale and La Forgia have argued that states' 'having actual knowledge of the particular violation at the time it was committed is not crucial.'[43] Rather, what mattered is the *general* knowledge of such actions being committed by non-state actors and the (deliberate) failure of the state to take any measures against such acts.[44] However, the CAT has not yet dealt with a case where there was 'only' general knowledge and it is therefore not clear whether it would follow this proposal. In both cases described above, the authorities were clearly aware of a specific risk

[40] *Hajrizi Dzemajl et al v Yugoslavia* [2002] Committee Against Torture CAT/C/29/D/161/2000, para. 9.2.

[41] *Francisco Dionel Guerrero Larez v Venezuela* [2015] Committee Against Torture CAT/C/54/D/456/2011, paras 6.3–6.6. See also Guercke (2022), p. 137.

[42] This is also reflected in case law dealing involving violence against women at the hands of private actors. On this, see Edwards (2006), p. 374.

[43] McCorquodale and La Forgia (2001), p. 206.

[44] Ibid.

and had the possibility to intervene in some way to prevent or stop the violations. Notably, the statement in General Comment No. 2 cited above refers to the knowledge of authorities that torture, or other forms of ill-treatment, 'are being committed', which suggests a difference between preventing the occurrence of torture or ill-treatment in the first place and intervening to stop it once it is already happening. A strict reading of the text would imply that only the latter would be equivalent to acquiescing to the torture or ill-treatment. The CED's definition of acquiescence in relation to disappearances overcomes this issue by referring to a 'risk of commission of enforced disappearance', thereby encompassing a failure to prevent the initial deprivation of liberty that constitutes the first element of an enforced disappearance. At the same time, the reference to a failure to act in light of a 'known pattern' of disappearances in paragraph 6 of the Statement seems to directly take up the CAT's definition of acquiescence and McCorquodale and La Forgia's argument regarding the sufficiency of general knowledge.

The Human Rights Committee and Acquiescence

The Human Rights Committee (HRC) dealt with the question of acquiescence in the cases of *Rosa Maria Serna et alt. v Colombia*[45] and *Carlos Moreno Zamora et alt v Mexico.*[46] The former case concerned a disappearance at the hands of paramilitary groups in Colombia, and the HRC found that the state had acquiesced to the victim's disappearance based on the state's relationship to paramilitary groups, who had received training and weapons from the Colombian army, as well as the state's failure to react to complaints made by the authors and investigate the paramilitary group.[47] In the case of *Carlos Moreno Zamora et alt v Mexico*, the authors had alleged that Jesús Israel Moreno Pérez, was a victim of an *enforced* disappearance even though he had been disappeared by unknown perpetrators. The authors' argument was based on authorities' failure to conduct an effective investigation not only by omission, but also by actively obstructing the investigation. For example, there was evidence to suggest that authorities had made up false testimonies and manipulated evidence.[48] The HRC, however, was not convinced by this argument:

[45] *Rosa María Serna et al v Colombia* [2015] Human Rights Committee UN Doc. CCPR/C/114/D/2134/2012.

[46] *Carlos Moreno Zamora et alt v Mexico* [2019] Human Rights Committee Communication No. 2760/2016, CCPR/C/127/D/2760/2016.

[47] Ibid., para. 9.3. In their concurring opinion, committee members Víctor Rodríguez Rescia and Fabián Omar Salvioli argued that the HRC should have been clearer in its reasoning for establishing the state's responsibility. More specifically, they held that 'The State's objective responsibility derives equally from its having established paramilitary structures and from its failure to effectively eliminate those structures; this created a situation of high and constant risk in the region where the authors were disappeared.' (*Rosa María Serna et al. v Colombia*, Individual opinion by Committee members Víctor Rodríguez Rescia and Fabián Omar Salvioli (concurring), para. 5). In addition, the Committee members stressed the importance of the general context (para. 6).

[48] *Carlos Moreno Zamora et alt v Mexico*, para. 12.2.

> [...] the Committee notes that, in the absence of any information pointing to a specific context of enforced disappearances in the place where the disappearance occurred, and in the absence of circumstantial evidence to substantiate the presumption of involvement, support or acquiescence of State agents in the disappearance, the Committee cannot conclude that the disappearance of Mr. Moreno Pérez is an enforced disappearance directly attributable to the State party.[49]

The HRC thus maintains a distinction between a failure to investigate a disappearance and acquiescence, even in cases where the state is actively involved in obstructing the investigation and tampering with evidence, thereby actively fuelling impunity.[50] This indicates a narrower understanding of acquiescence than that of the CED, particularly in relation to state inaction when there are 'known patterns' of disappearances, even if the latter are committed without any state involvement. This more narrow approach could relate to the difficulty of establishing foreseeability in relation to the initial deprivation of liberty, which is constitutive of an enforced disappearance.

Regional Bodies

The jurisprudence of the European and the Inter-American human rights courts is somewhat confusing and ambiguous in relation to acquiescence and does not provide clear answers to the questions of whether and how it overlaps with or differs from a failure to act with due diligence to prevent or respond to a disappearance committed by a non-state actor, or how it relates to the other attribution criteria.[51]

The European Court of Human Rights and Acquiescence

In the case of *Rantsev v Cyprus and Russia,* the ECtHR found that Cypriot authorities had 'acquiesced' in the deprivation of liberty of a trafficking victim.[52] In this case, the victim, a Russian national who had been trafficked to Cyprus under a specific visa scheme for 'artistes', had been briefly detained for immigration reasons at a police station. Once authorities had determined that her immigration status was regular, they refused to let her leave alone and called her employer. The employer took the victim to his apartment and kept her there against her will, which ultimately led to her death when she tried to escape from the apartment. The ECtHR first determined that the victim had been held in the apartment against her will and that this constituted a deprivation of her liberty contrary to Article 5 ECHR.[53] Subsequently, it found that Cyprus was directly responsible for this deprivation of liberty

---

[49] Ibid., para. 12.3.

[50] Guercke (2022), p. 136.

[51] For an overview of the confusing approach of the ECtHR to the question of "acquiescence and connivance", see Milanovic (2022).

[52] *Rantsev v Cyprus and Russia* [2010] European Court of Human Rights Application no. 25965/04.

[53] Ibid., paras 316–318.

because the Cypriot police had 'actively cooperated' in it, which led the Court to determine that authorities had *acquiesced* to the deprivation of liberty:

> Taken in the context of the general living and working conditions of cabaret artistes in Cyprus, as well as in light of the particular circumstances of Ms Rantseva's case, the Court considers that it is not open to the police to claim that they were acting in good faith and that they bore no responsibility for Ms Rantseva's subsequent deprivation of liberty in M.P.'s apartment. It is clear that without the active cooperation of the Cypriot police in the present case, the deprivation of liberty could not have occurred. The Court therefore considers that the national authorities acquiesced in Ms Rantseva's loss of liberty.[54]

Two elements are noteworthy in this statement: first, the relevance of context for determining that authorities were aware of a risk when they released the victim into the hands of her employer, which meant that they could not have been acting in 'good faith'. Second, the victim would not have been deprived of her liberty if it had not been for the 'active cooperation' of the authorities, which means that there was a causal link between the authorities' actions and the violation. The ECtHR's reasoning is also based on an actual possibility for authorities to intervene and prevent the deprivation of liberty, similar to the cases before the CAT and thus appears much narrower than the definition adopted by the CED.[55]

The Inter-American Court of Human Rights and Acquiescence[56]

In the jurisprudence of the Inter-American Court there are several cases involving disappearances at the hands of non-state actors where the IACtHR directly addressed the question of acquiescence. Initially, the Court seemed to clearly distinguish between acquiescence and a failure to prevent or respond to a disappearance committed by a non-state actor. Thus, in the case of *Velásquez Rodríguez*, the IACtHR indicated a difference:

> [...] What is decisive is whether a violation of the rights recognized by the Convention has occurred with the support or the acquiescence of the government, **or** whether the State has allowed the act to take place without taking measures to prevent it or to punish those responsible.[57]

---

[54] Ibid., para. 321.

[55] Note that in other disappearance cases the ECtHR did not examine acquiescence specifically, yet it also attributed responsibility for a disappearance after authorities had been in direct contact with the victim and his captors. For example, in *Medova v Russia* the Court reasoned: 'Therefore, while Mr Medov, K. and their captors were within the control of the authorities, the latter could have prevented the commission of an offence, but they released the six men, after which Mr Medov disappeared. [...] The Court considers that the authorities' decision to release the six men, which resulted in the disappearance of Mr Medov, constituted a breach of the positive obligation to take preventive measures to protect those whose life is at risk from the criminal acts of other individuals.' *Medova v Russia* [2009] European Court of Human Rights Application no. 25385/04, para. 99.

[56] The content in this section has previously been published in a slightly modified manner. See Guercke (2022).

[57] *Case of Velásquez-Rodríguez v Honduras (Merits)* [1988] Inter-American Court of Human Rights Ser. C No. 4, para 173. Emphasis added.

The disjunctive 'or' in this sentence indicates that 'support or acquiescence' and 'measures to prevent or punish' are not equal, although the IACtHR did not further elaborate on this distinction.[58] Following this reasoning, the IACtHR established acquiescence in cases where it found a direct relationship between state and non-state actors. An example of this approach is the case of *Blake vs Guatemala*:[59] the victims, two US-American journalists, had been detained by 'Civil Defense Committees' and disappeared. While the state argued that these civil patrols were voluntary community organisations, the IACtHR found that they had in fact 'acted as agents of the state'[60] because they had an 'institutional relationship' with the Guatemalan Army.[61]

In several cases concerning serious human rights violations committed by paramilitary groups in Colombia, the Inter-American Court established acquiescence (albeit not very explicitly so) on the 'support and collaboration' that these groups had received from the state[62] or on its finding that the state and paramilitary groups had acted 'in a coordinated, parallel or linked manner'.[63] Following the CED's definitions, in the former situation the attribution would be based on 'support' and only in the latter case on acquiescence. Moreover, the Inter-American Court has maintained the requirement of a 'relationship' between the state and non-state actor. For example, in the case of *Pueblo Bello*, which also concerned paramilitary activities in Colombia, the Court stopped short of establishing acquiescence and found that there was insufficient evidence to confirm a 'connection' between the Colombian Army and the paramilitary groups, as it had in similar cases. Instead, using the same language as in acquiescence cases, it found that Colombia held 'responsibility for the acts' committed by paramilitary groups due to its failure to prevent 'reasonably foreseeable' danger.[64] Based on the definition of acquiescence provided by the CED,

---

[58] The African Commission has taken up this sentence in its General Comment No. 3 on the right to life: 'A State can be held responsible for killings by non-State actors if it approves, supports or acquiesces in those acts *or* if it fails to exercise due diligence to prevent such killings or to ensure proper investigation and accountability.' African Commission on Human and Peoples' Rights (2015) General Comment No. 3 on the African Charter on Human and People's Rights: The Right to Life (Article 4), para. 9. Emphasis added.

[59] *Case of Blake v Guatemala (Merits)* [1998] Inter-American Court of Human Rights Ser C No 36.

[60] Ibid., para. 75.

[61] Ibid. paras 75–78. Vázquez Camacho has criticised the IACtHR's approach in this case, arguing that the Court confused acquiescence with a particular non-state actor acting as an agent of the state. See Vázquez Camacho (2013), p. 26; Guercke (2022), p. 139.

[62] *Case of the 19 Merchants v Colombia* [2004] Inter-American Court of Human Rights Ser C No. 109, para. 134.

[63] *Case of the "Mapiripán Massacre" v. Colombia*, para. 123. For an overview of the IACtHR's jurisprudence on acquiescence, see *Case of López Soto and others v Venezuela* [2018] Inter-American Court of Human Rights Series C No 362, note 233.

[64] *Case of the Pueblo Bello Massacre v Colombia* [2006] Inter-American Court of Human Rights Series C No. 140, para. 140; compare: *Case of the "Mapiripán Massacre" v. Colombia*, para. 122. I discuss the Inter-American Court's reasoning in the case of *Pueblo Bello* in more detail below (Sect. 3.2.1.3).

it is likely that the context in the case of *Pueblo Bello* would give rise to acquiescence due to the state's inaction.

The IACtHR has continued to connect acquiescence to a relationship between state and non-state actors but has added some unfortunate confusion in the case of *López Soto vs Venezuela*.[65] Linda Loaiza López Soto was kidnapped by a private individual and held in detention for several months where she was subjected to sexual torture and other forms of physical and mental violence. The Court reaffirmed that there was a distinction between a failure to prevent and acquiescence, in that the latter would imply a more 'direct' form of responsibility[66] because it 'signifies the State's consent to the action of a private individual, either by deliberate inaction or by its own actions that have created conditions that allowed the act to be executed by individuals.'[67] The IACtHR then distinguished between 'a general context of collaboration and acquiescence' and acquiescence linked to a particular case, holding that a general context was 'not sufficient' for establishing state responsibility.[68] Since there was no evidence of a relationship between authorities and the perpetrator, Venezuela was not *directly* responsible for the disappearance.[69] Rather, the Court found that the state had acquiesced in the sexual torture that Linda Loaiza López Soto was subjected to because authorities had not reacted when her disappearance was reported, even though the identity of the perpetrator was known to them.[70] The apparent requirement of *prior and specific* knowledge about the rights-violating conduct[71] in the case law of the IACtHR does not appear as such in the CED definition of acquiescence, which does not contain a reference to specific victims.

The approach by the Inter-American Court in *López Soto* is unfortunate and unnecessarily creates further confusion by introducing a distinction in levels of responsibility between different types of acquiescence, applying the same distinction that it had made in cases concerning a failure to prevent (discussed in the following section). Concerning acquiescence in particular, however, this statement by the IACtHR appears to impose a higher threshold for responsibility than that contained in the human rights instruments dealing with enforced disappearance

65 *Case of López Soto and others v. Venezuela*.

66 Guercke (2022), p. 139.

67 *Case of López Soto and others v. Venezuela*, para. 146. Part of this wording has now been incorporated in the CED's definition of acquiescence.

68 Ibid., para. 148 and cases cited in note 236.

69 Ibid., para. 169. Rather, the Court determined the Venezuelan state's international responsibility for failing to act with due diligence once authorities had been notified of Linda López' disappearance (and the identity of the perpetrator) and for 'tolerating acts that violated her rights to personal integrity, personal liberty, dignity, autonomy and privacy' (ibid., para. 170).

70 Ibid., paras 197–199.

71 On this, see also Vázquez Camacho, who argues that the jurisprudence of the IACtHR in relation to Colombia indicates a requirement for some level of what the author describes as 'intentionality'. Nonetheless, the author also recognizes that this position is controversial. See Vázquez Camacho (2013), pp. 29–30.

themselves. This is because according to the ICPPED, acquiescence is an attribution criterion for an enforced disappearance, which would automatically lead to a state's international responsibility. The IACtHR's reasoning, on the other hand, implies that there could be disappearances committed in a 'general context of acquiescence' that are not *enforced* disappearances. However, nowhere in the definition of enforced disappearance does it say that acquiescence needs to exist in relation to a specific victim or act. Rather, the definition refers to 'persons or groups of persons acting with the authorization, support or acquiescence of the State' (Article 2 ICPPED), which suggests that if a person, or group, is generally seen as acting with the acquiescence of the state, it would not be necessary to determine that the state had acquiesced in the deprivation of liberty of a specific individual. The CED's definition of acquiescence in paragraph 6 of the Statement, which refers to state failure to act in contexts of 'know patterns of disappearances' further supports this argument.[72]

A Failure to Investigate as Acquiescence[73]

The CED's definition of acquiescence contained in paragraph 6 of the Statement reflects arguments that a failure to investigate disappearances committed by non-state actors—independently of a failure to prevent the initial deprivation of liberty—could be read as acquiescence to this crime, especially in contexts where these disappearances are not isolated incidents and there is persistent impunity.[74] This argument is based on the refusal to provide information about the fate of the disappeared person as a constitutive element of the crime of enforced disappearance. Moreover, it resonates with General Comment No. 2 of the CAT cited above, which lists a failure to act with due diligence to investigate and prosecute an act of torture or ill-treatment as a basis for acquiescence. The IACtHR and the ECtHR have also both made statements in their jurisprudence suggesting that impunity, and a failure of the state to investigate disappearances (or other crimes) committed by private actors is a way of 'assisting' the perpetrators[75] because it can create an 'appearance of collusion in or tolerance of unlawful acts'.[76] Nevertheless, it is important to note that both

---

[72] Similarly, the CAT also does not refer to knowledge of torture of a specific individual but refers to the state's knowledge that 'acts of torture or other ill-treatment are being committed'. See Committee Against Torture (2008) General Comment No. 2: Implementation of Article 2 by States Parties. UN Doc. CAT/C/GC/2, para. 18.

[73] Parts this section have previously been published. See Guercke (2022).

[74] See Frey (2021).

[75] The IACtHR has used the words 'aid' or 'assist' in this context. See *Case of Velásquez-Rodríguez v. Honduras (Merits)*, para. 177; *Case of the Pueblo Bello Massacre v. Colombia*, para. 145; *Case of González et al ("Cotton Field") v Mexico* [2009] Inter-American Court of Human Rights Serie C No. 205, para. 291.

[76] *Buldan v Turkey* [2004] European Court of Human Rights Application No 28298/95, para. 84; *Varnava and Others v Turkey* [2009] European Court of Human Rights Applications nos. 16064/90, 16065/90, 16066/90, 16068/90, 16069/90, 16070/90, 16071/90, 16072/90 and 16073/90, para.

courts have made these statements to delineate the content and importance of the obligation to investigate, rather than as part of their reasoning to establish responsibility based on collusion or tolerance.

As I have argued elsewhere, the explicit obligation under Article 3 ICPPED to 'take appropriate measures to investigate' disappearances committed by non-state actors 'and bring those responsible to justice', implies that a failure to investigate and prosecute such disappearances would give rise to a violation of the obligations under Article 3 ICPPED. Thus, due to the existence of Article 3, it is more difficult to argue that under the ICPPED a failure to take appropriate investigative measures could also constitute acquiescence to the disappearance because such an approach would blur the distinction between Articles 2 and 3 even further.[77] Furthermore, due to the composite nature of the crime of enforced disappearance, and by extension disappearances that fall within the scope of Article 3 ICPPED,[78] acquiescence would have to relate to both the initial deprivation of liberty and the subsequent refusal to acknowledge it.

In its definition of acquiescence, the CED appears to have opted for a compromise in stating that a failure to 'take the measures necessary to prevent further cases of disappearances and to investigate the perpetrators and bring them to justice' amounts to acquiescence when there exists a 'known pattern of disappearances'.[79] In such cases, states clearly have awareness of risk of disappearances and, in failing to act, they contribute to their commission. At the same time, the CED Statement also upholds a distinction between impunity as acquiescence and a breach of obligations under Article 3 of the Convention in that it includes a separate paragraph in which it 'recalls that under international law, States have strict obligations with regard to due diligence when they have knowledge of a case of disappearance, or of a real and imminent risk of disappearance, perpetrated by a non-State actor.'[80] Therefore, the decisive criterion between acquiescence and a failure to act is the context surrounding disappearances that would normally fall within Article 3 ICPPED.

By including knowledge of a general pattern and failure to act in the definition of acquiescence, the CED takes up some more recent positions expressed by the WGEID and the Special Rapporteurship on Economic, Social, Cultural and Environmental Rights (REDESCA) of the Inter-American Commission on Human Rights

---

191; *Olewnik-Cieplińska and Olewnik v Poland* [2019] European Court of Human Rights Application no. 20147/15, para. 137.

[77] See Guercke (2022), p. 135. On the difference between the two articles, see also de Frouville (2021).

[78] Article 3 refers to 'acts defined in article 2 committed by persons or groups of persons acting without the authorization, support or acquiescence of the State' (Article 3 ICPPED). Therefore, disappearances that fall within the scope of Article 3 also must contain the composite elements of deprivation of liberty and concealment of the disappeared person's fate or whereabouts in line with Article 2 ICPPED.

[79] CED (2023) Statement on non-State actors in the context of the International Convention for the Protection of All Persons from Enforced Disappearances. UN Doc. CED/C/10, para. 6.

[80] Ibid., para. 22.

(IACHR). In its Report on Enforced Disappearance in the Context of Migration, the WGEID expressed the view that:

> [...] systematic situations of impunity regarding the abduction and detention of migrants by private actors, including smugglers or traffickers, could be considered in certain circumstances as a form of acquiescence and, as such, constitute enforced disappearance.[81]

The WGEID did not specify what would constitute 'certain circumstances', yet the reference to 'systematic situations' can be compared to the phrase 'known pattern' used in the CED Statement. Similarly, in their report on Inter-American standards on Business and Human Rights, the IACHR and REDESCA stated that prolonged failure by a state to respond to activities by businesses that threaten human rights and of which the state has knowledge, can constitute acquiescence for the purpose of direct attribution of responsibility to the state:

> For example, this could happen if a fundamental part of the lack of State response as a guarantor takes place as a consequence of the absence or lack of sustained diligence in the investigation and eventual punishment for serious and repeated violations of human rights involving the actions of a business entity.[82]

According to the IACHR, the criteria that would have to be considered for establishing tolerance or acquiescence in cases of a prolonged failure to investigate are 'the magnitude, seriousness, prolongation, and manifestations of the breach of the duties to prevent and investigate.'[83] Following this logic, where there is consistent and prolonged impunity and inaction by a state in a situation where non-state actors are known to perpetrate disappearances, this failure to respond would constitute acquiescence. The CED's definition reflects this understanding and broadens it because it does not include the word 'prolonged'.

The CED's definition of acquiescence thus reflects an amalgamation of different approaches taken by international and regional human rights bodies, including the most progressive ones. The definition could be criticised for going beyond existing jurisprudence because it encompasses not only situations where the state could directly intervene to prevent a disappearance, but also those where its actions or omissions are causally linked to a disappearance, albeit indirectly. First, where the state 'has created the conditions that allowed their commission', it can be considered as acquiescing to a disappearance that was foreseeable and imminent, without the need to establish a concrete failure to act.[84] Second, state inaction and impunity in the face of 'known patterns' can also be considered acquiescence without the need for separately establishing awareness and imminence of risk. In response to such

[81] Human Rights Council (2017) Report of the Working Group on Enforced or Involuntary Disappearances on Enforced Disappearances in the Context of Migration. UN Doc. A/HRC/36/39/Add.2, para. 42.

[82] Inter-American Commission on Human Rights and REDESCA (2019) Business and Human Rights: Inter-American Standards. OEA/Ser.L/V/II, CIDH/REDESCA/INF.1/19, para. 79.

[83] Ibid., para. 78.

[84] CED (2023) Statement on non-State actors in the context of the International Convention for the Protection of All Persons from Enforced Disappearances. UN Doc. CED/C/10, para. 5(d).

criticism, adopting a broader definition of acquiescence is warranted when it comes to disappearances because the characteristic lack of information inherent in the crime, regardless of the identity of the perpetrator, can only be overcome with the support of the state and its apparatus to search for victims and investigate the perpetrators. In that sense, and in view of the impact on relatives of not knowing the fate or whereabouts of the disappeared person,[85] and the influence of the state's actions or inaction on the suffering relatives experience, the former acquire great importance in all situations.

Importantly, while the CED's Statement on Non-State Actors maintains a distinction between a failure to prevent and acquiescence, it also equates them in some situations,[86] similar to the approach taken by the CAT, and blurring the distinction between attribution and breach. Consequently, in order to clarify the threshold of foreseeability and imminence contained in the definition of acquiescence, jurisprudence relating to state responsibility for a failure to prevent that does not amount to acquiescence, which I examine in the following section, can shed light on how knowledge of risk has been established.

3.2 Breach of an International Obligation

Once the question of attribution has been clarified, the second element of state responsibility is the existence of a breach of an international obligation. A breach can occur either by action or omission.[87] In the case of disappearances, if a disappearance committed by a non-state actor can be directly attributed to the state, for example because it can be shown that state agents acquiesced in the disappearance, the disappearance can be considered an enforced disappearance in line with Article 2 ICPPED. Given the prohibition of enforced disappearance in international law (see Introduction), the commission of this human rights violation always constitutes a breach of a state's international obligations and therefore entails the international responsibility of the state. Conversely, if a disappearance falls within Article 3 ICPPED, states may still incur international responsibility for failing to protect the rights of both the victims of disappearances, as well as their relatives, in line with their positive obligations to prevent and respond to acts committed by non-state actors (see Chap. 2). The previous section has shown that, especially with the adoption of a broad definition of acquiescence by the CED, the line between direct attribution based on acquiescence and responsibility for a failure to protect can be very thin in disappearance cases. However, the two do not always overlap. States

---

[85] See, for example, Finucane (2010).

[86] For an argument that acquiescence and a failure to prevent should always be considered as equal in the context of torture, see Bauer (2020).

[87] ILC (2001) Draft Articles on Responsibility of States for Internationally Wrongful Acts, with Commentaries. ILC Yearbook 2001, Vol. II, Part II, p. 35, para. 4.

can incur responsibility for breaching their obligations under Article 3 ICPPED to search and investigate, as well as to act with due diligence in situations where they have knowledge of a real and imminent risk of a disappearance.[88] Moreover, due to the particular nature of disappearances and beyond the ICPPED, states can incur responsibility for a number of other human rights violations that occur as a result of the disappearance. This section addresses how responsibility has been determined in jurisprudence involving a failure to prevent violations of rights by non-state actors, as well as how a failure to respond to a disappearance committed by a non-state actor can give rise to responsibility for violations of different rights.[89]

3.2.1 Responsibility for a Failure to Prevent[90]

States' preventive obligations regarding harm by non-state actors can be divided into general and specific obligations (see Chap. 2). The general obligation to take preventive measures encompasses putting in place effective legal frameworks to respond to acts by non-state actors that violate human rights, as well as adopting policies and programmes to counter such acts. Specific preventive obligations require states to take preventive 'operational' measures in particular situations where they are aware of an identifiable risk to someone's right.[91] Following the ARSIWA, a breach of either aspect of the obligation to prevent would give rise to state responsibility. This is because, according to Article 12 ARSIWA:

> There is a breach of an international obligation by a State when an act of that State is not in conformity with what is required of it by that obligation, regardless of its origin or character.[92]

According to the Commentary on Article 12, the notion of breach is broad and comprehensive, and does not require any type of distinction between 'categories of obligations'.[93] This also means that for the purpose of establishing the breach of an

[88] See CED (2023) Statement on non-State actors in the context of the International Convention for the Protection of All Persons from Enforced Disappearances. UN Doc. CED/C/10, para. 22.

[89] This section focuses mainly on jurisprudence from the ECtHR and IACtHR because there is very little case law by UN treaty bodies and in the African human rights system dealing with a failure to prevent. Moreover, UN treaty bodies generally do not include in-depth reasoning in published views, which makes it difficult to use their jurisprudence as guidance for understanding their reasoning. Where UN treaty bodies have come to similar conclusions as the ECtHR or IACtHR, this is mentioned in a footnote.

[90] The analysis presented in this section has previously been published in a summarised form. See Guercke (2021).

[91] This can, in some instances, overlap with the determination of acquiescence if the conditions specified in the CED's Statement on Non-State Actors (para. 5 a-d) are met.

[92] Article 12 ARSIWA.

[93] See ILC (2001) Draft Articles on Responsibility of States for Internationally Wrongful Acts, with Commentaries. ILC Yearbook 2001, Vol. II, Part II, p. 56, para. 6.

international obligation from the perspective of the law on state responsibility, it does not matter whether the obligation breached was one of means or one of result.[94]

However, in IHRL the determination of responsibility is slightly more nuanced. Thus, both the ECtHR and the IACtHR have found violations of an obligation to prevent only in relation to a failure to take *specific* preventive measures. This is because, in the words of the IACtHR, 'according to the Court's jurisprudence, it is evident that a state cannot be held responsible for every human rights violation committed between private individuals within its jurisdiction' and that therefore state responsibility in relation to acts committed by non-state actors is not 'unlimited'.[95] Moreover, both the Inter-American and the European human rights courts have emphasised that the obligation to prevent is a due diligence obligation of means and not of result,[96] which means that the occurrence of a human rights-violating act by a non-state actor does not automatically imply that a state failed to act with due diligence in trying to prevent it.[97] This is because obligations of due diligence require taking *reasonable* measures and therefore require an assessment of the reasonableness of the measures taken in order to establish a breach. Additionally, the obligation to take specific preventive measures depends on the circumstances of each case.[98] Consequently, in IHRL, in order for a human rights tribunal to establish the responsibility of a state for violating a particular victim's rights in cases where a non-state actor is the direct perpetrator, a 'test' is required to determine whether the state had specific preventive obligations vis-à-vis the victim or victims of the alleged violation and whether it acted with due diligence.

---

[94] See ibid., pp. 56–57, para. 11. See also Crawford (2013), pp. 219–220. On the question of due diligence and prevention obligations specifically, see ibid., pp. 226 ff.

[95] *Case of González et al. ("Cotton Field") v. Mexico*, para. 280.

[96] See, for example, *Osmanoğlu v Turkey* [2008] European Court of Human Rights Application no. 48804/99 [77]; *Olewnik-Cieplińska and Olewnik v. Poland*, para. 68; *Case of González et al. ("Cotton Field") v. Mexico*, para. 252; *Case of the Hacienda Brasil Verde Workers v Brazil* [2016] Inter-American Court of Human Rights Series C No. 318, para. 328; *Case of López Soto and others v. Venezuela*, para. 130.

[97] *Case of Velásquez-Rodríguez v. Honduras* (Merits), para. 175. The IACtHR also took this approach in the case of *López Soto v Venezuela*, where it applied this reasoning to the notion of acquiescence and distinguished between general acquiescence and acquiescence in a specific rights-violating act.

[98] See *Osman v The United Kingdom* [1998] European Court of Human Rights Application no. 23452/94, 1998–VIII, para. 116; *Mahmut Kaya v Turkey* [2000] European Court of Human Rights Application no. 22535/93, 2000–III, para. 86; *Mastromatteo v Italy* [2002] European Court of Human Rights Application no. 37703/97, 2002–VIII, para. 68; *Osmanoğlu v Turkey*, para. 73; *Medova v Russia*, para. 96; *Rantsev v. Cyprus and Russia*, para. 219; *Case of the Pueblo Bello Massacre v. Colombia*, para. 123; *Case of González et al. ("Cotton Field") v. Mexico*, para. 280; *Case of Luna López v Honduras* [2013] Inter-American Court of Human Rights Series C No. 269, para. 120; *Case of the Hacienda Brasil Verde Workers v. Brazil*, para. 323; *Case of López Soto and others v. Venezuela*, para. 138.

3.2.1.1 Criteria for Determining an Obligation to Take Specific Preventive Measures

There are three steps for determining whether a state failed in its obligation to prevent. First, it has to be established that a state had specific prevention obligations. Second, the state must have been able to take preventive measures. Finally, it must be shown that the state did not take such measures or failed to do so with due diligence.[99] In order to determine whether a state had an obligation to take specific prevention measures, the ECtHR and IACtHR have used a set of criteria. Although these criteria were developed in relation to the obligation to protect the right to life, they have since been applied to other rights, such as the right to be free from torture or ill-treatment[100] and from slavery or forced labour,[101] all of which could be infringed in the course of a disappearance committed by non-state actors. As outlined in Chap. 2 (Sect. 2.1.2.2), the criteria were first elaborated by the ECtHR in the case of *Osman v UK*.[102] In this case, a schoolteacher had developed an obsession for a pupil, Ahmet Osman, and began to stalk him. After over a year of reporting and filing complaints with the police and several measures taken (including the teacher's suspension from his job), the former teacher drove to the Osman's home, where he killed Ahmet Osman's father and injured Ahmet.[103] The European Court had to assess whether the United Kingdom (UK) failed in its obligation to protect the right to life of Ahmet Osman and his father. The ECtHR first established that an obligation to take preventive operational measures should 'not impose an impossible or disproportionate burden' on state authorities, which implied that 'not every claimed risk to life can entail for the authorities a Convention requirement to take operational measures to prevent that risk from materialising.'[104] Therefore, in order to determine whether a state had an obligation to take specific prevention measures, the European Court listed the following criteria:

> [...] it must be established to its satisfaction that the authorities *knew or ought to have known* at the time of the existence of a *real and immediate risk* to the life of an identified individual or individuals from the criminal acts of a third party and that they failed to take *measures within the scope of their powers which, judged reasonably, might have been expected to avoid* that risk.[105]

---

[99] See Ebert and Sijniensky (2015), pp. 347–348.

[100] See, for example, *Case of López Soto and others v Venezuela.*

[101] See, for the ECtHR and IACtHR, respectively, for example: *Rantsev v. Cyprus and Russia*; *Case of the Hacienda Brasil Verde Workers v. Brazil.*

[102] *Osman v. The United Kingdom.*

[103] The teacher also shot the deputy headmaster of the school where he had been a teacher and killed the latter's son, but this was not part of the complaint (see ibid., para. 56). According to the Court's description of the facts, when the former teacher was arrested, he asked the police '*"why didn't you stop me before I did it, I gave you all the warning signs?"*' (ibid., para. 57).

[104] *Osman v. The United Kingdom*, para. 116.

[105] Ibid. Emphasis added.

Additionally, the ECtHR specified that the standard to assess whether a state had failed in its obligation to take preventive measures was not one of 'gross negligence' or 'wilful disregard', as had been argued by the UK government, but rather that what needed to be shown on a case-by-case basis was that 'the authorities did not do all that could be *reasonably expected* of them to avoid a real and immediate risk to life of which they have or ought to have knowledge.'[106] Therefore, and in line with the objective determination of responsibility in IHRL generally, it is not necessary to demonstrate intent.[107]

The Inter-American Court of Human Rights has followed the ECtHR's approach in adopting these criteria and articulated them as follows in the case of *Pueblo Bello v Colombia*:

> [the State's] obligations to adopt prevention and protection measures for individuals in their relationships with each other are conditioned by the *awareness* of a situation of *real and imminent danger* for a *specific individual or group of individuals* and to the *reasonable possibilities of preventing* or avoiding that danger.[108]

Finally, the HRC articulated a similar standard in its General Comment No. 36 on the right to life:

> States parties are thus under a due diligence obligation to undertake *reasonable* positive measures, *which do not impose on them disproportionate burdens, in response to reasonably foreseeable threats to life* originating from private persons and entities, whose conduct is not attributable to the State.[109]

While the HRC does not mention the specificity of the risk in this statement, it did consider this element in one of the few cases where it dealt with state failure to protect. In the case of *Yelitze Lisbeth Moreno de Castillo v Venezuela*,[110] which concerned the death of a human rights defender, the Committee largely based its assessment on findings of the Inter-American Commission and Court, both of whom had previously dealt with the same case, and found that:

> [...] although at the time of the incidents in question human rights defenders, [...] were at risk by reason of the complex interactions occurring among a range of different actors, causes and interests, *that risk was not sufficiently specific in the particular circumstances of the case* to trigger the State party's legal responsibility for failing to take appropriate measures to protect a particular person, in this case Joe Luis Castillo.[111]

---

[106] Ibid. Emphasis added.

[107] The IACtHR has emphasised on several occasions that due to its nature as a human rights tribunal, it was not necessary to evidence intentionality in order to determine individual culpability or guilt. See, for example, *Case of the Pueblo Bello Massacre v. Colombia*, para. 112; *Case of Luna López v. Honduras*, para. 119.

[108] *Case of the Pueblo Bello Massacre v. Colombia*, para. 123. Emphasis added.

[109] Human Rights Committee (2019) General Comment No. 36: Article 6: Right to Life. UN Doc. CCPR/C/GC/36, para. 21. Emphasis added.

[110] *Yelitze Lisbeth Moreno de Castillo v Venezuela* [2018] Human Rights Committee UN Doc. CCPR/C/121/D/2610/2015.

[111] Ibid., para. 9.3. Emphasis added.

Based on these statements, the criteria for determining whether a state had an obligation to take specific preventive measures can thus broadly be summarized as follows:[112]

a) Awareness or knowledge[113]
b) Real and immediate risk
c) Directed at a specific/identified individual or group
d) Reasonable possibility of preventing the risk

Despite the apparent convergence (in principle) on these criteria across different human rights bodies, they are usually not assessed individually in existing jurisprudence and the assessment is not always consistent and at times unclear.[114] Moreover, the application of the test has changed over time, and especially the ECtHR has explicitly shifted its approach to include risks not just to identified individuals, but also to society as a whole.[115] This allows for a division into two main approaches to determining the existence of a specific prevention obligation, based either on the victim of the alleged violation ('victim-based approach'), or the source of the risk ('source-based approach').[116] These approaches can most clearly be identified in the case law of the ECtHR and, to a lesser extent, the IACtHR, which is why the following section focuses on case law of these bodies only. The section presents each approach and analyses its implications for the scope of responsibility in cases of disappearances at the hands of non-state actors.

3.2.1.2 The Victim-Based Approach

Where courts apply a victim-based approach, which most closely resembles the initial approach taken by the ECtHR in *Osman v UK*, the standard to be met is that authorities must have had knowledge that a particular victim, or group of victims, was at risk. Such awareness is often established on the basis of threats that the person received and reported prior to their assassination, torture, or disappearance.[117] In the

[112] See also Guercke (2021), p. 339.

[113] Such awareness can be objectively established in that the criterion is that the state was aware or 'ought to have known' (see *Osman v. The United Kingdom*, para. 116). The IACtHR has also reiterated this. See, for example, *Case of Luna López v. Honduras*, para. 124. For a discussion of the necessary level of knowledge, as well as other 'tests' applied by the ECtHR to determine the exact content of positive obligations, see Lavrysen (2016), p. 131 ff. For a more general discussion of these criteria, see Ebert and Sijniensky (2015); Monnheimer (2021), p. 116 ff.

[114] For an overview of the inconsistencies in the application of these criteria by both courts, see Ebert and Sijniensky (2015). For the ECtHR's approach to each of these criteria more specifically, see Lavrysen (2016).

[115] *Mastromatteo v. Italy*, para. 69.

[116] Guercke (2021).

[117] See, for example, respectively, *Case of Luna López v. Honduras*, paras 125–6; *Mahmut Kaya v. Turkey*, paras 88–90. Note however that this approach is not always taken. In the case of

absence of specific threats, in cases involving disappearances at the hands of non-state actors specifically, the awareness of a specific risk to the victim's rights to life, liberty, physical integrity and access to justice generally arises once the person has been reported as disappeared to the authorities. This however means that the initial deprivation of liberty is not included in the assessment of the state's responsibility.

The case that most clearly illustrates the victim-based approach involving disappearances is that of *González et al. v. Mexico*, also called the '*Cotton Field*' case, before the Inter-American Court. In this case the IACtHR dealt with the disappearance and brutal murder of three women in Ciudad Juárez, Mexico, whose bodies were found, together with another five bodies, in a cotton field near that city. The relatives of Laura Berenice Ramos Monárrez, Claudia Ivette González, and Esmeralda Herrera Monreal brought the case to the Inter-American Court, alleging the responsibility of the Mexican state for its failure to protect the lives of these women. In its analysis of the state's failure to protect the victims' right to life, the IACtHR made a distinction between two temporal moments for the purpose of establishing the state's responsibility based on a failure to prevent: first, the time prior to the disappearance, and second, the period between the report of the victims' disappearance to authorities and the discovery of their bodies.[118] While the IACtHR had found that during the first moment the Mexican state had not adopted effective preventive measures to counter the situation of violence against women in Ciudad Juárez and reduce general risk factors,[119] it held that

> [...] the failure to prevent the disappearance does not per se result in the State's international responsibility because, even though the State was aware of the situation of risk for women in Ciudad Juárez, *it has not been established that it knew of a real and imminent danger for the victims in this case.*[120]

However, once the victims had been reported as missing to the authorities, and in view of the general context of violence against women prevailing in Ciudad Juárez, the IACtHR found that the state was 'aware that there was a real and imminent risk that the victims would be sexually abused, subjected to ill-treatment and killed.'[121] This awareness gave rise to 'an obligation of strict due diligence' for authorities to conduct an exhaustive search and attempt to locate missing women.[122] As the authorities in this case had failed to respond promptly and diligently, the Mexican state was held responsible for its failure to prevent the victims' deaths and the abuse

---

Osmanoğlu v Turkey, for example, the ECtHR noted that the victim had received threats prior to his disappearance, but did not hold the state responsible for its failure to prevent the initial deprivation of liberty. See *Osmanoğlu v Turkey*, paras 75 ff.

[118] *Case of González et al. ("Cotton Field") v. Mexico*, para. 281.

[119] Ibid., para. 279.

[120] Ibid., para. 282. Emphasis added.

[121] Ibid., para. 283.

[122] Ibid.

they suffered.[123] The approach by the IACtHR in the *Cotton Field* case thus clearly distinguished between responsibility for violating general prevention obligations as opposed to specific obligations, suggesting that only the latter can give rise to the state's international responsibility.[124] Mexico was held responsible for its failure to act with 'strict due diligence' once the authorities had been notified of the disappearances, but not for its general failure to take effective measures to reduce the risk for women to become victims of fatal violence.

In subsequent case law, especially concerning cases of violence against women, the IACtHR similarly distinguished between the two moments for the purpose of establishing state responsibility for failing to prevent violations of the right to life[125] and physical integrity.[126] The ECtHR has followed a similar approach in a number of cases, although it has not made an explicit distinction between the two moments. An example is the case of *Rantsev v Cyprus and Russia*, mentioned above, which concerned the death of a human trafficking victim of Russian origin in Cyprus, who died when trying to escape her trafficker's apartment. The ECtHR examined the responsibility of both states for failing to protect the victim from human trafficking under Article 4 ECHR.[127] The Court found that Cyprus was responsible for a violation of Article 4 on the basis of its failure both to enact a protective legal framework against human trafficking,[128] and to take specific measures to protect the victim when she was at a police station, even though the officials were, or should have been aware, that she may have been a victim of human trafficking.[129] Conversely, the ECtHR found no violation of Article 4 by Russia on the basis of a failure

[123] The IACtHR thus found that the Mexican state had violated the victims' rights to life (Article 4.1 ACHR), humane treatment (Article 5.1 and 5.2 ACHR) and personal liberty (Article 7.1 ACHR) in connection with the obligation to guarantee under Article 1.1. ACHR, as well as of the obligations to prevent, punish and eradicate violence against women under Article 7(b) and (c) of the Inter-American Convention on the Prevention, Punishment and Eradication of Violence Against Women (Convention of Belém do Pará). See ibid., para. 286.

[124] These approaches have been criticised as not capturing the problem of structural issues that enable violations at the hands of non-state actors in the first place. For an overview of these criticisms, see Chap. 4, Sect. 4.2.2.1.

[125] See, for example, *Case of Véliz Franco et al v Guatemala* [2014] Inter-American Court of Human Rights Series C No. 277; *Case of Velásquez Paiz and Others v Guatemala* [2015] Inter-American Court of Human Rights Series C No 307. In the case of *Velásquez Paiz*, which concerned the disappearance and murder of a young woman, this approach also led the IACtHR to find a violation of the victim's right to life on account of the failure to act with strict due diligence once the victim was reported as disappeared.

[126] See, for example, *Case of López Soto and others v. Venezuela*. In this case the Court even made this distinction in relation to acquiescence (see discussion above). The IACtHR also took a similar approach in relation to the states' obligation to prevent slavery under Article 6 ACHR in the case of the *Hacienda Brasil Verde Workers v Brasil* (paras 322–328).

[127] Article 4 ECHR concerns the prohibition of slavery and forced labour. Therefore, the ECtHR first engaged in an analysis to determine whether human trafficking fell within the scope of Article 4 ECHR and found that it did. See *Rantsev v. Cyprus and Russia*, paras 272–282.

[128] Ibid., paras 291–293.

[129] Ibid., paras 296–298.

to take protective measures. The reason for this, according to the Court, was that even though Russian authorities were aware of a general risk of young women being trafficked abroad, it was 'insufficient, in order for an obligation to take urgent operational measures to arise, merely to show that there was a general risk in respect of young women travelling to Cyprus on artistes visa'.[130]

In cases concerning disappearances or kidnapping at the hands of unknown, or non-state actors, the ECtHR also used a similar threshold to determine violations of the right to life. In the case of *Osmanoğlu v Turkey*, the ECtHR could not establish the direct responsibility of Turkish authorities in the applicant's son's disappearance.[131] Nevertheless, it found that the Turkish state was responsible for a substantive violation of the victim's right to life under Article 2 ECHR on the basis of its failure 'to take the reasonable measures available to them to prevent a real and immediate risk to the life'.[132] The ECtHR found that Turkish authorities had sufficient knowledge of risk based on the fact that the victim disappeared in 'life-threatening' circumstances and had received threats prior to his disappearance.[133] Consequently, once his disappearance was reported, the ECtHR considered that 'following his disappearance, the life of the applicant's son was at more real and immediate risk than that of other persons at that time'.[134] Following this reasoning, the European Court assessed whether the state had taken operational measures to prevent a violation of the victim's right to life by investigating the kidnapping, rather than to prevent the initial disappearance that had already occurred.[135] In the case of *Olewnik-Cieplinska and Olewnik v Poland*, which involved the kidnapping and murder of Mr. Olewnik, the ECtHR found that kidnappings for ransom in Poland at the time of his abduction entailed a risk to his life and health.[136] Accordingly, once the authorities were aware of the kidnapping, they 'knew or should have known' of the existence of a real and immediate risk to his life and health. This awareness triggered the obligation of authorities to take reasonable measures to find the victim and investigate the case in order to identify the perpetrators.[137] Since the police committed a series of errors in their investigation of the kidnapping, the Court found that Poland did not comply with its obligation to safeguard the victim's right to life.[138]

---

[130] Ibid., para. 305.

[131] *Osmanoğlu v Turkey*, para. 71.

[132] Ibid., para. 84.

[133] Ibid., para. 75.

[134] Ibid., para. 76.

[135] Ibid.

[136] *Olewnik-Cieplińska and Olewnik v. Poland*, para. 122.

[137] Ibid., para. 125.

[138] Ibid., para. 131. See also Guercke (2021).

The Relevance of Context in the Victim-Based Approach

Notably, in the analysis of both Courts the awareness of an *immediate* risk to life following the disappearance in cases where a victim-based approach is applied, is often linked to the existence of a particular context, for example of widespread violence against women.[139] This suggests that, for these Courts, a disappearance at the hands of a non-state actor does not automatically give rise to the state's obligation to take more concrete preventive measures in all cases. For example, the majority of disappearance cases before the ECtHR, including the case of *Osmanoğlu v Turkey* cited above, concerned the conflict in south-eastern Turkey during the 1990s,[140] or the conflict in the Caucasus region of Russia,[141] as well as disappearances in Cyprus following the 1974 invasion by Turkish forces.[142] In these cases, all of which took place in contexts of armed conflicts, the European Court found that there existed a 'life-threatening context'.[143] This context was relevant for presuming that once a disappearance had occurred, the authorities were aware of an *immediate* risk to the victims' life. While the ECtHR did not clearly articulate any criteria for establishing the existence of a life-threatening context, the reasoning in the case of *Olewnik-Cieplińska and Olewnik v. Poland* discussed above, which concerned a kidnapping for ransom by non-state actors, suggests that it is not necessary for a disappearance to occur in the context of an armed conflict for it to be considered life-threatening.[144]

---

[139] For a discussion of the application of the immediacy criterion in the jurisprudence of both the ECtHR and IACtHR, see Ebert and Sijniensky (2015), pp. 358–360.

[140] See, for example, *Mahmut Kaya v. Turkey*; *Tahsin Acar v Turkey* [2004] European Court of Human Rights Application no. 26307/95; *Toğcu v Turkey* [2005] European Court of Human Rights Application no. 27601/95; *Osmanoğlu v Turkey*. All of these cases involved disappearances at the hands of unidentified actors. For an overview of enforced disappearance cases in Turkey before the ECtHR, see Scovazzi and Citroni (2007), pp. 189–211.

[141] See, for example, *Medova v Russia*; *Abdurzakova and Abdurzakov v Russia* [2009] European Court of Human Rights Application no. 35080/04; *Tsechoyev v Russia* [2011] European Court of Human Rights Application no. 39358/05; *Aslakhanova and Others v Russia* [2012] European Court of Human Rights Applications nos. 2944/06 and 8300/07, 50184/07, 332/08, 42509/10. Only in the cases of *Medova v Russia* and *Tsechoyev v Russia* did the ECtHR not find direct involvement of state actors. For an overview of the ECtHR's case law on enforced disappearances in this context, see Ibid., pp. 211–220.

[142] See *Cyprus v Turkey* [2001] European Court of Human Rights Application no. 25781/94; *Varnava and Others v. Turkey*.

[143] *Cyprus v. Turkey*, para. 133; *Toğcu v Turkey*, para. 112; *Medova v Russia*, para. 89.

[144] In this case, the ECtHR found that it was sufficient that the state knew that kidnappings for ransom in Poland at the time often involved '*particular torment, and included cases of damages to health, and cases of death of the victim*' (*Olewnik-Cieplińska and Olewnik v. Poland*, para. 122). This also meant that it was not necessary for the kidnappers to have made specific threats to harm the victim in order to establish the seriousness of the risk (ibid., para. 123). Similarly, in the case of *Medova v Russia*, the ECtHR found that the fact that Mr. Medov had been abducted by four armed men was sufficient to presume that his disappearance itself was life-threatening. See *Medova v Russia*, para. 90.

The IACtHR has also taken the context into consideration when determining whether a state had an obligation to act with due diligence and take preventive measures to prevent violations of the rights to life and physical integrity following a victim's initial disappearance. In the case of *Gutiérrez Hernández v Guatamela* for example, Mayra Gutiérrez had not come to work one day and had been disappeared ever since. It was suspected that an ex-partner of hers was responsible for her disappearance. Although the applicants alleged that the case involved an enforced disappearance, the Court considered that the evidence was insufficient to show direct state participation or acquiescence in the victim's disappearance.[145] Additionally, the IACtHR did not consider that authorities had an obligation of due diligence on the basis of a real and immediate risk to the victim once her disappearance was reported.[146] The reason for this was, according to the Inter-American Court, that at the time of the victim's disappearance authorities were not yet aware of a general context of increasing violence against women, which would have triggered their 'strict' due diligence obligations.[147] Following this reasoning, a report of a disappearance would not be sufficient to trigger strict due diligence obligations unless there existed a context of violence that would imply an *immediate* risk to the victim's life. Nonetheless, in the more recent case of *López Soto v Venezuela*, The IACtHR expressed a slightly different view and held that, in relation to women specifically,

> [...] the report of the kidnapping or disappearance of a women [sic] should activate the State's duty of *enhanced* due diligence, because this circumstance give [sic] rise to a scenario conducive to the perpetration of acts of violence against women, and entails a particular vulnerability to suffering acts of sexual violence that, per se, entail a risk to the life and the integrity of the woman, *regardless of a specific context*.[148]

This approach indicates a departure from the reasoning in *Gutiérrez Hernández* in relation to disappearances of women specifically, although the IACtHR did not elaborate on a potential difference between the notions of 'strict' and 'enhanced' due diligence.[149] Nevertheless, the Inter-American Court also maintained the distinction of awareness prior to the kidnapping or disappearance and after its

[145] *Case of Gutiérrez Hernández et al v Guatemala* [2017] Inter-American Court of Human Rights Series C No. 339, para. 136.

[146] Ibid., para. 141.

[147] Ibid., para. 139.

[148] *Case of López Soto and others v. Venezuela*, para. 145. Emphasis added. In its Statement on Non-State Actors, the CED also took up the notion of strict due diligence and emphasised that due diligence obligations are 'particularly strict where women or girls are involved'. See CED (2023) Statement on non-State actors in the context of the International Convention for the Protection of All Persons from Enforced Disappearances. UN Doc. CED/C/10, para. 22.

[149] In the Spanish originals of the cases the IACtHR equally uses different terms, referring to 'debida diligencia estricta' on the one hand (see *Caso González y otras ("Campo Algodonero") Vs México* [2009] Corte Interamericana de Derechos Humanos Serie C No. 205, para. 283; *Caso de Gutiérrez Hernández et al v Guatemala* [2017] Corte Interamericana de Derechos Humanos Serie C No 339, para. 139) and to 'el deber de debida diligencia reforzado' in the case of *López Soto* (see *Caso de López Soto et al v Venezuela* [2018] Corte Interamericana de Derechos Humanos Serie C No 362, para. 145).

occurrence for the purpose of establishing whether a strict or enhanced obligation of due diligence existed. In this sense, and considering the reasoning in *López Soto*, it can be assumed that if the disappeared victim is a woman, in the Inter-American system the risk to life will be considered as *immediate*. If a man were to be disappeared, however, the context might still play a role in determining the immediacy of risk and the state's responsibility for failing to act with due diligence once the disappearance has been reported.

As I have argued elsewhere,[150] the implication of the victim-based approach for cases involving disappearances committed by non-state actors is that the awareness of risk to a particular victim arises once the person has already disappeared, unless the victim had previously received threats and reported these to authorities. Therefore, a state can be held responsible for its failure to prevent violations of the rights to life, inhumane treatment, and liberty and security of the person, but not for the *initial* deprivation of liberty and thus for the disappearance itself. Moreover, a state cannot be held responsible for a general failure to prevent acts of violence, including disappearances, at the hands of non-state actors, because such a general failure cannot be linked to awareness of risk to a specific individual. Rather, the general failure to protect is part of the context that has been considered by both the IACtHR and the ECtHR as influencing the immediacy of risk and thereby also the urgency of a state's obligation to take preventive measures.

3.2.1.3 The Source-Based Approach

The second approach to determining whether a state had an obligation to take specific preventive measures focuses on the awareness by a state of a particular *source* of risk, rather than of a risk to a potential victim. This approach encompasses situations of risk that warranted measures by the state to protect society as a whole, or a group of people at risk from an identified source. Many of the cases where a source-based approach was used do not concern disappearances, but since they involve violations of the right to life, the reasoning can be applied by analogy to cases involving disappearances at the hands of non-state actors which can lead to a violation of the right to life. What is decisive in these cases is the state's awareness of a source of risk, as well as its ability to adopt reasonable measures to prevent the risk from materialising. Cases can be divided into two groups: the first dealing with cases where violations were committed by non-state actors, and the second concerning cases involving natural or industrial disasters or accidents.

[150] Guercke (2021), pp. 351–353. See also Abramovich (2010).

Source-Based Approaches and Non-State Actors

The first set of cases involves situations where non-state actors, either armed groups or private individuals, committed a rights-violating act. Before the ECtHR, these cases concerned the release of prisoners in the framework of alternative detention schemes, which meant that the respective states were considered as being directly involved in the creation of 'risk' to society.[151] In the cases of *Mastromatteo v Italy*,[152] *Maiorani et alt v Italy*[153] and *Choreftakis and Choreftaki v Greece*,[154] former prisoners, who had been serving long prison sentences for serious offences, were released from prison and subsequently committed murders. In the first of these cases, *Mastromatteo v Italy*, the European Court explicitly distinguished the case from that of *Osman v UK* and indicated that:

> The instant case differs from those cases in that it is not a question here of determining whether the responsibility of the authorities is engaged for failing to provide personal protection to A. Mastromatteo; what is at issue is the *obligation to afford general protection to society* against the potential acts of one or of several persons serving a prison sentence for a violent crime and the determination of the scope of that protection.[155]

The risk was thus 'a risk to life for members of the public at large rather than for one or more identified individuals'.[156] In order to determine whether the states had complied with their positive obligation to afford general protection to society, the ECtHR assessed both general and specific preventive measures. General preventive measures examined by the European Court included the content of the alternative detention schemes and whether these schemes included sufficient safeguards.[157] Subsequently, the Court analysed the application of those schemes and safeguards in practice in the specific cases.[158] According to the Court, the states possessed the necessary awareness of risk because the individuals had been sent to prison after committing very serious crimes, which in itself constitutes a form of protection to society.[159] In *Mastromatteo v Italy*, the ECtHR did not find a violation of Italy's obligation to protect the right to life for two reasons: first, Italy's alternative detention scheme did not raise issues under Article 2 because it provided 'sufficient

---

[151] According to Ebert and Sijniensky, in these cases the state had *contributed* to the creation of risk. See Ebert and Sijniensky (2015), p. 366, note 160.

[152] *Mastromatteo v. Italy*.

[153] *Maiorano and Others v Italy* [2009] European Court of Human Rights Application no. 28634/06.

[154] *Choreftakis and Choreftaki v Greece* [2012] European Court of Human Rights Application no. 46846/08.

[155] *Mastromatteo v. Italy*, para. 69. Emphasis added.

[156] Ibid., para. 74.

[157] Ibid., para. 72. See also *Choreftakis and Choreftaki v Greece*, paras 56–57.

[158] *Mastromatteo v. Italy*, paras 74–78; *Maiorano and Others v. Italy*, paras 113–121; *Choreftakis and Choreftaki v Greece*, paras 58–60.

[159] *Mastromatteo v. Italy*, para. 72; *Maiorano and Others v. Italy*, para. 108; *Choreftakis and Choreftaki v Greece*, para. 49.

protective measures for society'.[160] Second, it could not have been *reasonably foreseeable* for the authorities that the released individual would commit a crime that would result in the loss of life.[161] In this case, the person who was released from prison participated in a robbery and shot A. Mastromatteo, who was passing by in his car, because Mastromatteo refused to hand over his car to the bank robbers. The ECtHR reasoned that a simple causal test (that the murder would not have occurred had the perpetrator not been released from prison) was insufficient to establish the state's responsibility in this case, due to a lack of foreseeability.[162]

Conversely, in the case of *Maiorano and Others v Italy*, the person who committed the crime had been granted day-leave from prison despite numerous incidents of bad conduct, including the commission of further offences. The ECtHR reasoned that these incidents should have led to greater caution by the authorities in deciding whether to grant leave to this prisoner, who was serving time for 'extremely grave crimes'.[163] Consequently, the Court found that Italy had failed in its obligation to act with due diligence to protect the right to life in violation of Article 2 ECHR, even though the state could not have been aware of a risk to the specific victim.[164] In the case of *Choreftakis Choreftaki v Greece* the applicant's son had been stabbed to death by a former prisoner. The ECtHR engaged in the same analysis as in the cases of *Mastromatteo v Italy* and *Maiorano v Italy* and found that the Greek alternative detention system was, as such, compatible with Article 2 ECHR because it provided sufficient safeguards to society.[165] Nonetheless, in *Choreftakis Choreftaki v Greece* the European Court reasoned that, in the absence of a direct causal link between the

[160] *Mastromatteo v. Italy*, paras 72–73.

[161] Ibid., para. 76.

[162] Ibid.

[163] *Maiorano and Others v. Italy*, para. 115. The ECtHR formulated this as follows in the French original: 'Il n'en demeure pas moins que ces éléments positifs étaient contrebalancés par de nombreux éléments en sens contraire, qui, aux yeux de la Cour, auraient dû inspirer une plus grande prudence au moment de décider de donner ou non à une personne condamnée pour des crimes violents d'une gravité extrême la possibilité de passer la majeure partie de la journée en dehors du pénitencier et d'entrer en contact avec le monde libre.' The factors then considered by the ECtHR were the gravity of the crimes the perpetrator had committed and his autobiography in which he confessed to a number of violent crimes (ibid., para. 116), his non-exemplary conduct while in prison (ibid., para. 117), as well as breaches of the conditions of his day-leave (ibid., para. 119), all of which could, in the ECtHR's opinion, be considered indications that the prisoner posed a danger to society (ibid., para. 121).

[164] Ibid., para. 121.

[165] *Choreftakis and Choreftaki v Greece*, para. 56. Note that the European Court reached this decision despite certain temporal limitations in the Greek alternative detention system that prevented the competent judge from examining the entire disciplinary history of the prisoner (see ibid., paras 57–58). This was criticised in a dissenting opinion by Judge Sicilianos, joined by Judges Steiner and Lazarova Trajkovska, who disagreed with the majority's view, arguing that the way the Greek system was set up meant that certain alarming behaviour by the prisoner could not be taken into account at the time of consideration of his conditional release. See *Choreftakis and Choreftaki v Greece*, Opinion Dissidente du Juge Sicilianos, a Laquelle se Rallient Les Juges Steiner et Lazarova Trajkovska, paras 3–6.

application of the alternative detention system and the death of the applicant's son, the responsibility of the Greek state would only have been engaged if there had been a gap in the domestic legal framework.[166] Consequently, it found no violation of the right to life. The ECtHR's reasoning in these cases suggests that, in source-based approaches, the question of foreseeability of risk is relevant for the purpose of establishing state responsibility. However, in contrast to the victim-based approach, such foreseeability is determined in relation to the source of the risk—in these cases the behaviour of prisoners who had been released early—rather than a risk to a specific victim or group of victims.

The IACtHR used what can be considered a source-based approach in the case of the *Pueblo Bello Massacre*. In this case, falling short of establishing acquiescence as it had in other cases involving paramilitary groups in Colombia, the IACtHR attributed responsibility on the basis of the Colombian state's failure to prevent the abduction and disappearance of 43 men from the village of Pueblo Bello.[167] The IACtHR found that the state was aware of the 'possibility of specific danger owing to the activities of paramilitary groups or individuals that could materialize in situations that would affect the civilian population'.[168] This awareness was not based on specific threats received by the victims, but rather on the general threat posed by paramilitary groups operating in certain areas of the country. The state's awareness was evidenced by the fact that it had already taken legislative measures to outlaw and punish the activities of paramilitary groups and had deployed special army units to some areas of the country as a means of 're-establishment of public order'.[169] Despite these efforts, however, the state had failed to take effective measures to dismantle paramilitary structures and thereby 'deactivate' the danger that these groups posed.[170] In this case, it did not matter for the Court that the state did not have 'specific prior knowledge' of the attack, nor that there had not been any reports of threats to the community of Pueblo Bello.[171] The general awareness and the *systematic nature* of violence in certain areas which the state had declared to be emergency zones were considered as sufficient to give rise to 'accentuated' protection and prevention obligations[172] due to a 'reasonably foreseeable' dangerous situation.[173]

[166] *Choreftakis and Choreftaki v Greece*, para. 59. The ECtHR formulated this as follows in the French original: "Néanmoins, de l'avis de la Cour, *l'absence de lien de causalité direct et solide* entre les modalités d'application du système grec et la mort du fils des requérants, exigerait une défaillance évidente de la loi appliquée en l'espèce pour engager la responsabilité de l'Etat défendeur sur le champ de l'article 2 de la Convention." Emphasis added.

[167] *Case of the Pueblo Bello Massacre v. Colombia*, paras 140 and 151.

[168] Ibid., para. 125.

[169] Ibid.

[170] Ibid., para. 126.

[171] Ibid., para. 135.

[172] Ibid., para. 134.

[173] Ibid., para. 140.

As a result, the IACtHR reasoned that the ability of a paramilitary group to carry out a large-scale attack in an area where the military had established roadblocks, demonstrated the state's failure to act with due diligence to protect the population.[174] Moreover, the Inter-American Court established a direct causal link between the state's failure and the violations, holding that the massacre 'could not have been carried out if there had been effective protection for the civilian population in a dangerous situation that was reasonably foreseeable [...]'.[175] The Colombian state was thus held responsible for the violations of the rights to life, humane treatment and personal liberty enshrined in Articles 4.1, 5.1, 7.1 and 7.2 ACHR, read together with the obligation under Article 1.1 ACHR to respect and ensure these rights. In this particular case, a noteworthy aspect of the IACtHR's reasoning is its finding that the state had 'objectively created a dangerous situation for its inhabitants' by having initially encouraged the creation of paramilitary groups. Therefore, the persistence of the dangerous situation 'accentuates the State's special obligations of prevention and protection in the zones where the paramilitary groups were present'.[176] In this vein, where a state's actions or omissions can be shown to have 'objectively created' a particular risk, obligations of prevention are stricter and the attribution of responsibility for a failure to protect more likely.[177] Thus, the relationship between the state and the source of the risk, especially where the latter is a person or group of persons, may also be relevant for the assessment of the existence of a state's specific prevention obligations. The newly adopted definition of acquiescence by the CED takes up the IACtHR's approach in *Pueblo Bello* to establish awareness based on the source of risk, by including situations where 'the State has created the conditions that allowed [the commission of disappearances]'.[178]

Source-Based Approaches to Accidents and Disasters

The second type of cases that illustrate a source-based approach relate to environmental disasters or accidents. In these cases, states were aware of a risk resulting from specific dangerous activities or environmental issues and failed to take necessary steps to address these risks. The ECtHR has dealt with these types of cases on a number of occasions. For example, in the case of *Öneryildiz v Turkey*,[179] the

---

[174] Ibid., para. 139.

[175] Ibid., para. 140.

[176] Ibid., para. 126.

[177] On this, see Abramovich, who considers this approach by the Inter-American Court a middle-way between the establishment of complicity between state and non-state actors and a state's failure to take preventive measures. He terms this approach the 'created risk doctrine'. See Abramovich (2010), p. 175.

[178] CED (2023) Statement on non-State actors in the context of the International Convention for the Protection of All Persons from Enforced Disappearances. UN Doc. CED/C/10, para. 5 (d).

[179] *Öneryildiz v Turkey* [2004] European Court of Human Rights Application no. 48939/99, 2004-XII.

applicant had lost nine family members and his home because of a methane-gas explosion in a municipal rubbish tip in the outskirts of Istanbul. The ECtHR first affirmed that the positive obligations stemming from Article 2 ECHR where equally applicable to environmental issues[180] and 'public activities' relating to the management of waste.[181] The question to be examined by the European Court was whether the Turkish state had '[complied] with its duty to take all necessary measures to prevent lives from being unnecessarily exposed to danger and, ultimately, from being lost',[182] which the Court answered in the negative. The reasoning was based on the ECtHR's finding that the Turkish authorities were, or ought to have been aware, of the risks of a methane explosion in the rubbish tip. More specifically, the ECtHR found that

> [...] it was impossible for the administrative and municipal departments responsible for monitoring the relevant installations not to have known of the risks inherent in methanogenesis or of the necessary preventive measures, particularly as there were specific regulations in the area which, moreover, were not in any way complied with.[183]

Thus, not only were the authorities aware of a risk, but they also had obligations under existing regulations to address the risk of a gas explosion in a rubbish tip. The fact that no such preventive measures were taken was sufficient to show a 'causal link between, on the one hand, those negligent omissions and, on the other, the occurrence of the accident on 28 April 1993 and the ensuing loss of lives'.[184] Furthermore, the Turkish authorities failed in their obligation to provide information about the risks of a methane-gas explosion to the inhabitants of the area, which also meant that the latter could not take measures to protect themselves.[185] Both of these failures led the ECtHR to find a violation of the right to life under Article 2 ECHR.

The ECtHR took a similar approach in the case of *Budayeva and Others v Russia*,[186] which concerned the death of one person and loss of property following a mudslide. The European Court held that even though the authorities were aware of an increased risk of damage from a mudslide, they failed to take any measures to mitigate this risk or even to inform the inhabitants of its existence. While the ECtHR emphasized that states are afforded a wide margin of appreciation in relation to dealing with environmental hazards, it found that in this case authorities had opted for complete inaction.[187] This, however, was not justifiable in the Court's view,

[180] Ibid., para. 64.

[181] Ibid., para. 65.

[182] Ibid., para. 67.

[183] Ibid., para. 79.

[184] Ibid., para. 81.

[185] Ibid., para. 87.

[186] *Budayeva and Others v Russia* [2018] European Court of Human Rights Applications nos 15339/02, 21166/02, 20058/02, 11673/02 and 15343/02.

[187] Ibid., para. 156.

given that there existed a foreseeable danger to residents of the area.[188] Further, the ECtHR considered that

> [...] there was a causal link between the serious administrative flaws that impeded [the] implementation [of the land-planning and emergency relief policies in the hazardous area of Tyrnauz] and the death of Vladimir Budayev and the injuries sustained by the first and the second applicants and the members of their family.[189]

In both *Öneryildiz v Turkey* and *Budayeva and Others v Russia* the ECtHR thus determined state responsibility for a failure to take specific preventive measures on the basis of foreseeability of risk, as well as a causal link between the omissions of authorities and the violations of the victims' rights.

The IACtHR took up the ECtHR's approach in its judgement in the *Case of the Workers of the Fireworks Factory in Santo Antônio de Jesus and their Families v Brazil*, which dealt with an explosion in a fireworks factory in the Brazilian state of Bahía in 1998, in which 60 workers were killed and six survived with serious injuries. Some of the victims were children at the time.[190] The factory had operated with a permit, but without sufficient safeguards and with precarious working conditions for the employees.[191] The IACtHR found that the Brazilian state was responsible for violating the rights to life (Article 4.1) of the persons who were killed and of physical integrity (Article 5.1) of the survivors, as well as the rights of the child (Article 19) under the ACHR, on the basis that the state's failure to carry out inspections of the factory was causally linked to the explosion.[192] Drawing on its previous case law concerning regulatory obligations of states in relation to health services, the IACtHR held that states have positive obligations to regulate and inspect dangerous activities that pose a risk to life, including the production of fireworks.[193] It then established that Brazil had a sufficiently protective regulatory framework in place that required regular inspections of firework production sites.[194] Therefore, and in view of the fact that the fireworks factory had operated with a permit from the authorities, the IACtHR found that the state was aware of a risk to life to the factory workers and consequently should have carried out regular inspections.[195] As authorities failed to carry out any inspections of this sort, the IACtHR

---

[188] Ibid., para. 158.

[189] Ibid.

[190] *Case of the Workers of the Fireworks Factory in Santo Antônio de Jesus and their Families v Brazil* [2020] Inter-American Court of Human Rights Series C No. 407.

[191] Ibid., paras 68–73.

[192] Ibid., para. 139. The IACtHR also found that the state was responsible for violations of the right to equality before the law without discrimination (Article 24), the progressive development of economic, social, and cultural rights (Article 26), the rights to judicial protection (Articles 8 and 25), as well as the right to integrity (Article 5.1) of the relatives. An analysis of each of these violations lies beyond the scope of this book.

[193] Ibid., paras 118–121.

[194] Ibid., paras 124–132.

[195] Ibid., para. 133.

reasoned that the state had allowed the production of fireworks without verifying compliance with minimum safety standards. Insufficient safety measures caused the explosion in the factory, which meant that 'the omissive conduct of the state contributed to the occurrence of the explosion.'[196]

The foregoing overview of cases illustrates that the source-based approach focuses on the existence of causal links between the respective states' omissions and the ensuing risk and eventual loss of life. This can be either based on a state's direct contribution to the risk, as illustrated in the case of *Pueblo Bello* and the cases involving release of prisoners, or on its indirect contribution by failing to regulate particular harmful activities or to adopt measures to reduce a particular risk. While the source-based approach maintains the requirement of establishing the existence of more specific prevention obligations, it is broader than the victim-based approach and allows, to a certain extent, for a consideration of state actions and omissions that lead to the materialisation of a risk in the first place. In this sense, the source-based approach mediates the shortcomings of the victim-based approach in situations where actions and omissions by the state, despite the latter's awareness of the existence of a particular source of risk, *causally contribute* to the violation of human rights. By analogy, in cases involving disappearances at the hands of non-state actors, a source-based approach would allow for a finding of state responsibility for the disappearance in its entirety, that is, including the initial deprivation of liberty, if the perpetrator or perpetrators were known to authorities as potentially dangerous individuals and the authorities failed to take reasonable measures to prevent harm.

3.2.1.4 The Difference Between Acquiescence and a Failure to Prevent

The CED's definition of acquiescence reflects many of the criteria used in case law concerning prevention failure by the ECtHR and IACtHR where source-based approaches were taken, in the sense that it combines foreseeability of risk and a causal contribution by the state through action or omission. Interestingly, however, while a source-based approach to determining responsibility for a failure to prevent is still subject to considerations of reasonableness and proportionality of the measures adopted,[197] the CED's definition of acquiescence does not include such a requirement. This absence reinforces the argument that failing to act with due diligence and acquiescing to a disappearance continue to be different from one-another. At the same time, the lack of reference to reasonableness or proportionality in the definition of acquiescence is a particularly interesting development

[196] Ibid., para. 137. 'Por lo tanto, la conducta omisiva del Estado contribuyó a que se produjera la explosión'. Author's translation.

[197] In the case of *Budayeva and Others v Russia* for example, the ECtHR took into consideration the fact that the state had spent money on defence matters rather than environmental protection. See *Budayeva and Others v Russia*, para. 157.

because it suggests that establishing state responsibility on the basis of acquiescence could now require a lower threshold than establishing state responsibility for a failure to act with due diligence, even though the ensuing responsibility is greater in the former case. This is especially the case in relation to the final criterion listed by the Committee, which is the state's role in the creation of risk:[198] when read in a literal manner, it is sufficient to show that the state 'ought to have been aware' of a real and imminent risk of a disappearance and played a role in creating the conditions for this to occur, without having to show that the state's failure to take measures of due diligence to protect specific victims.

Additionally, while the Statement does not explicitly clarify whether the risk is general in nature—as it would be in a source-based approach—the lack of a reference to a specific victim or group of victims allows for such an interpretation. In view of the shortcomings of the victim-based approach in relation to disappearances committed by non-state actors discussed above, a source-based approach to establishing awareness of risk is generally more appropriate in situations where structural issues are at play because the state's role in the creation of risk implies a certain level of awareness that warrants effective action to be taken *before* a victim is deprived of liberty. This reasoning would be equally applicable to establishing risk awareness for the purpose of acquiescence. Importantly, even if a source-based approach were to be used, the CED's definition does not imply that acquiescence could be established in isolated cases of disappearances committed by non-state actors in which the state is indirectly involved, due to the requirements relating to state contribution to risk or the existence of patterns of disappearances, both of which indicate larger numbers of cases. The question that remains is where exactly the difference between a failure to prevent a disappearance committed by a non-state actor and acquiescence to such an act lies and it would be desirable for the CED to clarify the difference in future jurisprudence or reports to avoid confusion.[199]

3.2.2 Responsibility for a Failure to Respond

Once a disappearance has occurred, regardless of the perpetrator, states have an obligation to investigate and search for the disappeared person, as well as to provide a remedy (see Chap. 2). Failure to comply with these obligations constitutes a breach of a state's international obligations. For States Parties to the ICPPED, a failure to take appropriate measures to investigate and bring the perpetrators to justice in accordance with Article 3 ICPPED, will thus lead to their international responsibility for violating the obligations under this article—unless there was a 'known pattern' of

[198] CED (2023) Statement on non-State actors in the context of the International Convention for the Protection of All Persons from Enforced Disappearances. UN Doc. CED/C/10, para. 5(d).

[199] For a proposal on how to distinguish between a failure to act with due diligence and acquiescence based on the level of knowledge, see Fischer and Duhaime (2024).

disappearances, which would then lead to acquiescence and a different kind of responsibility.[200] Beyond the ICPPED, a failure to respond to a disappearance committed by a non-state actor can also constitute a breach of states' positive obligations to protect human rights. As discussed in Chap. 2, in addition to the separation into substantive and procedural aspects of different rights, which is particularly prominent in ECtHR case law, the obligation to investigate in cases involving disappearances committed by non-state actors is also viewed as part of the obligation to provide an effective remedy[201] and access to justice[202] by the ECtHR and the IACtHR, respectively. Due to this overlap, state responsibility for failing to investigate and to provide a remedy are generally examined together in cases involving disappearances at the hands of non-state actors. Indeed, since the majority of cases involving disappearances by non-state or unknown actors involve a failure by authorities to conduct an effective investigation and impunity, the issue of the provision of a judicial remedy or even reparations is usually not addressed.[203] In light of this, this section analyses state responsibility for a failure to comply with the obligation to investigate and to remedy together.[204]

In many cases involving a violation of the right to life by a non-state actor, state responsibility is established on the basis of the state's failure to conduct an effective investigation (procedural limb). In disappearance cases however, a failure to comply with this obligation has additional implications because a failure to investigate can amount to not just a breach of procedural obligations to protect life or obligations relating to ensuring an effective remedy, but also to a failure to prevent a substantive violation of the rights to life, liberty and physical integrity once a person has been reported as disappeared.[205] This overlap leads to a peculiar situation in relation to the

[200] Ibid., para. 6.

[201] Article 13 European Convention on Human Rights 1950 (ETS 5) (ECHR).

[202] Articles 8 and 25 American Convention on Human Rights 1969 (1144 UNTS 143) (ACHR).

[203] The ECtHR's approach to the obligation to provide an effective remedy has not been consistent, however. The ECtHR stopped examining allegations of violations of Article 13 (right to an effective remedy) in cases where it had already found a procedural violation of the right to life. See *Osmanoğlu v Turkey*, para. 111; *Tsechoyev v. Russia*, para. 159. This was a departure from previous cases, where the ECtHR had found violations of Article 13 in relation to the relatives of the disappeared persons, such as *Medova v Russia*, paras 129–130. The change in the ECtHR's approach raises some questions, especially because the ECtHR had previously held that the obligations under Article 13 were broader than the procedural obligations arising from Article 2 (see Chap. 2 Sect. 2.1.3.1). Moreover, the ECtHR generally established violations of Article 13 in relation to the relatives of the victim, whereas violations of the procedural limb of Article 2 only concern the victim herself. By omitting an analysis of a violation of Article 13, the ECtHR therefore misses an opportunity to establish the state's responsibility vis-à-vis the relatives of the disappeared person.

[204] The section addresses state failure to investigate and remedy in isolated cases.

[205] See, for example, *Mahmut Kaya v. Turkey*; *Osmanoğlu v Turkey*; *Medova v Russia*; *Olewnik-Cieplińska and Olewnik v. Poland*; *Case of González et al. ("Cotton Field") v. Mexico*; *Case of Velásquez Paiz and Others v Guatemala*; *Case of López Soto and others v. Venezuela*. Note, however, that this distinction between the substantive and procedural limbs of a given right is

determination of state responsibility because normally the obligations to investigate and prevent are distinct obligations and the former arises once a violation at the hands of a non-state actor has been committed. Before the ECtHR, the outcome of such an approach was particularly criticized by three dissenting judges in the case of *Osmanoğlu v Turkey*, who argued that the majority's finding of a violation of the substantive aspect of the right to life (Article 2) on the basis of the Turkish authorities' failure to investigate was confusing the substantive and procedural limbs of this right.[206] The IACtHR has taken up the ECtHR's distinction between substantive and procedural limbs of a particular right in some cases,[207] yet it has not done so consistently and generally did find violations of rights following a disappearance on the basis of a failure to investigate, especially in cases where, based on the context, the state had an obligation of strict due diligence to search for the victim and investigate the case.[208] This type of 'flexibility' in disappearance cases may be the most appropriate due to the peculiar nature of disappearances and the cruelty of not knowing what happened to the disappeared person, which is worsened by state inaction.

Thus, where a state does not comply with its obligations to respond to a disappearance committed by a non-state actor, which generally implies a failure to search and investigate, this constitutes a breach of its international obligations and violates the victim's right to an effective remedy and access to justice. Moreover, due to the unique nature of disappearances, the obligation to investigate and search for the disappeared person can effectively overlap with the obligation to take specific preventive measures, especially where a victim-based approach to the determination of this obligation is applied. Consequently, a failure to investigate and search for the disappeared person can also lead to violations of the substantive rights to life, liberty, and integrity of the disappeared person. In addition, the breach of the obligation to investigate and provide an effective remedy can lead to state responsibility vis-à-vis the relatives of victims of disappearances committed by non-state actors, which is examined in the next section.

---

explicitly made by the ECtHR in all these cases, whereas the IACtHR does not always elaborate on the distinction.

[206] See Joint Partly Dissenting Opinion of Judges Türmen, Vajić and Steiner in *Osmanoğlu v Turkey*. For a discussion of the dissent, see Vermeulen (2012), pp. 409–411. Vermeulen argues that such confusion is inevitable in disappearance cases due to the nature of the crime.

[207] See, for example, *Case of González et al. ("Cotton Field") v. Mexico*, paras 292–294.

[208] In the case of *Gutiérrez Hernández v Guatemala*, the Inter-American Court did not find a violation of the victim's right to life and integrity on the basis that the authorities were not aware of a 'real and immediate' risk to the victim's rights. See *Case of Gutiérrez Hernández et al. v. Guatemala*, para. 141. The IACtHR only found violations of the victim's and the relatives' rights to access to justice under Articles 8 and 5 ACHR in this case.

3.2.2.1 Violations of the Rights of Relatives

Due to the detrimental impact of disappearances on the relatives of the disappeared, the failure of states to react to a disappearance committed by a non-state actor can also lead to a violation of the rights of relatives. Specifically, a failure to investigate the case and search for the disappeared person can lead to state responsibility for the violation of the rights of relatives to an effective remedy and to integrity.[209] In the absence of a specific obligation to provide substantive reparations to the relatives of victims of disappearances committed by non-state actors (see Chap. 2), state responsibility for a violation of relatives' rights becomes an important question. This is because if a state can be held responsible for breaching its obligations vis-à-vis the relatives of disappeared persons, it has an obligation to provide reparations for harm caused to the victims, both in IHRL and under the law on state responsibility.[210]

Whereas both the ECtHR and the IACtHR have determined state responsibility for violations of the rights of relatives of disappeared persons, their approaches have differed throughout the years, especially in relation to violations of the right to humane treatment. For the ECtHR, the suffering of the relatives of a disappeared person can amount to a breach of the right to humane treatment under Article 3 ECHR, which is the direct result of the failure of authorities to take adequate measures to respond to a disappearance:

> [...] the essence of such a violation does not so much lie in the fact of the "disappearance" of the family member but rather in the authorities' reactions and attitudes to the situation when it is brought to their attention.[211]

Notwithstanding, the ECtHR has not consistently found violations of the relatives' right to humane treatment, even in cases clearly involving *enforced*

---

[209] See Article 13 ECHR and Articles 8 and 25 ACHR. Notably, one difference between the Courts' approaches is that the ECtHR has only found violations of the right to access to remedy in relation to the relatives of the disappeared person, rather than the disappeared person themselves, whereas the IACtHR usually finds violations of Articles 8 and 25 ACHR also in relation to the disappeared person.

[210] Human Rights Committee (2004) General Comment No. 31: The Nature of the General Legal Obligation Imposed on States Parties to the Covenant. UN Doc. CCPR/C/21/Rev.1/Add. 13, para. 16. Similarly, in the law on state responsibility, Article 30 ARSIWA stipulates that where an act of a state is in breach of an international obligation, the state must cease this act (if it is ongoing) and to 'offer appropriate assurances and guarantees of non-repetition, if circumstances so require' (Article 30 (b)). Moreover, Article 31 ARSIWA establishes that 'The responsible State is under an obligation to make full *reparation for the injury caused* by the internationally wrongful act.' Emphasis added.

[211] *Cyprus v. Turkey*, para. 156. See also *Tahsin Acar v. Turkey*, para. 238; *Osmanoğlu v Turkey*, paras. 96 and 98; *Abdurzakova and Abdurzakov v. Russia*, para. 119. The Special Chamber for Bosnia and Herzegovina has also found violations of Article 3 ECHR in relation to the relatives of the disappeared. On this, Baranowska (2021), pp. 143–144; Scovazzi and Citroni (2007), p. 240; Calvet Martínez (2015), p. 148.

disappearances.[212] Rather, the approach by the ECtHR has been to somehow 'measure' the suffering of relatives, depending on their relationship to the victim or the context of the disappearance, including whether the relatives had witnessed the victim's abduction.[213] This approach by the European Court is problematic because it can contribute to re-victimisation and runs counter to the definition of victim in the ICPPED, which encompasses 'the disappeared person and any individual who has suffered harm as the direct result of an enforced disappearance.'[214] In more recent cases involving disappearances at the hands of non-state actors, however, the ECtHR has found violations of Article 3 in relation to the relatives.[215]

The IACtHR on the other hand, has taken a broader approach. In cases involving enforced disappearances, as well as other grave human rights violations, the IACtHR has established that such violations impact the right to personal integrity of the relatives, shifting shifted the burden of proof to the state to show that these rights were not violated.[216] The IACtHR has interpreted the suffering of relatives as stemming both from the uncertainty about the fate of the loved person after the disappearance, as well as the actions of authorities. In the case of *Pueblo Bello v Colombia*, the Inter-American Court affirmed that

> […] in cases involving forced disappearance, the Court has stated that the violation of the right to mental and moral integrity of the next of kin of a victim is a direct consequence of this phenomenon; they suffer greatly as a result of the act itself, and their suffering is increased by not knowing the truth about the facts, which has the effect of ensuring partial impunity […].[217]

In addition, '[t]he absence of a complete and effective investigation into the facts and the partial impunity constitute an *additional source of suffering and anguish* for the next of kin.'[218] Moreover, in the *Cotton Field* case, the IACtHR also considered the context as a factor in the relatives' suffering:

---

[212] On this, see Scovazzi and Citroni (2007), p. 221. According to the authors, the ECtHR struggled with 'initial difficulties […] in understanding the essence of cases of enforced disappearance' (p. 195). For a more detailed discussion on the ECtHR's approach to Article 3 violations regarding the relatives of a disappeared person in cases of enforced disappearance, see Baranowska (2021), pp. 93–95.

[213] See, for example, *Tahsin Acar v. Turkey*, para. 238; *Toğcu v Turkey*, paras 127 ff. For a comparison between the approaches taken by the ECtHR and the IACtHR regarding the impact of disappearances on relatives and society as a whole and reparations, see Citroni (2012), pp. 66–67.

[214] Article 24, ICPPED.

[215] See *Osmanoğlu v Turkey*, para. 98; *Varnava and Others v. Turkey*, paras 200–202. Note that in the more recent case of *Olewnik-Cieplińska and Olewnik v. Poland*, which involved a kidnapping, the applicants did not allege a violation of their rights under Article 3 (or any other articles for that matter). It is therefore not clear how the ECtHR would have approached this question in such a case.

[216] *Case of Gutiérrez Hernández et al. v. Guatemala*, para. 197 and note 250.

[217] *Case of the Pueblo Bello Massacre v. Colombia*, para. 161.

[218] Ibid., para. 283. Emphasis added.

> […] the Tribunal finds that the violation of the personal integrity of the victims' next of kin stems from the circumstances suffered due to all the process that followed the disappearances […] and also by the general context in which the facts occurred.[219]

Conversely, in the case of *Gutiérrez Hernández*, referred to above, the IACtHR did *not* find a violation of either the victim's, or her relatives' rights to personal integrity. The reasoning of the IACtHR was that, since it had not found that the victim was a victim of *enforced* disappearance, its previous reasoning relating to the presumption of suffering of the relatives was not applicable. Consequently, the relatives should have provided evidence to demonstrate their suffering. Since neither their representatives nor the Inter-American Commission had provided such evidence, the IACtHR found itself unable to determine a violation of the relatives' right to personal integrity.[220] This approach by the IACtHR is problematic in light of its previous case law, and the approach to the suffering of relatives as a direct consequence of not knowing 'the truth about the facts'.[221] This is because by requiring the relatives of a victim who was disappeared by non-state actors to provide evidence of their suffering, the IACtHR effectively creates a distinction between the suffering of relatives depending on the perpetrator of the disappearance and omits the role played by authorities in exacerbating the suffering of relatives through inaction, regardless of the identity of the perpetrator.[222]

The ECtHR and the IACtHR have thus both held that the failure of authorities to carry out an effective investigation can amount to a violation of the relatives' right to humane treatment, not only due to the direct treatment received from authorities (such as revictimization or threats), but also due to the prolonged anguish of not knowing what happened to their relative.[223] However, neither Court has been

---

[219] *Case of González et al. ("Cotton Field") v. Mexico*, para. 424. The IACtHR then continued as follows, summarising the actions and omissions by authorities that caused suffering to the relatives: 'The irregular and deficient actions of the state authorities when trying to discover the whereabouts of the victims after their disappearance had been reported; the lack of diligence in determining the identity of the remains, the circumstances and causes of the deaths; the delay in the return of the bodies; the absence of information on the evolution of the investigations, and the treatment accorded the next of kin during the whole process of seeking the truth has caused them great suffering and anguish. In the Court's opinion, all the foregoing constitutes degrading treatment contrary to article 5(1) and 5(2) of the American Convention, in relation to article 1(1).'

[220] *Case of Gutiérrez Hernández et al. v. Guatemala*, para. 197.

[221] *Case of the Pueblo Bello Massacre v. Colombia*, para. 161.

[222] Some scholars may disagree with this assertion. For example, Baranowska points out that while all disappeared persons may 'suffer the same fate' regardless of the perpetrator, the families are more affected when the state is involved in an enforced disappearance because it is the state that holds all powers to investigate and provide information about the fate or whereabouts of the person. See Baranowska (2021), p. 31. This may hold true if it is assumed that in cases where the state is not directly involved, it will conduct an investigation because it is not actively hiding the victim's fate or whereabouts. However, a state might also not conduct searches or investigations for other reasons, which will then leave the families in a very similar position to those of victims of enforced disappearance.

[223] See, for example, *Osmanoğlu v Turkey*, para. 98; *Abdurzakova and Abdurzakov v. Russia*, para. 119; *Varnava and Others v. Turkey*, para. 200; *Case of the Pueblo Bello Massacre v. Colombia*,

entirely consistent in finding violations of the relatives' right to humane treatment or personal integrity, thereby leaving a small gap in relation to the protection of relatives.

The HRC has also found a violation of relatives' rights under Article 7 ICCPR (humane treatment). For example, with regard to the relatives of Jesús Israel Moreno Pérez, the HRC explained that the violation of the right to human treatment had occurred

> [...] owing to the fact that the serious omissions and obstructions in the investigation of the disappearance and the premature closure of the case by the authorities overseeing it have caused them great suffering, which exacerbates the loss of their loved one, and that the continuing uncertainty caused by the disappearance causes them "anxiety and stress and is a blight on their life".[224]

In this case, the HRC also found a violation of the right to life of the victim himself based on the state's failure to investigate once it had been made aware of his disappearance.[225]

3.3 Conclusion: Chapter 3

There are a variety of ways in which a state can incur international responsibility in relation to disappearances committed by non-state actors. Based on the law of state responsibility, the determination of state responsibility is a two-step process: first, it must be established which acts —or omissions— can be attributed to the state. Second, those acts and omissions that are attributable to the state must constitute breaches of the latter's international obligations. When it comes to violations of human rights obligations by non-state actors, a state can either be held responsible because disappearances by non-state actors are directly attributable to it, or because it failed to meet its positive obligations to prevent, investigate and redress such disappearances. For the purpose of direct attribution, in the case of disappearances, the definition of enforced disappearance in IHRL provides three attribution criteria that constitute *lex specialis* to the general rules of attribution: authorisation, support or acquiescence. After many years of uncertainty regarding the meaning of these terms, the CED's 2023 Statement on Non-State Actors delivered some much needed clarity by providing definitions for all of them. The definition of acquiescence reflects a broad range of existing case law and contemplates a variety of situations. Importantly, while acquiescence generally encompasses a failure to prevent a

---

paras 154 ff; *Case of González et al. ("Cotton Field") v. Mexico*, paras 412 ff; *Case of López Soto and others v. Venezuela*, paras 262 ff.

[224] *Carlos Moreno Zamora et alt v Mexico*, para. 12.9.

[225] Ibid., para. 12.7. For a more detailed discussion on the ECtHR's approach to Article 3 violations regarding the relatives of a disappeared person in cases of enforced disappearance, see Baranowska (2021), pp. 127–130.

disappearance committed by a non-state actor, a distinction between the two remains, albeit blurry. It is an important difference, however, because if inaction amounts to acquiescence rather than a 'mere' failure to prevent, the disappearance becomes an *enforced* disappearance, which directly impacts on the obligations of states, for example in relation to victims, and automatically means that the state bears responsibility. If a disappearance committed by a non-state actor is not directly attributable to the state, it can still incur responsibility for its failure to prevent such disappearances and respond to them. When it comes to a state's failure to act, the actions and, most prominently, omissions in question are unquestionably attributable to the state. Consequently, the assessment of responsibility centres on whether the state's actions or omissions constitute a breach of its international obligations.

A failure to investigate a human rights violations committed by non-state actors generally leads to state responsibility for a failure to meet procedural obligations. In disappearance cases, however, in addition to constituting a violation of Article 3 ICPPED, a failure to conduct an effective investigation can also constitute a violation of the substantive aspect of the rights to life, liberty, and personal integrity, due to the particular nature of disappearances that blurs the obligation to prevent violations beyond the initial deprivation of liberty with the obligation to investigate. Moreover, because of the detrimental impact of a disappearance on the relatives of the disappeared person, a failure to respond to a disappearance can also constitute a violation of the relatives' right to personal integrity, access to justice and an effective remedy. Establishing state responsibility for a failure to prevent is more complex, because it must be shown that the state had an obligation to take specific preventive measures in a particular case. The ECtHR and IACtHR use two approaches for determining the existence of such an obligation, which derives from the state's awareness of risk: the victim-based and the source-based approaches. When applied to cases involving disappearances, a victim-based approach often means that the state only had the necessary awareness once the victim was reported as disappeared, which means that the responsibility of the state does not encompass the initial deprivation of liberty. A source-based approach is broader because awareness is established in relation to the source of risk rather than the individual victim. While this difference may be subtle, it can have important consequences for the determination of reparations, given that these must be made for the 'harm caused' by a violation. The CED's definition of acquiescence is more similar to a source-based approach in that it considers a causal connection between a state's actions and omissions and the risk of a disappearance, thereby contemplating the state's contribution to the risk. This is an important development because it allows for a consideration of structural issues. Since the definition of acquiescence does not clearly state that the required foreseeability of risk needs to be established in relation to a specific individual or group of persons, it will be important for the Committee to take a clear position in this regard and not introduce a victim-based approach in practice. Moreover, other human rights tribunals should use the definition of acquiescence provided by CED in order to foster greater coherence in case law about the meaning of this particularly difficult concept and avoid protection gaps or contradictions in jurisprudence.

References

Abramovich V (2010) Responsabilidad estatal por violencia de género: comentarios sobre el caso "Campo Algodonero" en la Corte Interamericana de Derechos Humanos. Anuario de Derechos Humanos 6:167–182

Baranowska G (2021) Rights of families of disappeared persons: how international bodies address the needs of families of disappeared persons in Europe, 1st edn. Intersentia, Cambridge Antwerp Chicago

Bauer J (2020) Obscured by 'Willful Blindness': States' preventive obligations and the meaning of acquiescence under the convention against torture. Colum Hum Rights Law Rev 52:738–825

Calvet Martínez E (2015) Desapariciones forzadas y justicia transicional. La búsqueda de respuestas a través del derecho a la verdad, a la justicia y a la reparación. Dissertation, Universitat de Barcelona

Citroni G (2012) Measures of reparation for victims of gross human rights violations: developments and challenges in the jurisprudence of two regional human rights courts. Inter-Am Eur Hum Rights J 5:49–71

Crawford J (2013) State responsibility: the general part. Cambridge University Press, Cambridge

de Frouville O (2021) Criminalizing or trivializing enforced disappearances? The issue of 'Non-State Actors'. In: de Frouville O, Sturma P (eds) La pénalisation des droits de l'homme. Pedone, Paris

de Schutter O (2010) International human rights law: cases, materials, commentary. Cambridge University Press, Cambridge; New York

Ebert FC, Sijniensky RI (2015) Preventing violations of the right to life in the European and the Inter-American Human Rights Systems: from the Osman Test to a coherent doctrine on risk prevention? Hum Rights Law Rev 15:343–368. https://doi.org/10.1093/hrlr/ngv001

Edwards A (2006) The 'feminizing' of torture under international human rights law. Leiden J Int Law 19:349–391. https://doi.org/10.1017/S0922156506003359

Finucane B (2010) Enforced disappearance as a crime under international law: a neglected origin in the laws of war. Yale J Int Law 35:171–197

Fischer AR, Duhaime B (2024) "The Purloined Letter": migrant disappearances, systematic impunity, and States' Risk Awareness. Can Yearb Int Law/Annuaire canadien de droit international:1–52. https://doi.org/10.1017/cyl.2024.4

Frey BA (2021) Conceptualising disappearances in international law. In: Ansolabehere K, Frey BA, Payne LA (eds) Disappearances in the post-transition era in Latin America. British Academy Scholarship, London

Guercke L (2021) State responsibility for a failure to prevent violations of the right to life by organised criminal groups: disappearances in Mexico. Hum Rights Law Rev 21:329–357. https://doi.org/10.1093/hrlr/ngaa061

Guercke L (2022) State acquiescence to disappearances in the context of Mexico's 'War on Drugs'. In: Mandolessi S, Olalde Rico K (eds) Disappearances in Mexico: from the 'dirty war' to the 'war on drugs'. Routledge, Oxon, New York, pp 127–149

Guercke L (2025) Contemporary disappearances in Mexico: a conceptual challenge for the international framework on enforced disappearances. In: Baranowska G, Kolaković-Bojović M (eds) Enforced disappearances: on universal responses to a worldwide phenomenon. Cambridge University Press (forthcoming)

Huhle R (2013) Non-state actors of enforced disappearance and the UN Convention for the protection of all persons from enforced disappearance. HuV-I/JILPAC 26:21–26

Lavrysen L (2016) Human rights in a positive state: rethinking the relationship between positive and negative obligations under the European Convention on Human Rights. Intersentia

Mackenzie-Gray Scott R (2022) State responsibility for non-state actors: past, present and prospects for the future. Hart Publishing, Bloomsbury Publishing Plc, Oxford, UK

Marques Antunes NS (2006) Acquiescence. Max Planck Encyclopedias of International Law [MPIL]

McCorquodale R, La Forgia R (2001) Taking off the blindfolds: torture by non-state actors. Hum Rights Law Rev 1:189–218. https://doi.org/10.1093/hrlr/1.2.189

Milanovic M (2022) State acquiescence or connivance in the wrongful conduct of third parties in the jurisprudence of the European Court of Human Rights. In: Kajtár G, Çali B, Milanovic M (eds) Secondary rules of primary importance in international law: attribution, causality, evidence, and standards of review in the practice of International Courts and Tribunals. Oxford University Press, Oxford

Monnheimer M (2021) Due diligence obligations in international human rights law. Cambridge University Press, Cambridge

Scovazzi T, Citroni G (2007) The struggle against enforced disappearance and the 2007 United Nations Convention. Nijhoff, Leiden

Vázquez Camacho SJ (2013) La responsabilidad internacional de los estados derivada de la conducta de particulares o non-state actors conforme al sistema interamericano de promoción y protección de los derechos humanos. Comisión Nacional de los Derechos Humanos, Mexico City

Vermeulen ML (2012) Enforced disappearance: determining state responsibility under the international convention for the protection of all persons from enforced disappearance. Intersentia, Antwerp

Zach G (2019) Article 1 Definition of Torture. In: Nowak M, Birk M, Monina G (eds) The United Nations Convention against Torture and its Optional Protocol: a commentary, 2nd edn. Oxford University Press, Oxford, UK, pp 23–71

Chapter 4
State Responsibility for Disappearances Committed by Organised Criminal Groups

OCGs can infringe human rights in a number of ways, both directly and indirectly.[1] First, OCGs can engage in (organised) criminal activities that directly infringe on rights, such as human trafficking, which invariably impacts the right to be free from slavery or forced labour,[2] and can also lead to violations of the rights to life, the right to physical integrity, as well as the right to liberty and security of the person.[3] Similarly, the smuggling of human beings can lead to several human rights violations because it often involves precarious means of transportation that pose risks to persons' health and life, and can amount to inhumane or ill-treatment. Moreover, it heightens the vulnerability of persons being smuggled to become victims of different forms of exploitation.[4] Second, activities of OCGs can indirectly affect human rights, for example through corruption that leads to failure to provide certain services, or to impunity.[5] The connection between activities of OCGs and

[1] Noortmann and Sedman (2016), p. 412.

[2] See *Rantsev v Cyprus and Russia* [2010] European Court of Human Rights Application no. 25965/04, para. 282; *Case of the Hacienda Brasil Verde Workers v Brazil* [2016] Inter-American Court of Human Rights Series C No. 318, paras. 281–290. In these cases, the ECtHR and IACtHR established that human trafficking fell within the scope of Article 4 ECHR (prohibition of slavery and forced labour) and Article 6(1) ACHR (prohibition of slavery), respectively. For an analysis of human trafficking from an international legal perspective, see Gallagher (2010).

[3] Noortmann and Sedman (2016), p. 413. The authors mention the following rights enshrined in the International Covenant on Civil and Political Rights (ICCPR) as potentially violated by human trafficking: freedom from inhumane treatment, freedom from slavery, right to liberty and security, right to privacy, protection of family and children. Note that human trafficking can also include the issue of organ trafficking, which can entail a number of abuses. On this issue, see Budiani-Saberi and Columb (2013).

[4] For an overview of the human rights that can be affected as a result of smuggling, see Obokata (2005), pp. 400–402.

[5] On the direct and indirect impacts of corruption, see, for example, Human Rights Council (2015) Final Report of the Human Rights Council Advisory Committee on the Issue of the Negative Impact of Corruption on the Enjoyment of Human Rights. UN Doc. A/HRC/28/73, para. 29; Inter-

L. Guercke, *Failure of the State*, Interdisciplinary Studies in Human Rights 15,
https://doi.org/10.1007/978-3-031-83717-3_4

disappearances specifically is twofold:[6] on the one hand, both human trafficking and the smuggling of migrants can effectively result in the disappearance of victims, for example when they are held at an undisclosed location, or if they are abandoned in the desert or at sea and, when found dead, buried in mass graves without proper identification.[7] On the other hand, OCGs can be responsible for committing disappearances of persons in certain cases of kidnappings,[8] or if they secretly dispose of dead bodies (for example in a mass grave).[9] Therefore, disappearances committed by OCGs generally overlap with the commission of other crimes, which might or might not constitute autonomous human rights violations. For example, while human

American Commission on Human Rights (IACHR) (2019) Corruption and Human Rights in the Americas: Inter-American Standards. OEA/Ser.L/V/II., Doc. 236, paras 136–140.

[6]For an overview of different countries and contexts in which OCGs are involved in the commission of disappearances, see Global Initiative Against Transnational Organized Crime (2020). See also Barooah et al. (2024); Fortify Rights and SUHAKAM (2019). Relevant data are gathered by the UNODC Observatory on Smuggling of Migrants at https://www.unodc.org/unodc/en/data-and-analysis/observatory_som.html (accessed 30 October 2024) and the International Organisation for Migration's (IOM) Missing Migrants Project at https://missingmigrants.iom.int/ (accessed 30 October 2024). Note, however, that the IOM collects information about 'missing' migrants, which is a category that is broader than that of 'disappeared' migrants. For an explanation of the distinction between 'missing' and 'disappeared' migrants, see Committee on Enforced Disappearances (2023) General Comment No. 1 on Enforced Disappearance in the Context of Migration. UN Doc. CED/C/GC/1, para. 4.

[7]See Human Rights Council (2017) Report of the Working Group on Enforced or Involuntary Disappearances on Enforced Disappearances in the Context of Migration. UN Doc. A/HRC/36/39/Add.2, paras 14 and 34ff; UN General Assembly (UNGA) (2017) Report of the Special Rapporteur of the Human Rights Council on Extrajudicial, Summary or Arbitrary Executions: Unlawful Death of Refugees and Migrants, UN Doc. A/72/335, para. 9; Organization of American States (2018) Missing Women and Girls in the Hemisphere, General Recommendation of the Committee of Experts of the MESECVI (No. 2). OEA/Ser.L/II.7.10 MESECVI/CEVI/doc.250/18, pp. 8–9; Baranowska (2020), p. 19. On the issue of smugglers abandoning migrants specifically, see Human Rights Council (2017) Report of the Working Group on Enforced or Involuntary Disappearances on Enforced Disappearances in the Context of Migration. UN Doc. A/HRC/36/39/Add.2, paras 44–45. Additionally, organ trafficking can also be an effective cause of a disappearance if a person is killed in order to retrieve a vital organ. See Meshelemiah and Lynch (2019), p. 228.

[8]IACHR (2015) Situation of Human Rights in Mexico. OEA/Ser.L/V/II.Doc. 44/15, para. 100. Note, however, that kidnappings are not always disappearances, given that kidnappers generally acknowledge the deprivation of liberty of the victim. See Baranowska (2020), p. 19. Nevertheless, kidnappings can become disappearances if either no ransom is demanded, or ransom is paid and the person is not returned to their family. See, for example, IACHR (2013) Human Rights of Migrants and Other Persons in the Context of Human Mobility in Mexico. OEA/Ser.L/V/II. Doc. 48/13, paras 156–159.

[9]Such practices are discussed further in Chap. 5 on the situation in Mexico but are not necessarily unique to the Mexican context. For example, in relation to the issue of organised crime and violence against children, the IACHR stated that: 'Having noted the rise in the number of disappearances, the Commission observes that the practice of burying and concealing corpses has proliferated in several countries in recent years, as evinced by the increase in hidden graves and graveyards, making it more and more difficult to locate the corpses, identified the victims, and conduct a criminal investigation.' See IACHR (2015) Violence, Children and Organized Crime. OEA/Ser.L/V/II. Doc. 40/15, paras 329–330. See also Fortify Rights and SUHAKAM (2019).

trafficking *per se* is considered to violate a number of human rights, the smuggling of migrants is not.[10]

Despite the role played by OCGs in the commission of such human rights violations, there is, as yet, no jurisprudence at the regional or international level that has engaged with OCGs as perpetrators of disappearances and state responsibility in this regard. Consequently, in this chapter I explore how cases involving disappearances committed by OCGs —as a specific type of non-state actor— could and should be approached by human rights tribunals, in light of state obligations and approaches to establishing state responsibility discussed in the foregoing chapters. The chapter begins with an overview of state obligations under the international legal framework that is specifically aimed at the suppression of transnational organised crime and corruption[11] as a form of *lex specialis* to IHRL obligations to prevent and remedy human rights violations committed by OCGs. Subsequently, following the rules on state responsibility outlined in Chap. 3, I first examine the question of attribution and then turn to the question of breach and the determination of state responsibility for a failure to prevent disappearances committed by OCGs.

4.1 State Obligations in Relation to Disappearances Committed by OCGs

As discussed in Chap. 2, states must take measures at different levels (legal, policy, administrative and cultural) to ensure that individuals within their jurisdiction can enjoy their human rights. The positive aspect of state obligations encompasses taking measures to prevent and respond to abuses of human rights committed by non-state actors. While it is not possible to generate an exhaustive list of measures that states must take to prevent such abuses,[12] certain measures can be enumerated depending either on groups of persons who are particularly vulnerable to becoming victims of certain human rights abuses, or on the particular source of risk to the enjoyment of human rights (see Chap. 3). As argued in the previous chapter, if the

[10] Indeed, there has been criticism from the perspective of human rights on the criminalisation of smuggling activities at the international level because of the negative impact of such criminalisation on the protection of human rights. On the problematic nature of international crime suppression instruments from a human rights perspective due to their emphasis on the criminalisation of smuggling activities, which implicates a punitive focus that might run counter to a human rights approach, see Obokata (2005), p. 395.

[11] This framework includes the United Nations Convention Against Transnational Organised Crimes (UNTOC) and Protocols Thereto, 2000 (2225 UNTS 209), and the United Nations Convention Against Corruption (UNCAC), 2003 (2349 UNTS 41).

[12] See *Case of Velásquez-Rodríguez v Honduras (Merits)* [1988] Inter-American Court of Human Rights Ser. C No. 4, para. 175 and *Case of the Pueblo Bello Massacre v Colombia* [2006] Inter-American Court of Human Rights Series C No. 140, para. 116. See also Chap. 2.

source of risk relates directly to a non-state actor, it follows that preventive measures can focus not just on the actor's activities, but also on the non-state actor itself.

While no specific framework exists in relation to OCGs within IHRL, there does exist an international legal framework aimed at preventing and fighting transnational organised crime more generally.[13] This framework consists of the United Nations Convention against Transnational Organized Crime (UNTOC) and its Protocols,[14] as well as the United Nations Convention against Corruption (UNCAC),[15] all of which have been almost universally ratified.[16] These instruments are not part of IHRL and are aimed at countering transnational organised crime[17] rather than at protecting human rights, which is an important difference to keep in mind.[18] Nevertheless, they can be drawn upon as a body of *lex specialis* to establish the types of measures necessary to prevent risks to the enjoyment of human rights emanating from OCGs if these groups, or their activities, are considered to be a source of risk.[19] Given the preventive aim of UNTOC, its Protocols and UNCAC, it is possible to utilise their content to delineate preventive obligations in relation to

---

[13] Article 1 UNTOC.

[14] The Protocols comprise the following: Protocol to Prevent, Suppress and Punish Trafficking in Persons, Especially Women and Children, supplementing the United Nations Convention against Transnational Organized Crime 2000 (2237 UNTS 319) (Trafficking Protocol); Protocol Against the Smuggling of Migrants by Land, Sea and Air, supplementing the United Nations Convention Against Transnational Organized Crime 2000 (2241 UNTS 507) (Smuggling of Migrants Protocol); Protocol against the Illicit Manufacturing of and Trafficking in Firearms, Their Parts and Components and Ammunition, supplementing the United Nations Convention against Transnational Organized Crime 2001 (2326 UNTS 208).

[15] The Preamble of UNCAC makes reference to the link between corruption and organised crime: 'Concerned also about the links between corruption and other forms of crime, in particular organised crime and economic crime, including money laundering […]'.

[16] As of October 2024, the UNTOC had 192 States Parties 182 States were Parties to the Trafficking Protocol the UNCAC had 191 States Parties. The Smuggling of Migrants Protocol had slightly fewer ratifications with 152 States Parties. To contrast this, the ICCPR had 174 States Parties ICPPED had only 76 States Parties. Information retrieved from https://treaties.un.org/pages/ParticipationStatus.aspx?clang=_en. Accessed 21 October 2024.

[17] See Article 1 UNTOC; Article 1 UNCAC.

[18] See, for example, Gallagher (2001), p. 976: 'While human rights concerns may have provided some impetus (or cover) for collective action, it is the sovereignty/ security issues surrounding trafficking and migrant smuggling which are the true driving force behind such efforts.' Similarly, Noortmann and Sedman speak of a 'disconnect' between discourses of transnational crimes and human rights. They further point to the fact that UNTOC does not mention human rights at all. See Noortmann and Sedman (2016), pp. 408–410.

[19] A similar argument has been advanced by Anne Peters in relation to corruption and human rights specifically, although her main focus is on how the norms under the UNCAC itself can be strengthened by adding a human rights focus. See Peters (2018), p. 1260: '[…] if we interpret the UNCAC obligations in conformity with human rights law (Article 31(3)(c) of the Vienna Convention on the Law of Treaties), it becomes apparent that the measures mentioned here must in fact be taken in an effective way in order to fulfil the obligations to protect and to fulfil (including to prevent) grounded in human rights law.' For an overview of state obligations in relation to transnational organised crime, see Obokata (2010); Hauck and Peterke (2016).

disappearances committed by OCGs. For example, the UN Special Rapporteur on trafficking in persons, especially women and children (Special Rapporteur on Trafficking) has used the Trafficking Protocol to delineate the scope of 'prevention' measures relating to human trafficking.[20] In addition, certain obligations under UNTOC and its Protocols related to victims of crimes falling within these instruments could be drawn on to define the content of effective remedies as part of state obligations to respond.

Referring to UNTOC, its Protocols, and UNCAC to further delineate state obligations in relation to disappearances committed by OCGs, particularly for the prevention of such crimes, can aid the determination of state responsibility for a failure to prevent. This is because preventive obligations vis-à-vis acts committed by non-state actors are obligations of due diligence that are subject to several tests, including an assessment of reasonableness and proportionality (see Chap. 2). In relation to determining responsibility for a failure to act with due diligence, the reasonableness and proportionality of preventive measures taken are based on an acknowledgment of the need to balance the interests of the individual and society as a whole and make choices related to budgetary allocations.[21] The existence of specific obligations under another international legal framework is of great relevance in this regard because states who are parties to UNTOC, its Protocols, and UNCAC already have a legal obligation to take the measures stipulated in these instruments, which are not subject to balancing considerations. To exemplify, in its assessment of the 'burden' and proportionality of measures to protect victims of human trafficking in the case of *Rantsev v Cyprus and Russia*, the ECtHR relied on the Trafficking Protocol:

> It is relevant to the consideration of the proportionality of any positive obligation arising in the present case that the Palermo Protocol, signed by both Cyprus and the Russian Federation in 2000, requires States to endeavour to provide for the physical safety of victims of trafficking while in their territories and to establish comprehensive policies and programmes to prevent and combat trafficking.[22]

---

[20] See UNGA (2010) Report of the Special Rapporteur on Trafficking in Persons, Especially Women and Children. UN Doc. A/65/288, para. 17. The utility of drawing on other frameworks of international law for the purpose of defining the content of human rights obligations was confirmed by the IACtHR in its Advisory Opinion on The Environment and Human Rights, in which it drew on International Environmental Law standards to specify the 'meaning and scope' of obligations under the ACHR. See Inter-American Court of Human Rights (2017) Advisory Opinion on the Environment and Human Rights. OC-23/17, para. 44.

[21] The ECtHR has stated this in the following manner: 'In determining the scope of a State's positive obligations, regard must be had to the fair balance that has to be struck between the general interest and the interests of the individual, the diversity of situations obtaining in Contracting States and the choices which must be made in terms of priorities and resources. Nor must these obligations be interpreted in such a way as to impose an impossible or disproportionate burden.' *Ilaşcu and Others v Moldova and Russia* [2004] European Court of Human Rights Application no. 48787/99, 2004–VII, para. 332. See also Ebert and Sijniensky (2015), p. 344.

[22] *Rantsev v. Cyprus and Russia*, para. 287.

Following this reasoning, the measures corresponding to these obligations under UNTOC, the Trafficking and Smuggling of Migrants Protocols, and UNCAC cannot be considered as imposing a disproportionate burden on states.[23]

In drawing on this international framework as *lex specialis*, two caveats must be made: first, UNTOC is focused on 'transnational' organised crime, which may limit its applicability as *lex specialis* to define the content of state obligations towards all types of OCGs, as there could be OCGs without transnational ties involved in the commission of disappearances.[24] Nonetheless, the definition of 'transnational' in UNTOC is broad in that it includes crimes that are:

> (a) … committed in more than one State;
> (b) … committed in one State but a substantial part of its preparation, planning, direction or control takes place in another State;
> (c) … committed in one State but involves an organised criminal group that engages in criminal activities in more than one State; or
> (d) … committed in one State but has substantial effects in another State.[25]

Article 3(2)(c) can be read as including criminal organisations that launder profits in other countries, or that engage in international drug trafficking. Given that many OCGs today have transnational ties,[26] for the purpose of this argument it can be presumed that a large number of OCGs involved in the commission of disappearances can be considered as 'transnational'. Moreover, even if such OCGs were not transnational, the obligations under UNTOC could still be taken as guidance for the type of measures to be taken against purely national organised crime. Second, UNTOC and its Protocols have received criticism by human rights scholars due to their punitive focus, which can negatively impact on the protection of human rights.[27] This very valid critique is important to consider, and it must be emphasised that drawing on these instruments as a body of *lex specialis* is in no way intended to advocate for a more punitive approach to countering (organised) crime. In fact, in its General Comment on Enforced Disappearances in the Context of Migration, the CED explicitly called on states not to criminalise migrants or those who support

---

[23] The consideration of whether a state is party to instruments such as the Trafficking Protocol as a way of determining whether the state acted diligently has also been highlighted by the UN Special Rapporteur on Trafficking, Maria Grazia Giammarinaro, in her 2015 report on due diligence and human trafficking. See UNGA (2015) Report of the Special Rapporteur on Trafficking in Persons, Especially Women and Children. UN Doc. A/70/260, para. 14. See also Guercke (2021), p. 356.

[24] Indeed, Fijnaut and Paoli criticise the transnational focus of these international legal instruments as overlooking the local rootedness of many criminal organisations. They argue that this criticism is particularly important for the purpose of policymaking. See Fijnaut and Paoli (2008).

[25] Article 3(2) UNTOC.

[26] See, for example, European Parliamentary Research Service (2022). See also Kemp (2024) and Global Initiative Against Transnational Organized Crime (2023).

[27] See, for example, Noortmann and Sedman (2016), pp. 418–419. On the punitive nature of UNTOC and UNCAC and how this can raise issues from a human rights perspective, see also Boister (2002). For a criticism of these instruments in relation to the criminalisation of smuggling activities, see Obokata (2005), p. 395.

them. To avoid criminalising persons who assist migrants, the Committee clearly stated that states should ensure that terminology used in legislation against trafficking, smuggling, or terrorism is not abused for this purpose.[28]

4.1.1 The Obligation to Prevent[29]

Using UNTOC, its Protocols and UNCAC as *lex specialis* to further define the content of preventive measures that states should adopt in relation to human rights violations at the hands of OCGs is in line with the position of the CED expressed in its General Comment No. 1, which lists the implementation of obligations arising from these instruments (in addition to others) as a preventive measure against disappearances of migrants.[30] If persons can become victims of disappearances committed by OCGs either through a criminal activity, such as human trafficking, or after being abducted or killed by an OCG, it is also possible to envisage two ways of preventing disappearances by OCGs, either by preventing human trafficking or smuggling from occurring, or by taking measures against the groups themselves.

4.1.1.1 Preventing Human Trafficking

A first set of prevention measures related to disappearances committed by OCGs involve measures against trafficking in human beings.[31] These can be derived from the Trafficking Protocol directly and have been defined by the Special Rapporteur on Trafficking.[32] The Trafficking Protocol obliges states to criminalise trafficking in persons and related offenses (Article 5) and stipulates measures to be taken to assist and protect victims (Articles 6–8). Furthermore, it requires states to foster information exchange among their relevant authorities, such as law enforcement or immigration authorities, and provide training to these authorities (Article 10), and to

[28] Committee on Enforced Disappearances (2023) General Comment No. 1 on Enforced Disappearance in the Context of Migration. UN Doc. CED/C/GC/1, para. 30: '[…] States parties should review the terminology used in certain types of legislation, such as legislation on countering trafficking, smuggling and terrorism.'

[29] The subject of effective crime prevention lies beyond the scope of this research. The argument advanced here is focused on providing guidance for further defining the content of state obligations in relation to reducing the risk by OCGs in line with existing obligations under a more specific international legal framework than that of IHRL.

[30] Committee on Enforced Disappearances (2023) General Comment No. 1 on Enforced Disappearance in the Context of Migration. UN Doc. CED/C/GC/1, para. 28.

[31] See also Committee on Enforced Disappearances (2017) Concluding observations on the report submitted by Gabon. UN Doc. CED/C/GAB/CO/1, paras 19–20.

[32] See UNGA (2015) Report of the Special Rapporteur on Trafficking in Persons, Especially Women and Children. UN Doc. A/70/260.

ensure border and document controls (Articles 11–13). Article 9, which deals specifically with the prevention of trafficking requires states to adopt the following measures: 'Comprehensive policies and programmes' for the prevention of trafficking and the protection of victims; the gathering and dissemination of information about trafficking, for example through campaigns and the adoption of 'social and economic' initiatives, all of which should be designed in consultation with civil society; measures aimed at alleviating the root causes that make persons vulnerable to trafficking; and legislative, and other measures (educational, social, cultural) to discourage demand (Article 9.1–9.5).

The Special Rapporteur on Trafficking reiterated these obligations and emphasised the need to prevent human trafficking by addressing both 'supply and demand factors' that perpetuate this crime.[33] This includes addressing the root causes that make persons vulnerable to being trafficked in the first place;[34] reducing demand for the type of work where trafficking victims are often employed, including for sexual purposes and labour exploitation;[35] fostering opportunities for 'safe' migration and ensuring that existing strategies to ensure safe migration do not end up undermining the protection of human rights;[36] as well as adopting effective awareness-raising campaigns about the risks of trafficking.[37] All these measures should involve victims of trafficking in their design[38] and states should seek collaboration with the private sector in order to prevent trafficking.[39] Finally, states must collect data on the issue and continuously monitor and evaluate prevention programmes in order to assess and ensure their effectiveness.[40] At the same time, measures relating to prosecution are also important because they can constitute preventive measures.[41] These obligations were repeated in a later report by the Special Rapporteur on Trafficking concerning the meaning of due diligence in the context of human trafficking.[42]

The ECtHR has also confirmed that states have an obligation under Article 4 ECHR (prohibition of slavery and forced labour) to adopt 'a legislative and administrative framework to prohibit and punish trafficking'.[43] This obligation

---

[33] Ibid., para. 18.

[34] Ibid., paras 21–28.

[35] Ibid., paras 29–38.

[36] Ibid., paras 39–43. This has also been repeated by the CED as a preventive measure against disappearances of migrants in its General Comment on Enforced Disappearances in the Context of migration. Committee on Enforced Disappearances (2023) General Comment No. 1 on Enforced Disappearance in the Context of Migration. UN Doc. CED/C/GC/1, para. 27.

[37] UNGA (2015) Report of the Special Rapporteur on Trafficking in Persons, Especially Women and Children. UN Doc. A/70/260, paras 44–48.

[38] Ibid., paras 49–53.

[39] Ibid., paras 54–58.

[40] Ibid., paras 59–62.

[41] Ibid., para. 20.

[42] Ibid. Paras 19–23 address the issue of due diligence in the prevention of trafficking.

[43] *Rantsev v. Cyprus and Russia*, para. 285.

includes not just the provision of punishment for traffickers, but also the regulation of businesses that could be used to cover trafficking and the adoption of immigration rules that avoid the 'encouragement, facilitation or tolerance of trafficking'.[44] Finally, the ECtHR has also stated that states' preventive obligations in relation to human trafficking extend beyond putting in place such a legal and administrative framework, which it considered to be 'only one aspect of member states' general undertaking to combat trafficking'.[45] An example of how the Trafficking Protocol can be used by human rights tribunals is the ECtHR's approach in the case of *Rantsev v. Cyprus and Russia,* discussed in Chap. 3, which concerned the death of a victim of trafficking. In this case, the ECtHR used the Trafficking Protocol to define the content of the positive obligations arising from Article 4 ECHR.[46] The European Court held that at a general level, states must 'put in place a legislative and administrative framework to prohibit and punish trafficking'[47] and take preventive measures in accordance with the Trafficking Protocol. Moreover, the ECtHR affirmed that in certain circumstances states may also be required to 'take operational measures to protect victims, or potential victims, of trafficking.'[48] In this particular case, the ECtHR found that Cyprus had an appropriate legal framework against trafficking in place.[49] Nonetheless, there was also a particular visa regime for 'artistes' in place in Cyprus, which had been widely criticised for facilitating human trafficking by making the 'artiste' dependent on their employer or agent.[50] Moreover, the European Court found that this visa regime did not provide 'practical and effective protection against trafficking and exploitation',[51] in violation of Cyprus' obligations under Article 4 ECHR to put in place an effective legal and administrative framework, which reflects the general obligation to take legislative measures as one means of addressing harm by non-state actors, including OCGs (see Chap. 2, Sect. 2.1.2.1).

Like the ECtHR, the IACtHR has also derived obligations to prevent human trafficking from the prohibition of slavery and forced labour. In the *Case of the Hacienda Brasil Verde Workers,* the IACtHR dealt with the disappearance of two adolescents from a farm where they had been held in slave-like conditions and

---

[44] Ibid., para. 284.

[45] Ibid., para. 285.

[46] Ibid., para. 284.

[47] Ibid., para. 285.

[48] Ibid., para. 286. In the same manner as specific prevention obligations generally (see Chap. 2, Sect. 2.1.2.2), this obligation to take operational measures to protect is also subject to the state's awareness of 'circumstances giving rise to a credible suspicion that an identified individual had been, or was at real and immediate risk of being, trafficked or exploited within the meaning of Article 3(a) of the Palermo Protocol and Article 4(a) of the Anti-Trafficking Convention.' ibid. Upon having such awareness, authorities must then 'take appropriate measures within the scope of their powers to remove the individual from that situation or risk.' Ibid., para. 287.

[49] Ibid., para. 290.

[50] Ibid., paras 291–292.

[51] Ibid., para. 293.

assessed whether the Brazilian state was responsible for the violation of the prohibition of slavery (Article 6 ACHR). The Court first established that Article 6 ACHR imposed an obligation on states to prevent and investigate possible situations of slavery, servitude, human trafficking and forced labour.[52] It then used the same wording as in prior cases concerning violence against women, and reiterated the obligations to act diligently in response to cases of forced labour or trafficking, to ensure the existence of an appropriate legal framework and its effective implementation, and to adopt prevention policies to address the underlying risk factors and strengthen institutions in order to effectively respond to the phenomenon of contemporary slavery.[53] Thus, for the Inter-American Court, in contexts where there is either a particular group of victims that is at risk, or a specific practice known to endanger the rights of individuals (such as slavery, human trafficking or forced labour in this case), states have an obligation to adopt preventive strategies in addition to putting in place an appropriate legal framework.

4.1.1.2 Preventing the Smuggling of Migrants

The Smuggling of Migrants Protocol also requires states to criminalise the offence of smuggling (Article 6) and establishes measures for cooperation regarding the smuggling of migrants at sea in particular (Articles 7–9). Section III, which deals with preventive measures, includes information gathering (Article 10), measures relating to border control (Article 11) and the verification of documents (Articles 12–13), training of authorities (Article 14), as well as measures to raise awareness and to address the root causes of smuggling, including socio-economic realities that push people to migrate and seek out smugglers (Article 15). Further, states should adopt 'appropriate' measures to protect migrants from violence (Article 16(2)). Finally, Article 18 regulates the return of migrants.

Both the WGEID and the CED also consider measures against human trafficking and smuggling as constituting preventive measures against (enforced) disappearances in the context of migration. In its Report on Enforced Disappearance in the Context of Migration, the WGEID called on states to design their migration policies in such a way that these do not '[compel] migrants to resort to smuggling networks and thereby falling prey to trafficking networks, thus contributing to heightened risks of becoming victims of human rights violations'.[54] In the General Comment on

[52] *Case of the Hacienda Brasil Verde Workers v. Brazil,* para. 319.

[53] Ibid., para. 320.

[54] Human Rights Council (2017) Report of the Working Group on Enforced or Involuntary Disappearances on Enforced Disappearances in the Context of Migration. UN Doc. A/HRC/36/39/Add.2, para. 88 (a). This position was also taken by the UN Special Rapporteur on Extrajudicial, Summary and Arbitrary Executions in her report on arbitrary deaths of migrations, in which she emphasised the potentially detrimental impact of restrictive migration policies. See UNGA (2017) Report of the Special Rapporteur of the Human Rights Council on Extrajudicial, Summary or Arbitrary Executions: Unlawful Death of Refugees and Migrants. UN Doc. A/72/335, paras 9–13.

Enforced Disappearances in the Context of Migration, the CED included a long list of preventive measures, including urging states to adopt 'evidence-based policies to foster access to regular, safe and orderly migration', including, among others, working against smuggling of migrants and human trafficking (para. 27). Additionally, and with reference to the role played by non-state actors in the disappearance of migrants, the CED called on states to work together against exploitation and human trafficking and address human rights abuses that occur 'in the context of smuggling and corruption' (para. 28).

This brief review of the Trafficking and Smuggling of Migrants Protocols and jurisprudence indicates that obligations in relation to these specific criminal activities are very concrete measures related to border and document checks and training of authorities who might be in contact with victims of human trafficking. Additionally, they encompass more general and indirect measures that include not only awareness-raising, but also measures to address the root causes that make people vulnerable to becoming victims of trafficking or make them want to leave their countries of origin and take great risks by putting their lives into the hands of smugglers. Importantly, from a human rights perspective, none of these measures should be read as an excuse to enforce stricter border control measures, as these can themselves be conducive to human rights violations, for example by pushing smugglers to take more dangerous routes.[55]

4.1.1.3 Countering Organised Criminal Groups as a Form of Prevention

Disappearances committed by OCGs are not always linked to a specific organised criminal activity. In such cases, states must take measures against the groups themselves to reduce the risk to human rights that they represent. This is in line with the reasoning of the IACtHR in the case of *Pueblo Bello* discussed previously (Sect. 3.2.1.3), where the Inter-American Court considered Colombia's efforts to dismantle paramilitary groups as constituting a measure to reduce the risk posed by these groups to the enjoyment of human rights by the population.[56] Due to the growing role played by non-state actors in the commission of human rights abuses, there now exist more specific international standards to guide state behaviour vis-à-vis particular non-state actors who can be responsible for human rights violations, such as the United Nations Guiding Principles on Business and Human Rights

---

[55] See IACHR (2013) Human Rights of Migrants and Other Persons in the Context of Human Mobility in Mexico. OEA/Ser.L/V/II. Doc. 48/13, para. 91; UNGA (2017) Report of the Special Rapporteur of the Human Rights Council on Extrajudicial, Summary or Arbitrary Executions: Unlawful Death of Refugees and Migrants, UN Doc. A/72/335, para. 13; Human Rights Council (2017) Report of the Working Group on Enforced or Involuntary Disappearances on Enforced Disappearances in the Context of Migration. UN Doc. A/HRC/36/39/Add.2, para. 36; Committee on Enforced Disappearances (2023) General Comment No. 1 on Enforced Disappearance in the Context of Migration. UN Doc. CED/C/GC/1, paras 6 and 27.

[56] See *Case of the Pueblo Bello Massacre v. Colombia*, paras 125–127.

(Business and Human Rights Principles).[57] These soft law standards specify measures to be taken by both states and businesses to safeguard human rights, with a particular emphasis on the obligation of states to regulate and supervise the latter's activities in so far as they constitute a risk to the enjoyment of human rights.[58] Due to the illegal nature of OCGs, however, it is not really possible to conceive of these measures as being regulatory in nature, similar to those established in the Business and Human Rights Principles in relation to the activities of legal businesses. This is because the Business and Human Rights Principles require an official, legal relationship between the state and a business.[59] Since the operations by OCGs are, by definition, illegal and prohibited,[60] it would be difficult to imagine and also in contradiction to the obligations of states under UNTOC, to impose *regulatory* measures on them. Consequently, if any of their activities are to be curbed, including crimes such as disappearances that deprive victims of their human rights, then the group itself must be constrained effectively.[61]

This approach finds support in the HRC's General Comment No. 36 on the right to life, which lists as preventive measures not just addressing 'general conditions in society' that may create an environment conducive to violations of the right to life at the hands of non-state actors, including 'high levels of criminal and gun violence',[62] but also taking measures against groups that may be responsible for committing lethal violence:

---

[57] United Nations Office of the High Commissioner for Human Rights (OHCHR) (2011) Guiding Principles on Business and Human Rights: Implementing the United Nations "Protect, Respect and Remedy" Framework. HR/PUB/11/04.

[58] See ibid., Principles 1–10. On the obligations of states to guarantee, prevent, and supervise, see also IACHR and REDESCA (2019) Business and Human Rights: Inter-American Standards. OEA/Ser.L/V/II, CIDH/REDESCA/INF.1/19, paras 80–120. Similarly, there is growing development of standards relating to environmental protection as a means of safeguarding human rights, such as the Framework Principles on Human Rights and the Environment. These standards also encompass, among others, state obligations to 'regulate business enterprises to protect against human rights abuses resulting from environmental harm and to provide for remedies for such abuses.' See Commentary on Framework Principle 12, Human Rights Council (2018) Report of the Special Rapporteur on the Issue of Human Rights Obligations Relating to the Enjoyment of a Safe, Clean, Healthy and Sustainable Environment. UN Doc. A/HRC/37/59, para. 34.

[59] See OHCHR (2011) Guiding Principles on Business and Human Rights: Implementing the United Nations "Protect, Respect and Remedy" Framework. HR/PUB/11/04. The requirement of such a formal relationship is illustrated by the following measures established in the Guidelines: setting out clear expectations towards businesses (Principle 2), requiring reports to monitor business' compliance with laws and providing guidance (Principle 3), exercising of oversight (Principle 5), and promoting human rights in commercial transactions (Principle 6).

[60] UNTOC requires states parties to criminalise not just the actions of criminal groups, but also participation in such groups. See Article 5 UNTOC.

[61] This point is also made by Monica Hakimi, who lists fighting gang violence as a protective measure which states may have to take to comply with their duty to protect. See Hakimi (2014), p. 261.

[62] Human Rights Committee (2019) General Comment No. 36: Article 6: Right to Life. UN Doc. CCPR/C/GC/36, para. 26.

> States parties should also disband irregular armed groups, such as private armies and vigilante groups, that are responsible for deprivations of life and reduce the proliferation of potentially lethal weapons to unauthorized individuals.[63]

The HRC does not explicitly mention OCGs in this interpretation of the obligation to protect, and it could indeed be questioned whether OCGs could be considered 'irregular armed groups', as this term is most commonly used in the context of armed conflicts.[64] Nonetheless, if it could be established that OCGs were responsible for committing 'deprivations of the right to life' or disappearances in a particular context, and considering the protective aim of the international human rights regime, this provision of General Comment No. 36 should be read in such a way as to encompass obligations of states to constrain the (lethal) activities of OCGs as well.

The interpretation of positive obligations to protect persons from disappearances committed by OCGs by dismantling or constraining such groups is also reflected in the WGEID's Report on Enforced Disappearances in the Context of Migration, where it held that preventive measures could include:

> [...] those specifically tailored to address or mitigate factors that may increase the risk of enforced disappearances of migrants. For instance, *States should take all possible measures to combat criminal organizations which abuse or exploit migrants, notably trafficking networks* [...].[65]

The WGEID further recommended that states '[t]ake all possible measures to sanction criminal organizations which abuse or exploit migrants, notably trafficking networks.'[66] In its General Comment No. 1 the CED did not go quite as far as this. However, it did emphasise that states should implement their obligations under UNTOC and its Protocols, and UNCAC, which are aimed at preventing and countering organised criminal activities and constraining groups that engage in such activities.[67]

---

[63] Ibid., para. 21.

[64] A discussion of the question whether OCGs could indeed be considered as 'irregular armed groups' within the meaning of International Humanitarian Law (IHL) is beyond the scope of this research. For an overview of the possibilities of applying IHL to OCGs, see Peterke and Wolf (2016). The authors argue that in certain circumstances, where OCGs engage in direct and open armed confrontations with security forces, they might attain status, either on a collective or individual level, under IHL. However, the authors also highlight the vagueness of the criteria for the applicability of IHL, particularly in situations of non-international armed conflicts, and argue that current IHL is 'not yet able to address' situations where OCGs engage in violent conflict with the state (p. 405).

[65] Human Rights Council (2017) Report of the Working Group on Enforced or Involuntary Disappearances on Enforced Disappearances in the Context of Migration. UN Doc. A/HRC/36/39/Add.2, para. 65. Emphasis added.

[66] Ibid., para. 88 (c).

[67] Committee on Enforced Disappearances (2023) General Comment No. 1 on Enforced Disappearance in the Context of Migration. UN Doc. CED/C/GC/1, para. 28.

Obligations Under UNTOC

The first type of measures that states must take in order to counter organised crime in accordance with UNTOC relate to the creation of a legal framework that criminalises not only membership in an OCG (Article 5), but also certain activities in which OCGs engage, including money laundering (Article 6), corruption (Article 8), and obstruction of justice (Article 23). In addition to criminalising these acts, states must adopt measures to prevent and counter money laundering (Article 7) and corruption (Article 9) and ensure that both legal entities and natural persons are held liable for their involvement in such activities and sanctioned (Articles 10–11). Moreover, states must regulate the confiscation of proceeds and property from criminal activities (Articles 12–14). At the same time, states must ensure that they can exercise jurisdiction over the crimes covered by UNTOC and facilitate cooperation between law enforcement agencies in the investigation and prosecution of these crimes (Articles 15–22 and 24–27). States must also analyse trends in organised crime (Article 28), adopt training measures and provide technical assistance (Article 29), and cooperate in order to ensure the implementation of UNTOC, including through development cooperation (Article 30).

In addition to these general measures, Article 31 deals explicitly with prevention. The preventive measures listed include the development and evaluation of national projects to prevent transnational organised crime (Article 31(1)); the reduction of the possibility for criminal groups to participate in the legal economy through collaboration between the public and private sector; the adoption of integrity procedures and codes of conduct; the creation of registers and records on legal entities to avoid the 'misuse of legal persons' by criminal groups (Article 31(2)); the reintegration of offenders (Article 31(3)); the evaluation of existing instruments and practices (Article 31(4)); awareness-raising (Article 31(5)); as well as international cooperation and addressing root causes by 'alleviating the circumstances that render socially marginalised groups vulnerable to the action of transnational organised crime' (Article 31(7)). If viewed as *lex specialis* to the human rights obligations of states, these measures should be taken into consideration during an assessment of the types of preventive measures that a state should have taken, at a minimum, to counter activities committed by OCGs.

Obligations Under UNCAC

UNCAC does not contain a definition of corruption[68] and there is no agreed-upon definition of corruption at the international level.[69] The Inter-American Commission on Human Rights (IACHR) equally did not elaborate a definition of corruption, but described it as

> a phenomenon characterized by the abuse or misuse of the power entrusted, which may be public or private, that displaces the public interest for a private benefit (personal or for a third party).[70]

The relationship between human rights and corruption has received increasing attention in human rights scholarship in recent years.[71] However, it is a complicated relationship that raises multiple questions beyond the scope of this research, especially in relation to causation.[72] Corruption can negatively impact on the enjoyment of human rights in different ways, often indirectly, and this impact is most palpable in the realm of economic, social and cultural rights, for example if persons cannot access education or healthcare without having to pay a bribe, or when corruption in procurement leads to shortages of essential medical —or educational— supplies. However, it also has impacts on civil and political rights, especially (and most visibly so) in situations where bribes are required, for example in order for law enforcement and judicial authorities to take action.[73] When it comes to corruption and disappearances, the relationship is less visible and direct. The most obvious connection was highlighted by the WGEID in its Report on Enforced Disappearances in the Context of Migration: corruption can lead border officials to look the other way when traffickers or smugglers cross borders, which can directly implicate these officials in the disappearance (see Sect. 4.2.1.2 below).[74]

---

[68] Neither do the regional instruments such as the Council of Europe's Criminal Law Convention on Corruption 1999 (ETS No173), the Inter-American Convention Against Corruption 1996 (35 ILM 724). The African Union Convention on Preventing and Combating Corruption 2003 (43 ILM 5) also does not provide a separate definition of corruption, but rather defines corruption as 'the acts and practices including related offences proscribed in this Convention' (Article 1(1)).

[69] See Human Right Council (2015) Final report of the Human Rights Council Advisory Committee on the issue of the negative impact of corruption on the enjoyment of human rights. A/HRC/28/73, para. 5.

[70] See IACHR (2019) Corruption and Human Rights in the Americas: Inter-American Standards, OEA/Ser.L/V/II., Doc. 236, para. 3, citing IACHR Resolution 1/18.

[71] See, for example, Boersma et al. (2010); Nash Rojas et al. (2014); Peters (2015, 2018); Reyes (2019).

[72] On the difficulties relating to the question of causation when it comes to the link between corruption and human rights violations, see Peters (2024), pp. 10–13; Peters (2018), pp. 1267–1272.

[73] On the different ways in which corruption can impact on human rights, see, for example, Peters (2024), pp. 2–4; Peters (2018), pp. 1255–1257; Nash Rojas et al. (2014), pp. 26–29.

[74] See Human Rights Council (2017) Report of the Working Group on Enforced or Involuntary Disappearances on Enforced Disappearances in the Context of Migration. UN Doc. A/HRC/36/39/Add.2, paras 35–37; Duhaime and Thibault (2017), p. 584.

In this sense, in the same manner as measures to counter the activities of OCGs, anti-corruption measures can be viewed as preventive measures for the human rights abuses that may be facilitated by corrupt relationships between authorities and OCGs who commit them.[75] Chapter II of UNCAC deals specifically with the prevention of corruption. States have an obligation to adopt prevention policies and practices subject to regular evaluation (Article 5), yet the content of such policies is not specified in UNCAC. States are further obliged to create independent anti-corruption bodies (Article 6) and adopt regulations and codes of conduct for public officials (Articles 7–9), while making public sector employment and public procurement processes transparent (Article 9) and subject to reporting (Article 10). States must also ensure the independence of the judiciary and prosecution services (Article 11) and regulate the private sector (Article 12). The participation of society should be ensured, for example by raising awareness about corruption and transparency (Article 13). Finally, states should adopt measures to combat money-laundering, including the regulation of the banking and financial sectors (Article 14).

In addition to the preventive obligations established in Chapter II of UNCAC, Chapter III deals with the criminalisation of different forms of corruption and law enforcement measures, which can also be considered preventive measures in so far as they serve a deterrent function.[76] Relevant to acts committed by OCGs, in which officials may be involved through corruption, are the following crimes: bribery (Articles 15, 16, 21), trading in influence (Article 18), abuse of functions (Article 19), illicit enrichment (Article 20), laundering of proceeds (Article 23), concealment (Article 24), obstruction of justice (Article 25), and the participation or attempt to be involved in any of the previous activities (Article 27). Moreover, Chapter III also establishes obligations relating to the response to corrupt activities, which include measures relating to the prosecution of such offences (Articles 28–31), the protection of witnesses, victims and those who denounce corruption (Articles 23–33), as well as addressing the consequences of corruption and providing compensation for damage (Articles 34–35). Finally, states have to create specialised bodies and appoint

---

[75] This argument is also made by Anne Peters, who argues that the obligation to protect encompasses the reduction of 'structural human rights risks' and consequently, where corruption represents such a structural risk, measures to curb corruption. See Peters (2018), pp. 1259–1260. Similarly, Anne Gallagher has argued that addressing corruption and complicity related to human trafficking is an important component of acting with due diligence to prevent trafficking. See Gallagher (2010), p. 442ff. For an argument in favour of a human rights duty to prevent corruption, the content of which could be in part derived from UNCAC, see Reyes (2019), p. 334. In its report on 'Corruption and Human Rights in the Americas', the IACHR held that the obligation of states to guarantee human rights implies an obligation to counter corruption, especially where corruption itself constitutes a violation of human rights. See IACHR (2019) Corruption and Human Rights in the Americas: Inter-American Standards. OEA/Ser.L/V/II., Doc. 236, paras 225–258. See also Committee on Enforced Disappearances (2023) General Comment No. 1 on Enforced Disappearance in the Context of Migration. UN Doc. CED/C/GC/1, para. 28.

[76] The subsequent chapters of UNCAC deal with international cooperation (Chapter IV, Articles 43–50), asset recovery (Chapter V, Articles 51–59) and technical assistance and information exchange (Chapter VI, Articles 60–62).

persons for dealing with corruption, as well as to encourage and facilitate cooperation both with and among law enforcement authorities (Articles 36–42).

4.1.2 The Obligation to Respond

In addition to the preventive measures listed above, UNTOC, its Protocols, and UNCAC also contain provisions relating to the victims of crimes these instruments address. The corresponding obligations to investigate the respective crimes and to provide protection or damages to victims can be utilised to further delineate the content of states' obligation to respond. It must be noted that, with the exception of the Trafficking and Smuggling of Migrants Protocols, these measures are focused on responding to crimes related to organised criminal activities, or corruption-related crimes defined in UNCAC, rather than to potential human rights violations committed by OCGs.[77] Despite this limitation, however, certain measures can be understood as reinforcing state obligations vis-à-vis disappearances committed by OCGs.

4.1.2.1 Remedies for Victims of Human Trafficking

If a victim of a disappearance committed by an OCG is also a victim of human trafficking, the obligation to provide remedies under the Trafficking Protocol would be applicable. The Trafficking Protocol obliges states to 'ensure that its domestic legal system contains measures that offer victims of trafficking in persons the possibility of obtaining compensation for damage suffered.'[78] In addition to this procedural obligation to ensure access to a remedy, the Special Rapporteur on Trafficking has emphasised that where states have failed to act diligently to 'prevent and combat trafficking in persons',[79] the right to an effective remedy for victims of human trafficking goes beyond a right to compensation, but also 'encompasses recovery, restitution, satisfaction and guarantees of non-repetition.'[80] This is in line with IHRL standards outlined in previous chapters in that victims of human trafficking have a right to reparation when it can be shown that a state failed in its obligation to act with due diligence to prevent the crime. Importantly, the measures outlined by the Special Rapporteur on Trafficking in her report on effective remedies

[77] Moreover, the provisions of the Smuggling of Migrants Protocol are much narrower than those contained in the Trafficking Protocol and principally establish states' obligations to provide 'appropriate' protection and assistance to migrants who have been endangered as a consequence of smuggling. See Article 16 Smuggling of Migrants Protocol. Given this much narrower focus, these provisions are not analysed in depth.

[78] Article 6(6) Trafficking Protocol.

[79] See UNGA (2011) Report of the Special Rapporteur on Trafficking in Persons, Especially Women and Children. UN Doc. A/66/283, para. 12.

[80] Ibid., para. 13.

for victims of human trafficking presuppose that the victim has been found and liberated. In view of this, victims of human trafficking who have also been disappeared (and whose disappearance would fall within Article 3 ICPPED), have a right to reparation under the Trafficking Protocol. Nonetheless, this right would not extend to the relatives because it is limited to the person who was trafficked and would only be actionable once the victim has been found. In that sense, the Trafficking Protocol provides some additional protection for victims of disappearances committed by OCGs, but only in a limited manner.

4.1.2.2 Remedies Under UNTOC

Article 25 UNTOC is specifically concerned with '[a]ssistance to and protection of victims' and creates, in addition to provisions regarding assistance and protection, the obligation to 'establish appropriate procedures to provide access to compensation and restitution for victims of offences covered by this Convention.'[81] However, given the scope of UNTOC as relating to crimes committed by OCGs, whether Article 25 could be interpreted as establishing obligations for states vis-à-vis victims of disappearances committed by OCGs is questionable. According to Article 3 (1) UNTOC, the scope of application of the Convention includes 'serious crimes' committed by OCGs.[82] In turn, 'serious crimes' are defined in Article 2 (b) as 'conduct constituting an offence punishable by a maximum deprivation of liberty of at least four years or a more serious penalty.' While the UNTOC does not contain further specification of what constitute 'serious crimes', the preparatory works include a list of offences that could be considered as falling into this category. During the discussion of said list, a few delegations suggested including 'murder and other grave offences against the person' on it.[83] As disappearances committed by OCGs often overlap with murder or other serious violations of physical integrity rights, disappearances could be considered as 'serious' crimes. Moreover, while there is no standard penalty for disappearances, the ICPPED requires states to 'make the offence of enforced disappearance punishable by appropriate penalties which take into account its extreme seriousness.'[84] Accordingly, the requirement of a

[81] Article 25 (2) UNTOC.

[82] Article 2 (a) UNTOC defines 'organised criminal groups' as 'a structured group of three or more persons, existing for a period of time and acting in concert with the aim of committing one or more serious crimes or offences established in accordance with this Convention, in order to obtain, directly or indirectly, a financial or other material benefit.'

[83] United Nations Office on Drugs and Crime (2006) Travaux Préparatoires of the Negotiations for the Elaboration of the United Nations Convention against Transnational Organized Crime and the Protocols Thereto. General Assembly Res. 55/25, annex I, p. 33, note 41.

[84] See Article 7(1) International Convention for the Protection of All Persons from Enforced Disappearance 2006 (1726 UNTS 3) (ICPPED). Note however that, as explained in Chap. 2, Article 7 relates only to *enforced* disappearances and during the negotiations of the ICPPED there were no recorded discussions about the content of 'appropriate penalties'. However, in Mexico, for example,

penalty of at least four years included in the definition of 'serious crimes' would most likely be met. Given the gravity of the crime of disappearance, an argument can thus be made that it would fall within reach of the threshold of seriousness as required by UNTOC.

However, there are further limitations to the types of 'serious' crimes that can fall within the scope of the Convention. First, the crimes must be committed by an OCG 'in order to obtain, directly or indirectly, a financial or other material benefit'[85] and they must be 'transnational in nature.'[86] Can disappearing a member of a rival criminal group, or an own member who 'betrayed' the group, or a government official who refused to take a bribe, be considered 'a financial or other material benefit'? The definition of the specific purpose of the crimes was discussed at some length during the negotiations of the Convention and some delegations explicitly stated that murders committed by OCGs could be considered as indirectly contributing to the financial or other material benefit within the meaning of the article.[87] Following this line of argument, any crimes related to the operation of an OCG, including violent acts for the purpose of territorial control or ensuring discipline among group members, can be seen as indirectly linked to the ultimate purpose of the organisation to gain a financial or material benefit. This reasoning is also in line with scholarship on illicit markets and violence that indicates the strategic and selective use of violence for instrumental reasons related, among others, to market-control by drug-trafficking organisations.[88]

A final question to answer is whether disappearances could be considered *trans-national* crimes if they were perpetrated within the context of a single country. As cited above, Article 3 (2) UNTOC clearly establishes that a crime committed within a single state, by nationals of that state and against their co-nationals, cannot be considered transnational. Notwithstanding, where a crime is 'committed in one State but involves an organised criminal group that engages in criminal activities in more than one State',[89] it is also considered transnational. If an OCG launders money or otherwise operates in a different country, any of its crimes will thus fall within the

national legislation on disappearances (the General Law on Enforced Disappearance, Disappearance committed by Private Individuals and the National Search System) establishes the crimes of 'enforced disappearance' and 'disappearance committed by private individuals' with similarly severe penalties for both crimes. The crime of 'enforced disappearance' carries a penalty of 40 to 60 years in prison (Article 30) and the crime of 'disappearance committed by individuals' carries a penalty of 25 to 50 years (Article 34). See Ley General en Materia de Desaparición Forzada de Personas, Desaparición Cometida por Particulares y del Sistema Nacional de Búsqueda de Personas 2017 (DOF 17-11-2017). I discuss the Mexican context and legislation further in Chap. 5.

[85] Article 2(1) UNTOC.

[86] Article 3(1) ibid.

[87] United Nations Office on Drugs and Crime (2006) Travaux Préparatoires of the Negotiations for the Elaboration of the United Nations Convention against Transnational Organized Crime and the Protocols Thereto. General Assembly Res. 55/25, annex I, p. 12, note 16.

[88] See, for example, Andreas and Wallman (2009); Reuter (2009); Friman (2009); Snyder and Durán Martínez (2009).

[89] Article 3(2)(c) UNTOC.

scope of UNTOC. Considering the inherent difficulties of investigating cases of disappearances, especially if the victim was killed and the remains destroyed,[90] it may be difficult in practice to identify the perpetrators and, subsequently, demonstrate the transnational element of the crime. Nonetheless, as argued above, many OCGs can today be considered transnational. In that sense, a contextual analysis of disappearances in a particular region could indicate possible perpetrators, allowing an analysis of whether these groups have transnational ties. In the context of migration, the element of transnationality is most likely met in the majority of cases because groups of traffickers or smugglers would generally have transnational connections. Similarly, if criminal groups that participate in international trafficking of drugs or other goods are involved in the commission of disappearances, these would also be considered transnational, as would groups that are known to launder money outside of their country of origin or operation.

4.2 State Responsibility for Disappearances Committed by OCGs

As outlined in Chap. 3, two elements are crucial for the purpose of determining the responsibility of a state in accordance with the Articles on Responsibility of States for Internationally Wrongful Acts (ARSIWA):[91] attribution of conduct and the existence of a breach of an international obligation. Accordingly, this section first addresses the question of attribution of acts committed by OCGs, and second the question of breach, which then leads to the determination of state responsibility.

4.2.1 Attribution

The first question in relation to a state's responsibility for disappearances committed by OCGs is to establish whether such acts could be directly attributed to the state either based on the ARSIWA or on the IHRL criteria of authorisation, support or acquiescence.[92] One question that arises particularly in the case of OCGs is the extent to which connections between state officials and such groups through corruption could be a sufficiently strong link for direct attribution. Therefore, in this

[90] See Genovese and van der Wilt (2014), pp. 6–7.

[91] UNGA (2002) Articles on Responsibility of States for Internationally Wrongful Acts. UN Doc. A/RES/56/83 (ARSIWA).

[92] It must be noted that while this section examines the question of attribution in a general manner, whether or not acts of OCGs can be attributed to a state will always depend on the particular circumstances of each case. See Commentary on Article 8 ARSIWA. International Law Commission (ILC) (2001) Draft Articles on Responsibility of States for Internationally Wrongful Acts, with Commentaries. ILC Yearbook 2001, Vol.II, Part II, p. 48, para. 7.

section I first examine the extent to which acts committed by OCGs could be attributed to the state using the criteria established in the ARSIWA and the notion of acquiescence as defined by the CED in its Statement on Non-State Actors. Second, I assess how corruption can lead to direct attribution. The aim of this section is not to establish attribution criteria in the abstract, but rather to explore the questions that would need to be considered for attribution of acts by OCGs to a state, considering the characteristics of this non-state actor.

4.2.1.1 Attribution Based on the ARSIWA

The illegal nature of OCGs implies that any ties between the latter and authorities are generally not official or formalised in any way. This poses challenges for directly attributing the acts of such groups to a state, given the rather high standards for attribution established in the ARSIWA (see Chap. 3). For example, Articles 5 and 6 ARSIWA require formal empowerment of the non-state actor by the state to exercise governmental authority.[93] Articles 10 and 11 ARSIWA, which refer to the conduct of an insurrectional movement and the adoption of conduct as the state's own, respectively, are unlikely to be applicable. This is because it is questionable that OCGs, who exist for the purpose of obtaining 'a financial or other material benefit',[94] could be considered as insurrectional movements that would fall within the scope of Article 10 ARSIWA:[95] OCGs generally do not pursue political aims and often engage in violent confrontations with the state only to the extent that it serves their own economic purposes—for example through a policy change—, rather than with the aim of taking over the state.[96] Moreover, Article 11 ARSIWA, which covers 'conduct acknowledged and adopted by a state as its own', requires that the state '[identify] the conduct in question and [make] it its own'.[97] This, however, is unlikely to occur in relation to any acts committed by OCGs, including human rights violations, given that states officially make every effort to counter organised crime and address violence by criminal groups, and are legally bound to do so under UNTOC. Furthermore, states generally attempt to dissociate themselves both from criminal and human rights-violating conduct. Article 8 ARSIWA concerning 'conduct directed or controlled by a state' and Article 9 ARSIWA, concerning 'conduct carried out in the absence or default of the official authorities' may be relevant for attribution questions related to disappearances committed by OCGs. The other

---

[93] See Mackenzie-Gray Scott (2022), especially Chap. 2.

[94] Article 2(a) UNTOC.

[95] As I discuss below, Article 9 ARSIWA would be more suitable for situations where OCGs engage in activities that would normally be carried out by authorities.

[96] See, for example, Lessing (2015), pp. 1491–1492; Kalyvas (2015), p. 1520; Berti (2018).

[97] Commentary on Article 11 ARSIWA. ILC (2001) Draft Articles on Responsibility of States for Internationally Wrongful Acts, with Commentaries. ILC Yearbook 2001, Vol.II, Part II, p. 53, para. 6.

relevant article of the ARSIWA is Article 7, which refers to state agents acting *ultra vires*. This article is discussed separately (see below) because it does not actually concern the attribution of the conduct of a non-state actor to the state.

Attribution Based on Article 8 ARSIWA

Article 8 ARSIWA sets a rather high standard in that it requires a 'real link' between the non-state actor in question and the state.[98] This can result from an authorisation of the conduct of non-state actors who are employed as 'auxiliaries' to a state,[99] such as private military or security companies.[100] At the same time, where there is no official authorisation, the acts of non-state actors can be directly attributed to the state if they act 'under the direction or control' of the state.[101] While according to the International Court of Justice (ICJ) this standard requires that a state exercises 'effective control' over the acts of the non-state actor, and that such control must exist in relation to 'each operation in which the alleged violation occurred',[102] the wording of ARSIWA itself does not limit the attribution standard to 'effective' control and can therefore be read as allowing for a broader interpretation.[103] However, even if a more expansive interpretation were applied, for acts of OCGs to be attributable to a state in accordance with Article 8, in light of existing jurisprudence it would still have to be shown that these groups acted according to instructions of a particular state or carried out activities on its behalf. Although theoretically possible, it would likely be difficult to show that a criminal group carried out a particular human rights violation, including a disappearance, on orders of a state agent.[104] Possible examples of this might be criminal groups acting in collusion with state forces, which would still require evidence to show that the state agents involved gave the relevant instructions and not the other way around.[105] In this sense, even

[98] Commentary on Article 8 ARSIWA. Ibid., p. 47, para. 1. See also Chap. 3, Sect. 3.1.1.

[99] Ibid., para. 2.

[100] Crawford (2013), p. 115.

[101] See Article 8 ARSIWA.

[102] *Application of the Convention on the Prevention and Punishment of the Crime of Genocide (Bosnia and Herzegovina v Serbia and Montenegro)* [2007] ICJ Rep 43 (International Court of Justice), para. 400. This reasoning is based on the standard that the ICJ established in the *Nicaragua* case discussed in Chap. 3 (Sect. 3.1.1). See also the Commentary on Article 8 ARSIWA. ILC (2001) Draft Articles on Responsibility of States for Internationally Wrongful Acts, with Commentaries. ILC Yearbook 2001, Vol.II, Part II, p. 48, para 7.

[103] See Crawford (2013), pp. 156–157. This issue was particularly discussed in relation to the question of attribution of terrorist acts to states during the drafting of the ARSIWA. On the controversies around the 'effective control' standard, see also Mackenzie-Gray Scott (2022), pp. 74–81.

[104] On the difficulty of attributing acts or organised criminal groups to a state on the basis of the 'direction or control' standard, see also Decoeur (2018).

[105] This would then be attributable under Article 7, as discussed below.

situations of what Decœur terms 'state organised crime',[106] might not allow for the attribution of disappearances committed by OCGs if it cannot be shown that there was a direct link between a state's orders and the disappearances. It would however be possible to attribute the act on the basis of acquiescence in line with the CED's definition that includes 'connivance' between state and non-state actors, as discussed below.[107]

Attribution Based on Article 9 ARSIWA

Article 9 ARSIWA establishes that:

> The conduct of a person or group of persons shall be considered an act of a State under international law if the person or group of persons is in fact exercising elements of the governmental authority in the absence or default of the official authorities and in circumstances such as to call for the exercise of those elements of authority.[108]

The attribution of conduct committed 'in the absence or default of the official authorities' in accordance with Article 9 ARSIWA raises interesting questions in relation to OCGs. The article refers to exceptional situations in which 'a person of group of persons' carries out governmental functions without the explicit authorisation to do so.[109] Moreover, the functions engaged in must be 'called for'. Thus, Article 9 covers situations where there has been some form of 'collapse' of the state or loss of control over (parts of) its territory, and non-state actors have stepped in to provide necessary security to the population.[110] While there is very little ICJ case law dealing with Article 9[111] and it is therefore not clear what circumstances would trigger its applicability, it could be applicable—in theory—to situations where criminal organisations exercise certain control over particular areas and effectively engage in governmental functions in the face of state absence.

Recent examples of OCGs assuming certain state functions are OCGs and gangs in certain Latin American countries, including Brazil and El Salvador, who took it

[106] Decoeur defines 'state organised crime' as 'the use, by a public official in a position to shape or influence the actions of a state and acting in concert with a structured group, of the resources of the state to commit or facilitate the commission of acts criminalized in international law, in order to obtain a financial or other material benefit.' Decoeur (2018), p. 15. This criminological concept refers to a type of system criminality that is primarily aimed at obtaining a profit and involving high-level authorities (p. 6).

[107] See Committee on Enforced Disappearances (2023) Statement on non-State actors in the context of the International Convention for the Protection of All Persons from Enforced Disappearances. UN Doc. CED/C/10, para. 5 (c).

[108] Article 9 ARSIWA.

[109] See Commentary on Article 9 ARSIWA. ILC (2001) Draft Articles on Responsibility of States for Internationally Wrongful Acts, with Commentaries. ILC Yearbook 2001, Vol.II, Part II, p. 49, para. 1. See also Crawford (2013), pp. 166–170.

[110] Ibid., p. 169.

[111] Mackenzie-Gray Scott (2022), p. 68.

upon themselves to impose and enforce Covid-19 restrictions.[112] Further, in Colombia and Mexico, criminal organisations took advantage of the pandemic to provide support to poor communities by distributing food and medicine.[113] The question that arises in this regard is to what extent their exercise of authority can be deemed as 'called for', given the complexity of the contexts in which such groups may start exercising governmental functions.[114] Notably, the conduct that is attributable under Article 9 ARISWA must be directly related to the exercise of governmental authority,[115] which raises the question whether a disappearance committed by an OCG exercising such authority could be considered as attributable conduct. This would likely only be the case in a situation where an OCG assumed security functions and, in the exercise of these functions, committed a disappearance.

Attribution Based on Article 7 ARSIWA: Corruption

The issue of corruption by public officials is covered by Article 7 ARSIWA, which refers to so-called *ultra vires* acts, i.e. acts that are committed by an agent or organ of the state who '[acting] in that capacity, [...] exceeds its authority or contravenes instructions.'[116] Such acts are equally attributable to the state.[117] Corruption can fall within the scope of this article if, for example, a state official accepts a bribe.[118] The decisive criterion for attribution on the basis of Article 7 ARSIWA is that the official

[112] See Rivard Piché (2020); Hamid and Wouters (2021), pp. 2–3; International Crisis Group (2020), p. 10.

[113] See Tamayo Gomez (2020); International Crisis Group (2020), pp. 9–10.

[114] Cruz and others make the argument that macro-criminal networks operating at the highest level seek out legitimacy in the territory they operate in by providing goods or public services that would normally be provided for by the state. They list the criminal group 'La Familia Michoacana' as an example of such a network that engaged in community dispute resolutions and thereby superseded state institutions. Note, however, that such macro-criminal networks would involve state actors as well. See Cruz et al. (2024), pp. 17–20. On the complexities of relations between state and crime in the Mexican context, see also Le Cour Grandmaison's (2021) research on the Mexican state of Michoacán and the creation of self-defence groups. Initially created to counter the control exercised by criminal organisations, self-defence groups also allied with rival criminal groups. On the legal challenges surrounding the applicability of Article 9 ARSIWA, including the question of what 'governmental' means in this context, see Mackenzie-Gray Scott (2022), pp. 64–68.

[115] Commentary on Article 9 ARSIWA. ILC (2001) Draft Articles on Responsibility of States for Internationally Wrongful Acts, with Commentaries. ILC Yearbook 2001, Vol.II, Part II, p. 49, para. 3.

[116] See Article 7 ARSIWA.

[117] The Inter-American Court has similarly stated that '[i]t is a principle of international law that the State responds for the acts and omissions of its agents in their official capacity, even if they overstep the limits of their authority'. *Case of the Pueblo Bello Massacre v. Colombia*, para. 111.

[118] Commentary on Article 7 ARSIWA. ILC (2001) Draft Articles on Responsibility of States for Internationally Wrongful Acts, with Commentaries. ILC Yearbook 2001, Vol.II, Part II, p. 46, note 150.

acted 'in that capacity', which means that the official must have committed the act in the course of their official functions and not in a purely private capacity.[119] What is important to note is that it can be difficult to distinguish between 'official' and 'private' conduct, which means that this question must be assessed in light of the particular case.[120] However, in cases of corruption, if the latter is conceptualised as 'characterized by the abuse or misuse of the power entrusted, which may be public or private, that displaces the public interest for a private benefit (personal or for a third party)',[121] then by definition an official who engages in corruption is acting in his official functions (otherwise the act would not be considered corrupt). Following this line of reasoning, acts of authorities that are linked to corruption are attributable to the state. This is important for cases involving OCGs, given the close link between corruption and organised crime.[122] Nonetheless, what is being attributed in such cases is the act of the corrupt official, and not the act of the OCG itself. The following step of determining the existence of a breach of an obligation then raises complex questions about the causal connection between the corrupt act and the human rights violation that occurred. In view of the scarce scholarship and case law on this particular topic, it may be too difficult to establish this causal connection.[123] Rather, corruption may be a factor to establish acquiescence to a disappearance committed by an OCG, to which I turn next.

4.2.1.2 Attribution Based on Authorisation, Support or Acquiescence

The foregoing section has shown that it could, under certain —albeit very limited— circumstances, be possible to attribute disappearances committed by OCGs to a state on the basis of the general law on state responsibility. It is more likely, however, that such attribution would be made on the basis of the *lex specialis* criteria authorisation, support or acquiescence contained in the IHRL definitions of enforced disappearance. As mentioned above, in its Report on Enforced Disappearances in the Context of Migration, the WGEID considered how victims of human trafficking or smuggling can become victims of enforced disappearance through the acts and omissions of officials.[124] According to the WGEID, collusion and corruption can lead to officials turning a blind eye and a lack of sanctions for criminals, which implies

[119] Ibid., paras 7–8. Peters (2018), p. 1272ff; Crawford (2013), p. 137.

[120] See Commentary on Article 7 ARSIWA. ILC (2001) Draft Articles on Responsibility of States for Internationally Wrongful Acts, with Commentaries. ILC Yearbook 2001, Vol.II, Part II, p. 46, para. 8.

[121] IACHR (2019) Corruption and Human Rights in the Americas: Inter-American Standards. OEA/Ser.L/V/II., Doc. 236, para. 88.

[122] On the close link between corruption and organised crime, see ibid., paras 99–100.

[123] Peters (2024), p. 11; Guercke (2021), p. 356.

[124] Human Rights Council (2017) Report of the Working Group on Enforced or Involuntary Disappearances on Enforced Disappearances in the Context of Migration. UN Doc. A/HRC/36/39/Add.2, paras 36–37.

that the disappearances are committed 'with the implicit or explicit authorization, support or acquiescence of individuals operating in the capacity of State officials'.[125] Similarly, as discussed in Chap. 3 (Sect. 3.1.2.1), in the case of *Rantsev v Cyprus and Russia* the ECtHR found that Cypriot police officers had acquiesced in the deprivation of liberty of a trafficking victim by releasing her back into the hands of her trafficker.[126] Therefore, disappearances at the hands of OCGs that occur in a context of human trafficking or smuggling, can be directly attributed to the state through acquiescence in cases where there is direct contact between authorities and the traffickers, and the former's actions or omissions contribute to the victim's disappearance.

In its General Comment on Enforced Disappearances in the context of Migration, the CED also mentions collusion between state agents and criminal organisations, including trafficking groups, among the causes of migrant disappearances.[127] Moreover, in its definition of acquiescence adopted in 2023, the Committee included the state acting in 'connivance' with the perpetrators among the criteria for establishing acquiescence and explicitly listed 'persons involved in organized crime, in particular groups of smugglers or traffickers'[128] as one group of non-state actors to which the attribution criteria of Article 2 ICPPED could apply. The CED's view on the matter is also reflected in its report on the visit to Mexico, where the Committee found that 'persons involved in organized crime, with various forms of collusion and varying degrees of participation, acquiescence or omission by public officials, have become some of the main perpetrators of disappearances'.[129]

The challenge that arises with regard to acquiescence is establishing the necessary existence of risk and awareness that officials must have to be considered as 'acquiescing' to the disappearance. Examples provided in the WGEID Report on Enforced Disappearances in the Context of Migration to substantiate the argument that the involvement of corrupt officials can be considered as acquiescence are instances of collusion where authorities and traffickers or smugglers *directly* collaborated,[130]

[125] Ibid., para. 37. Gallagher similarly argues that in situations where officials turn a 'blind eye to suspicious movements' it would not be difficult to establish state responsibility. See Gallagher (2010), p. 226.

[126] *Rantsev v. Cyprus and Russia*, para. 321.

[127] Committee on Enforced Disappearances (2023) General Comment No. 1 on Enforced Disappearance in the Context of Migration. UN Doc. CED/C/GC/1, para. 6.

[128] Committee on Enforced Disappearances (2023) Statement on non-State actors in the context of the International Convention for the Protection of All Persons from Enforced Disappearances. UN Doc. CED/C/10, para. 8 (footnote omitted).

[129] Committee on Enforced Disappearances (2022) Report of the Committee on Enforced Disappearances on its visit to Mexico: Findings. UN Doc. CED/C/MEX/VR/1 (Findings), para. 13.

[130] See Human Rights Council (2017) Report of the Working Group on Enforced or Involuntary Disappearances on Enforced Disappearances in the Context of Migration. UN Doc. A/HRC/36/39/Add.2, paras 38–41.

implying direct knowledge of the crimes being committed. In the case of *Rantsev v Cyprus and Russia*, the necessary awareness of risk by authorities was determined on the basis of the 'context of the general living and working conditions of cabaret artistes'[131] in Cyprus at the time and the ECtHR's finding of acquiescence in the victim's deprivation of liberty was based on the authorities 'active cooperation' in the victim's deprivation of liberty, which meant that the latter would not have occurred if it had not been for the authorities' call to the victim's employer. Conversely, the ECtHR did not find that Cyprus was responsible for the victim's death, due to a lack of foreseeability.[132] Acquiescence thus appears to require not only a certain level of knowledge and foreseeability but also a direct (and causal) connection between the authorities and the trafficker. Following this logic, for acquiescence to arise, an official who turns a blind eye would have to be aware of the risk of a disappearance with regard to a specific individual and not just of a general risk.[133]

Conversely, the CED's definition of acquiescence included in the Statement on Non-State Actors, if read in a textual manner, does not contain the high threshold of awareness of risk regarding a specific individual. The definition requires foreseeability ('knew, had reasons to know, or ought to have known') and risk ('the commission of or [...] the real and imminent risk of commission'), in combination with four conditions (para. 5 a–d) that can be understood as establishing a causal link between the state and the non-state perpetrator. Notably, there is no explicit requirement for a *direct* causal link between the state's actions and/or omissions and the risk of a disappearance. Rather, the definition extends the possible situations in which a state could be considered as acquiescing to disappearances committed by OCGs. This is because in certain contexts it can be argued that a state has 'created the conditions' (para. 5 (d)) to allow for a disappearance by an OCG to occur (see below), has acted in 'connivance with the perpetrators' (para. 5 c) when there is direct collaboration between authorities and OCGs, has deliberately failed to take measures to prevent or respond to disappearances committed by OCGs (para. 5 (b)) or has explicitly or implicitly tolerated or accepted the situation (para. 5 (a)) by not reacting to reports of such disappearances. Alternatively, acquiescence arises in contexts of 'known patterns of disappearances' and state inaction (para. 6). Nowhere in the definition does it say that the state had to know of a risk to a specific individual of becoming a victim of a disappearance, which implies that the definition can be read as focusing on the source of risk rather than the victim.

Despite the focus on the state's connection to the risk, a main challenge that remains with regard to establishing acquiescence is that foreseeability must be established in relation to a risk of a *disappearance* rather than a general risk to life (or other human rights), which may not always be possible, especially in contexts where a disappearance overlaps with other crimes. Is awareness of risk of being a

---

[131] *Rantsev v. Cyprus and Russia,* para. 321.

[132] Ibid., paras 222–223.

[133] See Chap. 3, Sect. 3.1.2.1.

victim of human trafficking equal to awareness of risk of a disappearance? Does the latter have to be inferred from the context, for example if a state knew that particular trafficking networks do not let their victims communicate with their families and hide their whereabouts, thereby effectively disappearing them? Or that an OCG was known to engage in organ trafficking and killing victims (and hiding their bodies) after retrieving organs? In view of these persisting questions in relation to acquiescence, and the overlap between this assessment and the determination of responsibility for a failure to prevent, in the following section I focus on the determination of responsibility on the basis of a failure to prevent that, while involving similar reasoning, might fall short of reaching the threshold for acquiescence.

4.2.2 Responsibility for a Failure to Prevent Disappearances Committed by OCGs

As discussed in Chap. 3, there is a difference between the law on state responsibility and IHRL in relation to the establishment of state responsibility in that, under the former, a state incurs international responsibility for any breach of an international obligation that is attributable to it. Conversely, case law from human rights courts indicates that states can only be held responsible for a human rights violation if their acts and omissions are connected to the particular case before the tribunal and a specific victim or group of victims. To establish such responsibility, the state must have been aware of a risk or commission of a human rights-violating act and failed to act with due diligence to prevent or respond to it. As with acquiescence, responsibility for a failure to act with due diligence is conditioned on awareness of risk and a causal link between the state's omissions and the violation. Establishing awareness of risk is straightforward once a person has been disappeared and the disappearance has been reported, yet it is more complicated with regard to the initial deprivation of liberty of the victim.

Consequently, in this section I examine which of the approaches to determining responsibility on the basis of a failure to prevent outlined in Chap. 3[134] (*victim-based* or *source-based*) would be more appropriate in cases where OCGs perpetrate disappearances. Firstly, it is important to consider that an assessment of state responsibility in cases where any non-state actors are involved, always must be conducted in light of the circumstances of a particular case, as it is neither possible, nor desirable, to envisage all the different scenarios in which a state could be responsible for an act committed by a non-state actor.[135] This means that there

[134] Section 3.2.1.

[135] The Inter-American Court has stated this quite bluntly: 'Moreover, the attribution of international responsibility to a State owing to the acts of State agents or individuals must be determined on the basis of the characteristics and circumstances of each case, [...] and also on the corresponding special obligations of prevention and protection that are applicable. Although this attribution is

cannot be a single approach to dealing with all cases of disappearances committed by OCGs. Moreover, given the different ways in which acts by OCGs can lead to disappearances (such as human trafficking and other forms of forced labour, smuggling, killings), a single approach might not capture the nuances of each 'mode' of disappearance. Finally, OCGs vary greatly in terms of size, composition, organisational structure, mode of operation, among others,[136] which could also impact the assessment of state responsibility. Mindful of these limitations, I have argued elsewhere that a source-based approach would be most appropriate to determine state responsibility for a failure to prevent violations of the right to life committed by OCGs for two reasons: first, the shortcomings of the victim-based approach in contexts where there is a general identifiable risk; second, the reality that in many cases the state could be considered to have contributed to the creation of such risk.[137]

4.2.2.1 Shortcomings of the Victim-Based Approach

As outlined in the previous chapter, a victim-based approach to determining state responsibility for a failure to prevent implies that a state cannot be held responsible for the victim's initial deprivation of liberty, unless the victim had previously received and reported threats to the authorities. This is the case even if there is a context of private violence of which the state is aware. For example, in *Rantsev v Cyprus and Russia*, although the ECtHR found that Cypriot authorities had acquiesced in the victim's deprivation of liberty, it also found that Cyprus was *not* responsible for violating the victim's right to *life* because the Cypriot authorities could not have foreseen the victim's death when they released her back into the hands of her trafficker (see above).[138] The ECtHR explained its reasoning as follows:

> Although it is undisputed that victims of trafficking and exploitation are often forced to live and work in cruel conditions and may suffer violence and ill-treatment at the hands of their employers [...], *in the absence of any specific indications in a particular case, the general risk of ill-treatment and violence cannot constitute a real and immediate risk to life.*[139]

---

made on the basis of international law, the many different forms and characteristics that the facts may assume in situations that violate human rights makes it almost illusory to expect international law to define specifically – or rigorously or numerus clausus – all the hypotheses or situations – or structures – for attributing to the State each of the possible and eventual acts or omissions of State agents or individuals.' *Case of the Pueblo Bello Massacre v. Colombia*, para. 116.

[136] For an overview of different types of criminal organisations, see different chapters in Paoli (2014). See also Berti (2018).

[137] See Guercke (2021), pp. 353–356.

[138] See *Rantsev v. Cyprus and Russia,* paras 220–223.

[139] Ibid., para. 222. Emphasis added.

As a result, even though the authorities should have been aware of the possibility that the victim was a victim of trafficking, the ECtHR did not find that they should have equally been aware of a risk to her life and thus found no violation of the victim's right to life under the substantive limb of Article 2 ECHR.[140] Conversely, the Cypriot state was found to be responsible for failing to protect the victim from human trafficking, based on the insufficient guarantees of the regulatory framework in place (particularly in relation to visas for so-called 'artistes')[141] and the failure of authorities to verify whether the victim could have been a victim of human trafficking when she was at a police station, despite their awareness of an immediate risk of sexual exploitation.[142] The ECtHR did not find that Russia had violated its substantive obligations under Article 4 ECHR, because there was 'only' a general risk that women travelling on a particular type of visa to Cyprus might be victims of trafficking and Russia had taken general measures to warn about trafficking through the media.[143] Rather, Russia was found to have violated the procedural limb of Article 4 ECHR by failing to carry out an effective investigation into the part of the trafficking network that was based within its jurisdiction, as well as its recruitment mechanisms.[144] The ECtHR's reasoning in *Rantsev v Cyprus and Russia* thus illustrates a victim-based approach in so far that the European Court held that a 'general risk' was not enough to trigger more specific preventive obligations. Moreover, the direct contact between authorities and the victim played a crucial role in the ECtHR's reasoning, which suggests that if the victim had not been brought to the police station prior to her deprivation of liberty and death, the ECtHR might not have found Cyprus responsible for any substantive violations of her rights on the basis of a failure to take preventive measures.[145]

The approach by the ECtHR in *Rantsev v Cyprus and Russia* thus highlights one of the biggest shortcomings of the victim-based approach, which is its failure to account for more general risks. The reasoning behind the victim-based approach may be appropriate in isolated cases such as that of *Osman v UK* from which it

---

[140] Interestingly, the ECtHR found that there was no violation of Article 2 even though the Cypriot government, after initially rejecting the arguments by the applicants, had made a unilateral declaration in which it acknowledged that the decision by the police officers to release the victim back into the hands of her trafficker constituted a failure to comply with the positive obligation to take preventive measures arising from Article 2. See ibid., para. 187(a).

[141] Ibid., paras 290–293.

[142] Ibid., paras 295–298.

[143] Ibid., para. 305: 'It is insufficient, in order for an obligation to take urgent operational measures to arise, merely to show that there was a general risk in respect of young women travelling to Cyprus on artistes' visa. Insofar as this general risk was concerned, the Court recalls that the Russian authorities took steps to warn citizens of trafficking risks.'

[144] Ibid., paras 307–309.

[145] Note, however, that the ECtHR also found a substantive violation of Article 4 on the basis of a lack of a sufficiently protective legal framework in Cyprus (see ibid., paras 290–293). This approach is in line with the argument made by Monnheimer that certain positive obligations, including the requirement to adopt legislation, are obligations of result. See Monnheimer (2021), p. 56 ff.

originated, which dealt with a rather unique case of one schoolteacher's obsession with a pupil (see Chap. 3, Sect. 3.2.1.1). Following the reasoning of both the ECtHR and IACtHR that specific obligations to prevent should not impose a disproportionate or impossible burden on the state, the victim-based approach is appropriate in such isolated cases, including in a potential case where members of an OCG, that generally conducts its business without much violence, exceptionally abducted or killed a person and hid their whereabouts. However, where there exists an identifiable general risk, or what Ebert and Sijniensky term 'structural risks', such as persistent high levels of criminal violence, the victim-based approach falls short of capturing the full extent of the problem and the violation.[146] The failure of the victim-based approach to consider structural factors is problematic for two reasons: first, if a state is cannot be held responsible for its 'failure [...] to comply in general with its obligation of prevention' as reasoned by the IACtHR in the *Cotton Field* case,[147] or if a 'general risk of ill-treatment and violence' is insufficient to 'trigger' the obligation of states to take more specific measures to prevent violence by private actors, as suggested by the ECtHR in *Rantsev v Cyprus and Russia*, then, even though the state was aware of such a general situation of risk and failed to take preventive measures, it cannot be held responsible for this by a human rights court.[148] The impossibility of holding a state accountable for a general failure, however, contradicts the basic idea of IHRL and human rights courts as avenues for holding states accountable for failure to protect human rights within their jurisdiction, including from violations by private actors.[149] Moreover, and beyond IHRL, if 'obligations' and 'responsibility' in law are understood in a positivist manner as inherently linked to the possibility of incurring sanctions in cases of non-adherence to obligations,[150] the very existence of the legal obligation to take general preventive measures could be questioned.[151]

Second, applying the reasoning of the victim-based approach to situations of disappearances committed by OCGs specifically, the responsibility of the state is reduced to the period *after* the initial disappearance has been reported. This, however, overlooks the potential involvement of the state in the creation of risk in the first place, for example by not addressing structural issues that enable or facilitate the commission of human rights violations at the hands of non-state actors.[152] Abramovich makes this criticism in relation to the *Cotton Field* case. He points

---

[146] See Ebert and Sijniensky (2015). On the issue of risk creation, see especially pp. 356–357.

[147] *Case of González et al ("Cotton Field") v Mexico* [2009] Inter-American Court of Human Rights Serie C No. 205, para. 282.

[148] This is so even though, as shown in Chap. 3, from the perspective of the law on state responsibility, the state would be internationally responsible for having breached its general obligation to protect. See Guercke (2021), pp. 351–2.

[149] Ibid., p. 351.

[150] See Glanville (2011), p. 488.

[151] Ebert and Sijniensky (2015), p. 364; Guercke (2021), p. 351.

[152] Guercke (2021), p. 351. A similar argument has been made by Reyes in relation to state failure to counter corruption. See Reyes (2019).

out that in this case the disappearance of the victims prior to the discovery of the bodies made it possible to hold the state responsible for the failure to prevent a violation of the victims' right to life. However, if they had 'merely' been murdered and found immediately, the state would not have been held responsible for a violation of the victims' right to life because it did not have the necessary awareness of risk. The Mexican state's general failure to end widespread violence against women would not have been sufficient to establish responsibility for a failure to prevent. This, according to Abramovich, is problematic because it is clear that the state's actions and omissions contributed to the climate of generalised violence.[153] This criticism of the victim-based approach, which continues to be the dominant approach used by the IACtHR, was also voiced by Judge Ferrer Mac-Gregor Poisot in his Separate Opinion in the case of *Velásquez Paiz and Others v Guatemala*. In this case, the IACtHR conducted an analysis of the Guatemalan state's actions and omissions during two moments, prior to the victim's disappearance and once her disappearance had been reported, using the same approach as in the *Cotton Field* judgement. While the Court did find that the measures taken by Guatemala to address the general situation of violence against women in the country was 'insufficient',[154] it only established the state's responsibility for its failure to act with due diligence once the disappearance had been reported.[155] Judge Ferrer Mac-Gregor Poisot argued that it was a mistake that the Inter-American Court did not establish responsibility for the Guatemalan state's general failure to take preventive measures to protect women in the country, because this general failure was ultimately the cause of the failure to act with due diligence in the particular case.[156] Thus, Judge Ferrer Mac-Gregor Poisot argued that the IACtHR should have established Guatemala's responsibility also on the basis of the 'first moment' prior to the victim's disappearance.[157]

A state's failure to prevent a general risk to society can create the conditions for private acts of violence to be perpetrated and therefore affects society in its entirety.[158] For example, persistent impunity has been considered as encouragement for the perpetuation of violence committed by non-state actors (see Chap. 3, Sect. 3.1.2.1), and could now even give rise to acquiescence in line with the CED's Statement on Non-State Actors. According to IHRL, the state's primordial function vis-à-vis those within its jurisdiction is the protection of their human rights, especially the right to life as the most fundamental right. A consistent failure to take general measures to address structural issues would make it illusory to provide protection in individual cases, thereby questioning the fundamental function of the

---

[153] Abramovich (2010), p. 181.

[154] *Case of Velásquez Paiz and Others v Guatemala* [2015] Inter-American Court of Human Rights Series C No 307, para. 120.

[155] Ibid., paras 133–134.

[156] Ibid., Separate Opinion of Judge Eduardo Ferrer Mac-Gregor Poisot, paras 54–57.

[157] Ibid., para. 57.

[158] Guercke (2021), p. 352.

state.[159] Beyond this theoretical challenge, in a more 'practical' sense, not holding a state responsible for a general failure to prevent means that this failure cannot be taken into consideration for the determination of reparations, including guarantees of non-repetition: as a general principle of international law, states must provide reparations for the 'injury *caused by the internationally unlawful act*.'[160] Therefore, if a general failure to comply with the obligation to protect is not considered as a violation of the state's human rights obligations, strictly speaking it does not have to be remedied. Especially in cases of disappearances, where the necessary risk in victim-based approaches is generally only established once the initial disappearance occurred and has been reported (unless the victim received and reported threats prior to the disappearance), reparation measures will be limited to the state's failure to search for the victim and investigate the disappearance, not its failure to prevent the initial disappearance.[161]

These general criticisms of the victim-based approach in situations involving structural issues equally apply to contexts where OCGs are among the direct perpetrators of disappearances. Moreover, when it comes to OCGs specifically, such an approach would omit taking into consideration how the state's actions and omissions may have enabled these groups to commit violations.[162] If the state's main role is to protect the right to life of individuals within its jurisdiction, then its actions and omissions in relation to the existence of a particular non-state actor whose activities can pose a threat to this right should be considered for the purpose of assigning responsibility. As I have argued elsewhere, a failure to do so would create the legal fiction that non-state actors operate independently of state actions, which is an over-simplification that can lead to states' evading accountability.[163] A source-based approach is therefore more appropriate in cases involving OCGs, given that where the latter are known to engage in certain activities that risk the disappearance of persons, the state could reasonably be expected to take measures against this source of risk. This would be similar to source-based approaches described in Chap. 3 that involved environmental disasters or industrial accidents, and where the ECtHR and IACtHR assessed whether states, once aware of a potential source of risk and a specific group of victims, had taken precautionary measures (Sect. 3.2.1.3). Moreover, the existence of UNTOC and UNCAC as *lex specialis* to the obligations of states vis-à-vis acts committed by OCGs, further strengthens the

---

[159] See Hakimi (2010), p. 347; Glanville (2011), p. 487; Guercke (2021), p. 352.

[160] Article 31(1) ARSIWA. Emphasis added.

[161] *Case of González et al ("Cotton Field") v Mexico*, para. 463: 'The three gender-based murders in this case took place in a context of discrimination and violence against women. It does not correspond to the Tribunal to attribute responsibility to the State merely for the context; however, it cannot refrain from noting the extreme importance that the rectification of this situation signifies for the general measures of prevention that the State must adopt so that women and girls in Mexico can enjoy their human rights, *and it invites the State to consider this*.' Emphasis added. See also Guercke (2021), p. 352.

[162] See also Guercke (2021), p. 357.

[163] Ibid., p. 355.

argument for a source-based approach because states have clear obligations to take measures against this specific non-state actor.[164]

4.2.2.2 State Contribution to Risk

The second reason in favour of a source-based approach to disappearances committed by OCGs is the relationship between state agents and criminal groups and the subsequent involvement of the state in the creation of risk, which, as mentioned above, is generally not considered as decisive in victim-based approaches. The relationship matters, however, both for the purpose of attribution,[165] for example through acquiescence, as well as for assessing the capacity of the state to prevent the risk posed by a non-state actor.[166] For example, in the case of *Pueblo Bello*, the IACtHR considered the Colombian state's role in the creation of the risk posed by paramilitary groups as a factor that 'accentuated' the protection and prevention obligations of the state in relation to the risk emanating from these groups.[167] Based on the particular context, a similar approach could be envisaged for situations in which OCGs commit serious crimes without any consequences, for example because of widespread corruption. While in the Colombian case the state had actually allowed the creation of self-defence groups by law,[168] the toleration of corruption and ties between high-level government officials and OCGs could equally be seen as a risk-creating factor because it fosters impunity.[169] In this way, authorities may not officially—or legally—back criminal groups, yet corrupt links between the two actors imply that the latter are also not entirely independent actors or antagonistic.[170] While the type of ties between authorities and specific OCGs will vary from case to case, it is important to consider that, generally speaking, OCGs require certain connections to the state in order to function. Indeed, scholars of organised crime have pointed out that OCGs require a 'structural link to public and private authorities'[171] and that there exists an inevitable 'ontological association' between organised crime and the state because connections with the state are vital for

---

[164] Ibid., pp. 355–356.

[165] See Commentary on Article 8 ARSIWA. ILC (2001) Draft Articles on Responsibility of States for Internationally Wrongful Acts, with Commentaries. ILC Yearbook 2001, Vol.II, Part II, pp. 47–48.

[166] See *Genocide Case*, para. 430. For an in-depth discussion on how capacity to influence may trigger obligations to protect, see Hakimi (2014).

[167] *Case of the Pueblo Bello Massacre v. Colombia*, para. 126.

[168] See ibid., para. 95(1)-(3).

[169] For a similar argument, see Reyes (2019), p. 334.

[170] On the relationship between state and crime, see, for example, Decoeur (2018); Godson (2003). See also Chaps. 5–7 on the Mexican context.

[171] Author's translation. Olásolo Alonso and Galain Palermo (2018), p. 151. Olásolo and Galain further argue that, rather than taking advantage of legal loopholes, OCGs conduct their illicit transactions on the basis of relationships with authorities and jurisdictions.

crime to be considered 'organised'.[172] In that sense, a state's failure to curb state-crime relations, for example through countering corruption, impacts the power and capacity of OCGs to operate and, potentially, violate human rights.[173]

Furthermore, the manner in which a state approaches OCGs can also be of relevance for the level of violence exercised by such groups. Thus, where disappearances are not the result of the crime itself, as is the case in human trafficking, but for example caused by abandonment by smugglers or killings, state anti-crime policies may have contributed to these actions.[174] Additionally, scholarship on organised crime and illicit markets and violence more generally, has shown that OCGs, or illicit activities are not inherently violent,[175] but that violence is a means of settling disputes in illicit markets that lack access to legal means of conflict resolution.[176] Consequently, in addition to the awareness by a state of the risk posed by OCGs to the enjoyment of human rights, the state's actions or inactions in countering OCGs' activities could also be viewed as potentially contributing to the risk emanating from such groups.[177] Considering a state's contribution to risk is particularly relevant in light of the CED's definition of acquiescence, which contains the state's role in '[creating] the conditions that allowed [for the commission of a disappearance by a non-state actor]'[178] as one of the criteria for establishing acquiescence in instances of a foreseeable risk of the commission of a disappearance. While still subject to an analysis of foreseeability, in situations where an identified—or identifiable—OCG was involved in the commission of disappearances, it could be argued that a state created the conditions for this to occur if it failed to take effective measures against the group itself or against corruption as an enabling element. Such an approach could then lead to the state's responsibility for failing to act with due diligence to prevent a disappearance by countering the source of risk, or, if there was

[172] See Trejo and Ley (2020), p. 31. While this definition of organised crime differs significantly from the UNTOC definition, the argument is nonetheless worthy of consideration as it illustrates the connection between the state and organised crime more generally.

[173] See Guercke (2021), p. 354.

[174] See Committee on Enforced Disappearances (2023) General Comment No. 1 on Enforced Disappearance in the Context of Migration. UN Doc. CED/C/GC/1, paras 3, 7, and 27. See also Human Rights Council (2017) Report of the Working Group on Enforced or Involuntary Disappearances on Enforced Disappearances in the Context of Migration. UN Doc. A/HRC/36/39/Add.2, para. 36; UNGA (2017) Report of the Special Rapporteur of the Human Rights Council on Extrajudicial, Summary or Arbitrary Executions: Unlawful Death of Refugees and Migrants. UN Doc. A/72/335, paras 9–10.

[175] With the exception of those illicit activities that always entail some form of violence because the victims are human beings, such as human or organ trafficking.

[176] See sources cited in note 88 above. Trejo and Ley argue that uncertainty about the relations to state officials is a reason for increased violence by OCGs. See Trejo and Ley (2020), p. 59.

[177] This is particularly evident in the Mexican context, which I discuss further in the next chapter.

[178] Committee on Enforced Disappearances (2023) Statement on non-State actors in the context of the International Convention for the Protection of All Persons from Enforced Disappearances. UN Doc. CED/C/10, para. 5 (d).

sufficient foreseeability of a risk of a *disappearance* specifically, for an enforced disappearance on the basis of acquiescence.

4.2.2.3 The Question of Causation

The principal question in relation to determining responsibility on the basis of state contribution to risk in cases where OCGs are the direct perpetrators of crimes is that of causation. How does a state's failure to curb the activities of an OCG causally connect to the disappearance of a person? Causation and foreseeability of harm have received some attention in scholarship on state responsibility,[179] but very little in human rights scholarship or jurisprudence.[180] What, for example, is the link between an attributable corrupt act and a disappearance committed by an OCG that does not involve human trafficking? In cases involving victims of disappearances who were trafficked or smuggled and, during this process, crossed borders or were detained by immigration officials, the link between the actions and omissions of officials and the crimes committed is relatively straightforward (see above).[181] Yet, in other cases where OCGs commit disappearances as part of a terrorising strategy or in order to hide dead bodies, the connection between the authorities' acts and omissions and the crimes committed by OCGs is much weaker. Nonetheless, in view of the close links between organised crime and corruption, there often exists a connection between officials and OCGs. Peters argues that, based on the notion of causation in the ARSIWA, which is elaborated in Article 31 ARSIWA,[182] to establish cause in law between a corrupt act and a human rights violation, the latter has to be 'foreseeable and not too far removed from the corrupt public officials.'[183] Therefore, the creation of a permissive environment for the commission of crimes that infringe physical integrity rights through corruption, may be too remote from the specific act of violence.[184] However, if such crimes are committed in a regular manner by

[179] In particular in relation to shared responsibility as well as liability for lawful acts. See, for example: Stapleton (2001); Castellanos-Jankiewicz (2012); Murmann (2014); Gattini (2014); Plakokefalos (2015).

[180] The question of causation has received some attention in discussions of corruption and human rights violations. See, for example, Peters (2024), pp. 10–13; Peters (2019); Sepúlveda Carmona and Bacio-Terracino (2010), p. 25. See also Guercke (2021).

[181] However, even in these cases, it could be argued that the officials might have been complicit in the trafficking of victims, but not in their subsequent disappearance.

[182] Article 31 ARSIWA deals with reparations and establishes that:

1. The responsible State is under an obligation to make full reparation for the injury caused by the internationally wrongful act.
2. Injury includes any damage, whether material or moral, caused by the internationally wrongful act of a State.

[183] Peters (2018), p. 1268.

[184] Nonetheless, given that the obligation to prevent is a due diligence obligation, this does not necessarily present an obstacle, in view of the fact that a due diligence obligation can be breached even if the act did not occur. See Crawford (2013), p. 227.

identifiable OCGs, and there continue to exist links between the latter and corrupt officials, the causal link could be stronger and could now fall within the definition of acquiescence adopted by the CED if it can be established that there was a 'known pattern', or the state can be shown to be aware of the risk yet turning a blind eye (see above). Neither the European, nor the Inter-American courts have elaborated their causal analyses in detail in case law where source-based approaches were used, or engaged with questions of remoteness. However, it appears that, in such cases, a state's awareness of a particular source of risk and failure to take measures against it, would be sufficient to establish a causal link between the state's failure and the violation for the purpose of establishing responsibility. Further research is required to explore in more detail how the notions of foreseeability and proximity have been and should be applied in such cases.

4.3 Conclusion: Chapter 4

In situations where a particular non-state actor, or that actor's activities, pose a risk to the rights of individuals, states' preventive obligations can encompass measures to mediate this risk 'at the source' by constraining either the actor's activities, or the actor itself. Where the non-state actor is a legal entity, such as a business, this can be done through the regulation of activities. Yet, where the non-state actor is by definition illegal, as are OCGs, states must take measures to restrain the actor itself and counter its activities. In the case of OCGs, two aspects are important to consider for the purpose of determining state responsibility: first, the existence of an international legal framework which has the specific aim of preventing and fighting organised crime and corruption, which can provide guidance for the types of measures which states should take to address specific organised criminal activities that can lead to disappearances, such as human trafficking or smuggling, or OCGs themselves as a 'source' of risk. Second, the nature of the relationship between criminal organisations and the state, which is often not as antagonistic as it is portrayed. Using international crime suppression instruments, such as UNTOC, its Protocols, and UNCAC, as *lex specialis* to define the content of states' prevention obligations in relation to disappearances—and other atrocities—committed by organised crime, would broaden the spectrum of measures a state can reasonably be expected to take as part of its efforts to prevent human rights violations by OCGs.

Moreover, in view of the CED's definition of acquiescence, a state's failure to take such measures could be understood as contributing to creating the conditions in which OCGs can perpetrate disappearances, possibly leading to direct attribution of these crimes to the state. This widens the cases in which a state could be considered as acquiescing to disappearances committed by OCGs beyond those involving officials turning a blind eye to allow border crossings by human traffickers or smugglers, or situations where state authorities collaborate in some other direct manner with OCGs. The most challenging scenarios are those where officials and OCGs are connected through corruption but not in direct contact with the perpetrators at the time the violation occurs. The challenges with regard to directly attributing a disappearance through acquiescence, or establishing responsibility for a failure to prevent, centre around the foreseeability of risk and the causal link between a state's actions or omissions and the disappearance, even if the analysis focuses on OCGs as the source of risk. This is particularly challenging in relation to corruption: corrupt acts can always be attributed to the state because, by definition, corruption involves public officials, and it can therefore be argued that the latter are exercising their official functions when accepting a bribe. Nevertheless, the corrupt act might not be sufficiently causally connected to the disappearance of a victim. Further research is needed on these thresholds and to what extent corrupt ties between state actors the criminal organisations can be considered as 'contribution to risk' for the purpose of establishing responsibility for a disappearance.

References

Abramovich V (2010) Responsabilidad estatal por violencia de género: comentarios sobre el caso "Campo Algodonero" en la Corte Interamericana de Derechos Humanos. Anuario de Derechos Humanos 6:167–182

Andreas P, Wallman J (2009) Illicit markets and violence: what is the relationship? Crime Law Soc Change 52:225–229. https://doi.org/10.1007/s10611-009-9200-6

Baranowska G (2020) Disappeared migrants and refugees: the relevance of the International Convention on Enforced Disappearance in their search and protection. German Institute for Human Rights. https://www.institut-fuer-menschenrechte.de/fileadmin/Redaktion/Publikationen/Analyse_Studie/Analysis_Disappeared_Migrans_and_Refugees.pdf. Accessed 30 Oct 2024

Barooah R et al (2024) 'We just want to find our children': understanding disappearances as a tool of organized crime. Global Initiative Against Transnational Organised Crime. https://globalinitiative.net/analysis/disappearances-we-just-want-to-find-our-children/. Accessed 30 Oct 2024

Berti B (2018) Violent and criminal non-state actors. In: Draude A, Börzel TA, Risse T (eds) The Oxford handbook of governance and limited statehood. Oxford University Press, Oxford, UK, pp 272–290

Boersma M, Nelen JM, Rights UMC for H (2010) Corruption & human rights: interdisciplinary perspectives. Intersentia, Antwerp; Portland, OR

Boister N (2002) Human rights protections in the suppression conventions. Hum Rights Law Rev 2: 199–227. https://doi.org/10.1093/hrlr/2.2.199

Budiani-Saberi D, Columb S (2013) A human rights approach to human trafficking for organ removal. Med Health Care Philos 16:897–914. https://doi.org/10.1007/s11019-013-9488-y

Castellanos-Jankiewicz L (2012) Causation and international state responsibility. Amsterdam Law School Research Paper No. 2012-56

Crawford J (2013) State responsibility: the general part. Cambridge University Press, Cambridge

Cruz A, Enríquez JE, Guadarrama A, Niño JJ (2024) Redes de macrocriminalidad, desaparición de personas y construcción de paz: un estudio sobre el Estado de México. Heinrich Böll Stiftung, Mexico City

Decoeur H (2018) Confronting the shadow state: an international law perspective on state organized crime. Oxford University Press, Oxford, New York

Duhaime B, Thibault A (2017) Protection of migrants from enforced disappearance: a human rights perspective. Int Rev Red Cross 99:569–587. https://doi.org/10.1017/S1816383118000097

Ebert FC, Sijniensky RI (2015) Preventing violations of the right to life in the European and the Inter-American Human Rights Systems: from the Osman test to a coherent doctrine on risk prevention? Hum Rights Law Rev 15:343–368. https://doi.org/10.1093/hrlr/ngv001
European Parliamentary Research Service (2022) Understanding the EU response to organised crime. https://www.europarl.europa.eu/thinktank/en/document/EPRS_BRI(2020)652043. Accessed 30 Oct 2024
Fijnaut C, Paoli L (2008) Transnational organized crime. Max Planck Encyclopedia of Public International Law
Fortify Rights and SUHAKAM (Human Rights Commission of Malaysia) (2019) Sold like Fish': crimes against humanity, mass graves, and human trafficking from Myanmar and Bangladesh to Malaysia from 2012 to 2015. https://www.fortifyrights.org/reg-inv-rep-2019-03-27/. Accessed 30 Oct 2024
Friman HR (2009) Drug markets and the selective use of violence. Crime Law Soc Change 52:285–295. https://doi.org/10.1007/s10611-009-9202-4
Gallagher A (2001) Human rights and the new UN Protocols on trafficking and migrant smuggling: a preliminary analysis. Hum Rights Q 23:975–1004
Gallagher AT (2010) The international law of human trafficking. Cambridge University Press, Cambridge UK; New York
Gattini A (2014) Breach of international obligations. In: Nollkaemper A, Plakokefalos I (eds) Principles of shared responsibility in international law: an appraisal of the state of the art. Cambridge University Press, Cambridge, pp 25–59
Genovese C, van der Wilt HG (2014) Fighting impunity of enforced disappearances through a regional model. Amsterdam Law Forum 6:4–22
Glanville L (2011) On the meaning of 'responsibility' in the 'responsibility to protect'. Griffith Law Rev 20:482–504
Global Initiative Against Transnational Organized Crime (2020) Disappearances through organized crime. https://resiliencefund.globalinitiative.net/wp-content/uploads/2020/09/disappearances_OC_infographic.pdf. Accessed 30 Oct 2024
Global Initiative Against Transnational Organized Crime (2023) Global organized crime index: global overview and results. https://ocindex.net/report/2023/03-global-overview-results.html. Accessed 30 Aug 2024
Godson R (ed) (2003) Menace to society: political-criminal collaboration around the world. Transaction Publishers, New Brunswick
Guercke L (2021) State responsibility for a failure to prevent violations of the right to life by organised criminal groups: disappearances in Mexico. Hum Rights Law Rev 21:329–357. https://doi.org/10.1093/hrlr/ngaa061
Hakimi M (2010) State bystander responsibility. Eur J Int Law 21:341–385. https://doi.org/10.1093/ejil/chq037
Hakimi M (2014) Toward a legal theory on the responsibility to protect. Yale J Int Law 39:247–280
Hamid L, Wouters J (2021) Rule of law and areas of limited statehood: introduction and perspective. In: Hamid L, Wouters J (eds) Rule of law and areas of limited statehood: domestic and international dimensions. Edward Elgar Publishing, Cheltenham, pp 2–22
Hauck P, Peterke S (eds) (2016) International law and transnational organised crime. Oxford University Press, Oxford, New York
International Crisis Group (2020) Virus-proof violence: crime and Covid-19 in Mexico and the Northern Triangle. Report No. 83. https://www.crisisgroup.org/latin-america-caribbean/83-virus-proof-violence-crime-and-covid-19-mexico-and-northern-triangle. Accessed 30 Oct 2024
Kalyvas SN (2015) How civil wars help explain organized crime—and how they do not. J Confl Resolut 59:1517–1540. https://doi.org/10.1177/0022002715587101
Kemp W (2024) Time for a global strategy against organized crime. Global Initiative Against Transnational Organized Crime. https://globalinitiative.net/analysis/global-strategy-against-organized-crime/. Accessed 30 Oct 2024

Le Cour Grandmaison R (2021) Order, sovereignty, and violence in Mexico. Mexico Violence Resource Project. https://www.mexicoviolence.org/post/order-sovereignty-and-violence-in-mexico. Accessed 30 Oct 2024

Lessing B (2015) Logics of violence in criminal war. J Confl Resolut 59:1486–1516. https://doi.org/10.1177/0022002715587100

Mackenzie-Gray Scott R (2022) State responsibility for non-state actors: past, present and prospects for the future. Hart Publishing, Bloomsbury Publishing Plc, Oxford, UK

Meshelemiah JCA, Lynch RE (2019) The cause and consequence of human trafficking: human rights violations. The Ohio State University Pressbook, Ohio

Monnheimer M (2021) Due diligence obligations in international human rights law. Cambridge University Press, Cambridge

Murmann U (2014) Problems of causation with regard to (potential) actions of multiple protagonists. J Int Crim Justice 12:283–294. https://doi.org/10.1093/jicj/mqu018

Nash Rojas C, Aguiló Bascuñán P, Bascur Campos ML (2014) Corrupción y Derechos Humanos: Una mirada desde la Jurisprudencia de la Corte Interamericana de Derechos Humanos. Centro de Derechos Humanos, Facultad de Derecho Universidad de Chile, Chile

Noortmann M, Sedman D (2016) Transnational criminal organisations and human rights. In: Hauck P, Peterke S (eds) International law and transnational organised crime. Oxford University Press, Oxford, New York, pp 406–421

Obokata T (2005) Smuggling of human beings from a human rights perspective: obligations of non-state and state actors under International Human Rights Law. Int J Refugee Law 17:394–415. https://doi.org/10.1093/ijrl/eei013

Obokata T (2010) Transnational organised crime in international law. Hart Publishing, Oxford, Portland (OR)

Olásolo Alonso H, Galain Palermo P (2018) Los Desafíos del derecho internacional penal: atención especial a los casos de Argentina, Colombia, España, México y Uruguay. Tirant lo Blanch, Valencia

Paoli L (ed) (2014) The Oxford handbook of organized crime. Oxford University Press, Oxford, New York

Peterke S, Wolf J (2016) International humanitarian law and transnational organised crime. In: Hauck P, Peterke S (eds) International law and transnational organised crime. Oxford University Press, Oxford, New York, pp 381–405

Peters A (2015) Corruption and human rights. Basel Institute on Governance Working Paper No. 20. https://doi.org/10.2139/ssrn.2635443

Peters A (2018) Corruption as a violation of international human rights. Eur J Int Law 29:1251–1287. https://doi.org/10.1093/ejil/chy070

Peters A (2019) The risk and opportunity of the humanisation of international anti-corruption law: a rejoinder to Kevin E. Davis and Franco Peirone. EJIL: Talk! https://www.ejiltalk.org/the-risk-and-opportunity-of-the-humanisation-of-international-anti-corruption-law-a-rejoinder-to-kevin-e-davis-and-franco-peirone/. Accessed 30 Oct 2024

Peters A (2024) Human rights and corruption: problems and potential of individualizing a systemic problem. Int J Const Law. https://doi.org/10.1093/icon/moae038

Plakokefalos I (2015) Causation in the law of state responsibility and the problem of overdetermination: in search of clarity. Eur J Int Law 26:471–492. https://doi.org/10.1093/ejil/chv023

Reuter P (2009) Systemic violence in drug markets. Crime Law Soc Change 52:275–284. https://doi.org/10.1007/s10611-009-9197-x

Reyes J (2019) State capture through corruption: can human rights help? Am J Int Law 113:331–335. https://doi.org/10.1017/aju.2019.59

Rivard Piché G (2020) In El Salvador, criminal gangs are enforcing virus-related restrictions. Here's why. Washington Post. https://www.washingtonpost.com/politics/2020/06/01/el-salvador-criminal-gangs-are-enforcing-coronavirus-curfews-heres-why/. Accessed 30 Oct 2024

Sepúlveda Carmona M, Bacio-Terracino J (2010) Corruption and human rights: making the connection. In: Boersma M, Nelen H (eds) Corruption & human rights: interdisciplinary perspectives. Intersentia, Antwerp; Portland, OR, pp 25–50

Snyder R, Durán Martínez A (2009) Drugs, violence, and state-sponsored protection rackets in Mexico and Colombia. Colombia internacional 61–91. https://doi.org/10.7440/colombiaint70.2009.03

Stapleton J (2001) Unpacking "causation". In: Cane P, Gardner J (eds) Relating to responsibility: essays in honour of Tony Honoré on his 80th birthday. Hart Publishing, London, pp 145–186

Tamayo Gomez C (2020) Organised crime governance in times of pandemic: the impact of COVID-19 on gangs and drug cartels in Colombia and Mexico. Bull Latin Am Res 39:12. https://doi.org/10.1111/blar.13171

Trejo G, Ley S (2020) Votes, drugs, and violence: the political logic of criminal wars in Mexico. Cambridge University Press, Cambridge

Chapter 5
The Situation of Disappearances in Mexico

To ease the switch from 'law' to 'reality', this chapter introduces and describes the present-day situation of disappearances in Mexico, including a discussion of some of the legal questions the context raises, thereby setting the scene for the following chapters. In that sense, the chapter provides the necessary background information to the interviews with human rights professionals conducted for this research. Importantly, rather than providing an in-depth analysis of the complex phenomenon of disappearances, it gives a brushstroke overview of some of the main issues. The chapter includes not just a description of the phenomenon itself, but also of the Mexican legal framework aimed at addressing disappearances and providing protection and reparations for victims and relatives. Moreover, drawing on the analysis presented in previous chapters, I analyse the responsibility of the Mexican state for disappearances committed by OCGs from an international legal perspective.

5.1 The Phenomenon of Disappearances in Mexico

The phenomenon of disappearances in Mexico, has different historic and present-day dimensions,[1] but this research focuses primarily on the current dimension in the context of the so-called 'war on drugs.' This section briefly outlines the main characteristics of disappearances in Mexico, including the perpetrators and victims, possible causes, as well as the reaction by civil society and relatives of the disappeared.

[1] See Mandolessi and Rico (2022), especially chapters 2, 3, and 4.

L. Guercke, *Failure of the State*, Interdisciplinary Studies in Human Rights 15,
https://doi.org/10.1007/978-3-031-83717-3_5

5.1.1 The Legacy of Enforced Disappearances

Disappearances in Mexico are not a new phenomenon. From the late 1960s until the early 1980s, a period that is often referred to as the 'dirty war',[2] the Mexican government used repressive counter-insurgency tactics against social leaders and members of guerrilla groups, most prominently in the state of Guerrero.[3] While the regime in Mexico at the time was not a dictatorship,[4] it used similar tactics to those employed by military dictatorships in other Latin American countries in order to repress political opponents.[5] Disappearances that occurred during the 'dirty war' period in Mexico were thus 'traditional' enforced disappearances[6] that were carried out by state forces in a systematic manner against political opponents, especially members of rural and urban guerrillas.[7] According to the final report of the 'Mechanism for Truth and Historical Clarification' (MEH for its Spanish initials) in 2024,[8] 1166 persons were victims of enforced disappearance or 'temporary enforced

[2]Note that the term 'dirty war' to describe this period, while common, is not without controversy. In her doctoral thesis on the subject of memory of the disappeared in Mexico, Maria De Vecchi explains her reasons for not using this term given that it is 'ideologically charged'. See de Vecchi Gerli (2018), p. 15.

[3]See Karl (2014); Mendoza García (2015), p. 85; de Vecchi Gerli (2018), pp. 62–71.

[4]Mexico was ruled by a single party, the Institutional Revolutionary Party (Partido Revolucionario Institucional, PRI) for around 70 years throughout the twentieth century. The PRI's rule ended in 2000, when President Vicente Fox of the National Action Party (PAN for its Spanish initials) took office. While periodic elections were held during the one-party rule, political scientists have described the regime as 'authoritarian'. See, for example, Aguayo Quezada and Treviño Rangel (2006), p. 57. Today Mexico has been described as an 'illiberal democracy'. On this, see Trejo and Ley (2020), pp. 12–13.

[5]See Karl (2014), p. 728; González-Ocantos (2016), pp. 208–209; de Vecchi Gerli (2018), pp. 67ff; Mecanismo para la Verdad y el Esclarecimiento Histórico (2024a).

[6]For a description of such 'traditional' enforced disappearances, see, for example, Berman and Clark (1982).

[7]On the systematic manner in which persons were disappeared during this period, see, for example, Mecanismo para la Verdad y el Esclarecimiento Histórico (2024b). For an overview of the emergence of the guerrilla groups and the Mexican state's differentiated response to these groups during the 1960s–1980s depending on their rural or urban nature, see de Vecchi Gerli (2018), pp. 62–71.

[8]In October 2021, the Mexican government established the 'Commission for Access to Truth, Historical Clarification and the Promotion of Justice for Grave Human Rights Violations committed between 1965 and 1990' ('Comisión para el Acceso a la Verdad, el Esclarecimiento Histórico y el Impulso a la Justicia de las Violaciones Graves a los Derechos Humanos cometidas de 1965 a 1990', Truth Commission) to investigate serious human rights violations committed during the 'dirty war' period (and slightly beyond) and lay the groundwork for truth, justice, reparations, and memory. As one of the Truth Commission's mechanisms, the MEH was tasked with investigating political violence and human rights violations between 1965 and 1990 and communicating its findings with a new narrative based on the dignity of the victims. See https://comisionverdadyjusticia.segob.gob.mx/ and https://www.meh.org.mx/que-es-el-mecanismo-para-la-verdad-y-el-esclarecimiento-historico/. Accessed 4 November 2024.

disappearance'[9] between 1965–1990.[10] Despite the end of the 'dirty war' during the 1980s, there have to-date not been any large-scale efforts to search for the disappeared from that period. An initiative to clarify and prosecute these crimes was made in the early 2000s, when President Fox became the first president from an opposition party to take power after 70 years of rule by the Institutional Revolutionary Party (PRI, for its Spanish initials). What has been described as the 'Mexican solution to transitional justice'[11] involved the establishment of a Special Prosecutor's Office (FEMOSPP[12]) tasked with investigating and prosecuting a number of specific massacres, as well as crimes committed during the 'dirty war' period more generally.[13] Nonetheless, despite initial optimism, the FEMOSPP encountered numerous institutional problems and did not bring about the desired results, neither in the form of an official report of 'truth'[14] nor in that of convictions of perpetrators.[15] As a result, the majority of crimes remain in impunity and the disappeared have not been found. This includes Rosendo Radilla, for whose enforced disappearance the Mexican state was held to be responsible by the Inter-American Court of Human Rights (IACtHR) in 2009.[16] The *Radilla* case had a significant impact at the Mexican judicial level because it prompted an important pronouncement by the Mexican Supreme Court on the binding nature of IACtHR judgements, the need to interpret domestic norms in accordance with international human rights standards, as well as the lack of military jurisdiction over human rights violations.[17] Nevertheless,

[9] This is a concept adopted by MEH for persons who were subjected to enforced disappearance for a few days. Mecanismo para la Verdad y el Esclarecimiento Histórico (2024a), p. 196. According to international legal standards, there is no minimum duration period of detention for an enforced disappearance to occur. See Committee on Enforced Disappearances (2023) General Comment No. 1 on Enforced Disappearance in the Context of Migration. UN Doc. CED/C/GC/1, para. 17.

[10] Mecanismo para la Verdad y el Esclarecimiento Histórico (2024a), p. 95.

[11] Acosta and Ennelin (2006); Treviño Rangel (2012), pp. 67–68.

[12] The full title of the Prosecutor's Office was: The Special Prosecutors' Office for the Attention of Matters Allegedly Related to Federal Crimes Committed Directly or Indirectly by Public Servants Against Persons Linked to Social or Political Movements of the Past ('Fiscalía Especial para la Atención de Hechos Probablemente Constitutivos de Delitos Federales Cometidos Directa o Indirectamente por Servidores Públicos en Contra de Personas Vinculadas con Movimientos Sociales y Políticos del Pasado').

[13] See Acosta and Ennelin (2006), p. 103.

[14] The final report of the FEMOSPP was never officially released. However, a draft version of the report was circulated and has been available on the website of 'The National Security Archive' since 2006. See https://nsarchive2.gwu.edu/NSAEBB/NSAEBB180/index.htm. Accessed 4 November 2024.

[15] For an account of why the FEMOSPP failed and why prosecutions were ultimately unsuccessful, see, for example, González-Ocantos (2016), pp. 206–268; Treviño Rangel and Valdivia (2014); de Vecchi Gerli (2018), pp. 71–74; Mecanismo para la Verdad y el Esclarecimiento Histórico (MEH) (2024c), pp. 289–308.

[16] *Case of Radilla-Pacheco v Mexico* [2009] Inter-American Court of Human Rights Series C No. 209.

[17] See Suprema Corte de Justicia de la Nación (2010) Expediente Varios 912/2010. See also Inter-American Court of Human Rights (2013) Resolución de la Corte Interamericana de Derechos

searches conducted so far have not led to the recovery of Rosendo Radilla's remains and 50 years after his disappearance there has still not been a single conviction in the case.[18] In a similar vein, in its final report the MEH emphasised the institutional barriers to truth and justice that continue to this day, which include the refusal by certain key institutions to grant access to archives and documents.[19]

5.1.2 Present-Day Disappearances

Since 2006, the number of persons who have been disappeared in Mexico has increased exponentially. According to the official data, as of November 2024, 103,522 persons had disappeared or gone missing since December 2006.[20] Yet disappearances today, as well as other forms of violence, have acquired new dimensions, not just in terms of scale, but also with regards to their causes and dynamics.[21] While there exist continuities between disappearances during the different periods, the year 2006 is considered as a clear turning point in the phenomenon of disappearances in Mexico.[22] This is because it was in 2006 that then-incoming president Felipe Calderón declared a 'war' on drug-trafficking organisations and began deploying military forces to certain regions of the country in order to 'fight' such organisations and support or replace police forces.[23]

A number of factors have contributed to the upsurge of violence since 2006.[24] Among the key elements that have contributed to the exponential rise in violence

---

Humanos de 14 de Mayo 2013: Caso Radilla Pacheco vs. México—Supervisión de Cumplimiento de Sentencia, para. 5.

[18] AFADEM and Fundar (2024).

[19] Mecanismo para la Verdad y el Esclarecimiento Histórico (2024a), p. 37; Mecanismo para la Verdad y el Esclarecimiento Histórico (2024c), pp. 310ff. The annex of the report contains, among others, a list with the names of alleged perpetrators. See https://www.meh.org.mx/especial-informe-final/. Accessed 4 November 2024. Given the report's recent publication in August 2024, it is not yet clear what impact, if any, it will have on advancing accountability.

[20] Data retrieved from the National Register on Disappeared and Missing Persons ('Registro Nacional de Personas Desaparecidas y No Localizadas', RNPDNO): https://versionpublicarnpdno.segob.gob.mx/Dashboard/Sociodemografico. Accessed 4 November 2024.

These data aggregate 'disappeared' and 'missing' persons, which means that the number includes persons who may have gone missing for reasons other than the commission of a crime. If filtered for only 'disappeared' persons, the number is 94,662 persons disappeared between 1 December 2006 and 4 November 2024. Moreover, it is also important to note that there is a very high under-reporting rate of crimes in Mexico, which suggests that the real number could be much higher.

[21] See, for example, Ansolabehere and Martos (2022).

[22] See Vélez Salas (2016), p. 17; Mandolessi (2022).

[23] See, for example, Astorga Almanza (2015a), pp. 21–25.

[24] For an overview of several perspectives on the underlying causes of current violence in Mexico, see the contributions in the Journal of Conflict Resolution's 2015 Special Issue on Drug Violence in

across Mexican territory are the militarisation of public security and the attempt to dismantle criminal organisations by removing the top leadership.[25] The targeting of 'kingpins', or heads of drug-trafficking organisations, rather than leading to their disintegration, resulted in their fragmentation into smaller criminal organisations. The latter have expanded their criminal activities to include more predatory ones than drug-trafficking, such as extortion, which is considered to be an important factor in the rise of violence.[26] By late 2023 in addition to the over 100,000 persons who have been disappeared or gone missing since 2006, 392,000 persons had been internally displaced,[27] and there have been hundreds of thousands of violent deaths,[28] leading to what is considered to be a humanitarian and human rights 'crisis' in the country.[29]

Mexico: Shirk and Wallman (2015); Duran-Martinez (2015); Osorio (2015); Calderón et al. (2015); Lessing (2015); Kalyvas (2015). See also Trejo and Ley (2020); Justice in Mexico (2020). Some authors also point to the possibility of predatory economic interests as the overall drivers of violence, as well as disappearances more specifically. See, for example, Paley (2020); Pozos Barcelata (2018), pp. 192–193; Correa-Cabrera (2017). Recently, a few authors have also started to provide insight into the individual perpetrators' perspective. For the perspective of security forces, see Rea Gómez and Ferri (2019). For the perspective of former members of criminal organisations, see García Reyes (2019). These accounts provide an even more complex picture of the reasons behind both violence in general, and disappearances in particular, including, in the case of former members of the Zetas interviewed by Karina García Reyes, adherence to the Santa Muerte (Holy Death) cult.

[25] See, for example, Serrano (2017). On the impact of militarisation on the rise of human rights violations in Mexico, see also Guevara Bermúdez (2020). Another element emphasised by some authors is the transition in Mexico from a regime with authoritarian structures to an electoral democracy since the early 1990s, which reduced the ability of the State to control activities—and violence—of criminal organisations. This is one of the explanations for the increase of violence exercised by criminal organisations themselves from the 1990s onwards. However, it is important to note that prior to 2006 and the commencement of the 'war on drugs', homicide levels in the country had actually been decreasing overall. See, for example, Astorga Almanza (2015a), pp. 190–191; Rosen and Zepeda (2017). For an overview of the arguments of the 'democratisation model', see Shirk and Wallman (2015), pp. 1359–1362. For an account that further expands these arguments by including a political perspective, see Trejo and Ley (2020). For an account of the continuities between different periods of violence, see Allier Montaño et al. (2022).

[26] See Shirk and Wallman (2015); Rosen and Zepeda (2017), pp. 57–58; Justice in Mexico (2020), p. 5; International Crisis Group (2024), pp. 3–4.

[27] See Internal Displacement Monitoring Centre: https://www.internal-displacement.org/countries/mexico/. Accessed 4 November 2024. According to the IDMC, the figure is based on media reports and 'considered an underestimate due to a lack of systematic monitoring of violence displacements in the country'. See also Human Rights Council (2023) Visit to Mexico: Report of the Special Rapporteur on the human rights of internally displaced persons, Cecilia Jiménez-Damary. UN Doc. A/HRC/53/35/Add.2.

[28] According to official data from Mexico's National Statistical Institute (INEGI), between 2007 and 2023 there were 452,254 reported homicides. See INEGI (2024) Defunciones por homicidios. https://www.inegi.org.mx/sistemas/olap/proyectos/bd/continuas/mortalidad/defuncioneshom.asp?s=est. Accessed 31 October 2024. See also International Crisis Group (2024), pp. 1–4.

[29] Serrano (2017).

Within this overall context of violence and given the prevailing lack of investigations into disappearances that contributes to a shortage of information about the issue, it cannot be said with certainty why disappearances in particular have risen sharply.[30] However, available information indicates that there are a number of different reasons behind disappearances, ranging from criminal purposes such as human trafficking and forced recruitment into criminal organisations,[31] to terrorising the population as a means of securing territorial control,[32] as well as to 'simply' getting of rid of dead bodies.[33] This also implies that the modes of disappearing in the current Mexican context vary greatly.[34] In this sense, present-day disappearances in Mexico no longer fit within the traditional image of enforced disappearances.[35] Rather than being part of a clearly identifiable, top-down repressive policy, they are the outcome of different factors that are as yet insufficiently researched and understood.[36] Notwithstanding, despite the differences in disappearances during the 'dirty war' period and that of the 'war on drugs', impunity remains a connecting factor between both periods and across all types of disappearances, and regardless of which government holds power (see further below).[37]

5.1.2.1 Victims and Perpetrators of Disappearances[38]

Both victims and perpetrators of disappearances in Mexico today are heterogeneous groups and much remains unknown about them. In the absence of effective investigations that would provide insights into motives behind and patterns of disappearances, most available information has been collected, documented, and analysed by relatives of the disappeared themselves, civil society organisations, journalists, and academics. While no general conclusions can be drawn from this information

[30] According to Calveiro, the lack of information is also the result of the 'government's policy of concealment' through fragmentation of information and isolation of cases that is characteristic of enforced disappearances in Mexico. See Calveiro (2022), pp. 82–85. See also Allier Montaño et al. (2022), p. 63.

[31] See Guillén and Petersen (2019) and Quadratín (2020).

[32] This has particularly been documented in relation to the criminal group *Los Zetas*. See Open Society Justice Initiative (2016), pp. 93–96; Human Rights Clinic (2017); fidh et al. (2017), pp. 36–49; Open Society Justice Initiative (2018).

[33] This is illustrated by the existence of thousands of clandestine mass graves in the country. See Tzuc (2023a).

[34] See Yankelevich (2019), pp. 41–42; Calveiro (2022), pp. 85–92.

[35] See, for example, Robledo Silvestre (2015), p. 89; Mata Lugo (2017), pp. 43–45; Calveiro (2022), p. 80. Note, however, that there continue to be enforced disappearances committed for political reasons that correspond to the more 'traditional' understanding of the crime.

[36] See Yankelevich (2017), Ansolabehere and Martos (2022), Allier Montaño et al. (2022), and Calveiro (2022).

[37] Ansolabehere et al. (2021b), p. 13; Guevara Bermúdez and Chávez Vargas (2018); Allier Montaño et al. (2022).

[38] The content of this section will also be published elsewhere: Guercke (2025).

because it encompasses only a small number of cases in relation to the actual number of disappeared persons in Mexico, it nevertheless indicates variations across time and space in the modalities of disappearances, victims, and perpetrators.[39] Cognisant of the limitations in available data, this section summarises some of the available information with a view to illustrating the diversity of victims and perpetrators of disappearances in the country.

Victims

In a 2013 report on the issue of disappearances in Mexico, Amnesty International stated: '[a]nyone can be a victim of disappearance or enforced disappearance in Mexico.'[40] This statement, which illustrates the lack of a single unifying characteristic among victims, still holds true, although in some instances certain patterns have been identified.[41] Importantly, there is no evidence to support continued claims by authorities that most victims were in some way involved in criminal activities.[42] Despite this, criminalising attitudes and practices against victims and their relatives persist among authorities and society more generally.[43]

The vast majority of disappearances today cannot be tied to any form of political or social activism, but activists and social leaders also continue to be disappeared.[44] Additionally, breaking with the traditional—and legal—understanding that enforced disappearances are committed by agents of security forces, victims include police officers and members of the military.[45] In the north-eastern state of Nuevo León, for example, the first cases registered by the NGO Ciudadanos en Apoyo a los Derechos Humanos (CADHAC), were police officers who had disappeared.[46] In other cases, members of specific professional groups have become victims of disappearances, such as engineers, architects, or doctors,[47] and there are cases of collective disappearances, where entire groups of workers were disappeared.[48] In yet other cases,

[39] See, for example, Aguayo and Dayán (2017); ODIM (2017); Sánchez Valdés et al. (2018); IMDHD (2019a); Yankelevich (2019), pp. 41–42; IMDHD (2022). For a proposal of a typology of the different fates of victims of disappearances in the current context, see Pozos Barcelata (2018), pp. 149ff.

[40] Amnesty International (2013).

[41] See, for example, Ansolabehere and Martos (2022), p. 114. See also Committee on Enforced Disappearances (2022) Report of the Committee on Enforced Disappearances on its visit to Mexico: Findings. UN Doc. CED/C/MEX/VR/1 (Findings), para. 23.

[42] Committee on Enforced Disappearances (2022) Report of the Committee on Enforced Disappearances on its visit to Mexico: Findings. UN Doc. CED/C/MEX/VR/1 (Findings), para. 39.

[43] See Amnesty International (2013), p. 6; Human Rights Watch (2013), pp. 40–41; ODIM (2017), pp. 29–30.

[44] See Camacho Servín (2018). According to a joint investigation by three journalism networks published in October 2023, between 1 December 2006 and 1 August 2023, 93 land and environmental defenders have disappeared in Mexico. See Mongabay Latam et al. (2023).

[45] See Alzaga (2014); Proceso (2018); Calveiro (2022), p. 88.

[46] ODIM (2017), p. 25.

[47] See Martínez (2012); Amnesty International (2013), p. 5.

[48] See, for example, Coria (2015). For a more recent case, see Guillén (2024).

victims of ‘regular’ kidnappings are not liberated after the family has made the ransom payment, thus effectively converting the kidnapping into a disappearance.[49] In recent years, evidence has also come to light about forced recruitment by criminal organisations.[50] Conversely, there have been instances where disappearances appear to be linked to ‘social cleansing’, for example of persons with drug addictions who have disappeared from rehabilitation centres[51] or of members of the LGBTQI+ community, repeatedly after being held in ‘conversion therapy centres’.[52] Although most reported victims of disappearance are male,[53] women and girls are also being disappeared or go missing in rising numbers, often linked to human trafficking or gender-based violence (including femicide).[54]

Certain groups are in a situation of particular vulnerability with regard to disappearances and are also among the least visible victims of this crime. For example, poor and marginalised communities, often indigenous population, whose level of exclusion is such that disappearances are accepted as part of life and not reported.[55] Especially communities living in territories of certain economic or extractive interest often experience high levels of violence, including disappearances, which is also illustrated by disappearances of land and environmental activists.[56] Finally, an unknown number of migrants have disappeared on their journey through Mexico, for example because they become victims of human trafficking or kidnapping by criminal groups, who may act alone or in collusion with immigration authorities or security forces.[57]

49 See Román (2015); Calveiro (2022), p. 86.

50 Guillén and Petersen (2019).

51 Editorial Milenio (2018).

52 Committee on Enforced Disappearances (2022) Report of the Committee on Enforced Disappearances on its visit to Mexico: Findings. UN Doc. CED/C/MEX/VR/1 (Findings), para. 22.

53 Ibid., para. 14; Ansolabehere et al. (2021a, b); IMDHD (2022).

54 Committee on the Elimination of Discrimination against Women (2018) Concluding observations on the ninth periodic report of Mexico. UN Doc. CEDAW/C/MEX/CO/9, paras 23–24; Ansolabehere et al. (2021a, b); Ayala Martínez (2021); IMDHD (2022).

55 See Antillón Najlis (2018) and Hernández Castillo (2019).

56 See Pozos Barcelata (2018), pp. 192–193; Committee on Enforced Disappearances (2022) Report of the Committee on Enforced Disappearances on its visit to Mexico: Findings. UN Doc. CED/C/MEX/VR/1 (Findings), para. 21; Human Rights Council (2023) Visit to Mexico: Report of the Special Rapporteur on the human rights of internally displaced persons, Cecilia Jiménez-Damary. UN Doc. A/HRC/53/35/Add.2, para. 23; Mongabay Latam et al. (2023).

57 See Inter-American Commission on Human Rights (2013) Human Rights of Migrants and Other Persons in the Context of Human Mobility in Mexico, OEA/Ser.L/V/II. Doc. 48/13, para. 167; Citroni (2017); Fundación para la Justicia y el Estado Democrático de Derecho and TRIAL International (2018); Committee on Enforced Disappearances (2022) Report of the Committee on Enforced Disappearances on its visit to Mexico: Findings. UN Doc. CED/C/MEX/VR/1 (Findings), paras 19–20.

Perpetrators

Almost since the beginning of the 'war on drugs', there has been disagreement over the characterisation of violence. While subsequent Mexican governments have insisted that the vast majority of violence is committed by and among organised criminal groups,[58] human rights organisations have shown that both the armed forces and police forces of different levels (federal, state, municipal) are also involved in the commission of such crimes. This was confirmed by the IACtHR in the recent case of *Alvarado Espinoza and others v Mexico*, a case of an enforced disappearance committed by soldiers in the context of a special military operation in the northern Mexican state of Chihuahua.[59] The impunity which prevails in the vast majority of disappearance cases means that it is impossible to make any general statements about who the main perpetrators behind these crimes are. However, existing research, for example based on analyses of documented cases, has shown that both state agents and organised criminal groups are involved in disappearances, as are other private actors.[60] Importantly, these actors do not always act independently, but collude in the commission of crimes, including disappearances.[61] Indeed, given the complexity of violence and the pervasiveness of corruption (discussed further below), it is often difficult to draw clear lines between these actors, especially in relation to organised criminal groups and state actors.[62]

Two examples illustrate the complexity of state-crime relations in Mexico with regards to disappearances:[63] first, the Ayotzinapa case (see Chap. 1), while still not solved, clearly shows the links between state forces and criminal groups. The so-called 'historic truth' ('verdad histórica'), which refers to the official version of events as presented by the previous Mexican Administration of President Peña Nieto, claimed that the students had been detained by municipal police forces and handed over to a criminal group, allegedly on the orders of the mayor of the town of Iguala. The 'historic truth' was discredited following the investigation by the Interdisciplinary Group of Independent Experts (GIEI, for its Spanish initials), which was set up by the Inter-American Commission on Human Rights (IACHR)

---

[58] See Milenio (2010), Secretaría de Gobernación (2016) and AMLO (2019).

[59] *Case of Alvarado Espinoza and Others v. Mexico*, Inter-American Court of Human Rights, Series C No. 370, Judgment of 28 November 2018, paras 59–75.

[60] See, for example, Inter-American Commission on Human Rights (2015) Situation of Human Rights in Mexico. OEA/Ser.L/V/II.Doc. 44/15, paras 34–52; ODIM (2017), pp. 39–44.

[61] See Inter-American Commission on Human Rights (2015) Situation of Human Rights in Mexico. OEA/Ser.L/V/II.Doc. 44/15, paras 34–52; ODIM (2017), pp. 39ff; Open Society Justice Initiative (2018). This reality has also been recognised by the WGEID and the CED: Human Rights Council (2011) Report of the Working Group on Enforced or Involuntary Disappearances: Mission to Mexico. UN Doc. A/HRC/19/58/Add.2, paras 17–18; Committee on Enforced Disappearances (2022) Report of the Committee on Enforced Disappearances on its visit to Mexico: Findings. UN Doc. CED/C/MEX/VR/1 (Findings), paras 13, 22, 39.

[62] See Morris (2012), p. 29; Yankelevich (2019), p. 41.

[63] Parts of this section have also been published elsewhere: see Guercke (2021), pp. 346–347.

to provide assistance to the Mexican government in the clarification of the case.[64] Rather, the hypothesis proposed by the GIEI was that one of the buses commandeered by the students carried either drugs or money destined for the United States, and that their disappearance could have been the outcome of an effort to 'protect' the shipment.[65] Subsequent investigations by the Special Prosecutor's Office[66] for the case provided further evidence for this hypothesis.[67] What is noticeable is that even the state's cover-up story implied collusion between state forces and criminal groups, albeit not of all security forces. The investigations into the case and arrests warrants obtained indicate the involvement of police forces of all levels (municipal, state, federal, and ministerial), and the armed forces alongside an organised criminal group ('Guerreros Unidos'). The case thus raises questions about the nature and extent of the relationship between these actors, including that of who was working on the orders of whom.

The second example encompasses an attack on the towns of Allende and Piedras Negras in the north-eastern state of Coahuila, which was carried out by the criminal organisation 'the Zetas' over the course of 3 days in 2011.[68] This attack, which is commonly referred to as the 'Allende Massacre' is alleged to have been an act of 'vengeance' against three apparent 'traitors' who had collaborated with the United States Drug Enforcement Agency (DEA) and helped the latter get access to the phones of high-ranking Zetas. Once the DEA shared this information with Mexican police authorities, it was passed on to the Zetas' leadership. During the attack, anybody who was deemed to have a connection with the informants became a target. An estimated 300 persons were killed or disappeared in the span of 3 days, while police forces and firefighters received—and followed- instructions from the criminal group not to intervene. Following the attack, no investigations were carried out and relatives who tried to denounce the crimes were silenced with threats.[69] As a consequence, there was little or no public knowledge about these attacks until much later and the massacre was first reported on in early 2014.[70]

---

[64] See https://www.oas.org/en/IACHR/jsForm/?File=/en/iachr/giei/ayotzinapa/default.asp#. Accessed 26 November 2024.

[65] GIEI (2023), pp. 247 ff

[66] In 2019 a special unit was created within the General Prosecutor's Office to investigate and prosecute the Ayotzinapa case ('Unidad Especial de Investigación y Litigación para el caso Ayotzinapa'). In August 2022, the special prosecutor's office sought arrest warrants for 83 persons linked to the case, including 20 members of the military. Shortly afterwards, the General Prosecutor's Office cancelled at least 21 of these arrest warrants, which led the special prosecutor, Omar Gómez Trejo, to resign in protest. See Gibler (2023). In 2023, the prosecutor's office reactivated many of the arrest warrants. However, under the current leadership it is not considered as continuing a serious investigation. GIEI (2023), p. 181.

[67] Gibler (2023).

[68] Evans (2021).

[69] Several reports have documented this massacre. See, for example, Aguayo (2017), Aguayo and Dayán (2017), Human Rights Clinic (2017) and Thompson (2017).

[70] Aguayo and Dayán (2017), p. 34. On the efforts by civil society and local media to spread information despite government efforts to impede this, see ibid., pp. 32–34.

Other reports about the Zetas' activities in Coahuila have shown the extent of their influence and control over the police force and other authorities. For example, for several years the Zetas used a state detention facility in Piedras Negras as a base for their activities, including for killing and disintegrating or cremating bodies. At the same time, virtually the entire municipal police force of the town of Allende was on the payroll of the Zetas.[71] The Zetas are a criminal group that was originally established as the armed wing of the Gulf Cartel and was made up of former highly trained special forces of the Mexican Army.[72] After its split from the Gulf Cartel in 2010, the Zetas became one of the most powerful criminal organisations in the country and are generally associated with the exponential increase, as well as the particular brutality of violence during the following years.[73] As mentioned above, according to a number of reports, as part of their expansion strategy the Zetas employed disappearances in a systematic manner to terrorise local populations and establish control over territory. Additionally, the Zetas were involved in mass disappearances of migrants, especially in the state of Tamaulipas, which was only possible because of close ties to authorities.[74]

5.1.2.2 The Forensic Crisis as a Cause of Disappearances[75]

Not only is there a plurality of motives, perpetrators and victims of disappearance in Mexico today, but the disappearance crisis also causally overlaps with the country's forensic crisis.[76] This crisis stems from the incapacity of forensic authorities to identify dead bodies and remains, which is illustrated by over 72,100 unidentified bodies in the country[77] and numerous examples of authorities' mishandling of dead bodies. Many of these bodies were buried in official mass graves by overwhelmed and insufficiently trained forensic authorities who could not cope with the number of bodies they were receiving. In many instances, such inhumations did not follow adequate protocols and were conducted negligently and without proper

[71] See ibid.; Human Rights Clinic (2017). For details on payments received by police officers from Zetas, see Aguayo (2017), pp. 19–20.

[72] Correa-Cabrera (2017), pp. 21–22.

[73] Ibid., pp. 36–42.

[74] Turati (2023).

[75] A modified version of this section will also appear in a forthcoming book chapter: Guercke (2025).

[76] Some authors use the term 'administrative disappearance' in the Mexican context to describe this phenomenon. See, for example, Mata Lugo (2017), pp. 62 and 65. However, this concept still requires further development and has also been used in a slightly different manner by others, for example in reference to the failure by authorities to register cases as disappearances and the subsequent variations in official registers and statistics. See Antillón (2020).

[77] Tzuc and Sánchez (2024).

documentation, which has resulted in loss of information about the exact location of burial.[78] A lack of coordination among different institutions involved in the burials is another contributing factor to the effective loss of bodies.[79] Such malpractice came to light during exhumations, when bodies appeared that did not correspond to the persons indicated on registers or that were not listed in any official documentation.[80] Conversely, there have also been reports of identified bodies having been buried without notification to the families of those buried.[81]

Another stark example of the mishandling of remains are the actions of forensic authorities in the western state of Jalisco (home to one of Mexico's largest cities, Guadalajara), who cremated 1571 unidentified bodies between 2006 and 2015 without taking DNA samples from 1430 of those bodies prior to cremation.[82] Additionally, in 2018 a scandal erupted in the state of Jalisco when it became apparent that, due to a lack of space in the morgues, authorities had been storing 444 bodies in refrigeration trucks.[83] Similar storage practices due to lack of capacity have also been reported in other states.[84] In the northern state of Durango, during 2011 a number of clandestine mass graves were exhumed with backhoes, leading to the destruction of hundreds of bodies during the exhumation process.[85] Finally, forensic institutions in several states have sub-contracted private funeral homes to support them in handling bodies discovered in clandestine mass graves. Tasking private companies with conducting necropsies can also contribute to data loss.[86] In addition to these negligent practices by authorities in relation to bodies that arrived at forensic institutions, there are also thousands of clandestine mass graves spread across the Mexican territory, which implies an even greater forensic identification burden.[87] The fact that violence, including disappearances, has not stopped, also continuously adds to this burden and even if serious efforts were made to address it, it would take over a century to identify the bodies.[88] In response to the forensic crisis

78 See, for example, Rodríguez (2020). For an account of how this practice has its origins in the past, and the efforts by former staff members of the National Search Commission to identify persons buried in 'fosas comunes' (official mass graves) on a cemetery in Mexico City, see Nuño (2024).

79 Nuño (2024).

80 Tzuc and Turati (2020).

81 Tzuc (2023b) and Nuño (2024).

82 See CEPAD (2019), p. 9; Franco Migues (2019).

83 CEPAD (2019), p. 9.

84 See Sin Embargo (2018) and Tzuc and Turati (2020).

85 Quinto Elemento Lab (2020).

86 Vizcarra (2020).

87 Based on data provided by the National Search Commission, by April 2023 5696 illegal mass graves ('fosas clandestinas') had been discovered. See Tzuc (2023a).

88 Tzuc and Turati (2020). According to experts consulted by the CED during its 2021 visit to Mexico, it would take 120 years to identify the 52,000 unidentified bodies recorded at the time, not counting those added on a daily basis. See Committee on Enforced Disappearances (2022) Report of the Committee on Enforced Disappearances on its visit to Mexico: Findings. UN Doc. CED/C/MEX/VR/1 (Findings), para. 29.

an Extraordinary Forensic Mechanism (EFM) was created in late 2019 in order to support and speed up the identification of remains. Despite initial high hopes, it took almost 2 years for the mechanism's steering group ('grupo coordinador') to commence activities in mid-2021 and by mid-2023 all but one of the seven members had resigned amid uncertainties about contracts, concern over the Mechanism's lack of autonomy, and internal disagreements.[89] In early 2024, all funding to the EFM was halted by the National Search Commission.[90]

Improper handling of dead bodies and remains, as illustrated by the examples above, is thus another effective cause of many disappearances in Mexico today, even though it is quite different from the traditional —and legal— understanding of the crime of enforced disappearance and its aim to terrorise opponents.[91] Understanding the causes and dimensions of the phenomenon of disappearances in Mexico is thus further complicated by another element of the state's failure to protect persons from disappearances than those discussed in previous chapters. In this sense, the forensic crisis as a cause of disappearances raises additional legal questions, including whether cases of such 'administrative' disappearances could be considered as enforced disappearances, both under international law and domestic Mexican legislation (see below, Sect. 5.3.1.3).[92]

5.1.2.3 Impunity and Corruption as Facilitating Factors

Whereas the causes of disappearances in Mexico in the context of the 'war on drugs' are thus multiple, the unifying element among all disappearances is the impunity that surrounds them. At the same time, and in relation to disappearances committed by organised criminal groups specifically, another issue that must not be overlooked is corruption. The phenomenon of impunity in Mexico is too complex and multifaceted

[89] Cortez (2023).

[90] Tzuc (2024c). In August 2023, the head of the National Search Commission, Karla Quintana, resigned after an open dispute about the register of disappeared persons with President Andrés Manuél López Obrador. Her successor, Teresa Guadalupe Reyes Sahagún, assumed leadership in October 2023 after a selection process that was severely criticised by relatives and civil society organisations. See SitiosVerdad (2023).

[91] Reflecting on this aspect of the Mexican context, Javier Yankelevich proposes a conceptual distinction between the state of *being disappeared* and being the victim of the crime of disappearance. The latter can or cannot be the cause of the state of being disappeared. See Yankelevich (2020), p. 24. However, even if disappearances may not be committed with the aim of spreading terror, these crimes can, and do, still have a terrorising and possibly paralysing effect. I thank María de Vecchi Gerli for this comment.

[92] Yankelevich does not appear to think so. In his discussion of how different crimes overlap in cases where a homicide is committed and a person is subsequently not identified, he argues that a person can be considered disappeared for the purpose of search obligations under Mexican domestic law, even if they are not the victim of a crime of disappearance. See Yankelevich (2020), pp. 22–23.

to be examined in depth in this book, but it is a key factor to understanding some of the issues surrounding disappearances.[93] Estimated at 98%, enduring impunity in Mexico is viewed not only as one connecting element between crimes committed in the past and in the present, but also as a factor that perpetuates the commission of such crimes, both at the hands of state, as well as non-state actors.[94] In relation to disappearances specifically, while definitive numbers are difficult to come by, in 2021 the Mexican state reported to the CED that there had been 36 judgments in disappearance cases at the national level.[95] According to data obtained through freedom of information requests by one NGO, by 2023 22 convictions for the crime of enforced disappearance have been issued at the federal level since 2006 and 72 convictions at the state level since 2019, as well as 69 convictions for the crime of 'disappearance committed by private individuals' that I discuss below.[96] As mentioned above, impunity, including the lack of proper investigations, reduces the amount of information available about disappearances in the country because there is insufficient data to provide a clear picture of the problem, which also impacts the possibility of designing effective public policies to address the issue.[97] The lack of data is further aggravated by a general reluctance of persons to denounce crimes, due to lack of trust in authorities or fear, as indicated by an estimated under-reporting rate of 92.9% according to Mexico's National Statistics Institute.[98] Impunity in the Mexican context is thus composed of different elements: the non-reporting of disappearances, the failure to conduct effective investigations when cases are reported, as well as the lack of sanctions even where the perpetrators have been identified, which is exemplified not only by the low number of judicial sentences mentioned above, but also by the short duration of sentences.[99]

---

[93] Impunity is, of course, not only an issue in Mexico and represents a general problem in contexts where disappearances occur. On this, see the Human Rights Council (2020) Report of the Working Group on Enforced or Involuntary Disappearances on Standards and Public Policies for an Effective Investigation of Enforced Disappearances. UN Doc. A/HRC/45/13/Add.3. On general issues surrounding the conceptualisation of impunity, see Umaña (2017).

[94] See Inter-American Commission on Human Rights (2015) Situation of Human Rights in Mexico. OEA/Ser.L/V/II.Doc. 44/15, paras 63–68; CMDPDH et al. (2018), paras 10–12; Open Society Justice Initiative (2018).

[95] Committee on Enforced Disappearances (2022) Report of the Committee on Enforced Disappearances on its visit to Mexico: Findings. UN Doc. CED/C/MEX/VR/1 (Findings), para. 25.

[96] Impunidad Cero (2023), pp. 50–54. Author's own calculations based on data provided by Impunidad Cero: https://www.impunidadcero.org/articulo.php?id=196&t=impunidad-en-delitos-de-desaparicion-en-mexico-2023. Accessed 6 November 2024.

[97] See also Committee on Enforced Disappearances (2015) Concluding Observations on the Report Submitted by Mexico. UN Doc. CED/C/MEX/CO/1, para. 17. On the near absolute impunity in Mexico, see also Committee on Enforced Disappearances (2022) Report of the Committee on Enforced Disappearances on its visit to Mexico: Findings. UN Doc. CED/C/MEX/VR/1 (Findings), paras 24–27.

[98] This number is based on the National Institute for Statistics and Geography's (INEGI) 2024 annual survey on victimisation and perceptions on public security. See INEGI (2024).

[99] Yankelevich (2019), p. 48. For an in-depth analysis of existing sentences, see Serrano (2024).

Closely linked to the problem of impunity in Mexico, especially in relation to crimes committed by organised crime, is that of corruption.[100] Corruption in Mexico is widespread and deeply rooted and is particularly important to consider when it comes to the relationship between organised criminal groups and authorities. Indeed, in relation to drug-trafficking, Mexican authorities have historically been involved in such criminal activities, either indirectly by receiving a share of the profits, or directly.[101] Presently, however, pacts between officials and criminal groups no longer guarantee low levels of violence as they did previously. In fact, the dissolution of such pacts could be viewed as a factor that contributes to higher levels of violence generally, given that in fighting crime the state also needs to fight parts of itself.[102] Examples such as that of the Zetas' control over entire police forces in certain parts of the country indicate the potential impact of corruption and ensuing co-optation of security forces, which in turn contributes both to the commission of crimes, such as disappearances, and to the impunity that follows. Importantly, one of the arguments for militarisation used by Mexican governments is the continued perception that the military is not as corrupt as police forces in the country. However, high profile cases of military leaders charged for ties to organised crime, such as that of former Mexican Defence Minister General Cienfuegos, who was arrested in the United States in 2020, speak to the contrary.[103] The issuance of arrest warrants for several military officers in connection with the Ayotzinapa case, and the subsequent intervention by the federal government to cancel some of these arrest warrants, which ultimately lead to the dismantling of the special prosecutor's office for the case, also illustrates that the protection of certain interests involves the highest levels of the Mexican state.[104] Given the pervasiveness of corruption and its impact on the potential of obtaining effective responses from investigative and judicial authorities, especially at local level, civil society organisations in Mexico have called for an international mechanism to combat impunity.[105]

[100] On the interplay between impunity and corruption in Mexico, see especially Open Society Justice Initiative (2018). Mexico was ranked on place 126 of 180 countries scored (with a score of 31 out of 100) in Transparency International's 2023 corruption perception index. The score is equal to the previous years and higher than during the period of 2016–2019, but lower than during the years prior to 2015. See https://www.transparency.org/en/countries/mexico. Accessed 6 November 2024.

[101] See Pimentel (2003); Astorga Almanza (2015b); Olásolo Alonso and Galain Palermo (2018), pp. 156–159.

[102] See, for example, Morris (2012).

[103] However, the charges against Cienfuegos were dropped shortly after his arrest and he was able to return to Mexico, where a brief investigation exonerated him of all charges. See Golden (2022); International Crisis Group (2024), pp. 21ff.

[104] See Gibler (2023).

[105] See, for example, Open Society Justice Initiative (2018); CMDPDH et al. (2018), para. 54; IMDHD (2019b), pp. 4–9.

5.1.2.4 The Response by Relatives

Faced with inaction by authorities both in relation to search and investigative activities, many relatives of the disappeared have formed groups, so-called *colectivos* ('collectives'), in order to provide support to one-another and search for their loved ones.[106] There are now over 80 *colectivos* across Mexico and Central America that are part of the Movement for Our Disappeared in Mexico ('Movimiento por Nuestros Desaparecidos en México', MNDM).[107] Some of these groups are supported by and work closely with certain human rights NGOs and have become strong actors in their own right (e.g. FUUNDEC-FUNDEM in the northern state of Coahuila).[108] The *colectivos* have played a crucial role not only in drawing attention to the issue of disappearances, but also in demanding justice, truth and memory.[109] In recent years, especially after the disappearance of the 43 students from Ayotzinapa, some *colectivos* also started conducting their own searches for mass graves,[110] becoming increasingly specialised in forensic matters and search techniques.[111] This phenomenon is not studied in depth in this research but is an important aspect of the search for the disappeared and activism by relatives in Mexico today.[112] Notably, there are different ways in which relatives conduct searches: some work closely with authorities, while others do not receive any official support. Some *colectivos* are accompanied by NGOs, who also accompany searches, although this is not always the case given that the searches, when conducted without authorities, are controversial for many NGOs.[113] In the complex scenario of different perpetrators and victims, Yankelevich argues that the search and shared pain of relatives is the principal unifying factor among the heterogeneous groups of relatives.[114] Among the achievements of the relative movement was the adoption of

[106] On the topic of searches conducted by relatives' groups, see, for example, Martos and Jaloma Cruz (2017), pp. 84–89.

[107] Over 80 *colectivos* are now part of the Movement for Our Disappeared in Mexico, according to its website: https://movndmx.org/. Accessed 6 November 2024. However, not all *colectivos* are part of the Movement, which means that the actual number of *colectivos* is higher than 80.

[108] On the *colectivos* in Coahuila, for example, see Sánchez Valdés et al. (2018) and Verástegui González (2022).

[109] For a study of several different relatives' organisations and their memory practices, both in relation to victims of the 'dirty war' and victims of the 'war on drugs', see de Vecchi Gerli (2018). For a study of how the mobilisation of relatives has supported their efforts to challenge impunity, see Gallagher (2023).

[110] See, for example, Martos and Jaloma Cruz (2017), pp. 96–98.

[111] See, for example, Rea Gómez (2019). See also A Dónde van los Desaparecidos et al. (n.d.).

[112] The searches conducted by relatives are one of the main research subjects of the 'Research Group on Social and Forensic Anthropology' (Grupo de Investigación en Antropología Social y Forense), a research group made up of social scientists with the aim of understanding current violence in Mexico. See https://www.giasf.org/publicaciones-del-giasf.html. Accessed 6 November 2024.

[113] On the concerns of human rights NGOs in relation to the first National Search Brigade, see Martos and Jaloma Cruz (2017), pp. 103–104.

[114] Yankelevich (2019), pp. 41–42.

several laws aimed at securing the rights of victims and addressing the disappearance crisis, which I describe in the next section.

5.2 The Mexican Legal Framework

In response to the mobilisation of and pressure by relatives of disappeared persons and other victims of violence in the country, several laws have been negotiated and adopted in Mexico. In this section, I provide a brief overview of the applicable domestic legal framework around disappearances and victims at the national level.[115] In this, I particularly focus on how national legislation addresses the issue of disappearances committed by non-state actors and contrast it with the international standards discussed in previous chapters.

5.2.1 Background to the Domestic Legal Framework

Mexico is a federal country composed of 32 states and has three levels of government: federal, state and municipal.[116] In its report following a visit to Mexico in 2011, the Working Group on Enforced or Involuntary Disappearances (WGEID) highlighted a number of issues in the existing Mexican legal and institutional framework in relation to disappearances specifically. These included inadequate or non-existing definitions of the crime of 'enforced disappearance', as well as problems of coordination and a lack of clarity relating to competences between the different levels of government, which are the result of Mexico's complex federal structure.[117] Among the recommendations made by the WGEID in its report was the

[115] Since Mexico is a federal country, in many Mexican states there also exists legislation at the state level, relating both to disappearances generally, as well as regulating more specific issues, such as the 'declaration of absence'. An examination of the state-level legislation lies beyond the scope of this research. I also do not examine how Mexican legislation is applied in existing domestic jurisprudence, given that this research focuses on international human rights standards. The brief overview of the national legal framework is included because the interviews conducted for this research also cover the legal framework.

[116] Willey and Meyer (2024).

[117] Human Rights Council (2011) Report of the Working Group on Enforced or Involuntary Disappearances: Mission to Mexico. UN Doc. A/HRC/19/58/Add.2, paras 12–14. It is important to note that while these coordination issues were identified by the WGEID in 2011 and one of the reasons why the LEDDCPI was adopted, they continue today. For a more recent and detailed overview of the difficulties relating to coordination among different institutions and levels of government in relation to the search and investigation of disappearances, see Srovin Coralli (2021), pp. 77–78.

adoption of a 'comprehensive law on enforced or involuntary disappearance'.[118] This recommendation to adopt a 'general law that regulates all aspects of enforced disappearance covered by the Convention' was reiterated by the UN Committee on Enforced Disappearances (CED) in its Concluding Observations on the report submitted by Mexico in 2015,[119] as well as by the IACHR in its 2015 report on the Situation of Human Rights in Mexico.[120]

The recommendations from international and regional human rights mechanisms accompanied growing pressure from civil society for the adoption of a general law on disappearances.[121] This gained even more momentum after the disappearance of the 43 students from Ayotzinapa and the subsequent formation of the Movement for our Disappeared in Mexico, which is made up of relative groups and accompanying NGOs and individuals (see above). In 2015, a constitutional amendment was passed, which was necessary to provide Congress with the faculty to issue general laws for the creation of the following crimes and corresponding sanctions: kidnapping, enforced disappearance of persons, other forms of illegal deprivation of liberty, human trafficking, torture and other cruel, inhuman or degrading treatment, as well as electoral matters.[122] Although this amendment mandated the adoption of the corresponding general laws within a period of 180 days, it was not until late 2017 that the administration of President Enrique Peña Nieto adopted the Law on Enforced Disappearance, Disappearance committed by Private Individuals, and the National Search System (LEDDCPI/Law on Disappearances).[123] Before examining the details of the LEDDCPI, it must be noted that, as of October 2024, the regulations necessary to operationalise the Law ('reglamento') still have not been published. This omission was already criticised by the CED after its visit to Mexico in 2021.[124]

---

118 Human Rights Council (2011) Report of the Working Group on Enforced or Involuntary Disappearances: Mission to Mexico. UN Doc. A/HRC/19/58/Add.2, para. 86.

119 Committee on Enforced Disappearances (2015) Concluding observations on the report submitted by Mexico. UN Doc. CED/C/MEX/CO/1, para. 16.

120 Inter-American Commission on Human Rights (2015) Situation of Human Rights in Mexico. OEA/Ser.L/V/II.Doc. 44/15, para. 9. More precisely, the IACHR recommended that Mexico '[a] dopt a General Law regarding Disappearances and Forced Disappearances, and adopt all necessary measures to ensure that both at the federal and state level, the laws and practices comply with international standards on the subject.'

121 See Leyva Morelos Zaragoza (2019), p. 132; Serrano and de Pina Ravest (2021).

122 The constitutional amendment was published in Mexico's official gazette in July 2015: Diario Oficial de la Federación (DOF) (2015) DECRETO Por El Que Se Reforma El Artículo 73, Fracción XXI, Inciso a), de La Constitución Política de Los Estados Unidos Mexicanos.

123 Ley General en Materia de Desaparición Forzada de Personas, Desaparición Cometida por Particulares y del Sistema Nacional de Búsqueda de Personas. DOF 17-11-2017 (LEDDCPI).

124 Committee on Enforced Disappearances (2022) Report of the Committee on Enforced Disappearances on its visit to Mexico: Findings. UN Doc. CED/C/MEX/VR/1 (Findings), para. 58.

Table 5.1 Structure of the General Law on Enforced Disappearance, Disappearance Committed by Private Individuals and the National Search System (LEDDCPI)

General Law on Enforced Disappearance, Disappearance Committed by Private Individuals and the National Search System		
Section	Articles	Content
Section I	Articles 1–12	General Provisions
Section II	Articles 13–43	Crimes and Administrative Responsibilities
Section III	Articles 44–135	The National Search System
Section IV	Articles 136–157	The Rights of Victims
Section V	Articles 158–173	Prevention of Crimes
Transitory articles		Provisions that establish the timeframe for the implementation of the Law's provisions and specify what happens to existing institutions

5.2.2 *The General Law on Enforced Disappearance*

The extensive LEDDCPI, which is seen as an important achievement by the movement of relatives and civil society,[125] comprises 173 articles in five sections ('títulos'), which are in turn divided into chapters, as well as 21 'transitory' articles ('transitorios') (Table 5.1).

As a general law, the LEDDCPI must be applied in all Mexican states and at the three levels of government. Nonetheless, there remains a need for each state to adopt their own regulatory laws and protocols, as well as to create institutions to ensure the adequate application of the LEDDCPI.[126] For example, in relation to the National Search System, the LEDDCPI mandates the creation of a National Search Commission (CNB, for its Spanish initials), as well as local search commissions in each state with analogous competences to that of the CNB (Article 50). Furthermore, the National Prosecutor's Office (Fiscalía General de la República, FGR for its Spanish initials) and each local prosecutor's office are mandated to create special prosecutor's offices ('fiscalías especializadas') for the investigation and prosecution of the crimes established by the LEDDCPI (Article 68).[127] In the following sections I briefly outline how the LEDDCPI addresses the issue of different types of perpetrators of disappearances and, in some respects, goes beyond the international human

[125] See, for example, Serrano and de Pina Ravest (2021); Verástegui González (2022).

[126] For a detailed analysis of how the LEDDCPI regulates the search for the disappeared and the investigation of disappearance cases, see Srovin Coralli (2021), pp. 50ff.

[127] In May 2021, the Mexican Senate passed a new Law on the General Prosecutor's Office. This new law was described as a step backwards in relation to several matters, including the coordination with victims and participation in the National Search System. For a commentary on the law, see Delgadillo Pérez and Rojas Valdez (2021).

rights framework on enforced disappearances, especially in relation to the rights of victims. I then examine some of the challenges inherent in the LEDDCPI that might negatively impact on its effectiveness in protecting victims of disappearances.

5.2.2.1 How the LEDDCPI Deals with Different Types of Disappearances[128]

The LEDDCPI addresses the problem of state and non-state perpetrators of disappearances in several ways. First, as its title suggests, it creates two distinct crimes: 'enforced disappearance' and 'disappearance committed by private individuals'. Second, the Law explicitly creates an obligation to search for all disappeared and missing persons, regardless of the perpetrator (Article 89), and to conduct criminal investigations *ex officio* into all cases where a disappearance may be related to the commission of a crime (Article 13). At the time of adoption, the LEDDCPI thus went further than the international framework on enforced disappearances because, as discussed in Chap. 2, the ICPPED does not contain an explicit obligation to search for victims of disappearances falling within Article 3 ICPPED and the CED only took an unequivocal stance on this issue when it adopted the Statement on Non-State Actors in 2023. The LEDDCPI also overcomes some of the uncertainties that remained at the international level by establishing equal general obligations in relation to 'enforced disappearance' and 'disappearance committed by private individuals.'[129] Notably, there is an important difference in the definitions of the two crimes. Article 27 defines 'enforced disappearance' as follows:

> A public servant or private person acting with the authorisation, support or acquiescence of a public servant, commits the crime of enforced disappearance of persons if they by any means deprive a person of their liberty, followed by the abstention or refusal to acknowledge this deprivation of liberty, or to provide information about the person or the person's fate, destiny, or whereabouts.[130]

Conversely, 'disappearance committed by private individuals' is defined in Article 34 as

[128] A modified version of this section will also appear in a forthcoming book chapter: Guercke (2025).

[129] Articles 13–23 LEDDCPI. On how the LEDDCPI incorporates international standards on enforced disappearance in relation to investigation, see Leyva Morelos Zaragoza (2019), pp. 141–143.

[130] 'Comete el delito de desaparición forzada de personas, el servidor público o el particular que, con la autorización, el apoyo o la aquiescencia de un servidor público, prive de la libertad en cualquier forma a una persona, seguida de la abstención o negativa a reconocer dicha privación de la libertad o a proporcionar la información sobre la misma o su suerte, destino o paradero.' Author's translation.

> The crime of disappearance committed by private individuals is committed by anyone who deprives a person of their liberty with the aim of hiding the victim or the victim's fate or whereabouts.[131]

Thus, what distinguishes the definitions is not only the relationship to the state, but also the requirement of intent in the crime of 'disappearance committed by private individuals'.[132] The CED has criticised the difference between the two definitions because Article 3 ICPPED refers to 'acts defined in Article 2'.[133] According to the CED, this means that the definition of both crimes should be the same.[134] From a criminal law perspective, however, there is a logic to the definition because private individuals do not have an obligation to disclose information and do have a right not to self-incriminate.[135]

Another aspect in which the LEDDCPI clearly goes beyond the international legal framework relates to the recognition of *all* relatives of the disappeared as victims and their right to reparation. The LEDDCPI differentiates between 'direct' (the disappeared person) and 'indirect' (the relatives of the disappeared person) victims[136] even though no such distinction exists in the definition of victims contained in Article 24 ICPPED.[137] However, the LEDDCPI does not distinguish between relatives of victims of enforced disappearances and disappearances committed by private individuals, which is much broader than Article 24 that only mentions victims of *enforced* disappearance and does not apply to victims of disappearances falling within Article 3 ICPPED.[138] Thus, the relatives of victims of either crime have the right to participate in the search for the disappeared, to

[131] 'Incurre en el delito de desaparición cometida por particulares quien prive de la libertad a una persona con la finalidad de ocultar a la víctima o su suerte o paradero. [...]' Author's translation.

[132] This definition is more similar to that of the definition of enforced disappearance as a crime against humanity contained in the Rome Statute: 'Enforced disappearance of persons' means the arrest, detention or abduction of persons by, or with the authorization, support or acquiescence of, a State or a political organization, followed by a refusal to acknowledge that deprivation of freedom or to give information on the fate or whereabouts of those persons, *with the intention of removing them from the protection of the law for a prolonged period of time*.' Emphasis added. Article 7(2) (i) Rome Statute of the International Criminal Court 1998 (2187 UNTS 90).

[133] Article 3 International Convention for the Protection of All Persons from Enforced Disappearance 2006 (1726 UNTS 3) (ICPPED).

[134] See Committee on Enforced Disappearances (2018) Follow-up Observations on the Additional Information Submitted by Mexico under Article 29, Paragraph 4, of the Convention. UN Doc. CED/C/MEX/CO/R.1/Add.1, paras 10–11. In addition, the CED criticised the absence of a definition of enforced disappearance as a crime against humanity.

[135] González Espinosa (2024), p. 386.

[136] Article 137 LEDDCPI refers to the 'direct victims' of the crimes of enforced disappearance or disappearance committed by private individuals, whereas Article 138 LEDDCPI refers to the 'relatives of victims' of the two crimes. This is also in line with the definition of victims contained in the General Victims' Law discussed below.

[137] According to Article 24 (1) ICPPED, victims of enforced disappearance are 'the disappeared person and any individual who has suffered harm as the direct result of an enforced disappearance.' Consequently, there is no distinction between direct and indirect victims.

[138] See Chap. 2, Sect. 2.2.3.2.

access case files, to receive free photocopies of search dossiers, to receive different types of material and psychological support, assistance and protection, to request the intervention of independent experts, as well as to be diligently informed about any results of the search or investigation, among others (Articles 138–139).[139] When it comes to reparations, all victims covered by the LEDDCPI have a right to receive comprehensive reparation (Article 150). Nonetheless, Article 152 LEDDCPI retains a difference between victims: whereas the Federation and states have an obligation to provide comprehensive reparation to victims of 'enforced disappearance', their obligation to compensate harm caused to victims of 'disappearance committed by private individuals' is only subsidiary (Article 152).[140] This reflects current international standards on the obligations of states to provide reparations to victims of acts committed by non-state actors, which are also viewed as subsidiary in nature (see Chap. 2, Sect. 2.1.3.3).

Finally, the sections dealing with prevention (Articles 158–173) also do not differentiate between the crimes of 'enforced disappearance' and 'disappearance committed by private individuals' and therefore also go beyond the ICPPED in that they encompass preventive measures applicable to both crimes. These include the maintenance of accurate and disaggregate statistical information about the two crimes (Article 160); the exchange of information among specialised prosecutor's offices to facilitate the prosecution of perpetrators (Article 162); the design of collaboration mechanisms (Article 163); the coordination and design of programmes to combat the root causes underlying these crimes and marginalisation, such as poverty, community violence, the presence of criminal groups, trafficking networks, and social inequality (Article 164); the monitoring and evaluation of such programmes (Article 165); the annual and public submission by federal, state and local entities of information about the causes and incidence of both crimes; as well as the training and vetting of public officials in different institutions (Articles 167–173). Moreover, the National Search System is tasked with adopting information campaigns about the crimes, training search officials, carrying out programmes to incentivise the population to provide information, coordinating with civil society organisations, collecting data on both crimes, identifying circumstances that make persons particularly vulnerable to becoming a victim of either crime, providing information, exchanging information about prevention policies, and conducting research on the phenomenon of disappearances and related crimes as a basis for the adoption of policies (Article 161). All of these preventive measures are broadly in line with general preventive standards outlined in Chap. 2, yet go beyond them in

[139] Mexico's General Victims' Law contains similar provisions.

[140] 'La Federación y las Entidades Federativas, en el ámbito de sus respectivas competencias, son responsables de asegurar la reparación integral a las Víctimas por Desaparición Forzada de Personas cuando sean responsables sus servidores públicos o particulares bajo la autorización, consentimiento, apoyo, aquiescencia o respaldo de éstos.

La Federación y las Entidades Federativas *compensarán de forma subsidiaria el daño causado a las Víctimas de desaparición cometida por particulares* en los términos establecidos en la Ley General de Víctimas.*'* Emphasis added.

the sense that they are explicitly articulated in relation to the crime of 'disappearance committed by private individuals' in addition to the crime of 'enforced disappearance', whereas at the international level, the preventive standards relating to disappearances committed by non-state actors have to be inferred, with the exception of those relating to the prevention of disappearances of migrants in line with the CED's General Comment on Enforced Disappearance in the Context of Migration (see Chap. 2, Sect. 2.2.3.1).[141]

5.2.2.2 Challenges of the LEDDCPI

While the LEDDCPI has generally been welcomed and hailed as a success by many, there are also some criticisms in relation to its content and its complexity. For example, one aspect of the LEDDCPI that has received criticism is the inclusion of 'missing persons' ('personas no localizadas'). The LEDDCPI distinguishes between disappeared and missing persons as follows: disappeared persons are those whose whereabouts are unknown and where it can be presumed that their absence is related to the commission of a crime; conversely, missing persons are those whose whereabouts are unknown without any indications that their absence may be linked to a crime.[142] The authorities tasked with the search, according to the LEDDCPI, have to search for any person reported disappeared *or* missing (Article 89). This means that for the purpose of the search, the legal nature of the disappearance is irrelevant.[143] While this broad obligation to search was intended to overcome potential inaction by authorities on the basis of legal classifications, it also effectively blurs the distinction between disappeared and missing persons in this area. This creates the risk of authorities using the data of localised missing persons as a measure of success in the search for the disappeared.[144] Further, the inclusion of missing persons in the LEDDCPI could continue the practice of not investigating cases with little or no evidence, given that the LEDDCPI continues to require the presumption of a crime as a basis for the obligation to investigate.[145] Finally, and as mentioned above, the inclusion of both disappeared and missing persons in the LEDDCPI can create confusion as regards the statistical information about the phenomenon of disappearances.[146]

---

[141] See also Guercke (2025).

[142] See Article 4 (XV–XVI) LEDDCPI. For a critique of the inclusion of missing persons in the LEDDCPI, see Guevara Bermúdez and Chávez Vargas (2018), pp. 168–169.

[143] On this, see Yankelevich (2020), p. 26; de Pina Ravest (2021).

[144] De Pina Ravest (2021).

[145] Guevara Bermúdez and Chávez Vargas (2018), p. 169.

[146] In the report on its visit to Mexico, the CED expressed 'concern' about the National Register of Missing and Disappeared Persons and highlighted that it is not clear how many of the registered victims might be victims of enforced disappearance. See Committee on Enforced Disappearances (2022) Report of the Committee on Enforced Disappearances on its visit to Mexico: Findings. UN Doc. CED/C/MEX/VR/1 (Findings), para. 50.

Another potential issue in relation to the investigation and prosecution of the crimes, especially that of 'disappearance committed by private individuals', is the overlap that exists between this crime and other crimes both in federal and local criminal legislation. Due to this overlap, it will be possible to legally categorise a disappearance committed by a private individual as either this crime, the crime of kidnapping, or the crime of (illegal) deprivation of liberty.[147] Such categorisation has an impact not just on the manner in which the investigation is conducted, but also determines which unit deals with the case, which creates uncertainty around competencies.[148] In addition to this, the above-mentioned requirement to create new institutions for the search and investigation of disappearances at both federal and state level, all of which will have to coordinate with each other, may also lead to challenges in relation to competencies and thereby impact on the effectiveness of investigations. This is because the adequate functioning of this complex institutional structure requires a high level of coordination and collaboration, as well as sufficient funding.[149] Yet, in view of persistent problems surrounding the will of authorities to collaborate, this constitutes a particularly difficult aspect of the Law's implementation.[150] In practice, by early 2024, most states had adopted local laws on disappearances and victims, and created local search and victims' commissions, as well as special prosecutor's offices,[151] but coordination among them continues to be insufficient and, according to the CED, has impeded effective searches and investigations.[152]

5.2.3 The General Victims' Law

The General Law on Disappearance is not the only legal instrument adopted in Mexico that explicitly deals with the issue of disappearances. The General Victims' Law (Victim's Law/LGV for its Spanish initials), which was published in early 2013, was a first reaction by the Mexican government to the Movement for Peace with Justice and Dignity (MPJD for its Spanish initials). This movement, led by Mexican poet Javier Sicilia after the brutal assassination of his son in 2011, brought

[147] See Yankelevich (2020), p. 23. According to a report by the NGO Impunidad Cero, this kind of confusion between legal categories of crimes is already happening. See Impunidad Cero (2023), pp. 54–55.

[148] Yankelevich (2020), p. 25.

[149] See Leyva Morelos Zaragoza (2019), pp. 144–148.

[150] See Srovin Coralli (2021), pp. 64–80; Serrano and de Pina Ravest (2021); de Pina Ravest (2021).

[151] Cortez (2024).

[152] Committee on Enforced Disappearances (2022) Report of the Committee on Enforced Disappearances on its visit to Mexico: Observations and recommendations. UN Doc. CED/C/MEX/VR/1 (Recommendations), paras 26–32; Committee on Enforced Disappearances (2023) Concluding observations on the additional information submitted by Mexico under article 29 (4) of the Convention. UN Doc. CED/C/MEX/OAI/2, paras 21, and 37–38.

together different local movements, victims' groups and human rights organisations.[153] One of the most important aspects of the MPJD was the demand for all victims of violence, including victims of disappearances, to be recognised as victims. Recognition of victimhood was aimed at countering the stigmatising government discourse, according to which those who died or disappeared in the context of the 'war on drugs' were either collateral damage or involved in criminal activities, implying that they were somehow deserving of their fate.[154]

The LGV contains a very broad definition of 'victim', which includes anyone who has suffered economic, physical, mental or emotional harm or damage as a result of the commission of a crime or a violation of human rights. Relatives, or persons in charge of the victim, are considered 'indirect' victims.[155] In relation to disappearances in particular, the LGV establishes a number of obligations, mainly concerning the immediate search or release of disappeared persons.[156] The LGV also mandates the creation of victims' commissions, both at state and at federal level, as well as the establishment of a National System for Victims' Assistance (SNAV for its Spanish initials).[157] The implementation of the Victims' Law and the provision of effective assistance to victims has been plagued with challenges, in large part related to the structure and operation of the SNAV and the federal and local victims' commissions.[158] Victims face challenges and obstacles to access their rights as established by the LGV, from difficulties to be recognised as victims, to complicated bureaucratic processes, to insensitive and re-victimising treatment by staff of the victims' commissions.[159] The extent of delays and inaction by the federal Commission for Victims' Assistance (CEAV for its Spanish initials) is such that there are hundreds of complaints and judicial proceedings against the Commission.[160] Finally, while already struggling with insufficient funding, the proposed austerity measures introduced by the government of Andrés Manuel López Obrador in 2020 were such that the CEAV made a public statement warning that its operations would be completely paralysed.[161] The lack of effective protection of victims has also been highlighted as a point of concern by the CED on multiple occasions.[162]

---

[153] On the MPJD and the creation of the Victims' Law, see Gallagher (2012).

[154] See de Vecchi Gerli (2018), pp. 134–135.

[155] Article 4, Ley General de Víctimas. DOF 03-01-2017 (LGV).

[156] Articles 19, 21, 61, 73 (ii), 120 (xv), and 123 (ii) LGV.

[157] Articles 79–83 LGV.

[158] See, for example, Sánchez del Ángel and Dayán Askenazi (2016) and Angel (2018, 2020).

[159] Sánchez del Ángel and Dayán Askenazi (2016), pp. 17–19.

[160] See, for example, Angel (2020) and I(dh)eas (2020).

[161] Comisión Ejecutiva de Atención a Víctimas (2020), Avilés (2020) and Angel (2021b).

[162] Committee on Enforced Disappearances (2015) Concluding observations on the report submitted by Mexico. UN Doc. CED/C/MEX/CO/1, paras 38–39; Committee on Enforced Disappearances (2022) Observaciones finales sobre el informe presentado por México en virtud del artículo 29, párrafo 1, de la Convención. UN Doc. CED/C/MEX/FU/1, paras 37–38; Committee on Enforced Disappearances (2022) Report of the Committee on Enforced Disappearances on its

The domestic legal framework in Mexico thus provides wide-ranging measures of protection to victims of disappearances, both of 'enforced disappearance' and 'disappearance committed by private individuals', as well as to their relatives. However, due to the many setbacks in the implementation of the Victims' Law and the LEDDCPI, as well as the different institutions and bodies created to support the search for and identification of victims, much of the initial optimism has turned to frustration as institutions and mechanisms are grossly underfunded and cannot operate. Open conflicts between heads of the institutions and the government, which led to resignations by heads and members of several of these institutions, have further undermined progress. These include the resignations of two heads of the CEAV in 2020 and 2021,[163] the special prosecutor for the Ayotzinapa case in 2022,[164] and the head of the National Search Commission in 2023 amidst a dispute over the number of disappeared persons within the administration of former president López Obrador, who ordered a recount by census of all disappeared persons.[165] The government's new register, presented in December 2023, was heavily criticized by relatives whose disappeared loved ones were no longer included.[166] Additionally, the appointment of new a CNB Commissioner without following protocols and consulting with civil society in 2023, and the subsequent dismissal by the newly appointed Commissioner of most of the staff in early 2024, impacted on existing efforts to search for the disappeared.[167]

5.3 Disappearances in Mexico from an International Legal Perspective

Mexico has signed and ratified the vast majority of international and regional human rights instruments and has been a party to the ICPPED since 2008.[168] As discussed in previous chapters, according to the definitions contained in regional and

visit to Mexico: Observations and recommendations, UN Doc. CED/C/MEX/VR/1 (Recommendations), paras 76ff.

[163] Angel (2021a) and Ferri (2020).

[164] See GIEI (2023), pp. 294 ff; Inter-American Commission on Human Rights (2022) Tercer Informe del Mecanismo Especial de Seguimiento al Asunto Ayotzinapa (MESA): Avances y seguimiento del cumplimiento de la Medida Cautelar MC/409/14, paras 244–255.

[165] A dónde van los Desaparecidos (2023).

[166] Tzuc (2024b).

[167] Tzuc (2024a).

[168] In September 2020 Mexico accepted the jurisdiction of the CED to hear individual cases but it has not accepted the interstate communication procedure under Article 32 ICPPED. On Mexico's ratification status of international human rights treaties, see https://tbinternet.ohchr.org/_layouts/15/TreatyBodyExternal/Treaty.aspx?CountryID=112&Lang=EN (accessed 6 November 2024). For Mexico's ratifications of instruments in the Inter-American system, see http://www.cidh.org/annualrep/2004eng/annex1.htm. Accessed 6 November 2024.

international human rights instruments, for a disappearance to be considered 'enforced', it has to be committed by a state actor, or 'by persons or groups acting with the authorization, support or acquiescence of the State'.[169] Moreover, according to Article 3 ICPPED, disappearances committed by non-state actors who act fully independently of the state, must be distinguished from enforced disappearances.[170] Therefore, from an International Human Rights Law (IHRL) perspective, disappearances in Mexico today comprise both enforced disappearances and disappearances falling within the scope of Article 3 ICPPED.

As discussed in Chap. 2, states have a number of obligations in relation to disappearances committed by non-state actors, both under Article 3 ICPPED, as well as under more general human rights instruments. The most explicit of these is the obligation to investigate, which is established in Article 3 ICPPED. The obligation of the Mexican state to investigate all disappearance cases has been reiterated on numerous occasions by different international (and regional) human rights mechanisms.[171] For example, in the report on its visit to Mexico in 2011, the WGEID stated that it was not possible to know exactly how many disappearances were *enforced* and that unless proper investigations were carried out, cases could not be ruled out as enforced disappearances.[172] The CED has taken a similar stance by accepting Urgent Actions from Mexico in cases where there was no clear information about the perpetrators.[173] Moreover, in its views on the individual communication *Berrospe Medina*, the CED noted that, when there are sufficient elements to show state involvement in a disappearance, the burden of proof is reversed and it is the state that must show that it was not directly or indirectly involved in the disappearance through a diligent investigation.[174] This was in response to the Mexican state's argument that it had not found any operations by state forces related to the case and therefore investigated the disappearance as 'false imprisonment that was most likely committed by an organized crime group'.[175] It is therefore clear that by failing to effectively investigate cases of disappearances committed by non-state actors, Mexico is violating its obligations under the ICPPED, as well as obligations relating to other rights that can be violated as a result of a disappearance.

---

[169] Article 2 ICPPED.

[170] Committee on Enforced Disappearances (2023) Statement on non-State actors in the context of the International Convention for the Protection of All Persons from Enforced Disappearances. UN Doc. CED/C/10, para. 18.

[171] Committee on Enforced Disappearances (2022) Report of the Committee on Enforced Disappearances on its visit to Mexico: Findings. UN Doc. CED/C/MEX/VR/1 (Findings), paras 40–41.

[172] Human Rights Council (2011) Report of the Working Group on Enforced or Involuntary Disappearances: Mission to Mexico. UN Doc. A/HRC/19/58/Add.2, para. 18.

[173] Committee on Enforced Disappearances (2014) Report of the Committee on Enforced Disappearances. UN Doc. A/69/56, paras 61–62; Committee on Enforced Disappearances (2017) Report of the Committee on Enforced Disappearances. UN Doc. A/72/56, pp. 57–58.

[174] *Berrospe Medina and Mendoza Berrospe v. Mexico* [2023] Committee on Enforced Disappearances CED/C/24/D/4/2021, para. 7.3.

[175] Ibid., para. 4.2.

The *Cotton Field* case before the IACtHR,[176] which I discussed in previous chapters (see Chap. 3, Sect. 3.2.1.2), deals with exactly this issue, albeit in the context of widespread violence against women in Ciudad Juárez during the 1990s and thus prior to the beginning of the 'war on drugs'. Nonetheless, many of the shortcomings in investigations identified in that particular case, continue to occur today in relation to disappearances of both female and male victims.[177] Yet the current context, the particular role played by organised criminal groups as perpetrators of violence generally, and of disappearances more specifically, as well as the scale of the atrocities committed and the forensic crisis, raise additional questions from an international legal perspective. The first concerns the scope of the Mexican state's responsibility for disappearances committed by non-state actors; the second concerns ongoing discussions about the characterisation of the violence as a non-international armed conflict (NIAC) or as crimes against humanity, which would broaden the international legal regimes applicable to the Mexican situation. In the following sections I highlight and examine these questions in turn, without aiming to provide definitive answers.

5.3.1 The International Responsibility of the Mexican State[178]

Regarding the Mexican state's international responsibility in relation to disappearances, two questions stand out: first, and considering high levels of impunity, the extent to which the state can be considered as acquiescing to, or responsible for failing to prevent all disappearances committed by organised criminal groups —or other private actors— in the country. Second, whether 'administrative' disappearances, in which the state is *de facto* responsible for the disappearance of the person, could be considered enforced disappearances. In what follows, I discuss each of these questions in turn.

5.3.1.1 Acquiescence

As discussed in previous chapters, up until the adoption of the CED's Statement on Non-State Actors in 2023, there was no clear definition of 'acquiescence' and no in-depth legal analysis of the concept in jurisprudence, leaving doubts about whether

[176] *Case of González et al ("Cotton Field") v Mexico* [2009] Inter-American Court of Human Rights Serie C No. 205.

[177] On the lack of progress in relation to disappearances of women despite the measures ordered in the *Cotton Field* case, see Inter-American Commission on Human Rights (2015) Situation of Human Rights in Mexico. OEA/Ser.L/V/II.Doc. 44/15, paras 181–184.

[178] Some parts of this section are published elsewhere: Guercke (2021, 2022, 2025).

and how acquiescence differed from a failure to prevent, among others. The most clear-cut cases were those where acquiescence was established on the basis of a relationship between state and non-state actors. In relation to disappearances committed by OCGs in Mexico, in cases where there was direct collaboration between authorities and criminal organisations, or clear evidence of authorities standing by, such as the disappearance of the 43 students from Ayotzinapa or the massacres carried out by the criminal group the Zetas in northern Coahuila (see above), there would be, at a minimum, acquiescence by authorities.[179] In these cases, it was evident that authorities had both knowledge of the crimes that were being committed and that their actions and omissions enabled the commission of the crimes by criminal groups as direct perpetrators. However, not all cases of disappearances in Mexico reach the scale, organisation, or visibility of cases like 'Allende' or 'Ayotzinapa', making it much more difficult to show the participation of state forces. Yet, although state forces are not always as directly involved as in these emblematic cases, there may be links between them and the perpetrators (for example through corruption) that facilitated the disappearance. Likewise, their failure to react to disappearances, search for the disappeared person, and conduct a proper investigation into the case, creates a permissive climate for such crimes to be committed and causally connects authorities to all disappearances. In view of this, scholars working on Mexico have called for reconsidering the separation between enforced disappearances and 'mere' disappearances in contexts where state and crime cannot be distinguished[180] and for viewing systematic impunity as a form of acquiescence.[181]

As I have argued elsewhere, existing case law leaves some doubt as to whether the above arguments would be accepted and taken up by courts.[182] Nonetheless, as discussed in Chap. 3, the CED's broad definition of acquiescence now opens the possibility to argue —from an international legal perspective— that a large number of disappearances in Mexico today could be considered *enforced* disappearances on the basis of acquiescence.[183] This is especially so because the CED definition refers to situations where there is a 'known pattern of disappearances of persons and the State has failed to take the measures necessary to prevent further cases of disappearance and to investigate the perpetrators and bring them to justice'.[184] This definition can be read as referring to the consequences of impunity and therefore reflects the argument that 'systematicity' or the structural nature of impunity in Mexico should

[179] Guercke (2022), p. 141.

[180] Gallagher (2020).

[181] See Frey (2021). I have engaged with this argument previously: Guercke (2022).

[182] Guercke (2022).

[183] Guercke (2025).

[184] Committee on Enforced Disappearances (2023) Statement on non-State actors in the context of the International Convention for the Protection of All Persons from Enforced Disappearances. UN Doc. CED/C/10, para. 6.

be considered as acquiescence.[185] However, it is not entirely clear whether systematicity of impunity necessarily implies the required awareness, which would have to relate to 'known patterns' of disappearances. To answer this question, it must be clarified what it means to be aware of 'known patterns' and whether there could be such a thing as 'retroactive' acquiescence. For example: would it be possible to argue that the Mexican state is acquiescing to disappearances that occurred in the early years of the war on drugs, when the issue was still not very well-known, or documented? This argument could be made based on the continuous nature of disappearances and the ongoing failure of the state to investigate effectively, including an analysis of broader criminal patterns. An objection to retroactive acquiescence would be that acquiescence necessitates a causal link between a failure to prevent and the initial deprivation of liberty (see Chap. 3, Sect. 3.1.2.1). Additionally, as patterns of disappearances in Mexico shift across time and space, it is questionable whether the same reasoning could be applied to all disappearance everywhere in the country, and it would not apply to individual perpetrators without ties to OCGs. In that sense, the CED definition does not yet provide definitive answers to all questions surrounding acquiescence in the Mexican context. In view of this and with a view to avoiding different treatment among victims, as I argue elsewhere, it might be most appropriate to apply a presumption of acquiescence that shifts the burden of proof to the state to show that it did not acquiesce.[186]

5.3.1.2 Responsibility for a Failure to Prevent

If acquiescence cannot be established, a second question concerns the possibility of determining the Mexican state's responsibility based on a failure to prevent disappearances at the hands of OCGs or other private actors. This question could have been addressed as a hypothetical scenario by the IACtHR in the case of *Alvarado Espinoza and Others v Mexico* mentioned above.[187] The case concerned the disappearance of three members of a family in the northern state of Chihuahua in the context of the 'war on drugs' and military activities conducted as part of the

[185] Already in 2014, the UN Special Rapporteur on extrajudicial, summary or arbitrary executions referred to 'systematic and endemic impunity' in Mexico. See Human Rights Council (2014) Report of the Special Rapporteur on extrajudicial, summary or arbitrary executions, Addendum, Mission to Mexico. UN Doc. A/HRC/26/36/Add.1, para. 11. The CED more recently referred to the impunity being a 'structural feature' in Mexico. Committee on Enforced Disappearances (2022) Report of the Committee on Enforced Disappearances on its visit to Mexico: Findings. UN Doc. CED/C/MEX/VR/1 (Findings), para. 27.

[186] Guercke (2025).

[187] While it is of course not a requirement of the Inter-American Court to engage in hypothetical scenarios, it did so in the seminal case of *Velásquez Rodríguez v Honduras*, which is now one of the most widely cited judgments in relation to states' obligations in relation to acts committed by non-state actors. See *Case of Velásquez-Rodríguez v Honduras (Merits)* [1988] Inter-American Court of Human Rights Ser. C No. 4, paras 181–182.

'Operativo Conjunto Chihuahua'.[188] The argument presented by the defence of the Mexican state was that the perpetrators were not soldiers, as alleged by the applicants, but rather criminals using fake military uniforms.[189] The Inter-American Court found this argument unconvincing and determined that there was sufficient evidence to show that members of the Mexican Army had abducted the victims. As a result, the Mexican state was found to be directly responsible for the enforced disappearance of Nitza Paola Alvarado Espinoza, José Ángel Alvarado and Rocío Irene Alvarado Reyes.[190] Based on this finding, the IACtHR did not engage further with the question of criminal groups committing disappearances and the potential implications for state responsibility of such practices. Nonetheless, given that there exists evidence of use of (fake) military uniforms by criminal groups in Mexico, for example by the Zetas in Coahuila,[191] it would have been interesting if the Inter-American Court had engaged with this question in more detail.[192] For example: what, if any, is the implication on state responsibility of the ability and practice by OCGs to manufacture and use military uniforms? What reasonable measures would a state have to take in order to protect human rights in such a situation?

The Mexican context supports the argument made in Chap. 4 and elsewhere[193] that source-based approaches to determining state responsibility would be more appropriate in contexts involving OCGs because the crimes in question are committed by an identifiable 'source' of which the state was aware. In Mexico, consecutive governments have stated that most of the violence, including disappearances, is committed by OCGs.[194] While the veracity of such assertions, particularly in relation to disappearances, can be questioned due to the insufficiency of available statistical information, it nevertheless demonstrates the state's awareness of the source of risk. In addition to this, and as outlined above, the exponential increase in violence in Mexico, as well as its persistence, has been directly connected to the security strategies adopted by the past and current administrations. An argument could therefore be made that the state not only failed to address the source of the risk, but also contributed to the creation of risk emanating from OCGs.[195] This

[188] *Case of Alvarado Espinoza and Others v. Mexico* [2018] Inter-American Court of Human Rights Ser. C No. 370, paras 72–75.

[189] Ibid., para. 162.

[190] Ibid., paras 190–191.

[191] The report on the Zetas' control of a prison in northern Coahuila lists as one of the activities that this group was engaged in the manufacturing of military uniforms. See Aguayo and Dayán (2017), p. 15.

[192] Guercke (2022), p. 132.

[193] Guercke (2021).

[194] See above, note 58.

[195] Guercke (2021). Moreover, as mentioned above, the criminal group the Zetas was initially composed of former members of the Mexican Army. One of the reasons given to explain why criminal groups in Mexico adopted military-style tactics (including of psychological warfare and terrorisation) is the military training of the Zetas. See, for example, Correa-Cabrera (2017), pp. 89–91.

contribution to risk, if the reasoning of the IACtHR in the case of *Pueblo Bello* were followed (see Chap. 3, Sect. 3.2.1.3), would heighten the state's preventive and protection obligations in areas where OCGs were known to operate.[196] Moreover, in light of the CED Statement on Non-State Actors, it could even be considered as acquiescence in certain circumstances.[197] Consequently, in order to determine the state's responsibility for a failure to prevent disappearances, the reasonableness and effectiveness of specific measures adopted by the Mexican state against OCGs could be assessed as a means of determining the state's diligence. At the same time, as discussed above, the current phenomenon of disappearances in Mexico has become incredibly complex and perpetrators also include non-state actors who are not OCGs, for example private individuals (especially in the context of gender-based violence) or small gangs. In these cases, the argument in favour of a source-based approach would not be applicable, unless the individual perpetrator had been known to the authorities. Consequently, under the current IHRL framework, the Mexican state is not equally responsible for failing to prevent all types of disappearances, even if a source-based approach were applied.

5.3.1.3 Mishandling of Dead Bodies and Remains as Enforced Disappearances[198]

Considering Mexico's ongoing forensic crisis and the examples of gross negligence by forensic and investigative authorities mentioned above, a third question that could arise is whether disappearances that result from such bad practice could be considered *enforced* disappearances. An example would be a homicide committed by a criminal group, where the victim's body is not buried in an illegal mass grave but left on the street and taken to a morgue. Authorities cannot identify the victim immediately and decide to send the body to the local cemetery to be buried in a mass grave, but they fail to take a DNA sample or record other identifying information. They also fail to properly register where the body was buried. When the family comes to the morgue to ask about their relative, authorities deny that the person was ever in the morgue because they have no records. To the family, their relative has been disappeared. In cases such as this, the lack of information about the person's fate or whereabouts, which in practice constitutes the disappearance, is the result of actions or omissions by state agents, even if the initial crime of homicide may have been committed by a non-state actor. To recall, the definition of enforced disappearance in IHRL contains three elements: deprivation of liberty, involvement of state

[196] See *Case of the Pueblo Bello Massacre v Colombia* [2006] Inter-American Court of Human Rights Series C No. 140, para. 127.

[197] Committee on Enforced Disappearances (2023) Statement on non-State actors in the context of the International Convention for the Protection of All Persons from Enforced Disappearances. UN Doc. CED/C/10, para. 5 (d).

[198] An extended version of this section is forthcoming: Guercke (2025).

agents, and negation of information about the fate or whereabouts of the victim.[199] In cases of 'administrative disappearances', which result from negligent behaviour of forensic and investigating authorities, state agents are clearly involved (second element) and there is negation of information about where the person is buried or what happened (third element). However, with regard to the first element, the deprivation of liberty, the matter becomes more complicated.[200]

According to the Human Rights Committee (HRC), 'liberty' within the meaning of Article 9 International Covenant on Civil and Political Rights (ICCPR) (liberty and security of the person) refers to the 'freedom of confinement of the body'.[201] In this sense, the deprivation of liberty includes different forms of restrictions to a person's ability to move freely by confining the person to a particular space or transporting her without her will.[202] This would suggest that in order for a person to exercise their right to liberty, the person must be alive and, consequently, the mishandling and eventual 'loss' of a dead body would not constitute a deprivation of liberty.[203] Hence, it is unlikely that negligent practice by forensic and/or investigative authorities could constitute an enforced disappearance on its own, given that the first element of the disappearance, the deprivation of liberty, would be lacking. Nonetheless, the scale of Mexico's forensic crisis challenges the legal definition of enforced disappearance and poses questions for legal scholarship concerned with this human right violation. This is because the mishandling of the remains by state agents of thousands of persons in Mexico is the effective cause of their disappearance or, in cases where bodies were exhumed from illegal mass graves and subsequently lost, their second disappearance. Establishing the state's responsibility for such disappearances only on the basis of its failure to react does not fully capture this reality. This is especially the case in view of the impact that such an 'administrative disappearance' has on the relatives of the disappeared and the fact that the international legal framework concerned with the missing and the disappeared was

[199] Scovazzi and Citroni (2007), pp. 271–272; Calvet Martínez (2015), pp. 76 ff. Note that Vermeulen interprets the definition as containing four elements, the fourth being the removal from the protection of the law. However, she also acknowledges and describes that it is debatable whether this fourth element is a constitutive element or rather the effect of a disappearance. See Vermeulen (2012), pp. 53–58.

[200] I thank Grażyna Baranowska for bringing my attention to this issue.

[201] See Human Rights Committee (2014) General Comment No. 35: Article 9 (Liberty and Security of Person). UN Doc. CCPR/C/GC/35, para. 3.

[202] Ibid., para. 5.

[203] This is in line with the reasoning of the IACtHR, which has stated on numerous occasions that the right to life is the basis for the enjoyment of all other rights. See, for example, *Case of the Pueblo Bello Massacre v Colombia* [2006] Inter-American Court of Human Rights Series C No. 140, para. 120. Note, however, that while such practices might not constitute a 'deprivation of liberty', they nevertheless constitute violations of the State's obligations relating to the handling of remains and respect for the dignity of the deceased, as well as the obligations towards the relatives of the disappeared. See Article 24(3) ICPPED and Principle 2, Committee on Enforced Disappearances (2019) Guiding Principles for the Search for Disappeared Persons. UN Doc. CED/C/7. See also Scovazzi and Citroni (2007), p. 369; Baranowska (2017).

primarily created to address the detrimental impact on relatives of not knowing what happened to their loved ones.[204]

5.3.2 *Open Legal Discussions Around Mexico's 'War on Drugs'*

Beyond these questions relating to the international responsibility of the state from an IHRL perspective, there are two additional legal questions surrounding the 'war on drugs' in Mexico on which there is no clear consensus and that could have an impact on both the state's obligations and responsibility. The first question is whether it would be possible to characterise the situation in Mexico as one of an internal armed conflict, which would make International Humanitarian Law (IHL) applicable and open the possibility of categorising some of the atrocities committed as war crimes. The second question omits discussions about the existence of an armed conflict and relates to the commission of crimes against humanity. This section briefly outlines both discussions, which have mainly been driven by non-governmental organisations in Mexico and have not received much international scholarly attention.[205]

5.3.2.1 The Existence of an Armed Conflict for the Purpose of IHL

The question of whether the 'war on drugs' in Mexico is a 'war' in the sense of being an armed conflict under international law has gained some attention over the past decade. While conflict research centres have long categorised the situation in Mexico as a war,[206] and the numbers of executions, disappearances and forcibly displaced persons are comparable to those of an armed conflict,[207] whether the conflict can be considered a NIAC under international law is not certain.[208] Those who have argued

[204] For a discussion of the origins of the international legal framework on enforced disappearances, see Finucane (2010).

[205] Some of the fairly recent international legal scholarship on organised crime addresses similar questions. See, for example, Hauck (2016) and Peterke and Wolf (2016). Moreover, in 2023 the International Committee of the Red Cross (ICRC) published an issue of the International Review of the Red Cross with a focus on organised crime and International Humanitarian Law: International Committee of the Red Cross (ICRC) (2023).

[206] See, for example, Heidelberg Institute for International Conflict Research (2011) and Voronkova (2017).

[207] OHCHR (2015); Lambin (2018), p. 85.

[208] For an overview of the discussions and arguments on this matter, see Guevara Bermúdez (2019), pp. 152–155; Padin (2023). For arguments in favour of the existence of a NIAC in Mexico, see Bergal (2011) and Wotherspoon (2012). For arguments against this, see, for example, Nill Sanchez (2013); Rodiles (2018) and, more generally, Kalmanovitz (2023).

that there exists a NIAC in Mexico, have usually done so with great caution, emphasising that there is no consensus as regards the qualification of violence in Mexico as a NIAC.[209] Moreover, the authors have not argued in favour of the existence of a NIAC in the entire Mexican territory, but rather during certain periods of time and between the Mexican government and certain criminal groups, given the latter's complexity and their changing nature and capacity.[210] The categorisation of the situation in Mexico as a NIAC would have a number of implications. On the one hand, it would mean that some of the crimes committed could be considered war crimes.[211] On the other hand, it would provide a clearer mandate for humanitarian assistance in the country, which is crucial in view of the large number of displaced and disappeared persons.[212] Furthermore, states have obligations relating to the search of missing persons under IHL (see Chap. 2, Sect. 2.1.3.2), which would also be applicable.

Proponents of categorising the situation in Mexico as one of a NIAC argue that the application of IHL would provide greater clarity in relation to applicable regulations on the use of force by the Mexican armed forces.[213] Nonetheless, there remain many discussions in IHL itself in relation to non-international conflicts in particular,[214] which raise questions about whether the application of this body of law would truly bring the desired clarity. Indeed, some even argue that the concurrent application of IHL and IHRL standards would do more harm than good by creating confusion and effectively lowering the protection of human rights.[215] This is because while IHL and IHRL ultimately have the same aim of protecting lives, and IHRL continues to apply in contexts of armed conflicts,[216] IHL presumes that some taking of lives is acceptable. As a result, from a purely legal perspective, the existence of an armed conflict can potentially complicate situations further by opening up additional legal questions, which, while theoretically interesting, will not necessarily contribute to more effective human rights protection in practice.

---

[209] See, for example, Lambin (2018), p. 86.

[210] Ibid., pp. 86–91; CMDPDH and Instituto Tecnológico y de Estudios Superiores de Occidente (ITESO) (2019), pp. 235–236.

[211] Lambin (2018), p. 91; CMDPDH and ITESO (2019), p. 178, para. 47.

[212] Guevara Bermúdez (2019), pp. 151–152.

[213] Ibid.

[214] For discussions of the applicability of IHL standards to organised crime more generally and the questions raised by in this context, see, for example, Peterke and Wolf (2016), Kalmanovitz (2023), Muggah (2023), Freeman and Casij Peña (2023) and Redaelli and Arévalo (2023).

[215] Rodiles (2018), pp. 279–280; Padin (2023), p. 793.

[216] See Doswald-Beck (2006), p. 881.

5.3.2.2 The Commission of Crimes Against Humanity

Independently of the discussion around the existence of an armed conflict in Mexico, another legal question raised by the scale of present-day violence in Mexico is the extent to which some of the crimes committed constitute crimes against humanity for the purpose of applying an ICL lens to crimes such as disappearances. In recent years, arguments in favour of this have gained traction in some parts of Mexican civil society, and a number of communications have been presented to the International Criminal Court (ICC) with the hope of the latter's opening a preliminary examination into the situation in Mexico.[217] Proponents of the existence of crimes against humanity argue that there is a need to analyse violence in Mexico not at the national, but rather at a regional level,[218] and that the scale and patterns of violence in certain regions of the country and at certain times evidence the existence of atrocity crimes, including torture, extrajudicial executions, and enforced disappearances.[219]

From an ICL perspective, the situation in Mexico raises different issues.[220] The most prominent of these is whether an organised criminal group could be considered an 'organisation' for the purpose of the Rome Statute.[221] According to Article 7(1) of the Rome Statute, crimes against humanity are defined as follows:

> For the purpose of this Statute, 'crime against humanity' means any of the following acts when committed as part of a widespread or systematic attack directed against any civilian population, with knowledge of the attack.

Paragraph 2(a) of Article 7 further clarifies the meaning of 'attack' as used in this definition:

> Attack directed against any civilian population' means a course of conduct involving the multiple commission of acts referred to in paragraph 1 against any civilian population, pursuant to or in furtherance of a State or organizational policy to commit such attack.

One question thus raised by the Mexican context is the extent to which the acts of criminal organisations, or other non-state actors, could be considered as constituting an 'organisational policy'.[222] A second question is at which point a 'policy' can be

[217] See CMDPDH and fidh (2019) and fidh and I(dh)eas (2021). See also Open Society Justice Initiative (2016), CMDPDH et al. (2018) and fidh and I(dh)eas (2020). The NGO Reporters Without Borders has also requested the ICC to open examinations into Mexico in relation to the high numbers of journalists that have been killed or disappeared in Mexico in recent years. See Reporters without Borders (2020). For an analysis of how a preliminary examination by the ICC could be beneficial for the process of judicial reform at the domestic level, see Saenz (2017), pp. 104 ff.

[218] See, for example, fidh and I(dh)eas (2020), p. 4.

[219] See Open Society Justice Initiative (2016), p. 15; CMDPDH et al. (2018), p. 6, para. 7.

[220] For an overview of these issues, see, for example, Robinson (2015).

[221] On this, see de Frouville (2021) and Wolffenbuttel (2021).

[222] For an argument that the criminal group of Zetas could be considered an 'organisation' for the purpose of Article 7 Rome Statute, see Open Society Justice Initiative (2016), pp. 89ff. For an argument that certain criminal organisations in Mexico meet the necessary organisational

said to exist, and whether the widespread failure of the Mexican state to respond to crimes committed either by its own forces or by non-state actors, i.e. impunity, could constitute such a policy, as is also argued by a number of NGOs in Mexico.[223] In some of the communications to the ICC presented by civil society organisations, the latter allege that crimes against humanity were not only committed by state forces, but also the criminal group the Zetas.[224] This is noteworthy, given that in no other human rights NGO publications on the situation in Mexico is the issue of criminal organisations as perpetrators of e.g. disappearances dealt with in any depth.[225] A final aspect of relevance to the topic of disappearances specifically is that, according to the Rome Statute, enforced disappearances as crimes against humanity require the intentionality of removing the victim 'from the protection of the law for a prolonged period of time'.[226] According to some authors, this requirement makes the prosecution of enforced disappearances as crimes against humanity particularly difficult.[227]

There is as yet very little academic discussion on these issues[228] and the ICC has thus far not made any announcements in relation to opening preliminary examinations beyond Phase 1 into Mexico.[229] The Mexican state, for its part, has not accepted the existence of crimes against humanity in its territory.[230] In its response to allegations of crimes against humanity, the Mexican State did not engage with the question of whether organised criminal groups could be responsible for the commission of crimes against humanity, despite its insistence that 'in Mexico, the vast majority of violent crimes have been committed by criminal organisations'.[231] Notably, in the discussions concerning the Draft Articles on Prevention and

---

characteristics to fall within the remit of Article 7(1) Rome Statue, see also Olásolo Alonso and Galain Palermo (2018), pp. 167–168.

[223] See Open Society Justice Initiative (2016), pp. 60–65; CMDPDH et al. (2018), paras 10–12; fidh and I(dh)eas (2020), p. 15. A deliberate failure to act can indeed constitute a state or organisational policy within the meaning of ICL. See, for example, Robinson (2014); Rodenhäuser (2018), pp. 262–263.

[224] See Open Society Justice Initiative (2016), pp. 89ff; fidh et al. (2017), pp. 43ff.

[225] Organised crime groups are always mentioned as perpetrators, as is the issue of collusion, yet neither issue is engaged within any depth. This is most likely due to the state-centred nature of IHRL and the specific aims and constraints of human rights NGOs.

[226] See Article 7 (2) (i) Rome Statute.

[227] See, for example, Anderson (2006), p. 259; Scovazzi and Citroni (2007), pp. 275–277. This, however, is not a view that is shared by all ICL scholars, and some argue that the temporal element will not be an obstacle. See International Law Commission (2019) Fourth Report on Crimes against Humanity. UN Doc. A/CN.4/725, para. 77 and note 177.

[228] See Robinson (2015).

[229] According to the ICC Office of the Prosecutor's Policy Paper on Preliminary Examinations, the latter do not formally commence until Phase 2. See Office of the Prosecutor (2013), para. 80. Mexico is thus not yet officially considered as a situation under preliminary examination. For a list of all preliminary examinations, see https://www.icc-cpi.int/pages/pe.aspx. Accessed: 7 November 2024.

[230] See Monroy and Langner (2016) and Secretaría de Gobernación (2016).

[231] Secretaría de Gobernación (2016). Author's translation.

Punishment of Crimes Against Humanity, the Mexican state commented on the notion of 'organisational policy' as a requirement for the existence of an 'attack directed against a civilian population' and expressed the opinion that it should be made clear that the organisations committing such a policy should be 'state-like'.[232] This suggests that if the state were to respond to these allegations, it would likely try to argue that organised criminal groups cannot be considered as 'state-like'.

5.4 Conclusion

The phenomenon of disappearances in Mexico in the context of the 'war on drugs' is highly complex given the multiplicity of factors which influence the commission of such crimes and the heterogeneity of both perpetrators and victims. While it is thus different from the enforced disappearances committed during the 'dirty war' period in Mexico, which were aimed at repressing guerrilla movements and political opposition, widespread impunity connects the two periods. Structural problems of impunity and corruption fuel the perpetuation of violence, while at the same time making it more difficult to grasp due to a lack of reliable information. From an international legal perspective, the co-existence of state and non-state perpetrators, especially organised criminal groups, as well as the often blurry lines between these actors, raise several questions in relation to the characterisation both of violence generally, and specific crimes particularly. The General Law on Disappearance, which was adopted in late 2017, was aimed at overcoming legal uncertainties by creating two crimes, 'enforced disappearance' and 'disappearance committed by private individuals', and establishing wide-ranging search and investigative obligations for both crimes. In this aspect, the Mexican domestic legal framework goes beyond the international legal framework on enforced disappearances and provides more explicit protection to victims of 'disappearance committed by private individuals' and their relatives than the ICPPED. However, the LEDDCPI is also a highly complex law that requires the creation of different institutions at different levels of government, which will require much coordination and resources. Victims and their relatives in Mexico are even 'doubly' protected due to the existence of the General Victims' Law, which also establishes certain obligations in relation to disappearances, yet the difficulties in the Victims' Law's implementation highlight the challenges awaiting the implementation of the General Law on Disappearance. From an international human rights perspective, the situation in Mexico raises several questions, especially in relation to the legal implications of persistent impunity and contribution to risk as acquiescence, or as a basis for responsibility for a failure to prevent. The state's direct contribution to *de facto* disappearances by improperly handling dead bodies highlights yet more questions for how to

[232] See International Law Commission (2019) Fourth Report on Crimes against Humanity. UN Doc. A/CN.4/725, para. 69.

conceptualise the state's responsibility vis-à-vis victims of such disappearances and their relatives. Despite some important developments at the legal level in Mexico, there continue to exist several grey areas which have to be dealt with in the fight against disappearances. The question as to how human rights practitioners who work on the issue of disappearance in Mexico experience these challenges arising from such a practically and legally complex scenario is the main subject of the empirical research for this research, the analysis of which is presented in the following chapters.

References

A Dónde van los Desaparecidos (2023) Renuncia comisionada de búsqueda Karla Quintana; fue por presiones "de arriba". A dónde van los desaparecidos. https://adondevanlosdesaparecidos.org/2023/08/24/renuncia-comisionada-de-busqueda-karla-quintana-fue-por-presiones-de-arriba/. Accessed 6 Nov 2024

A Dónde van los Desaparecidos, Imer Noticias, Quinto Elemento Lab (n.d.) Camino a encontrarles: Historias de Búsquedas. Quinto Elemento Lab. https://quintoelab.org/project/camino-encontrarles-historias-busquedas-desparecidas-mexico. Accessed 6 Nov 2024

Acosta M, Ennelin E (2006) The "Mexican solution" to transitional justice. In: Mariezcurrena J, Roht-Arriaza N (eds) Transitional justice in the twenty-first century: beyond truth versus justice. Cambridge University Press, Cambridge, pp 94–119

AFADEM (Asociación de Familiares de Detenidos Desaparecidos y Víctimas de Violaciones a los Derechos Humanos en México), Fundar, Centro de Análisis e Investigación (2024) Verdad y Justicia: La Deuda de 50 Años del Estado Mexicano con Rosendo Radilla y las víctimas del terrorismo de Estado. In: Fundar, Centro de Análisis e Investigación. https://fundar.org.mx/verdad-y-justicia-la-deuda-de-50-anos-del-estado-mexicano-con-rosendo-radilla-y-las-victimas-del-terrorismo-de-estado/. Accessed 4 Nov 2024

Aguayo S (2017) En el desamparo: Los Zetas, el Estado, la sociedad y las víctimas de San Fernando, Tamaulipas (2010), y Allende, Coahuila (2011). El Colegio de México, Mexico City

Aguayo S, Dayán J (2017) El Yugo Zeta: Norte de Coahuila, 2010-2011. El Colegio de México, Mexico City

Aguayo Quezada S, Treviño Rangel J (2006) Neither truth nor justice: Mexico's De Facto Amnesty. Latin Am Perspect 33:56–68. https://doi.org/10.1177/0094582X05286085

Allier Montaño E, Vicente Ovalle C, Granada-Cardona JS (2022) Recasting history to cast off shadows: state violence in Mexico, 1958–2018. In: Mandolessi S, Olalde Rico K (eds) Disappearances in Mexico: from the 'dirty war' to the 'war on drugs'. Routledge, Oxon, New York, pp 50–72

Alzaga I (2014) Defensa Nacional Busca a 242 Militares Desde 2010. Milenio. http://www.milenio.com/policia/defensa-nacional-busca-242-militares-2010. Accessed 4 Nov 2024

AMLO (2019) Versión Estenográfica de La Conferencia de Prensa Matutina Del Presidente Andrés Manuel López Obrador. https://lopezobrador.org.mx/2019/02/04/version-estenografica-de-la-conferencia-de-prensa-matutina-del-presidente-andres-manuel-lopez-obrador-37/. Accessed 8 Nov 2024

Amnesty International (2013) Confronting a nightmare: disappearances in Mexico. AMR 41/025/2013. https://www.amnesty.org/en/documents/amr41/025/2013/en/. Accessed 4 Nov 2024

Anderson K (2006) How effective is the international convention for the protection of all persons from enforced disappearance likely to be in holding individuals criminally responsible for acts of enforced disappearance. Melb J Int Law 7:245–277

Angel A (2018) Las víctimas se multiplican, pero los apoyos no. Animal Político. https://www.animalpolitico.com/2018/10/comision-victimas-menos-personal-dinero/. Accessed 6 Nov 2024

Angel A (2020) Comisión de Víctimas, con personal insuficiente y 476 denuncias por maltrato y acoso. Animal Político. https://www.animalpolitico.com/2020/01/comision-victimas-maltrato-acoso/. Accessed 6 Nov 2024

Angel A (2021a) Encargado de la CEAV renuncia tras seis meses en el cargo y sin que haya aún nuevo titular. Animal Politico. https://animalpolitico.com/2021/01/encargado-ceav-renuncia-tras-seis-meses-en-el-cargo-aun-sin-nuevo-titular. Accessed 6 Nov 2024

Angel A (2021b) CEAV operará en 2022 con déficit de más de mil 600 millones; peligran pagos y contrataciones. Animal Político. https://animalpolitico.com/sociedad/ceav-2022-deficit-peligran-pagos-contrataciones. Accessed 6 Nov 2024

Ansolabehere K, Martos A (2022) Violence regimes and disappearances: some reflections from the north-east region of Mexico. In: Mandolessi S, Olalde Rico K (eds) Disappearances in Mexico: from the 'dirty war' to the 'war on drugs'. Disappearances in Mexico. Routledge, Oxon New York, pp 97-124

Ansolabehere K, del Cid J, de Pina Ravest V et al. (2021a) Nombrarlas para encontrarlas: Contexto, dinámicas y respuestas en torno a la desaparición de mujeres en el centro de México. Observatorio sobre Desaparición e Impunidad. https://www.flacso.edu.mx/wp-content/uploads/2022/01/flacso-nombrarlasencontrarlas-17112021-compressed.pdf. Accessed 8 Nov 2024

Ansolabehere K, Frey BA, Payne LA (2021b) Introduction. In: Ansolabehere K, Frey BA, Payne LA (eds) Disappearances in the post-transition era in Latin America. British Academy Scholarship, London

Antillón X (2020) La cuenta de los que (nos) faltan. Animal Político. https://animalpolitico.com/analisis/organizaciones/res-publica/la-cuenta-de-los-que-nos-faltan-2. Accessed 6 Nov 2024

Antillón Najlis X (ed) (2018) Yo sólo quería que amaneciera impactos psicosociales del caso Ayotzinapa. Fundar, Centro de Análisis e Investigación. http://ayotzinapa.fundar.org.mx/wp-content/documentos/DocAyotziFINAL.pdf. Accessed 8 Nov 2024

Astorga Almanza LA (2015a) ¿QUÉ QUERÍAN QUE HICIERA? Inseguridad y delincuencia organizada en el gobierno de Felipe Calderón. Grijalbo, Mexico City

Astorga Almanza LA (2015b) Drogas sin fronteras. Debolsillo, Mexico City

Avilés E (2020) Atención a víctimas: austeridad y presupuesto son la punta del iceberg de los problemas estructurales que ha arrastrado la CEAV desde su creación. Comisión Mexicana de Defensa y Promoción de los Derechos Humanos. http://cmdpdh.org/2020/06/cp-atencion-a-victimas-austeridad-y-presupuesto-son-la-punta-del-iceberg-de-los-problemas-estructurales-que-ha-arrastrado-la-ceav-desde-su-creacion/. Accessed 6 Nov 2024

Ayala Martínez A (2021) Buscando mujeres desaparecidas en vida: entre trata de personas y violencia de género. A dónde van los desaparecidos. https://adondevanlosdesaparecidos.org/2021/03/04/buscando-mujeres-desaparecidas-en-vida-entre-trata-de-personas-y-violencia-de-genero/. Accessed 8 Nov 2024

Baranowska G (2017) Advances and progress in the obligation to return the remains of missing and forcibly disappeared persons. Int Rev Red Cross 99:709–733. https://doi.org/10.1017/S181638311800036X

Bergal C (2011) The Mexican drug war: the case for non-international armed conflict classification note. Fordham Int Law J 34:1042–1088

Berman MR, Clark RS (1982) State terrorism: disappearances. Rutgers Law J 13:531–577

Calderón G, Robles G, Díaz-Cayeros A, Magaloni B (2015) The beheading of criminal organizations and the dynamics of violence in Mexico. J Confl Resolut 59:1455–1485. https://doi.org/10.1177/0022002715587053

Calveiro P (2022) Disappearance and governmentality in Mexico. In: Mandolessi S, Olalde Rico K (eds) Disappearances in Mexico: from the 'dirty war' to the 'war on drugs'. Routledge, Oxon, New York, pp 75–96

Calvet Martínez E (2015) Desapariciones forzadas y justicia transicional. La búsqueda de respuestas a través del derecho a la verdad, a la justicia y a la reparación. Dissertation, Universitat de Barcelona

Camacho Servín F (2018) En 11 años han desaparecido 151 luchadores sociales. La Jornada. https://www.jornada.com.mx/2018/05/17/politica/016n2pol. Accessed 10 March 2025

CEPAD (Centro de Justicia para la Paz y el Desarrollo) (2019) Incineraciones de Cuerpos No Identificados. Crímenes Sin Justicia. https://mx.boell.org/es/2019/01/30/incineraciones-de-cuerpos-no-identificados-en-jalisco-crimenes-sin-justicia. Accessed 6 Nov 2024

Citroni G (2017) The first attempts in Mexico and Central America to address the phenomenon of missing and disappeared migrants. Int Rev Red Cross 99:735–757. https://doi.org/10.1017/S1816383118000346

CMDPDH (Comisión Mexicana de Defensa y Promoción de los Derechos Humanos), fidh (International Federation for Human Rights) (2019) De la estrategia de seguridad a los crímenes de lesa humanidad en México (Informes presentados a la Corte Penal Internacional). http://cmdpdh.org/publicaciones-pdf/cmdpdh-estrategia-de-seguridad-a-crimenes-de-lesa-humanidad.pdf. Accessed 8 Nov 2024

CMDPDH (Comisión Mexicana de Defensa y Promoción de los Derechos Humanos), Instituto Tecnológico y de Estudios Superiores de Occidente (ITESO) (2019) The situation of drug-related violence in Mexico from 2006-2017: a non-international armed conflict? 1st edn. Instituto Tecnológico y de Estudios Superiores de Occidente (ITESO), Guadalajara

CMDPDH (Comisión Mexicana de Defensa y Promoción de los Derechos Humanos), World Organisation Against Torture, International Federation for Human Rights et al (2018) Crimes against humanity in the war on drugs: submission for Mexico's Third Universal Periodic Review. https://www.cmdpdh.org/publicaciones-pdf/cmdpdh-epu-crimenes-de-lesa-humanidad-en-el-marco-de-la-lucha-contra-las-drogas-en.pdf. Accessed 8 Nov 2024

Comisión Ejecutiva de Atención a Víctimas (2020) Decreto De Austeridad Paralizará Funcionamiento De La Ceav. Gobierno de México. http://www.gob.mx/ceav/prensa/decreto-de-austeridad-paralizara-funcionamiento-de-la-ceav. Accessed 6 Nov 2024

Coria C (2015) Desaparecen 7 trabajadores en Chihuahua; gobierno estatal anuncia búsqueda. Excélsior. https://www.excelsior.com.mx/nacional/2015/10/31/1054459. Accessed 4 Nov 2024

Correa-Cabrera G (2017) Los Zetas Inc.: criminal corporations, energy, and civil war in Mexico. University of Texas Press

Cortez E (2023) El Mecanismo Extraordinario de Identificación Forense: Un Proyecto Trunco. Instituto Mexicano de Derechos Humanos y Democracia (IMDHD). https://www.imdhd.org/comunicacion/blog/el-mecanismo-extraordinario-de-identificacion-forense-un-proyecto-trunco/. Accessed 8 Nov 2024

Cortez E (2024) A seis años de la Ley General de Desaparición, ¿Dónde estamos? Red Lupa. https://imdhd.org/redlupa/avance-de-la-ley-general-de-busqueda/a-seis-anos-de-la-ley-general-de-desaparicion-donde-estamos/. Accessed 6 Nov 2024

de Frouville O (2021) Criminalizing or trivializing enforced disappearances? The issue of 'non-state actors'. In: de Frouville O, Sturma P (eds) La pénalisation des droits de l'homme. Pedone, Paris

de Pina Ravest V (2021) How to create a search mechanism for disappeared persons: lessons from Mexico. In: Ansolabehere K, Frey BA, Payne LA (eds) Disappearances in the post-transition era in Latin America. British Academy Scholarship, London

de Vecchi Gerli M (2018) ¡Vivxs lxs Queremos! The battles for memory around the disappeared in Mexico. Doctoral dissertation, University College London

Delgadillo Pérez AL, Rojas Valdez E (2021) Fiscalía General de la República: el recuento de los daños. Proceso. https://www.proceso.com.mx/opinion/2021/5/20/fiscalia-general-de-la-republica-el-recuento-de-los-danos-264330.html. Accessed 6 Nov 2024

Doswald-Beck L (2006) The right to life in armed conflict: does international humanitarian law provide all the answers? Int Rev Red Cross 88:881–904. https://doi.org/10.1017/S1816383107000823

Duran-Martinez A (2015) To kill and tell? State power, criminal competition, and drug violence. J Confl Resolut 59:1377–1402. https://doi.org/10.1177/0022002715587047

Editorial Milenio (2018) ¿Dónde está Elvis Axell? Milenio. https://www.milenio.com/opinion/humberto-rios-navarrete/cronicas-urbanas/donde-esta-elvis-axell. Accessed 8 Nov 2024

Evans M (2021) The Allende Massacre in Mexico: a decade of impunity. National Security Archive. https://nsarchive.gwu.edu/briefing-book/mexico/2021-03-18/allende-massacre-decade-impunity. Accessed 8 Nov 2024

Ferri P (2020) La comisionada de atención a víctimas en México renuncia por los recortes. El País. https://elpais.com/sociedad/2020-06-24/la-comisionada-de-atencion-a-victimas-en-mexico-renuncia-por-los-recortes.html. Accessed 6 Nov 2024

fidh (International Federation for Human Rights), Centro Diocesano para los Derechos Humanos Fray Juan de Larios, Familias Unidas en Búsqueda y Localización de Personas Desaparecidas (2017) Mexico Coahuila: ongoing crimes against humanity. https://www.fidh.org/IMG/pdf/angmexico_coahuila_ongoing_crimes_against_humanity_fidh-final_a_revisar-1.pdf. Accessed 7 Nov 2024

fidh, I(dh)eas (2020) Situation of impunity in Mexico. Report no. 750a. https://www.idheas.org.mx/wp-content/uploads/2020/05/Mexique750ang-1.pdf. Accessed 8 Nov 2024

fidh, I(dh)eas (2021) Mexico: criminal structure within the Public Prosecutor's Office of the State of Nayarit and crimes against humanity. Report no. 769a. https://www.fidh.org/IMG/pdf/fidh-idheas_-_nayarit_report_english_.pdf. Accessed 8 Nov 2024

Finucane B (2010) Enforced disappearance as a crime under international law: a neglected origin in the laws of war. Yale J Int Law 35:171–197

Franco Migues D (2019) Desaparecer Hasta Volverse Cenizas. Quinto Elemento Lab. https://quintoelab.org/project/volversecenizas. Accessed 6 Nov 2024

Freeman M, Casij Peña M (2023) Negotiating with organized crime groups: questions of law, policy and imagination. Int Rev Red Cross 105:638–651. https://doi.org/10.1017/S1816383122000649

Frey BA (2021) Conceptualising disappearances in international law. In: Ansolabehere K, Frey BA, Payne LA (eds) Disappearances in the post-transition era in Latin America. British Academy Scholarship, London

Fundación para la Justicia y el Estado Democrático de Derecho; TRIAL International (2018) Informe presentado al Comité contra la Desaparición Forzada en vista del dialogo de seguimiento con respecto a México, en ocasión de la 15ª sesión. https://trialinternational.org/wp-content/uploads/2018/11/Full-report-to-the-Committee-on-Enforced-Disappearances-Spanish.pdf. Accessed 8 Nov 2024

Gallagher J (2012) Mobilization in Mexico in 2012: the movement for peace and the struggle for justice. Anuario del Conflicto Social 2:1235–1260

Gallagher J (2020) (Enforced) disappearances – when state and criminal perpetrators blur. Völkerrechtsblog. https://voelkerrechtsblog.org/articles/enforced-disappearances-when-state-and-criminal-perpetrators-blur/. Accessed 6 Nov 2024

Gallagher J (2023) Bootstrap justice: the search for Mexico's disappeared. Oxford University Press, New York

García Reyes K (2019) Violence within: understanding the use of violent practices among Mexican drug traffickers. Justice in Mexico Project working paper series 16. https://justiceinmexico.org/wp-content/uploads/2019/11/GARCIA_Violence-Within.pdf. Accessed 7 Nov 2024

Gibler J (2023) Cómo el gobierno dinamitó la investigación del caso Ayotzinapa. Quinto Elemento Lab. Quinto Elemento Lab. https://quintoelab.org/project/ayotzinapa-gobierno-instruccion-investigacion-iguala-normalistas. Accessed 6 Nov 2024

GIEI (Grupo Interdisciplinario de Expertos Independientes) (2023) Ayotzinapa VI: Hallazgos, avances, obstáculos y pendientes. https://centroprodh.org.mx/wp-content/uploads/2023/07/Informe-Ayotzinapa-6-web.pdf. Accessed 6 Nov 2024

Golden T (2022) Dropping the charges against general Cienfuegos was William Barr's call. ProPublica. https://www.propublica.org/article/william-barr-mexico-cartels-cienfuegos-case. Accessed 6 Nov 2024

González Espinosa R (2024) Desafíos del Derecho Penal en México. El tipo penal de desaparición forzada de persona cometido por particulares. In: Montalvo Velásquez C, Zuluaga Taborda J, Astrain Bañuelos L (eds) Desafíos actuales del Derecho penal y la Política criminal en Alemania y Latinoamérica. Eckhaus Verlag, Würzburg, pp 381–394

González-Ocantos EA (2016) Shifting legal visions: judicial change and human rights trials in Latin America. Cambridge University Press, New York

Guercke L (2021) State responsibility for a failure to prevent violations of the right to life by organised criminal groups: disappearances in Mexico. Hum Rights Law Rev 21:329–357. https://doi.org/10.1093/hrlr/ngaa061

Guercke L (2022) State acquiescence to disappearances in the context of Mexico's 'war on drugs'. In: Mandolessi S, Olalde Rico K (eds) Disappearances in Mexico: from the 'dirty war' to the 'war on drugs'. Routledge, Oxon, New York, pp 127–149

Guercke L (2025) Contemporary disappearances in Mexico: a conceptual challenge for the international framework on enforced disappearances. In: Baranowska G, Kolaković-Bojović M (eds) Enforced disappearances: on universal responses to a worldwide phenomenon. Cambridge University Press (forthcoming)

Guevara Bermúdez JA (2019) Preface. In: The situation of drug-related violence in Mexico from 2006-2017: a non-international armed conflict? 1st edn. Instituto Tecnológico y de Estudios Superiores de Occidente (ITESO), Guadalajara, pp 149–156

Guevara Bermúdez JA (ed) (2020) Entre la Brutalidad y la Impunidad: los crímenes atroces cometidos al amparo de la estrategia de seguridad militarizada (2006-2018). Comisión Mexicana de Defensa y Promoción de los Derechos Humanos, Mexico City

Guevara Bermúdez JA, Chávez Vargas LG (2018) La impunidad en el contexto de la desaparición forzada en México = Impunity in the context of enforced disappearance in Mexico. Eunomía Revista en Cultura de la Legalidad, pp 162–174. https://doi.org/10.20318/eunomia.2018.4161

Guillén B (2024) Una ola de secuestros masivos pone en jaque a Nuevo León. El País. https://elpais.com/mexico/2024-04-23/una-ola-de-secuestros-masivos-pone-en-jaque-a-nuevo-leon.html. Accessed 4 Nov 2024

Guillén A, Petersen D (2019) El regreso del infierno: los desaparecidos que están vivos. A dónde van los desaparecidos. https://adondevanlosdesaparecidos.org/2019/02/04/los-desaparecidos-que-estan-vivos/. Accessed 4 Nov 2024

Hauck P (2016) Transnational organised crime and international criminal law. In: Hauck P, Peterke S (eds) International law and transnational organised crime. Oxford University Press, Oxford, pp 448–469

Heidelberg Institute for International Conflict Research (2011) *Conflict Barometer 2011*. No. 20. University of Heidelberg. https://hiik.de/conflict-barometer/bisherige-ausgaben/?lang=en. Accessed 6 Nov 2024

Hernández Castillo A (2019) Las múltiples ausencias de los indígenas desaparecidos en México. A dónde van los desaparecidos. https://adondevanlosdesaparecidos.org/2019/04/25/las-multiples-ausencias-de-los-indigenas-desaparecidos-en-mexico/. Accessed 4 Nov 2024

Human Rights Clinic (2017) 'Control…Over the Entire State of Coahuila'. An analysis of testimonies in trials against Zeta members in San Antonio, Austin, and Del Rio, Texas. The University of Texas School of Law

Human Rights Watch (2013) Mexico's disappeared: the enduring cost of a crisis ignored. https://www.hrw.org/report/2013/02/20/mexicos-disappeared/enduring-cost-crisis-ignored. Accessed 4 Nov 2024

I(dh)eas (2020) Juez admite amparo contra la CEAV por incumplimiento de recomendación de la CNDH en caso de desaparición forzada. https://www.idheas.org.mx/comunicaciones-idheas/sala-de-prensa-idheas/comunicados/juez-admite-amparo-contra-la-ceav-por-incumplimiento-de-recomendacion-de-la-cndh-en-caso-de-desaparicion-forzada/. Accessed 6 Nov 2024

IMDHD (Instituto Mexicano de Derechos Humanos y Democracia) (2019a) Dignificando la Memoria: la Desaparición de Personas en Veracruz. https://www.imdhd.org/dignificando-la-memoria/category/descargas/. Accessed 7 Nov 2024

IMDHD (Instituto Mexicano de Derechos Humanos y Democracia) (2019b) Propuesta ciudadana para la construcción de una política sobre verdad, justicia y reparación a las víctimas de la violencia y de las violaciones a derechos humanos. http://imdhd.org/wp-content/uploads/2019/01/Consolidado-JAG-Modelo-JVRP-4-elementos_20-enero-2019.pdf. Accessed 8 Nov 2024

IMDHD (2022) Diagnóstico de mujeres desaparecidas. https://www.imdhd.org/publicaciones/diagnosticos/diagnostico-de-mujeres-desaparecidas/. Accessed 7 Nov 2024

Impunidad Cero (2023) Impunidad en Delitos de Desaparición en México. https://www.impunidadcero.org/uploads/app/articulo/196/contenido/1701870164C42.pdf. Accessed 8 Nov 2024

INEGI (Instituto Nacional de Estadística y Geografía) (2024) Encuesta Nacional de Victimización y Percepción sobre Seguridad Pública (ENVIPE) 2024. Comunicado de prensa número 562/24. https://www.inegi.org.mx/contenidos/saladeprensa/boletines/2024/ENVIPE/ENVIPE_24.pdf. Accessed 6 Nov 2024

International Committee of the Red Cross (ICRC) (2023) Organized crime. Int Rev Red Cross 923

International Crisis Group (2024) The Generals' Labyrinth: crime and the military in Mexico. Latin America report 106. https://www.crisisgroup.org/sites/default/files/2024-05/106-crime-military-mexico.pdf. Accessed 7 Nov 2024

Justice in Mexico (2020) Organized crime and violence in Mexico: 2020 special report. Justice in Mexico, University of San Diego, San Diego, CA

Kalmanovitz P (2023) Can criminal organizations be non-State parties to armed conflict? Int Rev Red Cross 105:618–636. https://doi.org/10.1017/S1816383122000510

Kalyvas SN (2015) How civil wars help explain organized crime—and how they do not. J Confl Resolut 59:1517–1540. https://doi.org/10.1177/0022002715587101

Karl S (2014) Rehumanizing the disappeared: spaces of memory in Mexico and the liminality of transitional justice. Am Q 66:727–748. https://doi.org/10.1353/aq.2014.0050

Lambin J (2018) Mexico: armed gang violence sliding into armed conflict? In: Bellal A (ed) The war report: armed conflicts in 2017. Geneva Academy of International Humanitarian Law and Human Rights, Geneva, pp 83–91

Lessing B (2015) Logics of violence in criminal war. J Confl Resolut 59:1486–1516. https://doi.org/10.1177/0022002715587100

Leyva Morelos Zaragoza S (2019) The Mexican law on the forced disappearance of persons, disappearances committed by individuals and the national missing persons system: how many steps forward? Mexican Law Rev XII:125–154. https://doi.org/10.22201/iij.24485306e.2019.2.13641

Mandolessi S (2022) Introduction—Disappearances in Mexico: From the 'dirty war' to the 'war on drugs'. In: Mandolessi S, Olalde K (eds) Disappearances in Mexico. Routledge, Oxon, New York, pp 1–27

Mandolessi S, Rico KO (eds) (2022) Disappearances in Mexico: from the 'dirty war' to the 'war on drugs'. Routledge, London

Martínez P (2012) Esclavos del narco: Profesionistas forzados. Animal Político. https://www.animalpolitico.com/2012/10/esclavos-del-narco-los-esclavos-especializados/. Accessed 4 Nov 2024

Martos A, Jaloma Cruz E (2017) Desenterrando el dolor propio: Las Brigadas Nacionales de Búsqueda de Personas Desaparecidas en México. In: Yankelevich J (ed) Desde y Frente al Estado: Pensar, atender y resistir a la desaparición de personas en México. Suprema Corte de la Justicia de la Nación, Mexico City, pp 75–128

Mata Lugo DO (2017) Traducciones de la 'idea de desaparición (forzada)' en México. In: Yankelevich J (ed) Desde y Frente al Estado: Pensar, atender y resistir la desaparición de personas en México. Suprema Corte de la Justicia de la Nación, Mexico City, pp 27–74

Mecanismo para la Verdad y el Esclarecimiento Histórico (2024a) Fue el Estado (1965-1990) - Volumen 1: Presentación, resumen y recomendaciones del Informe Final del Mecanismo para la Verdad y el Esclarecimiento Histórico. Secretaría de Gobernación, Mexico City

Mecanismo para la Verdad y el Esclarecimiento Histórico (2024b) Fue el Estado (1965-1990) Volumen 2, Parte 1 ¿Qué pasó? Violaciones graves a derechos humanos y sus consecuencias (1965-1990). Secretaría de Gobernación, Mexico City

Mecanismo para la Verdad y el Esclarecimiento Histórico (2024c) Fue el Estado (1965-1990) - Volumen 5: ¿Por qué sigue ocurriendo? Factores de persistencia de la violencia estatal tras 1990. Secretaría de Gobernación, Mexico City

Mendoza García J (2015) Memoria de las desapariciones durante la guerra sucia en México. Athenea Digital Revista de pensamiento e investigación social 15:85–108. https://doi.org/10.5565/rev/athenea.1446

Milenio (2010) Cuarto Informe de Gobierno: Mensaje completo de Calderón. Vanguardia. https://vanguardia.com.mx/cuartoinformedegobiernomensajecompletodecalderon-544810.html. Accessed 5 Nov 2024

Mongabay Latam, Quinto Elemento Lab, A Dónde Van los Desaparecidos (2023) Especial: Defensores desaparecidos. Quinto Elemento Lab. https://quintoelab.org/project/especial-defensores-territorio-ambiente-desaparecidos. Accessed 4 Sept 2024

Monroy J, Langner A (2016) En México No Se Cometen Crímenes de Lesa Humanidad, Responde El Gobierno. El Economista. https://www.eleconomista.com.mx/politica/En-Mexico-no-se-cometen-crimenes-de-lesa-humanidad-responde-el-gobierno-20160607-0096.html. Accessed 7 Nov 2024

Morris SD (2012) Corruption, drug trafficking, and violence in Mexico. Brown J World Aff:29–43

Muggah R (2023) Organized crime in armed conflicts and other situations of violence. Int Rev Red Cross 105:569–574. https://doi.org/10.1017/S1816383123000036

Nill Sanchez A (2013) Mexico's drug war: drawing a line between rhetoric and reality note. Yale J Int Law 38:467–510

Nuño A (2024) Desaparecer en una fosa común, desde la 'guerra sucia' hasta hoy. A dónde van los desaparecidos. https://adondevanlosdesaparecidos.org/2024/02/14/desaparecer-en-una-fosa-comun-desde-la-guerra-sucia-hasta-hoy/. Accessed 7 Nov 2024

ODIM (Observatorio sobre Desaparición e Impunidad) (2017) Informe sobre Desapariciones en el Estado de Nuevo León con información de Cadhac. https://odim.juridicas.unam.mx/sites/default/files/Observatorio%20-%20Informe%20NL%20%28Final%29.pdf. Accessed 7 Nov 2024

Office of the Prosecutor (2013) Policy paper on preliminary examinations. International Criminal Court. https://www.icc-cpi.int/sites/default/files/2023-11/OTP-Policy_Paper_Preliminary_Examinations_2013-ENG.pdf. Accessed 7 Nov 2024

OHCHR (2015) Statement of the UN High Commissioner for Human Rights, Zeid Ra'ad Al Hussein, on His Visit to Mexico, October 7th, 2015. Office of the United Nations High Commissioner for Human Rights Press Release. https://www.ohchr.org/EN/NewsEvents/Pages/DisplayNews.aspx?NewsID=16578&LangID=E. Accessed 7 Nov 2024

Olásolo Alonso H, Galain Palermo P (2018) Los Desafíos del derecho internacional penal: atención especial a los casos de Argentina, Colombia, España, México y Uruguay. Tirant lo Blanch, Valencia

Open Society Justice Initiative (2016) Undeniable atrocities: confronting crimes against humanity in Mexico. Open Society Foundations, New York

Open Society Justice Initiative (2018) Corruption that kills: why Mexico needs an international mechanism to combat impunity. Open Society Foundations, New York

Osorio J (2015) The contagion of drug violence: spatiotemporal dynamics of the Mexican war on drugs. J Confl Resolut 59:1403–1432. https://doi.org/10.1177/0022002715587048

Padin JF (2023) Opening Pandora's box: the case of Mexico and the threshold of non-international armed conflicts. Int Rev Red Cross 105:772–794. https://doi.org/10.1017/S1816383122000571

Paley DM (2020) Guerra Neoliberal: Desaparición y búsqueda en el norte de México. Libertad bajo palabra, Mexico

Peterke S, Wolf J (2016) International humanitarian law and transnational organised crime. In: Hauck P, Peterke S (eds) International law and transnational organised crime. Oxford University Press, Oxford, pp 381–405

Pimentel SA (2003) Mexico's legacy of corruption. In: Godson R (ed) Menace to society: political-criminal collaboration around the world. Transaction Publishers, New Brunswick, pp 175–198

Pozos Barcelata AA (2018) El Cuerpo Ausente como Sujeto Político: el Proceso de Construcción de la Desaparición de Personas en México como un Problema de Acción Política (1969-2018). Doctoral dissertation, Université du Québec à Montréal

Proceso (2018) '¿Les ha quedado grande el cargo?', lanza madre de militar desaparecido a Peña y Cienfuegos. Proceso. https://www.proceso.com.mx/533346/les-ha-quedado-grande-el-cargo-lanza-madre-de-militar-desaparecido-a-pena-y-cienfuegos. Accessed 4 Nov 2024

Quadratín (2020) Campos de trabajo forzado del narco son la nueva esclavitud en Guerrero. Quadratín Guerrero. https://guerrero.quadratin.com.mx/campos-de-trabajo-forzado-del-narco-son-la-nueva-esclavitud-en-guerrero/. Accessed 4 Nov 2024

Quinto Elemento Lab (2020) Las Fosas de Durango: Cuando Las Máquinas Desmembraron a Los Muertos. Quinto Elemento Lab. https://quintoelab.org/crisisforense/las-fosas-de-durango-cuando-las-maquinas-desmembraron-a-los-muertos/. Accessed 6 Nov 2024

Rea Gómez D (2019) ¿Cómo hablar científicamente de un familiar que se desintegra en el desierto? Pie de Página. https://piedepagina.mx/como-hablar-cientificamente-de-un-amor-que-se-desintegra-en-el-desierto/. Accessed 6 Nov 2024

Rea Gómez D, Ferri P (2019) La tropa: por qué mata un soldado, Primera edición. Aguilar, Mexico City

Redaelli C, Arévalo C (2023) Targeting drug lords: challenges to IHL between *lege lata* and *lege ferenda*. Int Rev Red Cross 105:652–673. https://doi.org/10.1017/S1816383123000024

Reporters without Borders (2020) RSF asks ICC to investigate crimes of violence against journalists in Mexico. Reporters without Borders. https://rsf.org/en/news/rsf-asks-icc-investigate-crimes-violence-against-journalists-mexico. Accessed 7 Nov 2024

Robinson D (2014) The draft convention on crimes against humanity: what to do with the definition? Queen's University legal research paper no. 2015-013. https://ssrn.com/abstract=2531530

Robinson D (2015) Mexico: the war on drugs and the boundaries of crimes against humanity. EJIL: Talk!. https://www.ejiltalk.org/mexico-the-war-on-drugs-and-the-boundaries-of-crimes-against-humanity/. Accessed 7 Nov 2024

Robledo Silvestre C (2015) El laberinto de las sombras: desaparecer en el marco de la guerra contra las drogas. Estudios Políticos (Medellín):89–108. https://doi.org/10.17533/udea.espo.n47a06

Rodenhäuser T (2018) Organizing rebellion: non-state armed groups under international humanitarian law, human rights law, and international criminal law. Oxford University Press, Oxford

Rodiles A (2018) Law and violence in the global south: the legal framing of Mexico's 'NARCO WAR'. J Confl Secur Law 23:269–281. https://doi.org/10.1093/jcsl/kry003

Rodríguez F (2020) Desaparecer Dos Veces: La Burocracia Que Pierde Cuerpos. Quinto Elemento Lab. https://quintoelab.org/crisisforense/desaparecer-dos-veces-la-burocracia-que-pierde-cuerpos/. Accessed 6 Nov 2024

Román JA (2015) Familia veracruzana pagó rescate por un hijo y perdió a dos de sus miembros. La Jornada. http://www.jornada.com.mx/2015/11/02/politica/005n2pol. Accessed 4 Nov 2024

Rosen JD, Zepeda R (2017) Una década de narcoviolencia en México: 2006-2016. In: Benítez Manaut R, Aguayo Quezada S (eds) Atlas de la Seguridad y la Defensa de México 2016. Instituto Belisario Domínguez del Senado de la República and Colectivo de Análisis de la Seguridad con Democracia, A. C. (CASEDE), Mexico City, pp 55–66

Saenz RD (2017) Confronting Mexico's enforced disappearance monsters: how the ICC can contribute to the process of realizing criminal justice reform in Mexico. Vand J Transnatl Law 50:45–112

Sánchez del Ángel D, Dayán Askenazi J (2016) Anexo 7: Recomendaciones hacia la Verdad, la Justica y la Reparación Integral. In: En el Desamparo: Los Zetas, el Estado, la sociedad y las víctimas de San Fernando, Tamaulipas (2010) y Allende, Coahuila (2011). El Colegio de México, Mexico City

Sánchez Valdés VM, Pérez Aguirre M, Verástegui González J (2018) Formación y Desarrollo de los Colectivos de Búsqueda de Personas Desaparecidas en Coahuila: Lecciones Para el Futuro. El Colegio de Mexico, Mexico City

Scovazzi T, Citroni G (2007) The struggle against enforced disappearance and the 2007 United Nations Convention. Nijhoff, Leiden

Secretaría de Gobernación (2016) Posición del Gobierno Mexicano respecto al informe de la Organización Open Society Justice Iniciative. Press Release. http://www.gob.mx/segob/prensa/posicion-del-gobierno-mexicano-respecto-al-informe-de-la-organizacion-open-society-justice-iniciative. Accessed 5 Nov 2024

Serrano M (2017) Mexico: a humanitarian crisis in the making. In: Pansters WG, Smith BT, Watt P (eds) Beyond the drug war in Mexico: human rights, the public sphere and justice. Routledge, New York, pp 53–75

Serrano S (2024) Hacia la responsabilidad de los perpetradores: las sentencias por desaparición de personas. In: Ansolabehere K, Serrano S, Martos A (eds) Desapariciones y regímenes de violencia. Lecciones desde México, 1st edn. Universidad Nacional Autónoma de México (UNAM), Instituto de Investigaciones Jurídicas (IIJ), Mexico City, pp 137–162

Serrano S, de Pina Ravest V (2021) The legal framework on disappearances in Mexico: from demands to the law and back to demands. In: Ansolabehere K, Frey BA, Payne LA (eds) Disappearances in the post-transition era in Latin America. British Academy Scholarship, London

Shirk D, Wallman J (2015) Understanding Mexico's drug violence. J Confl Resolut 59:1348–1376. https://doi.org/10.1177/0022002715587049

Sin Embargo (2018) Milenio: son 12 tráilers con cadáveres los que rondan por al menos 6 ciudades del país. SinEmbargo MX. http://www.sinembargo.mx/25-09-2018/3476009. Accessed 6 Nov 2024

SitiosVerdad (2023) Perfil y proceso de designación de nueva titular de la Comisión Nacional de Búsqueda, preocupante: MNDM. Movimiento por Nuestros Desaparecidos en México. https://movndmx.org/perfil-y-proceso-de-designacion-de-nueva-titular-de-comision-nacional-de-busqueda-preocupante-mndm/ Accessed 8 Nov 2024

Srovin Coralli A (2021) Coordination between the search and criminal investigations concerning disappeared persons. Swisspeace. https://www.swisspeace.ch/assets/publications/downloads/Reports/Coordination-between-the-search-and-criminal-investigations-concerning-disappeared-persons.pdf. Accessed 6 Nov 2024

Thompson G (2017) Anatomía De Una Masacre. ProPublica. https://www.propublica.org/article/allende-zetas-cartel-masacre-y-la-dea. Accessed 6 Nov 2024

Trejo G, Ley S (2020) Votes, drugs, and violence: the political logic of criminal wars in Mexico. Cambridge University Press, Cambridge

Treviño Rangel J (2012) Policing the past: transitional justice and the special prosecutor's office in Mexico, 2000–2006. Doctoral dissertation, The London School of Economics and Political Science

Treviño Rangel J, Valdivia M (2014) Gobernando el Pasado: el Proceso de Justicia Transicional en México, 2001-2006. Foro internacional 54:31–75

Turati M (2023) San Fernando: última parada: Viaje al crimen autorizado en Tamaulipas. AGUILAR, Mexico City

Tzuc E (2023a) México rebasa las 5,600 fosas clandestinas. A dónde van los desaparecidos. https://adondevanlosdesaparecidos.org/2023/10/09/mexico-rebasa-las-5600-fosas-clandestinas/. Accessed 4 Nov 2024

Tzuc E (2023b) Cruce de datos: la clave para localizar a miles de personas desaparecidas. A dónde van los desaparecidos. https://adondevanlosdesaparecidos.org/2023/01/23/cruce-de-datos-la-clave-para-localizar-a-miles-de-personas-desaparecidas/. Accessed 6 Nov 2024

Tzuc E (2024a) Acometen despidos masivos en la CNB… y dan direcciones a funcionarios sin experiencia. A dónde van los desaparecidos. https://adondevanlosdesaparecidos.org/2024/01/11/acometen-despidos-masivos-en-la-cnb-y-dan-direcciones-a-funcionarios-sin-experiencia/. Accessed 6 Nov 2024

Tzuc E (2024b) Tiene censo de AMLO otros datos… equivocados. A dónde van los desaparecidos. https://adondevanlosdesaparecidos.org/2024/01/22/tiene-censo-de-amlo-otros-datos-equivocados/. Accessed 6 Nov 2024

Tzuc E (2024c) Adiós al Mecanismo Extraordinario de Identificación Forense; cierra en marzo. A dónde van los desaparecidos. A dónde van los desaparecidos. https://adondevanlosdesaparecidos.org/2024/02/26/adios-al-mecanismo-extraordinario-de-identificacion-forense-cierra-en-marzo/. Accessed 6 Nov 2024

Tzuc E, Sánchez M (2024) Cierra sexenio con más de 72,100 cuerpos sin identificar. A dónde van los desaparecidos. https://adondevanlosdesaparecidos.org/2024/09/24/cierra-sexenio-con-mas-de-72100-cuerpos-sin-identificar/. Accessed 7 Nov 2024

Tzuc E, Turati M (2020) Un País Rebasado Por Sus Muertos. Quinto Elemento Lab. https://www.quintoelab.org/crisis-forense/un-pais-rebasado-por-sus-muertos/. Accessed 6 Nov 2024

Umaña C (2017) Impunity: in the search of a socio-legal concept elucidations from a state crime case study. Doctoral dissertation, University of Ottawa

Vélez Salas A (2016) Narrativas interdisciplinarias sobre desaparición de personas en México. Comisión Nacional de los Derechos Humanos, Mexico City

Verástegui González J (2022) The right to search in the case of disappeared persons: a right constructed from below. In: Mandolessi S, Olalde K (eds) Disappearances in Mexico: from the 'dirty war' to the 'war on drugs'. Routledge, Oxon, New York, pp 187–209

Vermeulen ML (2012) Enforced disappearance: determining state responsibility under the international convention for the protection of all persons from enforced disappearance. Intersentia, Antwerp

Vizcarra M (2020) Crisis Forense: Cuando Las Funerarias Suplieron al Semefo. Quinto Elemento Lab. https://quintoelab.org/crisisforense/crisis-forense-cuando-las-funerarias-suplieron-al-semefo/. Accessed 6 Nov 2024

Voronkova A (2017) Is Mexico really in a state of conflict? International Institute for Strategic Studies. https://www.iiss.org/online-analysis/online-analysis/2017/05/mexico-state-conflict/. Accessed 6 Nov 2024

Willey G, Meyer C (2024) Mexico. Encyclopedia Britannica. https://www.britannica.com/place/Mexico. Accessed 8 Nov 2024

Wolffenbuttel AR (2021) Enforced disappearances: applicable to political organizations? Virginia J Int Law Online 61:159–174

Wotherspoon MT (2012) Mexico's drug war, international jurisprudence, and the role of non-international armed conflict status. J Int Humanit Leg Stud 3:291–321. https://doi.org/10.1163/18781527-00302008

Yankelevich J (2017) Introducción. In: Yankelevich J (ed) Desde y Frente al Estado: Pensar, atender y resistir la desaparición de personas en México. Suprema Corte de la Justicia de la Nación, Mexico City, pp xi–xxi

Yankelevich J (2019) Un concepto comunicativo de la desaparición de personas y dos notas jurídicas al respecto. Revista Mexicana de Ciencias Penales 2:37–55

Yankelevich J (2020) El concepto de persona desaparecida. In: Yankelevich J (ed) Manual de Capacitación para la Búsqueda de Personas. La Voz de la Academia. Comisión Nacional de Búsqueda, pp 19–28

Chapter 6
Uncertainty, Pragmatism, and Frustration: the Experiences of Human Rights Practitioners Working on Disappearances in Mexico

The previous chapters provided an analysis of the general international legal framework on disappearances committed by non-state actors and introduced the Mexican context. They have illustrated the grey areas in the legal framework—some of which have recently been addressed by the Committee on Enforced Disappearances—and how present-day disappearances in Mexico exemplify these grey areas and raise new questions from a theoretical perspective. But what happens in practice? How do human rights professionals work in a legal grey area? What—if any—are the challenges of working in a context where disappearances are committed by organised criminal groups in practice? How relevant are the legal questions in this work and how do they impact it, if at all? This chapter contrasts the theoretical legal perspective of the preceding chapters with an 'insider' perspective by presenting a description of the experiences of human rights practitioners who work on the issue of disappearances in Mexico and whom I interviewed for this research.[1] Interviews took place in Mexico City and in the states of Chihuahua, Nuevo León, Coahuila, Jalisco and Guerrero, where I spent a week each with a local human rights organisation. This allowed me to broaden my understanding of the realities of human rights practitioners in different parts of the country and taught me that the experiences of working on the issue of disappearances in Mexico varies depending on the geographical context. Therefore, before presenting general themes across all interviews,

[1]The interviews were conducted in 2019 and since violence in Mexico is ongoing, some of the information shared with me might have changed in the meantime. The research findings were presented to some of the participants in 2021 and some updates have been added in footnotes based on feedback received during the presentations. I edited the English translations of the quotes slightly for readability and clarity. The Spanish original quotes are retained in footnotes, with very minor edits. Interviews are identified by number only and additional details have been omitted for reasons of confidentiality.

L. Guercke, *Failure of the State*, Interdisciplinary Studies in Human Rights 15,
https://doi.org/10.1007/978-3-031-83717-3_6

I first clarify and discuss some differences between the realities of practitioners working in 'the states'[2] and those working in Mexico City.

6.1 A Note on Geographic Differences

NGOs based in the states receive much higher numbers of cases and aim to provide comprehensive support to all persons, which includes not just legal support, but also support with humanitarian needs, such as helping victims and relatives with obtaining economic or social assistance, as well as providing psychological support.[3] The high number of cases and relatively broad mandate, combined with limited institutional capacity, were described by participants working for NGOs based in states as significant challenges, as well as impediments to engaging in complex litigation.[4] In contrasting their own work with that of NGOs based in Mexico City, most of these participants expressed the view that Mexico City NGOs focus on a handful of cases per year, while they support hundreds of cases annually, given that the vast majority of disappearances occur outside of Mexico City.[5] At the same time, there is more contact and access to authorities in most of the states that I visited than at the federal level.[6] One participant, who has worked both in Mexico City and in different states, spoke about what they described as the great difference between working in the capital or in the states, reflecting also about the responsibility of NGOs based in Mexico City towards those who work in situations of 'much greater emergency'. The participant outlined the differences:

> … [here] there is no filter, as there would be in Mexico City [or] when you go to international organisations, there are filters to receive people. Here [in the state] the people just arrive directly, so there is daily urgency. So now let's say, you just arrived [at work], well-prepared, you had your to-do-list with three tasks, [thinking] 'today I will do these tasks', right

[2]This shorthand is used to refer to the other states visited during the research. Mexico City is a federal entity as well, but as it is the country's capital city, it is understood as different from 'the states' ('los estados').

[3]This is not to say that NGOs based in Mexico City do not provide psychological support or assist relatives in accessing economic support. However, the number of relatives that NGOs based in Mexico City supports is generally much smaller. In this sense, in the states the support function of NGOs is much more visible and takes much more prominence (in terms of time dedicated) than in Mexico City.

[4]For example, interviews 11, 13, 15, 16, 22, 23, 28. This does not mean that NGOs based in states have not engaged in complex litigations—for example, two of the NGOs that I visited have brought and litigated cases before the Inter-American Court of Human Rights. Moreover, the choice not to focus on litigation is not always restricted to budgetary or capacity considerations but can also be based on the NGO's understanding of their own role and aim of their work (interview 15). In this sense, the different approaches by NGOs can be viewed as complementary. (Interview 15 and comment during presentation on June 10, 2021.

[5]For example, interviews 12, 13, 15, 22, 23, 24.

[6]Interview 24.

> [laughs] - and then a woman arrives who is fleeing because her husband will do something to her, then a man arrives who is reporting that his son disappeared, something like that, then a human rights defender arrives who has just been threatened with something - right? I mean, that was your day.[7]

During the time I spent with NGOs based in different states, I was able to experience the fast-paced rhythm of work,[8] witnessing for example relatives coming in spontaneously to talk about their case or other issues they may be facing, meetings with authorities to follow up on investigations and searches, the organisation of public events, travelling to other parts of the state for meetings, interviews or workshops, as well as the reception of new cases, some of which had only just occurred, which meant that there was a higher probability to find the victim alive if search mechanisms were activated with a sense of urgency. During the week I spent with one NGO, for example, a disappearance was reported, and a staff member started calling authorities in order to immediately activate the search for the person.

In this sense, the work done by human rights NGOs based in states appeared to be less 'strategically' oriented,[9] but rather dominated by the need to respond to everyday matters related to large numbers of victims, or in the case of disappearances, their relatives, who turn to the organisations for support. Thus, especially during the weeks I spent in the states, I got the strong impression that theoretical legal questions were far removed from and not particularly relevant to the day-to-day reality of human rights professionals, especially since the vast majority of cases remains at an investigative stage.[10] This distance was also reflected in the types of responses I received from participants in relation to certain questions, such as the challenges they face in their work, questions relating to state responsibility that I had thought of in legal terms, as well as questions about reparations. The work of human rights NGOs based in the states is thus much closer and more directly connected to the daily reality of victims and relatives,[11] and is also driven by the day-to-day urgency of victims' and relatives' needs rather than strategic objectives.

---

[7] '... allá es... , como no hay un filtro, no, como puede ser en la parte de la Ciudad de México y luego cuando te vas a otras organizaciones internacionales, pues hay filtros, filtros para poder atender a la gente. Acá te llega la gente directamente. Entonces es la urgencia diaria, es la urgencia diaria. Entonces ahora te llegó no sé quién que, una señora, tu llegabas, muy bonita, tenías tu lista de tres temas de pendientes, hoy voy a hacer estos pendientes, no [ríe], y resulta que llega una señora que está huyendo de que su marido la va a no sé qué no sé cuánto, que llega un señor que te está denunciando que... lo... su hijo, desaparecido no sé qué no sé cuánto, que llega un defensor de derechos humanos que lo están amenazando por no sé qué, ¿no? Este, o sea, esa fue tu día. No, ese fue tu día.' Interview 24.

[8] This included at times back-to-back meetings with no breaks in between, working after hours and during weekends, new cases coming in throughout the day, among others.

[9] This is not to be understood as a criticism. I understand 'strategically' to refer to work based on mid- or long-term advocacy strategies, possibly including strategic litigation. As mentioned previously, this can also relate to the general orientation of the NGO.

[10] Field diary, 1 and 19 September 2019.

[11] I distinguish between victims and relatives because not all relatives consider themselves to be victims. Participants sometimes spoke about 'victims' and sometimes about 'relatives' or 'families'. Therefore, by separating the terms I omit a discussion of whether all relatives should be considered as victims.

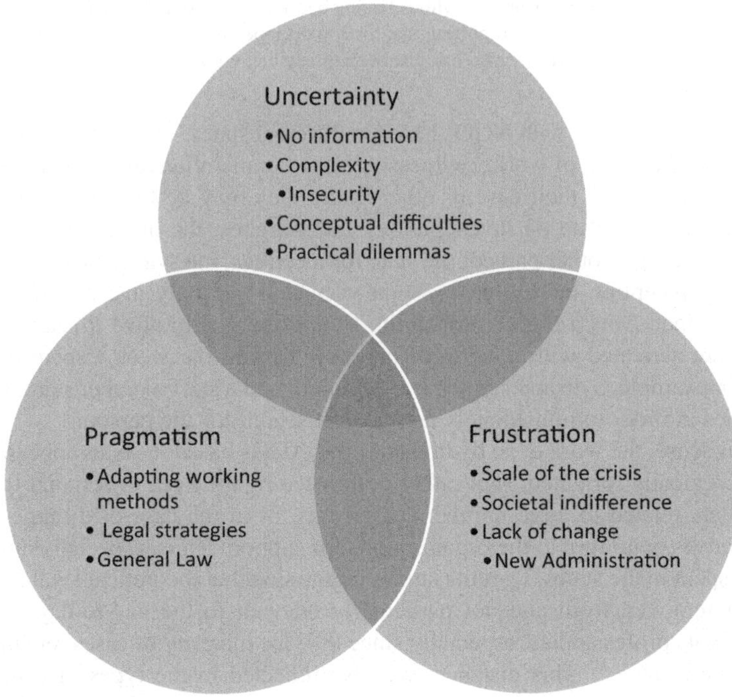

Fig. 6.1 Dimensions of participants' experiences (elaborated by author)

6.2 Themes

Nonetheless, despite these differences, there remained common experiences among the participants. Based on a thematic analysis,[12] I focus on three predominant themes in the data: uncertainty, pragmatism, and frustration. Broadly speaking, each theme corresponds to a dimension of the participants' experience: the *context* in which they work (uncertainty), the *actions* that they have taken and continue to take (pragmatism), and their *emotional* reactions (frustration).[13] Notably, the themes are all interrelated and cannot be separated entirely from one-another. I illustrate the different themes and how they overlap in Fig. 6.1. The centre of the diagram, where all themes intersect, encompasses the actions and omissions by the state which can be considered as connecting the three dimensions of the participants' experience.

In what follows, I describe each theme in turn, beginning with the theme of uncertainty, which is divided into a number of sub-themes: the lack of information, the complexity of the situation, which includes ongoing insecurity, as well as

[12] See Chap. 1, Sect. 1.2.2.1.

[13] Where there were notable differences in the participants' experiences as regards any of these, I mention this in the text.

conceptual difficulties that include the legal classification of crimes and grasping the state's responsibility. Finally, uncertainty leads to several practical dilemmas. Second, the theme of pragmatism describes the adaptation of working methods by participants, principally in response to the needs of relatives of the disappeared. While the adaptation of working methods differs in nature between NGOs working in states and those based in Mexico City, the pragmatic attitude towards the creation of two crimes in the General Law on Enforced Disappearance, Disappearance Committed by Private Individuals and the National Search System (General Law on Disappearances) is similar.[14] Finally, the theme of frustration describes the emotional reaction by participants to the context in which they work, the scale of the crisis, the perceived indifference by society, and the absence of tangible change in reality despite significant achievements at legal and institutional levels. I conclude the chapter by summarising the themes and briefly discussing how they relate to each other.

6.2.1 *Uncertainty*

The context in which participants work is one of uncertainty. This uncertainty is composed of a number of different elements: the lack of information regarding perpetrators and individual cases, the complexity of the phenomenon of disappearances in Mexico, its dimensions, the physical insecurity that exists in many parts of the country, and the (initial) uncertainty relating to the legal classification of disappearances. This context of uncertainty gives rise to practical dilemmas that were mentioned by a number of participants. I address each of these issues below.

6.2.1.1 Lack of Information

A first element that creates uncertainty in the participants' work on disappearances, especially where the disappearances are committed by OCGs (or other private actors), are several unknowns about the perpetrators of these crimes. This is due to various reasons: first, some participants who work in states with high numbers of disappearances spoke about the total absence of any trace of some disappeared persons.[15] As one participant based in a state explained:

---

[14] For a description of the General Law on Disappearances and the two crimes it creates ('enforced disappearance' and 'disappearance committed by private individuals'), see Chap. 5, Sect. 5.2.2.

[15] The absence of information is generally an inherent characteristic of the crime of disappearance, whether it is committed by state or non-state actors. See for example de Frouville (2021). However, in the absence of an organised repressive campaign or information about patterns of disappearances in the Mexican context, this inherent characteristic is further compounded by the lack of certainty regarding the perpetrators, which I described in the previous chapter (Interview 34). I discuss this problem further in Chap. 7 (especially Sect. 7.1.3).

> There is a segment… of disappeared persons about which nothing is known, there is no trace. Neither who took them, nor when, nor where.[16]

In some instances, participants linked this absence of information to the manner in which perpetrators, especially criminal groups, operated—or continue to operate—in certain parts of the country, for example by burning or otherwise disintegrating bodies.[17] Second, a few participants mentioned that where criminal actors were involved in a disappearance, it was much more difficult to determine who the perpetrator might be than when state actors were involved.[18] At the same time, however, and more prominently, participants connected the absence of information about the disappearances to the lack of effective or careful investigations by authorities and the ensuing loss of evidence and information.[19] This was summarised by one participant working for an NGO in Mexico City:

> […] and (then there are) other cases where, exactly because of this lack of investigation, it is not clear who the people responsible for the disappearance are and there remains this ambiguity of whether it was state agents or private individuals, or private individuals with some sort of collaboration of state agents. But what I mean is there it is the investigation itself, or the omissions in the investigation, that lead us to this point of not knowing.[20]

In addition to not knowing who the perpetrators of disappearances are in individual cases, at a more general level some participants also mentioned the problem of not having reliable statistics about the (dimensions of the) phenomenon of disappearances, for example because not all disappearances are investigated as such and rather classified as different crimes.[21]

A final reason for the lack of information that participants spoke about is the severe under-reporting of crimes in many areas of the country as a result of the population's fear and distrust in authorities.[22] Consequently, much of what is happening in the country, especially in certain areas, remains unknown. This is

---

[16] 'Hay un segmento, hay un segmento de desaparecidos que no se sabe nada, no hay rastros. Ni quién se los llevó, ni en qué momento, ni dónde. Ahí no sabemos'. Interview 10.

[17] Interviews 14 and 22.

[18] For example, interviews 12, 23, 29.

[19] Interviews 1, 6, 8, 12, 13, 15, 17, 18, 19, 22, 24, 29, 32. The lack of effective investigations is also one of the aspects that contributes to impunity, which many participants described as one of the main challenges that they are facing in their work (interviews 1, 2, 6, 10, 12, 16, 17, 18, 19, 22, 23, 29, 32).

[20] 'y otros casos donde justo, pues, por la misma falta de investigación, pues aún no está claro quiénes son, los responsables de la desaparición, y pues ese está en esa ambigüedad sobre si fueron agentes del estado o particulares, o particulares con algún tipo de colaboración de agentes del estado, en fin, no, pero, digamos, ahí la propia investigación, o las omisiones en la investigación nos llevan a ese punto donde no sabemos, no.' Interview 8.

[21] Interviews 7, 17, 21, 22, 27, 28. The inadequate classification of crimes continues to be a major challenge, as was pointed out during the presentation of the themes to participants (10 June 2021). Note that during the interviews, one participant mentioned the problem of wrong classification even by the National Human Rights Commission (CNDH). Interview 2.

[22] Interviews 2, 6, 10, 13, 26, 18, 19, 21, 22, 24, 28, 30.

illustrated by the reflection of one participant based in Mexico City, who spoke about the lack of information as one of the biggest challenges in relation to their work. To exemplify this, the participant spoke about not learning of the 'Allende massacre' carried out by the Zetas in Coahuila in 2011 (see Chap. 5, Sect. 5.1.2.1) until more than 2 years after it had occurred:

> And for a long time, I had doubts about the stories that came out of there, because it was just too much. Then we started hearing about people being cremated in the Piedras Negras prison and again the level of horror was such that it seemed to us impossible that this was not known, that people did not find out about all of this. So then, at the beginning, this made me ask: what is happening in Tamaulipas? And I still wonder about what we do not know about Tamaulipas, what we do not know about Guerrero... what we still have to find out about Veracruz, and then, little by little, when victims' organisations started to form, the information started to come out. Although I think that we do not even know half of what is really happening in this country.[23]

This quote shows that even persons who are working on the issue of disappearances and human rights violations may not be informed about atrocities until much later and cannot truly estimate the scale of crimes that continue to occur. The result of this, according to the participant, is that there are 'information black holes' in certain areas of the country.[24] Similarly, some participants spoke about the 'silence' that prevails in some regions.[25] In these areas relatives might be too afraid in the context of ongoing violence to report the disappearance of a loved one and are forced to 'cry in silence'.[26] Moreover, even when relatives do turn to an NGO to report a disappearance, they sometimes do not want to follow up on the case (especially at the investigative or judicial stages) because they are afraid of reprisals.[27]

---

[23] 'Y por mucho tiempo he tenido dudas sobre las historias, los relatos que salían de allá, porque era demasiado. Después empezamos a escuchar de gente cremada en en la prisión de Piedras Negras, y de nuevo el nivel de horror era tan alto que nos parecía imposible que no se sabe, que no se, que la gente no se enteró, de todo esto. Así que, esto al inicio me hizo preguntar ¿qué pasa en Tamaulipas? Y aún me hace preguntar lo que no sabemos de Tamaulipas, lo que no sabemos de Guerrero, lo que no sabemos, lo que aún tenemos que averiguar de Veracruz, no... Y y después, poco a poco, a medida que las las organizaciones de víctimas empezaron a formarse, la información empieza a salir. Aunque yo creo que no sabemos ni la mitad de lo que realmente está pasando en este país.' Interview 26.

[24] Interview 26.

[25] Interviews 7, 19, 22, 26, 30, 31.

[26] 'Tienes que llorar en silencio.' (Interview 30) The participant spoke about victims that are not acknowledged at all due to an interplay of structural discrimination, violence, and fear.

[27] Interviews 11, 10, 12, 13, 29, 30. Such reprisals do happen and relatives who report the disappearance of a loved one have been subject to threats and attacks (see, for example, Interviews 1, 6, 8, 10, 12, 13, 14, 21, 23, 30). Several mothers have also been killed during the search for their children. See for example the widely reported cases of Marisela Escobedo and Miriam Rodríguez, both of whom were killed in trying to obtain justice for the death or disappearance of their daughters. See BBC News (2010); Ahmed (2020). During a thematic hearing before the Inter-American Commission on Human Rights (IACHR) in February 2024, relatives and organisations presented a list of 21 killings and one disappearance of relatives of disappeared persons since the killing of Marisela Escobedo in 2010. See Sandoval (2024).

The fear and reluctance by relatives to report disappearances was explained by a number of participants as resulting from high levels of corruption and collusion among state actors or institutions and criminal groups, which means that, in the word of one participant who has worked in different parts of Mexico 'if it is not the bad guys [responsible for the disappearance] then it is those who were supposed to be the good guys and that are meant to protect you'.[28] In a similar vein, virtually all participants spoke about the 'blurry lines'[29] between 'state' and 'crime' and several participants mentioned that, particularly in rural areas, entire local security forces are working for criminal groups and are therefore seen as untrustworthy,[30] making it difficult to distinguish 'who is working for whom, if organised crime is using the state for its purposes, or the state using organised crime for its state aims, such as public security, control…'.[31] One participant based in Mexico City spoke about the difficulties of working in states where collusion between the state and criminal actors is so high that it seems to lead to a 'discourse of state absence' because prosecuting authorities, even if they wanted to, would not be able to do anything about a case. The participant then gave the example of the state of Nayarit: the former governor is wanted for illicit activities and the former state attorney general has been sentenced to prison for criminal activities and, according to the participant, had been personally involved in disappearances. The participant described the effect this has for those living in the state:

> So, think of a prosecutor who is a drug-trafficker, and a governor who is part of that process. With the notaries who work for him, with control over all repressive structures and the agents of the prosecutor's office ('ministerios públicos') that can prosecute you and send you to jail, with control over the prisons – what do you do? You go away, leave, displaced. Who will stay there and raise their voice about what is happening? Total silence, there is nothing. There are no stories.[32]

---

[28] 'si no son los malos, van a ser los que se suponía que tienen que ser los buenos, y que te tienen que proteger.' Interview 24.

[29] Interview 26.

[30] Interviews 1, 5, 6, 7, 8, 10, 12, 13, 14, 15, 16, 18, 21, 22, 23, 24, 25, 26, 29, 30, 31, 33, 34. Note that the participants in interviews 13 and 14 spoke of such collusion in the past tense. The impossibility of distinguishing between state and criminal forces was also repeated and emphasised during the presentations to participants (June 10 and 14, 2021). One participant also mentioned that there is certain information that will never be known.

[31] 'Ya no sabes quién trabaja para quién, si es el crimen organizado usando al estado para cumplir sus fines, o el estado usando al crimen organizado para cumplir fines de estado, que es seguridad pública, control… nunca sabes.' Interview 25.

[32] 'Entonces, tú ponte a pensar un fiscal, que es narcotraficante, con un gobernador que es parte del proceso. Con los notarios que trabajan para él, con toda la estructura de represión y ministerios públicos que te pueden perseguir y meter a la cárcel, con el control carcelario, ¿qué haces? Te vas de ahí, sales, desplazado. Quién se va a quedar ahí, levantando la voz diciendo aquí pasa esto, no. Silencio absoluto, no hay nada. Hay una ausencia de historias construidas. No hay, no hay historias.' Interview 19. This issue was also mentioned by a participant during the presentation of themes in June 2021, who spoke about how civil society has to adapt strategies and working methods to the particular conflict dynamics of each state and adjust to the particular security situation (14 June 2021).

This quote highlights the difficulties of obtaining accurate information from particular geographic regions. At the same time, it also touches upon an issue raised by a few participants in relation to the lack of investigation, or even reaction, by local authorities who work in these contexts. Infiltration of security forces and institutions at the local level also means that authorities who may have the intention to do their job properly, will risk their lives if they do so.[33] Fear and reluctance to risk their lives was described by some participants as reasons for inaction by individual authorities, even in relation to very basic tasks, such as responding to calls for help[34] or giving testimony in court.[35]

6.2.1.2 Complexity

In addition, according to a number of participants, uncertainty arises from the complexity of violence. This is because the dynamics of violence generally, and disappearances specifically, vary from one state to the next, or even across different regions within one state, as well as across time.[36] This complexity was outlined by one participant based in Mexico City, who spoke about the need for civil society to document more information on a regional basis in order to gain a better understanding of the phenomenon. In this, the participant also mentioned that Mexico was more complicated than other contexts with large numbers of disappeared persons:

> I: And how is the Mexican case more complicated than others?
>
> P: I think it's because of the number of actors. So, you not only have disappearances as a result of a conflict, for example, but also disappearances as a result of human trafficking. Or you have disappearances because of territorial disputes, or disappearances resulting from a settling of scores between criminal groups. So, the number of variables surrounding disappearances in Mexico is much higher than those of cases such as Argentina, Bosnia, Guatemala, or Peru, where there were two main actors, the Shining Path and the state. In the Mexican case, the combination of actors, even regional ones, varies a lot, there are very small groups that are also committing disappearances and this complicates (our) understanding tremendously. [...] In Veracruz, for example, [...] the testimonies refer more to participation by actors from the state of Veracruz than by organised crime groups, so this means that those who mainly committed disappearances were the state police. In Coahuila the municipal police, in other places organised crime in cooperation or together with the state. In the Ayotzinapa case, it is clear that everybody was involved. In Tamaulipas, for example, there is, even though there is not much information, what we know from

---

[33] For example, interviews 10 and 13. This was also reaffirmed by participants during the presentation of the themes (10 June and 14 June 2021). Moreover, one participant pointed out that it is not always a risk to the official's life, but officials who take initiative might be demoted or otherwise removed from office, as was the case in Veracruz, where some advances had been made to convict a former state prosecutor and police officers for enforced disappearance (June 14, 2021).

[34] Interview 12.

[35] Interview 11.

[36] For example, interviews 1, 4, 7, 12, 16, 17, 25, 26, 27, 29, 30, 33. This was also reiterated by participants during the presentations of themes in June 2021.

> newspaper articles is that there is a lot of participation in the commission of disappearances by federal actors. And so this complicates the understanding tremendously, we need to understand (the situation) at a regional level, and not necessarily at the national level.[37]

This quote illustrates a number of aspects of the complexity of the situation in Mexico: the participation of different security forces of the state (federal, state, municipal), regional differences in the dynamics of disappearances, as well as the participation of OCGs, acting both independently and in cooperation with state forces. At the same time, it also indicates how the lack of information and complexity of the situation together contribute to great uncertainty, not only in terms of a lack of knowledge, but also in terms of understanding the phenomenon of disappearances.[38] A final aspect of this complexity, which was mentioned by a few participants, is the entanglement of interests behind the crimes, which includes not just the state and organised crime, but also businesses.[39]

---

[37] 'I: ¿Y cómo es que es más complicado el caso mexicano que otros?

P: Yo reo que por la cantidad de actores. Es decir, no nada más tienes desapariciones producto de un conflicto, por ejemplo, sino también tienes desapariciones producto de redes de trata. O tienes desapariciones por casos de ejecuciones de conflictos de tierra, o tienes desapariciones por ajustes de cuenta entre grupos criminales. Es decir, la cantidad de variables que hay alrededor de la desaparición en México, son por mucho mayores a los casos, repito, argentino, el bosnio, el guatemalteco, el peruano, donde había dos grandes actores, no, Sendero y el estado. Si en el caso mexicano, el cruce de actores, incluso regionales, varía mucho, hay bandas muy pequeñas que también están haciendo desapariciones, entonces, complica tremendo el entendimiento, sí. Entonces, por ejemplo, en Veracruz tienes una mayor... responsabilidad de la policía estatal, por ejemplo. Pero en Coahuila, eran más municipales que estatales, porque la dinámica criminal era otra. Y algunos otros estados, tendrás mucho más participación... por ejemplo, incluso en Veracruz hay más participación, los testimonios hablan más de participación de actores del estado de Veracruz, que de grupos del crimen organizado. Es decir, quien operaba la desaparición, en su mayoría era policía estatal. En Coahuila era la policía municipal, en otros lados es el crimen organizado, en cooperación, o en conjunción con el estado, el caso Ayotzinapa es muy claro la participación de todo mundo, sí, en Tamaulipas, por ejemplo, hay, aunque no hay mucha información, lo que tenemos por notas periodísticas es mucha participación de actores federales en las desapariciones. Y eso entonces complica tremendamente el entendimiento, necesitamos entendimientos regionales, no necesariamente nacionales.' Interview 7. In interview 9, the participant also compared the dynamics of disappearances in Mexico to those in other countries.

[38] See also interviews 2 and 25.

[39] For example, interviews 1, 18, 21, 23, 26, 30. The participants connected this issue to the notion of 'macro-criminality'. The complexity of the nexus between these three groups and the need for further research on the topic was also pointed out during the presentations of the themes to participants on 10 and 14 June 2021. Dynamics of macro-criminal networks have been analysed in several recent studies. See, for example, Cruz et al. (2024), Espinal-Enríquez et al. (2023), and Vázquez (2019).

6.2.1.3 Ongoing Insecurity

An additional aspect of complexity that was pointed out by some participants is the ongoing nature of violence in Mexico.[40] On the one hand, this contributes to the lack of information about the phenomenon, as described above, because of insufficient security to report and share stories.[41] On the other hand, as violence continues, patterns change, which further increases the difficulty of understanding the phenomenon. One participant based in Mexico City described this difficulty as follows, referring to the territorial expansion of disappearances, including the rising number of disappearances in Mexico City:

> It does not stop and the patterns are moving as well - it is very complicated. You think that you have a good understanding of certain aspects of disappearances during one period, but that is not enough to understand, for example, those [disappearances] that are now happening in Mexico City.[42]

This quote suggests that due to the ongoing and changing nature of the phenomenon, its complexity further increases, creating even more difficulty in characterising what is happening. Moreover, some participants pointed to the difficulty of taking, or even contemplating, measures to address the phenomenon while disappearances continue to occur.[43] One participant who worked for an institution in Mexico City, described this challenge as follows:

> [...] the situation is further complicated by the fact that it is a problem that is ongoing... so you do not have the space for different institutions to decide: what do I address first? That what happened in the past? what happens right now? what happened 40 years ago? the girl who disappeared just now, the one who disappeared five years ago, the one who disappeared ten years ago, the one who disappeared 40 years ago?[44]

This quote points out some of the dilemmas that exist in terms of addressing disappearances in Mexico in the face of ongoing violence. It reflects the position of other participants, who emphasised that the first necessary step towards change was to stop disappearances from happening, as expressed by this participant, who was also based in Mexico City:

---

[40] For example, interviews 7, 11, 17, 23, 25, 27.

[41] The lack of security was also mentioned by some participants as an obstacle for truth-finding mechanisms, such as truth commissions. See, for example, interviews 7 and 26.

[42] 'No para y se ha vuelto, se están moviendo los patrones, también es bien complicado. Tu crees que ya tienes como bien comprendida ciertas cosas de la desaparición en un periodo, pero pues eso ya no te da para leer, por ejemplo, las que están pasando ahorita aquí en la Ciudad de México.' (Interview 25)

[43] For example, interviews 5, 25, 27.

[44] 'pero complejiza la situación que estemos todavía, o sea, es un problema que que sigue pasando, que sigue pasando, entonces no tienes el espacio desde las diferentes instituciones, de decir: ¿qué atiendo primero, lo de atrás, lo de ahorita, lo de hace 40 años, lo de la muchacha que acaba de desaparecer ahorita, la que desapareció hace cinco años, la que desaparición hace diez, la que desapareció hace 40?' Interview 27.

> I think we have to focus much more on how to design strategies to stop [disappearances] from occurring. Until then, I think we cannot understand anything else…. I mean, there is no way that we can deal with the consequences if we do not turn the page [first]. Otherwise, we will continue to live in an emergency room every day. For example, with the forensic discussion,[45] the aim is to create a forensic programme to deal with the existing backlog and the forensic crisis, but we have to determine a specific period, because more bodies accumulate every day. So, if we create an instrument like that, a programme with those characteristics, how do we ensure that we do not just attend the daily urgencies? That is a dilemma everywhere, for all issues. If we do not stop what is happening, we cannot deal with what happened in the past, we are just administering it and suffering human rights violations on a daily basis. The correct approach is: this has to stop.[46]

This quote illustrates how, at a more general level, the continued rise in disappearances and violence makes it very difficult to think about broader mechanisms for justice, or even for the humanitarian identification of remains. At the same time, continued physical insecurity also poses a number of challenges for the day-to-day work of participants, which I describe further below (see Sect. 6.2.1.5).

6.2.1.4 Conceptual Difficulties

Due to the complexity of the context and the number of actors involved, participants also mentioned conceptual difficulties that have arisen in relation to both the legal classification and the communication of violence, including disappearances. Several participants spoke about how the complexity of the situation makes it challenging to create a coherent narrative about what is happening and explain it to victims, relatives, Mexican society more generally, as well as towards outside actors. I provide a number of examples below.

Legal Classification of Crimes

Several participants mentioned conceptual difficulties with legal classification and characterisation. Reflecting on their initial reaction to the sudden rise in violence and disappearances, participants, especially those based in states, spoke about

[45] This refers to the discussion about how to address the forensic crisis in the country (discussed in Chap. 5, Sect. 5.1.2.2) and the creation of an extraordinary forensic mechanism to identify the thousands of unidentified bodies and remains in the country.

[46] 'Yo creo que tenemos que enfocarnos mucho más a diseñar estrategias para que deje de suceder. Mientras, yo creo que no podemos entender nada más, si no detenemos lo que pasa hoy. O sea, no hay manera de atender las consecuencias, si no le damos la vuelta a la página. Si no vivimos en una sala de emergencias todos los días, todos los días, con la discusión forense, por ejemplo, si se quiere establecer un programa de atención forense, que atienda el rezago que hay y la crisis forense, pero tenemos que ponerle un periodo, porque todos los días se siguen acumulando cuerpos. Entonces si hacemos un instrumento de estas, un programa de estas características, cómo hacemos para no quedarnos atendiendo lo de todos los días, ese es un dilema en todos lados, para todos los temas. Si no detenemos lo que pasa, no podemos atender lo que ya pasó, no estamos administrando eso y sufriendo en lo cotidiano las violaciones a derechos humanos. El enfoque correcto es: esto debe parar.' Interview 5.

themselves as human rights defenders, as well as authorities, not being 'prepared'[47] for what was happening and not really knowing what to do when violence 'exploded'.[48] Some related this to the new disappearances being conceptually different from the 'traditional' ones that some participants (or the NGOs they work for) had previously dealt with or knew of,[49] which meant that they initially 'did not really know what they were, nor what to call them'.[50] For example, one participant, who works for an NGO based in a state, explained how they dealt with the new 'types' of disappearances that did not correspond to the traditional understanding of enforced disappearances:

> So, what we did was first to document the cases. Because these cases did not show the same patterns as the cases of disappearances for political activism ('militancias políticas'). We could say that here they were disappearing average people who, for the most part, had nothing to do with the kind of motives we knew historically, which was that they were opposed to the political regime. So, we had to start working in different ways because you could not just do what we would normally do in cases of disappearances of a political or social activist. There it was like we knew the ABC, and here you could not place the families at risk because we were confronting new actors who… who killed. So, it was not as simple as saying 'today I will report the crime, [request] some precautionary measures, I will send the case to the Inter-American Commission and so forth'. But on top of that, we could not show that the persons who were disappearing were, [that their disappearance] was linked to the direct participation of state actors.[51]

This quote illustrates the difficulties for human rights professionals to respond to new types of disappearances, which, in the absence of clear information about who the perpetrators were or whether there were any connections to state officials, did not fit within existing legal categories that presuppose state involvement. Domestically, this created challenges for NGOs because authorities refused to open criminal investigations into these crimes.[52] Moreover, externally, it was also difficult for NGOs to 'convince' regional and international human rights bodies that

[47] Interview 14.

[48] Interview 26; see also interviews 9, 14, 15, 21, 23, 24, 30, 34.

[49] For example, interviews 3, 9, 15, 23, 30, 32, 34.

[50] 'Sí, al principio, nos sabíamos qué era, no sabíamos cómo nombrarlas.' Interview 3.

[51] 'Entonces lo que hicimos fue… primero documentar los casos. Porque… estos casos no tenían el patrón de los casos de desaparición por… por militancias políticas. Estamos hablando de que aquí estaban desapareciendo gente de a pie que no tenía nada que ver, en la mayoría de los casos, con una razón que era la que teníamos histórica que era ser opositoras al régimen político. Y entonces la manera en como que teníamos que trabajar implicaba otros modos porque no podías hacer lo que hacíamos normalmente cuando había una desaparición de un militante social o político. Como que el ABC ya lo sabíamos, y acá no podías arriesgar a la familia, a las familias, porque nos estábamos enfrentando con nuevos actores, que… que mataban. No, o sea que no… no eran tan simple como 'hoy voy a presentar la denuncia, alguna medida cautelar, mando el caso de la Comisión Interamericana y no sé qué'. Pero además nosotros no podíamos comprobar que las personas que estaban desapareciendo tenían eh, la naturaleza tenía que ver con participación directa de entidades estatales.' Interview 15.

[52] For example, interviews 2, 6, 10, 13, 14, 16, 30. Note that this is by no means a thing of the past and authorities continue to open investigations for crimes other than disappearances. Additionally, despite the creation of specialised prosecutor's offices for disappearances following the adoption of the General Law on Disappearances, not all disappearance cases are transmitted to these specialised units (comments during presentation on 10 June 2021).

the disappearances were a human rights issue and warranted their attention. These difficulties were explained by one participant, who directed an NGO working principally on the topic of disappeared migrants, and whose staff had documented around 350 cases of disappeared migrants. They first talked about the fact that the issue of disappeared migrants in Mexico was absent from discussions, which also illustrates that certain groups of disappeared persons are less visible than others (see Chap. 5, Sect. 5.1.2.1). Then they continued:

> But on top of that, you had to deal with, for example, sometimes the United Nations organs who came to do their reports on disappearances, saying: 'okay, tell me how many cases of enforced disappearances of migrants you have'. And I would present the 350. And they would say: 'listen, but [these do not fall] within the traditional concept of enforced disappearances, no'. And I would answer that we do not know, because the information that we have about a migrant in transit is minimal. [...] So why should I determine which one is enforced disappearance and which one is not, in what kind of context the state allowed this happen or not? But it was difficult for us to make even the United Nations understand that these cases could fall within the logic of enforced disappearance.[53]

Similarly, to define and explain the scope of the state's responsibility from an international perspective is complicated, especially when it comes to aspects related to the state's failures to act.[54] This was described by a number of participants, especially participants based in Mexico City who engage more frequently with regional or international human rights mechanisms. One participant based in Mexico City spoke about this as a problem for international law to 'understand' the Mexican conflict:

> [I]t has also been a problem for international law itself to understand our conflict. I mean, it is a mixture between problems of state and non-state actors, where the state has different degrees of responsibility. Even the Committees on Torture and Disappearances had to change their logic and say that even if they are committed by private individuals you [the

[53] 'Pero además, eh, tu tenías por ejemplo a veces a los órganos de Naciones Unidas que venían a hacer sus informes sobre desaparición, y te decían: a ver, dime cuantos casos de migrantes bajo desaparición forzada tienes. Y yo presentaba los 350, no. Y me decían: 'oye, pues no, o sea, estos, bajo el concepto tradicional de desaparición forzada pues no'. Y yo les decía:' pues no sé, o sea la información que se tiene de una persona migrante en tránsito es mínima'. Aquí logras tener más información, un poquito más, porque hay una red local que te ayuda para ir armando el caso. Entonces por qué yo voy a decir yo cuál es desaparición forzada, cuál no, en que contexto el estado permitió que esto pasara o no, o sea... Pero nos costó mucho, que también incluso desde Naciones Unidas se entendiera que estos casos podían caber bajo la lógica de desaparición forzada.' Interview 32. During the presentation of the themes (10 June 2021), one participant indicated that by now the Inter-American human rights institutions and UN treaty bodies have 'understood' the situation and have no doubts in relation to the Mexican State's obligations to respond to all disappearances. This, according to the participant, is also reflected in the Guiding Principles for the Search for Disappeared Persons that were adopted by the CED in 2019 and that I discuss in Chap. 2 (Sect. 2.2.2).

[54] The problem of responsibility for a failure to act is discussed further in Chaps. 3 and 7.

> state] are also responsible. Less so, because you did not prevent, and when they occur you have to investigate, sanction, and repair.[55]

Another participant who worked for an international NGO described the experience of trying to explain the responsibility of the Mexican state to regional and international mechanisms, as well as the strategy for communicating, as follows:

> [...] So yes, it has been difficult to communicate that we are saying that something very serious is happening, but at the same time we are not saying that there are 40 thousand disappearances committed by state agents, but we are saying that there is state responsibility, so that is complicated. Generally, we frame it in this way: we do not know [how to classify these disappearances] because they are not investigated, and they continue to occur because there is a violation of the general obligation to prevent. There are no measures to stop them from happening, so [...].[56]

This quote illustrates the difficulties of communicating the state's responsibility due to the number of perpetrators and shows how NGOs have addressed this problem by focusing on the state's failure to prevent and respond, as well as to its responsibility to clarify who is responsible. The difficulty for human rights bodies to accept the situation of disappearances in Mexico as falling within their remit was also confirmed by another participant, who at the time when disappearances started to rise in the context of the 'war on drugs', was a member of an international body working on enforced disappearances:

> [...] we were caught off-guard, even those of us who supposedly were experts on the topic. You know, we were saying 'no no no, these are not disappearances, these are disputes between cartels [...].[57]

Despite these initial difficulties, some participants spoke about how, for example by relying on Article 3 of the International Convention on the Protection of All Persons from Enforced Disappearance (ICPPED),[58] they were able to insist on the state's

[55] 'O sea, ha sido un problema también para que el propio... derecho internacional entienda nuestro conflicto. No, o sea, es una mezcla entre problemas de actores estatales y actores no-estatales, donde el estado tiene diferentes grados de responsabilidad, no. Hasta que los comités de tortura y de desaparición han tenido que cambiar su lógica de decir, cuando son cometidas por particulares también tienes responsabilidad. Menor, no, porque no previniste, luego cuando ya suceden tienes que investigar, sancionar y reparar.' Interview 25.

[56] '[...] Entonces sí ha sido difícil comunicar que estamos diciendo que está pasando algo muy grave, y al mismo tiempo no estamos diciendo que hay cuarenta mil desapariciones cometidas por agentes estatales, pero sí estamos diciendo que hay responsabilidad del estado, entonces eso es complicado. O sea, generalmente lo enmarcamos en eso: no sabemos qué son, porque no son investigados, y sigue ocurriendo porque hay una violación del deber general de prevención. No hay medidas para evitar que se cometan, entonces...' Interview 3.

[57] 'nos agarró desprevenido, incluso a los que se suponía que éramos especialistas en el tema. Sabes que no no no no, decíamos, estas no son desapariciones, estas son pleitos entre carteles y...'. Interview 9.

[58] Article 3 of the ICPPED establishes the obligations of states to 'adopt appropriate measures to investigate disappearances committed by non-state actors acting without the authorisation, support or acquiescence of state agents, as well as to bring perpetrators to justice.' See Chap. 2, Sect. 2.2.

obligation to investigate all cases of disappearances.[59] Indeed, it did not appear that participants continued to view the existence of different perpetrators as a challenge from a legal-definitional perspective at the domestic level, especially since the adoption of the General Law on Disappearance and the creation of two crimes by this Law, 'enforced disappearance' and 'disappearance committed by private individuals', which cover all types of disappearances.[60]

Nonetheless, despite general agreement among participants that the General Law on Disappearance was an important legislative achievement that helped to bring more visibility and recognition to the issue of disappearances,[61] there continued to be different views among participants about whether all disappearances committed by OCGs, or even all disappearances (including those committed by any private individual), could be considered *enforced*. When asked about this particular point, two participants explained the different views as reflecting a difference between a political stance and a legal one.[62] The former refers to the position that the state bears ultimate responsibility because of its historic role in the commission of enforced disappearances, and its current actions and omissions that perpetuate the crisis, whereas the latter refers to a narrow legal interpretation of the definition of enforced disappearance in international law and the difference between Articles 2 and 3 of the ICPPED discussed in previous chapters.

Some participants emphasised that it was important to maintain a separation between the two crimes, believing that *enforced* disappearances are qualitatively worse than those committed by private actors, principally due to the state's protective function.[63] One participant, who works for an NGO based in Mexico City that specialises in strategic litigation, even expressed the view that conflating the two crimes into one was 'dangerous' in the sense that it created confusion among relatives and 'perverted' the meaning of what an enforced disappearance was.[64] Others, however, emphasised the role of the Mexican state in creating the conditions that allow disappearances to occur, or the fact that collusion in certain parts of the country makes it virtually impossible to distinguish between state and criminal

---

[59] For example, interviews 3, 9, 15.

[60] For example, interviews 3, 4, 15, 19, 29. Rather, participants described the issues as lying with the implementation of the General Law on Disappearances, as well as the continued problems with authorities' not classifying cases correctly, even after the creation of the two crimes (comments during presentation, 10 June 2021).

[61] Interviews 1, 4, 6, 8, 9, 10, 11, 15, 16, 17, 22, 23, 24, 25, 28, 29, 33, 34.

[62] Interviews 8 and 19. I specifically asked about participants' views on the possibility of distinguishing between enforced disappearances and those committed by non-state actors. This question was based on previous research and informal conversations with human rights practitioners in Mexico, which had indicated to me that this was a controversial issue. During the presentation of the themes, participants also indicated that the position might depend on the role of the person who holds it. For example, a relative might have a different view than a lawyer working for an NGO (10 June 2021).

[63] Interviews 9, 12, 19, 24, 28.

[64] Interview 19.

actors.[65] Thus, some participants explained that especially where OCGs were involved in disappearances, as soon as one 'scratches the surface'[66] ties between criminal organisations and state officials begin to show, which makes it very difficult to differentiate between them.[67]

At the same time, a number of participants also explained that for them a distinction between types of disappearances was possible and 'warranted',[68] because there were indeed some disappearances committed with neither involvement of state actors, nor organised crime groups.[69] In this vein, one participant based in Mexico City explained that the phenomenon of disappearances in Mexico had become so complex that to argue that all disappearances are enforced would over-simplify the issue:

> Nevertheless, I think that we now have a more complex phenomenon [...] in Mexico. I think that it is perhaps an oversimplification to argue that all disappearances are enforced disappearances because there is necessarily this permission by authorities... I think that there are enforced disappearances also committed by criminal groups that are not necessarily part of organised crime, or by people who might not necessarily be a part of any criminal group, who commit disappearances – and these disappearances, even though they are not part of this complex phenomenon, are also not investigated. For example, a case where a robbery goes bad and the thieves end up killing and disappearing the person. [This is] not the type of case that we are used to hearing about, but that nevertheless does happen, and that would be like simplifying the phenomenon of disappearances. So impunity has made the phenomenon of disappearances more complex [...] I think that it is organised crime acting with permission, or that authorities do not do anything to prevent these crimes, which is at the heart of the issue, I think that that is what has devasted Mexico the most in relation to the phenomenon of disappearances, but that these are not the only cases.[70]

---

[65] Interviews 7, 14, 15, 16, 22, 23, 34.

[66] Interviews 5 and 33.

[67] For example, interviews 5, 16, 19, 23, 26, 29, 33.

[68] Interview 32.

[69] For example, interviews 3, 16, 25, 33. In this vein, one participant also spoke about disappearances having become a normalised practice that went beyond disappearances committed on the orders of a criminal leader. Interview 3.

[70] 'yo creo que sí se puede distinguir, aunque en la mayoría de casos, o sea, hay casos complejos en donde la desaparición si bien es ejecutada por un grupo del crimen organizado, sabemos que siempre, o casi siempre, hay una colusión entre crimen organizado y autoridades estatales, no, y no solo en la práctica de la desaparición, en la práctica de masacres, por ejemplo, o en la práctica de torturas, no, o de detenciones arbitrarias a veces. [...] Ehm sin embargo, creo que en México ya tenemos un fenómeno más complejo que eso, o sea, creo que decir que todas las desapariciones son desapariciones forzadas porque necesariamente hay esa permisión de las autoridades, es tal vez simplificar el fenómeno [I: ok]. Yo creo que hay desapariciones forzadas también ejecutadas por grupos criminales que no necesariamente son del crimen organizado, o por personas que no necesariamente son grupos criminales, no, que ejecutan desapariciones y que esas desapariciones, aunque no son parte de este fenómeno complejo, tampoco se investigan. Eh por ejemplo algún caso de un robo que a los ladrones les salen mal y terminan matando a la persona y la desaparecen. En ese caso, ese caso no es un caso como el que estamos acostumbrados a oír, no, pero que ocurren, y que sería como simplificar el fenómeno de la desaparición. Y es que el fenómeno de la desaparición debido a la impunidad se ha vuelto eh... más complejo digamos [...] Creo que ese es el, creo que es el que crimen organizado con permisión o eh las autoridades no hacen nada para prevenir esos hechos creo que es el corazón del asunto, no, creo que lo que más tiene este digamos azotado a

In addition to illustrating the complexity of the phenomenon of disappearances in Mexico today and its implications for the classification of disappearances, the participant also touches upon another issue, which is the role of impunity, and thereby the state's omissions. This was also expressed by another participant based in Mexico City, who similarly emphasised the difficulty of categorising what is happening in Mexico in neat boxes, and thus the complexity:

> So, what I have seen [is] that for these academics, researchers who come from other countries, and we even experienced this with the United Nations, ... well, it is very difficult for them [because] they want to see things in boxes: this is this, this is that, this is organised crime, these are state actors, this is disappearance... we have a hotch-potch of everything here. And I think that what is important in all of this is not to take our eyes off the state, even if it is about organised crime.[71]

This quote not only highlights the difficulty of making neat distinctions between types of disappearances in the current Mexican context, but indirectly touches upon the question of the state's role in the matter, which the previous quote also indicates. These conceptual differences were further reflected in participants' views on the responsibility of the Mexican state in relation to the phenomenon of disappearances, which I discuss in more depth in Chap. 7 (Sect. 7.1).

6.2.1.5 Practical Dilemmas

In addition to the conceptual challenges which arise in the Mexican context from a legal perspective, the context of uncertainty and insecurity in which the participants work, especially those who are based in states or who accompany *colectivos* (relatives' groups) in states, creates a number of practical dilemmas for their work. Ongoing violence and physical insecurity affect the participants' work in several ways, both directly and indirectly. Indirectly, fear and distrust impact on the amount of information available about what is happening in certain parts of the country, given that many relatives choose not to report disappearances. Participants also have to consider their own security, especially those working directly in areas with high levels of insecurity.

Regarding the security of relatives, moreover, some participants based in Mexico City described how persistent insecurity in some parts of the country meant that even though relatives might have been *willing* to provide information, the participants

México si hablamos del fenómeno de la desaparición en sí, pero creo que no son los únicos casos.' (Interview 2)

[71] 'Entonces, yo lo que veo es que para estos académicos, estudiosos, incluso nos pasó con Naciones Unidas, que vienen de otros países, pues se les hace muy difícil, no, y entonces quieren ver las cosas en cajones, no. Esto es esto, esto es esto, esto es esto, esto es crimen organizado, estos son actores estatales, esto es desaparición... tenemos una mezcolanza de todo. Y yo creo que lo importante de todo esto es no dejar de ver la mirada del estado, aunque sea un tema de crimen organizado.' Interview 32.

could not document the cases because it would put relatives at too much risk.[72] One participant based in Mexico City described this in the following manner:

> I mean there are places where it is very complicated to go to, even though we know that grave violations are being committed – not because we cannot go, but because if you go, you get the information and leave, but the people will stay there at great risk. And you cannot do that, right, so it is also a matter of assessing where it is possible to document in a reasonably safe manner for the people and also have an impact.[73]

This quote illustrates how important it is for NGOs to weigh the risks involved in documenting or reporting cases in order not to place relatives at greater risk. For NGOs based in states, this also concerns decisions about whether to follow-up on certain cases, which are taken in consideration of the potential risk to relatives.[74] One participant working for an NGO in a state spoke about the carefulness with which the organisation approaches disappearances cases in view of the possibility of collusion between authorities and criminal groups:

> I: And a while ago you mentioned that here you can see the collusion much more [...] How does that affect the work that you do as civil society?
>
> P: [inhales] Oh God, well, I mean, of course that it scares you, it scares you a lot.... the fact that you are in the same territory, as the people whom you are accusing, I think that places you at a different level of risk. And not just that, but I mean, honestly, even going to the prosecutor's offices ('fiscalías') in certain areas always scares you, right, to know that perhaps they are watching you. And, on top of that, we have had a number of cases where they also threaten the family, and then they do not want to continue the search. It depends, right, there are some relatives who say 'they threatened me and I want nothing more to do with this' [...] the [situations] where I have been scared were related to disappearances, coming out of a hearing, being in a particular place, that kind of stuff. So of course, that impacts on how you do your job ... you weigh a lot what legal actions you will take, you weigh a lot what you will say publicly, you consult with the family a lot – because one thing is what you want to do, but another thing is what the family wants... you think about it more than in other cases where you just say 'well, legally this is what we have to do, period'. Right, in cases of [violence against] women, it's like 'okay, the man did this, so we have to report this, we have to request parental custody,' and that's it, there isn't more you can do. And [in disappearance cases] you have to think [carefully about what you could do and discuss the consequences and ask] the family: 'listen, you have not received any threats, nobody has said anything to you? Okay, if not, then okay, we agree, consensus, [name of colleague] do you agree, do you think this is [a good way to go]? Okay, come on then, let's go with that.' Right, like these types of things [laughs] ... but, I mean to this day nothing has happened to us.[75]

---

[72] For example, interviews 31 and 33.

[73] 'o sea hay lugares donde, aunque sepamos que está habiendo graves violaciones, es muy complicado ir – no porque no podamos ir, sino porque vas, eh, sacas la información, te regresas, pero la gente se queda ahí, se queda en mucho riesgo. Y eso tampoco puedes hacer eso, no, entonces también viendo dónde se puede documentar de una manera razonablemente segura para las personas, y que pueda tener un cierto impacto, también en ese sentido, no.' Interview 33.

[74] For example, interviews 10, 12, 30.

[75] 'I: Y hablabas hace rato de que acá justamente se ve más la colusión. [P: Aja] Eso, ¿cómo afecta el trabajo que hacen desde la sociedad civil?

This quote illustrates not only the care with which cases are taken on in view of the security of relatives, but also the need for NGOs to consider their own security. The extent to which this is the case varies between different parts of the country and changes over time. This is illustrated by the experience of participants working for NGOs in certain regions of the country, who described security concerns and violence as prominent in the past, but less so in the present.[76] Conversely, in other states that I visited, or certain states that participants mentioned during the interviews, such as Chihuahua, Veracruz, Tamaulipas, Michoacán, Nayarit, Jalisco and Guerrero, physical security continues to be a major concern, especially in relation to travelling to particular areas.[77] Where insecurity is still high, participants spoke about ensuing restrictions on their ability to travel to certain states, or areas within some states, where cases that they accompany are based. Moreover, working with certain authorities could also constitute a risk if the latter are a target. The following statement from one participant working for an NGO in a state, who spoke about the consequences of infiltration or control of security forces by criminal groups, illustrates how insecurity and fear affects the work and movement of human rights organisations themselves:

> I: And does this [infiltration] in any way affect the work that you do as a human rights organisation?
>
> P: Well yes because we cannot go to certain areas because we are afraid. […] Yes of course, I mean… to live in a territory controlled by a criminal group restricts everybody's freedom. Including ours. We can no longer go to places during the night. Personally, I do not travel by night. Only by day, … before I could have slept next to the highway, just stop and … Now you cannot even travel […] because they have also imposed a schedule ('horario'): during the day there is no problem, but the night is ours. And the night is theirs alone, the highways

---

P: [inhala] Ay dios, pues eso, no, claro que te da miedo, mucho miedo. Este… uno, eso, o sea, te digo, el estar en el mismo territorio, este, que donde, que las personas que estás acusando creo que te pone, pues, en otro nivel de riesgo. Y no solo ahí, sino digo la verdad hasta ir a la fiscalía de ciertos lugares, de ciertos lugares, siempre te da temor, no, saber que a lo mejor… te están viendo, te están… así. Y, porque además, nos ha tocado varios casos de… de familias que las amenazan también, y luego ellas ya no quieren seguir la bús… depende, no, ha habido familias que dicen me amenazaron, ya no quiero nada. […] No, entonces te digo siempre las cosas que me han dado miedo tienen que ver con desaparición, salir de una audiencia, estar en un lugar, o sea, como cosas así. Entonces claro que eso tiene un impacto en cómo efectúas tu trabajo, pues claro. Este… mides mucho el tema de las acciones legales, mides mucho lo que públicamente dices, preguntas mucho a la familia porque también una cosa es lo que tu quieras hacer, pero otra lo que la familia quiera, este… la piensas más que en otras cosas que, pos que no, que no lo piensas, que dices tu, en otros casos dices 'ah, jurídicamente hay que hacer esto y punto'. No, en el caso de las mujeres es como 'ah el hombre hizo esto, ah aquí hay que presentar una denuncia, hay que pedir la guarda y custodia, o sea, y ya, no hay más, pum, esto es'. Y acá hay que como decir 'bueno, pues sí, pudiéramos hacer esto, pero, si hacemos esto, a decir que sí lo hacemos' o 'oiga cómo ve, y la familia, oiga ¿no ha recibido amenazas, no le han dicho nada?' 'Bueno, si no okay okay, acuerdo, consenso, diga sí sí sí, ¿[nombre de colega de la organización], sí está de acuerdo, piensa que está bien?' '¿Oigan ustedes también?' 'Bueno, órale pues, vámonos con esto'. No, o sea como cosas así [ríe] que, pero pues no, también al día de hoy no nos ha pasado nada pues.' Interview 12.

[76] For example, interviews 13, 14, 15 and fieldnotes, 21 August 2019; field diary, 28 August 2019.

[77] For example, interviews 1, 2, 10, 12, 13 18, 21, 22, 23, 28, 29, 30.

> are deserted, the highways, only they use them. So [...]it has limited our actions, our activities.[78]

Similarly, most participants who spoke about the implications of insecurity spoke about this in relation to travelling to particular places or restricting activities on certain cases in order not to endanger relatives. Some participants related this to the difference in levels of collusion between criminal groups and authorities, which was described as much higher, or at least much more visible, in rural areas or outside of capital cities.[79] Notably, participants associated risks to themselves (and relatives) mainly with criminal organisations, or authorities acting in collusion with the latter, rather than with the state in general.[80] The difference in participants' experiences of insecurity and fear depending on levels of collusion between authorities and criminal groups also reflects the complexity of the Mexican context. Thus, two participants based in Mexico City spoke about their experience of accompanying searches in other states, where they were accompanied by federal security forces to ensure protection from criminal groups and local security forces, who were seen as colluded.[81] One participant reflected on this experience in the following manner:

> So, it has happened, that we have gone to really ugly places, but with security. Let the state ensure this security. And here for example a black-and-white logic with the state is not useful either, for example to say all the soldiers are bad; or the National Guard – they're all bad, or the gendarmes - they are not all bad, because it is they [laughs] who have gone to protect us in the field. So, I mean when you go into the field with two Marine patrols [laughs], then that is also, those discourses that are sometimes very urban [and] sound nice [when you are here], but there [laughs], it is they who will protect us because there is nothing we can do. And it has happened, I mean, incidents and so forth, and it is they who put their bodies (on the line). And who have the preparation and so on.[82]

---

[78] 'I: ¿Y eso afecta de alguna forma el trabajo que hacen ustedes como organización de derechos humanos?

P: Pues sí, pues porque no podemos ir a determinados lugares porque tenemos temor. [...] Sí, desde luego, o sea, no... vivir en un... vivir en un territorio dominado por un grupo criminal pues restringe las libertades de todo mundo. Y de nosotros. Yo... nosotros ya no podemos salir en la noche a los lugares. Yo personalmente no viajo en la noche. Solo de día, porque... antes yo me podía quedar a dormir a media carretera. Nada más pararme y... No ahora ni siquiera viajar, pues, porque no sabe uno, pues porque ellos han puesto horarios también. En el día no hay problema, pero la noche es nuestra. Y la noche es de ellos y nada más y carreteras solas, las carreteras, pues, solo ellos se ven. Entonces la... nos ha limitado nuestra acción, nuestra actividad.' Interview 10.

[79] For example, interviews 10, 12, 28, 30.

[80] For example, interviews 2, 10, 12, 21.

[81] Interviews 1 and 21.

[82] 'Ahora, sí ha pasado, en lugares muy feos, donde hemos ido, pero llevamos seguridad, no. Que el estado garantice esa seguridad. Eh, e incluso las lógicas con el estado de blanco y negro tampoco son buenas, por ejemplo, decir: eh, no pues todos los militares son malos. O la Guardia Nacional – todos son malos. O los gendarmes, no, todos son malos, porque ellos son los que nos han ido a cuidar en terreno. O sea, llevas a un cuerpo de dos patrullas de marinos, [ríe] en terreno, entonces esa es también, esos discursos de, a veces son muy de ciudad, no, de ah sí aquí muy bonito, pero allá, cuando [ríe] vamos a ir, ellos son los que nos van a cuidar, porque no tenemos nada que hacer. Y sí ha pasado, pues, incidentes y demás, y ellos son los que, pos ponen el cuerpo, no. Y los que tienen la preparación y, y demás.' Interview 21.

This reflection illustrates the complexity of working in a context where some, but not all, security forces are colluding with criminal groups and committing atrocities, and state forces continue to be the main provider of security. Similarly, prior to one interview that I conducted in a state, when discussing confidentiality and Informed Consent, the participant asked me if I really thought that the criminals ('malandros') up in the mountains would be reading what I published. Further, referring to a meeting with authorities we had attended the day before, the participant asked me if these officials seemed to me as posing a threat to the NGO and pointed out that at times these authorities provide protection to NGO members.[83]

At the same time, the experience of participants working for an NGO that is based in an area with high levels of collusion between criminal organisations and authorities is markedly different from that described by other participants: in addition to concerns about travelling and general safety, 'regular' human rights complaints, which are not related to disappearances or activities of criminal groups, can lead to threats against the NGO from such groups because accused officials turn to local criminal leaders for support against 'those human rights [people]' in order to avoid a negative human rights record.[84] Thus, any formal complaint against authorities can lead to backlash by criminal groups. One participant gave an example of the dilemmas that arise for human rights actors in the course of their work: members of the NGO had evidence in a case involving the disappearance of a woman, yet the family was too afraid to report the disappearance and fled town. The body of the disappeared woman was found a few days later. The participant described how difficult it is to make work-related decisions in this type of context:

> Now, what do you do when the family flees? And you have the evidence? [B]ut you are also facing a hostile environment where you have to ask yourself if you report, what do you report? I mean, judicially you cannot. Well, you could say 'here is the [evidence]', but if the family does not want to, because they might be afraid for their own security, you are faced with an ethical dilemma of choosing what you should do, what we should do in the face of this situation of decomposition, of collusion, of crime, between state and non-state authors. So then sometimes, well you are on a knife's edge, and you don't know what to do. I mean, we are situated in such a crude reality, so cruel, so bloody, that you just feel overwhelmed. And you do not know what it is you should do. So, it is not easy at all, because on top of that your own security is on the line, and there is also the fact that victims want justice, but they are afraid. […] So, this is a huge problem for us now, faced with this situation, well, we have to adapt to what the victim wants, to, well, stay silent, to find other ways of protecting the victims or to report crimes, and also to protect ourselves. Because we are in a hostile environment, of fear.[85]

[83] Fieldnotes, 15 August 2019.

[84] Interview numbers omitted for security reasons.

[85] 'Ahora, ¿cómo denuncias cuando se huye la familia? ¿Y cuando tienes la evidencia? Y… pero también ves un ambiente hostil, donde dices bueno, si denuncias, ¿qué denuncias? O sea, tu no, jurídicamente no puedes. Bueno, puedes decir 'aquí está [la evidencia]', pero… mientras la familia no quiera, porque teme por su seguridad, pues ahí es donde entras en un dilema ética de decir qué te toca hacer, qué nos toca hacer, ante esta situación de descomposición, de colusión, de crimen, entre autores estatales y no-estatales. Entonces a veces, pues te sientes en el filo de la navaja y no sabes qué hacer, no. O sea, estamos interpelados por una realidad tan cruda, tan cruel, tan sangrienta, que

This quote touches upon another dilemma mentioned by several participants, which is that especially at the state level, where there is much more direct contact with authorities (see above), it is often not clear with whom one is working.[86] Given the risks related to confronting criminal organisations, it is of practical relevance to know whom one is accusing of having committed a disappearance and what implications this could have. In certain areas of the country, this means that whether or not an NGO actively pursues a particular case has to be carefully weighed against the risk this might entail, and it is not always possible to really know this. The participant who discussed the ethical dilemmas arising from relatives' fear (see previous quote), also spoke about this uncertainty:

> So, it is very difficult now because you ask yourself, when you speak to an authority, you do not know what relationship this authority has to crime, and so you cannot be sure that you can actually report or ask authorities to intervene or… right? You can't. Because you need to have a very fine grasp of the information, of the scheme of alliances between the political actor, between the police and this crime group, between this 'halcón'[87]… I mean, we now need to become experts in organised crime in order to effectively defend human rights. But we do not feel that we have the right profile for that, it creates risks for us, it means venturing into the lion's den and say 'me, in order to defend human rights, I need to know about all this mess of criminal interests'. But the fact that you want to go into this and do some research in order to assess which intervention would be the most appropriate, then they will say that you are working against them, and they will say, well, this is a traitor. So, this is a very serious issue, very serious. And, well, we survive, in these situations with great difficulty. I mean you cannot, even if you know things you cannot report them. Because [authorities] will not respond. Because if you tell the public official, he will tell the criminal, because the criminal holds power, and enjoys impunity.[88]

---

te sientes desbordado. Y que no sabes qué tienes que hacer. O sea, no es tan sencillo, porque además está de por medio tu seguridad, y está de por medio, pues también el hecho de que, pues, las víctimas quieren justicia, pero tienen miedo. Pero por otra parte estás ante una institucionalidad que no funciona, o sea, no funcionan las instituciones, hay instituciones fallidas que le están fallando al ciudadano. Entonces en un mundo real dices, no sabes, no hay, no hay recursos jurídicos, eh, eficaces que protejan los derechos de las víctimas, o por lo menos garanticen que se investiguen estos hechos, no hay. Porque está un aparato… ya muy podrido, donde un funcionario no te va, no va a comprometerse a investigar, porque sabe que está atrapado en esta red. Entonces, es un problema muy grande que ahora nosotros, ante esta situación, pues, tenemos que… adaptarnos a lo que pida la víctima, a tener, pues, guardar silencio, a tener que buscar otras formas de cómo proteger a las víctimas o de cómo interponer denuncias, y también cómo auto-protegernos. Porque estamos en un ambiente hostil, no, de miedo.' Interview number omitted for reasons of confidentiality.

[86]For example, interviews 6, 8, 11, 12, 15, 16, 24, 27, 30, 31, 34.

[87]Word for somebody on the lookout for criminal groups.

[88]'Entonces, es muy difícil ahora, porque entonces tu dices, si hablas con una autoridad, no sabes cuál es el vínculo de esa autoridad con los del crimen, entonces dices pues es que esto no te da certeza de que puedas denunciar, o que puedas pedir la intervención o que, ¿no? No puedes. Porque necesitas tener como muy fino la… cómo se dice, la información, de cómo está el tinglado de las alianzas que hay entre este actor político, entre este policía, entre este grupo de la delincuencia, entre este halcón… o sea, necesitamos ahora especializarnos en delincuencia organizada, para poder hacer eficaz la defensa de los derechos humanos. Pero pues eso, para eso sentimos que… no da nuestro perfil, nuestro, nos pone en riesgos, es meterte a la boca del lobo y decir 'es que yo, para que

While collusion between state and criminal actors creates a number of dilemmas for NGOs in relation to the uncertainty about whom they are dealing with, some participants also spoke about how insecurity can affect authorities themselves in the sense that they are too afraid to go to certain places to investigate or search.[89] This in turn was described by one participant working for an NGO in a state as creating additional dilemmas for them as a human rights organisation. The participant shared the story of a relative whose brother had disappeared. The agent of the prosecutor's office told the relative that she knew who might be responsible, but did not dare touch them, as that would mean risking her life. Moreover, she said that if the relative decided to report her for not acting, she doubted that another officer would dare go to the area. The relative could understand the officer's position. The participant then continued:

> And there are many other cases like this where (we) say 'listen, we have to do another search there' and (the authorities) tell us 'it's very dangerous there, we cannot just go there […]' – 'well, do what you have to do to be able to go'. But sometimes in concrete cases like this one, of agents of the prosecutor's office like this woman who was an investigating officer and who was saying 'I also have children […] and I cannot go'. And there you also ask yourself okay, and what now? As an organisation what do you do, do you report her? What are you going to get from that? Just to get her fired. But will you achieve that another official will go […]? I mean, that also raises other dilemmas where you say well, yeah, what do you do?[90]

This quote is interesting in that the participant refers to a certain level of understanding by relatives, yet also by the participant, towards authorities who are equally affected by insecurity and may be unwilling to risk their lives.[91] Moreover, as the

---

defienda los derechos humanos necesito saber toda esta maraña de, de intereses del crimen'. Pero el hecho de que te quieras meter, en términos de hacer un trabajo de investigación para ver qué intervención es la más adecuada, pues entonces van a decir que tu estás haciendo un trabajo en contra de ellos y decir bueno, este, este es un traidor. Entonces es un asunto muy grave, no, muy grave. Y que, pues, sobrevivimos, en en estas situaciones de manera muy difícil, no, muy difícil. O sea, no puedes, o sea, a pesar de que sepas las cosas, no las puedes denunciar. Porque no te van a hacer caso. Porque, eh, si le dices al funcionario ese, se le va a decir al delincuente, porque el delincuente tiene poder, no, goza de impunidad.' Interview number omitted for reasons of confidentiality.

[89] Interviews 10, 11, 12, 13.

[90] 'Y así como ese hay muchos otros casos de decir 'es que hay que ir hacer otro rastreo allá' y que nos dicen 'oye pero es que está bien cabrón allá, allá no podemos ir en cualquier, hay que especialmente, no sé qué', bueno, 'pues hagan lo que tengan que hacer para que vayan'. Pero a veces en casos concretos así de los ministerios públicos, a veces te dicen, digo esa era una mujer una ministerio público la que decía 'yo también tengo hijos y no se qué y no puedo ir', y ahí también dices tu '¿bueno y luego?' ¿Como organización que haces también, la denuncias? ¿Qué vas a ganar? Pues que la corran no más. Pero ¿vas a ganar que otro sí vaya, que otro…? O sea, te plantea también como otros dilemas que dices tu pues sí, ¿qué haces?' Interview 12.

[91] Similarly, during my fieldwork stay I attended a government consultation with civil society for the National Human Rights Programme on the right to memory, truth, justice and reparations (field notes, 27 August 2019). The forum was split up into four different groups to discuss each of these rights, and I sat in on the discussion on guarantees of non-repetition. During this discussion, the issue of lack of resources came up and a woman (relative) expressed the view that if police officers earn 6000 MXN a month, have a tiny gun and do not receive bulletproof vests, it is no surprise that

participant mentions, knowing that many officials are equally afraid and unwilling to risk their lives implies that reporting the official for not doing her job would most likely not result in any change for the better.

6.2.2 Pragmatism

The theme of pragmatism[92] encompasses participants' descriptions of how they, or the organisations they work for, have adapted to the present-day context of disappearances in Mexico by changing their 'traditional' manner of working. This pragmatic adaptation refers to general adjustments to organisations' traditional ways of working and overlaps to some extent with the previous theme in that pragmatism can be understood as a way of responding to uncertainty. However, pragmatism comprises general changes to strategies and working methods rather than more *ad hoc* decisions related to trusting certain authorities or assessing the level of risk involved in a particular activity. What characterises the adaptation differs somewhat between NGOs based in Mexico City and those based in the states. Moreover, there are also differences between the states, depending on the security situation and the political climate in which they operate. Despite the differences, however, a common element in participants' description of how they have adapted their work was that they related these changes to the needs of relatives of the disappeared, as well as the latter's growing organisation and strength over the course of the past 15 years.

---

when there is a shooting the officers will hide under the next car. This also seemed to me to indicate a certain understanding of the reality in which police officers work (field notes, 27 August 2019).

Importantly, however, I mentioned this point specifically during one of the presentations to participants in June 2021 and asked whether they shared the view that there could exist some understanding of inaction by authorities—during one meeting, one participant pointed out that even though the lack of resources is a fact that affects the work of police officers or agents of the prosecutor's office, there are nevertheless differences between officers and there are some who try despite all odds, whereas others simply do not seem to care and perhaps use the lack of resources as an excuse (10 June 2021). Similarly, during the second meeting one participant told me that they had absolutely no understanding for the lack of action by authorities and others seemed also to be skeptical of this (14 June 2021). Therefore, while in the quoted interview there appeared to be some understanding, or at least consideration of the difficult reality in which certain state officials work, it is important to point out that this does not reflect the general position of most participants. At the same time, a number of participants did also speak about the very real limitations and lack of resources of security forces or prosecutors, especially in view of the caseload they have.

[92] I use the term 'pragmatism' in the sense of the ordinary meaning of the word: 'the quality of dealing with a problem in a sensible way that suits the conditions that really exist, rather than following fixed theories, ideas, or rules' and not in the philosophical sense of the term. See https://dictionary.cambridge.org/dictionary/english/pragmatism. Accessed 28 October 2024.

6.2.2.1 Adapting Working Methods

For participants working for NGOs based in the states who are confronted with the everyday urgencies of large numbers of relatives,[93] adapting their working methods has meant, where possible, starting to collaborate with authorities towards whom several NGOs previously had a much more confrontational stance. For some NGOs based in Mexico City, who engage in more strategic litigation and generally receive fewer cases, it has meant moving beyond their traditional single-case-based model of work to providing advice and training to *colectivos* and, in some cases, to accompany these groups during searches. I describe these phenomena below.

Adaptation by NGOs in States

Some participants working for NGOs based in the states described how they have adapted their ways of working by emphasising changes in relation to their work with authorities. A number of NGOs that I visited have started formal collaborations with authorities and *colectivos* as a way of following up on the large number of cases, for example by holding regular meetings between (investigative) authorities, *colectivos*, and the NGOs.[94] Importantly, at the search and initial investigation stage of cases, participants explained that no difference was made between different types of disappearances, or perpetrators. Such differences were only made at a judicial stage, if it was reached, which is rarely the case.[95] For some of these NGOs this meant a significant change to their previous stance vis-à-vis authorities, historically marked by distrust and mutual prejudices.[96] One participant from an NGO based in a state described the decision to collaborate with authorities, and how they began doing so, in the following way:

> It was a pretty complex process where we realised that we could not do it on our own. [Name of the NGO] was not going to be able to do this alone. [W]e realized that the families also would not be able to do it on their own. So we had to include those who knew how to conduct search and investigative work, right, and that was the prosecutor's office ('fiscalía'). And that was the moment when, thanks to Sicilia in 2011,[97] we began to work together,

---

[93] As mentioned in the introduction, much of the work by NGOs at state-level focuses on supporting relatives with their daily needs beyond the search for their loved ones, such as economic and psychological support or helping them obtain a declaration of absence ('declaración de ausencia').

[94] Some of these collaboration experiences have also been documented. For Coahuila, see Sánchez Valdés et al. (2018) and Ríos Vega and Spigno (2018). For Nuevo León, see CADHAC (2014). For Jalisco, see CEPAD (2018).

One NGO in Mexico City that works with *colectivos* from the state of Veracruz also engaged in such a collaboration in that state (Interview 18).

[95] For example, interviews 10, 11, 12, 13, 14, 15, 16, 22, 23, 24. This was also mentioned by participants based in Mexico City who accompany *colectivos*. Interviews 18 and 21. Note however that two participants also mentioned that there are certain differences with regards to what can be done legally and that there are more possibilities in cases of enforced disappearances. Interviews 12 and 24.

[96] Interviews 14, 22 and 23.

[97] This refers to the Movement for Peace with Justice and Dignity, led by the poet Javier Sicilia after the killing of his son in 2011. The Movement included a caravan across Mexico (and all the way to

> which was something that took us a number of months to try out, working with a lot of difficulty because prejudice was in the way. We had clashes amongst each other. It was not until we focused on the search of the disappeared person as the main issue that families started to give a little more information, because sometimes they wouldn't give it, and the authorities to trust more, and for us to be more attentive to the processes that were developing. But this process started because we had no other option. I mean, we could not work on our own, because we would not have gotten anywhere, [name of the NGO] had for a long time been an organisation that was shouting, bashing ('golpeando'), accusing, very rebellious, but when this process with Javier Sicilia started and we went to the Prosecutor's Office and the attorney general at the time told us 'I will investigate', of course none of us believed him, but then we started seeing in practice that they actually started investigating. So then our attitude as an organisation changed. From shouting and accusing to sitting down at the table and investigate, search, and ask questions.[98]

The quote illustrates both the reasons for and the initial difficulties of collaborating with authorities based on mutual prejudices between NGO members, relatives and authorities, yet it also contains a positive reflection about this experience.[99] Moreover, the participant pointed out that during the years of collaboration with authorities, the NGO received fewer threats than before.[100] The overall positive assessment of the collaboration expressed by this participant, despite the fact that many of the disappeared still have not been found ('We searched. We searched and searched, we did not find anything, but we searched'[101]) is, however, not necessarily shared by other participants based elsewhere who have collaborated, or continue to do so, with authorities.[102] Nonetheless, even where the collaboration experience was not

---

the US) and resulted in the adoption of the Victims' Law in Mexico in 2012. For an overview of the Movement and its impact on Mexican legislation, see Gallagher (2012).

[98] 'Entonces fue un proceso bastante complejo en donde vimos que solas no podíamos. Solo [nombre de la organización] no iba a poder con eso. Eh… vimos que las familias solas tampoco iban a poder, y ellos sin nosotros tampoco. Entonces teníamos que incorporar a quienes sabían hacer el trabajo de la búsqueda e investigación, no, y esa fue la fiscalía. Y ese fue el momento, en donde gracias a Sicilia en 2011, empezamos un trabajo junto que, que duró varios meses tratando, trabajando con mucha dificultad, porque los prejuicios no nos dejaban. Entre unos y otros, los tres actores nos chocábamos, no. Fue hasta que pusimos en el centro que lo que buscábamos era a la persona desaparecida, que empezó a las familias a dar un poco más de información, porque luego no la daban, y las autoridades a confiar más, no, y nosotros estar más atentas a los procesos que se iban dando. Pero este proceso se dio porque no nos quedó otra. O sea, no era, no podíamos trabajar solos, porque no íbamos a avanzar a ningún lado, [nombre de la organización] había sido una organización durante mucho tiempo que había estado gritando, golpeando, diciendo, muy contestataria, pero cuando se da este proceso con Javier Sicilia, y que vamos a la Procuraduría y que el entonces procurador dice voy a investigar, por supuesto nadie le creímos, pero empezamos a ver en los hechos que se empezó a investigar. Entonces nuestra actitud también como organización cambió. De estar gritando y diciendo, a sentarnos en la mesa a investigar, a buscar, a preguntar.' Interview 14.

[99] Notably, another participant in this interview also mentioned that when the NGO first began collaborating with authorities, they were criticised by other NGOs for doing so because the government was traditionally seen as bad. Interview14.

[100] Interview 14.

[101] 'Buscamos. Buscamos buscamos, no encontramos, pero buscamos.' Interview 14.

[102] Interviews 15, 16 and 22; field diary 29 August 2019.

necessarily described as positive, participants still spoke about the need to continue working with authorities in order to be able to, at a minimum, know and document what authorities are, or are not, doing.[103]

Notably, the examples of collaboration with authorities, whether described as positive or not, also seemed fragile in that they were described as enabled by the political interests of particular government employees. Thus, two organisations who had established collaborations with officials described how this changed after elections, or how it was electoral interests that enabled collaboration in the first place.[104] One participant who works for an NGO in a state spoke about their experience: in this case, the collaboration was made possible by the political ambitions of the prosecutor, who wanted to run for governor of the state. This was a significant change for the NGO that had not had any option to engage in dialogue with authorities before because it had actively litigated against a state prosecutor, leaving the state and NGO on bad terms. The participant explained:

> […] the issue of disappearances was not even acknowledged and then, when the prosecutor started talking about the issue and appropriated it, it was really interesting to see how his discourse changed. Because in 2016, he had been saying that in [name of state] there were no enforced disappearances – there is actually a newspaper article […] where he says that there are no enforced disappearances, just a couple in [name of city] where there are a few municipal police officers involved, but those were not enforced disappearances. That's it. But then he changed his discourse completely and started talking about the pain and suffering of victims, and 'I want to help' - I mean, just a few months later he was a person… who had done a 180-degree turn [laughs]. That was pretty interesting.[105]

In this sense, adaptation in the form of collaboration with authorities is not only based on decisions by the NGO and needs of relatives, but also on the political opportunity of collaborating.

The importance of the political climate and willingness by authorities is also highlighted by the experience of the members of an NGO based in another state, who described a total absence of trust in authorities due to their collusion with organised crime.[106] Their form of adapting to this 'hostile' environment[107] is to report cases outside of the municipality where they occurred, either at the level of the state, or even at the federal level, as a means of avoiding reprisals by criminal groups and

---

[103] Interview 16.

[104] Interviews 13, 14, 22, 23.

[105] '[…] no se reconocía nada situación de desapariciones y lo que decía el fiscal que se apropió ese tema como suyo, fue muy interesante ver también su cambio de discurso. Porque en el año 2016 decía, eh, en [estado], no hay desapariciones forzadas – de hecho, hay una nota, […] de que no hay desapariciones forzadas, nada más hay algunas en [ciudad], donde hay algunos policías municipales involucrados, pero no es desaparición forzada. Ya. Pero luego cambió por completo el discurso, y como que dolor y sufrimiento de las víctimas, yo quiero ayudar, o sea, unos meses después fue una persona… pues de 180 [ríe] grados de cambio. Fue como interesante.' Interview 22.

[106] In this particular state, there is no collaboration with authorities at all and even advocacy efforts are rarely directed at the state authorities because engaging with them is not seen as of any use. Interview 28.

[107] Interview number omitted for reasons of confidentiality.

increasing the possibility of action by authorities who are not colluding with these groups. This so-called 'federalisation' was described by a number of participants as a way of avoiding interactions with corrupt local authorities[108] or in the hope that investigations might advance.[109] Another reason for federalisation, according to a number of participants, is the failure of the System for Assistance to Victims, discussed in Chap. 5 (Sect. 5.2.3), which was especially the case at the local level. Thus, relatives try to take their cases to the federal level as a means of getting the support to which they are entitled as indirect victims.[110] Federalisation is then a pragmatic way of dealing with three issues: security considerations, refusal to investigate, and access to assistance measures.[111] Nonetheless, even though federal authorities may be perceived as less corrupt or colluded and cases are brought to the federal level because of this, a few participants pointed out that, in reality, the conduct of investigations at federal level has no advantage in terms of results and can be even worse than at local level.[112] According to one of these participants, this is partially due to the greater barriers to access to federal (as opposed to local) authorities, which makes it more difficult to exert pressure on them and follow-up on cases.[113]

Adaptation by NGOs in Mexico City

Participants working for NGOs based in Mexico City described their adaptation in a slightly different manner.[114] While several of the NGOs based in Mexico City whom I spoke to engage in strategic litigation and therefore select only a few emblematic cases to litigate, some have adapted this traditional way of working in response to the large number of victims and relatives. Thus, some Mexico City-based NGOs now try to support *colectivos* who are based in other states with no or few local human rights NGOs, such as Veracruz or Nayarit. The process of adaptation was described as

---

[108] Interviews 21, 28, 29, 30, 32. Additionally, one participant also described their use of '*triangulation*' in order to obtain a response or reaction from state authorities by appealing to members of the federal government to exert pressure on the former. Interview 28.

[109] For example, interviews 1, 3, 24.

[110] For example, interviews 1, 21, 27.

[111] One participant based in Mexico City also mentioned that they took cases to the Federal Prosecutor's Office for practical reasons of access, given that the NGO is based in Mexico City, but the case occurred in the north-east of the country. Interview 32.

[112] Interviews 24, 27, 32. Indeed, federalisation was also discussed during one of the presentations of themes, and one participant who works for an NGO based in a state explained that their NGO, and the relatives with whom they work, prefer to keep cases at the local level because there is a greater chance of cases advancing and because local authorities are perceived as more open (10 June 2021). This indicates that the practice of federalisation depends very much on local circumstances.

[113] Interview 24.

[114] This is likely related to several factors. For example, as discussed above, NGOs based in Mexico City are (traditionally) more focused on strategic litigation of a few cases, and the majority of disappearances occur outside of Mexico City. Perhaps for the same reason, many of the NGOs based in Mexico City started working on the issue of disappearances in the context of the 'war on drugs' several years after NGOs based in the states.

follows by one participant who works for a human rights NGO based in Mexico City that traditionally conducted strategic litigation of individual cases but has now broadened its approach:

> I: Earlier you mentioned that reality caught you off-guard - what did you mean by that?
>
> P: I think that [I meant] that our traditional capacity is based on individual cases, which means that if I am going to work on a case, and I will take it upwards ('subir'), as we say, and I will be the lawyer on that case, I need to know every last detail, so I need to have read the case file and every single element. But if you are supporting a *colectivo* that is impossible. I mean, you cannot have this level of knowledge because you do not have the capacity, you would need 50 lawyers. We are six in our area, six full staff and six volunteers, so, as much as one would want to, that is not going to happen. … and that, for example, we also cannot support many *colectivos*, it is not like we will be supporting ten *colectivos*, or five, not even five I would think. So, our traditional approaches [ended] up being outdated. That's more what I meant and that therefore we have to adjust our work, and we have to come up with new methods for support, design templates so that the families can do their own follow-up work. Now, in a meeting with the *colectivo* we designed the forms and gave them to everybody so that they know who their prosecutor's office agent is and how their inquiry is going, where their DNA sample is, and we are always trying to make sure our work is rigorous, but conscious that the previous level of going into every detail, not missing a single letter, will probably have to change. Because otherwise you have less capacity, and it is not like the families will wait for you, the victims have a different notion of time than we do. If you spend too much time reviewing the file, they will just move on.[115]

At the same time, the participant reflected on how, despite these changes, the work of NGOs outside of Mexico City is different from theirs, making a direct comparison with NGOs in the states who work side-by-side with certain *colectivos* and who

---

[115] 'I: Y, hace rato mencionabas que la realidad les tomó malparados. [P: mhm] ¿a qué te referías con eso?

P: Yo creo que a más como que nuestra capacidad tradicional estaba basada en casos individuales, es decir: si yo voy a, a trabajar en un caso y lo voy a subir, como decimos, voy a ser el abogado de ese caso, necesito tener todos los detalles dominados, no, es decir, tener leído el expediente, todos los elementos. Pero cuando tu acompañas a un colectivo eso no se puede. O sea, tu no puedes tener ese nivel de conocimiento porque no te da la vida, o sea, necesitarías 50 abogados. Eh, en el área somos seis, seis personas contratadas y seis, seis voluntarias, no, entonces… uno por más que quiera, eso no va a pasar, no. Eh… y que, por ejemplo, también no podemos acompañar a muchos colectivos, no es que no sí vamos a acompañar a diez colectivos o a cinco, ni siquiera cinco pensaría, no. Entonces que nuestras reflexiones tradicionales se pueden, se quedaron o se pueden quedar desfasadas. Más a eso me refiero, no, eh, y que entonces tenemos que ajustar nuestro trabajo, no, y tenemos que generar nuevos métodos de acompañamiento, generar formatos para que las propias familias hagan su propio seguimiento, ahora en, en una reunión con el colectivo ya fue hacer formatos y entregarle a cada quien para que sepan quién es su MP y cómo va su averiguación, dónde está su, su muestra de ADN, eh, cuidando la seriedad del trabajo, pero sabiendo que el nivel anterior, no, de ir al detalle, no perderte una letra, probablemente tenga que cambiar, no. Eh… porque ya no se… si no, reduces tu capacidad, y como que las familias no te van a esperar, los tiempos de las víctimas no son nuestros tiempos. No, si tu te quedas revisando el expediente, ellas se van.' Interview 21.

almost become synonymous with these *colectivos* to outsiders, even though they do engage in other activities.[116]

NGOs in Mexico City have not just started to support certain *colectivos* with following up on their cases, but also with searches conducted by relatives. This aspect of adaptation by NGOs in Mexico City, which was mentioned by a few participants there, was related to the growing strength and assertiveness of relatives' groups vis-à-vis human rights organisations.[117] Thus, a number of participants based in Mexico City spoke about their initial hesitation, or even rejection of relatives conducting their own searches and their gradual realisation that for many relatives the participation in such searches was a necessity. For example, one participant based in Mexico City spoke about the separation and, to some extent, liberation of relatives' groups from NGOs:

> And that was also an important change, it was an important rupture that taught us as organisations big lessons. For example, on the topic of searches. That families would go out to dig - you have no idea how that shocked us at the beginning. We were like: 'what? what do you mean they will go [and search]? Apparently, they take their picks and shovels and go, and just imagine the risk, they go and ask the people of the community because they always know who has ties to organised crime.' To me this is like a restorative justice exercise - they go and ask people 'look, we won't do anything to you, we will not prosecute you, we will not open proceedings against or report you, nothing, we just want you to tell us where you know that they buried them.' [...] Wherever they tell them, they use their pick and find something. So, we were saying 'but it is really dangerous to talk to members of organised crime, or somebody who used to be a member, or knows criminals. The mothers, the families go there without any protection and if they find something, then what? There are no DNA databases, whom are they going to find, there is no chain of custody, they don't know' – you have no idea how this shocked us. Until they told us 'we will do it with or without you because we are fed up'.[118]

[116]For example, CADHAC also works on topics related to security in communities and monitoring police forces and defends unjustly incarcerated persons. See https://cadhac.org/que-hacemos/. Accessed 10 March 2025. CEDEHM in Chihuahua works with women who are victims of gender-based violence and also on the issue of human rights defenders. See https://cedehm.org.mx/es/#enfoques. Accessed 10 March 2025.

[117]For example, interviews 1, 3, 4, 8, 21. This was not at all mentioned by NGOs based in states, who at most mentioned tensions between certain *colectivos* and the NGO or different positions.

[118]'Y eso también es un cambio importante, fue un quiebre importantísimo que nos dio grandes lecciones a las organizaciones. En el tema, por ejemplo, de las búsquedas. O sea, el que sean las familias que salgan a excavar, o sea, al principio no sabes como nos escandalizaba. Decíamos ¿cómo?, ¿cómo van a ir?, dicen que salen con su pico y pala, que van, además qué riesgos, van y preguntan a la gente de la comunidad, porque ahí se sabe, siempre quiénes son los que estaban ligados a crimen organizado. Van, que a mi me ha parecido un tema de justicia restaurativa, no, van, mira, preguntan a la gente:' mira no te vamos a hacer nada, no vamos a proceder en contra de ti, ni vamos a iniciarte un proceso ni te vamos a denunciar, nada, solo queremos que nos digas en dónde sabías que los enterraban'. Tal, tal, y tal. En donde les dicen, clavan pico y encuentran. Entonces decíamos, pero qué peligroso hablar con la gente del crimen organizando, o que era integrante o que conoce la gente del crimen organizado. Van las mamás, van las familias, sin ningún, ninguna medida de seguridad, y luego ya qué, si encuentran ¿qué?, no hay bancos de ADN, van a encontrar a qué gente, o sea, no hay cadena de custodia, no saben – no sabes cómo nos escandalizaba. Hasta que nos dijeron, o sea, 'con o sin ustedes, lo vamos a hacer, porque estamos cansadas'.' Interview 4.

The participant then went on to explain that it was quite understandable that relatives had had enough of officials searching for their relatives 'on paper', which is what they had been doing for years. And continued:

> Today, well, the organisations have become more conscious [and adjust to what the families want]. And rather [we ask them] how we can help, if they want us to help - perhaps if they have to talk to state prosecutor's offices, ensure that there are experts present, ensure that the bodies are brought to a certain place, that the inhumations are done in a particular way. That's what [the families] told us: 'If you want to. And if not, we'll do it anyway'.[119]

Nowadays, some NGOs actively accompany searches and try to mediate between authorities and relatives, as well as to ensure that authorities provide protection to relatives. Moreover, they try to support relatives in obtaining information about the whereabouts of their loved ones, including by appealing directly to the population of certain areas or criminal organisations.[120] One participant based in Mexico City reflected on this:

> Because the information comes from many places. […] I mean the information comes from the criminals […] to the point that we have taken people, who work for some group, to search missions ('diligencias') so that they could show us places. And I think that in a different moment, with a black-and-white logic this… you know, when they interviewed me here when I started working for [name of NGO], if they had told me that I would be interviewing criminals, well… I am sure I would have said no [laughs], with a black-and-white vision, good people and bad people – 'no way, under no circumstances would I do that'. But the realities of this broken country make you obtain information from wherever you can, to… find.[121]

Speaking directly to criminal groups as a means of obtaining information is not the approach taken by all organisations, however, and the question of whether to support relatives' groups in leading searches is not one on which all participants agreed. Especially participants based outside of Mexico City voiced opposition or doubts about this, emphasising the danger this poses to relatives, but also the responsibility of authorities to conduct searches.[122] Indeed, a number of participants, based both in

[119] 'Hoy, pues ya las organizaciones pues un poco más sensibilizadas, no, también, pues es como, como digan. Y más bien cómo apoyamos, quieren que apoyemos, pues, a lo mejor y si hay que hacer interlocuciones con la fiscalía de los estados, garantice que haya peritos ahí, garantice que se lleven los cuerpos a tal, o sea, que las inhumaciones se hagan de tal forma, o sea, así nos dijeron: 'si quieren. Y si no, lo vamos a seguir haciendo.' Interview 4.

[120] For example, Interview 1.

[121] 'Porque la información llega de muchas, de muchas maneras. […] o sea la información llega del crimen, llega del crimen, por ejemplo, no, eh, a grado de que hemos llevado, pues, personas que – que trabajan con algún grupo, a diligencias, para que nos señalan puntos. No, y, y creo que en otro momento, bajo una lógica como ahí de blanco y negro, eso… sabes de cuando me dijeron aquí, aquí me entrevistaron cuando entré a trabajar a [organización] y yo iba a entrevistar a criminales, pues… seguro habría dicho que no [ríe], bajo una visión muy, eh, sí, de blanco y negro, buenos y malos – 'cómo crees, no, yo, eso bajo ninguna circunstancia'. Pero las realidades de este país tan descompuesto te llevan a obtener información de donde sea, no, para… encontrar.' Interview number omitted for reasons of confidentiality.

[122] For example, interviews 13, 14, 15, 30.

states and in Mexico City, emphasised that it was the state's obligation to search for the disappeared and not that of the families.[123] The difference in positions on this matter was described by one participant based in Mexico City in the following way:

> … and lastly, I would say that we have seen that there are different positions among *colectivos*, and even among organisations. So that means that there are organisations that believe that families should not go out onto the ground ('a terreno'), that they should not go out and search and that the state should do this, and there are others that basically say that the state should stay out of it, that the families know [how to do it]. And I think we are in a more intermediate position, that if they want to go (and search) that is their right, and that the state has an obligation to search - because one also should not relieve [the state] of that obligation.[124]

The difference in positions could be linked to the different nature of the relationship between NGOs and *colectivos*, as NGOs in Mexico City do not generally accompany one particular *colectivo* (as some of the NGOs based in states do) and therefore might take a more pragmatic stance and support multiple *colectivos* in their activities, rather than just leaving them to conduct searches on their own. Furthermore, as already described, in some of the states that I visited there are existing efforts to collaborate with authorities in the search, whereas this is not the case in other states.[125] Moreover, the particular security situation in each state also plays a role in whether or not NGOs support searches by relatives.[126] Some participants also raised doubts about supporting the searches for other reasons, noting that the ongoing forensic crisis in the country means that exhuming remains without adequate facilities for storing them could be counterproductive.[127] The dilemmas associated with balancing the needs of relatives to search for their loved ones in the face of inaction by authorities with the very real limitations in terms of forensic capacity, was described as follows by one participant based in Mexico City:

> And then, the people who are searching, there is also a difficult dilemma: are we going to continue digging out bodies? Just randomly? And to hand them over to the state that will put them who knows where?… I mean, me, if they ask me, I would answer as a closed-minded lawyer: 'well no, we should wait …'. [But] the families will continue to do this as long as they do not see any changes: 'better dig them out.' […] But at some point there will be a

[123]For example, interviews 9, 14, 15, 22, 23, 24.

[124]'Eh… y, y de último diría que hemos visto que sí hay posiciones distintas entre colectivos, incluso entre organizaciones. Es decir, hay organizaciones que creen que las familias no deberían ir a terreno, no, que no deberían salir a buscar y que el estado solo debe hacerlo, y hay otras que dicen que prácticamente el estado no debería meterse, no, que ya las familias lo saben. Y nosotros creo que estamos más como en una posición intermedia, no, que, que si quieren ir es un derecho, y que el estado tiene la obligación de buscar, no, tampoco es que hay que quitarles esa, esa obligación.' Interview 21.

[125]Note that there are also *colectivos* in the states that I visited who conduct their own searches, but these are not the *colectivos* accompanied by the NGOs that I visited.

[126]For example, interviews 15 and 30.

[127]For example, interviews 17 and 25.

> conflict there between the government and the families. So, I am worried about this, and they are digging and digging and digging out bodies and we do not know where they are.[128]

This quote illustrates the difficult position of NGOs who are conscious of both the needs of relatives and their distrust in authorities, but also the risks associated with taking matters into one's own hands both in terms of security as well as in relation to loss of evidence and exhumed bodies.

6.2.2.2 Changes to Legal Strategies

A second aspect of pragmatism relates to the adaptation of strategies in relation to *legal* work specifically. Thus, in addition to responding to the needs and actions taken directly by relatives of the disappeared, some participants, especially those working for NGOs based in Mexico City, also adjusted some of their previous strategies in light of the complexity of the situation. For example, a number of participants spoke about a move away from strategic litigation at the regional or international level towards domestic efforts.[129] This was explained in different ways, for example in reference to the complexity and heterogeneity of disappearances in the country and the resulting futility of selecting an exemplary case to take to the regional or international level.[130] Another reason was the over-saturation ('drowning',[131] 'collapsed'[132]) of the Inter-American human rights system and the general length of proceedings before regional and international mechanisms.[133] In addition to this, a number of participants spoke about the limited impact of such litigation in terms of producing actual change (see Sect. 6.2.3.3). However, this view was not shared by all participants. Rather, some spoke about their continued efforts in the realm of strategic litigation and the importance of such litigation to increase visibility of the situation in Mexico and exert (external) pressure on the Mexican state, albeit in different fora than the Inter-American system. Thus, for example, some NGOs are

[128] 'Y luego las, pues la gente que busca, no, o sea, que ya hay por ahí… un dilema como muy duro, no, o sea, ¿vamos a seguir sacando cuerpos? ¿a lo wey? ¿y entregándoselos al estado para que los ponga quién sabe dónde?… pero, o sea, yo, te digo, cuando a mí me preguntan, yo digo, yo diría, te digo desde muy cerrada abogada, pues no, hay que esperar … o sea, las familias hasta que no vean un cambio van a seguir haciendo esto: mejor los saco. O sea, o se van a perder toda la información, no sé si esto va a cambiar, se va a inundar, va a explotar, no. Pero, pues, va a llegar un momento que va a haber conflicto ahí… entre gobierno y, y familia, no. Entonces a mí, a mí me preocupa, y se están sacando y sacando y sacando cuerpos y no saben, no sabemos donde están.' Interview 25.

[129] Interviews 1, 2, 4, 21, 31, 32.

[130] Interviews 7 and 25.

[131] Interview 19.

[132] Interview 2.

[133] Interviews 2, 6, 8, 13, 15, 19, 28, 31. A few participants spoke about the creation of the GIEI for the Ayotzinapa case as an example of how to make better and more timely use of international mechanisms. Interviews 8 and 28.

now focussing more on United Nations treaty bodies.[134] Conversely, participants working for NGOs based outside of Mexico City, mentioned that they were only just beginning to explore sending cases to the regional or international level.[135]

At the same time, due to the scale of the crisis of disappearances, and other human rights violations in the country, a few participants expressed doubts about the utility of the international human rights framework for addressing the situation. In one participant's view, the number of cases meant that the Mexican context 'surpassed' the international human rights framework that is focused on individual cases.[136] Others spoke about International Human Rights Law (IHRL) as being 'insufficient',[137] or 'outdated'.[138] In relation to this, some participants mentioned the need to move away from IHRL and towards International Criminal Law (ICL) as a tool for 'understanding'—and responding to—the current situation in Mexico. This is exemplified by the following statement from one participant based in Mexico City who worked for an international organisation:

> So, when all of this exploded, we started asking whether, faced with a phenomenon of this magnitude, International Criminal Law was not better equipped to respond to what is really happening and explain what is really going on in Mexico, or at least in certain parts of Mexico, during certain periods [laughs] - to avoid generalising.[139]

This quote also reflects the complexity of the Mexican situation in that the participant mentions and simultaneously qualifies the utility of ICL for understanding what happens in Mexico, as it will depend on the region and time period (see also Chap. 5, Sect. 5.3.2.2).[140]

6.2.2.3 The Creation of Two Crimes in the LEDDCPI

The last example of pragmatism relates to the creation of two crimes in the General Law on Disappearances. As mentioned above (Sect. 6.2.1.4), participants expressed different opinions about the possibility of distinguishing between enforced

---

[134] For example, interview 19.

[135] Interviews 13, 14, 15, 16, 22, 23.

[136] Interview 7.

[137] Interview 31.

[138] Interview 21.

[139] 'Entonces cuando todo esto explotó, nosotros nos pusimos, no, nos pusimos la pregunta si frente a un fenómeno de tan magnitud, eh, el Derecho Penal Internacional no está mejor equipado para responder a lo que realmente pasa y para explicar, no, lo que realmente pasa en México, o al menos en ciertas partes de México, en ciertos periodos [ríe], no, para no no generalizar, no.' (Interview 26) See also interviews 7 and 31.

[140] Note that not all participants spoke about this and there were also different stances regarding the communications sent to the ICC. For example, one participant explained that the NGO that they work for does not support the communications to the ICC based on the concern that by accusing both state forces and criminal organisations of committing crimes against humanity, the responsibility of the state might end up being diluted. Interview 21.

disappearances and those that are not, especially where disappearances are committed by organised crime. Nevertheless, most participants agreed that it was necessary and important to have created the two crimes in the General Law on Disappearances. Some argued that this was necessary because enforced disappearances have a particular gravity and should therefore be considered as a separate crime from those disappearances that are committed by private persons.[141] Others, however, explained the decision to create two separate crimes as a pragmatic necessity in response to the particularities of the Mexican context, the need to ensure that authorities had an explicit legal obligation to investigate *all* disappearances, as well as reasons related to the procedure of establishing criminal liability under Mexican law.[142] For one participant based in Mexico City, who had previously worked for an NGO in a state, this showed that the General Law on Disappearances was a 'product of distrust':

> I: And I understand that the creation of the two crimes was one of the aspects that created a lot of difficulty during the process [of negotiation of the General Law].
>
> P: Look, the law, I have said time and again, is a product of distrust. [...] [For example], the reason for the proposal to create a Search Commission that is separate from the prosecutor's office ('fiscalía') is because nobody trusts that the prosecutor's offices will investigate, they have already shown us that they won't. So, we needed to create something else. [...] What we imagined was a decentralised institution not controlled by the prosecutor's office that could obligate the prosecutor's office to provide information. It is a complex scheme because, ideally, the prosecutor's office that conducts the investigation would investigate both: where the disappeared person is and where the person who committed the disappearance is. But the lack of trust in the investigating authorities led to the creation of a separate institution. The other part was that of the crimes, and the reason that [the crime of disappearance] committed by private individuals was included, in the context in which we in Mexico are living, is because we did not want to provide the agent of the prosecutor's office with an excuse not to record a disappearance simply because he initially did not see that authorities were involved. So, the way to oblige them to investigate, no matter who took them, and to begin an investigation, was to include two very similar crimes. And then later down the path see if it can be established that there was state responsibility or not.[143]

[141] Interviews 9, 12, 17, 19, 24.

[142] For example, interviews 3, 5, 8, 15, 25, 28, 29.

[143] 'I: Y entiendo que la parte de la creación de tos tipos penales fue como una de las cosas que generaron bastante dificultad en el proceso.

P: Mira, la Ley, yo he insistido, es producto de la desconfianza. [...] si se sugirió una Comisión de Búsqueda separada de la fiscalía, es porque no hay confianza en las fiscalías para hacer investigaciones, eso ya nos lo demostraron. Entonces necesitábamos crear otra cosa. [...] entonces lo que imaginamos fue un órgano descentralizado, que estuviera fuera del control de la fiscalía, pero que obligara a la fiscalía aportar información. Es un esquema complejo, porque lo mejor es que la fiscalía que haga la investigación, haga la investigación de las dos cosas: dónde está la persona desaparecida, y dónde está el responsable que lo cometió, pero te digo que la desconfianza en las procuradurías motivó a crear una instancia por separado. Lo otro fue los dos delitos, y si se puso por particulares, en el contexto en el que vivimos en México, es porque no se quería prejuzgar, nuevamente, no queríamos dejar al Ministerio Público el pretexto de no calificar desaparición simplemente porque a primera, en primera instancia no veía a autoridades involucradas. Entonces la manera de obligarlos a investigar, no importa quien se los llevó, y de iniciar la investigación, era

This quote indicates that the creation of the two crimes was more of a practical necessity than a theoretically-driven decision. Another participant based in Mexico City similarly explained this choice as guided by 'pragmatism' in order to avoid reinforcing the state's denial of the problem of disappearances. While the participant recognised that the creation of two crimes could contribute to the state's evasion of responsibility for disappearances by not investigating the ties between private individuals and authorities, ultimately this risk was seen as the lesser of two evils when faced with the possibility of leaving victims of disappearances with no clear connection to the state without 'legal protection':

> Because if we leave them [cases with no clear state involvement] without any such [legal] protection, yes, of course we understand the power of the political vindication of saying that they are all enforced disappearances, but in legal and procedural terms this would end up strengthening the denial of the crimes and the search for... well, technicalities to avoid opening investigations into enforced disappearances.[144]

Thus, although some participants were not convinced by the creation of two crimes on a more 'principled' level, they nevertheless accepted and supported it in practice. As one participant based in state summarised: 'I honestly do not think that [the crime of disappearances committed] by private individuals should exist, but right now we need it.'[145]

6.2.3 *Frustration*

In contrast to the previous themes, frustration reflects the emotional aspect of participants' experience and has a more negative 'undertone', encompasses doubts, and evokes an impression of bleakness.[146] While some participants explicitly spoke about their frustration with the overall lack of change in the behaviour of authorities

---

poniendo dos tipos muy similares. Y ya en el camino ver si se desprende que hay o no responsabilidad estatal.' Interview 5.

[144] 'Porque si los dejamos sin esa protección, sí, entendemos la fuerza de la reivindicación política de decir son desapariciones forzadas, pero en términos jurídicos y procesales eso lo que haría es reforzar la postura de negar los hechos y buscar... eso, no, tecnicismos para evitar que se abrieran investigaciones por desaparición forzada.' Interview 8. Additionally, one reason given for this pragmatic decision, and which was mentioned again during the first presentation of themes, was the difficulty of evidencing state involvement in a disappearance in a criminal trial, where the evidentiary standard is much higher than in IHRL where responsibility is objectively determined (10 June 2021).

[145] 'Eh, yo, sinceramente, creo que no debería de haber la de particulares, pero la necesitamos ahorita.' Interview 15.

[146] Field notes, 2 August and 22 September 2019. The word I used in my notes for the picture that was described to me in these interviews was 'devastating'. Additionally, during the transcription process I made the following note (29 January 2020): 'Some interviews (7 and 18, for example) are quite disheartening to listen to. The sensation I had while listening to them, as well as during the transcription process, is one of despair and hopelessness. In Interview 3 this also comes through,

despite legal and institutional changes in favour of broader human rights protection,[147] others expressed this more indirectly in speaking about the enormity of the issues and the continued failure of authorities to act.

6.2.3.1 The Scale of the Crisis

The scale of the crisis seemed to contribute to frustration in the sense that the numbers of cases and lack of adequate response from authorities are such that addressing the issue seems almost impossible. One participant who works for an NGO based in a state, described this as follows when asked about the main challenges in their work on disappearances.[148] After outlining the lack of effective investigations, including resources and training to search for the disappeared, the participant continued:

> … well, it [the challenges] is basically everything [laughs] - when you ask something like that – we have nothing. We have nothing and 44,000 disappeared persons in the country[149] and tons of mass graves and nobody is searching for the thousands of disappeared. That is why the relatives have to go and search on their own.[150]

This quote illustrates quite bluntly how negative some participants viewed the situation in view of insufficient efforts by the state to address the crisis.

The frustration at the continuation of violence and disappearances, as well as institutional inertia, was described as overwhelming and draining not just for relatives, but also for NGOs themselves,[151] who are left with a feeling of 'impotence'.[152] The reflection of one participant working for an NGO based in Mexico City, who spoke about the devastating and self-perpetuating effects of violence on society, reflects this:

> P: … I think we are in a circle of violence [and] there does not seem to be a way out. I hope that there will soon be an answer to get out of this circle of violence. Because people cannot live like this, we cannot live in a circle of violence. It will drive us insane. Really, people will go crazy, so much violence. Then we will be living in a constant state of fright. […] I mean, it is excessive violence… we try to do something [laughs sarcastically] in spite of this.

---

when the participant asks 'what do you do with this?'- in reference to the inability of solving the enormous number of cases and the structures that lie beneath them.'

[147] Interviews 12, 15, 18, 19, 25.

[148] Note that this NGO does not collaborate with authorities.

[149] The interviews were conducted in 2019, when the official number of disappeared persons was around 44,000. As discussed in Chap. 5, the official number of disappeared persons in Mexico reached over 100,000 in May 2022. See OHCHR (2022).

[150] '… pues es que es como que es todo, no [ríe], cuando pre-, cuando hacen esas preguntas, que no tenemos nada. Verdad, no tenemos nada y 44,000 desaparecidos en el país y muchísimas fosas y no se está buscando, los miles de desaparecidos. Por eso los familiares, ellos tienen que buscar por su cuenta.' Interview 29.

[151] Interviews 1, 15, 18, 25, 32.

[152] Interview 21.

> I: And, and does this exacerbated violence also have an impact on civil society?
>
> P: Mmm yes, in the sense that the challenges are huge. And so we no longer know what route to take, how to move forward and with what. And who supports us. Yes yes yes, it impacts on civil society, yes it does. Because we want to do things, we want to contribute. But we also do not have unlimited capacity to do so. We are also not that many organisations and the challenge is tremendous, the problem is enormous, enormous, enormous, so case by case we will not get anywhere.[153]

This quote expresses the difficulties faced by NGOs who are working on the issue of disappearances, or human rights violations more generally, in the face of the scale of the crisis and its complexity, which also means that there is no 'magic formula'[154] to address the issue.[155] In this sense, the quote also overlaps with the views expressed by some participants that there is a need to move beyond the IHRL framework and adopt collective approaches to deal with the large numbers of cases (see above, Sect. 6.2.2.2).

6.2.3.2 Societal Indifference

At the same time, several participants spoke about what they perceived as societal indifference, either referring to Mexican society as a whole, or to the particular state in which they worked, and emphasised the need to create a narrative that would foster 'societal empathy'.[156] The following statement from a participant from an NGO based in Mexico City illustrates this point:

> But the general population in Mexico doesn't know, is not aware of the situation. And I think that this would be essential to be able to heal the social fabric that is so broken at the moment.[157]

---

[153] 'Creo que estamos en un círculo de violencia en el cual parece que no hay una salida. Espero que pronto haya alguna propuesta para salir de este círculo de violencia. Porque la gente no puede vivir de esta manera, no podemos nosotros vivir en un círculo de violencia. Nos vamos a volver locos. De verdad que la gente se va a desquiciar, tanta violencia. Entonces, vamos a vivir atemorizados todo el tiempo. [...] o sea, es una violencia exacerbada. ... Intentamos hacer algo [ríe], a pesar de eso.

I: Y, y esa violencia exacerbada ¿también tiene un impacto en la sociedad civil?

P. Mmm sí, en el sentido de... los retos son mayores. Y entonces ya no sabemos, o sea, por dónde seguimos, cómo seguir, con qué seguir. Y quién nos apoya, no. Sí sí sí, tiene un impacto, por supuesto... en la sociedad civil, sí lo tiene. Porque sí queremos hacer cosas, queremos contribuir a ello. Pero tampoco tenemos toda la capacidad para hacerlo. Ni somos tantas organizaciones... el reto es mayúsculo, el problema es enorme, enorme enorme, entonces caso por caso no vamos a llegar a ningún lado.' Interview 18.

[154] Interview 4.

[155] This was particularly reflected in participants' answers to the question about what they would change if they could change how the issue of disappearances is addressed. For example, interviews 4, 6, 13, 21, 25, 26, 27, 28, 29.

[156] Interview 7. Also interviews 3, 6, 13, 19, 22, 23, 24, 25, 26, 30.

[157] 'Pero en México, en general la población, no lo sabe, no está consciente de la situación. Que me parece que sería indispensable para sanar como ese tejido social que tenemos hoy en día como tan fracturado.' Interview 6.

Not only was society described as not aware of the situation, an issue mentioned by several participants was the continued stigmatisation or even criminalisation of victims and relatives, especially where the victims were apparently disappeared by criminal groups, despite certain achievements by relatives throughout the years to change these attitudes.[158] One participant also spoke about the internalisation of these stigmatising attitudes by relatives themselves, especially in marginalised communities, who accept the disappearances as something that happened because their relative was involved 'in something' (most likely a criminal activity).[159] A few participants also connected the lack of empathy to a lack of memory among Mexican society, including of the 'dirty war' period.[160]

6.2.3.3 Lack of Change

In addition to the magnitude of the issue and the lack of support from society, several participants expressed frustration or disillusionment with the lack of change despite certain achievements at legal and institutional levels, as well as, in some cases, collaborative efforts with authorities. As indicated in Sect. 6.2.2.1 above on collaboration with authorities, these efforts can be rather fragile and depend on the political climate. Moreover, even where there has been some institutional change and NGOs have made some progress in collaborating with authorities, this does not guarantee finding the disappeared person or changing the behaviour of all authorities. The frustration at the continuation of bad practices by authorities despite such achievements, was expressed as follows by one participant who works in a state where collaboration with authorities has been considered as rather 'successful':

> Yes, sure, we have many laws, we have working groups and fora and models that the government and [name of educational institution] sell as successful models, but… we could not even rescue [name] whose mother already identified him on the basis of forensic information and who was killed on the same day he disappeared and now the prosecutor's office will probably say that it is a regular homicide, a matter of local jurisdiction ('fuero común'). And this after the agents of the prosecutor's office lost the homicide investigation file and left the mother suffering for four years while looking for this goddamned file that could contain some information about her son and that, once we had found the file and she recognised the dead body of her boy in the photographs they tell us that they cannot exhume the body because they do not know in which part of the cemetery he is buried. Actually, they do not even know if he is in the cemetery. They had the body. They had it in their custody. They are also responsible for [name's] disappearance. I mean they could have returned the body to the mother on the same day that they found it.[161]

---

[158] For example, interviews 7, 8, 10, 13, 15, 22, 24, 25, 30, 34.

[159] Interview 30.

[160] Interviews 7, 11, 13, 23.

[161] 'No, sí tenemos muchas leyes, tenemos… mesas y foros y modelos que vende el gobierno y la [nombre de institución de educación] como modelos exitosos, pero… no pudimos ni siquiera rescatar a [nombre de persona desaparecida], que su madre ya lo identificó en la información pericial, y que lo mataron el mismo día que lo desaparecieron y ahora seguramente va a decir la

This quote illustrates how difficult it is to translate changes at a legal or institutional level to 'the ground', especially where the problems involve negligent actions by authorities and the disappearance itself is actually the outcome of such negligence.[162] At a more general (national) level, the participant from Mexico City who was previously quoted speaking about the enormity of the crisis also reflected on the issue that despite the creation of institutions in response to recommendations from international human rights mechanisms, there has not been any tangible change:

> And our task becomes more and more [inhales] difficult, it costs energy, a lot of energy, because, at the same time, you have worked for so many years and you do not see any progress. And you ask yourself: well, what have I been doing all these years? Nothing. Well yes, there has been progress with some laws, but these laws are not applied as they should be, institutions have been created, but these institutions end up being very bureaucratic... yes, we have made progress, well, on some things, but... these legal or institutional instruments have not worked.[163]

The last part of this quote touches upon what was expressed by most participants in relation to the large gap between law and reality in Mexico and their experience of authorities acting in the same ways as before despite training and new regulations.[164] In this sense, for most participants the main issue they were facing was the lack of political will to actually change things.[165] For one participant the continued lack of will was also directly related to the absence of societal empathy and the resulting lack of a 'political cost' of the issue of disappearances.[166] In view of this inertia, a

---

fiscalía ahí es homicidio común, es del fuero común. No, después de que los ministerios públicos perdieron la carpeta de investigación de homicidios, que tuvieron a la mamá más de cuatro años sufriendo por encontrar esa puta carpeta donde podía haber alguna información de su hijo, y que, ya que encontramos la carpeta y que ella lo reconoce por fotografías el cuerpo sin vida de su niño, este, nos digan que no pueden exhumar porque no saben en qué parte del panteón está. Es más, que ni siquiera saben si está en el panteón. El cuerpo lo tuvieron ellos. Lo tuvieron bajo su custodia. Ellos son culpables también de la desaparición de [nombre de persona desaparecida]. No, pudieron haber entregado el cuerpo a su madre ese mismo día que recuperaron el cuerpo.' Interview 15.

[162] See also interview 2. For a description of the forensic crisis and mishandling of remains, see Chap. 5, Sect. 5.1.2.2.

[163] 'Y nuestra tarea cada vez es más [inhala] difícil, nos quita energías, muchas energías porque también, has trabajado tantos años y no ves avances, no. Y dices: bueno, pues ¿qué he hecho en todos estos años? Nada. Bueno sí, se ha avanzado con algunas leyes, pero esas leyes no se aplican como deberían de aplicarse, se han creado órganos, pero luego esos órganos se vuelven burocráticos... o sea, sí hemos avanzado, pues, en algunas cosas, pero... es, esos instrumentos legales o institucionales no han funcionado, no.' Interview 18.

[164] Interviews 3, 4, 5, 6, 7, 8, 9, 12, 13, 14, 16, 18, 19, 22, 23, 25, 28, 29, 30, 31, 33. In relation to this, during the presentation of themes in June 2021, one participant spoke about their concern about the focus on training officials to treat victims respectfully and well rather than to do their job and investigate more effectively. While the correct treatment is of course necessary and important, according to two participants, it risks becoming a 'containment' strategy and to serve as an excuse not to work (the better the treatment, the worse the outcome) (14 June 2021).

[165] Interviews 2, 4, 6, 7, 8, 9, 10, 11, 12, 13, 14, 15, 17, 18, 19, 21, 22, 23, 24, 25, 26, 28, 29, 30, 31, 32, 33, 34.

[166] Interview 25.

few participants self-critically questioned their own (legal) approach of '[trying] to fix the country on paper'.[167] Additionally, some participants spoke about how legal negotiations were exhausting for relatives[168] and that even advances in terms of convictions would not necessarily bring 'justice' to relatives.[169] One participant based in Mexico City, who had previously worked and accompanied relatives and searches, described this as follows:

> So, really, what did we gain from spending so much time coming up with the perfect criminal construct ('tipo penal'), if that will not have implications in terms of getting the families closer to justice? … to the truth? They would say: sometimes we want a perfect law, I mean, the experts want a perfect law, but this perfection does not mean justice for the families – sometimes, for the families, justice does not even mean a conviction because they still do not know where their relative is.[170]

The example given in this quote of relatives still not knowing where their loved one is despite criminal convictions of perpetrators, was also mentioned by two other participants, who worked for an NGO that had achieved a conviction of the perpetrator without obtaining information about the whereabouts of the victim.[171]

Another aspect of the lack of change and ensuing frustration is illustrated by the experience of participants who have been engaged in litigation at the domestic level. One major issue encountered in domestic litigation is the refusal by authorities to comply even with their most basic obligations, such as sharing photocopies of case files with relatives, to which the latter are entitled.[172] Consequently, some NGOs have spent years in litigation to obtain access to photocopies, as illustrated by the experience of a participant based in Mexico City, who directed an NGO that has engaged in a lot of such litigation:

> So, the first challenge for us was to get photocopies of the files, because even though the families were authorised as victims […] and we were their representatives, the PGR[173] systematically refused to provide us with copies of the files. The first time that they authorised the copies was after like five, six years of litigation. And that is not to say that once we had the judgment, we immediately received the copies. The PGR still reinterpreted the judgment and wanted to give us only what they wanted. It took us another two years, one year and a half more for the court to say that to the PGR that it meant copies of the entire file. Because since it concerns organised crime, what if you pass on the information and spoil the

[167] Interview 25. See also interviews 8, 12, 15.

[168] Interviews 4 and 15.

[169] Interview 24.

[170] 'O sea, quien, en realidad, ¿de qué valió, estarle metiendo tanto tiempo a perfeccionar un tipo penal, si eso no va a tener implicaciones de acercar a la justicia a las familias? [I: sí] ¿a la verdad? Ellas decían: a veces nosotros, o sea nosotros queremos una Ley perfecta, o sea los técnicos quieren una Ley perfecta, pero eso perfecto no implica la justicia para las familias, a veces para las familias la justicia ni siquiera es que lo condenen porque ni siquiera saben en donde está su familiar.' Interview 1.

[171] Also interviews 12 and 24.

[172] On the issue of obtaining photocopies, see interviews 13, 16, 22, 23, 32.

[173] Procuraduría General de la República (Federal Prosecutor's Office). After a reform in 2018, this institution is now the Fiscalía General de la República (Federal Attorney General's Office).

> investigation, which has not brought any results. I mean this is just completely illogical. All the copies that we have obtained have been through an 'amparo' [habeas corpus proceeding]. All of them. All of them. Some five, six, seven years just to get [the copies].[174]

As a result of these challenges, according to the participant, 'we have not even started to argue about substantive issues.'[175] Thus, much litigation continues to focus on the most 'basic' things, which also means that more 'sophisticated' legal questions have not yet been addressed.[176]

Finally, a number of participants also spoke about the existence of numerous judgments against Mexico by the Inter-American Court of Human Rights, some of which have led to important institutional reforms. Yet the absence of any tangible change in relation to the effective protection of human rights, both in relation to the issue of disappearances, as well as, for example, to that of violence against women,[177] made them question law as a means of effecting change.[178] For example, in addition to international judgments, some participants mentioned that over the past decades Mexico has received countless recommendations from regional and international human rights bodies on what issues to address, such as impunity, yet it continues to have the same structural problems as 20 years ago.[179] Notably, despite these rather negative views, many participants, including some of those who expressed doubts about the utility of law, also emphasised the continued importance of international legal standards for their work, as well as for law generally.[180] In the words of one participant based in Mexico City, law is 'all that we have got'[181] to try

---

[174] 'Entonces el primer reto para nosotros fue conseguir las copias de los expedientes, porque aunque las familias estaban autorizadas como víctimas, eran víctimas, y nosotros éramos sus representantes, la PGR se negó sistemáticamente a entregarnos copias de los expedientes. O sea, la primera vez que nos autorizaron las copias fue después cómo de cinco, seis años de litigo. Y no quiere decir que inmediatamente se logró la sentencias, se nos dieran las copias. Todavía la PGR, reinterpretó la sentencia y nos quiso entregar lo que ellos quisieron. Nos llevaron dos años, un año y medio mas, para que la corte le dijera a la PGR son las copias de todo el expediente. Porque como es crimen organizado, no sea que tu vayas a pasar la información y me vayas a frustrar la investigación, que no ha dado ningún resultado. O sea, el colmo de lo ilógico, no. Todas las copias que hemos conseguido, tienen un amparo de por medio. Todas. Todas. Algunas cinco, seis, siete años para conseguirlas.' Interview 32.

[175] Interview 32. Field diary, 5 October 2019.

[176] Interview 24.

[177] Interview 12.

[178] Some participants also spoke about law as a political tool rather than an instrument of justice, whose value lies in the recognition of the issue and the creation of standards with which to pressure authorities (interviews 1, 12, 15, 16, 23).

[179] For example, interviews 8, 25, 32. This issue was also touched upon during the presentations of themes in June 2021, also in relation to the lack of prioritisation of the issue of disappearances (and serious human rights violations generally) and the example of the forensic crisis, which was described as the Mexican state shooting itself in the foot because if it had followed recommendations from treaty bodies years ago, it might have been able to avoid the current scale of the crisis (14 June 2021).

[180] This was also repeated during the presentation of the themes to participants (10 June 2021).

[181] Interview 5.

and counter human rights violations and the disrespect for law that prevails in the country, including by authorities.

The AMLO Administration

Lastly, frustration was expressed by several participants in relation to the administration of President Andrés Manuel López Obrador (AMLO), who held office from late 2018 until September 2024. Even though they were not asked about the (then) new administration, quite a few participants began to speak about it and one participant even expressed surprise at my not asking about it.[182] The participants shared that there had been a lot of hope among civil society that the AMLO administration would bring change and expressed their disillusion or negative surprise about the administration's failure to meet its campaign promises. One aspect of this disillusion was that, despite the AMLO administration's increased recognition of the problem and its scale, as well as a general change in rhetoric, participants did not see this reflected in practice, for example in increased budgets. Moreover, they voiced concerns about the continuation of previous policies, especially the militarisation of public security, the lack of clarity about the administration's human rights programme, as well as its rather confrontational stance towards civil society.[183] One participant based in Mexico City voiced specific concerns about the prioritisation of certain cases by the new administration:

> […] at least from what we have seen so far, in this six-year term there will not be any change either. [From] the roundtable discussions between the government and civil society that began in September and finished in December [of 2018], […] well, the comments we received from the authorities that in relation to justice there won't be much, they won't accept an extraordinary mechanism [against impunity], they want the General Prosecutor's Office to solve emblematic cases, Ayotzinapa being one of them – of course it is important that Ayotzinapa is solved, yes, it's very important that Ayotzinapa is solved, but if Ayotzinapa is solved in order to not solve the rest, then that is very perverse. Or if Ayotzinapa is solved together with another three or four emblematic cases, and we know which ones matter to the state, Tierra Blanca, Veracruz, the one of the Marines in Tamaulipas, which appear to be the ones that they want to deal with. [But] to solve emblematic cases and with that cover up the justice deficit to me is worrying, perverse, and something that will produce more problems than solutions.[184]

---

[182] Interview 26.

[183] Interviews 4, 6, 7, 8, 10, 25, 26, 19, 15, 28, 32. This confrontational stance continued until the end of the AMLO administration in 2024 and the overall situation worsened in the years after the interviews were conducted.

[184] 'sí, porque digo, de menos por lo que se ve en este sexenio, tampoco va a haber cambio. [De] las mesas de diálogo entre el gobierno y sociedad civil, que empezaron en septiembre y terminaron en diciembre, […] pues, los comentarios que había por parte de las autoridades era en temas de justicia que, no va a haber gran cosa, no van a aceptar un mecanismo extraordinario, quieren que la Fiscalía General de la República resuelva casos emblemáticos, el caso de Ayotzinapa uno de ellos, que es importante que se resuelva Ayotzinapa, sí es muy importante que se resuelve Ayotzinapa, pero si se resuelve Ayotzinapa para no resolver el resto, entonces es muy perverso. O si se resuelve Ayotzinapa y otros tres o cuatro casos emblemáticos, que sabemos incluso cuáles son los que al estado le importan, Tierra Blanca, Veracruz, la de los marinos en Tamaulipas, que aparentemente

This quote highlights both distrust and scepticism by participants in relation to the AMLO administration, which, according to participants, continued to pursue approaches that have not brought about necessary changes or addressed the scale of the crisis, thereby not offering a solution to the many problems.[185] Hence, in addition to the practical and conceptual challenges related to uncertainty, the enormity of the crisis and the difficulties of addressing it appear to contribute to doubts and frustration among participants. Notably, these aspects are not necessarily connected to the existence of organised crime, but mainly to what some participants described as the 'inertia' of the state[186] and the lack of change.

6.3 Conclusion

The three predominant themes across the interviews analysed for this research are uncertainty, pragmatism and frustration. *Uncertainty* describes the context in which the participants work, which comprises a lack of information, the complexity of actors and their relationship, ongoing violence and insecurity, as well as conceptual difficulties relating to the legal categorisation and communication of the crimes, all of which pose challenges to their work. Moreover, not always knowing which authorities one can trust and what actions are safe to take, both for relatives and for NGOs themselves, creates a number of practical dilemmas. Against this background, and in consideration of the urgent needs of relatives of the disappeared, *pragmatism* describes how participants have adapted their means of working to the context, including the demands and needs of relatives of the disappeared. Rather than following established approaches, or even their own convictions, participants have pragmatically adjusted their work to the situation and started collaborating with authorities, accompanying searches, using different (international) legal frameworks, and supporting the creation of two crimes in the General Law on Disappearance. Finally, *frustration* highlights the emotional dimension of participants' experience that relates to the enormity of the crisis and the lack of tangible change despite significant progress on legislative and institutional levels. For some participants this also leads to doubts about the possibilities of change and their own current approaches. Within each theme, there are certain differences between participants who are based in Mexico City and interact more regularly with regional and international human rights mechanisms, and participants based in the states of

son sobre las cosas que quieren ir, resolver casos emblemáticos y tapar con eso el déficit de justicia, me parece preocupante, perverso, y generará más molestias que soluciones.' Interview 7.

[185] For example, interview 4. The frustration and disappointment with the AMLO administration was also voiced again by one participant during the presentation of themes in June 2021, who spoke about the fact that 2 years after the interviews there had been no change, impunity continued as high as before, and recent electoral violence clearly showed the ties between crime and state. Another participant told me that things were even worse than in 2019 (14 June 2021).

[186] Interviews 8, 11, 31.

Chihuahua, Coahuila, Guerrero, Jalisco, and Nuevo León, or those who have experience working at the state level. For example, while participants based in Mexico City spoke more about conceptual (or even legal) challenges, participants based in states spoke much more about practical challenges related to security, collusion, and the number of cases that they are dealing with. This also reflects the general differences between participants based in states and those in Mexico City outlined at the beginning of the chapter.

The three themes are not mutually exclusive, and, in some cases, there is significant overlap. For example, the scale and complexity of the crisis do not just create uncertainty but are also a reason why NGOs have chosen more pragmatic approaches and adapted their working methods and strategies. Coupled with the lack of action by authorities, they also give rise to frustration and doubts about what else to do. At the same time, frustration arose for some participants after having adapted their ways of working to collaborate with authorities, yet not achieving concrete changes. Moreover, across all themes the importance of relatives and their needs is noticeable, in that the work that all participants engage in is ultimately about supporting the relatives. Another cross-cutting issue that connects all themes are the actions and omissions of authorities, especially their failure to investigate. The failure by authorities to investigate is one of the main reasons for the continued lack of information, which includes not knowing which authorities are colluded with criminal groups, or who is working for whom. It is also the reason for NGOs' adaptation of strategies in the face of inaction or the slowness of investigations, either by directly working with authorities and relatives to follow up on cases, or by training relatives to do their own follow-up work, as well as by accompanying searches. However, the lack of action continues and manifests in an overall lack of change that is at the heart of the frustration expressed by many participants. Taken together, the themes illustrate the complexity of working in a context where disappearances are committed by state actors and members of OCGs and show that the core of the issue is a broad, or even complete failure by the state to provide protection, which I discuss in the next chapter. One key aspect of this complexity from the perspective of human rights work is the difficulty of distinguishing between perpetrators and defining the exact role of the state in the commission of disappearances and other crimes. This has an impact in practical terms in that it is often not possible to know whom one is working with, as well as in conceptual terms for the purpose of communicating the situation. Furthermore, the theme of frustration suggests the impact of working in such a context on participants in a more emotional sense and paints a discouraging image of the situation. Nonetheless, their pragmatic adaptation highlights the ways in which participants continue to try responding to the needs of relatives, even if this means moving away from more traditional ways of working.

References

Ahmed A (2020) She stalked her daughter's killers across Mexico, one by one. The New York Times, 13 December 2020. https://www.nytimes.com/2020/12/13/world/americas/miriam-rodriguez-san-fernando.html. Accessed 28 Oct 2024

BBC News (2010) Mexico murder protest mother Escobedo killed. BBC News, 17 December 2010. https://www.bbc.com/news/world-latin-america-12023345. Accessed 28 Oct 2024

CADHAC, Ciudadanos en Apoyo a los Derechos Humanos (2014) Desaparición de personas en Nuevo León. Sistematización de experiencias en búsqueda de la justicia y la verdad

CEPAD, Centro de Justicia para la Paz y el Desarrollo (2018) Informe sobre el Proceso de Creación e Implementación de la Fiscalía Especializada en Personas Desaparecidas. ¿El camino hacia la Verdad y la Justicia? https://repositorio.colmex.mx/concern/books/wm117p84r?locale=es. Accessed 28 Oct 2024

Cruz A, Enríquez JE, Guadarrama A, Niño JJ (2024) Redes de macrocriminalidad, desaparición de personas y construcción de paz: un estudio sobre el Estado de México. Heinrich Böll Stiftung, Mexico City

de Frouville O (2021) Criminalizing or trivializing enforced disappearances? The issue of 'Non-State Actors'. In: de Frouville O, Sturma P (eds) La pénalisation des droits de l'homme. Pedone, Paris

Espinal-Enríquez J, Isunza E, Isunza A, Vázquez D (2023) Redes de poder y gobernanza criminal. Dinámicas regionales en Veracruz (2004-2018), 1st edn. Heinrich Böll Stiftung, Mexico City

Gallagher J (2012) Mobilization in Mexico in 2012: the movement for peace and the struggle for justice. Anuario del Conflicto Social 2:1235–1260

OHCHR (2022) Bachelet calls on Mexico to step up efforts as tragic milestone reached of more than 100,000 disappearances. Office of the High Commissioner for Human Rights, 17 May 2022. https://www.ohchr.org/en/press-releases/2022/05/bachelet-calls-mexico-step-efforts-tragic-milestone-reached-more-100000. Accessed 28 Oct 2024

Ríos Vega LE, Spigno I (2018) El Grupo Autónomo de Trabajo en Coahuila: un modelo de interlocución entre familiares de personas desaparecidas, gobierno y sociedad civil. Academia Interamericana de derechos Humanos, Saltillo

Sánchez Valdés VM et al (2018) Formación y Desarrollo de los Colectivos de Búsqueda de Personas Desaparecidas en Coahuila: Lecciones Para el Futuro. El Colegio de México, Mexico City

Sandoval R (2024) Buscar no debe costar la vida. Animal Politico, 10 March 2024. https://animalpolitico.com/analisis/invitades/madres-buscadoras-desaparecidos-asesinadas. Accessed 28 Oct 2024

Vázquez D (2019) Captura del Estado, macrocriminalidad, y derechos humanos, Primera edición. Facultad Latinoamericana de Ciencias Sociales, Sede México, Fundación Heinrich Böll e.v., Universidad Nacional Autónoma de México, Instituto de Investigaciones Jurídicas, Mexico City

Chapter 7
Mexico's Protection Failure

The experiences of human rights practitioners working on the issue of disappearances in Mexico, as described in the previous chapter,[1] can be drawn on to think critically about the protective capacity of International Human Rights Law (IHRL) in relation to disappearances committed by organised criminal groups (OCGs). The themes of uncertainty, pragmatism and frustration described in Chap. 6 indicate that, even though this research focused primarily on disappearances committed by OCGs, the participants' experiences are closely linked to the *state's* actions and omissions in what can be described as an overall 'protection failure' if viewed from the perspective of IHRL.[2] While this may relate to the identity of the participants as individuals who work in the field of human rights and whose main interlocutor continues to be the state,[3] the interviews suggest that this is not the only reason: on the one hand, based on widespread collusion between state and criminal actors, it is often not possible to make a clear distinction between state and non-state actors. On the other hand, there are practical impediments for trying to focus directly on OCGs, due to the risks associated with confronting such groups which, in the words of one

[1] As in the previous chapter, I edited the English translations of the quotes included in this chapter slightly for readability and clarity.

[2] For the notion of 'protection failure', I draw on the 'respect, protect, fulfil' framework employed by the United Nations as a way of characterising the nature of human rights obligations, which I discussed in Chap. 2. See Chap. 2, Sect. 2.1.1. While from the perspective of the 'respect, protect, fulfil' framework the notion of human rights *protection* is particularly relevant in contexts involving non-state actors as perpetrators, it also reflects the aim of IHRL more generally to ensure the protection of rights through the rule of law, as expressed in the Preamble of the Universal Declaration of Human Rights: 'Whereas it is essential, if man is not to be compelled to have recourse, as a last resort, to rebellion against tyranny and oppression, that human rights should be protected by the rule of law'. See Universal Declaration of Human Rights (UDHR) 1984 (UN Doc A/RES/3/217 A).

[3] This was explicitly stated by one participant. Interview 2.

L. Guercke, *Failure of the State*, Interdisciplinary Studies in Human Rights 15,
https://doi.org/10.1007/978-3-031-83717-3_7

participant, 'no organisation is prepared to take'.[4] Thus, it is not only a matter of the state being the natural and main 'target' of human rights NGOs' activities based on the IHRL framework, but also because of the danger involved in directly confronting OCGs, who 'kill'.[5] Moreover, given that participants described impunity as one of the main obstacles to change and reasons for the perpetuation of violations by all actors,[6] and a lack of political will as the reason for the continuation of this impunity,[7] focusing on the state remains crucial.

Consequently, in this chapter I focus on the state's protection failure and its implications for the protective ability of IHRL, rather than OCGs as perpetrators. I begin by highlighting some dimensions of the state's protection failure that I consider to be of particular relevance for the analysis and which are based on the participants' views on the question of state responsibility. Building on this description, I then introduce different and interdisciplinary analytic perspectives to critically engage with the protective capacity of IHRL, drawing on compliance scholarship and the concept of 'areas of limited statehood', socio-legal scholarship concerning over-legalisation, and Stanley Cohen's concept of interpretive denial. Finally, I return to the international legal realm and argue that there is a need to critically re-examine state responsibility from an international legal perspective, taking into consideration the potential 'intentionality' behind a lack of capacity to protect human rights and state unwillingness. Given the limitations of IHRL specifically, the law on state responsibility may provide greater possibilities of thinking about intentionality of omissions and a lack of will, for example by revisiting the concept of 'state criminality' and contemplating concepts of 'state gross negligence' and 'state recklessness'.

7.1 Dimensions of Protection Failure

This section describes several noteworthy aspects of the Mexican state's protection failure drawing on the themes described in Chap. 6, as well as participants' views on the responsibility of the state more specifically. These aspects constitute the basis for the following sections, in which I engage with theoretical literature from different disciplines.

---

[4] '… si denuncias al cartel de los Zetas o al Cartel Jalisco Nueva Generación, ellos no te van a difamar en medios de comunicación, no, sería otro tipo de riesgo que la organización no está preparada para asumir, *y creo que ninguna organización de derechos humanos en el país está preparada para eso*.' Interview 2.

[5] Interview 15.

[6] See also Chap. 5 (Sect. 5.1.2.3) on impunity as a perpetuating factor.

[7] See Chap. 6, Sect. 6.2.3.3.

7.1.1 The All-Encompassing Nature of the State's Failure to Protect

The first aspect of the Mexican state's protection failure is its all-encompassing nature, which was clearly reflected in participants' views on the state's responsibility. When asked about this matter, a number of participants spoke about the state's indisputable role in the rise of disappearances, and violence more generally. Indeed, some participants expressed the view that the state's responsibility was 'everything'.[8] One participant based in Mexico City summarised the different facets of the state's responsibility as follows:

> it is crystal-clear that there is a legal responsibility, a political responsibility, a moral responsibility, a social responsibility that has many facets, but all of these are linked to the state, right. [...] But the responsibility is everything, the responsibility is a state policy to have brought the military out onto the streets, a policy of the state that is complicit, corrupt, of federal police, the military, municipal, state police. Together with, in this relationship with organised crime. The omission, negligence, incapacity of the state in the face of reports by the families, the historic contempt, ignorance, mockery, denial, absence of prioritisation [...].[9]

This quote also illustrates the complexity of the Mexican state's responsibility and that it can perhaps be thought of as consisting of different levels.[10] At a general level, many participants spoke about the militarised security strategy implemented by former President Felipe Calderón and the 'war on drugs' as the origin of violence and mass human rights violations because of militarisation.[11] Moreover, a number of participants spoke about the role of the Mexican state in allowing criminal organisations to become as powerful as they are,[12] as well as its failure to provide general security to its citizens, which is evident from the sheer numbers of disappearances in the country.[13] One participant working for an NGO in a state put this bluntly:

---

[8] Interviews 7, 11, 29.

[9] 'Hm, pues está clarísimo que hay una responsabilidad jurídica, una responsabilidad política, una responsabilidad ética, una responsabilidad social que tiene muchas aristas, pero que, que en todas está vinculado al estado, no. [...] Pero la responsabilidad es toda, la responsabilidad es una política de estado de haber sacado el ejército a las calles, una política de estado cómplice, corrupta, de los policías federales, del ejército, los policías municipales, estatales, no. En la conjunción en este binomio con la delincuencia organizada, no. La omisión, negligencia, incapacidad, del estado frente a las denuncias de las familias, el histórico desdén, desconocimiento, burla, negación, ausencia de priorización [...].' Interview 19.

[10] See also interviews 3, 25.

[11] I 2, 4, 6, 9, 10,11, 13, 15, 16, 18, 19, 21, 30. For a discussion of disappearances in the context of the 'war on drugs', see Chap. 5, Sect. 5.1.2. In addition, a few participants went even further, speaking about the state's overall failure to secure rights, including a failure to provide proper education or even basic infrastructure (for example, interview 23).

[12] Interviews 12, 13, 25, 30, 32.

[13] For example, interviews 10, 11, 15, 23, 25, 26, 33, 34.

> First of all, they are responsible for the disappearances. [W]e are talking about more than 40,000[14] disappeared persons – I beg your pardon. I mean, they cannot just say that this is all the bad guys' fault because they are bad, poor bad guys. That the state does not know what to do. So, there is a responsibility of the state, and individual responsibilities of state officials in this tragedy that we are living.[15]

In addition to the state's direct or indirect involvement in the crisis, many participants spoke about the failure of the state to react to violence and, for a long time, its refusal even to acknowledge what was happening, or the extent of the problem.[16] One participant based in Mexico City linked the responsibility of the state directly to the lack of recognition of the issue throughout the years:

> Well, the state is the main responsible in this. There was lack of response of the state to the phenomenon of disappearances from the start of the crisis, let's say from 2006, 2007 onwards, [when] the first reports were ignored. But I believe that there is more. First, for a long time, the state ignored the phenomenon. Then it tried to hide the phenomenon. Then it was slow to adopt measures to address the phenomenon. And when it finally took, recognised in some way the phenomenon, it did so half-heartedly. It did so with reservations. It did so while keeping up a protective wall around the state and federal forces, especially around the military.[17]

These quotes highlight how the state's actions and omissions at different stages are understood by participants as making the state the principal responsible for the phenomenon of disappearances in the country and the scale it has reached. The actions comprise the policies adopted, the direct commission of disappearances, as well as the close ties between state and criminal forces that make it difficult to distinguish between these two actors. Conversely, omissions encompass the lack of prevention and response to disappearances.

---

[14] As mentioned in Chap. 5, the official number of disappearances in Mexico continues to increase, which is partly due to new forms of data gathering. During my fieldwork in mid-2019, the official number was 40,000 disappeared, whereas now this number stands at over 100,000.

[15] 'Primero son responsable por la desaparición. No…están hablando de más de cuarenta mil desaparecidos, perdón. O sea, no pueden estar hablando de que los malos fueron los que hicieron esto nada más porque son malos, pobrecitos malos. Que el estado no sabe qué hacer, no. Entonces, hay responsabilidad del estado, y con responsabilidades individuales de funcionarios del estado, en… en toda esta tragedia que estamos viviendo.' Interview 15.

[16] Interviews 1, 4, 6, 7, 8, 9, 10, 16, 25, 19, 22, 24, 29, 33. For an analysis of the official discourse of the Calderón administration and its denial of the existence of human rights violations, see Treviño Rangel (2018).

[17] 'Bueno, el estado es el principal responsable en… en esto. Hay una falta de respuesta estatal al fenómeno de desapariciones desde el inicio de, de la crisis, decimos, desde 2006, 2007, los primeros informes han sido ignorados. Pero hay más, yo creo. El estado primero, y mucho tiempo, ha ignorado el fenómeno. Después ha intentado ocultar el fenómeno. Después ha intentado minimizar el fenómeno. Después ha tardado tomar medidas para el fenómeno. Y cuando ha tomado finalmente, ha tomado, ha reconocido de cierta medida el fenómeno, ehm, lo ha hecho a media medida, no. Lo ha hecho con reservas. Lo ha hecho, … manteniendo un muro de protección para las fuerzas estatales, federales, y en particular para los militares, no.' Interview 26.

7.1.2 The Blatancy and Slipperiness of Protection Failure

One particular aspect of the all-encompassing nature of the protection failure is its blatancy, which manifests not only in the scale of the crisis discussed previously (Chap. 6, Sect. 6.2.3.1), but also in the perceived 'absence' of the state in certain parts of the country.[18] Participants also spoke of a 'state vacuum',[19] 'abandoned' communities,[20] 'lost territories',[21] or a loss of the 'monopoly of legitimate use of violence',[22] all of which evoke an image of the state's incapacity to exert control and protect its population in certain parts of the country. Moreover, the protection failure is also particularly blatant when it comes to the state's lack of response to crimes committed either by state agents or OCGs. This is not only illustrated by the forensic crisis described in Chap. 5, which was also mentioned by several participants during the interviews,[23] but also the continuity of bad and negligent practices by authorities, to which many participants referred when they expressed their frustration about either the scale of the issue or the lack of change.

The inertia of both individual authorities and the 'state' in a more abstract sense, also means that many of the obstacles faced by participants in relation to their legal work continue to relate to the most 'basic' of matters.[24] The implication for this research is that many of the more substantive legal questions relating to OCGs as perpetrators of disappearances, such as those identified in the first chapters of this book, play a much less prominent role in the daily work of most participants.[25] One participant, who has worked for NGOs in Mexico City and in different states, explained this as follows:

> [...] the context is too crude, it's not sophisticated enough to be able to say 'we are missing standard number three [laughs]'. That is the truth, we are in a situation of such barbarity, that... I think we have not even achieved to get the most basic things done. So, I mean, hopefully, hopefully at some point we will be able to tell you 'we should further develop these standards because we realised...' but I think that at the moment the situation is: 'listen, be sensitive with the victims, do not give them this information, or give them this information, how are you treating these plastic bags that just appeared,[26] do you have the capacity or not?' I mean, these things that, I insist, are the most basic ones -but it is what we are living here in Mexico. The access and real participation of victims, providing them with photocopies of the investigations, which is super difficult – it is not even about checking on what page are they saying something or other, well no, they do not even let you read the page

[18] Interviews 1, 3, 10, 19, 21, 23, 31.

[19] 'vacíos del estado'. Interview 1.

[20] Interview 21.

[21] Interviews 21 and 31.

[22] Interview 28.

[23] Interviews 2, 5, 7, 8, 13, 15, 17, 21, 22, 24, 25, 33.

[24] Interview 32.

[25] Interviews 24 and 32.

[26] This refers to the discovery of over 120 plastic bags with human remains that were found in the state of Jalisco (close to the capital Guadalajara) in September 2019. See Gutiérrez (2019).

> because it is completely redacted. That is what we have to deal with. I cannot imagine anything sophisticated that we could... no, truthfully no [laughs]...[27]

The refusal to provide photocopies, despite a legal obligation to do so, or the insensitive treatment of relatives constitute a clear failure of the state to comply with its obligations to investigate and provide access to an effective remedy to victims and relatives, which I discussed in Chap. 2 (Sect. 2.1.3.3).[28] The persistence of such practices means that more complex legal questions rarely come up in practice, especially not for those litigating at the domestic level.

7.1.2.1 The Difficulty of Pinpointing Responsibility

While the failure of the Mexican state to protect is thus clear, the extent of this failure, which includes actions and omissions by state agents at all levels, could also be viewed as making the question of responsibility 'slippery' in the sense that, while it is clear that there is an overall responsibility of the abstract 'state', it becomes difficult to narrow down this responsibility to any particular actor.[29] This is especially so because the line between those who are directly responsible for a disappearance and those whose actions and omissions indirectly contribute to it is difficult to trace. The following reflection by one participant based in a state illustrates this:

> And whose fault or responsibility is it that drug-trafficking organisations have proliferated across the country? Of course, it is the state's. And whose fault is it that they not only proliferated, but also acted with impunity? Well, of course, it's the state's. But whether that means that it is then in that moment directly responsible for a disappearance, well, yes and

[27] 'O sea, pero lo que quiero decir es que el contexto es tan burdo, que tampoco hay tal sofisticación para que tu dijeras nos falta el estándar número tres, no [ríe], este... eh, es la verdad, o sea, estamos en una situación de, de tanta... eh, como barbarie, que... yo creo que es como lo básico, que ni siquiera se ha logrado hacer pues, no. Entonces... yo, yo, ojalá, ojalá que después te digamos ay te podemos desarrollar este estándar porque nos hemos dado cuenta que aquí... pero creo que ahorita la situación es oiga, pues, este, sea sensible con las víctimas, no diga, no de esta información, o de le esta información, no, este, cómo está tratando usted estas bolsas que aparecieron, tiene capacidad o no, o sea, esas cosas que, insisto, son las básicas, no, las básicas, pero que son lo que estamos viviendo aquí en México, no. Mhm. El acceso de la participación real de las víctimas, el dar copias de las investigaciones, que dificilísimo que es, este, no, o sea, todas esas cosas que son natu-, ya ni siquiera es a ver es que en la foja no sé qué están diciendo, pues no, ni siquiera te dejan leer la foja, no, porque está toda testada. Eh... o sea, eso es lo que, con lo que estamos lidiando, no, ehm, mhm. Entonces... yo creo que ahorita, te digo, no imagino algo sofisticado que podríam- no, la verdad que no. Sí [ríe]...' Interview 24.

[28] For example, interviews 24 and 32.

[29] In individual cases, this is of course possible if a proper investigation is conducted. An example is the investigation of the Ayotzinapa case by the special prosecutor's office, which led to arrest warrants against high-ranking military officials and the former Attorney General of Mexico. See Gibler (2023).

> no, at the international level there is an international responsibility, yes, but not for example a criminal liability or something like that, well no.[30]

In addition to the difficulty of translating an overall responsibility to individual criminal liability, the uncertainty described in Chap. 6 further adds to this 'slipperiness', given that while the state is clearly failing in its obligations and can be viewed as responsible, many details of its failure are unknown. This includes for example the question of who is working for whom, or what motives lie behind the commission of crimes or the inaction by individual authorities. These questions are further complicated by Mexico's federal structure,[31] and the heterogeneity of actors involved in the commission of disappearances. As a result, as described by some participants, the complexity of the Mexican context makes it difficult not only to pinpoint responsibilities, but to create a narrative to explain what is happening (see Chap. 6, Sect. 6.2.1.4).

One aspect of this difficulty that some participants touched upon either directly or indirectly is understanding the reasons for inaction, or for obstructive actions, by authorities. As mentioned in Chap. 6 (Sect. 6.2.3.3) virtually all participants mentioned that one of the main, if not *the* main obstacle to change, was the lack of will by the Mexican state, either as a whole or as 'embodied' by individual authorities. Nonetheless, some participants also spoke about capacity-related issues as reasons for inaction or lack of progress. For example, some participants explained inaction by local authorities in reference to their ignorance and lack of training, or the conditions in which they work.[32] In regard to the latter, the experiences shared by participants illustrate how the Mexican state, as a whole, is also failing its own agents, for example by not providing them with sufficient funds, personnel, and, ultimately, security.[33] Thus, not only are police officers and soldiers among the disappeared,[34] but they are also left unequipped to confront criminal groups[35] or to

---

[30] 'Y ¿de quién es culpa o responsabilidad, este, que se haya, que haya proliferado el narcotráfico en el país? Pues por supuesto del estado. Y ¿de quién es culpa no solo su proliferación sino la impunidad con la que actuó? Pues, por supuesto del estado. Pero sí, como tal por una desaparición ya en ese momento directamente sea totalmente responsable, o sea, sí y no, como a nivel internacional hay una responsabilidad internacional sí, pero no por ejemplo para una responsabilidad penal o algo así, pues no.' Interview 12. A similar comment was made by one participant during the presentation of themes in June 2021, who spoke about the difference between the objective responsibility under IHRL and the subjective individual criminal responsibility, which is much more difficult to evidence (10 June 2021).

[31] For example, interviews 1, 25, 26, 32 and comment during presentation of themes on 10 June 2021.

[32] For example, interviews 3, 4, 6, 8, 10, 11, 12, 13, 16, 17, 18, 19, 22, 23, 24, 29, 31, 33.

[33] See Chap. 6.

[34] See Chap. 5 (Sect. 5.1.2.1) and interviews 13 and 14.

[35] Interview 12.

withstand the temptation of corruption because they are underpaid.[36] As a result, municipal police forces were described as controlled by or at least collaborating with criminal groups in certain areas of the country.[37] This can lead to seemingly paradoxical situations, for example where security forces from a different state or a different level (for example, federal police instead of state or municipal police) are brought in to protect investigating and forensic authorities, relatives and NGOs during search operations, including from local security forces.[38]

Moreover, investigative authorities in most parts of the country are chronically understaffed.[39] Not only is there a severe problem of case overload but, in certain parts of the country, authorities who *do* want to do their job correctly put themselves at great risk and may receive threats.[40] The consequences of the work overload is captured in this reflection by one participant, who self-critically wondered why they, as civil society organisations, were not putting more emphasis on demanding higher budget allocations:

> ... let's say that, all of a sudden, with the help of a magic wand, we all get up tomorrow and all the investigating officers and police officers that deal with disappearances, all of them, by some divine miracle, are sensitive, know about human rights, and are not corrupt. What is that going to change? Well yes, okay, perhaps that some people are less frustrated because now they are being treated very well, now the guy knows tons about human rights and tells them 'oh yes, that's really terrible' – but how is that going to have a real impact on the substantial progress of the investigations? It won't have any because they will continue to be paralysed. Well, perhaps they will advance with a few cases, I mean, they will say 'okay, well, let's advance in ten cases because we already know a lot about them', but they have 400, or 500, in some places they have 600 [cases].[41]

This quote illustrates the reality of insufficient capacities of those in charge of investigating crimes. However, the participant also mentioned this issue to

---

[36] For example, interview 10. On the low salaries received by Mexican police forces as lack of capacity, see also Anaya-Muñoz (2019), p. 453. According to Anaya, members of police forces generally have low levels of education, and police salaries are so low that the vast majority of Mexican police officers lives under or barely above the poverty line.

[37] For example, interviews 1, 5, 7, 10, 12, 13, 14, 15, 16, 21, 22, 23, 29, 30.

[38] Interviews 1 and 21. And Chap. 6, Sect. 6.2.1.5.

[39] Mexico has less police officers than the international average. Similarly, prosecuting officers (ministerio público) and forensic officers are also low paid (albeit better than police officers) and have excessive workloads, while lacking adequate equipment. See Anaya-Muñoz (2019), pp. 452–455.

[40] Interviews 10, 13, 18.

[41] 'pero vamos a decir que ya, con una barrita mágica nos levantamos mañana y todos los ministerios públicos y policías que se dedican a desaparición, todos por un milagro divino son sensibles, saben de derechos humanos y no son corruptos. Eso: ¿qué va a hacer? Ah bueno, pues que alguna gente este menos frustrada porque ahora lo tratan muy bien, que el wey ya sepa un chingo de derechos humanos y diga ay sí, pero está bien cabrón, pero eso ¿cómo va a tener un impacto real en el avance sustantivo de las investigaciones? No lo va a tener porque van a poder seguir imposibilitados, bueno, a lo mejor va a sacar poquitos casos, te digo, va a decir bueno, pues, saca diez casos, porque ya sabemos mucho [de ellos], pero tiene 400, tiene 500, habrá lados donde tiene 600.' Interview 12.

emphasise the need for more resources and to show the lack of *will* at the federal level to prioritise the issue economically and politically. In this sense, while capacity-related problems were mentioned when participants spoke about local authorities, this was not so when they spoke about the state as a whole or the federal level, where a lack of will was described as the main issue.

7.1.2.2 The Question of Intentionality

In addition, the blatancy of the state's failure and its persistence are such that they can appear intentional. Thus, for some participants the persistence of the state's failure to protect human rights combined with the existence of some very strong and well-functioning institutions, indicates an intentionality behind the protection failure.[42] While it may be difficult to provide evidence of intentionality behind impunity,[43] certain actions and omissions by the Mexican state mentioned by some participants during the interviews could be taken as indications that impunity is not just casual. One example is the lack of change despite countless recommendations by regional and international human rights bodies, international judgements against the Mexican state, as well as numerous legal and institutional reforms at the domestic level. Yet, not only does 'everything get lost in implementation',[44] but there appears to be active obstruction of progress. Thus, for example, human rights NGOs have had to continue litigating domestically after obtaining international judgements or orders because authorities refuse to act in compliance with them and question their bindingness.[45] The blatancy of impunity that is illustrated by NGOs having to litigate the adherence to international judgements or sharing of photocopies, as previously described, could thus also be understood as intentional obstruction.

[42] For example, interviews 6, 7, 8, 21, 33, 34. As mentioned in Chap. 5 (Sect. 5.3.2.2), some NGOs are arguing that the Mexican state is pursuing a *policy* of impunity (interviews 2, 4, 8). However, the argument made by these organisations does not deal with the question of intent but is based on the objective failure of the state to investigate. See, for example, Open Society Justice Initiative (2016), pp. 61–67.

[43] On this subject, see also Anaya, Cavallaro and Cruz Marin's work on 'active impunity' in Mexico: Anaya-Muñoz et al. (2021).

[44] Interview 25.

[45] For example, in the case of *Radilla Pacheco v Mexico* before the Inter-American Court of Human Rights (IACtHR), which concerned an enforced disappearance during the 'dirty war' period, the IACtHR ordered, among others, the search for Rosendo Radilla. However, further litigation was necessary for authorities to actually start the searches (interview 2). This reflects the general response of the Mexican state to international judgements or orders, which has included questioning whether such decisions are legally binding. As a result, several cases have been litigated before the Mexican Supreme Court, which has pronounced that the decisions by the IACtHR are binding (see Chap. 5, Sect. 5.1.1). More recently, the Supreme Court also held that Urgent Actions of the Committee on Enforced Disappearances are binding. See I(dh)eas (2021).

7.1.3 Meta-Uncertainty

A final aspect of the state's protection failure in relation to *disappearances* committed by OCGs specifically, which the participants' experiences highlight, is the prevailing context of uncertainty. As described in Chap. 6, the failure of the state to act and investigate, but also to prevent, creates different types of uncertainty—factual, in relation to the disappeared persons' fate and whereabouts, but also in relation to, for example, the legal classification of crimes because it is difficult to know whether and how private actors, such as OCGs, and state actors are connected to each other and whether they were involved in the disappearance in first place. The latter produces further uncertainty regarding what specific actions to take in a situation where the consequences are not clear. The foregoing adds to the uncertainty inherent in the crime of disappearance: uncertainty about the fate of the person, which includes the person's whereabouts, the circumstances of their disappearance, and the identity of the perpetrators, is one of the crime's main characteristics and the reason for its grave impact on relatives.[46] This is reflected in the definition of enforced disappearance in IHRL, which includes as one of the constitutive elements of this crime the 'refusal to acknowledge the deprivation of liberty or [...] concealment of the fate or whereabouts of the disappeared person'.[47] As discussed in Chaps. 2–4, from a jurisprudential perspective, it is not entirely clear whether the failure by authorities to react to the large number of disappearances in Mexico could be considered as constituting acquiescence, although the definition provided by the CED could now be interpreted in this way.[48] Beyond this technical legal question, however, the role played by the Mexican state in allowing disappearances to occur, for example by not investigating them, seems quite apparent. This was expressed by an international expert who has worked on Mexico in different capacities:

[46] See, for example, Scovazzi and Citroni (2007), pp. 191 and 272; Finucane (2010); Vermeulen (2012), pp. 124–127; Calvet Martínez (2015), pp. 41–42; Baranowska (2021). This inherent characteristic of enforced disappearances has also been reaffirmed by the IACtHR: 'According to this Court's case law, one of the characteristics of forced disappearance, contrary to extrajudicial execution, is that it includes the refusal of the State to acknowledge that the victim is under its control and to provide information in this regard, *in order to create uncertainty about his or her whereabouts, life or death, so as to intimidate and to suppress rights*'. *Case of Alvarado Espinoza and Others v Mexico* [2018] Inter-American Court of Human Rights Series C No. 370 [200]. Emphasis added.

[47] See Article 2 International Convention for the Protection of All Persons from Enforced Disappearance 2006 (1726 UNTS 3) (ICPPED).

[48] See Chap. 3 in general, Chap. 4 in relation to OCGs, and Chap. 5 on the situation in Mexico specifically.

[49] '[…]porque hay aquiescencia en la no-búsqueda, no, o en el ocult- no en el ocultamiento activo si quieres [ríe], pero en el, en la negación de esa realidad, no, eso tiene que generar una responsabilidad, no. Es que si no estamos así abriendo la puerta a más impunidad todavía […].' Interview 34.

> […] because there is acquiescence in not-searching -, perhaps not in the active concealment if you will [laughs briefly], but in the denial of this reality [and] that should also generate a responsibility. Otherwise, we will be opening the door for even more impunity […].[49]

Currently the prevailing impunity and the ensuing lack of clarity about not just the whereabouts of disappeared persons and the circumstances of their disappearances, but also the underlying motives and mechanisms that could explain their occurrence, as well as the lack of certainty regarding who can be trusted (for both relatives and NGOs), could be viewed as creating a 'meta-uncertainty' surrounding the phenomenon of disappearances in the country. This 'meta-uncertainty' is the outcome of the state's failure to investigate, not just individual cases of disappearances, but also the underlying patterns and constellations, including of collusion between state and criminal actors. As mentioned in Chap. 6, the persistence of such uncertainty poses significant challenges to establishing a narrative and explanations about what is happening, which in turn is crucial for relatives to make sense of the disappearance of a loved one.[50] The cruelty of the prevailing 'meta-uncertainty' thus raises the question whether the perpetuation of uncertainty through state negligence should be considered as constitutive of acquiescence due to the suffering it causes to the relatives of the disappeared person.[51] The CED's definition of the term appears to support this argument somewhat by including a combination of state inaction and knowledge of risk in situations where there are patterns of disappearances committed by non-state actors.[52]

To summarise, the dimensions of the Mexican state's protection failure, especially as described by participants during the interviews in relation to their views on the responsibility of the state, highlight the state's overall responsibility for what is happening in the country, regardless of individual perpetrators. In view of the blatancy of failure and the direct and indirect involvement of state agents at all levels, the responsibility can also be seen as 'slippery' in the sense that it is difficult to pinpoint, especially when thinking about individual actors. An additional aspect is the apparent intentionality behind the protection failure, which is illustrated by the persistent lack of change and active obstruction by the state not just of investigations themselves, but also of legal efforts made by human rights NGOs. Finally, the consistent failure by the state to respond to and investigate disappearances and the

---

[49] '[…]porque hay aquiescencia en la no-búsqueda, no, o en el ocult- no en el ocultamiento activo si quieres [ríe], pero en el, en la negación de esa realidad, no, eso tiene que generar una responsabilidad, no. Es que si no estamos así abriendo la puerta a más impunidad todavía […].' Interview 34.

[50] For example, interview 34.

[51] For an argument that the international legal framework against enforced disappearances is fundamentally based on the suffering of relatives, see Finucane (2010). For a similar argument on the need to broaden the notion of enforced disappearance so as to be able to hold states accountable for the context in which present-day disappearances occur, see Frey (2021) and Gallagher (2020).

[52] Committee on Enforced Disappearances (2023) Statement on non-State actors in the context of the International Convention for the Protection of All Persons from Enforced Disappearances. UN Doc. CED/C/10, para. 6. See also Chap. 5.

underlying patterns of criminality that motivate them, creates a 'meta-uncertainty' around the disappearances, which adds to the inherent uncertainty of the crime. The state's role in creating this meta-uncertainty supports arguments for a broader reading of the notion of acquiescence, as has now been included in the CED's definition.

7.2 The Mexican Protection Failure and Areas of Limited Statehood

One aspect of the state's protection failure, as described by some participants, is the relationship between 'state' and 'crime' and the blurry lines between them. Indeed, some participants spoke about the 'absence' of the state in certain areas of the country (see above). Such absence points to the analytic notion of 'areas of limited statehood' (ALS), a concept that has recently gained attention in human rights compliance scholarship. In this section, I connect two aspects of the Mexican state's protection failure to discussions in scholarship on ALS and human rights compliance: the blurry lines between 'state' and 'crime', and the underlying lack of will that was described by many participants as the ultimate reason for the lack of adherence to human rights obligations and the implementation of domestic standards.

7.2.1 The Concept of Areas of Limited Statehood

ALS scholarship departs from the 'empirical reality' that within Westphalian states that are considered 'sovereign' from the point of view of international law, there can be areas where the state does not exercise the level of control that this 'legal fiction' would suggest.[53] Börzel, Risse and Draude define ALS as 'those parts of a country *in which central authorities (governments) lack the ability to implement and enforce rules and decisions and/or in which they do not command a legitimate monopoly over the means of violence*'.[54] Such ALS exist across the globe in different regimes and are not unique to states that are perceived as 'weak'. Moreover, scholars in this field emphasise that the existence of ALS does not necessarily imply a lack of governance in such areas, which is a crucial distinction between this concept and that of 'state failure'.[55]

Much of the ALS scholarship focuses on questions of governance, and, more specifically, on questions of effectiveness and legitimacy.[56] In this sense, as regards

[53] See Krieger (2018), p. 544; Börzel et al. (2018b), p. 8.

[54] Börzel et al. (2018b), p. 6. Emphasis in original.

[55] Ibid., pp. 4–5.

[56] See, for example, Börzel et al. (2018a) and Hamid and Wouters (2021a).

non-state actors, the questions addressed by ALS scholars are to what extent such actors can exercise effective governance and what this means for international law,[57] or the rule of law, both domestically and internationally.[58] This is based on the recognition that a binary distinction between state and non-state actors does not reflect reality because the latter may also exercise governance functions.[59] In relation to human rights protection, ALS scholarship makes two propositions: first, limited statehood does not automatically imply less protection of human rights and it is therefore possible to examine the extent to which non-state entities that exercise control in ALS might actually be protecting human rights;[60] second, the existence of ALS challenges one of the underlying assumptions of the so-called 'spiral model' of human rights compliance proposed by Risse, Ropp and Sikkink, which was that the main obstacle to compliance with human rights was the lack of *willingness* by states to protect human rights. However, as Börzel and Risse point out, this is different in states with ALS, where, while there might also be a lack of will, the main issue is considered to be a lack of *capacity*, including, for example, the judicial capacity to take effective measures against corrupt members of police forces.[61]

7.2.1.1 International Law and ALS

From an international law perspective the existence of ALS is problematic because international law is based on the legal fiction of a sovereign state that has full authority over its territory.[62] According to Krieger, thinking about ALS from an international legal perspective raises questions of external intervention if a state cannot fulfil its governmental role.[63] While such a perspective risks abuse to justify military interventions and therefore needs to be treated with great caution,[64] to some extent the idea of a non-military external intervention resonates with the demands of human rights organisations in Mexico and the views expressed in some interviews in relation to the need for an international mechanism to address impunity in Mexico.[65] This demand also aligns with findings by Börzel and Risse about the factors that

[57] Krieger (2018).

[58] See Hamid and Wouters (2021c).

[59] Börzel et al. (2018b), p. 8.

[60] See, for example, Börzel and Risse (2013), Berger et al. (2018) and Hamid and Wouters (2021a).

[61] See Börzel and Risse (2013). Indeed, in situations where ALS are fully under the control of '*de facto* regimes', Hamid and Wouters argue that in order to enhance the international rule of law—and with it the protection of human rights—it is necessary to engage with *de facto* governors and explore routes for holding the latter accountable for human rights violations, rather than to continue focusing on the 'parent state'. See Hamid and Wouters (2021b).

[62] On this, see Krieger (2018).

[63] See ibid.

[64] Ibid.

[65] See, for example, Open Society Justice Initiative (2018); CMDPDH et al. (2018), para. 54. See also, for example, interviews 2, 3, 5, 7, 9, 23, 26, 29, 30.

positively impact on greater human rights protection in countries with ALS. These factors include the strengthening of domestic (judicial) institutions with foreign assistance, for example to fight corruption that undermines the effectiveness of the rule of law.[66]

7.2.2 Mexico and ALS Scholarship

Based on the definition of ALS given above, such areas can be said to exist in Mexico. However, due to the difficulty of distinguishing between 'state' and 'criminal' actors in many parts of the country, as well as the apparent intentionality of 'failure' by the state, I posit that the situation in Mexico highlights additional questions for ALS scholarship.

7.2.2.1 Blurry Lines Between Crime and State

As discussed in Chap. 6, the difficulty of distinguishing between state and criminal actors was mentioned by most participants, a number of whom pointed out that even where OCGs were the apparent perpetrators of a disappearance, as soon as one started to 'scratch the surface',[67] the connections to authorities would appear. One participant based in Mexico City explained this as follows:

> [...] because if you, even in your thesis, if you just stick to the issue of non-state actors and you do not look at the state, I mean, you are leaving a great gap because the non-state actors exist because the state has allowed this, and because the state has fostered them, and because the state has been a part of them.[68]

This quote also reflects research about the relationship between state and crime in Mexico, which illustrates that it is not possible to conceptualise OCGs as fully separable from the state. For example, in a recent study on macro-criminal networks, Vázquez found that in most of these networks, the state actually played a crucial and organising role.[69] More precisely, in Mexico 'it is also the state that captures the

---

[66] See Börzel and Risse (2013), p. 83. On the potential positive effects for enhancing accountability by supporting local judicial institutions in ALS, see also Lake (2014). Note, however, that Lake also cautions about potential unintended consequences of foreign support of local institutions and that further scholarship is required to assess whether foreign involvement should necessarily be considered as a positive thing. See ibid., pp. 523–524.

[67] See Chap. 6, Sect. 6.2.1.5.

[68] '[...] porque si tu te quedas solamente con el tema de, incluso en tu tesis, yo me quedo solamente con el tema de actores no-estatales, y no miro al estado, o sea, estás dejando un gran vacío porque los actores no-estatales existen porque el estado lo ha permitido, y porque el estado los ha promovido, y porque el estado ha formado parte de ellos.' Interview 32.

[69] Prologue by Bartelt in Vázquez (2019), p. 14.

state.'[70] From a different perspective, in his article on caciques and the crime-governance nexus in Mexico, Pansters shows how 'informal orders' in Mexico worked long before the 'narco' became a main issue, and argues that these historic informal governance structures lie at the heart of why criminal organisations have been able to become so powerful.[71] Furthermore, based on his work on criminal organisations in the state of Michoacán, Le Cour Grandmaison argues that the relationship between state and crime should be considered as 'a fluid process' that does 'not necessarily indicate the capture, weakening, or failure of the state.'[72] These findings also align with more general literature about the relationship between organised crime and state authorities, as discussed in Chap. 4.

Similarly, Schmidt and Spector have proposed the concept of 'authorised crime' to describe and explain present-day violence in Mexico, based on the argument that OCGs in Mexico do not operate in a vacuum created by state absence, but rather in association with state agents.[73] Thus, OCGs in Mexico did not 'take over' or 'capture' the state as independent actors. Rather, this 'capture' emerged out of historic relationships and involvement of ruling elites in criminal activities. Finally, in their recent work on the rise of criminal violence in Mexico, Trejo and Ley depart from the 'fuzzy' borders between state and organised crime in the Mexican context, as well as in some other countries, arguing that it is impossible to conceptualise organised crime as independent of the state because there needs to be some level of government protection for organised crime to function as such.[74] The complexity of entanglements between different political, private, and criminal interests in Mexico has also been illustrated in recent Mexican elections in June 2021 (local) and 2024 (presidential and local), during which hundreds of political candidates were killed.[75]

The experiences of the participants, as well as scholarship that challenges the divisibility of state and crime in Mexico, is in line with the argument made by Berti, who has written on the issue of OCGs and ALS.[76] According to Berti, 'violent and criminal non-state actors' constitute a particular group of non-state actors that is

---

[70] Author's translation: 'En este sentido es también el Estado el que captura al Estado'. Ibid., p. 12.

[71] See Pansters (2018). Pansters lists several additional factors that contributed to the increasing power of Mexican drug-trafficking organisations, such as the change in cocaine trade and consumption, the implementation of neoliberal policies, and the democratisation of politics in Mexico. See ibid., pp. 322–324.

[72] See Le Cour Grandmaison (2020).

[73] See Schmidt and Spector (2017). The authors' concept of authorised crime is somewhat similar to that of 'state organised crime' proposed by Decoeur. See Decoeur (2018). The notion was also used by journalist Marceli Turati in her work on organised crime and violence in the state Mexican of Tamaulipas. See Turati (2023).

[74] Trejo and Ley (2020), pp. 36–37.

[75] See Kloppe Santamaría (2021) and Pellegrini and Breda (2024). During the presentation of themes in June 2021, several participants also mentioned the elections that had just occurred as an example of the levels of collusion between state and criminal actors, as well as the state's use of organised crime for its political interests (June 10 and 14, 2021).

[76] Berti (2018).

'especially diverse, fluid, and elusive',[77] which mirrors the heterogeneity of the Mexican reality. Moreover, she also posits that where such groups are profit-oriented, as OCGs would be by definition,[78] the nature of the relationship between the group and the state varies.[79] As a result of these variations among groups, whether or not they will seek to exercise governance depends on the circumstances. At the same time, 'the link between profit, politics, control, and governance is often complex, multi-layered and difficult to deconstruct'.[80] Consequently, Berti argues that it is virtually impossible to think about OCGs in a decontextualised manner and that a strict division between state and non-state actors in the context of organised crime seldom reflects reality.[81] This argument is supported by views expressed in some interviews (see Chap. 6, especially Sect. 6.2.1). In the Mexican context, therefore, if ALS is to be used as an analytical framework, further research is needed to assess who is exercising governance for and with whom, considering the differences across regions with regards to dynamics of violence and the relationship between state and criminal actors.[82]

7.2.2.2 The Intentionality of Failure

Despite these caveats, the concept of ALS is analytically more useful for the Mexican context than that of 'state failure'.[83] This is in line with the view of some participants, who expressly addressed the question of state failure during the interviews and argued that Mexico could not be considered a 'failed state' given that the state has many strong and well-functioning institutions.[84] When reflecting on the issue of state failure,[85] participants immediately brought up the question of intentionality in the Mexican context. Thus, one participant based in Mexico City explained that Mexico was 'not a failed state, in the sense that there is no state, but rather that it is a state that does not want to do its job - and that is very

[77] Ibid., p. 272. Note however that the author does not provide an explanation of how she distinguishes between violent and criminal groups, or whether she sees them as being part of the same type of non-state actors. It appears as though the latter is the case.

[78] This is the case if the definition of OCGs in the UNTOC is used: 'a structured group of three or more persons, existing for a period of time and acting in concert with the aim of committing one or more serious crimes or offences established in accordance with this Convention, *in order to obtain, directly or indirectly, a financial or other material benefit*'. Article 2(a) United Nations Convention against Transnational Organized Crime 2000 (2225 UNTS 209). Emphasis added.

[79] Berti (2018), p. 273.

[80] Ibid., p. 276.

[81] Ibid., p. 284.

[82] Examples of such research are recent studies published by the Heinrich Böll Foundation on macro-criminal networks in certain Mexican states. See Vázquez (2019), Espinal-Enríquez et al. (2023) and Cruz et al. (2024).

[83] See also Kenny and Serrano (2012), pp. 9 ff; Serrano and de Pina (2021).

[84] Interviews 7, 21, 33, 34.

[85] I did not ask about the notion about 'state failure'. However, a few participants brought this question up when I asked them about the state-crime relations and the difficulty of distinguishing between crime and state.

different'.[86] In a similar vein, another participant, also based in Mexico City, expressed the view that 'Mexico is a failed state where it wants to be, and where it needs to be, and where it doesn't, it isn't'.[87] Both of these quotes touch upon the issue of intention of the state to not act and, in this sense, challenge both the notion of state failure and the underlying assumption in ALS scholarship that the main obstacle for compliance with human rights obligations is one of capacity.

The idea of intentionality behind failure is not unique to Mexico. In his more recent work on ALS, Risse acknowledges that there might be states where elites promote weakness and lack of capacity in order to serve their interests.[88] In this regard, Risse picks up the notion of 'cunning states' developed by Randeria in relation to India. Randeria defines cunning states as those states 'which capitalize on their perceived weakness in order to render themselves unaccountable both to their citizens and to international institutions.'[89] She argues that cunning states strategically and intentionally ('cunningly') use their alleged weakness as a way of justifying the adoption of certain policies and the non-adoption of others, such as the protection of human rights, towards citizens and international actors. Thereby, they avoid intervention from outside in unwanted areas.[90] Notably, Randeria listed Mexico, alongside Russia and India, as an example of a cunning state as early as 2007.[91] The following description of a 'double-discourse' employed by the Mexican government given by one participant based in Mexico City, illustrates how the Mexican state actively engages in such cunning evasion of responsibility:

> [T]he Mexican state can tell you openly and with a straight face 'I cannot guarantee the security of people in that place in Guerrero, or in that place in Chihuahua, in that place in Tamaulipas'. And it tells you this in order to not go and protect these people, in order to not prevent for example disappearances or other grave human rights violations. So then you say 'okay, well if you cannot do it, international law provides other mechanisms, because international law does not like it if there are empty territories, with the exception of Antarctica [laughs]. So if you cannot do it, why not just recognize it? why don't you recognise that you are incapable of maintaining control over areas of your territory? And then you can ask for international assistance with this problem'. But they refuse to recognise this publicly, while in private they use it to tell you 'no, I cannot protect these people. You are telling me that they are attacking this village in... Guerrero but I cannot send anybody because it is too dangerous. Period.' So there is a very serious double-discourse in this sense. Of course this is a double-discourse of the state, which has to do with whose discourse it is. The discourse of whoever has to actually go there and send police officers, soldiers, and

86 '[...] no es un, no es un estado fallido, en el sentido de que no exista estado, si no que es un estado que no quiere hacer su trabajo, que es muy diferente'. Interview 33.

87 'México es un estado fallido donde quiere serlo y donde necesita serlo y donde no, no lo es.' Interview 7.

88 Risse (2017), p. 142.

89 Randeria (2003), pp. 27–28.

90 Randeria (2007), pp. 6–7.

91 Ibid., p. 6.

so forth, is much more cautious and tells you 'no, I cannot enter there, I cannot enter, and I do not care what happens there because I cannot do anything about it'.[92]

This quote not only illustrates the different facets of the 'state' in the Mexican context, but also indicates how the apparent limited statehood in certain areas can be strategically used by the state to justify its failure to protect human rights and guarantee security to its citizens.[93] Moreover, the continued involvement by different levels of the state in macro-criminal structures alongside a discourse of having to fight organised crime, suggests that the state only selectively recognises the issues it is facing.[94] While Risse does not discuss the implications of a deliberate promotion of weakness for ALS scholarship in depth,[95] the Mexican context highlights that further research on this issue is required, even if the existence of limited statehood is viewed as a merely empirical matter. One way of dealing with 'cunning' states in this body of scholarship is to continue focusing on willingness and its relationship to the lack of capacity, which I discuss next.

[92] '[...] el estado mexicano, te puede decir con toda la cara 'no puedo garantizar la seguridad de las personas en tal lugar de Guerrero o en tal lugar de Chihuahua, en tal lugar de Tamaulipas'. Y te lo dice para no ir y proteger a esas personas, para no prevenir, por ejemplo desapariciones u otras graves violaciones a derechos humanos. Entonces tu le dices 'bueno, pues ustedes no pueden, el derecho internacional tiene otros mecanismos, porque al derecho internacional no le gusta que haya territorios vacíos, salvo en Antárctica no [ríe], entonces si ustedes no pueden, ¿por qué no lo reconocen así? O sea, ¿por qué no reconocen que son incapaces de mantener el control sobre zonas de su territorio? Y buscan la asistencia internacional para atender ese problema'. Pero se niegan a reconocer eso, públicamente, mientras que en privado lo usan para decirte 'no, yo no puedo proteger a esas personas. Sí tu me estás diciendo que están atacando a tal pueblito en... en Guerrero, pero yo no voy a enviar a nadie porque es demasiado peligroso. Punto.' Entonces hay un tema de un doble discurso muy fuerte, muy grave en este sentido. Obviamente un doble discurso por parte del estado que tiene que ver con quien da discurso, no. El discurso de quien tiene que ir allí a poner policías, soldados y demás, es mucho más cauto y te dice 'no pues ahí no puedo entrar, yo no puedo entrar, me da igual lo que ahí suceda, porque yo no puedo hacer nada con ello.' Interview 33.

[93] During the presentation of themes on 14 June 2021, some participants also touched upon this matter, highlighting that the Mexican state is very capable of deploying hundreds of police officers to suppress protests, but apparently not to counter criminal groups.

[94] According to Vázquez, such selective recognition is part of the 'institutional denial' that persists in what he terms 'Democracia a la Mexicana' ('Mexican style democracy'), resulting in an overall 'lack of recognition of the problems that effectively exist in Mexico'. See Vázquez (2018), pp. 196–197.

[95] Risse focuses on his main argument that limited statehood does not automatically mean a lack of governance or governability. He argues that it is an empirical question whether limited statehood is the result of a lack of capacity or willingness and holds that limited statehood is the basis for elites' deciding to maintain a weak state. See Risse (2017), p. 143.

7.2.3 The Continued Importance of Willingness

The reality described by participants throughout the interviews, as well as the above-cited scholarship on state-crime relations in Mexico, thus highlight several questions for ALS and human rights scholarship. Both the role of the state in its own capture (see above), as well as the apparent intentionality of 'failure', pose the question whether the application of the concept of ALS could not be misleading, or even provide the state with an excuse for non-compliance, especially if the underlying issue is one of willingness rather than capacity.[96] While an in-depth analysis of the causal relationship between a lack of will and a lack of capacity lies beyond the scope of this research, most participants expressed the view that the main obstacle to change at the level of the Mexican state as a whole, was an absence of will. Even though the reality of a lack of capacity by local authorities was also mentioned, the persistence of such incapacity was linked to an overall lack of will, as reflected in the lack of budget allocations at both local and federal levels. Moreover, the examples of collaboration with authorities given by some participants, which at times were described with disbelief,[97] indicate that the opportunity for such collaborations to occur was related to particular political interests. In this sense, the interviews also illustrate that where there is will, for whatever reason ('I don't know, well, we achieved or we were lucky, fortunate, the stars aligned, however you want to put it, that the CNDH (National Human Rights Commission) and the Prosecutor's Office of [state's name] handed over their files to us'[98]), there is also capacity to make progress. Finally, and as already mentioned above, the issue of corruption and its persistence can be viewed as a manifestation of unwillingness because it presupposes the involvement of political actors who benefit from existing structures. This is so at the macro-level, but some participants also mentioned collusion and corruption as reasons for inaction by individual authorities.[99]

A similar argument has recently been made by Anaya-Muñoz, who draws on Mexico as a 'crucial' case to highlight the under-theorisation of the notion of 'willingness' in human rights compliance scholarship.[100] Additionally, he advances

---

[96] A similar argument is made by Anaya and Saltalamacchia, who argue that an over-emphasis on the alleged lack of capacity as an obstacle to compliance could be used by the state for the purpose of denial. See Muñoz and Saltalamacchia (2018), p. 226. I discuss the issue of denial more specifically in Sect. 7.3.3 below.

[97] For example, interviews 7 and 22.

[98] 'Se tuvo la suerte, no sé, bueno, el trabajo o la suerte, la fortuna, se alinearon los astros, como lo quieras decir, para que CNDH y las Fiscalía de [...] entregaran expedientes.' Interview 7. This was the participant's response to my question about how a truth-finding project that was part of a collective reparation in one of the states through the Executive Commission for Assistance to Victims (CEAV) came about. The project involved several institutions granting researchers access to files. The quote illustrates how the effective collaboration by some institutions (because not all institutions did collaborate) is by no means taken for granted.

[99] For example, interviews 8, 13, 16, 23, 24, 29, 31, 32, 33.

[100] See Anaya-Muñoz (2019) and Muñoz and Saltalamacchia (2018).

a proposal on how to conceptualise and operationalise the notion of willingness, based on a series of indicators to measure 'political will' in relation to anti-corruption efforts.[101] Such an 'objective' operationalisation of willingness is important in that it avoids the more complex question of underlying reasons, or the need to establish causal relations between lack of will and lack of capacity.[102] Nonetheless, based on the entanglements between state and criminal actors, and the apparent intentionality behind the state's protection failure, further research should also examine the underlying reasons for unwillingness, which may include in-depth analyses of macro-criminal structures.[103] Such research could contribute to reducing the uncertainty about underlying interests that might either be leading to the direct commission of human rights violations, including disappearances, or to the lack of reaction. This is especially the case if ways for reducing unwillingness are to be found.

To summarise, the existence of powerful criminal organisations and collusion between these and state actors indicate the existence of ALS in which the Mexican state, as a whole, does not exercise full, legitimate command over the means of violence. However, much of the ALS scholarship concerned with the protection of human rights is based on the notion that, for the state, one of the main obstacles to such protection in ALS is the lack of capacity to provide it. Consequently, the question of whether a state is willing to protect rights is no longer viewed as the main issue. Nonetheless, as I have discussed in this section, the idea of 'self-capture' by the state and the resulting entanglement between 'state' and 'crime', as well as the apparent 'cunning' intentionality behind the Mexican state's incapacity, point back to questions of willingness, rather than capacity. This highlights the need for better understanding of the interplay between will and capacity across different levels of the state, as well as more research on existing macro-criminal relations as a way of uncovering the interests that may lie behind apparent incapacity.

[101] The indicators are: (1) 'locus of initiative', referring to whether a particular initiative was proposed by a government or by domestic or external actors; (2) 'analytical rigour', referring to the conduct of an in-depth analysis of the issue to be addressed; (3) 'mobilisation of support', referring to how participative and inclusive the initiative is; (4) 'application of credible sanctions', referring to the prosecuting and sanctioning of individuals involved in unlawful activities; and (5) 'continuity of effort', referring to the allocation of a sufficient budget and the existence of a long-term perspective in the design of the initiative. See Anaya-Muñoz (2019), pp. 449–450.

[102] See ibid., p. 461. Moreover, an objective determination would reflect IHRL standards that do not require showing intent. See, for example, Crawford (2013), pp. 60–62. The IACtHR has also explicitly stated the irrelevance of individual motives or intent by individual agents. See for example *Case of Velásquez-Rodríguez v Honduras (Merits)* [1988] Inter-American Court of Human Rights Ser. C No. 4, para. 173.

[103] Another analysis is advanced by Serrano and de Pina, who argue that the issue is not merely one of willingness, but rather one of *tolerance* for non-compliance, which is based on a political decision and therefore also hints at a form of intentionality. See Serrano and de Pina (2021).

7.3 The Limits of Legal Solutions

A second aspect of Mexico's protection failure based on the participants' experiences is that the potential of legal solutions should not be over-estimated. This is illustrated by the following: first, the humanitarian needs of relatives of the disappeared and subsequent adjustment of working methods by NGOs; second, the potential 'trap' of (over)legalisation; and third, the plausible deniability of responsibility that arises from an emphasis on legal binaries, each of which is discussed in turn.

7.3.1 The Humanitarian Needs of Relatives

First, and particularly in relation to disappearances, the pragmatic changes that practitioners made to their work on disappearances (see Chap. 6, Sect. 6.2.2) are based on the needs of relatives. Initially, the latter relate primarily to the search for their loved ones and addressing the immediate economic, social and psychological consequences of the disappearance—and not necessarily to accountability or justice.[104] One participant based in Mexico City, whose organisation works primarily on cases involving disappeared migrants and supports *colectivos* in Central America, explained this as follows:

> There are times where one would like to do more things, as part of a strategic litigation, but the thermometer of how much we can do are definitely the families.... I'll give you an example: when we started with disappearance cases, some of them from Central America, of course we wanted to start working on the aspect of justice in parallel to the search, right, and that was impossible. For the families the issue of justice was - and by justice. I mean to go and start litigating the case file, the question of who was responsible, the question of the role of the state - for the families that was not on their map, they had absolutely no interest in anything to do with responsibilities. For them the issue was the search, so that is how... well, you deconstruct your training as a more traditional lawyer, to understand that the case is built collectively.[105]

[104]This is not to suggest that justice is not important for the relatives, but it may not be the most urgent priority.

[105]'Hay ocasiones en las que uno quisiera hacer más cosas, no, como parte de un litigio estratégico, pero el termómetro de cuanto podemos hacer definitivamente son las familias. Por ejemplo, te pongo un ejemplo: cuando empezamos con casos de desaparición, algunos de Centroamérica, obviamente que nosotros queríamos también empezar a ver paralelamente el tema de justicia con el de búsqueda, no, y eso era imposible. O sea, para las familias el tema de justicia estaba... justicia me refiero a... ir a hacer un litigio en el expediente, el tema de los responsables, el tema del papel del estado, o sea para las familias eso estaba fuera del mapa, o sea no, a ellas no les interesaba absolutamente nada que tuviera que ver con responsabilidades. Para ellas el tema era la búsqueda, no, entonces de esa forma es como... digamos, pues, deconstruyes de una formación de abogado más tradicional, no, para entender que el caso se construye colectivamente.' Interview 32.

As this quote illustrates, and as I have already discussed in Chap. 6, relatives of the disappeared and their needs play an important role in 'directing' the work of many NGOs, leading those that were traditionally more focused on strategic litigation to adapt their working methods. This relates to the characteristics of disappearances and their effect on relatives of disappeared persons, but also to the scale of the problem in the Mexican context specifically. The latter was emphasised by several participants when they spoke about the necessary solutions, or the question of reparations, and mentioned that the scale of the problem required large-scale solutions that would move beyond individual cases.[106] Consequently, in situations involving disappearances, due to the particular nature of these crimes, traditional legal approaches can fall short of meeting the needs of relatives. In the Mexican context, due to the scale of the issue, a strictly legal approach that would require the judicialization of every single case is unrealistic, which means that additional, alternative ways of obtaining 'justice' will have to be found.[107]

7.3.2 *The Trap of Over-Legalisation*

Second, the lack of change despite important legal and institutional reforms, as well as the existence of judgements and countless recommendations by regional and international human rights bodies, has driven some of the participants to question the efficacy of legal approaches, as discussed in Chap. 6 in relation to frustration (Sect. 6.2.3). In this vein, many participants emphasised the gap between law and reality and some reflected (self-)critically on the utility of creating new laws and institutions as a way of achieving meaningful change.[108] One participant based in Mexico City expressed the view that, while law itself was not the problem, 'one could achieve better things with less law.'[109] Similarly, as mentioned, most participants pointed out that the main issue was one of a lack of political will, rather than a lack of legal instruments, or even capacity. The question this raises is whether, especially in contexts where a state is not willing to comply with its human rights obligations, an over-emphasis on legal 'solutions', or approaches, can also trap human rights practitioners, and with them the victims of human rights violations themselves, in a

[106] See Chap. 6, Sect. 6.2.3.1.

[107] In this vein, at the beginning of the administration of President López Obrador, there were several proposals for the adoption of transitional justice mechanisms in Mexico. However, no such measures have been taken. See, for example, Centro de Investigación y Docencia Económicas (CIDE) (2018) and IMDHD (2019). More recently, see also Hernández et al. (2020).

[108] Interviews 8, 13, 22, 23, 25. At the same time, however, many participants still emphasised the importance of (international) legal standards to legitimise their demands and serve as a tool to exert pressure on the state (see further below).

[109] 'cosas mejores con menos ley'. Interview 26.

vicious cycle of 'trying to fix the country on paper'.[110] This is not to suggest that the work of human rights practitioners is futile. However, it is important to carefully reflect on where the main efforts are focused and what implications the emphasis on legal changes has in practice, also in terms of what it means for both human rights NGOs and victims. For example, a few participants spoke about the process of negotiating the General Law on Disappearances (LEDDCPI) as being 'exhausting' for relatives and warned of further divisions among the relatives' movement if another law had to be negotiated.[111]

This aspect of participants' experiences resonates with more general critiques of (over-)legalisation of human rights, which highlight two things: first, the excessive focus on IHRL in much of human rights scholarship, and second, the emphasis on *legal* measures to ensure the implementation of human rights norms at the domestic level.[112] In relation to the second criticism and from a sociological perspective, Woodiwiss argues that effective enforcement of human rights requires 'ordinary respectfulness' and, beyond the incorporation of human rights norms into domestic legislation, 'it must mobilize the supportive elements and/or processes present within the social routines of everyday life'.[113] The importance of such 'ordinary respectfulness' was also highlighted by some participants who spoke about the challenges posed by the high tolerance for the disrespect for law in Mexican society generally[114] and the apparent indifference by most of society towards the issue of disappearances more specifically.[115] In addition, some participants mentioned the fact that law does not mean justice.[116]

Despite recognising potential gaps between law and justice, much of the activities by civil society in Mexico continue to be focused on legal changes. This may relate to the characteristics of the participants as members of NGOs that engage in litigation and 'legal' human rights work, as well as to their sources of funding.[117] At the same time, it may also relate to the scale and complexity of the problem of disappearances, which requires systemic changes that lie far beyond the capacity of

---

[110] Interview 25. On this, see also Serrano and de Pina (2021). The authors argue that an excessive focus in Mexico on processes, rather than outcomes, can end up becoming an obstacle for achieving truth, justice and reparations when it comes to human rights compliance. The creation of new institutions can effectively become a 'trap'.

[111] For example, interview 15.

[112] See Çali and Meckled-García (2006); Freeman (2006); Fraser (2020), pp. 7–12.

[113] Woodiwiss (2006), p. 34. Similarly, according to Fraser, there is a need for human rights to become accepted as 'societal norms'. See Fraser (2020), p. 11.

[114] Interviews 5, 23, 25.

[115] Especially interviews 7, 13, 19, 22, 23, 24, 25, 26.

[116] Interviews 1, 15, 16, 23. Indeed, according to Donnelly, '[l]aw, necessarily, falls short of justice' because it is impossible for law to capture every aspect of either suffering or human needs. See Donnelly (2006), p. 71.

[117] Interview 7. On the general issues in relating to funding for NGOs in Mexico, see Frey (2015).

civil society to address.[118] Additionally, becoming 'experts in organised crime'[119] to promote alternative means of justice could greatly increase the risks practitioners might face. The problem of an approach that places too much emphasis on the law, and change through law, lies in the risk of making false promises about the possibility of change because it omits a consideration of the politics behind the problems it aims to solve.[120] In the Mexican context, one could add to this that beyond politics, there are diverse private interests fuelling the continuation of violence, which have not yet been much explored and which would also need to be considered when seeking to end violence.[121] Moreover, as the theme of frustration illustrates, a continued focus on legal changes without tangible change in practice can lead to self-doubts and frustration among human rights practitioners in the long run.[122] In this sense, it is important to critically reflect on the benefits and drawbacks of directing efforts towards legal changes and, in parallel, explore alternative and complementary, pathways towards justice for victims.

7.3.2.1 The Shortcomings of (Legal) Centralisation in the Mexican Context

Additionally, in the Mexican context specifically, it is important to think about the potential limitations, or even drawbacks, of *centralised* discussions about legal and institutional reforms. During my stay in Mexico and the time I spent with NGOs working in states, I had the strong impression that if change were to occur, it would have to start at the local level.[123] As discussed in Chap. 6, at the local level there have been much greater advances in relation to collaboration with authorities, which, in some cases, was described by participants as having brought about positive results. One participant who has worked both in Mexico City and in different states, also spoke about the greater proximity to authorities at local level and the advantages of that in comparison to the experience of cases based at the federal level (PGR, now

[118] Nor is it the role of civil society to address these issues. Some comments in this regard where also made during the interviews, when participants pointed out that they, as civil society, or relatives themselves, were actually doing the state's job. For example, interviews 2, 9, 10, 13, 21.

[119] See interview cited in Chap. 6, note 88.

[120] On this, see Kennedy (2002), pp. 116–117.

[121] Very few authors have begun to attempt to study the connections between businesses and violence in certain parts of the country. See, for example, Correa-Cabrera (2017) and Paley (2020). A further example to illustrate possible connections between business interests and human rights violation are the killings and disappearances of land and environmental defenders in Mexico, many of whom were protesting against large mining projects. See, for example, Global Witness (2024), p. 16; Nuño (2023).

[122] The emotional impact of this on human right practitioners is an area for further research.

[123] Field diary, 19 September 2019.

FGR), where access was much more restricted.[124] Moreover, organisations that are based in states have a much greater and in-depth understanding of the dynamics of their state, which is crucial in view of the heterogeneity of actors and violence dynamics in Mexico.

These impressions resonate with Gallagher's argument that local judicial institutions should be thoroughly examined in order to understand how to improve access to justice and rights protection for the population.[125] Based on her research on such local judicial institutions, she argues that it is unhelpful to view 'the state as a coherent unitary actor'.[126] However, many of the policy discussions and political negotiations on the issue of disappearances continue to occur at the federal level in Mexico, which can create not only logistical challenges for NGOs based in states but also additional work for them.[127] Thus, when I interviewed participants based in the states, they spoke about the value of the General Law on Disappearances because it mandates the creation of nation-wide DNA databases and registers of disappeared persons, which are seen as important. Nonetheless, in most of the states that I visited there had also already been legislative advances at the local level. Once the LEDDCPI was adopted, NGOs at the state level had to start working on updating the local legal framework and creating new institutions in line with the new general law. As expressed by one participant based in a state:

> [...] but then suddenly these general laws arrive and then sometimes it does not matter [laughs] what you might have achieved here, because there comes the general law to change things.[128]

While it was not mentioned as a significant issue by the participants based in states, having to update local laws and institutions in order to reflect changes in nationally applicable legislation could also be seen as contributing to 'trapping' practitioners in legislative and procedural reforms.[129]

7.3.3 Plausible Deniability

If the underlying issue is one of will, rather than capacity, and the state acts 'cunningly', then an over-emphasis on legal solutions can also end up being used by the state for evasion of responsibility.[130] This is because the state can utilise legal nuances to deny responsibility for human rights violations. Drawing on Cohen's

---

[124] Interview 24.

[125] See Gallagher (2018), p. 256.

[126] Ibid.

[127] Field diary, for example 16 August 2019, 19 September 2019.

[128] '[...] pero luego de pronto llegan estas leyes generales que ya a veces no importa [ríe] lo que hayas ganado acá, porque viene la ley general a cambiar, a cambiar las cosas.' Interview 12.

[129] On this topic, see Serrano and de Pina (2021).

[130] Interviews 8, 15, 25.

theory of denial,[131] the situation in Mexico and the presence and participation of OCGs in the commission of human rights violations lends itself very well to 'interpretive denial'. Cohen describes this particular form of denial as giving facts 'a different meaning from what seems apparent to others', rather than outrightly denying their occurrence.[132] According to Cohen, 'legalism' in general can be utilised for interpretive denial, due to the nature of law and legal categories, which often leave room for interpretation.[133] This is particularly prevalent in the context of human rights, and is difficult to counteract because it creates 'an opaque moat between rhetoric and reality'.[134] In this sense, the difficulty of fitting the situation of disappearances in Mexico in neat legal boxes[135] can be used to engage in this form of denial.[136] In the interviews, some participants, especially based in Mexico City, expressed the view that the Mexican state strategically used its failure to address impunity, corruption, and organised crime more generally, as a way of evading (international) accountability.[137]

To exemplify this, one participant described the apparent intentionality behind the protection failure of the Mexican state as a 'political decision to generate impunity, [a part of which] includes fostering or perpetuating a chronic state of incapacity'.[138] According to the participant, the motivation behind the decision to foster incapacity is that the responsibility for failing to investigate a disappearance is a less serious form of responsibility for the state at the international level.[139] If this is the case, then an 'admission' by the State of its responsibility based on a failure to investigate, can also be connected to the notion of interpretive denial in the sense that the state offers a particular interpretation of its failure to meet its human rights obligations. In line with this are also the views of some participants who spoke about the almost cynical use of the apparent absence of the state in certain parts of the country as a justification for continued inaction and evasion of responsibility (see

[131] Note that Treviño has similarly used Cohen's theory of denial to analyse the discourse of the government of former president Felipe Calderón. However, he does so mainly in relation to the denial of human rights violations committed directly by state agents. See Treviño Rangel (2018).

[132] See Cohen (2001), p. 7.

[133] Ibid., pp. 107–109.

[134] Ibid., p. 108.

[135] Interview 32.

[136] These views also resemble the above-mentioned argument by Vázquez on 'institutional denial' in Mexico, which, according to him represents the default response by authorities to any form of criticism or scrutiny, including reports by UN special rapporteurs on human rights issues. See Vázquez (2018), pp. 196–197.

[137] For example, interviews 8, 9, 33, 34.

[138] 'porque hay una decisión política de generar impunidad. Y que parte de esa decisión política de generar impunidad, pasa por propiciar o perpetuar un estado de incapacidad crónico.' (Interview 8) A similar argument is made by Schmidt and Spector in relation to their proposed concept of 'state authorised crime'. The authors argue that it is quite possible that the government deliberate intervened to curb institutional checks, leading to a 'planned inefficiency'. See Schmidt and Spector (2017).

[139] Interview 8.

above).[140] Such use by the state of its own incapacity to exercise control in certain parts of the country in order to evade responsibility can be understood as an clear example of interpretive denial as explained by Cohen.[141] In addition to this, the comments made by some participants about the administration of President López Obrador illustrate the difficulties of countering interpretive denial. Thus, one participant described how the official acknowledgement of responsibility for past human rights violations by the AMLO administration made it harder for civil society to denounce violations in the present, especially when trying to convince other countries to exert pressure on Mexico.[142]

In summary, the general limitations and even potential pitfalls of a predominant focus on legal or institutional solutions can be connected to the discussion of the previous section and the lack of willingness of the state to comply with its human rights protection obligations. First, focusing on legal solutions when the underlying issue is one of a lack of will leads to exhaustion and disillusion among both relatives and practitioners, who may begin questioning their own approaches. Given that Mexico is a federal state and in view of the heterogeneity of the context, there are also certain limitations to *centralised* legal approaches. Second, focusing on legal matters facilitates interpretive denial by the state because the latter can use the existence of non-state actors and its apparent incapacity as a means to deny its responsibility in the situation. Nonetheless, despite these limitations, many participants emphasised the continued importance of (international) legal standards as tools and guidance for their work. In the following section I return to these international legal standards themselves.

7.4 Revisiting Protection Failure from the Perspective of International Law

In this final section I reflect on the IHRL framework and its protective capacity in light of the foregoing discussion. While cognisant of the limitations and potential pitfalls of legal approaches discussed in the previous section, the experiences of participants in Mexico nevertheless also indicate a need to critically re-examine state responsibility from an international legal perspective, taking into consideration the scale of failure and the unwillingness—and possible 'intentionality'—behind an apparent lack of capacity. If willingness is a key factor for enhancing the protection

[140] Interviews 8, 9, 33.

[141] Cohen (2001), p. 109. Cohen here specifically refers to blaming other forces that 'supposedly have nothing to do with the government and are beyond its control'.

[142] Interview 4. Note that this is not the only reason why it is difficult for civil society to convince other countries to take action against Mexico. A number of participants mentioned the economic importance of Mexico and the subsequent reluctance of other states to put actual pressure on the Mexican state. For example, interviews 4, 23, 33.

of human rights, even in so-called ALS, then avenues need to be explored to incentivise willingness.[143] One such avenue could be to respond to a lack of will, as illustrated by either the systematicity of or the intentionality behind protection failure, by conceptualising the latter at the legal level. This is because if pressure is to be exerted on a state to make changes, a legal framework, albeit not a solution in itself, can prove useful in so far as it clearly delineates the obligations and responsibility of the state, thereby helping to counter interpretive denial. This is not only in line with arguments about the normative force of IHRL,[144] but also reflects the views of participants as 'users' of these standards. In the following sections, I outline why international standards continue to be of relevance for the protection of human rights and discuss the challenges of dealing with the intentionality of failure from an IHRL perspective. Finally, I argue that in order to fully capture an overall protection failure, the notion of state criminality might have to be revisited.

7.4.1 The Continued Relevance of International Standards

As mentioned in the previous chapter, despite the frustration expressed by some participants about the gap between law and reality, the interviews also indicate the continued relevance of law and international legal standards. Thus, despite doubts expressed by some participants about the utility of law, or international human rights standards as a means of addressing the phenomenon of disappearances or obtaining tangible change,[145] many participants nevertheless spoke about the importance of law for providing guidance or serving as a 'tool' to put pressure on governments.[146] To illustrate the relevance of international standards, a few participants spoke about the Ayotzinapa case (see Chap. 1), where pressure exerted both domestically and internationally in response to the 43 students' disappearance—and the government's attempted denial of responsibility—led to the creation of a new *ad hoc* international mechanism. The participants described the creation of the Interdisciplinary Group of Independent Experts (GIEI) as important because its work highlighted the structural problems in criminal investigations in Mexico with great detail, which can guide future changes and reforms.[147] Moreover, a number of participants emphasised that

[143] I thank Prof. Alexa Koenig for highlighting this point.

[144] See, for example, Donnelly (2006), p. 73. On the normative effects of IHRL, as well as a criticism of too much focus on compliance in much human rights scholarship, see also Howse and Teitel (2010).

[145] For example, interviews 8, 13, 15, 18, 22, 23, 25.

[146] For example, interviews 2, 3, 4, 5, 12, 13, 18, 19, 22, 23, 32, 33.

[147] For example, interviews 1, 25, 28, 34. Moreover, the investigation conducted by the first special prosecutor for the Ayotzinapa case showed that it is possible to conduct effective criminal investigations and obtain arrest warrants against high-ranking officials when officials want to do their work and have the resources to do so. Indeed, this investigation, and the resignation of the prosecutor based on interference with his work, further underscores that willingness is crucial to

international standards are essential because they provide guidance and legitimacy to their demands.[148]

Considering the above, in order to retain their utility as a tool to support demands on governments, it is important for international legal standards pertaining to the protection of human rights—and their interpretation—to be as progressive as possible and respond to reality. In this manner, they can constitute aspirational standards that provide for broad and all-encompassing protection of human rights, rather than being cynically used by states to evade accountability on the basis of legal nuances. This is especially the case where, as illustrated by the Mexican context, an apparent lack of capacity actually stems from a lack of willingness to address structural issues and widespread corruption, and where a plurality of private interests may be involved.[149] In that sense, human rights mechanisms should pay attention to the interplay of willingness and capacity because if they fail to do so they risk perpetuating certain narratives that may ultimately lead to evasion of accountability by the state. While this argument may be based on a utopian vision of international law,[150] if human rights protection is understood as being inherently aspirational and utopian, it follows that international human rights standards should be interpreted in such a way as to provide the maximum legal 'protection' possible. In the following section I therefore examine to what extent IHRL, or the broader international legal framework, can capture an overall protection failure by establishing state responsibility.

7.4.2 The Limitations of IHRL

In the first part of this chapter, I outlined the all-encompassing nature of the Mexican state's protection failure, which illustrates the overall responsibility of the state. However, delineating the *legal* responsibility of the state for this protection failure is more complicated than affirming it from a moral or political perspective. For most participants, the Mexican state's responsibility was clear in relation to its failure to comply with its obligations to search for the disappeared and investigate all cases, which corresponds to the legal standards discussed in previous chapters.[151] This clarity of obligations is also reflected in the participants' approach to dealing with the

counter impunity. For an overview of the work the of the special prosecutor's office, see Gibler (2023).

[148] For example, interviews 1, 9, 10, 11, 12, 15, 16, 17, 32, 33. These views are also in line with scholarship on transnational advocacy networks and their role in promoting international norms and adherence to them. For example, Risse and Sikkink listed as one of the purposes of transnational advocacy networks that '[they] empower and legitimate the claims of domestic opposition groups against norm-violating governments, and they partially protect the physical integrity of such groups from government repression.' Risse and Sikkink (1999), p. 5.

[149] On the interplay of capacity and willingness, see Anaya-Muñoz (2019).

[150] See Koskenniemi (2011), p. 39.

[151] Interviews 3, 4, 5, 6, 7, 8, 9, 12, 13, 14, 16, 17, 18, 21, 22, 23, 24, 25, 27, 28, 30, 33, 34.

complexity of the Mexican context and the difficulty of communicating the state's responsibility in legal terms, for example by focusing on its obligation and failure to investigate (see Chap. 6, Sect. 6.2.2.3). Additionally, a number of participants pointed out that authorities are clearly aware of what is happening, which means that they have an obligation to act and take preventive measures against future violations by non-state actors.[152]

At the same time, the difficulty of determining legal responsibility on the basis of omissions generally, and the existence of OCGs as perpetrators of disappearances alongside state forces, leave room for interpretive denial in the Mexican context and some participants described the state's failure to act as legally and conceptually challenging. Additionally, as previously mentioned, several participants based in Mexico City spoke about the apparent intent of the state to remain incapable, which reflects the notion of the 'cunning state' described above. According to the participant who spoke about the Mexican state's decision to generate 'chronic incapacity' (cited above), the intentionality of failure creates a dilemma because it is a situation that has not as yet been addressed by international human rights standards—or in international jurisprudence:

> Now, from the perspective of international [legal] standards, this responsibility is much more difficult to determine, it is very difficult to frame [...] in the traditional schemes of state responsibility and of international standards. Because ultimately, if I go and litigate before the Inter-American Court, then how do I explain to the Court, how do I translate that the state took a deliberate political decision to stay incapable? Ultimately [the Court will ask me] to translate this in terms of what generic obligation I am referring to - [the obligation to] respect or guarantee -, and then to link this to a particular right. So then this will end up being personal liberty, access to justice, life, etcetera ... But this part where the state takes a political decision is very difficult to translate in legal terms. ... I guess in that sense it would be interesting to see how you analyse this topic in your thesis. I mean, if the international standards are sufficient to capture, or to reflect, the responsibility that arises from this. If you look at the definition of impunity, in the international standards [...] the legal definition of impunity translates to an absence of consequence or sanctions or responsibility for the perpetrators. But it is defined as an omission, as an absence of. And here what we are talking about is that impunity is not just an omission. It is an action, a decision.[153]

---

[152] For example, interviews 18, 32, 33, 34. These comments relate to the obligation of the state to take preventive measures once it is aware of a risk, as discussed in Chaps. 2–4.

[153] 'Ahora, yo lo que creo es que... desde los estándares internacionales, o sea, como que esta responsabilidad es muy difícil de asir, o sea, sí es como muy difícil de encuadrarla, digamos, en... en los esquemas tradicionales de responsabilidad del estado y de estándares internacionales. O sea, porque al final si yo voy a litigarlo ante la Corte Interamericana, yo cómo le explico a la Corte, ¿cómo le hago la traducción, de que un estado tomó una decisión política deliberada de mantenerse en incapacidad? Al final lo que voy a pedir a la Corte que esto lo traduzca en términos de a qué obligación genérica me estoy refiriendo, es respeto o garantía, y que eso lo vincule con un derecho en particular. Pues que ahora termina siendo, pues, libertad personal, acceso a la justicia, vida, etcétera. ... pero esta parte donde un estado toma esa decisión política es muy difícil de traducirlo en términos jurídicos, pues. No sé... supongo que ahí ya más bien interesará conocer el análisis que hagas en tu tesis sobre el tema. O sea, si los estándares internacionales nos dan para captar, o para reflejar, no, la responsabilidad que se genera. O sea, si tu miras la definición de impunidad, de los estándares internacionales, está principalmente, digamos, con ciertas variaciones, pero la definición

This quote elucidates the conceptual challenges faced by human rights practitioners when it comes to capturing the overall responsibility of the Mexican state from an international legal perspective and raises the question whether IHRL is equipped to capture the complexity of what is happening in Mexico, including relations between 'state' and 'crime', as well as the apparent intentionality behind impunity.[154]

To what extent can IHRL capture overall responsibility and/or intentionality? As discussed in Chaps. 3 and 4, certain developments in IHRL jurisprudence, including source-based approaches to determining state responsibility for failing to prevent human rights violations by non-state actors and the CED's definition of acquiescence relating to disappearances specifically, are a step in the direction of capturing general failure. Moreover, the definition of acquiescence provided by the CED includes contexts in which '[t]he State has *deliberately and in full knowledge*, by action or omission, failed to take measures to prevent the crime and to investigate and punish the perpetrators',[155] which encompasses a subjective element. This wording could thus be seen as reflecting intentionality behind inaction, such as that described by some participants in the Mexican context. However, without further clarification by the CED of the precise meaning of 'deliberate' failure, it is not clear whether and how such deliberateness will be established and applied by human rights bodies in cases that involve possible state acquiescence, if at all. Indeed, the inclusion of deliberateness unnecessarily introduces a criminal law notion to an IHRL definition, thereby arguably raising the evidentiary threshold.[156] This is because the determination of state responsibility in IHRL, and in international law more generally, is 'objective'[157]—in contrast to individual criminal responsibility—which means that, as a general rule, the motives behind a violation of human rights or breach of obligation are not taken into consideration.

---

jurídica de impunidad se traduce en ausencia de consecuencia o sanción o responsabilidad para los perpetradores. Pero, o sea, está definido como una omisión, como una ausencia de. Y acá de lo que estamos hablando, es que la impunidad, no es solamente una omisión. Es una acción, una decisión.' Interview 8.

[154] A similar argument is made by Allier et alt., who argue that the state's omissions when it comes to the identification of bodies and investigation of disappearances are intentional and part of the state's strategy to hide the ties between state and criminal actors: 'Far from being an error, these omissions and lack of transparency suggest an intention of maintaining the political and the criminal as indistinct. Perpetrators of violence can thus operate in uncertain territory, making it difficult to shed light on the political motivations of violence, the state embedded criminality, and the overlap between them.' Allier Montaño et al. (2022), p. 65.

[155] Committee on Enforced Disappearances (2023) Statement on non-State actors in the context of the International Convention for the Protection of All Persons from Enforced Disappearances. UN Doc. CED/C/10, para. 5(b). Emphasis added.

[156] The most likely scenario is that the term 'deliberately' will be applied in situations where state agents were literally standing by when a disappearance occurred, taking into consideration case law discussed in Chap. 3, where authorities failed to intervene directly in a situation when they could have done so. The deliberateness of the act could then be inferred from the fact that the agents were watching something unfold and decided—for whatever reason—not to interfere.

[157] See Crawford (2013), pp. 60–62.

Even if the 'deliberate' failure to act by a state were included in an analysis of acquiescence, or other forms of state responsibility, it is important to remember that, without a connection to a particular victim, a state's active and deliberate role in fostering impunity or failing to protect rights is currently insufficient for holding a state accountable in a human rights court. As the analysis in Chaps. 3 and 4 has highlighted, the current approach by the European and Inter-American Human Rights Courts, and to a lesser extent the Human Rights Committee, does not allow determining state responsibility for a *general* failure to prevent violations of human rights at the hands of non-state actors, unless this general failure is based on the absence of sufficient *legal* protection of the right in question.[158] This was especially illustrated in the case of *López Soto*, where the IACtHR did not find that the Venezuelan state was responsible for the victim's initial kidnapping, despite finding that it happened within a general context of *acquiescence*.[159] In that sense, even a source-based approach or the CED's broad definition of acquiescence that does not necessarily require foreseeability in relation to a specific victim (see Chap. 3), would likely fall short of accounting for broader and more systemic protection failures because in a case before a human rights tribunal a causal link to the violation of a specific individual's (or group of individuals') right needs to be established.

The Mexican context, however, illustrates the conceptual problem of not holding a state responsible for a general failure to prevent and respond to disappearances committed by non-state actors. This is because a determination of responsibility based on a failure to respond in an individual case fails to fully capture the role of the state in perpetuating the issue.[160] Furthermore, it appears contradictory that a state can be held responsible for a violation of a right if it fails to adopt preventive legislation, yet it cannot be held responsible if it fails to adopt policies to prevent the violation because the necessary causal link is missing or the risk is deemed as not sufficiently foreseeable.[161] Not only does such an approach raise questions about the *legal* nature of an obligation for whose breach a state cannot be held responsible (see Chap. 4, Sect. 4.2.2.1),[162] but it also seems counter-intuitive in light of the object and purpose of IHRL, especially in contexts where the failure of the state to protect rights occurs on such a large scale as it does in Mexico. Additionally, if failure is intentional, which could also be understood as part of a state's unwillingness to protect rights, the ensuing accountability gap can be cynically—or cunningly—

[158] See Chap. 3 (Sect. 3.2.1.2), discussing *Rantsev v Cyprus and Russia*.

[159] *Case of López Soto and others v Venezuela* [2018] Inter-American Court of Human Rights Series C No 362, para. 148. See also Chap. 3, Sect. 3.1.2.1.

[160] This argument is in line with the criticism voiced by Judge Ferrer Mac-Gregor Poisot in his separate opinion in the case of *Velásquez Paiz et al. v Guatemala*, which I discuss in Chap. 4 (Sect. 4.2.2.1).

[161] This contradiction might stem from the fact that due diligence obligations are subject to availability of resources, which, arguably, would not be a problem when it comes to adopting legislation, but could be a determinant in relation to policies.

[162] On the necessity of responsibility for the existence of legal obligations, see also Pellet (2010), pp. 3–4. I have also made this argument in Chap. 4 and elsewhere: Guercke (2021), p. 351.

employed by the state vis-à-vis outside actors, while trapping victims and human rights advocates in endless legal reforms.

7.4.3 Capturing Protection Failure Beyond IHRL

The determination of responsibility in IHRL thus has a somewhat narrow scope because regional and international human rights tribunals require a link between the failure of a state to comply with an obligation and the violation of the alleged victim's right. In other words, a state cannot be held responsible for an overall failure to comply with its obligations in situations that involve non-state actors as direct perpetrators, without a connection to a specific victim or group of victims through foreseeability of risk and preventive capacity, or state contribution to risk. Conversely, as I have discussed in Chap. 3, according to the Articles on Responsibility of States for Internationally Wrongful Acts (ARSIWA), a state bears international responsibility if it breaches its primary obligations and it is not necessary to link this breach to a particular victim, as it is in IHRL.[163] This means that, in theory, from the perspective of the law on state responsibility, a state would be internationally responsible for breaching any type of obligation, whether general or specific.[164] The difference in accountability raises the question whether in contexts where non-state actors are involved and the failure of the state is of a more general nature, it would be more suitable to explore accountability routes beyond IHRL and within the law on state responsibility. As argued by Fletcher, the latter could be more useful to furthering the type of structural changes needed to address systemic issues.[165] This is because, in line with the rules on state responsibility, once a state has breached its obligation, it must not only end the breach, but also provide reparations for the harm caused.[166] In view of the scale of an overall protection failure and considering apparent intentionality, one avenue towards accountability might be to re-visit the notion of state criminality, as proposed by Fletcher.[167]

When the failure of a state to protect is generalised and a state acts 'cunningly', reconsidering the notion of state criminality would allow to think about a general protection failure that is causally linked to serious human rights violations as an

[163] See Fletcher (2016), p. 514. Additionally, as pointed out by Koskenniemi, even though there is a special IHRL regime, this 'does not mean that state responsibility is inapplicable to human rights breaches.' Koskenniemi (2010), p. 47.

[164] In practice, however, there is no rule on state responsibility regarding state failure to act with due diligence in relation to acts committed by non-state actors, which means that there is also a gap in the international legal framework on state responsibility when it comes to consequences for such failure. See Mackenzie-Gray Scott (2021); Mackenzie-Gray Scott (2022), chap. 7.

[165] See Fletcher (2016), p. 515.

[166] Articles 30 and 31 ARSIWA.

[167] See Fletcher (2016), p. 515.

instance of 'state gross negligence',[168] or, if the intention behind omissions is to be reflected, 'recklessness'.[169] Both notions would go beyond a secondary rule on breaches of due diligence obligations, such as that proposed by Mackenzie-Gray Scott,[170] in that they would reflect a more serious breach of such obligations. Gross negligence could encompass a repeated and prolonged failure to act, including a lack of actual implementation of recommendations for change, whereas recklessness would include an assessment of whether the failure to act was in some way deliberate. This proposal is not as far-fetched as it may seem: the ARSIWA already contain a rule relating to 'aid or assistance in the commission of an internationally wrongful act' (complicity), which contains a subjective element,[171] and previous drafts of the Articles contained the notion of international *crimes* of state. The latter was dropped in the final version of the Articles and was replaced by a rule concerning the consequences for 'serious' breaches of international obligations deriving from peremptory norms of international law.[172] Such serious breaches, as defined in Article 40 ARSIWA, involve 'gross or systematic failure [by a state] to fulfil its obligation' under a peremptory norm, also known as *jus cogens*. Human rights obligations, especially those from which no derogation is possible, are generally considered to be part of *jus cogens*[173] and the African Commission on Human and Peoples' Rights has recognised 'the prohibition of enforced disappearance and the corresponding obligations to investigate and punish those responsible' as *jus cogens*.[174] To what extent positive obligations of states concerning violations committed by non-state actors would be included as peremptory norms, continues

[168] Gross negligence implies negligence on a very serious scale, meaning a breach of a duty of care that had very serious consequences (such as the death of a victim in domestic law) and should therefore be considered a crime. See Law (2022a).

[169] Recklessness is a criminal law concept that describes a mental state between negligence and intention in that it entails awareness of risk and an unreasonable decision to take the risk. See Law (2022b).

[170] See Mackenzie-Gray Scott (2021); Mackenzie-Gray Scott (2022), chap. 7. Mackenzie-Gray Scott's argument is based on the aim to increase unity and coherence in international law, given that due diligence is among the 'most ambiguous' concepts, as well as on the need to hold states to account for all types of wrongdoing in connection to acts committed by non-state actors, including failing to act with due diligence (p. 204).

[171] Article 16 ARSIWA. According to the Commentary on Article 16, for responsibility under this article to arise, the aid or assistance must be given with knowledge of the wrongful act, and 'with a view to facilitating the commission of that act', which implies deliberate assistance. See International Law Commission (ILC) (2001) Draft Articles on Responsibility of States for Internationally Wrongful Acts, with Commentaries. ILC Yearbook 2001, Vol. II, Part II, p. 66, paras 3, 5, 7. Note, however, that complicity is generally established based on actions and not omissions. See Mackenzie-Gray Scott (2021), pp. 368–369.

[172] See Luban (2011), p. 79; Crawford (2013), pp. 390–392; Fletcher (2016), pp. 470–473; Scobbie (2009), pp. 274–276; Zimmermann and Teichmann (2009), p. 303.

[173] See, for example, den Heijer and van der Wilt (2016), pp. 8–14.

[174] African Commission on Human and Peoples' Rights (2022) Guidelines on the Protection of All Persons from Enforced Disappearances in Africa, Preamble, p. 9. On state practice regarding the prohibition of enforced disappearance as *jus cogens*, see also Shelton (2021), pp. 76 ff.

to be a subject of debate that lies beyond the scope of this research.[175] What matters for present purposes is that the ARSIWA already contemplate certain consequences for serious breaches of norms that were originally conceptualised as 'international crimes of state'.[176]

Independently of the discussion around peremptory norms, exists the notion of obligations *erga omnes*, which states hold on the basis of fundamental community interests and towards the international community as a whole.[177] These obligations also include 'the basic rights of the human person'.[178] *Erga omnes* obligations are addressed in Article 48 ARSIWA, which establishes that any state can invoke the responsibility of another state if 'the obligation breached is owed to the international community as a whole.'[179] Re-visiting the notion of crimes of state and thinking about concepts of 'state gross negligence' or 'state recklessness' that could be considered breaches of *erga omnes* obligations could be a way to address the current accountability gap. Such an approach may better reflect the underlying values at stake, taking Mexico as an example: if a state that is not involved in an armed conflict or 'failed' permits that thousands of people are displaced, disappeared, and killed, and, in addition, fails to identify tens of thousands of bodies or punish any of the perpetrators despite having received recommendations and reprimands by regional and international bodies for its inaction for decades, it would be counter-intuitive to argue that this situation does not affront the values of the international community as reflected in international human rights instruments. Given states' obligations to act diligently to protect human rights from violations committed by non-state actors, a consistent failure to comply with these obligations should be viewed as a violation of fundamental rights whose protection is in the interest of all states because they concern the fundamental rights of human beings. Developing concepts that could capture the gravity of the failure beyond a 'mere' lack of due diligence, would be one way to encompass the overall nature of the Mexican state's failure to protect, including the apparent intentionality behind its omissions.[180] As *erga omnes* obligations are based on the values of the international community as a

[175] den Heijer and van der Wilt (2016), p. 10.

[176] ILC (2001) Draft Articles on Responsibility of States for Internationally Wrongful Acts, with Commentaries. ILC Yearbook 2001, Vol. II, Part II, p. 111, para. 5.

[177] See, for example, Carli (2023). Note that *jus cogens* and *erga omnes* obligations are at times equated. The origins and content of these notions, however, are different. For an overview of the differences, see Picone (2011).

[178] International Law Commission (ILC) (2001) Draft Articles on Responsibility of States for Internationally Wrongful Acts, with Commentaries. ILC Yearbook 2001, Vol. II, Part II, p. 112, note 640.

[179] Article 48 (1) (b) UN General Assembly (2002) Articles on Responsibility of States for Internationally Wrongful Acts. UN Doc. A/RES/56/83 (ARSIWA).

[180] For an overview of 'due diligence' (indirect state responsibility) in the preparatory works of the ARSIWA and how it was ultimately excluded, see Mackenzie-Gray Scott (2022), pp. 179–205.

whole, their breach enables all states to take action,[181] which would carve additional paths to exert pressure on the state who is in breach of the obligation.

7.5 Conclusion

The experiences of human rights practitioners working on the issue of disappearances in Mexico described in Chap. 6 illustrate the all-encompassing nature of the state's failure to protect. The totality of the protection failure, as described by participants, and the meta-uncertainty surrounding the issue of disappearances in Mexico indicate that, even where disappearances are committed by OCGs, the actions and omissions by the state play a key role. In this sense, when thinking about the protective capacity of IHRL vis-à-vis victims of disappearances committed by OCGs, and their relatives, it continues to be important to focus on the state. This is not only because at present OCGs cannot be held directly accountable before a human rights court or body. Rather, the Mexican context suggests that 'taking the eyes off the state'[182] would not be an adequate reflection of reality. At the same time, the interviews highlight the complexity of the Mexican state's protection failure and its 'slipperiness', based on the uncertainty that surrounds much of it - including the underlying reasons: is it a lack of will or a lack of capacity, or both? Is it the same across the entire country or does it differ from state to state? What exactly are the relationships between state and criminal actors? And who is in charge of whom? As I have argued in this chapter, the different aspects of this protection failure raise several questions of importance for international human rights scholarship. From the perspective of human rights compliance scholarship, at first sight the situation in Mexico appears to be one where 'areas of limited statehood' exist, which would suggest that one of the main issues standing in the way of effective human rights protection, understood as compliance with human rights obligations, is the capacity of the state. However, in considering the role of the state in its own 'capture' in the Mexican context, as exemplified by deep-rooted state-crime relations, the willingness of the state to protect human rights remains important in thinking about why human rights continue to not be protected. This is in line with recent arguments by scholars working on the issue of compliance in the Mexican context and is further supported if Mexico is thought of as a 'cunning' state.

Yet if a lack of willingness is one of the fundamental obstacles to (effective) human rights protection in Mexico, then this also raises questions about the adequacy of legal approaches to dealing with the issue of disappearances, echoing scholarship that is critical about over-legalisation in the human rights space. In the case of disappearances, legal 'solutions' are inherently limited, due to the urgent, manifold and often non-legal needs of the relatives of the disappeared whom human

[181] International Law Institute (2005).

[182] Interview 32.

rights practitioners accompany. At the same time, the lack of tangible change that gives rise to frustration raises doubts about the utility of legal approaches and the question whether an (over-)emphasis on legal and institutional change might not be playing into the hands of the state. Such doubts resonate with the notion of 'interpretive' denial, for which the situation in Mexico lends itself due to the existence of OCGs and the great uncertainty that surrounds the phenomenon. Furthermore, given the federal nature of the Mexican state and the many differences between regions, the centralisation of legal efforts may not always be the best approach. Finally, returning to the international legal framework, while cognisant of the limits of legal approaches, participants confirmed that international legal standards continue to play an important guiding and legitimising function and can be used as a tool. It is therefore important to continue thinking about the extent to which IHRL can 'capture' the scale of the state's protection failure and reflect the all-encompassing nature of its responsibility. At present, the IHRL framework is not quite able to capture the full dimension of the state's protection failure. Due to the individual-centred nature of IHRL, this body of law contains inherent limitations that lead to an unfortunate accountability gap for general failures of the state to protect human rights, even with the expanded definition of acquiescence adopted by the CED and source-based approaches to determining state responsibility outlined in previous chapters. Nonetheless, as the Mexican context illustrates, the question of unwillingness to comply with human rights obligations, which may encompass an *intention* not to protect rights, plays an important role in the lack of change and, ultimately, the perpetuation of human rights violations by state and non-state actors alike. The totality of the state's protection failure, and the view expressed by some participants that this failure is intentional, taken together with the limitations of current human rights jurisprudence on questions of protection failure, suggest that re-visiting the concept of state criminality in the law on state responsibility might offer additional pathways to state accountability, as it would forego the need to focus on individual cases. The gravity of the state's failure to act, and perhaps even the apparent intentionality behind it, could be encompassed by notions such as 'gross state negligence' or 'state recklessness', respectively, which could fall within the scope of either peremptory norms of international law or, at a minimum, *erga omnes* obligations, whose breach enables all other states to react and invoke responsibility. This would not only better reflect reality, but also open up additional avenues for exerting pressure on a state from outside the IHRL framework (with a view to incentivising will), for example by highlighting the obligations of other states to act.

References

Allier Montaño E, Vicente Ovalle C, Granada-Cardona JS (2022) Recasting history to cast off shadows: state violence in Mexico, 1958–2018. In: Mandolessi S, Olalde Rico K (eds) Disappearances in Mexico: from the 'dirty war' to the 'war on drugs'. Routledge, Oxon, New York, pp 50–72

Anaya-Muñoz A (2019) Bringing willingness back in: state capacities and the human rights compliance deficit in Mexico. Hum Rights Q 41:441–464

Anaya-Muñoz A, Cavallaro J, Cruz-Marín P (eds) (2021) La impunidad activa en México. Cómo entender y enfrentar las violaciones masivas a los derechos humanos. ITESO, Tlaquepaque, Jalisco

Baranowska G (2021) Rights of families of disappeared persons: how international bodies address the needs of families of disappeared persons in Europe, 1st edn. Intersentia, Cambridge

Berger T, Lake M, Berger T, Lake M (2018) Human rights, the rule of law, and democracy. In: Draude A, Börzel TA, Risse T (eds) The Oxford handbook of governance and limited statehood. Oxford University Press, Oxford, pp 415–437

Berti B (2018) Violent and criminal non-state actors. In: Draude A, Börzel TA, Risse T (eds) The Oxford handbook of governance and limited statehood. Oxford University Press, Oxford, pp 272–290

Börzel TA, Risse T (2013) Human rights in areas of limited statehood: the new agenda. In: Sikkink K, Ropp SC, Risse T (eds) The persistent power of human rights: from commitment to compliance. Cambridge University Press, Cambridge, pp 63–84

Börzel TA, Draude A, Risse T (2018a) The Oxford handbook of governance and limited statehood, Oxford University Press, Oxford

Börzel TA, Risse T, Draude A (2018b) Governance in areas of limited statehood: conceptual clarifications and major contributions of the handbook. In: Draude A, Börzel TA, Risse T (eds) The Oxford handbook of governance and limited statehood. Oxford University Press, Oxford, pp 2–26

Çali B, Meckled-García S (2006) Human rights legalized - defining, interpreting and implementing an ideal. In: Meckled-García S, Çali B (eds) The legalization of human rights: multidisciplinary perspectives on human rights and human rights law. Routledge, London, pp 11–31

Calvet Martínez E (2015) Desapariciones forzadas y justicia transicional. La búsqueda de respuestas a través del derecho a la verdad, a la justicia y a la reparación. Dissertation, Universitat de Barcelona

Carli E (2023) Community interests above all: the ongoing procedural effects of erga omnes partes obligations before the international court of justice. EJIL: Talk! https://www.ejiltalk.org/community-interests-above-all-the-ongoing-procedural-effects-of-erga-omnes-partes-obligations-before-the-international-court-of-justice/. Accessed 15 Nov 2024

Centro de Investigación y Docencia Económicas (CIDE) (2018) Estudio para elaborar una propuesta de política pública en materia de Justicia Transicional en México. CIDE, Centro de Investigación y Docencia Económicas, Mexico City

CMDPDH (Comisión Mexicana de Defensa y Promoción de los Derechos Humanos), World Organisation Against Torture, International Federation for Human Rights et al (2018) Crimes against humanity in the war on drugs: submission for Mexico's third universal periodic review. https://www.cmdpdh.org/publicaciones-pdf/cmdpdh-epu-crimenes-de-lesa-humanidad-en-el-marco-de-la-lucha-contra-las-drogas-en.pdf. Accessed 8 Nov 2024

Cohen S (2001) States of denial: knowing about atrocities and suffering. Polity, Cambridge

Correa-Cabrera G (2017) Los Zetas Inc.: criminal corporations, energy, and civil war in Mexico. University of Texas Press, Austin

Crawford J (2013) State responsibility: the general part. Cambridge University Press, Cambridge

Cruz A, Enríquez JE, Guadarrama A, Niño JJ (2024) Redes de macrocriminalidad, desaparición de personas y construcción de paz: un estudio sobre el Estado de México. Heinrich Böll Stiftung, Mexico City

Decoeur H (2018) Confronting the shadow state: an international law perspective on state organized crime. Oxford University Press, Oxford

den Heijer M, van der Wilt H (2016) Jus cogens and the humanization and fragmentation of international law. In: den Heijer M, van der Wilt H (eds) Netherlands yearbook of international law 2015: jus cogens: quo vadis? T.M.C. Asser Press, The Hague, pp 3–21

Donnelly J (2006) The virtues of legalization. In: Meckled-García S, Çali B (eds) The legalization of human rights: multidisciplinary perspectives on human rights and human rights law. Routledge, London, pp 67–80

Espinal-Enríquez J, Isunza E, Isunza A, Vázquez D (2023) Redes de poder y gobernanza criminal. Dinámicas regionales en Veracruz (2004-2018), 1st edn. Heinrich Böll Stiftung, Mexico City

Finucane B (2010) Enforced disappearance as a crime under international law: a neglected origin in the laws of war. Yale J Int Law 35:171–197

Fletcher LE (2016) A wolf in sheep's clothing? Transitional justice and the effacement of state accountability for international crimes. Fordham Int Law J 39:447–531

Fraser J (2020) Social institutions and international human rights law implementation: every organ of society. Cambridge University Press, Cambridge

Freeman M (2006) Putting law in its place: an interdisciplinary evaluation of national amnesty laws. In: Meckled-García S, Çali B (eds) The legalization of human rights: multidisciplinary perspectives on human rights and human rights law. Routledge, London, pp 49–64

Frey BA (2015) Uneven ground: asymmetries of power in human rights advocacy in Mexico. In: Pruce JR (ed) The social practice of human rights. Palgrave Macmillan US, New York, pp 121–139

Frey BA (2021) Conceptualising disappearances in international law. In: Ansolabehere K, Frey BA, Payne LA (eds) Disappearances in the post-transition era in Latin America. British Academy Scholarship, London

Gallagher J (2018) The judicial breakthrough model: transnational advocacy networks and lethal violence. In: Anaya-Muñoz A, Frey B (eds) Mexico's human rights crisis. University of Pennsylvania Press, Philadelphia, pp 250–272

Gallagher J (2020) (Enforced) disappearances – when state and criminal perpetrators blur. Völkerrechtsblog. https://voelkerrechtsblog.org/articles/enforced-disappearances-when-state-and-criminal-perpetrators-blur/. Accessed 14 Nov 2024

Gibler J (2023) Cómo el gobierno dinamitó la investigación del caso Ayotzinapa. Quinto Elemento Lab. Quinto Elemento Lab. https://quintoelab.org/project/ayotzinapa-gobierno-instruccion-investigacion-iguala-normalistas. Accessed 6 Nov 2024

Global Witness (2024) Missing voices: the violent erasure of land and environmental defenders. Global Witness. https://www.globalwitness.org/en/campaigns/environmental-activists/missing-voices/. Accessed 15 Nov 2024

Guercke L (2021) State responsibility for a failure to prevent violations of the right to life by organised criminal groups: disappearances in Mexico. Hum Rights Law Rev 21:329–357. https://doi.org/10.1093/hrlr/ngaa061

Gutiérrez EM (2019) Jalisco: localizan más restos humanos en La Primavera, Zapopan. Milenio. https://www.milenio.com/policia/jalisco-localizan-restos-humanos-primavera-zapopan. Accessed 14 Nov 2024

Hamid L, Wouters J (2021a) Rule of law and areas of limited statehood: introduction and perspective. In: Hamid L, Wouters J (eds) Rule of law and areas of limited statehood: domestic and international dimensions. Edward Elgar, Cheltenham, pp 2–22

Hamid L, Wouters J (2021b) De facto regimes in areas of limited statehood and the international rule of law. In: Hamid L, Wouters J (eds) Rule of law and areas of limited statehood. Edward Elgar, Cheltenham, pp 47–72

Hamid L, Wouters J (eds) (2021c) Rule of law and areas of limited statehood: domestic and international dimensions. Edward Elgar, Cheltenham

Hernández M, Guadarrama A, Correa C (2020) Reflections on transitional justice in Mexico: paradoxes and possible processes. International Center for Transitional Justice. https://www.ictj.org/publication/reflections-transitional-justice-mexico-paradoxes-and-possible-processes. Accessed 15 Nov 2024

Howse R, Teitel R (2010) Beyond compliance: rethinking why international law really matters: beyond compliance. Glob Policy 1:127–136. https://doi.org/10.1111/j.1758-5899.2010.00035.x

I(dh)eas, Litigio Estratégico en Derechos Humanos (2021) En una decisión histórica, la SCJN de México reconoció que las Acciones Urgentes emitidas por la ONU son vinculantes y obligatorias para todas las autoridades encargadas de la búsqueda e investigación de las personas desaparecidas. idheas. https://www.idheas.org.mx/comunicaciones-idheas/sala-de-prensa-idheas/comunicados/en-una-decision-historica-la-scjn-de-mexico-reconocio-que-las-acciones-urgentes-emitidas-por-la-onu-son-vinculantes-y-obligatorias-para-todas-las-autoridades-encargadas-de-la-busqueda-e-investigacion/. Accessed 14 Nov 2024

IMDHD (2019) Propuesta ciudadana para la construcción de una política sobre verdad, justicia y reparación a las víctimas de la violencia y de las violaciones a derechos humanos. http://imdhd.org/wp-content/uploads/2019/01/Consolidado-JAG-Modelo-JVRP-4-elementos_20-enero-2019.pdf. Accessed 8 Nov 2024

International Law Institute (2005) Resolution on *erga omnes* obligations. https://www.idi-iil.org/app/uploads/2017/06/2005_kra_01_en.pdf. Accessed 28 Nov 2024

Kennedy D (2002) International human rights movement: part of the problem? Boundaries in the field of human rights. Harv Hum Rts J 15:101–126

Kenny P, Serrano M (2012) Introduction: security failure versus state failure. In: Mexico's security failure: collapse into criminal violence. Routledge, New York, pp 1–26

Kloppe Santamaría G (2021) Mexico's recent election violence can't be blamed on organized crime gangs alone. openDemocracy. https://www.opendemocracy.net/en/democraciaabierta/mexico-recent-election-violence-cant-be-blamed-on-organized-crime-gangs-alone/. Accessed 15 Nov 2024

Koskenniemi M (2010) Doctrines of state responsibility. In: Crawford J, Pellet A, Olleson S, Parlett K (eds) The law of international responsibility. Oxford University Press, New York, pp 45–51

Koskenniemi M (2011) The politics of international law. Hart Publishing, Oxford

Krieger H (2018) International legal order. In: Draude A, Börzel TA, Risse T (eds) The Oxford handbook of governance and limited statehood. Oxford University Press, Oxford, pp 542–563

Lake M (2014) Organizing hypocrisy: providing legal accountability for human rights violations in areas of limited statehood. Int Stud Q 58:515–526. https://doi.org/10.1111/isqu.12144

Law J (ed) (2022a) Gross negligence. In: A dictionary of law. Oxford University Press

Law J (ed) (2022b) Recklessness. In: A dictionary of law. Oxford University Press

Le Cour Grandmaison R (2020) Order, sovereignty, and violence in Mexico. Mexico Violence Resource Project. https://www.mexicoviolence.org/post/order-sovereignty-and-violence-in-mexico. Accessed 15 Nov 2024

Luban D (2011) State criminality and the ambition of international criminal law. In: Isaacs T, Vernon R (eds) Accountability for collective wrongdoing. Cambridge University Press, Cambridge, pp 61–91

Mackenzie-Gray Scott R (2021) Due diligence as a secondary rule of general international law. Leiden J Int Law 34:343–372. https://doi.org/10.1017/S0922156521000030

Mackenzie-Gray Scott R (2022) State responsibility for non-state actors: past, present and prospects for the future. Hart Publishing, Bloomsbury Publishing Plc, Oxford

Muñoz AA, Saltalamacchia N (2018) Factors blocking the compliance with international human rights norms in Mexico. In: Anaya-Muñoz A, Frey B (eds) Mexico's human rights crisis. University of Pennsylvania Press, Philadelphia, pp 207–226

Nuño A (2023) Desaparecen a defensores de Aquila tras amenaza de minera y persecuciones, acusan comuneros. A dónde van los desaparecidos. https://adondevanlosdesaparecidos.org/2023/01/31/desaparecen-a-defensores-de-aquila-tras-amenaza-de-minera-y-persecuciones-acusan-comuneros/. Accessed 15 Nov 2024

Open Society Justice Initiative (2016) Undeniable atrocities: confronting crimes against humanity in Mexico. Open Society Foundations, New York

Open Society Justice Initiative (2018) Corruption that kills: why Mexico needs an international mechanism to combat impunity. Open Society Foundations, New York

Paley DM (2020) Guerra Neoliberal: Desaparición y búsqueda en el norte de México. Libertad bajo palabra, Mexico

Pansters WG (2018) Drug trafficking, the informal order, and caciques. Reflections on the crime-governance nexus in Mexico. Glob Crime 19:315–338. https://doi.org/10.1080/17440572.2018.1471993

Pellegrini S, Breda T (2024) Five key takeaways from the 2024 elections in Mexico. ACLED. https://acleddata.com/2024/07/02/five-key-takeaways-from-the-2024-elections-in-mexico/. Accessed 15 Nov 2024

Pellet A (2010) The definition of responsibility in international law. In: Crawford J, Pellet A, Olleson S, Parlett K (eds) The law of international responsibility. Oxford University Press, New York, pp 3–16

Picone P (2011) The distinction between jus cogens and obligations erga omnes. In: Cannizzaro E (ed) The law of treaties beyond the Vienna Convention. Oxford University Press, Oxford, pp 411–424

Randeria S (2003) Cunning states and unaccountable international institutions: legal plurality, social movements and rights of local communities to common property resources. Eur J Sociol 44:27–60. https://doi.org/10.1017/S0003975603001188

Randeria S (2007) The state of globalization: legal plurality, overlapping sovereignties and ambiguous alliances between civil society and the cunning state in India. Theory Cult Soc 24:1–33. https://doi.org/10.1177/0263276407071559

Risse T (2017) Human rights in areas of limited statehood: from the spiral model to localization and translation. In: Snyder J, Vinjamuri L, Hopgood S (eds) Human rights futures. Cambridge University Press, Cambridge, pp 135–158

Risse T, Sikkink K (1999) The socialization of international human rights norms into domestic practices: introduction. In: Sikkink K, Ropp SC, Risse T (eds) The power of human rights: international norms and domestic change. Cambridge University Press, Cambridge, pp 1–38

Schmidt S, Spector C (2017) Crimen autorizado. Una revisión. H ideas 11. https://doi.org/10.24215/23139048e002

Scobbie I (2009) Assumptions and presuppositions: state responsibility for system crimes. In: Nollkaemper A, van der Wilt H (eds) System criminality in international law. Cambridge University Press, Cambridge, pp 270–297

Scovazzi T, Citroni G (2007) The struggle against enforced disappearance and the 2007 United Nations Convention. Nijhoff, Leiden

Serrano S, de Pina V (2021) Perdidos en el proceso: La Desaparición De Personas en México. In: Serrano S, Vázquez D (eds) Crisis de estatalidad y violaciones a derechos humanos, 1st edn. FLACSO-México, Mexico City, pp 113–164

Shelton D (2021) Jus Cogens. Oxford University Press, Oxford

Trejo G, Ley S (2020) Votes, drugs, and violence: the political logic of criminal wars in Mexico. Cambridge University Press, Cambridge

Treviño Rangel J (2018) Silencing grievance: responding to human rights violations in Mexico's war on drugs. J Hum Rights 17:485–501. https://doi.org/10.1080/14754835.2018.1487777

Turati M (2023) San Fernando: última parada: Viaje al crimen autorizado en Tamaulipas. AGUILAR

Vázquez D (2018) Democracia a la Mexicana: a framework conducive to human rights violations. In: Anaya-Muñoz A, Frey B (eds) Mexico's human rights crisis. University of Pennsylvania Press, pp 187–206

Vázquez D (2019) Captura del Estado, macrocriminalidad, y derechos humanos, Primera edición. Facultad Latinoamericana de Ciencias Sociales, Sede México, Fundación Heinrich Böll e.v., Universidad Nacional Autónoma de México, Instituto de Investigaciones Jurídicas, Ciudad de México

Vermeulen ML (2012) Enforced disappearance: determining state responsibility under the international convention for the protection of all persons from enforced disappearance. Intersentia, Antwerp

Woodiwiss A (2006) The law cannot be enough: human rights and the limits of legalism. In: Meckled-García S, Çali B (eds) The legalization of human rights: multidisciplinary perspectives on human rights and human rights law. Routledge, London, pp 32–48
Zimmermann A, Teichmann M (2009) State responsibility for international crimes. In: Nollkaemper A, van der Wilt H (eds) System criminality in international law. Cambridge University Press, Cambridge, pp 298–313

Chapter 8
Conclusion

The purpose of International Human Rights Law (IHRL) is to protect the inherent dignity of all human beings by establishing legally binding obligations on states to safeguard human rights.[1] If a state fails to comply with these obligations, IHRL provides certain supra-national accountability mechanisms that victims can turn to in order to obtain redress for violations of their rights.[2] When actors who are not states violate human rights, this state-centric protective framework quickly encounters obstacles.[3] The issue of disappearances committed by organised criminal groups (OCGs) is but one example among many situations where non-state actors effectively violate human rights, albeit a particularly heinous one because of the detrimental impact that a disappearance has on the relatives of the disappeared person. For the relatives, and the suffering they endure because they do not know what happened to their loved ones, it might not matter who was responsible for the disappearance, at least not while they are desperately searching for their loved one.[4] However, from a legal perspective it matters who committed the disappearance. This is because under IHRL, there is a difference between *enforced* disappearances, which must be committed by an agent of the state, or by a non-state actor acting with the 'authorisation, support or acquiescence' of a state agent, and other kinds of disappearances with no such state involvement that would fall within Article 3 of the International Convention for the Protection of All Persons from Enforced Disappearance (ICPPED).

While enforced disappearances are considered as one of the gravest human rights violations, to the extent that some consider their prohibition as having attained *jus*

[1] Guercke (2021), p. 329.

[2] See https://www.un.org/en/about-us/udhr/foundation-of-international-human-rights-law. Accessed 17 November 2024.

[3] See Klabbers (2009).

[4] This is of course not the case for all relatives, and each experience is different. Moreover, the demands can also change over time.

L. Guercke, *Failure of the State*, Interdisciplinary Studies in Human Rights 15,
https://doi.org/10.1007/978-3-031-83717-3_8

cogens status under international law (see Chap. 1), disappearances committed by non-state actors do not have the same status. Moreover, the exact obligations of states in relation to these crimes, as well as their victims, are less clear than those pertaining to victims of enforced disappearances and have, until now, not received a thorough examination in legal scholarship. Furthermore, under positive international law, only states can be held legally accountable before regional or international human rights bodies. In this sense, even where non-state actors are the direct perpetrators of a human rights violating act, the—extent of—the responsibility of the state continues to be a crucial question because it constitutes the basis for seeking justice and reparations before international or regional human rights bodies.[5]

Based on the normative premise that IHRL *should* protect victims of all types of disappearances, especially in view of the severe suffering caused to relatives by the disappearance of a loved one, in this book I have explored the protective capacity of IHRL vis-à-vis victims of disappearances committed by OCGs, and their relatives. To do so, I drew on the disciplinary and methodological tools of both law and social sciences and combined doctrinal legal research with qualitative interviews with human rights practitioners who work on the issue of disappearances in the context of Mexico's 'war on drugs'. This combination of disciplinary approaches provides 'internal' and 'external' perspectives to the issue of disappearances committed by OCGs in IHRL, contrasting the international legal questions with the reality of those who use international legal standards in their work. The decision to merge two disciplinary lenses into a single piece of research was motivated by the perception that purely legal research in the field of human rights is often too removed from reality (see Chap. 1).

In Chaps. 2–4, I examined the obligations of states vis-à-vis victims of disappearances committed by non-state actors and the ways in which states can be held responsible for such disappearances based on an analysis of instruments and jurisprudence of the African, European, and Inter-American human rights systems, as well as UN treaty bodies. I then examined the issue of disappearances committed by OCGs more specifically. With regard to the determination of state responsibility, in Chap. 3 I outlined how, beyond the rules of state responsibility, a state can be held responsible either by establishing acquiescence to disappearances committed by non-state actors, or on the basis of a failure by the state to prevent or respond to the disappearance. Existing jurisprudence concerning disappearances—or other human rights violations—committed by non-state actors leaves some doubts in relation to the difference between acquiescing to a particular conduct and failing to prevent it and even the CED Statement on Non-State Actors that provides a long-awaited definition of acquiescence maintains a very thin separation between the two. While a blurry boundary between failure to prevent and acquiescence may not be problematic with regard to other types of human rights violations, in cases of disappearances the distinction is important because acquiescence 'converts' a disappearance that would otherwise fall within Article 3 ICPPED into an *enforced*

[5] Guercke (2021), p. 330.

disappearance, leaving no doubt about the state's responsibility. Furthermore, as discussed in Chap. 2, states have clearer and broader obligations regarding enforced disappearances, especially towards the victims of such crimes, who, in the case of an enforced disappearance, include the relatives of the disappeared person in accordance with Article 24 ICPPED. This further underlines the importance of distinguishing between acts that amount to *enforced* disappearances, especially in view of the newly adopted definition of acquiescence, and those which fall within Article 3 ICPPED. At the same time, it highlights the importance of examining state responsibility beyond the ICPPED with a view to protecting victims.

Given the complex nature of disappearances, where a state fails to respond to such a crime it can incur responsibility for a number of substantive human rights violations, even if the disappearance was committed by a non-state actor. The rights that can be violated by state omissions following a disappearance include the rights to life, liberty, integrity and access to justice of the disappeared person, as well as the rights to integrity and access to justice of relatives. However, responsibility for a failure to prevent a disappearance at the hand of a non-state actor is more complex and initially requires a determination of whether a state had a specific obligation to take preventive measures so as to avoid creating unreasonable expectations on a state. There are two approaches for this determination in the jurisprudence of the ECtHR and IACtHR, based either on the (potential) victim, or the source of the risk. As I argue in Chap. 4 and elsewhere,[6] when it comes to disappearances committed by OCGs, a source-based approach should be applied to establish responsibility. This is because the international legal framework against transnational organised crime and corruption can be used as *lex specialis* to further specify a state's due diligence obligations to prevent such disappearances by taking reasonable measures against the 'source' of the risk. In addition, due to the specific nature of OCGs, there often exists a relationship between the state and this non-state actor, for example through corruption, which could be considered as a contribution by the state to the risk emanating from such groups, if not acquiescence. These elements could and should also be taken into consideration when determining whether a state acquiesced to disappearances committed by OCGs in line with the CED's definition. The doctrinal analysis indicates that IHRL provides some protection to victims of disappearances committed by OCGs, and their relatives. However, if these disappearances fall within Article 3 ICPPED, the protection falls short of that afforded to victims of enforced disappearances. Consequently, questions about attribution through authorisation, support or acquiescence become particularly important and some issues, such as the way in which corruption can be causally linked to a disappearance, require further research. Moreover, it will be up to human rights tribunals to take up and apply the CED's definition of acquiescence and not to use a too narrow victim-based approach to determining responsibility for a failure to prevent in cases involving OCGs as perpetrators.

---

[6]Guercke (2021).

In Chaps. 5–7, I focused on the specific situation of disappearances in the context of Mexico's 'war on drugs', which began in late 2006. Since then, over 103,500 persons have officially disappeared or gone missing in a complex context of state and criminal violence (see Chap. 5). While much remains unknown about individual perpetrators and motives behind the disappearances, it is generally agreed that the main perpetrators of disappearances are state forces and OCGs. However, these actors can often not be clearly distinguished, as is illustrated by many instances of collusion between state and criminal forces, such as in the case of Ayotzinapa. Moreover, as discussed in Chap. 5, which introduced the phenomenon of present-day disappearances in Mexico, another reason for the large number of disappearances is the ongoing forensic crisis in the country, with currently at least 72,000 unidentified bodies and thousands of official and clandestine mass graves around the country. While such 'forensic disappearances' are not likely to fall within the definition of enforced disappearance under IHRL, they raise questions for IHRL and legal scholarship as regards the extent of state responsibility.[7] The Mexican domestic legal framework in some ways goes beyond IHRL as regards the obligations in relation to victims of disappearances committed by non-state actors. For example, the General Law on Disappearances (LEDDCPI), adopted in 2017, and the General Victim's Law, adopted in 2013, establish a right to reparation for direct and indirect victims (such as relatives) of disappearances. Moreover, the LEDDCPI creates two crimes, 'enforced disappearance' and 'disappearance committed by private individuals', and creates equal prevention and response obligations for both crimes. In addition to the issue of 'forensic disappearances', the situation in Mexico raises several questions for international legal scholarship, which I highlighted in Chap. 5. These include whether all disappearances could be considered as enforced disappearances on the basis of impunity as acquiescence; whether the violence could be characterised as a non-international armed conflict; and if some or all of the disappearances could be considered crimes against humanity within the meaning of International Criminal Law.

Building on the general description provided in Chap. 5, in Chaps. 6 and 7 I presented and analysed the interviews conducted with human rights professionals working on the issue of disappearances in Mexico. In Chap. 6, I described three main themes that I identified across the interviews analysed for this research: uncertainty, pragmatism, and frustration. Uncertainty refers to the context in which the participants work; pragmatism to the way in which they have adapted their (traditional) ways of working to the particular challenges arising from the phenomenon of disappearances in the country and the needs and demands of relatives; and frustration to an emotional aspect of their experiences related to the scale of the issue and the general lack of change. The themes are not mutually exclusive and overlap to a certain degree. Moreover, collectively, they point to the actions and omissions of the state, even where disappearances may be committed by OCGs. First, at a more general level, the state's militarised security strategy and ongoing impunity were

[7] I also discuss these questions in a forthcoming publication: Guercke (2025).

described to be among the main reasons for high levels of violence, as well as its continuation in the country. Second, corruption and collusion, and a general lack of effective investigations, lead to difficulties in clearly distinguishing between 'state' and crime, allowing OCGs to control entire security forces, and fostering distrust in authorities. This distrust, coupled with ongoing insecurity, also contributes to under-reporting and thereby a lack of information, thus creating a cycle of uncertainty. Third, the failure of authorities to act has led relatives to take matters into their own hands and conduct searches, and NGOs to adapt their habitual working methods to respond to the needs of relatives and find new ways of pressuring authorities into doing their jobs. Finally, the historic and continued lack of tangible change, despite important achievements and advances at legal and institutional levels, foster self-doubts expressed by some participants and give rise to frustration.

While prevailing uncertainty implies that there is no single or definitive explanation for continued inaction and lack of change, and the interviews suggest that reasons may vary between different levels of 'the state' (municipal, state, federal), most participants voiced the opinion that the main obstacle to change was an overall lack of political will. One important aspect of the interviews to highlight, especially for participants who work in states where violence and disappearances were —or continue to be— most prevalent, is that international legal questions appear distant from and almost irrelevant to their day-to-day reality of working with relatives of disappeared persons. This is especially the case because due to the general lack of effective investigations, only very few cases have reached a judicial stage and because of the many practical challenges faced by relatives and organisations. In this sense, asking about 'protection' by international legal standards in the sense of guidance for local litigation, may be a few steps ahead of reality.

Drawing on the legal framework examined in Chaps. 2–4, in Chap. 7 I argued that the themes presented in Chap. 6 illustrated a complete 'protection failure' by the Mexican state. This failure has several dimensions: its all-encompassing nature; its blatancy and 'slipperiness' when it comes to assigning individual responsibilities; and the meta-uncertainty it produces. Drawing on these dimensions, I then connected the analysis to existing human rights scholarship and identified possible routes for further analysis. One salient aspect of the protection failure is that it highlights the difficulties of addressing the 'state' as a coherent entity, as international law does and requires: not only are the lines between 'state' and crime blurry, but state officials themselves are affected by the lack of protection by the state, which creates certain paradoxes in the Mexican context. For human rights practitioners this creates dilemmas because, by definition, they have to work with 'the state'. At the ground level, practitioners must work with authorities because it is the latter who must conduct investigations and searches for the disappeared, yet it is not always clear whether such collaboration could create more problems and risks than it solves. On the other hand, at the federal level, where there is less contact with individual authorities and the 'state' seems more abstract, it is difficult to create a coherent narrative about what is happening. The federal structure of the Mexican state adds another layer of complexity. The interviews reflect a difference between explanations for inaction at the level of the abstract 'state', where participants spoke about the state's strategy to maintain incapacity and evasion strategies, and explanations at a more direct level of individual authorities, which can relate to lack of training, lack of will, collusion, or also fear and lack of resources. This underscores the importance of thinking critically about the meaning of 'the state' and to what extent an international legal approach creates certain unhelpful 'legal fictions'.[8]

The opaque relationship between state and crime pushes the boundaries of what can be captured by existing legal concepts. At the same time, it points back to the importance of considering the 'willingness' of the state to comply with its human rights obligations. As a result, in engaging with current scholarship on human rights protection in 'areas of limited statehood' (ALS), I argued that the Mexican context highlights the need to ask whether the state is not in full control because it 'lost' the ability to exercise it, or whether it did so willingly and in a 'cunning' manner. Other scholars who have worked on the Mexican context have made similar arguments and emphasised the importance of not overlooking the question of willingness in ALS and how a lack of capacity and a lack of will might be intertwined. Adding to these calls, I argue that where OCGs are the non-state actor that apparently exercises control in ALS, further scholarship is needed to unpack what this actually means, considering the relationship and dynamics between 'state' and 'crime'.[9] Conversely, the question of willingness is also crucial in view of the potential pitfalls of an (over-)emphasis on legal solutions to the issue of disappearances, which was highlighted in the interviews. This is because legalisation lends itself to being (ab)used to evade accountability by means of 'interpretive denial', which the Mexican state appears to engage in. Yet, rather than interpreting the gap between law and reality as rendering international legal questions unnecessary or irrelevant, the participants' experiences also highlight the continued importance of critically reflecting on the capacity of international legal standards to capture the all-encompassing nature of the Mexican state's protection failure. This is because these standards still represent tools to exert pressure and guide action. One important question is whether the apparent intention behind the state's failure to protect, as blatantly shown by the pervasiveness of impunity, can be taken into consideration in the process of determining state responsibility. The CED's definition of acquiescence provides an opportunity to do so by including the 'deliberate' failure by a state to prevent and respond to a foreseeable and imminent risk of a disappearance at the hands of non-state actors, yet it is not clear how a court would approach this matter. Moreover, the IHRL framework's focus on violations of individual rights and cases leaves an

[8] I have come to realise, and perhaps this represents the basis of the disconnect that I felt between my initial research ideas and the reality in which participants work, that my initial 'hunches' that came from my previous knowledge were based on what Risse terms the 'common blind spot in human rights research': the assumption that the states being studied are 'fully functioning Weberian states that enjoy a monopoly over the means of violence and/or the capacity to implement and enforce central decisions'. See Risse (2017), p. 135.

[9] In addition to the relationship between state and criminal actors, the notion of macro-criminality which was mentioned by a number of participants, suggests a need to add economic actors to this analysis. This was also emphasised during the presentation of themes to participants in June 2021.

accountability gap when it comes to a general and structural failure of the state to protect human rights. As a result, I argued that, in order to fully capture an overall protection failure by a state, such as that of Mexico, the law on state responsibility might be better suited to hold a state accountable. To reflect the gravity of a structural failure to protect human rights, I suggested to revisit the concept of crimes of state in the law on state responsibility and exploring the notion of 'state gross negligence' and 'state recklessness'.

8.1 Concluding Reflections

What is the protective capacity of IHRL vis-à-vis victims of disappearances committed by OCGs, and their relatives? This question has several answers. On the one hand if IHRL standards are interpreted in such a manner as to allow for a determination of state responsibility that takes into consideration the complexity of the connections between states and OCGs, they can provide a certain level of protection—the definition of acquiescence adopted by the CED is an example of this approach, which should be taken up by human rights tribunals and not be interpreted too narrowly. As the study on the Mexican context, and the experiences of human rights practitioners working there suggests, the actions and omissions by the state continue to be of high relevance, even where disappearances are committed by OCGs. This points to a continued importance of exploring state responsibility, especially in grey areas that involve corruption. At the same time, the empirical research indicates that the vast majority of challenges faced by human right practitioners in the Mexican context are not of a legal nature, thereby highlighting the limits of thinking about 'protection' from a purely legal perspective. Indeed, an overemphasis on legal approaches can be a 'trap' that does not lead to actual change and facilitates interpretive denial by the state. Moreover, the study on Mexico highlights that 'the state' has many different facets and cannot be seen as a single entity. This raises the question to what extent international law's fiction of the coherent, unified state may actually be counterproductive because it fails to account for internal complexity.

During the interviews, some participants reflected on the evasion techniques of the Mexican state and the problem of the state's —apparently cynical— use of its own incapacity to evade responsibility. This happens on two levels: on the one hand, the state admits to failures to investigate crimes committed by non-state actors, which effectively hides the underlying role of the state in allowing the non-state actor to do as it pleases. On the other hand, it engages in a double discourse of arguing that it has not lost control over its territory towards the outside, while internally saying that it cannot go into certain areas of the country. The reason the state is able to engage in these 'evasion games' is because international law at present does not contain concepts that would allow for capturing the extent of the Mexican state's protection failure, especially in relation to the underlying lack of will or intentionality. In the absence of a notion of state criminality in present international law, the question of intent is not part of the determination of state responsibility for human rights violations. Indeed, not having to demonstrate intent is an important feature of the human rights system that represents less of an evidentiary hurdle than international criminal law. This question might be important, however, especially in relation to state omissions in situations where non-state actors are involved in the commission of crimes, as illustrated by the CED's inclusion of 'deliberate' inaction in its definition of acquiescence.

Despite acknowledging the limitations of the law, the experiences of participants also indicate that international legal standards and questions, while not solutions in and of themselves, remain important because they provide legitimacy to demands and can serve as tools to exert pressure on the state. In relation to this, the empirical research indicates that where disappearances are committed by OCGs in a context of complete protection failure by the state, based on a lack of will more than a lack of capacity, the current IHRL framework falls short of capturing the all-encompassing nature of the state's responsibility. Exploring ways of how more attention could be paid to the question of intention in the determination of state responsibility also beyond IHRL could be one way of mediating this shortcoming. A return to the notion of crimes of state might allow for the development of concepts such as 'state gross negligence' and 'state recklessness', which could encompass the overall and sustained protection failures and possible intent underlying structural omissions.

8.2 Avenues for Further Research

8.2.1 Legal Research

- The argument for a broader form of responsibility that would reflect a general failure to prevent and how accountability could be achieved in practice requires further attention and elaboration. Additionally, the question of whether IHRL, or the law on state responsibility, can capture the intentionality behind impunity, or behind a failure to protect more generally, requires additional research. This includes further development, from the perspective of the law on state responsibility, of the concepts of 'state gross negligence' and 'state recklessness' proposed in this research. Both could be thought of as aggravated forms of breaches of due diligence obligations and could therefore be developed on the basis of an existing proposal for a corresponding secondary rule in international law, such as that advanced by Mackenzie-Gray Scott.[10]
- After the CED's adoption of a definition of acquiescence, further research is needed to assess how human rights bodies, including CED itself, apply this definition and address the difference between a failure to prevent a disappearance by a non-state actor and acquiescing to it. Especially for contexts such as Mexico,

[10] Mackenzie-Gray Scott (2021, 2022).

where impunity is persistent and contributes to the perpetuation of disappearances by non-state actors, it will be important to define at what point it is possible to speak of 'known patterns' of disappearances for the purpose of establishing acquiescence.

- The question of the type of reparations for victims of disappearances committed by non-state actors, as well as their relatives, also requires further research. For example, an open question is what type of measures would be adequate to repair the harm caused by a general protection failure. This is particularly important in relation to the adoption of guarantees of non-repetition. In view of the limitations of purely legal approaches discussed in this book, these questions go beyond the legal realm.
- The role and responsibilities of other states should also be further explored. Given that the empirical literature has shown that pressure and (non-military) intervention from outside is most effective to both induce 'will' but also improve respect for human rights where capacity is limited, then the behaviour of other states becomes equally relevant, as do questions about whether other states might have *obligations* to act. While one might argue that it is a political rather than a legal question whether other states will exert pressure, and in practice economic interests are considered to be a major obstacle to political pressure on Mexico,[11] if other states held legal obligations to respond to what is happening in Mexico (or elsewhere), then this could in turn be leveraged to pressure those states into action.
- There is a clear gap in IHRL, and in IHRL scholarship, on the problem of corruption and collusion in relation to the protection of human rights. While it is a difficult field to conduct research on because many corrupt ties are hidden, it is also the state's obligation to investigate these ties—not directly under IHRL, but certainly under UNTOC and UNCAC. One could argue that this obligation also exists under IHRL indirectly, to the extent that states have an obligation to prevent.[12] Future research could explore how to incorporate an obligation to prevent and fight corruption within IHRL, for example by drawing on the 'precautionary principle' in International Environmental Law, which establishes that states must take precautionary measures and avoid activities that could potentially be hazardous for the environment, even when there is no scientific certainty about its environmental impact.[13] Such a precautionary principle would also overcome the need to establish causal links between systemic issues and an individual rights violation.

[11] Interview 4.

[12] See, for example, Reyes (2019). See also Peters (2024), pp. 13–14.

[13] See Schröder (2014).

8.2.2 Empirical Research

The empirical research highlights some of the challenges faced by human rights practitioners in Mexico in their work towards ensuring the protection of human rights. While this research is based on the single context of disappearances in the context of Mexico's 'war on drugs', and therefore only provides a glimpse into the reality of human rights practitioners, it nevertheless points to several areas of further research in human rights scholarship and policy development.

- In support of arguments made by Anaya-Muñoz and Serrano and de Pina, the empirical research indicates the need to place greater attention to the question of state willingness and unwillingness, or tolerance of non-compliance, and how these relate to matters of capacity. This is particularly the case where non-state actors are involved in the commission of human rights violations, such as disappearances, and even more so where these non-state actors are OCGs, due to their complex and often non-antagonistic relationship to the state. At the same time, my research suggests that the notion of 'the state' itself is not a coherent one. Existing research has shown that outside intervention to strengthen domestic judicial institutions can make an important contribution to increasing state capacity where one of the underlying issues is corruption.[14] This reflects proposals by Mexican civil society for the creation of an international mechanism against impunity. If a lack of will is at the heart of the issue, and the state is not a unitary actor, how can willingness be induced? And who must be willing to make the necessary changes? In a state as complex and heterogenous as Mexico, is attention to the federal level misguided and could more change be achieved at local level, considering the specificities of the locality? These are important questions to consider in future research on human rights compliance.
- Several matters surrounding human rights organisations in Mexico more generally could also be the subject of further research. First, as discussed in Chap. 6, the theme of frustration suggests a rather bleak picture of the situation. This raises the question how NGOs working in the Mexican context address and foster resilience, given that the issue of disappearances will require attention for many years to come. A second issue that came up only tangentially during the interviews, but nevertheless caught my attention, is the question of who funds the work done by human rights practitioners and to what extent the funding they receive constrains, and perhaps even directs, their work. Moreover, in the Mexican context particularly, there is significant discrepancy in capacity between NGOs based in Mexico City and those working in states, despite the fact that most human rights violations occur outside of Mexico City (and the most tangible progress has been made at the state level). During the course of my fieldwork, it became apparent to me that sustainable change could only happen at local level, partly due to the complexity of the country. The size of the country poses real challenges for

[14] See Börzel and Risse (2013).

coordination, and the centralisation of discussions and negotiations around laws and policies constitute logistical problems. While there appears to be growing awareness generally of issues related to '*chilangocentrismo*' (the centralisation of funding and attention to Mexico City),[15] further research should explore the dynamics and models of collaboration (if these exist at all) between human rights NGOs based in states and those based in Mexico City and identify best practices and areas of improvement.[16] This could also be useful for donors, who should consider that much more tangible change can be achieved at the local level where NGOs and relative groups have managed to build —albeit tenuous— relationships with local authorities that have led to some progress.[17] Furthermore, and in view of the inherent limitations and doubts expressed by participants about the utility of emphasising legal and institutional reforms, such research could also explore links between more traditional human rights NGOs for which the participants in my research work and other civil society organisations with a less legal focus.

- The existence of ties between state and criminal actors, as well as the involvement of the private sector with criminal actors and how it may be involved in fuelling violence, are in need of further exploration.[18] For human rights NGOs, the existence of such ties also means a need to re-adjust their traditional means of working, which is another area that merits more research and consideration by donors. This is because some traditional means of defending human rights, such as naming and shaming, do not work with criminal actors who have no interest in being perceived as adhering to legal standards, let alone respect or protect rights. Further research should explore the implications for human rights work and how organisations working in such can contexts be supported effectively.
- A final issue that requires further research is the matter of societal indifference, which was touched upon by a number of participants and mentioned as one of the biggest challenges. This needs to be overcome, for example to put pressure on politicians to make actual changes. How can society be compelled to mobilise on an issue (beyond the short-term)? What strategies could civil society employ to create sufficient empathy and indignation for society to engage with the issue of

[15] A term used by some participants during interviews. 'Chilango' is a term to refer to all things from Mexico City, so the term could be loosely translated as 'Mexico City-bias' (see also Chap. 1, Sect. 1.2.2.2).

[16] When I asked participants about the existence of a common strategy during the presentation of themes in June 2021, I was told that no such overarching strategy exists, but that NGOs collaborate and support each other's work on a more *ad hoc* basis and have learned from each other's experiences. A number of participants expressed interest in hearing more about what I learned during my stays with NGOs in different states and their working methods—while this is something that my research did not focus on, the interest expressed during the presentations also highlights the need for further research on this matter.

[17] On this, see also the findings by Gallagher (2023).

[18] This point was also emphasised by a number of participants during the presentation of themes in June 2021. Recent studies on macro-criminal networks in Mexico are an example of such research. See Vázquez (2019), Espinal-Enríquez et al. (2023) and Cruz et al. (2024).

disappearances? Such research could explore processes in other countries to understand what is needed for mobilisation efforts to succeed and be sustained over time. Moreover, it could also study previous experiences in Mexico that contributed to positive change or failed to do so.

8.2.3 Research Methods

- The findings relating to the differences in experiences of interview participants based in Mexico City and the states also raise methodological questions for researchers in relation to the type of knowledge that can be gained from conducting interviews depending on the location of these interviews in a capital city or outside of it, especially in federal countries. The 'surprises' I encountered at the local level in the different states that I visited, greatly added to my capacity to comprehend the complexity of the issue of disappearances in Mexico and impacted on my analysis. This shows the inherent limitations of conducting research only in capital cities, where access might be easier, but where the experiences of individuals working there might be very different from those who work in other parts of the country. This difference could equally apply to urban and rural experiences.[19] Indeed, the type of NGOs I interviewed, are usually based in capital cities of the states, which also means that their experience differs from that of activists in rural areas.[20]
- More research that combines internal and external perspectives on law is needed to support the development of common methodologies to guide interdisciplinary research projects and establish standards for evaluation of such research.

8.3 Final Remark

This book is a slightly updated version of my doctoral thesis. I began the research in 2017, 3 years after the disappearance of the 43 students from Ayotzinapa. As I finish the book manuscript in November 2024, the 10-year anniversary of their disappearance has already passed. To ensure publishing a book that is as up to date as possible, I updated information, added sources, and increased numbers. When I began my PhD research, the official number of disappeared persons in Mexico was around 27,000. Today, the official register counts over 115,000 disappeared or missing persons. Although all these numbers must be taken with a large measure of salt, they

[19] I thank Prof. Stephan Parmentier for drawing my attention to this point.

[20] This was also mentioned by the participant in Interview 12. Furthermore, I also experienced the differences between rural and urban settings myself when visiting the NGO Tlachinollan, which is based in Tlapa, a rural mountain town in the state of Guerrero.

are still staggering. When I conducted the interviews for this research, in 2019, participants expressed their frustration over the lack of tangible progress. Since then, institutions that represented hope to families and organisations have been starved of funding and support, to the point that some individuals who were genuinely concerned about findings answers and dedicated to their work, have resigned from the various mechanisms. It is disheartening to witness from far away and only underscores the need for critical research and thought about how local human rights practitioners can be supported in a sustained manner.

References

Börzel TA, Risse T (2013) Human rights in areas of limited statehood: the new agenda. In: Sikkink K, Ropp SC, Risse T (eds) The persistent power of human rights: from commitment to compliance. Cambridge University Press, Cambridge, pp 63–84

Cruz A, Enríquez JE, Guadarrama A, Niño JJ (2024) Redes de macrocriminalidad, desaparición de personas y construcción de paz: un estudio sobre el Estado de México. Heinrich Böll Stiftung, Mexico City

Espinal-Enríquez J, Isunza E, Isunza A, Vázquez D (2023) Redes de poder y gobernanza criminal. Dinámicas regionales en Veracruz (2004-2018), 1st edn. Heinrich Böll Stiftung, Mexico City

Gallagher J (2023) Bootstrap justice: the search for Mexico's disappeared. Oxford University Press, New York

Guercke L (2021) State responsibility for a failure to prevent violations of the right to life by organised criminal groups: disappearances in Mexico. Hum Rights Law Rev 21:329–357. https://doi.org/10.1093/hrlr/ngaa061

Guercke L (2025) Contemporary disappearances in Mexico: a conceptual challenge for the international framework on enforced disappearances. In: Baranowska G, Kolaković-Bojović M (eds) Enforced disappearances: on universal responses to a worldwide phenomenon. Cambridge University Press (forthcoming)

Klabbers J (2009) (I can't get no) recognition: subjects doctrine and the emergence of non-state actors. In: Bianchi A (ed) Non-state actors and international law. Ashgate, Surrey, pp 37–56

Mackenzie-Gray Scott R (2021) Due diligence as a secondary rule of general international law. Leiden J Int Law 34:343–372. https://doi.org/10.1017/S0922156521000030

Mackenzie-Gray Scott R (2022) State responsibility for non-state actors: past, present and prospects for the future. Hart Publishing, Bloomsbury Publishing Plc, Oxford

Peters A (2024) Human rights and corruption: problems and potential of individualizing a systemic problem. Int J Constitutional Law. https://doi.org/10.1093/icon/moae038

Reyes J (2019) State capture through corruption: can human rights help? Am J Int Law 113:331–335. https://doi.org/10.1017/aju.2019.59

Risse T (2017) Human rights in areas of limited statehood: from the spiral model to localization and translation. In: Snyder J, Vinjamuri L, Hopgood S (eds) Human rights futures. Cambridge University Press, Cambridge, pp 135–158

Schröder M (2014) Precautionary approach/principle. Max Planck Encyclopedia of Public International Law

Vázquez D (2019) Captura del Estado, macrocriminalidad, y derechos humanos, Primera edición. Facultad Latinoamericana de Ciencias Sociales, Sede México, Fundación Heinrich Böll e.v., Universidad Nacional Autónoma de México, Instituto de Investigaciones Jurídicas, Mexico City

The manufacturer's authorised representative in the EU is Springer Nature Customer Service Centre GmbH, Europaplatz 3, 69115 Heidelberg, Germany. If you have any concerns regarding our products, please contact ProductSafety@springernature.com

Printed and bound by CPI Group (UK) Ltd, Croydon, CR0 4YY
30/09/2026
02225589-0013